PN6112.
B45   The Best plays
Be

68-7847

JUL   2000

Date Due

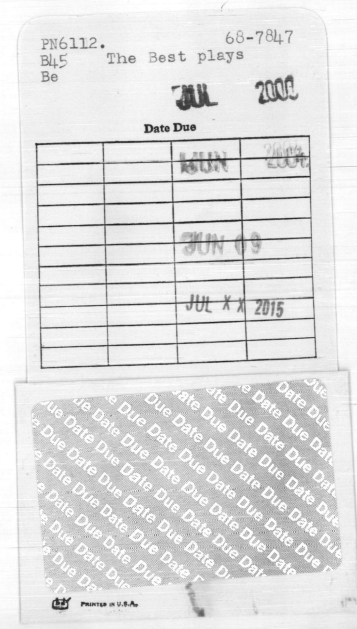

		JUN	2004
		JUN 09	
		JUL X X 2015	

PRINTED IN U.S.A.

THE BEST PLAYS OF 1966-1967

THE

BURNS MANTLE

YEARBOOK

JOEL GREY IN
"CABARET"

THE BEST PLAYS OF 1966-1967

THE
BEST PLAYS
OF 1966-1967

EDITED BY OTIS L. GUERNSEY JR.

Illustrated with photographs and
with drawings by HIRSCHFELD

DODD, MEAD & COMPANY

NEW YORK • TORONTO

68-7847

"A Delicate Balance": by Edward Albee. Copyright © 1966 by Edward Albee. Reprinted by permission of the Author and Atheneum Publishers. All rights reserved. See CAUTION notice below. All inquiries concerning rights for professional and amateur stock production should be addressed to: William Morris Agency, Inc., 1350 Avenue of the Americas, New York, N.Y. 10019. All other inquiries should be addressed to the publisher: Atheneum House, Inc., 162 East 38th Street, New York, N.Y. 10016.

"The Killing of Sister George": by Frank Marcus. Copyright © 1965 by Frank Marcus. Reprinted by permission of Random House, Inc. See CAUTION notice below. All inquiries should be addressed to the publisher: Random House, Inc., 457 Madison Avenue, New York, N.Y. 10019.

"Hamp": by John Wilson. Copyright © John Wilson 1966. Reprinted by permission of the Author and Evans Plays. See CAUTION notice below. All inquiries should be addressed to the publisher: Evans Plays, Evans Brothers Ltd., Montague House, Russell Square, London, WC1, England.

"Cabaret": by Joe Masteroff, John Kander and Fred Ebb. Lyrics Copyright © 1966 Sunbeam Music Corp. Used by permission of Tommy Volando. All rights reserved. Picture captions for "Cabaret" are paraphrased from the complete play text published by Random House, Inc. and used by permission. See CAUTION notice below. All inquiries concerning the lyrics should be addressed to: Sunbeam Music Corp., 22 West 48th Street, New York, N.Y. 10036. All other inquiries should be addressed to the publisher: Random House, Inc., 457 Madison Avenue, New York, N.Y. 10019.

"The Apple Tree": by Jerry Bock and Sheldon Harnick. Text Copyright © 1967 by Jerry Bock and Mayerling Productions Ltd. Lyrics Copyright © 1966 by Appletree Music Company. Reprinted by permission of Random House, Inc. See CAUTION notice below. All inquiries should be addressed to the publisher: Random House, Inc., 457 Madison Avenue, New York, N.Y. 10019.

"America Hurrah": by Jean-Claude van Itallie. Copyright © 1966, 1967 by Jean-Claude van Itallie. Reprinted by permission of Coward-McCann, Inc. See CAUTION notice below. All inquiries should be addressed to the publisher: Coward-McCann, Inc., 200 Madison Avenue, New York, N.Y. 10016.

"The Homecoming": by Harold Pinter. Copyright © 1965 and 1966 by Harold Pinter. Reprinted by permission of Grove Press, Inc., See CAUTION notice below. All inquiries should be addressed to the publisher: Grove Press, Inc., 80 University Place, New York, N.Y. 10003.

EDITOR'S NOTE

IN EACH succeeding volume in the *Best Plays* series our aim is to hold one theater year in sharp focus, however the areas of activity may change color and intensity, like a mosaic of lights glowing now here and now there: London, Paris, Los Angeles, Broadway, off Broadway, off off Broadway, etc.

Thus, our statistical material, our essays and even our selection of the ten Best Plays quite naturally take on the characteristics of the season itself. 1966-67 was a good year off Broadway, so there are three off-Broadway scripts on the Best list. A grand display of British playwriting talent? Four British plays on the Best list. Ever-growing importance of the musical stage? Three musicals on the list. A lack of "serious" theater? Only one drama among the Best Plays—and so it goes, inevitably, as the theater itself goes on.

Our effort to reflect a theater year in its full breadth as well as in detail always seems to mean expanded coverage from volume to volume, as we go after the new without relaxing our attention elsewhere. For example, New York's "off off Broadway" is sending more and more bubbles to the surface—one of 1966-67's Best Plays, *America Hurrah,* was gestated in experimental productions before it finally surfaced off Broadway. Accordingly, within this volume's chapter on "The Season in New York" are two special reports on off off Broadway, one on a section of its Establishment (the Equity Theater) and one on its experimentation in the cafes and churches. At the same time, we hold to our customary total coverage of the Broadway and off-Broadway scenes, reviewing all accomplishments and missteps, listing all production facts and credits and summarizing the on- and off-Broadway years in handy one-page references. To increase the usefulness of the *Best Plays* series in the musical theater, musical revivals in the "Plays Produced on Broadway" section will carry either a *Best Plays* volume and page reference for the musical's song numbers, or will list those numbers in the revival entry.

The American regional theater year is described in essays by artists, critics and educators writing about play production in various parts of the United States. Los Angeles, far more prolific in its theater activity than other cities, is treated as a special case in a resume of its program highlights. The ANTA Directory of 1966-67 productions in the professional regional theater covers almost 300 programs in 36 major centers of activity (last year there were only 30). Programs of the major summer festivals, mostly Shakespeare, are listed together with a progress report on Stratford, Ontario, by a member of its staff. The London and Continental seasons are scrutinized both critically and factually. Our photo sections picture the highlights and acting bests of the New York theater year. Outstanding examples of scenic and costume design are shown in photos of sketches, with the kind permission of the designers. One of the Best Plays—*Cabaret*—is synopsized in pictures in order to capture the total "look" of a 1966-67 Broadway show. The total look of Broadway as a whole is reproduced with total perception in the Hirschfeld drawings. Each year Al Hirschfeld creates a set of drawings of how the theater ought to look, and by the end of the season it has just about managed to look that way.

Obviously this volume is the work of many hands, the dedication of many efforts. To the authors of the signed articles and introductions many, many thanks on behalf of theater lovers everywhere who will enjoy this book much more because of their generous contribution of time and talent. Among those who helped to assemble and process the wealth of information in these pages were the many patient, helpful members of Broadway and off-Broadway production staffs, particularly in the press offices; and my one and only patient, helpful wife. This book is an extraordinary editorial accomplishment by Jonathan Dodd of Dodd, Mead & Company; Rue Canvin of the *World Journal Tribune* (off-Broadway productions and Shakespeare festivals); Elizabeth Rivers of the Dramatists Guild (prizes, publications and necrology); Ella A. Malin of ANTA (Directory of Professional Regional Theater); Ossia Trilling (European Editor); Dale Olson (Los Angeles highlights); Bernard Simon (bus-truck tour information); and others including Hobe Morrison of *Variety* lending a hand over some of the rougher spots. My own heartfelt thanks are only a small part of what *The Best Plays of 1966-67* owes to their efforts.

OTIS L. GUERNSEY Jr.

June 1, 1967

CONTENTS

Drawings by HIRSCHFELD

SUMMARIES
OF THE
SEASONS

THE SEASON IN NEW YORK

By Otis L. Guernsey Jr.

"THE BRITISH are coming, the British are coming!" the teen-agers warned us with their cries of rapture, and did we listen? No—most of us laughed when first the Beatles stepped off the boat, but soon it was too late to prevent the British from swarming all over the era with reinforcements like Tom Jones, James Bond, Vidal Sassoon, miniskirts and the Redgrave girls. Now they are here in strength, both feet planted in the center of American culture, not to be budged. Even the New York theater has fallen under their influence, their domination. The very best plays of the 1966-67 season in New York were written by Elizabethan playwrights—subjects of Queen Elizabeth II.

The year's best play was Harold Pinter's challenging *The Homecoming*. The year's best-*made* play was Frank Marcus's *The Killing of Sister George*. The year's funniest play was Peter Shaffer's *Black Comedy*. The best drama by far was John Wilson's *Hamp* off Broadway. Distinction in the area of the musical comedy/play continued to be a monopoly of American authors, who came up with *The Apple Tree, Cabaret* and (off Broadway) *You're a Good Man Charlie Brown* for the list of Best Plays. The excellent work of American authors in Edward Albee's *A Delicate Balance*, Robert Anderson's *You Know I Can't Hear You When the Water's Running* and (off Broadway) Jean-Claude van Itallie's *America Hurrah* was nevertheless overshadowed by the British presence.

1966-67 was the second dismal year in a row for American playwriting. Volume was off significantly, even alarmingly—19 new plays and 8 new musicals as compared with 25 and 11 in 1965-66 and 25 and 10 in 1964-65. American writers didn't even chalk up a significant record of disappointment. Most of our previously successful playwrights (I was going to say "well established," but there's no such thing as a well established playwright) were missing from the Broadway scene in 1966-67, so that the failure of Frank D. Gilroy's *That Summer—That Fall* after 12 performances stood out as an event. Foreign authors kept grabbing the limelight even in the matter of disappointment, notably with Peter Weiss's *The Investigation* (a financial success but a ponderous theatrical effort) and Brian Friel's *The Loves of Cass McGuire*, both of which failed to stir up anything like the excitement of, respectively, the same authors' *Marat/Sade* and *Philadelphia, Here I Come!* of last season.

Paradoxically, there were about the same number of stage programs offered on Broadway—78 as compared with 76 last season and 81 the season before.

3

The 1966-67 Season on Broadway

PLAYS (19)

A DELICATE BALANCE
We Have Always Lived in the Castle
Under the Weather
Don't Drink the Water
We Comrades Three
Those That Play the Clowns
My Sweet Charlie
Agatha Sue I love you
The Star-Spangled Girl
Come Live With Me
The Paisley Convertible
Love in E-flat
Of Love Remembered
The Natural Look
YOU KNOW I CAN'T HEAR YOU WHEN THE WATER'S RUNNING
That Summer—That Fall
A Warm Body
Little Murders
The Girl in the Freudian Slip

MUSICALS (8)

THE APPLE TREE
CABARET
Walking Happy
I Do! I Do!
A Joyful Noise
Sherry
Illya Darling
Hallelujah, Baby!

SPECIALTIES (4)

A Hand Is on the Gate
The Threepenny Opera
At the Drop of Another Hat
Hello, Solly!

REVIVALS (32)

Guys and Dolls
Show Boat
Annie Get Your Gun
Dinner at Eight
The Country Girl
The Rose Tattoo
Elizabeth the Queen
The Consul
Lincoln Center Rep:
  The Alchemist
  Yerma
  Galileo
D'Oyly Carte:
  The Pirates of Penzance
  The Mikado
  Ruddigore
  H.M.S. Pinafore
  Patience
APA-Phoenix:
  The School for Scandal
  Right You Are
  Measure for Measure
  Hamlet
  Romeo and Juliet
  Finian's Rainbow
  The Sound of Music
  Wonderful Town
National Repertory:
  The Imaginary Invalid
  A Touch of the Poet
  Tonight at 8:30

Carousel
Marat/Sade
Bristol Old Vic:

FOREIGN PLAYS IN ENGLISH (10)

Help Stamp Out Marriage!
The Investigation
THE KILLING OF SISTER GEORGE
The Loves of Cass McGuire
The East Wind
How's the World Treating You?
Hail Scrawdyke!
THE HOMECOMING
The Astrakhan Coat
BLACK COMEDY and *White Lies*

The Wild Duck
You Can't Take It With You
War and Peace

FOREIGN-LANGUAGE PRODUCTIONS (5)

Gilbert Becaud on Broadway
Let's Sing Yiddish
The Apparition Theater of Prague
Les Ballets Africains
Sing Israel Sing

HOLDOVER SHOWS WHICH BECAME HITS DURING 1966-67

Man of La Mancha
Half a Sixpence
Mame
Philadelphia, Here I Come!
Sweet Charity
Wait a Minim!

Categorized above are all the plays listed in the "Plays Produced on Broadway" section of this volume.

Plays listed in CAPITAL LETTERS have been designated Best Plays of 1966-67.

Plays listed in **bold face type** were classified as hits in *Variety*'s annual list of hits and flops publishd on June 7, 1967.

Plays listed in *italics* were still running on June 1, 1967.

But this total figure includes a huge number of revivals—32—exactly double the 16 revivals in 1965-66. With the Music Theater and the Repertory Theater of Lincoln Center, the City Center doing straight plays as well as musicals, visits from the D'Oyly Carte, the Bristol Old Vic, the National Repertory Theater and the APA-Phoenix, as well as other individual revival enterprises, it was a banner year for those who enjoy seeing the theatrical past evoked on the living stage.

Also paradoxically, business was tremendous, with record grosses on Broadway, and with attendance greatly improved off Broadway thanks to a large number of fine shows. There were fewer new Broadway shows, but the holdovers were running longer. The new smash hits like *Cabaret* ($12 top) and *I Do! I Do!* ($9.90 top) added their audience-pulling power to the many popular holdovers: *Barefoot in the Park* (at a $6.75 top in its fourth year), *Cactus Flower* ($7.50 in its second year), *Fiddler on the Roof* (third year, $9.90), *Funny Girl* (fourth year, $9.60), *Hello, Dolly!* (fourth year, $9.90), *Mame* (second year, $9.90), *Man of La Mancha* (second year, $8.50), *The Odd Couple* (third year, $7.25) and *Sweet Charity* (second year, $9.50).

Into this theatrical supermarket the New York show-shopper poured a total 1966-67 gross of $55,056,030 (according to *Variety* estimate), topping the fifty million mark and breaking the record for the third straight year (previous records were set in 1964-65 with $50,462,765 and in 1965-66 with $53,862,187). The number of playing weeks (if 10 shows run 10 weeks, that's 100 playing weeks) in 1966-67 was 1,269, third-highest behind 1,295 in 1965-66 and 1,325 in 1947-48. In this statistic the fall-off in activity was very slight, indicating that the reduced number of new productions is being nearly balanced by the longer runs of the successes. It should also be noted in passing by the box office that Christmas Week, 1966, brought in the highest single week's gross in Broadway history: $1,519,636, the first such gross of record (according to *Variety*) to go over the million-and-a-half mark. Touring Broadway shows also did exceptionally well at the box office ($43,572,-116, more than $10 million better than last year) with a whopping increase in activity to 916 playing weeks from 699 in 1965-66.

In 1966-67 Broadway was a Neil Simon festival. Simon came up with still *another* comedy hit—*The Star-Spangled Girl*. Add this one to *Barefoot in the Park, The Odd Couple* and *Sweet Charity,* and you reach the astonishing but inescapable conclusion that Simon had *four* hit shows running simultaneously on Broadway in 1966-67, and they were still running, *all of them,* at season's end. Simon's best combined week's gross, it is estimated, topped $200,000. Of course David Merrick, who does not write his shows himself, did better than that. Merrick's weekly gross for *Hello, Dolly!, Cactus Flower, Don't Drink the Water, I Do! I Do!* plus sundry holdovers and short-run new plays that didn't make it ran as high as $325,000. Merrick's *Dolly* has already passed the $30,000,000 level in worldwide grosses. Another big continuing Broadway success story is that of *Fiddler on the Roof,* which has already earned $2,580,000 in distributed profits and is still going strong—three repertory companies, three, are doing the show in *Finland.*

Lots of cash at favored box offices, British playwrights, revivals, Neil Simon, David Merrick—these were the peaks of the 1966-67 theater season. The deepest valley was the fall-off in new-play production, and there were others, notably the depressions dug by big musicals that failed to make it: *A Joyful Noise* (closed after only 12 performances with a deficit of $500,000), or *Breakfast at Tiffany's* which folded in previews leaving Merrick out $425,000. The musical *Chu Chem* folded in tryout, as did three plays mounted in New York for Broadway: *The Hemingway Hero, Two Weeks Somewhere Else* and *What Do You Really Know About Your Husband?* In the talent department Ruth Gordon, Alan Webb, Saul Bellow, Shelley Winters, Michael Stewart, Alfred Drake, Louis Gossett, Ray Walston, George Abbott, John Raitt, Roddy McDowall, Soupy Sales, Marsha Hunt, Norman Krasna, Ingrid Thulin, Frank D. Gilroy and others made the Broadway effort this season only to find that effort largely wasted.

Stand far enough away from the 1966-67 season and you cannot help concluding that it was as thin and gaunt in the creative department as it was fat and sassy at the box office. It is hardly worth mentioning any more that the volume of plays dealing in dramatic form with "serious" subjects is hardly worth mentioning. I say dramatic in *form* because there is much "serious" content and intent with the comic form of our theater. In fact, there are times when it seems that our trans-Atlantic theater is a soap box for those who feel certain that all Creation is a colossal joke on the human race, and who are striving to launch the newest, most acutely ironic laugh as the cosmos pulls the chair out from under yet another unfortunate, just-about-to-sit Job.

There is no lack of "serious" material in our theater, only of "serious" dramatic form. If *The Killing of Sister George*—in which the leading character is brought to practise mooing like a cow in order to survive—was for laughs alone, then who needs something to cry over? There's much to be said for conveying criticism and agony by indirection, and indeed the old definitions of "comedy," "drama" and "comedy-drama" are graying out in works like *A Delicate Balance* and *The Homecoming*.

It is argued that in the second half of the 20th century everything in general has become so uncomfortable, or at least so complex, that it can be faced *only* with laughter. Tears would be a kind of surrender. But even if all the special pleading is justified, and ours is indeed an especially trying age, you wouldn't guess it from the "serious" jokes in the Broadway comedies. Even if our festering problems of overpopulation, the bomb, the scientific adventure, etc., are ready to be sliced with satire and ridicule, that's not what's happening onstage, baby. What's happening—or what happened in 1966-67—was repetitious sardonic laughter in the time-traveled areas of sexual prowess, impotence and deviation. If the big kick is irony, the big hang-up is sex, not the state of the universe. The total annihilation of the human race may be the second-biggest joke in contemporary comedy, but if so it is running a very poor second.

The big best-seller among theater forms, however, remains the American musical comedy/play. Among the ten Best Plays of 1966-67, three are musicals, inevitably. As more and more creative effort is concentrated in this area a bigger proportion of our best theater work takes place within it. We have developed this form to the danger point of near-perfection where we can machine-make it—almost. Many of the musicals which turn up nowadays, even some of the most popular ones, are canned goods, taking some proven high-quality material from a novel or play and processing and packaging it in musical form. From a point of bias toward original creative forces, it's hard to decide whether in the long run it's better for the theater when this canning machinery works (as in *I Do! I Do!*, based on *The Fourposter*) or when it doesn't (as in *Sherry!*, based on *The Man Who Came to Dinner*). But canned or creative, the musical theater made still another strong season with the pulling power of new attractions and the staying power of the old ones; it is the equal of the ironic comedies in attracting attention and their superior in attracting audiences.

Admittedly, it was a most disappointing theater year on various levels, but within it were fine examples of writing, acting, directing and design to be described hereinunder, play-by-play. Flowers bloomed in the desert of 1966-67; there were songs to sing, and chills of irony, and not all of the laughter on the stage or in the auditorium was hollow.

Hits and Bests

In the theater, the tight meaning of the word "hit" is a show that pays off its production cost. No amount of cocktail party conversation, prizes or rave reviews can paste the "hit" label on a show that doesn't make it at the box office. But in recent seasons some of the overtones around the word have been fading. For example, it no longer means as much to achieve hit status by season's end; in fact, the May 31 hit list often includes shows which paid off early, not because of a high degree of popularity, but because of special production circumstances. Shows are costing more to produce, so they don't earn hit classification as quickly as they used to; but they are running longer and are earning more in the long pull. The smash success musical *Cabaret* did not make the 1966-67 hit list by May 31, but its backers are not worried. More and more frequently the major and most popular productions aren't achieving hit status until the *following* season (note the six 1965-66 holdovers so listed in the one-page Broadway summary).

Accordingly, in summarizing the 1966-67 record we list below not only *Variety's* annual May 31 estimate of Broadway hits; we also add our own guess at "probable hits"—shows still running June 1 which (we think) had a good chance of paying off—or coming very close to it—as they continued to run on into the 1967-68 season.

Shows whose titles appear in CAPITAL LETTERS were also Best Plays:

Hits (*Variety* Estimate)

At the Drop of Another Hat	*The Star-Spangled Girl*
A DELICATE BALANCE	YOU KNOW I CAN'T HEAR YOU
The Investigation	WHEN THE WATER'S RUN-
THE KILLING OF SISTER	NING
GEORGE	

Probable Hits

BLACK COMEDY	THE HOMECOMING
CABARET	I Do! I Do!
Don't Drink the Water	

At the Drop of Another Hat was a two-man performance by Michael Flanders and Donald Swann, British satirists in their second popular Broadway program of musical caricatures of animals, people and events. To a certain extent all British importations are special cases. Already mounted, cast, directed and rehearsed—or, at the very least, blocked out and perfected before London audiences—they cost relatively little in money and effort to bring to the point of a Broadway opening night, as compared with starting from scratch with a raw script. But the 1966-67 British plays were special cases of excellence, too, and it is a pleasure to note that they all approached hit level, with audiences attracted even to the perplexing mysteries of *The Homecoming.*

Harold Pinter consolidated his position as one of the world's leading playwrights of the absurdist or any other school with his much-debated *The Homecoming,* the year's best play and the Tony and Critics Award winner. Its setting (by John Bury) was the living room and hallway of a lower-middle-class London home; gray, drafty, the back wall knocked out to make a bigger archway, exposing the support beam and looking as though it had been raped and left for dead. Within this forbidding environment live a shouting, sometimes domineering father, his vapid brother who is a chauffeur, and his two sons. One of these sons is an indifferent boxer, and one is a pimp. Another is a Ph.D. (listen to the change in key), the eldest, a professor at a California university. He comes home for a visit, bringing his wife. After meeting her, the father and his two younger sons decide that they could use a woman around the house, for their sport and convenience. The Ph.D.'s wife would suit them very well, and she looks as though she could earn her own keep moonlighting as a prostitute in Greek Street (another change in key?). Calmly setting her own terms, the wife accepts this offer from her brothers and father-in-law to share their dubious hospitality (another change?). Her imperturbable teacher-husband departs for California, alone, never losing his cool, leaving his family competing and begging for his wife's favor (another?).

What does all this *mean?* audiences and critics have asked themselves. They also asked Pinter, who refused to elucidate, referring all questions back to the script. Two can play at that game. Before making any comment on *The Home-*

coming I will present here the unedited notes which I scribbled in the dark during the performance. I am not a note-taker, and in the case of no other play during the 1966-67 season did I jot more than one or two words of reminder. But in the case of *The Homecoming* I found the following observations scrawled in my program:

> Corpses . . . cool . . . gallows humor but the trap never drops.
> Futile break in widepants cuffs.
> Fear in a cheese sandwich. Not a raised eyebrow but everything is sardonic.
> Utter destruction with injections of water and air.
> This may be the best playwriting there is.

Let Harold Pinter try to figure out what *that* means. Certainly I do not know what *The Homecoming* means any better than Pinter says he does, but I can tell from looking over these notes that it had a very strong impact upon me as it was taking place before my senses in the theater.

Pinter, I feel, was dramatizing simultaneously the conscious and the subconscious. He cannot pretend in external reality that the father of this family suddenly turns to his educated son and proposes that his wife become the family prostitute. What is happening—it seems to me—is that Pinter's characters begin a scene as people operating consciously in external reality; then in the course of the scene they blurt out and personify their subconscious drives, fears, longings. For example, the wife—played with fearful control by Pinter's own wife, Vivien Merchant, in this production—is at first merely the wife of a college professor, a bit ill at ease in the unfamiliar environment of her husband's boyhood home. But in the next beat (like a sudden change of key in a musical composition) she starts to personify everyone's sexual drives including her own.

This technique—or characteristic, if I am wrong about it being a deliberate effect by the playwright—is at times confusing and at times extremely effective. From the opening scene, dread underlies this play like a psychosis, dread often expressed in the characters' attitudes but never in their words. Finally this dread comes out into the open as though Pinter had slowly turned his characters inside out so that they begin acting not rationally but subconsciously, emotionally, atavistically. They hardly ever raise their voices, but they are on the gallows of life; there is fear even in their cheese sandwiches; the air they breathe, the water they drink, is destroying them. They are alive, and there is no greater peril than that.

After a London season in production by the Royal Shakespeare Company as directed by Peter Hall, *The Homecoming* arrived on Broadway perfect in performance and style. Paul Rogers, who played the father, was so caught up in his role that (he stated in an interview) he scrubbed up like a surgeon every night before going on because the old man (says the script) is fanatically neat. Ian Holm as the pimp-son cut a streak of cruelty through the play. The notation "futile break in widepants cuffs" refers to a telling wardrobe detail of John Normington as Sam, the chauffeur-brother, a perfect study in futility.

There are dead spots in the script of *The Homecoming* which, paradoxically, may be caused by its very originality. This play is an exploration in dramatic art, a new form of expression which changes key like a musical composition. In its rush toward breakthrough it trails flaws and exposes problems: for example, many of the key-changes in *The Homecoming* take longer than necessary for its audience to grasp that the key *has* changed, so that in many places the audience is ready to move ahead before the script is. But the sudden thought in the dark expressed in the note "This may be the best playwriting there is" doesn't mean merely, there is this season. Obviously (to me) *The Homecoming* was the best of the season. The note signifies there is, period. This may be the best kind of playwriting to go on with into the future.

A second distinguished visitor (and a palpable hit) was *The Killing of Sister George* by Frank Marcus, the British drama critic and playwright, who made his Broadway debut with this script. (In his character of drama critic, Marcus reviews the 1966-67 London season in an article in this volume.) His *Sister George* was a well-made explicit comedy about an actress who plays a soap opera heroine: the ever-helpful visiting nurse "Sister George" in a BBC serial idealizing British country life. Now Sister George must be "killed" in the soap opera story in order to attract new public attention to the program. And in the play there is another "death" taking place at the same time that Sister George is being "killed." In the play's "real life," the actress who plays Sister George is a swaggering, cigar-smoking, take-charge type who lives with a pale young woman roommate she calls "Childie." Their private emotional relationship is being wracked and destroyed at the same time that the actress's role is being eliminated from the serial—leaving her, finally, alone on the stage, practising mooing. All she hopes to salvage from the wreck of her personal and professional life is the role of a cow in a forthcoming BBC idiocy.

In one of the season's top performances Beryl Reid portrayed the actress as a gallant creature; something of a bully who enjoys disciplining her weak-willed roommate; but standing up bravely to attempted bullying by a tailored woman executive from the BBC. In another standout performance Eileen Atkins became an angular symbol of arrested development and total selfishness as the babyish but not so innocent "Childie." The neurotic, doomed relationship between these two women may be part of the human comedy, but Marcus was not laughing *at* them in his excellent play. He has great sympathy for them in their emotional predicament; along with the laughter, his play both exposed and evoked strong feelings.

Last season Peter Shaffer was represented on the Best list by the philosophical-historical ironies of *The Royal Hunt of the Sun*. This season he was represented by the year's funniest play, the one with the punning title *Black Comedy*, a third jewel in Britain's triple-crown championship of Broadway.

Like *Charley's Aunt, Three Men on a Horse* and such, *Black Comedy* spins off from a single comic proposition, to wit: the fuses have blown so that the action takes place in pitch black darkness (but the reality of the lighting is reversed, so that when the setting appears blacked-out to the characters it appears brightly lighted to the audience). The characters are cardboard—designedly so—in a cutout situation. A fumbling young artist and his debutante fiancee have swiped the neighbor's elegant furniture to impress a millionaire who is coming to the studio to look at the artist's sculptures. The two-level setting designed by Alan Tagg (a stairway at right leads to a bedroom above) was deliberately cluttered to make it an obstacle course for characters in total "darkness" serving drinks, flirting and trying to sneak the furniture back while its rightful owner is in the room.

John Dexter's direction encouraged caricature in the acting of Michael Crawford as the harassed young artist, Lynn Redgrave as the waddling debutante, Peter Bull as her blowhard father, a colonel, and Donald Madden as the delicate young man who owns the furniture. In the dark, fears become exaggerated; secret repressions are secretly released (but the audience could see), in a very funny show which had all the earmarks of a comedy classic-to-be.

Black Comedy was commissioned by Britain's National Theater and was first performed by them (though not with this cast). Its action is continuous in a long one-act form, and Shaffer wrote a companion piece, the shorter *White Lies,* as a curtain-raiser for *Black Comedy* on the Broadway program. *White Lies* studied a fading fortune teller (Geraldine Page) victimized by a vicious young client; it was a little droplet of acid not quite so searing as its author had hoped. It suffered, too, from the handicap of standing in the deep shadow of its illustrious companion piece. Audiences came to the theater programmed by critical and word-of-mouth raves to laugh at *Black Comedy.* Sometimes they started laughing right away, as soon as the curtain rose (no point in not getting your full money's worth)—and often it took them a while to get over their preconceived *Black Comedy* notions before they could settle down to the rather more serious matter of *White Lies.*

The best American play of the Broadway year was Edward Albee's *A Delicate Balance* which was a hit and won Albee his first Pulitzer Prize. (A 1963 Pulitzer for *Who's Afraid of Virginia Woolf?* was voted by the jurors but withheld by the trustees.) Like *The Homecoming, A Delicate Balance* resists old definitions of theater. It is a comedy which coexists with nameless terror. Asked about his own definitions, Albee replied in an article in *Diplomat* magazine: "There's quite a difference between comedy and humor. *Virginia Woolf* was a comedy in the sense that everybody ended up with what they wanted (I'm being just slightly ironic). That's the definition of comedy: everybody ending up with what they want, or what they *think* they want. Now, serious theater must accomplish two things. The serious play has got to say something about the nature of the play as an art form itself; it has got to try to advance, to change that art form. It must also try to change the spectator in some fashion; alter his point of view, his view of reality, his view of the theater. This is the double responsibility of serious theater, and good intentions are never enough . . . I suppose *Virginia Woolf* was a serious comedy . . . Not everybody ends up with what they want, or what they think they want, in *A Delicate Balance.*"

By this definition, it would be possible to regard Albee's *A Delicate Balance* as a drama; yet I would prefer to class it with *Virginia Woolf* as a "serious comedy" because, at the end, the delicate balance upset by the events of the play is restored. All is exactly as it was at the beginning of the play (almost). Albee ends *A Delicate Balance* with his unflappable suburban housewife resuming a conversation that was interrupted as the play began.

What happened in between certainly challenged the spectator to search himself with two questions: what obligations do we assume in accepting friendship and love? and what rights do we acquire in giving them? The arena for Albee's examination of these realities is a suburban household delicately balanced within all the proprieties: the husband Tobias (Hume Cronyn) toying with his after-dinner anisette, the wife Agnes (Jessica Tandy) exercising a delicately articulated control over all. The pressures in this household are controlled pressures, balanced pressures until a neighboring couple—Agnes' and Tobias' best friends—move right into the guest room without either invitation or explanation, seeking refuge from a fear they cannot describe or understand, a fear that descended on them suddenly as they were sitting at home in the void of their lives.

Seeking sanctuary at the same time is the daughter of the house, running home to mother after her fourth unsuccessful marriage. So here are two spearheads of need—friend and family—converging, clashing, competing for attention. How much consideration do Agnes and Tobias owe their friends in exchange for having enjoyed their friendship? These are friends who have nowhere else to go because they have no *other* best friends. And how much do Agnes and Tobias owe their daughter simply because she *is* their daughter? That is the tangle that Albee's play weaves and then unweaves, with tolerant Tobias and articulate Agnes acted with total comprehension by the Cronyn-Tandy husband-and-wife team. Like Albee's *Tiny Alice, A Delicate Balance* had a relatively short (132 performances) first run on Broadway. But *Tiny Alice* has since enjoyed several distinguished productions elsewhere; it is growing in stature with each appearance. *A Delicate Balance,* too, is a new root planted in the theater, and its continuing growth as part of the stage repertory of the 1960s seems inevitable.

The other three American playscripts hovering above or near the hit line were all comedies. Robert Anderson (whose article on the American Playwrights Theater appears in "The Theater Around the United States" section of this volume) rejoined the ranks of hit playwrights with *You Know I Can't Hear You When the Water's Running,* a program of four one-acters, all on the periphery of sexual matters. It was directed by Alan Schneider (who also staged *A Delicate Balance*) so as to tune up the many ironic laughs in Anderson's script without tuning out his deep bass notes beneath the humor. The first playlet, *The Shock of Recognition,* presented a playwright who would show a naked man on the stage for all sorts of noble artistic reasons but is himself embarrassed by an eager actor stripping off his clothes in an attempt to grab the part. The second, *The Footsteps of Doves* exhibited a middle-aged married couple at the Rubicon of changing from a double to twin beds. The third, *I'll Be Home for Christmas,* was bitter fruit, as a middle-aged husband

JESSICA TANDY, HENDERSON FORSYTHE, CARMEN MATHEWS,
HUME CRONYN, MARIAN SELDES AND ROSEMARY MURPHY IN
"A DELICATE BALANCE"

and wife expose the meaninglessness of their own marriage in discussing their children's sex problems: he with affection and understanding; she coldly and relentlessly "practical." The fourth playlet, *I'm Herbert,* is the muddled conversation of an old couple boasting of past love affairs but now unable to remember exactly who loved whom and when.

In his program of one-acters, Anderson was almost always laughing but not always joking. The characters were brilliantly served by an excellent cast: Martin Balsam as the eager-beaver actor and the middle-aged husbands; Eileen Heckart as the three wives, two middle-aged and one old; and George

Grizzard as the playwright and the old roue. The Anderson plays were part of a banner one-act year in the New York theater, distinguished also by Peter Shaffer's long one-acter *Black Comedy,* Jerry Bock's and Sheldon Harnick's one-act musicals in *The Apple Tree,* Jean-Claude van Itallie's biting one-acters off Broadway in *America Hurrah,* together with Anderson's notably entertaining foursome.

In full-length and good-humored comedy, Neil Simon made the hit list again for the fourth straight time with his *The Star-Spangled Girl,* a bit of fluff about swinging young San Francisco intellectuals, and he did it in a season when it was very hard to sell love's young dream in wedlock, in flaming illicit romance or on twofers. In this one Simon presented two roommates (Anthony Perkins and Richard Benjamin, a young specialist at dead-pan comedy acting) editing a rebellious little magazine and competing for the beautiful girl (Connie Stevens) who moves in next door. The jokes and the sight gags flew thick and fast from Simon's supremely gifted imagination, almost hiding the fact that his comedy never got off the mark of its opening situation, and had nowhere much to go anyhow. *The Star-Spangled Girl* was witty (like all Simon scripts) and volatile (like all comedies directed by George Axelrod), but, finally, an incompleted sketch.

The third American comedy close to the hit line was Woody Allen's *Don't Drink the Water,* a heaping platter of corn buttered with one-liners in a script about a Newark caterer on a European vacation with his wife and daughter in an Iron Curtain country, wrongly suspected of being a spy and forced to take refuge in the American embassy, a Florida shirt among the morning coats. The play was just one big, overfed American folk joke; yet every year, it seems, Broadway has a "fluke" success like *Don't Drink the Water* (last season's was *The Impossible Years*). Nobody likes it but the audience. It appears to be merely a vehicle for some special performer (in this case Lou Jacobi, every feather indignantly ruffled as the bruised and innocent caterer). But the contemptible play runs on and on, defying all critical cliches and major casting changes. Obviously *Don't Drink the Water* was more than just a fluke; the character jokes about the impossible spy, the inept young American left to run the embassy in the ambassador's absence, momma in the embassy kitchen, the one-track-minded Communist policeman, etc., got plenty of laughs, an advantage that can't be laughed off so easily. A large segment of the regular Broadway theatergoing audience my feel a bit sheepish in their enjoyment of such fantasies as this. Never mind, *Don't Drink the Water* was a very funny situation comedy, and Allen richly deserved any success he could find with it.

Peter Weiss's *The Investigation* (English version by Jon Swan and Ulu Grosbard, who also directed the production) was remarkable as the only no-doubt-about-it-serious theater success of the Broadway season. It is a drama in the journalistic genre (like *The Deputy*) which not only contemplates a real event—the murder of 4,000,000 people in the German concentration camp at Auschwitz—but also borrows the words from reality to describe it. Weiss took the transcript of the Frankfurt trial of Auschwitz criminals and

JILL HAWORTH (WITH PHONE), JOEL GREY, BERT CONVY,
JACK GILFORD AND LOTTE LENYA IN "CABARET"

condensed it, adding nothing, but telescoping the testimony of accusers and
accused, telescoping the people into composites, until there remained a highly
distilled but uniformly factual account of a major horror. As a play (which,
incidentally, was sold to NBC for about $450,000 for a color TV tape), *The
Investigation* was not so much the experience of a tragedy as the examination
of a tragedy after the fact, like an inquest held to fix responsibility for the

death of Hamlet. It was grievous, but not challenging; terrible to contemplate but not dramatically terrible. *The Investigation* was bitter medicine which after all did nothing for our chronic illness, our continuing shock at this damnable turn of events in human history; nor did it much advance the cause of serious drama.

The steady stream of popular musicals upon which Broadway depends so heavily for both income and excitement continued, with *Cabaret* and *I Do! I Do!* approaching hit status and others not too far below it. *Cabaret* (orchestra $12 and $10 a seat; boxes $10; front mezzanine $7.90, $8.90 on Friday and Saturday nights; rear mezzanine $6.90, $5.90, $4 and $2) was a typical Broadway smash, high in price, popularity and quality. Also typically in the 1960s, it was cut from a pattern; it musicalized material from Christopher Isherwood stories about a young writer and a night-blooming girl who lives with him in hedonistic, pre-Hitler Berlin—material previously dramatized successfully in John van Druten's *I Am a Camera*. It has been converted successfully into a musical with flair and flavor in the adaptation, the score, the acting, the staging and the design.

The edge-of-darkness mood was deepest in the performance of Joel Grey as the Emcee, the compere of this sepulchral Berlin night spot, and by extension the symbol of the city's doom. He was a death-clown, hair plastered down, makeup emphasizing the skull behind the grin as he bids the customers "Willkommen" or suggests a new game in "Two Ladies." Joe Masteroff's book conjured up a Nazi bully who makes himself fairly unpleasant. But it isn't blows from the bully that shove this pleasure-seeking society over the cliff of the Nazi era, it is the soothing little nudges of the smirking Emcee. Grey combined his abilities as a mime, an actor and even as a makeup artist to produce an unforgettable negative of human nature.

Cabaret dipped love, hospitality, loyalty, patriotism in acid throughout its book, its Fred Ebb lyrics, its John Kander score, its staging and performances. Even the Boris Aronson settings contributed mightily to the irony—the cabaret "audience" was sometimes the theater's audience reflected in a huge trapezoidal mirror upstage. We were all in this *Cabaret*—or could have been, or could be again if we don't watch out. It was a good show about Berlin in 1929-30 in the full tradition of the American musical theater in 1966-67.

The season's second near-hit (as of May 31) musical was *I Do! I Do!* ($9.90), straight from the cannery and founding its popularity on musical and acting virtuosity. It was based on Jan de Hartog's *The Fourposter* about a marriage weathering the years and the storms. As a play and now as a musical this show had only two characters—no chorus line, no scene changes, no mirrors, nothing but a husband and wife and a double bed. It was still the same play, with holes cut out by Tom Jones and Harvey Schmidt for musical intervals, songs whose very titles form a precis of the plot: "I Do! I Do!", "I Love My Wife," "Something Has Happened," "Nobody's Perfect," "Flaming Agnes," "The Honeymoon Is Over," "When the Kids Get Married," "The Father of the Bride." With Robert Preston and Mary Martin playing the couple and singing the songs, the musical was the season's most attractive star turn. She can sing a little better than he can; he can act a little better than she can; they worked extremely well together, never exploiting an advantage, lending support over the rough spots. The Martin Preston stint was a virtuoso duet, a show in itself.

Those were the hits, the almost-hits, the about-to-be-hits of 1966-67. Their number was small (11) but roughly the same as in other recent seasons. There is a steady appetite, it seems, for the best that is available in the theater in and around New York, either in vintage or non-vintage years.

If a show's box office success is a right-now measure of its popularity, can conclusions be drawn from scanning the 1966-67 hit list? Certainly it was not overloaded with musicals (only 2 out of 11) in a theater which seems dominated by their presence because the hits keep on running year after year. It included one example of wholly "serious" theater. There was good patronage for every shading of comedy from *Don't Drink the Water* to *The Homecoming*. Movie and TV sales and other special circumstances accounted for the success of some of the 11 hits, rather than regular attendance, but there are no rules about how a show should make money (and it should be remembered, in passing, that many a non-hit turns into a mighty profitable item in stock, repertory and other future production). In my opinion, the 1966-67 hit list proves, for the nth time, that there are no boundaries around the tastes of the New York theatergoer. The vision of the producer is sometimes limited; likewise that of the critic; but seldom that of the audience. I am tempted to go further and say that *any* show of unusual merit will *always* find some kind of a hearing on Broadway if it gets past producers and critics—I am tempted to say it because it is almost true. The exceptions are so conspicuous that they become causes celebres like last year's *The Lion in Winter*. Whatever the faults of the 1966-67 Broadway season, it included no such case of artistic neglect; it did not fail a single one of its worthier playscripts.

New on Broadway

In the theater, as elsewhere on this planet, immediate popularity is not the only measure of success. The ultimate sign of theater success (we insist) is selection as a Best Play in this volume. Such selection is made with the script itself as the primary consideration, for the reason that the script is the very spirit of the theater. It is not only the quintessence of the theater's present, it is also most of what endures into the future. The Best Plays are the best scripts, giving as little weight as is humanly possible to comparative production values, and with no regard whatever for a play's type—musical, comedy or (sigh!) drama—for its origin on or off Broadway, or for its popularity at the box office or lack of same.

The Best Plays of 1966-67 were the following, listed in the order in which they opened (an asterisk * with the performance number signifies the play was still running on June 1, 1967):

A Delicate Balance
(hit; 132 perfs.)
The Killing of Sister George
(hit; 205 perfs.)
The Apple Tree
(260* perfs.)
America Hurrah
(off B'way; 234* perfs.)
Cabaret
(221* perfs.)

The Homecoming
(168* perfs.)
Black Comedy
(125* perfs.)
You're a Good Man Charlie Brown
(off B'way; 98* perfs.)
Hamp
(off B'way; 101* perfs.)
You Know I Can't Hear You, etc.
(hit; 92* perfs.)

Last season, eight of the Best Plays were in some respect a debut for their authors. This season there was one Broadway debut (Frank Marcus's *Sister George*), one Broadway "first" (the book of *The Apple Tree*), one off-Broadway debut (John Wilson's *Hamp*) and one professional theater debut (Clark Gesner's *Charlie Brown*). As has been noted previously, three are musicals; three are from off Broadway; three are already hits; three are probable.

The Apple Tree ($9.90) ran strongly all through the season. Certainly it was a triumph for Jerry Bock and Sheldon Harnick, a song writing team which came up not only with the best and wittiest score of the season but also, I believe, with its best book in their first try at writing a Broadway libretto themselves. *The Apple Tree* was not one musical, but three musicals, each a one-acter. The three playlets are based on two stories—Mark Twain's *The Diary of Adam and Eve* and Frank R. Stockton's *The Lady or the Tiger?* —and Jules Feiffer's cartoon story *Passionella*. The book material is of course second-hand; but here, at least, the stories consumed were of a different literary species, not cannibalized from the theater itself. They were adapted as though they were born in a trunk, however; and the three separate ideas— one of Adam and Eve discovering the world, one of clawing jealousy and one of Hollywood glamor—looked as though they were born triplets. One whispers *(Diary)* and one shouts *(Passionella);* one was plain *(Diary)* and one was fancy *(Lady or Tiger).* But all three were played in much the same key of comic irony, with the last two items reshaped, somewhat, to match the Twain manner.

A high level of ironic comment was maintained in Mike Nichols' staging and in the caustic asides of a narrator (Larry Blyden). Between them, they never for a moment let any of the characters get away with an affectation, or the actors with a meaningless gesture. Barbara Harris's performance as Eve, Princess Barbára and Ella-Passionella was the season's musical best. The way she sang about wanting to be a mo-o-o-vie star may make it impossible for anyone to speak that word again without using at least three o's. Alan Alda, too, came on strong as Adam, Sanjar and Flip opposite Miss Harris's three poses. *The Apple Tree's* ups were high on the scale of musical entertainment. It was the season's best as a whole and in many of its parts—for example, Tony Walton's costumes, which solved the problem of clothing Adam and

Eve by using some brown, nondescript fabric; then broke out into camp with Passionella's golden gown (see sketches in photo section).

On the 1966-67 Broadway musical stage as a whole, there were 10 new shows mounted. Of these, one died in tryout—*Chu Chem,* about a Jewish family taking up Chen Buddhism. Another, *Breakfast at Tiffany's,* based on the Truman Capote novel, folded in New York previews after a change of titles (from *Holly Golightly*), directors, (from Abe Burrows to Joseph Anthony) and adapters (from Burrows to Edward Albee) in the course of production.

Two of the 10 musicals were almost-hits at press time, as previously noted. Of the remainder, the one that fared worst (only 12 performances) was *A Joyful Noise,* a show in folk-song style, based on a novel about a modern minstrel driven out of a Tennessee town by the father of the girl he loves, then making it big as a pop music idol. The show had a lively contemporary sound in the score by Oscar Brand and Paul Nassau and a brash contemporary air about it, but it was panned brown by the New York critics. John Raitt, in the leading role of the wandering minstrel, replied with an outstanding exhibition of gallantry under fire. On the second night, with all the wounds still fresh, Raitt nevertheless came out fighting in a solid, swinging performance. His show not only went on; it came on strong. Raitt's courage and professionalism seemed all the more admirable in a season when, all too frequently, the theater news carried announcements of fatigue, defection and other sighful disengagements on the part of Broadway performers.

One of the musical no-hitters, *Walking Happy* was this season's *Half a Sixpence.* Its book based on *Hobson's Choice* had a British flavor in its tale of a humble shoemaker's apprentice who marries the boss's daughter. *Walking Happy* became a vehicle for Norman Wisdom, the British comedian, a runty wizard of song and dance who filled every scene with his presence. And the Danny Daniels dances, expressing various stages of the apprentices's breakout, were one of the highlights of the season. Another shortlived musical, *Sherry!* was an amiable canning of the Moss Hart-George S. Kaufman comedy *The Man Who Came to Dinner,* with Clive Revill in the Monty Woolley role—pleasant enough both comically and musically but dated in its satire of the Alexander Woollcott-Harpo Marx-Gertrude Lawrence era.

A pair of musicals bearing stars and still running at the end of the season was *Illya Darling* and *Hallelujah, Baby!* *Illya* musicalized the movie *Never on Sunday,* with the shapely Greek actress Melina Mercouri in her celebrated performance of a congenial Piraeus prostitute (the material suffered in transition from screen to stage, but not Miss Mercouri). In *Hallelujah,* Leslie Uggams turned on her charm and her full singing voice for the story of a Negro girl determined to get out of the kitchen (in 1910), making it in show business (in the 1920s and 1930s), becoming civil-rights conscious (in the 1940s to 1960s). The years go by as indicated, but the characters do not age in this Arthur Laurents book (nor do they really come to fruition as personalities, that's one of the problems with the show). Laurents' work was remarkable, though, as the season's only original musical libretto. He deserves

INGRID THULIN IN "OF LOVE REMEMBERED"

a special commendation and citation for keeping invention alive, for growing fresh material in a cannery year.

Turning to the so-called "serious" theater, drama had not disappeared entirely from Broadway in the season of 1966-67. But a home-grown attempt to tackle a pressing sociological problem onstage met with little success. David Westheimer's first Broadway play, *My Sweet Charlie,* was adapted from his own novel about a Negro lawyer (Louis Gossett) who has killed a man in a civil rights brawl, and a poor-white-trash girl (Bonnie Bedelia) who is pregnant and hopes to have her baby in secret. Both take refuge in an abandoned Gulf Coast summer cottage (one of the season's more effective designs, by Jo Mielziner). Their wary mutual mistrust at the beginning of the play works better in this script than their growing rapport and his final self-sacrifice to save her life. Another drama, *Of Love Remembered,* spanned two continents with its tale of a Scandinavian femme fatale migrating from Norway to Minnesota—but even with Ingrid Thulin in the lead it couldn't get its arms around the audience. *We Comrades Three* was an earnest effort by APA-Phoenix to present Walt Whitman and some of his works onstage, but even with Helen Hayes in the cast it lacked definition and force.

A most ambitious and highly respected effort of serious theater this season was Frank Gilroy's *That Summer—That Fall,* a transposition of the Phaedra tragedy to an Italian family in America today. Irene Pappas came over from Greece to play the darkly beautiful wife who develops a fatal passion for her husband's handsome young illegitimate son. Gilroy's dialogue was understated, almost coded; his characters flamed without losing their cool, if such a thing is possible—but perhaps it wasn't. It didn't work, but it was a worthy try in an admirable but generally unfelt example of serious drama (and here again, Mielziner's design was a standout).

Even in the form of thrillers, drama found hard going. Hugh Wheeler's adaptation of Shirley Jackson's novel *We Have Always Lived in the Castle,* about a teen-ager who has poisoned her family in a fit of rage, almost worked but not quite, though capably staged by Garson Kanin. A British thriller, *The Astrakhan Coat* by Pauline Macaulay, benefited from good performances by Brian Bedford (as an elegant young gang leader who steals and kills for kicks) and Roddy McDowall (as a numbskull waiter who is made the fall guy) under Donald McWhinnie's direction. But the play failed to stir up excitement, mostly because the victim was no match for his oppressor, and no object for strong sympathy.

With a scarcity of good new drama, the gray area between bright laughter and solemn agony became more eagerly explored, more populated with plays in the good-to-excellent class. This season, 12 new Broadway plays were billed in their programs as "comedies"; but I am not speaking only of them, or of black comedy, or camp, or other forms of cynical abrasion; nor does the expression "high comedy"—carrying as it does the comedy-of-manners image of a teacup slowly lowered to register severe shock—serve to encompass and include all this genre. I am speaking also of just-barely-comedy and perhaps-not-quite-comedy like this season's *The Homecoming* and *A Delicate Balance;* like last season's *Marat/Sade* and *Philadelphia, Here I Come!;* comedy that stings, that will do for serious drama until the drama snaps out of its doldrums; that will do perhaps *too* well because it offers the drama too much competition, like a too-competent understudy.

1966-67 brought a solid block of these gray plays from foreign sources (the foreign-play average tends to be high in comparison with American scripts, of course, because they are pre-tested on their home grounds; likewise the performances of foreign casts, who may have played together a year or more and are competing for "bests" with American actors who may just be getting the feel of the parts at award time). An interesting British entry (classified by its own author as a "comedy") was *How's the World Treating You?* in which a born loser (James Bolam) fails in the army, courtship and marriage and finally attempts suicide. It was a promising playwriting debut for Roger Milner, who made his West End and Broadway debuts with these caustic comments about how we fall victim to the whims and ambitions of others. A less auspicious British debut was David Halliwell's with *Hail Scrawdyke!* about a young painter who organizes an outrageous revolt. This play made a noise in Dublin and London (but lasted only 20 performances there) under the title *Little Malcolm and His Struggle Against the Eunuchs.* At least we were spared that title on a Broadway marquee. Renamed, recast and restaged by Alan Arkin, it lasted only 8 performances.

A couple of foreign plays in the just-barely-comedy category which did *not* enjoy the benefit of long previous practise were Brian Friel's *The Loves of Cass McGuire* and Leo Lehman's *The East Wind.* Both scripts were having their world premieres on Broadway, the first produced by the David Merrick Arts Foundation and the second by Lincoln Center Repertory. In *Cass McGuire,* as in last season's *Philadelphia, Here I Come!,* Friel was writing rue-

IRENE PAPPAS IN "THAT SUMMER—THAT FALL"

fully of family conflict. His Cass McGuire is an adventuress (a swagger role for Ruth Gordon under Hilton Edwards' direction) who has spent and mis-spent a full life in America, all the while sending money home to help her family. Returning home to Ireland, she is a disturbing influence on her family and is pushed off into a home for the aged, supported by her own money saved through the years by a family who didn't want it, either. This "You can't go home again" theme also turned up as part of *The East Wind,* also in its world premiere, the first new work offered by the Repertory Company of Lincoln Center in its Vivian Beaumont Theater. This was a human comedy played out by two refugees from the same small European town, one yearning for home and the other yearning to explore the world, winding up as partners in a London delicatessen. The homesick one returns for a visit and finds himself a stranger; the other never quite finds a home anywhere else. Both *The Loves of Cass McGuire* and *The East Wind* achieved moments of intense sympathy within unsatisfactory dramatic structures. They were songs rather than stories of pity.

On this side of the Atlantic, the cartoonist-satirist Jules Feiffer wrote a play, and instinctively his hand moved like a ouija-board platen into designs of black comedy. Feiffer's *Little Murders* was about a family headed by a fretful father (Heywood Hale Broun in an aggressive phase) who is worried. His son is effete, his daughter is marrying a hulking odd-ball pacifist, and people are shooting at him through the windows. The city has him surrounded (in Ming Cho Lee's brooding set) and eventually he and his family will feel the need to shoot back. There are a few whiplash vignettes, like the arrival of a psychedelic minister to perform the wedding ceremony. On the whole, though, seeing *Little Murders* was a bit like reading cartoon captions with your hand over the drawings. You got the impression that something fascinating might be taking place, but you were never entirely clear just what it was or what it meant.

Dark, too, was much of the humorous comment in Saul Bellow's program of three one-act plays—*Out From Under, The Wen* and *Orange Souffle*—which came to Broadway under the portmanteau title *Under the Weather* after previous stagings in Glasgow, Spoleto and London. There was no mystery about Bellow's subjects, however, in his second less-than-successful attempt to break out into the commercial theater. The first play was broadly farcical, about a widower's ruses to put off re-marriage. The weather clouds up in the second playlet about a Nobel Prize winner obsessed with a wen he once saw on an intimate part of a childhood playmate's body. The third, most carefully developed and longest of the one-acters, described the friendship of an 87-year-old industrialist and a prostitute—for ten years he's been visiting her, but when she finally tries to establish a close personal relationship, she fails.

Except for the hit and near-hit described previously, box office prospects were dark at the lighter end of the comedy scale. George Abbott staged his 107th and 108th shows to little avail. They were the British import *Help Stamp Out Marriage!*, a sex comedy with two couples, one married and one not, milling around the same apartment; and *Agatha Sue, I love you*, co-produced by Abbott's daughter Judith, the Broadway playwriting debut of a former stagehand, Abe Einhorn, in a farce about two gamblers and a pretty folk singer living cozily in a hotel.

Then there were the two doctor comedies about young interns, one married (in Harry Cauley's *The Paisley Convertible*) with tangled in-law problems, and one not (in Norman Krasna's *Love in E-flat*) but jealously monitoring each other's apartments with listening devices. Both plays were set on New York's East Side. The most remarkable feature of either of them was Donald Oenslager's two-level set for *Love in E-flat* with its dizzyingly high upstairs apartment, along whose naked striding edge the actors gamboled with seeming nonchalance.

Finally, in the sly romance department, not even the presence of TV comedian Soupy Sales in the leading role could save *Come Live With Me* from swift extinction, with its tale of a writer bedeviled in his London apartment by too many women including his wife—the Broadway debut of its authors, Lee Minoff and Stanley Price. William F. Brown's *The Girl in the Freudian Slip*, about psychiatrists and their personal sex problems, came along in late May as the caboose of the 1966-67 season but lasted only three performances. Two shows made an appearance of only one performance each: Lee Thuna's *The Natural Look*, her first Broadway effort, about a husband, a working wife and the advertising business; and Lonnie Coleman's *A Warm Body*, about a knowing archeologist in the apartment of a skeptical lady newspaperman for a night of chit-chat and other divertissements. This was a bad year also for at least one unusual idea around which Michael Stewart wrote his *Those That Play the Clowns*, starring Alfred Drake, but lasting only 4 performances In this one, a group of strolling players are interrupted in their routine procedures when they are asked to put on a very special performance —by a prince named Hamlet at a castle called Elsinore.

Among the year's specialty shows was *A Hand Is on the Gate,* a collection of prose excerpts, poems and songs by Negro authors in various keys from warm affection to outraged protest, representing various phases of American life and history. The ninety-five separate excerpts spoken and sung by a cast of eight are fully listed under this play's entry in the "Plays Produced on Broadway" section of this volume.

Among other specialties were two Yiddish musicals—*Let's Sing Yiddish* and *Sing Israel Sing*—and a revue facetiously entitled *Hello, Solly!* with occasional dialogue in English but with many Yiddish punch lines on the jokes. Foreign specialties included the Republic of Guinea's *Les Ballets Africains; The Apparition Theater of Prague,* a scenic illusion of free-floating, moving objects carried by actors dressed in black and "invisible" against a black background; *Gilbert Becaud on Broadway* with a program of his own songs; and the Stockholm Theater of Fantasy marionette version of *The Threepenny Opera.* These marionettes were not puppets or any other kind of dolls. They were living actors in costumes and masks who moved about the stage but nevertheless did not speak or sing their own lines. The voices were done by other performers.

Such were the new shows—19 American plays, 8 musicals, 10 foreign plays in English, 5 foreign-language productions and 4 specialties—which made up the 1966-67 Broadway season of 46 new works. Could anyone call it a great year without blushing? Sure—Joel Grey could call it a great year, and so could many other individuals who put their best foot forward. It was the art itself that was out of step, not they, not the playwrights, actors, directors, designers, composers, lyricists, choreographers and others who did their best work in 1966-67. No overall statistic, no sweeping critical evaluation can take away from their achievement.

It remains only to list the very, very bests (as I saw them), and in this connection I would like to comment on the category of "supporting" actors and actresses. It is hard to make clear distinctions between "leading" or "starring" and "supporting" roles. Sometimes they are blurred by technicalities. For example: was Joel Grey still a "supporting" player in *Cabaret,* after he was given star billing? Was Vivien Merchant in a "leading" role in *The Homecoming* because she was the only woman in the cast, and/or because her role was a pivotal element of the plot?

In an attempt to do away with technicalities and arbitrary classifications, I would like to divide the acting into "primary" and "secondary" roles—a primary role being one which carries a play; one which might cause a star to inspire a revival just to appear in that role. All others, however important, are classed as secondary in this consideration of the year's bests. Here they are:

Plays

BEST PLAY: *The Homecoming* by Harold Pinter
ACTOR IN A PRIMARY ROLE: Hume Cronyn as Tobias in *A Delicate Balance*
ACTRESS IN A PRIMARY ROLE: Beryl Reid as June Buckridge in *The Killing of Sister George*
ACTOR IN A SECONDARY ROLE: Robert Salvio as Hump in *Hump*
ACTRESS IN A SECONDARY ROLE: Vivien Merchant as Ruth in *The Homecoming*
DIRECTOR: Alan Schneider for *A Delicate Balance* and *You Know I Can't Hear You When the Water's Running*
SCENERY: Jo Mielziner for *My Sweet Charlie* and *That Summer—That Fall*
COSTUMES: James Hart Stearns for *The Alchemist, Galileo* and *Yerma*

Musicals

BEST MUSICAL: *The Apple Tree,* by Jerry Bock and Sheldon Harnick
ACTOR IN A PRIMARY ROLE: Robert Preston as Michael in *I Do! I Do!*
ACTRESS IN A PRIMARY ROLE: Barbara Harris as Eve, Princess Barbára and Ella-Passionella in *The Apple Tree*
ACTOR IN A SECONDARY ROLE: Joel Grey as Master of Ceremonies in *Cabaret*
ACTRESS IN A SECONDARY ROLE: Reva Rose as Lucy in *You're a Good Man Charlie Brown*
DIRECTOR: Mike Nichols for *The Apple Tree*
SCENERY: Boris Aronson for *Cabaret*
COSTUMES: Tony Walton for *The Apple Tree*
CHOREOGRAPHY: Danny Daniels for *Annie Get Your Gun* and *Walking Happy*
SCORE: Jerry Bock and Sheldon Harnick for *The Apple Tree*

32—Revivals, Count 'Em—32

There was a time when the Broadway theatergoer could complain that he was being cheated of his heritage. The older glories evaporated from the scene under the heat of the new productions massed in the playhouses. Well, in the 1966-67 season we enjoyed as liberal a helping of our theater heritage as anyone could readily absorb. Within what we term the "Broadway" theater, which includes the two Centers, City and Lincoln, there were *five* repertory companies operating at one time or another, plus many one-shot revivals, bringing the total of musicals and plays revived to 32—surely a modern Broadway record.

This year found our local repertory group, the Repertory Company of Lincoln Center, still a long way from finding itself as an ensemble, or acquiring a definite character within the New York theater's scheme of things. Its existence had yet to be justified; it seemed to be waiting for a match to start a fire. Its work was good but not exceptionally stimulating. It marked time with a production of Ben Jonson's *The Alchemist,* attractively designed and dressed by James Hart Stearns and featuring yet another Michael O'Sullivan villain. It pondered dark pools of marital hatred and frustration among Spanish peasants in Lorca's *Yerma.* It came up with a new play—the aforementioned *The East Wind* by Leo Lehman—its first under the Jules Irving-Herbert Blau management; unfortunately for the many American authors aching to be heard, a foreign script, and an indifferent one.

Lincoln Center's revival of Bertolt Brecht's *Galileo* was its best work to date. It provided a sturdy framework for a bravura performance by Anthony Quayle of the 17th century astronomer (and for another fine display of design and stagecraft in Lincoln Center's versatile play-machine). *Galileo* is a drama of ideas (science vs. faith, the individual vs. the establishment, reason vs. rote). It neglects the emotional, personal side of Galileo's confrontation with Rome, in which he denied his own astronomical findings in order to escape the Inquisitor's instruments of torture. The play does not much care how Galileo felt when faced with this terror (the incident doesn't take place on the stage). It is interested in him principally as a symbol of truth. This *Galileo* was an adequate repertory item which nevertheless set no fires in this viewing.

No, Lincoln Center didn't find itself this year; in fact it lost a little bit of itself when Herbert Blau resigned as co-director on January 13, leaving Jules Irving to carry on alone. The Blau-Irving operation has functioned not so much as a true repertory company building a backlog of productions as it goes along, with its own company of actors learning a repertory of roles; rather, the Blau-Irving regime has offered what amounts to a series of one-shots with special players imported for the leads: O'Sullivan for *The Alchemist,* Gloria Foster for *Yerma,* Quayle for *Galileo.* The Lincoln Center management has renewed Irving's contract as sole director, so it must have full confidence in his future plans. It is certainly to be hoped that such plans will include the production of American scripts, both new and old. If American playwrights have not written and/or are not writing scripts worthy of production by an American company, then we had better give up the whole New York permanent repertory experiment right now and give the Vivian Beaumont Theater to the Cafe La Mama.

The Association of Producing Artists Repertory Company (APA-Phoenix) put one toe into Broadway last season with the revival of *You Can't Take It With You,* found conditions warm and hospitable, and so spent this entire season there. Both in the choice and performance of its plays, APA demonstrated the kind of taste, ensemble skill and occasional individual flair that should be at first expected and finally demanded of any repertory company seeking to make lasting friends. The APA company has stayed together and played together since its formation in 1960 by its director, Ellis Rabb. Mr. Rabb, his wife Rosemary Harris, Keene Curtis (who presents an actor's-eye-view of APA in an article in "The Season Around the United States" section of this volume) and Dee Victor have been with APA from the very beginning; Donald Moffat and Nicholas Martin joined in the fall of 1960; Clayton Corzatte in 1961. Others came to stay over the years and seasons as APA began making its mark in the United States, in Europe, in New York—at first off Broadway under the auspices of the Phoenix Theater and now on Broadway as a combined APA-Phoenix venture.

There's no question of stars drifting in and out of this company for special performances. When Helen Hayes joined for the 1966-67 season she came to play, and play she did—as Mrs. Candour in *The School for Scandal* (the hit of this repertory), Signora Frola in *Right You Are* and Mother in *We Comrades Three* (the New York debut of an adaptation of Walt Whitman that didn't quite work on the stage). The company also offered *The Wild Duck*, their vest-pocket spectacular *War and Peace* and their American comedy hit *You Can't Take It With You*. They had the skill and assurance of a group that has been performing these works long enough so that now they could give lessons—*Right You Are* since 1960 and *The School for Scandal* since 1961. Miss Hayes has signed up for another season and, yes, Broadway is lucky, the APA-Phoenix will be back next season.

One of the three other repertory visitors was ANTA's touring troupe, the National Repertory Theater offering Molière, Noel Coward and Eugene O'Neill *(A Touch of the Poet)* for two weeks of a less-than-distinguished New York appearance. England's D'Oyly Carte made an American tour this year, stopping at Broadway with its productions of Gilbert & Sullivan operettas. The fifth of the season's repertory groups was also from England: the Bristol Old Vic with skillful revivals of *Measure for Measure, Hamlet* and *Romeo and Juliet*.

Side by side with the repertory there were 13 one-at-a-time revivals during the season. Peter Weiss's *Marat/Sade* appeared in a re-staging, a curious example of the revival of a play only one season after its first run. There was an all-star Broadway presentation of the George S. Kaufman-Edna Ferber comedy *Dinner at Eight* reflecting the new interest in Kaufman's work inspired by last season's APA production. This season we had Kaufman's *The Butter and Egg Man* off Broadway, the musical *Sherry!* (based on Kaufman and Hart's *The Man Who Came to Dinner*) as well as *Dinner at Eight*. The latter is about dinner guests preparing to gather for a party given by a hostess who will let nothing stop her from going through with it, not even the suicide of one of the prospective guests, nor her husband's imminent ruin and physical collapse. Performed by Walter Pidgeon, Ruth Ford, Arlene Francis, June Havoc, Darren McGavin and others of similar acting calibre, the Kaufman-Ferber work had a touch of old-fashioned Broadway glamor about it. It's curious to note, too, that these guests were dining at 8 p.m. and yet expected to be taken to a musical where they would arrive only a *little* late for the first-act curtain. Ah, 1932!

The success in recent seasons of *You Can't Take It With You* and *The Glass Menagerie* in Broadway revivals adds force to the argument that New York can supply an audience for the American straight-play library, but not a theater. This season the City Center moved to fill the need. In addition to its regular program of musical revivals, it offered three expertly produced plays: Clifford Odets' *The Country Girl*, with Jennifer Jones, Rip Torn and

Joseph Anthony; Maxwell Anderson's *Elizabeth, the Queen,* with Anne Meacham; and Tennessee Williams' *The Rose Tattoo,* with Maureen Stapleton in the role she created in the original Broadway production. The latter was the biggest success of the three and moved to the Billy Rose Theater to continue its run following the City Center engagement. Here's how the purpose of this new City Center enterprise was explained in a program note:

> The City Center Drama Company, under the direction of Jean Dalrymple, has made long-range plans for theater seasons which will be devoted exclusively to the works of leading American playwrights.
>
> In opera, ballet and musicals the City Center has continued to emphasize American productions. Now this policy has been extended to the drama. Although our cultural roots in the performing arts stem from Europe, there has been a high level of literate and significant plays by American writers since World War I, which should be seen again and viewed in their proper perspective.
>
> Miss Dalrymple will make her choices from the plays of Eugene O'Neill, Robert E. Sherwood, Sidney Howard, Maxwell Anderson, Elmer Rice, Lillian Hellman, Sidney Kingsley, Clifford Odets, George S. Kaufman and Moss Hart, Tennessee Williams, William Inge, Paddy Chayefsky, Howard Lindsay and Russel Crouse, Arthur Miller and others. In taking this step we believe that the City Center again is filling an important role on the American scene.
>
> These drama seasons will be sponsored and assisted by George T. Delacorte, the John Golden Fund, Rita Allen and the Dorothy and Lewis S. Rosenstiel Foundation.
>
> MORTON BAUM
> Chairman, Board of Directors

In addition, of course, Miss Dalrymple and her City Center Light Opera Company kept reminding us of the American musical theater's glorious heritage with a season full of revivals: *Guys and Dolls, Carousel, Finian's Rainbow, The Sound of Music* and *Wonderful Town.* New York City Opera did Gian Carlo Menotti's *The Consul* again. And the New York State Theater of Lincoln Center, under Richard Rodgers' guidance, offered a handsome summer production of *Show Boat* and brought *Annie Get Your Gun*—with Ethel Merman—to Broadway in the fall after its spring debut at Lincoln Center and summer tour. This *Annie* was revived so effectively, with so much valuable new material, that it received one vote as the best musical of 1966-67 in the New York Drama Critics Circle voting (from Henry Hewes).

This was a disproportionately large revival year, to be sure, with 32 productions alongside only 19 new American plays and 8 new musicals on Broadway. But it served many purposes, some better than they have been served in recent seasons. The past paraded by in works by Shakespeare, Sheridan, Pirandello, Ibsen, Jonson, Lorca, Molière. And, for a change, in the American parade with Rodgers & Hammerstein, with Loesser and Kern there were some straight play writers, too: Kaufman, Odets and Maxwell Anderson, O'Neill and Tennessee Williams.

Off Broadway

The 1966-67 season off Broadway amounted to 69 productions of record, as compared with 66 last year and 75 two years ago. These broke down into 29 plays, 8 musicals, 8 foreign plays in English and 5 revues (a total of 50 new works as compared with 40 a season ago), plus 10 revivals, three foreign-language productions and 6 specialty shows. By "off Broadway" we mean a production which employs a professional Equity cast, invites criticism at a designated opening and has a regular schedule of public performances. (We exclude productions for special segments of the audience, like Yiddish-language plays, or productions staged only for children, and we make allowances in the case of visiting troupes.) Even with technical definitions, however, production levels vary so widely off Broadway that you can't tell anything very much from over-all statistics until you look closer to see what *kind* of shows these were. For example, the revival of the musical *By Jupiter* was a fully mounted production; in another off-Broadway offering the "Equity cast" consisted of two people, one of whom was the producer's wife.

The number that really counts off Broadway is the number of exciting shows, and in this respect 1966-67 tested very high. Three off-Broadway productions made the Best Plays list and others were close. In recent seasons, off Broadway seemed to be relying on revivals of its "standards"—Albee, Beckett, Pinter, Ionesco, Genet—or to be merely toying with sensation. 1966-67 was the season it went back to work.

Jean-Claude van Itallie's *America Hurrah* was a program of one-acters which made the Best Plays easily in this one-act year, and which was Kerr's and Nadel's first-choice play in the Critics Voting. Its author subtitled it "Three Views of the U.S.A.", but indeed it was only one view expressed three ways: the view that certain elements of American life in which some take great pride may cause others the most acute anguish; a view expressed with powerful irony and most inventive stage style. The first playlet, *Interview,* was a fugue of four job-seekers and four interviewers which expands out of the employment agency to include many of the painful brush-offs of city life (including city death). The second, *TV,* showed three viewers at a rating organization slowly swallowed by the TV programs they are paid to watch, like rabbits going down the throat of a boa constrictor.

The third, *Motel,* was a masque of three dolls: a motel-keeper house-proud of her establishment, and two guests who rent a room only to wreck it. The three "characters" were larger-than-life papier-mache figures worn by three actors. Their grotesque appearance with huge grinning, nodding heads was matched by grotesque behavior in which the guest dolls, a man and a woman, make love and scrawl obsenities—raw, subway-men's-room obscenities—in large, easy-to-read letters and drawings on the motel room walls before they pull these same walls down. They do this as a lark, grinning and nodding,

The 1966-67 Season off Broadway

PLAYS (29)

Undercover Man
Until the Monkey Comes
Command Performance
Match-Play and A Party for Divorce
A Whitman Portrait
Who's Got His Own
This Here Nice Place
AMERICA HURRAH
Three Hand Reel
Javelin
Viet Rock
The Infantry
The Ox Cart
Night of the Dunce
The Displaced Person
Kicking the Castle Down
The Deer Park
Sometime Jam Today
The Rimers of Eldritch
MacBird!
Fortune and Men's Eyes
Not a Way of Life
Chocolates
Gorilla Queen
Harold and Sondra
The Party on Greenwich Avenue
The Death of the Well-Loved Boy
To Bury a Cousin
A Time for the Gentle People

MUSICALS (8)

My Wife and I
Autumn's Here!
Man With a Load of Mischief
The Penny Friend
The Golden Screw
Shoemakers' Holiday
YOU'RE A GOOD MAN CHARLIE BROWN
Follies Burlesque '67

REVUES (5)

Below the Belt (cabaret)
Mixed Doubles (cabaret)
Skits-oh-Frantics!
An Evening with the Times Square Two
Absolutely Free

REVIVALS (10)

American Savoyards
The Mikado
Trial by Jury and H.M.S. Pinafore
Mardi Gras!
The Long Christmas Dinner, Queens of France and The Happy Journey
The Butter and Egg Man
Antigone
By Jupiter
Dynamite Tonite
To Clothe the Naked
The Coach with the Six Insides

FOREIGN PLAYS IN ENGLISH (8)

The Kitchen
Eh?
When Did You Last See My Mother?
The Wicked Cooks
HAMP
Carricknabauna
The Experiment
Drums in the Night

FOREIGN-LANGUAGE PRODUCTIONS (3)

Les Femmes Savantes
Die Brücke
Les Fourberies de Scapin

SPECIALTIES (6)

The Israeli Mime Theater
Blitzstein!
Baird Marionettes: *People Is the Thing That the World Is Fullest Of*
Davy Jones' Locker
The Harold Arlen Songbook
The Diary of a Madman

Categorized above are all the plays listed in the "Plays Produced Off Broadway" section of this volume.
Plays listed in CAPITAL LETTERS have been designated Best Plays of 1966-67.
Plays listed in *italics* were still running on June 1, 1967.

while the motel-keeper doll continues to advertise her place in glowing terms, and lights flash and a siren shrieks warning. Thus the American motel *ideos*— the concept of mass-produced convenience—contains the seeds of its own destruction. Creature comforts appeal not to the best within us, but to the bestial *creature,* van Itallie seemed to be saying as he lifted a corner of the veil for a glimpse of what the creature looks like. All three of these highly imaginative one-acters were to some extent contraptions, and their directors— Joseph Chaikin for *Interview* and Jacques Levy for *TV* and *Motel*—deserve extra credit for a smooth and potent production.

Clark Gesner's musical adaptation of the Charles M. Schulz comic strip "Peanuts" was a risky undertaking—"Peanuts" addicts might have lynched the perpetrator of a merely adequate rendition. But Gesner won his dare handsomely with *You're a Good Man Charlie Brown,* a wonderful show which is easily a Best Play and received several citations in the Critics Circle voting for best musical.

You're a Good Man Charlie Brown was a series of episodes in which Charlie Brown (the born loser), Snoopy (a canine superstar), Lucy (the shrew), Schroeder (the Beethoven fancier), Linus (hugging his blanket) and Patty (blonde and bubbleheaded) cope with baseball, the Red Baron, Lucy's tantrums, kite flying, a book report on "Peter Rabbit," a glee club rehearsal and each other. These are matters familiar to readers of the comic strip, and in the show they varied in length just as printed episodes do. Some were fully developed scenes (like a Sunday page), others were one-panel blackout skits. All were in perfect key with our image of six-year-old Charlie Brown and his gang. Reva Rose made her face do exactly what Lucy's does on paper, with voice to match, in an uncanny performance. Bill Hinnant wore no special costume or makeup, but while he was on stage he became a dog—the very dog Snoopy who yearns to be a jungle animal but is chained emotionally to his supper dish. Joseph Hardy's direction should be credited for evoking these and the other excellent performances, and Alan Kimmel's set was simple and versatile: a white background to pick up changes of colored lights on a stage dressed with geometrical shapes, capable of being arranged to represent anything from a schoolroom to a doghouse. I don't see how *You're a Good Man Charlie Brown* could have been better; why, it was almost as good as "Peanuts."

John Wilson's *Hamp* is a third off-Broadway script in this year's list of Best Plays. *Hamp* completed the British sweep of the New York theater season; it was by far the best drama. It reached way back for its subject to the Battle of Passchendaele in 1917, in the story of a British soldier who is tried, convicted and shot for desertion. In the eye of this somewhat familiar moral storm Wilson has found the heart of the conflict between group and individual needs and responsibilities. It raised every question: should Hamp have been a soldier in the first place? Once a soldier, should he have deserted under any circumstance? Having deserted, should he receive mercy? Or should he be sacrificed to the needs of the group? *Hamp* dramatized both sides of these questions, and it also faced the physical horror of execution; the blood penalty that must be paid; the ritualism of this form of killing which helps to impersonalize it for everyone except the victim. The performances were painfully convincing, notably those of Michael Lipton as the defense attorney and Robert Salvio as poor left-footed Hamp. This lean, unremitting, rending and tearing drama was seen in New York previously in a movie version entitled *King and Country,* in the season of 1963. It has lost no force in the passage of time. Its symbols may be borrowed from World War I, but its moral dilemmas remain to trouble us this very hour.

There were many other 1966-67 achievements in the smaller playhouses. The first act of *Fortune and Men's Eyes* was high up among the season's best work, in an account of homosexuality in prison among four cellmates: a dyed-blond "queen" (played by Bill Moor with no quirks barred), his idealistic young victim, a tough gangster-type who likes to protest that he is no "pansy" and a farm boy (Terry Kiser) who becomes one of them through experience with each. John Herbert, the author, once spent six months in a Canadian prison, and his subject matter, appalling though it may have been, was expressed in such a way that it did not directly exploit sensationalism. It was a commendable effort, unfortunately vitiated in the second act in shouting and loss of clear purpose or resolution.

Another off-Broadway standout wasn't sensational *enough:* the much discussed *MacBird!* Its author, Barbara Garson, used Shakespearean parody as a magnifying glass to lampoon the political scene, with MacBird (an LBJ-like figure in the drawling person of actor Stacy Keach, a ragged eagle) instigating the murder of his chief "John Ken O'Dunc," a murder which is then avenged by John's brother "Robert Ken O'Dunc" (played by William Devane to resemble, uncannily, the junior Senator from New York). The savagery of *MacBird's* opening attack was exciting, so far outside any consideration of truth or taste that it could not possibly give offense. But the joke became tangled in its own tricks and parallelisms, both Shakespearean and Johnsonian, losing its momentum and even its spirit of total irreverence.

Also promising a good deal more than it was able to perform was Norman Mailer's *The Deer Park.* Its avowed intention (in the opening scene) was to reveal sin in high Hollywood places (or maybe, the script suggested, the setting was not really Hollywood but some sort of dream-world limbo). Most of its sinning (happily heterosexual) was pretty mild stuff compared with the off-Broadway average.

One of the year's most attractive off-Broadway productions was the musical *Man With a Load of Mischief,* an innocent, almost operetta-like concept. Set in an inn in 19th century England, this one sang a troubadour's tale of a nobleman in a secret romantic escapade with the Prince's mistress. But the lady, it turns out, prefers the nobleman's valet (played by Reid Shelton in excellent voice). John Clifton's music for *Man With a Load of Mischief,* like Ben Tarver's book, had great charm. Other musical highlights of the off-Broadway year were *Autumn's Here!* (a musicalization of the Ichabod Crane story) and *Dynamite Tonite,* a comic opera with emphasis on acting by Arnold Weinstein and William Bolcom, previously produced off Broadway by the Actors Studio in 1964, reworked in a staging at Yale Drama School, and, in this production, attracting one citation in the Critics Circle voting (from Martin Gottfried). Out of the past came a successful revival of the Richard Rodgers-Lorenz Hart musical *By Jupiter*, plus *Blitzstein!* (a program of his works) and *The Harold Arlen Songbook*. The outstanding revue attractions were both cabaret and both by Rod Warren: *Below the Belt* and *Mixed Doubles*.

Causes pleaded stridently off Broadway included the anti-war protest, most conspicuously expressed in *Viet Rock*, which made ironic comment and presented adverse examples in a persuader-device of theatrical production. Also polemic was the war-is-hell message of *The Infantry*. The little man's fight for identity against the establishment was celebrated in the British comedy *Eh?* about an employee who deliberately pushes all the wrong buttons in a dye works. One of the season's more sensational experiments was *Gorilla Queen*, a comedy which explored the subject (and some of the possibilities) of sex deviation in the story of a female ape-goddess and the men who worship her.

In a somewhat nobler spirit of experimentation, the Messrs. Edward Albee, Clinton Wilder and Richard Barr—under the banners of Theater 1967 and Albarwild Theater Arts Inc., and with the assistance of a Rockefeller grant—put on a series of five American play programs. Two were revivals: an evening of Thornton Wilder one-acters and a production of George S. Kaufman's *The Butter and Egg Man*. Three were new works: Frank Gagliano's *The Night of the Dunce*, Lanford Wilson's *The Rimers of Eldritch* and Grandin Conover's *The Party on Greenwich Avenue*. All were received with respect (particularly *Rimers*, about narrow-mindedness and injustice in a small town) but none achieved ranking among the season's leaders in popularity. The same was true of three major European importations: Arnold Wesker's *The Kitchen*, Günter Grass's *The Wicked Cooks* and Christopher Hampton's *When Did You Last See My Mother?*

Dorothy Raedler's perennially competent American Savoyards were present off Broadway in 1966-67, complementing Broadway's visiting D'Oyly Carte. Bil and Cora Baird's marionette theater was a standout entertainment. Off Broadway also had its Brecht (the American premiere of *Drums in the Night*), its revival success (Jean Erdman's return with her *The Coach With the Six Insides*, inspired by *Finnegans Wake*) and even its Joel Grey performance—in Guy Lombardo's Jones Beach musical *Mardi Gras!*

Such parallels might embarrass devotees of off Broadway who balk at any suggestion that it might become a "little Broadway," a scale model of the commercial theater. Nevertheless, in 1966-67 off Broadway has rivaled Broadway with the quality of its work, and, in some ways, beaten it. Off Broadway came up with two *new* authors on the Best Play list (Gesner and Wilson; van Itallie was previously produced in the program *6 from La Mama*), whereas Broadway found only one. Off Broadway came up with a musical, *You're a Good Man Charlie Brown*, to equal anything uptown, at least in imagination; it came up with a black, contemporaneous, inventive *America Hurrah;* it came up with the only "serious" play in serious contention for this year's bests. Broadway not only couldn't find a drama the equal of *Hamp;* it couldn't even assimilate *Hamp* itself, apparently, because this London script could have been acquired for production uptown just as well as downtown. So, in 1966-67, off Broadway has done what Broadway could or would not do, and has done it extremely well—and surely that is one of off-Broadway's highest aims, achieved.

Off Off Broadway

Side-by-side with the elegant formalities of the Broadway theater; mixed in with the Equity casts and regular performance schedules off-Broadway; tucked away out of sight of most critics in converted churches, libraries, cafes—and sometimes even in theaters—is a form of tributary stage activity which for want of a better name has come to be known as "off off Broadway." The name is unsatisfactory, if only for the reason that it is a put-down; the use of the word "off" twice tends to assign it a level below other theater activity. The truth is, its fermentation rate is the highest in town, and sometimes it raises its head above Broadway itself: for example, two-thirds of *America Hurrah* surfaced from off off Broadway. And as a Best Play of 1966-67, *America Hurrah* can be said to have o'ercrowed no fewer than 67 Broadway and 66 off-Broadway productions.

In many ways off off Broadway is a way of life both for the artists who create it and the critics and reporters who cover it. It is surveyed here in two guest reports. The first by R.J. Schroeder, editor of off-off-Broadway anthologies, takes up the highlights of the disorganized year in the scattered production centers. The second, by George Freedley, consultant curator of the Theater Collection of the New York Public Library, views a form of off-off-Broadway Establishment (if it can be called that) in his report on one of its oldest and firmest experimental organizations: the Equity (formerly Equity Library) Theater.

Here are the two special reports:

THE 1966-67 OFF-OFF-BROADWAY SEASON IN NEW YORK

By R. J. Schroeder

Editor, *The New Underground Theater* (Bantam Books)

The outstanding characteristic of the 1966-67 off-off-Broadway season in New York was the amazing number of productions. Never, I am sure, have so many new playwrights in one city had so many opportunities to stage so many new plays. There was a time when the Judson Poets' Theater and the Caffe Cino were almost the only platforms for the untried but aspirant dramatist. By this season, at least six coffee houses, nearly a dozen churches and perhaps another couple of dozen assorted lofts, nooks and crannies had become theaters-of-sorts for playwrights-of-sorts. Over 300 new plays were produced this season in non-commercial, non-Equity undertakings—new plays written by some fifty or sixty commercially unknown playwrights.

Consequently, the mean average of quality went down. That is, while this abundance of experimental activity gave large numbers of would-be writers, directors and actors heretofore unavailable opportunities for theater experience, and may be assumed to bode well for the theater's future, increased quantity has not meant increased quality so far as today's product is concerned. The off-off-Broadway theatergoer in 1966-67 suffered a great many dismal evenings for each of his evenings of discovery and delight. But of the relatively few nights of discovery and delight, I have much that it is a pleasure to report.

For example, there evolved this season a troupe who announced that they had gone beyond the theater of the absurd to the positively ridiculous, and that they were proud to so identify themselves. The new Playhouse of the Ridiculous's director was John Vaccaro, and its authors were Ron Tavel and Charles Ludlem. *Lady Godiva* was their first offering, and it was followed by *Indira Gandhi's Daring Device, The Life of Juanita Castro, Kitchenette, Screen-Test* and *Big Hotel*. If you will imagine the most absurd of the absurdist plays starring and directed by Olsen and Johnson of *Hellzapoppin'* in a specially-adapted performance for an American Legion stag party, you'll grasp some of the flavor of the Vaccaro-directed productions of the Playhouse of the Ridiculous. These productions were the life of the off-off-Broadway season, but the troupe appears to be out of business at this writing.

The reason for its demise was the only international incident any segment of the American theater can claim to have provoked this season. *Indira Gandhi's Daring Device* was a campy and thoroughly disrespectful satire which took India's population-feeding problems as the point of departure for some trenchant and Aristophanean comments upon the human condition. The Indian government learned of the production and complained to our State Department. There followed a series of ludicrous events culminating in steps taken by officials of the City of New York which made it impossible for the troupe to continue to perform.

If the life of the 1966-67 off-off-Broadway party was the Playhouse of the Ridiculous, the greatest charm was provided by two musicals which occupied the stage of the Caffe Cino for most of the summer of 1966. *Dames at Sea, or Golddiggers Afloat* was a spoof of the Ruby Keeler-Dick Powell movies, and of the Busby Berkeley choreography. Perfectly cast and directed by Robert Dahdah, the postage-stamp musical was an absolute delight. Its book and lyrics were by George Haimsohn and Robert Miller, and its music by James Wise. The same George Haimsohn did the book and lyrics for the follow-up *Psychedelic Follies,* this time with music by John Amon. A satire on the Village drug scene, it, too, was a delightful show.

The coffee-houses, as always, presented numerous authors, but this year the successes were equally those of the playing ensembles and directors. Just as the performing and directing of the Cino musicals were tremendously important to their success, the acting of the La Mama troupe, directed by Tom

O'Horgan, came to play an increasing role in the La Mama Experimental Theater Club's better-received productions. This troupe has been taking American coffee-house plays to European audiences in recent seasons, and its exposure to European acting and directing has resulted in increasing experimentation with the ensemble expressionistic techniques of Peter Brook of England, the Berliner Ensemble of East Germany and Grotowski's Polish Lab Theater. The La Mama troupe's ensemble-oriented productions of Rochelle Owens' *Futz,* Paul Foster's *Tom Paine* and of revivals of several coffee-house "standards" from previous seasons excited considerable critical interest.

Perhaps the crowning achievement of the always-provocative Judson Poets' Theater at Judson Church in the Village was Al Carmines' opera *Song of Songs,* an opera-with-dance version of the Biblical passage. Carmines has been moving toward this sort of beautifully imaginative expression for several seasons and has achieved in *Song of Songs* what may be off off Broadway's most esthetically fulfilled offering to date. The choreography of Aileen Passloff and Remy Charlip was inseparably important with Carmines' own direction to the success of the presentation.

The other most active church-based group, the Genesis Theater at St. Marks-in-the-Bowery, had an existentialist season. Murray Mednick, with his *Sand, Mark of Zorro* and *Guidelines,* displayed the kind of manic monologuery that Sam Shepard had pioneered in previous seasons, but with a contrary nihilistic bitterness that was typical of the Genesis offerings. Grant Duay's *Fruit Salad* was, like *Mark of Zorro,* a mixed-media presentation, with some action on stage and some on screen, and perhaps outdid even Mednick in intentionally repulsive nihilism.

Three groups offered seasons of plays in a more traditional vein. The Second Story Players and a troupe called Thresholds continued their presentations of a series of rarely-performed plays, and continued to grow in perception and ensemble achievement. A new group, Gene Feist's Roundabout Theater, performed Strindberg, Maeterlinck, Molière and *Pins and Needles* in a season-long repertory, and in so doing made a creditable contribution to the off-off-Broadway season.

At the Greenwich Mews, a praiseworthy series of Spanish and Puerto Rican theater took place. Andres Castro's robust production of *Yerma* easily outpointed that at Lincoln Center, and his version of the classic *La Celestina* was theater at its best. A modern Puerto Rican drama, Rene Marques' *The Ox Cart,* was also given an effective rendition by the same producing group. There are indications that these productions for New York's large Spanish-speaking population will lead to an expanded repertory next season.

I believe that just as much of quality emerged from the 1966-67 off-off-Broadway season as had come out of any previous season. But the quantity of shows produced off off Broadway has risen to such a degree that it has become increasingly important to exercise knowledgeable selectivity if one is to avoid a less-than-entrancing evening in the coffee-houses, the churches and the lofts.

EQUITY (LIBRARY) THEATER

By George Freedley

Consultant curator of the Theater Collection of The New York Public Library

In the spring of 1943 Sam Jaffe and I were lunching at the Algonquin and discussing the plight of the young actor. The six theaters that did experimental plays had been declared "off limits" to members of the Actors Equity Association. Sam said that if playhouses could be found, Equity's council would grant permission for productions in which young performers might test their talents. I immediately spoke of the little theaters built by the WPA in the basements and top floors of branches of The New York Public Library in the height of the Great Depression. The stages were simple and the floors ungraded, but Sam liked the idea and presented it to the Equity council. They asked that a committee be formed to investigate. It included the late Dudley Digges, Aline MacMahon, Alexander Clark, the late Phillip Loeb, Sam Jaffe and myself.

On an extremely hot day in June the committee set forth to inspect the auditoria. We used the West Side IRT and after visiting two or three branch libraries the committee members began to disappear one by one. We were reduced to just Aline, Sam and me when we reached the Fort Washington Branch at 179th St., having started at the Hudson Park Branch at 77 Seventh Ave. South. We found that simple reversible screens could be used and that most scenic changes could be accomplished with lighting. We discouraged painting of the screens, since the choice of color of one director might not suit the next. In addition to guests of Equity Library Theater, the neighborhood readers of the branch libraries would be invited to attend the productions without cost. There was no money allotted to the productions. The actors and directors took up a collection among themselves to pay the then $2 custodial fee and for the mimeographed programs. With the usual difficulties of mounting productions, frictions arose between the theatrical companies and their host. People *would* smoke in the auditoria—and, despite a rule to the contrary, the casts would occasionally hold parties in them.

The first bill presented on February 20, 1943 at the Hudson Park Branch consisted of John Millington Synge's *Edge of the Glen* and Noel Coward's *Fumed Oak*. In the latter play was Louisa Horton, later to triumph in the Boston and West Coast companies of *The Voice of the Turtle*. The audience received both plays warmly, but it was difficult for the actors to get agents and producers to come and see them in anything as unfamiliar as a library. The neighbors took mightily to the project, and seats were divided on a percentage basis between the libraries and the actors.

Five more productions were mounted before the heat of summer, which came early in 1943, forced the season in the un-air-conditioned auditoria to close.

Realizing that some funds had to be found to continue and that an Executive Secretary for ELT would have to be hired, Sam Jaffe and I made an appeal to the producer, John Golden, who had just established a foundation with assets of $100,000. Walter Greaza, the assistant executive secretary of Equity, went with us. John grinned at us as we approached hat in hand and saw no reason why he shouldn't give us a grant—but not as much as we had hoped for. At least we would be able to pay our executive secretary $45 a week. The first person to fill the post was Anne Girlette (Mrs. George Voskovec). In the following season 27 separate bills were offered, and the number was later to reach the impressive sum of 56 in a single season.

When Anne Girlette left us Teresa Hayden took over and was invaluable to the committee and ELT. Her good looks, amiable disposition and compulsive drive to do good for others carried us through many dark times. Getting permission to do plays without royalty was always a struggle. Equity's council ruled that only plays previously produced in New York and recognized classics could be staged. No new plays could be performed. ELT focused its attention on actors, directors, stage managers. Although most of the aspiring performers seen at ELT were relatively unknown to the general public, occasionally a more celebrated star would appear with the company. I managed to persuade Louis Kronenberger of *P.M.* and Lewis Nichols of the *Times* to take the long subway ride to the Fort Washington Branch on 179th St. to view a production. They were not too impressed, but were kindly in their critiques.

One production that was particularly successful was John Reich's staging of Goethe's *Faust Part I,* which Richard Watts Jr. of the *Post* praised in his review. *Anatol,* the series of one-acters by Schnitzler, was staged by Mady Christians and costumed by Lucinda Ballard. It was a very successful production and established Carmen Matthews as a comedy actress. Previously she had been typed only as a player of tragedy. In addition to Mr. Watts, Willella Waldorf and Vernon Rice were generous in their coverage of ELT productions.

In the fall of 1947, Gov. Thomas E. Dewey made state aid available to rehabilitate the libraries which in the war years had fallen into rack and ruin. Unfortunately, the libraries chosen for the state government program took three out of the four of the most used auditoria out of circulation. It was then decided to find other places closer to Broadway in which to present ELT productions. At this point I resigned as co-chairman and Sam Jaffe served as chairman alone, still leaning heavily on John Golden for advice and finances. When it was finally accepted that ELT was strictly an Equity project Golden withdrew and ELT was sponsored by Equity alone except for small gifts from interested friends.

In November 1966 Equity Theater (as it had become known) returned to the Library by presenting a series of experimental "Informal" productions in the Auditorium of the Library and Museum of Performing Arts at Lincoln Center. It has now come around full circle and is again a part-time project of the Library.

In addition to nine 1966-67 revivals presented at Equity Theater's perma-

nent home, The Master Theater, 103d St. and Riverside Drive, it presented
nine "Informal" productions at the Library. The Informals were under the
capable supervision of Moreen Moran.

The Informals presented this season have another element of fulfillment
besides marking ELT's return to the Library. The idea for them was developed
by Davey Marlin-Jones, former managing director, and Frederick C. Williams,
the present one, three years ago after seeing a production of Paul Shyre's
adaptation of John Dos Passos' *Inside USA*. Mr. Shyre appeared in the leading role of Whistler in the Informal Production entitled *The Gentle Art of
Making Enemies*.

In 1959 ELT reorganized to the present managing director system. Filling
that post since then have been Lyle Dye Jr., Patrick McGinnis, Davey Marlin-
Jones, Shepard Traube, and Mr. Williams. Dorothy Sands is the current president of Equity Theater's board.

A complete listing of 1966-67 Equity Theater revivals and Informals, together with the programs of other off-off-Broadway "establishment" groups
such as American Place, ANTA Matinees and the Blackfriars' Guild, appears
at the end of the "Plays Produced Off Broadway" section of this volume.

Offstage

Behind the scenes, 1966-67 was a year in which the New York theater
watched newspaper after newspaper go under; a year in which small steps were
taken toward the solution of some of the theater's more pressing institutional
problems; a year in which Richard Maney, theater press agent, historian,
raconteur and all-purpose eminence—who inspired the character Owen
O'Malley in the hit comedy *Twentieth Century* by Ben Hecht and Charles
MacArthur—retired with the following characteristic comment to his many
Broadway friends and associates:

> Of course I'm going to miss the theater.
> But at 75 plus, I thought it the better part of valor to go AWOL while
> I still had a few of my marbles. If I've learned anything in the theater
> it is that everyone stays on too long: playwrights, musical saw players,
> acrobats and David Merrick.
> I'm one of the theater's fortunates. Rarely have I been idle for more
> than a week or two in the last 40 years. Few stars can make such a
> boast.
> I raise my glass to you, Sirs!
>
> RICHARD MANEY

While Maney was calling it quits, some of his best friends on the papers
were finding themselves quite unwillingly disfranchised. As the season of
1965-66 ended, an ominous silence had fallen upon many New York presses.
The *Herald Tribune*, *Journal-American* and *World-Telegram & Sun* had
ceased publication April 24, 1966 pending the working-out of union agree-

ments re their proposed merger. Historically, as their names indicate, they were the accumulation of seven newspapers. To the theater, as of the end of the 1965-66 season, they represented three drama critics—Walter Kerr, John McClain and Norman Nadel—and three outlets for theater news, advertising and reporting.

The original plan to come back with three papers proved unworkable. On August 15, 1966, the *Herald Tribune* folded, not with a bang—not in the full agony of a final edition with all editorial flags flying—but silently, in suspended publication, with a whimper about the generic problems that face *all* newspapers: union intractability, rising costs, competition from other media. The *Trib's* value to the New York theater was inestimable and, as far as can be seen now, irreplaceable. It was the Other Voice. In past decades it offered Broadway producers a versatile instrument (as opposed to the *Times's* inflexible format) for bringing their shows to the attention of the public. Under the direction of the late Arthur H. Folwell and those who succeeded him, its New York theater coverage spoke through the typewriters of such as Percy Hammond, Richard Watts Jr., Howard Barnes, Lucius Beebe, Bert McCord, William K. Zinsser, Walter Kerr, Stuart West Little, Judith Crist and myself. The *Trib* was no easy publicity mark, but it was steadily *interested* in the theater, and, with its passing, Broadway lost a loyal friend.

No sooner had the *Trib* folded, when a reshuffling took place at the *Times*. Stanley Kauffmann departed and Walter Kerr, Supercritic, took over drama criticism's superjob on a *Times* which now did not even have the *Trib's* competing voice to reckon with. The shopping-service aspects of this position; its almost absolute life-and-death power over individual productions, could be only an enormous embarrassment to a critic determined to fulfill his highest artistic function. An attempt to mitigate this monstrous economic side-effect of *Times* criticism is planned for next season. The job is to be split in two. Instead of writing both daily and Sunday, Walter Kerr will write Sunday criticisms only, and Clive Barnes—the *Times's* present dance critic—will do the daily reviews. In the meantime, the policy instituted by Stanley Kauffmann of attending shows at their last preview performance, to give him more time to consider his review, was abandoned. As one *Times* insider expressed it, "We're through with all of *that*."

The newly-merged afternoon-and-Sunday paper finally began publishing in the fall, with Norman Nadel as its drama critic. The late John McClain, who had been highly and warmly regarded in drama criticism (at the *Journal-American*) as a spokesman for the man-about-town, ceased writing play reviews. The new *World Journal Tribune* lasted almost as long as the drama season, then folded on May 5, 1967. With its demise the last traces of seven daily New York newspapers—the *World, Telegram, Sun, Journal, American, Herald* and *Tribune*—simply vanished. Broadway, which had begun the year with six daily newspaper critics (Kauffmann, Kerr, Nadel, McClain, John Chapman of the *Daily News* and Richard Watts Jr. of the *Post*) ended it with three (Kerr, Chapman and Watts).

The advantage to the theater of having as many critics as possible (if you are going to have any at all) seems obvious. The clamor is louder when you have a hit, and wide divergence of opinion sometimes acts as a net when you don't. The influence of the TV critics has been growing steadily, and it is possible that in coming seasons they will perform some of the function of differing opinion once performed by their newspaper colleagues. An infallible sign of the T V commentators' growing stature was the banning of one of them by David Merrick from his opening-night press list. The target of Merrick's opprobrium was the exceedingly perspicacious and entertaining Edward Newman of WNBC-TV. Otherwise, for the most part, Merrick took it easy on the critics this season—mellowed, no doubt, by the success of his shows including Carol Channing's *Hello, Dolly!* tour which lasted 1,272 performances from November 18, 1963 through June 11, 1967, grossing a total of $17,015,018 including $310,000 for one 10-performance week in Oklahoma City.

Three other people got mad enough at critics this season to make a public outcry. In London John Osborne, nettled at the reviews of his play *A Bond Honored,* telegraphed this fair warning to his tormentors: "The gentleman's agreement to ignore puny theater critics as bourgeois conventions that keeps you pinned in your soft seats is a thing that I fall in with no longer. After 10 years it is now war." Edward Padula, who wrote, produced and directed the harshly criticized *A Joyful Noise* on Broadway, voiced his displeasure: "I feel that the public accepted unanimously what I had to offer. But I find that the critics did not sense what I thought we had to give." Jules Feiffer, smarting from the attack on his first Broadway effort, *Little Murders,* damned the whole commercial theater system.

As an organization, the critics altered the requirements for membership in their New York Drama Critics Circle. Membership in the Circle had been limited to critics of non-trade New York City publications. The rules were relaxed to admit George Oppenheimer of *Newsday,* Harold Clurman of *The Nation,* Hobe Morrison of *Variety* and William Raidy of the Newhouse Papers.

In other theater organizations, the Dramatists Guild moved to new headquarters in the former Shubert penthouse atop the Sardi Building at 234 West 44th Street. The League of New York Theaters elected Richard Barr president to succeed Harold Prince at the expiration of his term. Prince is credited with major influence in starting the new special bus service between the theater district and the East Side for evening performances. The Legitimate Theater Exploratory Commission, of which John F. Wharton was consultant-director, studied the possibility of using a computer to improve the circumstances of ticket sales. The Committee also took under advisement many suggestions in all phases of theater activity, including one by a Brooklyn taxi driver to stagger evening curtain times: musicals at 8:15, straight plays at 8:45.

George Freedley's retirement as curator of the Theater Collection of the New York Public Library, for reasons of health, became effective May 1. Freedley will continue the association as consultant curator. The Society of Stage Directors and Choreographers negotiated a basic agreement off Broadway: $500 for directors and $375 for choreographers, with royalties on a sliding scale. Actors Equity doesn't negotiate a new contract with the League of

New York Theaters until 1968, but there was some agitation this season over the employment of foreign actors in New York shows. Forty-eight actors picketed Lincoln Center in February, protesting the casting of Margaret Leighton in a revival of *The Little Foxes* and Anthony Quayle as *Galileo*. Equity members held a meeting on this foreign-actor issue and voted 491 to 2 to demand that permission to hire a foreign (except Canadian) actor on Broadway or at Lincoln Center be required from a majority of Equity's own 72-member council. Meanwhile, British actors offered the information that in the past seven years British Equity's record of employment of American actors in England has been "Yes" 524 times and "No" only 18 times. Another piece of Actors Equity business last season was the grading of resident theaters into four categories with weekly minimums for actors as of the close of the 1966-67 season. Examples are as follows: class A ($135) Minnesota Theater Company and the Stratfords; class B ($120) the Arena Stage in Washington; class C ($100) Center Stage, Baltimore, and Charles Playhouse, Boston; and class D ($90) Alley Theater, Houston, and Theater Company of Boston, Inc.

Also in the matter of organizations, the Metropolitan Opera Company opened triumphantly in its new theater in the Lincoln Center complex. The acoustics were fine and the theater handsome and comfortable, so the move was a success—except for a few gremlins like unexpectedly large deficits and a couple of dressing rooms walled up by mistake during construction and discovered by accident. The installation is so large and complex that a Pentagon-like security system of passes controls the coming and goings of Metropolitan Opera personnel, and few have Q clearance for the entire building. Meanwhile, highly-publicized efforts to save the old Met failed—it was scavenged by souvenir hunters and then reduced to a heap of rubble.

The Ziegfeld Theater, too, disappeared from its familiar chunk in the Sixth Avenue skyline, razed because it was economically inefficient to operate. And at season's end it was disclosed that interests including the Rockefellers and Time Inc. had bought The Playhouse; ominously, tenants of offices in the theater's building were notified that the space would no longer be available.

On a more positive note, the New York Shakespeare Festival's new year-round headquarters on Lafayette Street were progressing toward completion; their new, 300-seat Anspacher Theater was expected to be ready for the autumn opening of a series of seven new American playscripts. The headquarters will include a second 300-seat theater and other facilities.

An effort to organize a cross-country audience for Broadway musicals aimed for 300,000 subscribers in 25 cities. Called the American Musical Theater Club, it failed to get anywhere near that many supporters and found it necessary to close the four musical productions it had sent out: *Funny Girl, On a Clear Day You Can See Forever, Where's Charley?* and *The Desert Song.*

The 1966-67 season saw the publication, under the auspices of the Twentieth Century Fund, of another major study on the performing arts in America, prepared by William J. Baumol and William G. Bowen, both of Princeton, and entitled *Performing Arts—The Economic Dilemma.* Its particular hang-up was what it called the "income gap" between rising costs and relatively static

earnings in live performances (there's no way, the report reasoned, significantly to reduce the cost-per-performance of a live string quartet by automation, which is the answer to rising costs in other areas of activity). The total
performing-arts income gap has now reached $25,000,000 (the report esti-
mates) and is growing—except on Broadway which, the study admitted, is
holding its own economically. The study also offered a per-seat estimate of the
Broadway situation. Musicals (average cost per performance, $6,509) cost
$4.90 a seat to put on; straight plays (averaging $3,077) cost $2.83. The
cost of the theater tickets, the report added, is only 53 per cent of the cost
of a Broadway evening.

The $25 million income gap must be closed, of course, by subsidy. In 1966-
67, grants from the government's National Foundation on the Arts were scattered thinly over the theater around the United States to help put on a production there or encourage a new playwright here. There were several examples of private subsidy, too, like the Ford Foundation's $1,400,000 added to
its previously-matched $1,000,000 for the new Alley Theater building in
Houston. Direct subsidy of Broadway has not been in the cards, however,
because there is not yet an "income gap" in the commercial theater, however
wide the good-play gap may seem. But a step in the direction of eventual assistance of the commercial theater in especially sensitive situations was taken
by the creation of a so-called Theater Development Fund. This Fund is to be
established with the help of a small grant from the Twentieth Century Fund to
defray the cost of incorporation. It is to be supported by pledged contributions from the various branches of the theater, from private non-profit organizations, from individuals, even (possibly) from government arts funds. The
Theater Development Fund would use this money (a hoped-for $250,000 the
first year) to subsidize worthwhile Broadway plays; to help shows which have
already helped themselves through the risk and agony of Broadway production but which might need a little extra time to build up some momentum at
the box office; shows of conspicuous quality like *The Subject Was Roses, Poor
Bitos* or last year's *The Lion in Winter.* The Fund could be used to purchase
tickets for distribution to students and other special audiences, to give a play
a longer viewing or encourage it to hold on until it begins to attract audiences
on its own.

So—let the curtain come down on the 1966-67 season, but no need to hurry
out into the night to avoid a final comment, as though there were nothing encouraging to be said. 1966-67 wasn't especially creative, no, but it brought
over *The Homecoming* and mounted *America Hurrah.* How was it in the
matter of involvement? Well, it didn't spill its controversies out into the
streets, but it tried to get involved with *The Investigation, Viet Rock, Mac-
Bird!* even with *Little Murders.* No, it wasn't an exceptionally productive year
—quite the contrary. But it did produce 32 revivals for special-interest audiences and (we blush to repeat) it grossed an all-time high of more than $55
million.

In any fall-off of production it is mostly flops that are missing. When a thaw sets in, *this* iceberg melts much faster on the bottom than it does on the top. To illustrate, four decades ago the prolific season of 1926-27 brought forth 188 new plays and 49 new musicals as compared with 66 and 16 (off Broadway included) in 1966-67. Here were the Best Plays of that 1926-27 season, as chosen by Burns Mantle: *Broadway, Saturday's Children, Chicago, The Constant Wife* (foreign), *The Play's the Thing* (foreign), *The Road to Rome, The Silver Cord, The Cradle Song* (foreign), *Daisy Mayme* and *In Abraham's Bosom.*

Well, was the Best Plays list of that 237-show season three times as interesting as the one in this volume's 82-show season? Certainly not. Forty years ago they had Robert E. Sherwood, Sidney Howard, Maxwell Anderson, George Kelly; Somerset Maugham and Ferenc Molnar. Today we have Edward Albee, Jerry Bock and Sheldon Harnick, *Robert* Anderson; Harold Pinter and Peter Shaffer. They had George Abbott on that 1926-27 Best Play list, true, but we may have him on ours *next* year. The top of our iceberg is solid and bright—so what if the bottom is much smaller?

In sum, 1966-67 may have been a defensive year in the New York theater— but the position was well defended. The theater functioned; it *was;* it introduced new work worthy of its past traditions, and it held the door wide open for a future that seems, now more than ever, illimitable.

THE SEASON AROUND THE UNITED STATES

with

A DIRECTORY OF PROFESSIONAL REGIONAL THEATER

Compiled by the American National Theater and Academy

INTRODUCTION

By Norman Nadel

Drama critic, New York *World Journal Tribune*

IN THE ANNALS of regional theater, 1966-67 appears likely to be remembered as the season of crisis. From Seattle to Philadelphia, bills mounted up, budgets collapsed, business managers resigned, directors were fired, boards split over the theater of the absurd vs. an operating economy of the absurd, the public went along with some experimental theater but shunned campy Shakespeare, and most of the happy money doled out by foundations somehow got used up faster than anybody had expected.

Significantly, the season of crisis followed by only a year or two the time of highest expectations. But the various crises have proved to be more real—and in the long run, more beneficial—than all the previous optimism. Regional theater was due for a moment of truth, and '66-67 seems to have provided it. What remains is for the various enterprises across the land to assess what has been happening, in their own back yards as well as elsewhere, and turn the experience to future advantage.

Of course, the year just passed wasn't the only critical year; regionally or in New York, every year is one of crisis—this seems to be the normal state of the living theater. Nevertheless, problems reached a peak, for reasons which date back into the 19th century in some cases, and in others are strictly of the present. Government support of the arts—theater included—first was proposed to the Congress as long ago as the 1880's, even if nothing concrete was accomplished until we had a president as culturally enlightened as the late John F. Kennedy. Regional theater didn't have to wait that long. In fact, there were professional resident theater companies in cities all across the United States years ago, before motion pictures gradually wooed away the audiences. So the current movement is less a birth than a rebirth, despite the fact that the old acting companies were quite different in operation and—hopefully—standards of play selection than those of today. Now we are somewhat less influenced by box office prospects and more by intrinsic dramatic worth, though to claim this as more than a vague tendency would imply a Utopia which does not as yet exist.

Anyway, and in defense of the old stock companies, they had to earn their keep, which meant one eye on the box office at all times. Only within the past few years have substantial monies been available from government as well as private sources to enable regional and educational theater to expand and develop as they have. The suddenness of this affluence has more than a little to do with the upheavals of the past year. Not every theater management—business as well as artistic—was prepared to dispense these funds as prudently as good sense dictated. And somehow everybody expected that the income in one year would be equaled or exceeded in the next. The same naivete led them to believe that audiences would either hold the same or increase in equal proportion. Neither assumption proved reliable.

They might have benefitted from a careful study of the period when municipal symphony orchestras were starting to spring up across the land—this about fifteen to thirty years ago; some of us still bear the scars of that noble (and ultimately triumphant) battle. The first year or so of a new orchestra often would look quite encouraging—big civic drive, a proclamation from the mayor, editorials in the newspapers, and so forth. Society would turn out, give some money—not enough, but some—and the audience would nearly fill the hall. But this relatively happy time almost inevitably was followed by a decline, when some citizens decided they weren't that enthusiastic about good music, the venture proved less newsworthy, and the gifts fell off. That period had to be endured, while a devoted, loyal nucleus was being built in the community—a nucleus which eventually was to become large and strong enough to support an enduring music tradition.

Regional theater is just about at that in-between point now. Some projects will fail, and a few have, but for the majority the forward course will continue to be onward and upward, if erratically. Company managements have realized they made mistaken estimates about income, expense, popular support or audience taste. Several are learning that you don't inculcate a total theater culture overnight. And all are discovering that no single rule determines what is good repertory. There is no question that the nucleus of popular as well as official support has been formed in a number of cities, providing a security for the future which is better than endowment money in the long run.

Another reason why this current need for realistic reappraisal occurred was the unduly optimistic predictions which accompanied the start of the regional theater movement less than ten and more like three or four years ago. Only that recently, some critics were predicting the death of the commercial theater (they would say "Broadway," contemptuously) and the rise of regional theater as the salvation of the American stage. These, however, were mostly academic observers, taking their myopic view of the drama in America from their study window overlooking the campus, or New York-based magazine critics who never venture beyond the shores of Manhattan. Actually, only a few critics really move around to look at theater across the country. Howard Taubman of the New York *Times* is one, Henry Hewes of *Saturday Review* is another, and I believe I can count myself a third. Martin Gottfried of *Women's Wear Daily* visited a number of outlying theaters this past season on a grant, but he was very impatient with anything less than his concept of perfection, and he did not seem to understand the complex and subtle problems which dictate a slow growth rather than sudden blooming. Those of us who have worked in the field (I was a drama critic in Columbus, Ohio, for a number of years) know how deliberate the pace of cultural growth can be— and how rewarding it is, in the long run, to be at least a little bit patient.

The truth is that the New York theater—commercial, educational, experimental and in all its other facets—probably will continue to be the most resourceful in America for many years, if not indefinitely, and that regional theater will not displace it but already is augmenting it. Nevertheless, ill-informed predictions led directors, actors, managers and boards of directors to assume they were "in like Flynn," and that merely by working hard and with a God-given sense of purpose they would succeed. It has taken until now for them to realize how difficult their job is.

Also, some of the companies which made news in one way or another have proved to be less worthy, in solid achievement, than others whose operation was quieter and less spectacular. A case in point is the Cleveland Play House, which happens to be the oldest (over half a century) professional repertory theater in the United States. *Best Plays* in the past hasn't even included a report on that city by a Cleveland critic and didn't bother to list the Play House at all when it referred to a half-dozen professional regional theaters in 1960, though the volume has an essay on Houston, which accomplishes far less, theatrically, despite the fine vigor of its Alley Theater.

The Cleveland Play House operates three theaters, has a children's program, tries new and worthy plays and serves its community better than almost any other regional theater in the United States. Most important, instead of being content with this situation, the Play House board is restless. Currently it is searching for new ways to broaden the cultural horizon, new ideas to envigorate their theater and new daring in the selection and staging of plays. In a talk with some of the Play House board I proposed that they commission a play each year, or offer an annual prize for a new play, with a guaranteed production, and the ideas were enthusiastically received.

One main issue in the past year—or years—of crisis has been artistic standards. Directors *tend* to be experimental; theater governing bodies *tend* to be cautious. Too much of the time, communication between them breaks down, and then you have the sort of upheaval which was occurred twice in two years in Pittsburgh, for example. Without going into the issues, charges and countercharges on both sides (an observer would be out of his mind to try), it must be admitted that the talented William Ball, director of the American Conservatory Theater which did part of a season in Pittsburgh, isn't the world's smoothest diplomat. And the clever young John Hancock, who followed him this past season, isn't as seasoned a director as he hopefully will become. On the other side, the board of the Pittsburgh Playhouse was bullheaded at times, as well as inconsistent. Financial pledges made at the start of the season did not match the money which actually came forth, which is why the Playhouse had its financial crisis last November and early December. It survived the fiscal storm, but lost Richard Hoover, its managing director for the past twenty years, and jettisoned young Hancock.

On the other hand, these upheavals frequently were followed by new and encouraging beginnings. Stuart Vaughan, after parting company with the Seattle Repertory Theater, found a home with the brand new Repertory Theater, New Orleans, an enterprise which is receiving warm and enthusiastic support from the community, and which includes such remarkably talented young artists as costume designer Gordon Micunis in its company. Right from the start, New Orleans has implemented a school program, touring its troupe through Jefferson and Orleans Parishes' public and parochial schools, that already has allowed 38,000 youngsters to discover the stage. This program and one in Providence, R. I., are jointly financed by the National Endowment for the Arts and the U. S. Office of Education.

If statistics give you reassurance, there are figures to show that regional theater is gaining—number of operations (38 in 36 cities in 1966-67, compared with 33 in 30 cities last season), total audience, sums expended and earned, and number of productions (more than 275). Statistics, however, can be less meaningful than the more subtle and less easily measured indices of acceptance. Talking with directors, you realize that there is a gradually increasing enlightenment, curiosity and sense of adventure in audiences—in communities where, only a short time ago, there weren't stage audiences at all. Nothing has been more encouraging this season than this evidence of acceptance for dramas and comedies unconventional in structure, acting style, language or subject matter. People have been known to sit still for plays so candid that they would have started an outraged exodus as little as ten years ago. Moral standards have not relaxed, but audiences have accepted the fact that exposure to a straightforward play does not necessarily constitute a moral hazard. They can like or thoroughly dislike a play, without becoming indignant at the director or at the theater for putting it on.

Audiences are not becoming sheep; on the contrary, as their theater experience grows, so does their assurance and orientation as critics. Where once they'd say they didn't like a play, now they're more inclined to point out exactly why, or what should be done to make it better.

Generally, whenever one problem has been solved in a community theater, another pops up to take its place, but the pros are less apt to go into panic at each successive setback. I recall a chat with one theater managing director. With the placidity of a man inured to hardship, he casually stated: "We had a staff of twenty-two last year, counting the pickets from the stagehands' union."

The following accounts from individual cities provide the specifics of the 1966-67 season across the nation, the sometimes abrupt changes of personnel and policy, and the tabulation of plays and playwrights represented on each stage. Taken collectively, they also represent more actors, directors, designers and other theater craftsmen professionally employed and getting invaluable experience than could possibly be the case without regional theater, or with less of it. All this points back to one inescapable truth: that no segment of American theater can exist by itself. As regional theater gains in artistic stature, so does the New York theater, and educational theater, and amateur theater, because the interchange of talent among them is an inevitable and natural process. Despite the upheavals, the reversals and the bitter re-examinations of this past year, regional theater has continued to mature. The prospect ahead might be no less stormy, but thanks to all regional theater has been through, it can be more clearly seen, and more sanely weathered.

AMERICAN PLAYWRIGHTS THEATER:

more than 50 productions coast to coast

By Robert Anderson

Playwright and teacher, author of the APT choice play *The Days Between* and of the 1966-67 Best Play *You Know I Can't Hear You When the Water's Running.*

THE AMERICAN Playwrights Theater, the brainchild of playwrights Jerome Lawrence and Robert E. Lee, was incorporated in 1964. The idea of the project is to make available to college and community theaters new and hitherto unproduced plays by "established" playwrights, and to provide these same playwrights with a new and stimulating and profitable field for production.

The idea is eagerly supported by the American National Theater and Academy, the American Educational Theater Association, and Ohio State University, where APT has its offices, with David H. Ayers as executive director.

The organization was designed to meet two problems which have previously thwarted similar attempts along this line. First, college and community theaters have been reluctant, by and large, to do new plays, since most often the new plays offered were by unknown playwrights, and audiences have proved less than eager to come to see new plays by new playwrights. (I am glad to say this situation is gradually changing.) Second, at the same time, "established" playwrights, who work two or more years on a play and depend on the returns for a living, were reluctant to let their new plays be done by just a few college or community theaters, which might take the newness off the plays and at the same time not provide any real financial return.

APT has made an effort to solve both these problems. It offers new plays by known playwrights whose reputations might be expected to create some audience interest. And by offering a playwright the possibility of over 180 productions across the country, it can hold out the hope for some kind of national impact for his work—as well as good financial returns. Now that APT has a grant from the National Council on the Arts, the possible returns are more than doubled.

The method of procedure is as follows: APT asks for plays from "established" playwrights. (The term "established" is, of course, ridiculous, since no playwright is ever secure enough to consider himself "established," but nobody has come up with a more acceptable word.) The submitted play is read by an advisory committee, made up of the non-playwright members of the APT board from college and community theaters. They advise the writer and the other members of the board whether or not they feel a particular play would arouse the enthusiasm of enough subscribers to make its submission worth while. (A play must be accepted by at least twenty-five theaters to be "activated"). If this committee feels that the play is likely to get more than twenty-five acceptances, it submits the play to the full committee. If there is more or less general agreement, the play is then sent to the more than 180 member theaters. When twenty-five have agreed to produce the play, the play is "activated." At this point, the writer receives $10,000.00 from the National Council on the Arts. In addition, each theater deciding to do the play pays a minimum royalty of $200.00 as an advance against possibly larger royalties based on standard percentages. The National Council on the Arts will also match the royalties from APT theaters up to the amount of $15,000.00.

Now the playwright, with the advice of the board of APT, chooses from among whatever theaters may offer to present the first or "pilot" production of his play. He goes to the chosen theater and works with the director and cast very much as he would work during rehearsals of a play on Broadway. After the "pilot" production, which is usually in the spring or summer, the playwright makes whatever changes he wants in his script, and the subsequent productions are based on that revised script. He can then sit back and just read the dozens of reviews which come in over the year, or he is most welcome to attend any or all the productions, to confer, re-write, suggest, encourage, applaud, despair, or whatever he feels like doing. The APT subscribers have the exclusive rights to do the play in the United States for one year. After that, all rights revert to the playwright.

My play, *The Days Between,* was the first play to be "activated." It was accepted by fifty theaters for the 1965-66 season. The previous season, too few subscribers elected to produce the plays submitted by the board, and they were not activated.

My play had been under option to both Leland Hayward and Alfred de Liagre. The problems of casting had been overwhelming and discouraging (as usual). There is no need to detail the various "almosts" and succeeding changes of mind or schedule which finally left me feeling frustrated and disheartened.

At the annual board meeting of APT, it appeared that we had no play for the coming season, and we felt that if we failed to get off the ground for two seasons running, the future of APT might well be in doubt. For various reasons I felt that my play was inappropriate for college and community theater production, but the board felt otherwise, and we submitted the play to the subscribers.

I am sure that some of the fifty theaters which accepted the play for production did so more out of enthusiasm for the APT project than for my play. They, too, were eager to get the project off the ground, and if my play left something to be desired, still it would at least be serviceable, and better things might follow. I am grateful to all the theaters for their sporting cooperation.

The "pilot" production of my play took place at Paul Baker's Theater Center in Dallas in May, 1965. For me it was an exciting and heartening event. I worked with Baker and the cast for two weeks, getting the script and the production the way we wanted it. The opening received extensive local and national attention. The Dallas audience responded vigorously and made our opening a theatrical "event—and APT was launched. In the succeeding year I was in touch with many of the theaters which did the play, and I attended twelve productions, sometimes arriving just in time for the opening, other times coming for a few days or a week of rehearsals.

Naturally, the critical reactions to the play varied widely. But the important point is, no matter what the various critics and audiences felt about my play, they all seemed to welcome the excitement as well as the risk of producing a new play. Without exception, they all put their money on the line, to see the next season's play. In addition, the event brought to some theaters more local attention than they had ever had before.

How did I, as a kind of guinea pig playwright, feel about the project? Enthusiastic. I enjoyed the kind of picnic spirit which prevailed. "I'll bring the play, and you bring the cast." In New York, we rightly spend months and months trying the cast just the "right" person for each part. It is an exhausting and frustrating experience.

It is also a disturbing experience, of course, to go to some APT theaters and meet casts which you think at first glance are not quite right. But you quickly realize that your thinking is conditioned by casting in New York; you realize that the local audience comes together with the understanding of the degree of experience of the actors, and more often than not, the show "works."

Of course, some plays work better than others under these circumstances. In the case of my play, I think a number of 19-year-old college girls found it quite a challenge to act a 37-year-old wife whose marriage was going on the rocks for complex reasons. This same girl would have found no trouble in acting something like the Madwoman in *The Madwoman of Chaillot*. Certain of our contemporary "under-written" plays require actors of great personal dynamism and inventiveness to give the silences and pauses the meaning and overtones the playwright intended.

I hasten to add that I saw many effective and moving productions of my play in both the college and community theaters, and I was enriched by my contact with so many eager young people for whom theater was still total excitement and promise.

This last season, 1966-67, the APT play has been George Sklar's *And People All Around,* based on the murders of the civil rights workers in Mississippi. This has proved to be a dynamic choice for APT, even bringing out the Ku Klux Klan to try to break up one performance in Maryland. Critics across the country have called it "A stunning experience" (Boston Traveler), "A memorable evening about heroes of our time" (Bozeman, Montana), "Bold, bitter blistering play. Potentially a Broadway blockbuster" (Columbus Dispatch), "A play that commands respect" (Los Angeles Times).

George Sklar has written: "For a secluded novelist, I'm the travelingest playwright. I must say I'm enjoying it all. Whatever the future of this play, it's doing a job on audiences who see it. And I keep thanking my stars there's an APT to get it to these kids in the universities."

The play for the 1967-68 season will be *Ivory Tower* by Pulitzer Prize winner Jerome Weidman and James Yaffe. It is a fascinating trial play based on an incident in the life of a celebrated poet similar to Ezra Pound.

So APT is well on its way, thanks to a certain amount of giving and taking on all sides, and to the extraordinary talents of the executive director, David H. Ayers, whose industry and tact and dedication have kept the difficult project moving forward.

APT has now established itself as a producer with a wide range of theaters and audiences ready, willing and able to handle new plays. The problem, as with all producers, is how to find the plays. For many years, in one capacity or another, I have read a fair sampling of new plays from a wide range of playwrights. The truth is there are just not a great number of produceable plays written each year. And it is almost inevitable that a playwright, after spending a year or two writing a play, will head for Broadway production first.

Does this mean that APT is going to get only Broadway rejects? I think not. As APT becomes a theater in being with more and more audiences across the country, playwrights may very well aim certain plays specifically for this audience. And . . . a more important point . . . Broadway rejects are not necessarily poorer plays. Managers produce or do not produce plays for a wide variety of personal and public reasons. All playwrights have had plays turned down by a great number of producers only to have them saved from the waste paper basket at the last minute and subsequently turned into hits.

I was asked repeatedly if my play *The Days Between* was going on to Broadway. In one way, I suppose the greatest boon to APT would have been to have the play go on to Broadway and become a success. But I'm not sure. I don't think APT should be regarded as a Broadway try-out circuit. I think it must have enough self-confidence to make its own hits on its own terms, to be proud that it is presenting an effective evening which may be experienced only in an APT theater.

A few years ago I evolved a catch phrase: "I wish the playwright could make a living in the theater and not just a killing." On Broadway it is usually a hit or a flop. But APT offers the playwright (only one or two a year, to be sure) a chance to make this living, a chance to write occasionally for a more stable theater. His play *will* be done in twenty-five to 180 theaters. Opening night in Dallas will not effect opening night in Rochester. The play will have a life before hundreds of audiences, and not die ignominiously after an unfortunate premiere on Broadway.

So what is important is that a new theater of nationwide scope has been brought into being. It has managed to provide audiences for two plays of some value. It has provided new plays for audiences who have rarely experienced the excitement of seeing new plays, and it has given directors and actors the pleasure (and the pain) of working on material before patterns have been set by Broadway production. Other attempts of this kind have failed for one reason or another. I do not think APT will fail. Perhaps the timing is right this time. Theaters across the country seem to be hungry for new experiences, and with production problems greater than ever in New York City, playwrights are eager for new and different opportunities to see their plays produced. As with everything else in life, there will be good times and bad times, success and failure. But the important thing is that the idea is right and, therefore, should be able to survive the difficulties.

ANN ARBOR and ELSEWHERE with the APA

By Keene Curtis

Actor who joined the Association of Producing Artists (APA) Repertory Company for its first production in 1960 and has remained. His roles during the APA-Phoenix engagement on Broadway during the 1966-67 season were Sir Oliver in *The School for Scandal*, Sirelli in *Right You Are*, Boris in *You Can't Take It With You*, Napoleon and Pierre (alternating) in *War and Peace* and Molvik and Balle (alternating) in *The Wild Duck*. Before spending the season on Broadway, the APA made its customary visits to Los Angeles, Toronto, and, of course, the University of Michigan at Ann Arbor, where it often originates and polishes its new repertory productions as part of the university's Professional Theater Program.

1966-67 WAS APA-PHOENIX'S first full season of repertory on Broadway. In fact, it was the first full season of repertory on Broadway since 1948, when Eva Le Gallienne's American Repertory Theater held forth at the International Theater.

This season, we did six plays at the Lyceum Theater: *The School for Scandal, Right You Are, We Comrades Three, The Wild Duck, You Can't Take It With You* and *War and Peace*. Except for *We Comrades Three*, which was not a critical or popular success and was subsequently dropped from the New York repertory (a luxury made possible in a repertory situation since success or failure does not depend on a single hit or miss), all plays were performed in rotation throughout the season.

Repertory, incidentally, is a term often misapplied. Doing a series of plays in succession, finishing one before doing the other, is not repertory; it is stock. It is well to understand the difference, because they do not make the same demands of the actor. Being a member of the APA Repertory Company has meant a season playing and alternating seven roles in five plays. It has meant a steady if not remarkable income, and lots of hard work fifty-two weeks out of the year. Our rehearsal process is never-ending. We rehearse five hours a day on days when we have an evening performance, and it is not uncommon to be rehearsing two or three shows a week—two new plays, perhaps, and one old one for which you are being groomed as an alternate. There may also be a brush-up rehearsal for a play that has been out of the repertory for four or five weeks; and possibly an hour's private session with either Edith Skinner, our voice coach, who is attempting valiantly to establish a uniform method of speech for the company—or Rhoda Levine, our movement coach, who is trying to make us aware of our bodies, both our misuse of them and our extension of them. Neither is an easy task, particularly for American actors who tend to neglect both.

Our week begins with a look at the call board and is often so complicated we dare not look past the first day. The poor stage management staff needs a computer to keep it all sorted out. And if I'm ever asked I am usually at a loss to know what I'm playing week to week, or with whom. On more occasions than one we have been caught by our fellow actors putting on the wrong make-up, or searching frantically for a costume and wig only to realize that play isn't being done this week. It almost comes down to the familiar story of the old character actor touring the provinces whose only question upon entering the stage door was, "Where's the stage and what's the play?".

The only way you get a rest is by having a play off. Then you have the afternoons off when that play is rehearsing and the evenings off when it is playing.

Wouldn't it be simpler, my friends ask, to do a single Broadway show where—once you have opened—rehearsing is over, your time is your own, you only have one part to learn, and where you probably make a great deal more money per week? Well, I've been with APA since its founding in 1960 and I'm still with it. So, granted a choice, my answer is obviously "No." Why? I can best explain by going back to the beginnings of APA and the reasons for its founding.

The first hope of anyone believing himself tinged with talent is to have that belief confirmed through some form of certified recognition—from the High School drama coach, the community theater director, the local critic, anyone waving a banner of authority—giving him a stamp of approval to go out into the world and prove himself an honorable competitor or very possibly to make a fool of himself. But once the commitment has been made, the second hope of the artist is to be allowed unencumbered growth—the opportunity to fulfill his creative potential. It was because of a lack of such opportunity (and I'm speaking specifically now of the Broadway "professional theater") that APA was conceived. Ellis Rabb, the founder of APA, and many of his fellow workers including myself, nearly all of us active in the Broadway theater—as active as it was possible to be in a gradually diminishing area of activity—found that the chance to develop our craft was becoming increasingly difficult, if not impossible. The commercial aspect of theater diminishes daring. The lack of daring breeds mediocrity. And mediocrity breeds dull theater. A by-product of this is a theater which only sporadically takes chances and rarely innovates. Actors, as a result, usually remain that which they were "in the beginning."

Let me explain. On Broadway, as a rule, any actor who makes a "name" for himself is stamped as a commodity—boxed, labeled, and advertized as that which he appeared to be at the moment in his career when he received his first noticeable public and critical acclaim. As with any commodity, a good seller bears repeating or at least copying. The actor, therefore, is usually called upon to repeat or copy himself. Whereupon his image becomes "set" in the eyes of the public, the producers, the directors, and not infrequently himself, until the point is reached where the pattern is irreversible. The dumb blonde is called upon to play all the dumb blondes, the good looking juvenile all the Romeos. The villain of this play will surely be hissed at in the next. If you make an audience laugh doing pratfalls you'd better invest in a foam rubber cushion for your dressing room. You'll be needing it ever after. If your commodity stays in favor you stand the chance of making lots of money, having your image stamped in gold in Hollywood, living happily ever after. But if your commodity falls out of favor or is not needed this season you will be neatly left upon the shelf collecting dust and unemployment until you *are* needed, or forgotten forever.

So what does the theater end up with? Lost or partially explored talent. Actors whose reach is from A to C, or if you like, X to Z—or personality performers. Let me quickly say that I do not mean in any way to belittle actors who are a product of this system. Nor do I question their ability. There are many actors who play ABC or XYZ roles brilliantly, being specialists in their field, and I for one am always happy to buy tickets to see them. And I am no less enthusiastic about "personality" performers. But for any actor who would like to get off the shelf, to have a determining voice in his own future, to stretch himself beyond C to, say, F and eventually and hopefully to Z, the hurdles are staggering. APA was specifically formed to surmount them. Ellis Rabb, the motivating force behind APA, was prompted by a paragraph in a Tyrone Guthrie book which said that if American actors were tired of the prevailing situation they should stop screaming and go out and do something about it. He did.

Before proceeding, since I have been disparaging Broadway, it would be well to emphasize that every generality has its exceptions. You can have brilliant Broadway as well as bad repertory. You have actors who *have* broken the Broadway typecasting mold and proven themselves in a variety of extraordinary vehicles without the help of repertory, and you have actors in repertory who will *never* lose their limitations no matter how long they are prodded by opportunity. No, there is no battle between Broadway and repertory. The best of each is beneficial to both. It's just that repertory has staked out a new lot next door and is building its own kind of house. Hopefully, the cups of sugar will still be borrowed—freely and happily as with all good neighbors.

So much for the "why" of APA. What about the "how"? To develop our craft we must work with the best tools. In our case, they are the great plays, both past and contemporary. Without great roles you cannot have great actors. With the Broadway emphasis on musicals and domestic sex comedies, the opportunities to stretch one's self there are limited. Three years of *John Loves Mary* may put money in the bank but it won't add a great deal to your ability. I don't mean that *John Loves Mary* is not worth doing. It can stand up and be counted in any respectable company. But while you're doing a *John Loves Mary* you'd better take a serious look at the big league boys: Shakespeare, Chekhov, Pirandello, Molière, Shaw, Gorki, Sheridan, Giraudoux, yes, and Kaufman and Hart, Williams, Miller, Albee, Ionesco, de Ghelderode, Pinter, etc. They are the ones who will test your strength, give you a field of vision beyond your own, excite you to exploration, demand dimension. To know them is to find the task both easy and difficult: easy because they give you characters you do not have to fake, and difficult because the characters, being real, have their own mystery. In other words, they demand as much of you as you are capable of giving, which is never enough. Therein lies their sneaky genius.

How successful you are varies from character to character, and play to play; but hopefully you improve from season to season. You see, we don't do a play once and then shelve it. It may remain in the repertory two or three seasons, or it may be done one year, dropped for two, and re-done the fourth. For instance we have done four different productions of *A Midsummer Night's Dream,* three of *The Seagull,* two of *Man and Superman,* three of *The School for Scandal*—sometimes with different directors, nearly always with variations in casting. We ourselves may play different roles in the same play from season to season. It is not uncommon for us to juggle three or four roles in each play. In a season like the current one consisting of six productions, it is likely that you will have to be on top of an average of eight to twelve roles, not counting new ones you may be rehearsing for the coming season. Certainly there is no chance to get rusty, and unequaled opportunity to improve work in progress. The mistakes you made last year can be rectified, the interpretation you found so illusive the first time around may fall easily into place the second. With familiarity and confidence, a role may enrich itself in that surprising way that is the marvel of inspiration. Not that we allow ourselves to be less than our best. We don't. Or at least we try not to. No artist does. Nor does any artist ever believe that he cannot be better. In that lies what Martha Graham calls the "agony of creation." We are simply trying in APA to provide the haven where the creative process can best function.

What happens to "type casting" when you try to do that many roles? Nothing, fortunately. If we were to type-cast our plays, most of us would have to sit in the wings and watch—or be fired. We all have our limitations, as do directors, writers, etc; some imposed (there is little you can do if you are seven feet tall and skinny, or five feet tall and fat); some psychologically inherent (the way your mind works, your emotional climate, your personality projection). And all of these things affect how you are cast, of course; but our area of freedom is much greater in repertory. For instance, this season I played a grey-haired English uncle in *The School for Scandal,* a dark wispy-haired Italian in *Right You Are,* a gray frizzy-haired but balding Russian in *You Can't Take It With You,* and Napoleon, spit curls and all, in *War and Peace.* I emphasize the coiffure because I am in fact bald. In the commercial Broadway theater, chances are that I would never have been cast in any of these roles. I would have been stopped at the casting director's gate by a switchboard operator telling me I was not the type. Come back, she would say, when we are looking for someone bald, your age, and your build (to the inch, very likely). Back on the shelf, you see.

Another characteristic of repertory is the fact that you work with the same people over an extended period of time. This can be an enormous advantage in the preparation of a new play. As Rosemary Harris pointed out the last time she did a Broadway play outside the APA-Phoenix, the first week of a rehearsal is spent getting acquainted, proving to your fellow actors that you are worthy to be in their company. The second week is spent discovering how they work. Only in the last two weeks do you settle in to a concentrated productive rehearsal period. In repertory, all the preliminary folderol is eliminated. You *know* how your fellow actors work. Also, there is no star system in APA-Phoenix, and a wide range in size of parts you are asked to play. Rosemary Harris will play the lead, Natasha, in *War and Peace* one night and a ten-line walkon the next as Signora Ponza in *Right You Are.* Helen Hayes plays Signora Frola in *Right You Are* juxtaposed to the much smaller part of the Grand Duchess in *You Can't Take It With You.* Thus, there is no competitive axe to grind. Efforts are concentrated in making the *play* work rather than in upstaging your fellow actor.

A friend asked me if there wasn't a danger of complacency as a result of this cozy family atmosphere. Possibly, but there are things that work against it. One is the alternate system, devised to spread the work load (if an actor has a heavy rehearsal schedule during a particular week his alternate might play the evening performances, and vice versa) and to allow more actors to study the major roles. But it also generates a kind of healthy competition which precludes apathy. Another way of stimulating the company is to invite outside directors to participate, and encourage the most respected actors of our time to join us in a one or two-year residency. Miss Hayes came for this season, and to our delight has decided to stay for another. Melvyn Douglas *would* have been with us this past year, had it not been for an unexpected illness. We are looking forward to his rejoining. Every actor of stature brings his own coloring to the company. It gives us all added dimension. Also, if we are offered an exciting opportunity to work outside the company—on Broadway, in films or TV—every effort is made, short of disrupting the continuity of the program, to allow us to do it.

Is it all working as planned, then? Well, the first miracle of APA is its survival. It has been a long, sometimes tortuous path with obstacles so formidable we could see no way over or around them. I can't tell you how many times we have layed the bier for APA, gathered the flowers and lit the candles. But somehow, some way, there was always a rescue. Like the *Perils of Pauline* serials, we managed to survive for another reel. There are still perils, mostly monetary, but we are more hopeful now than we have ever been. We believe that our original premise about the value of a repertory company is still sound. We know we have made many mistakes and that we are still making them. With no precedent to follow, they come easily. But we believe they are fewer now than they were. We are growing, we feel, both individually, as an ensemble, and as an organization. We have no formal statement of policy to make, no platform to expound, and we stand on no political forum. What we are is what we do. The public and the critics will define us. Our trust is that we may carry on the best tradition of all good theater and serve our public by entertaining it.

BOSTON

By Elliot Norton

Drama critic, Boston *Record American* and *Sunday Advertiser*

IN RETROSPECT, every theater season seems pretty grim: there are so many dreary shows, so many sadly inept ones, so many that are imperfect, in proportion to the few that have a glimmer of truth or of true dramatic excitement, that the impression which remains with the playgoer at year's end is one of frustration. Yet the Boston theatrical year of 1966-67 had some high points and even a peak or two. There were some reasons to be pleased, or even to rejoice. Not many, but some.

In tentative support of that point of view, the records can be adduced. These will demonstrate that, for better or worse, almost every new show which found a following on Broadway had its first performances here. That some of these were less than scintillating during the Boston test term is a matter of fact; that others were never very good even after repairs is a matter of opinion. In any case, the Back Bay public got a first look at such as *The Homecoming* by Harold Pinter, which was brilliant in concept and in performance; *Black Comedy,* by Peter Shaffer, which was entertaining; *At the Drop of Another Hat,* in which Michael Flanders and Donald Swann were completely delightful; also *I Do! I Do!* which its director, Gower Champion, was later to describe as "a bomb in Boston"; *Cabaret,* which was not a masterpiece of the drama; *The Apple Tree,* which was wonderfully well played by Barbara Harris and the others; and *Don't Drink the Water,* a terrible play which was, nevertheless, kinda funny.

One dreadful musical became a kind of case history: *Holly Golightly* was so bad that David Merrick closed it here and ordered it rewritten by Edward Albee as *Breakfast at Tiffany's,* but the televiewers of Boston either didn't know or didn't care. Since two of their stars—Mary Tyler Moore and Richard Chamberlain—were in it, they besieged the Shubert Theater, bought out every seat and enthused mightily, like passengers who didn't understand that the ship was sinking.

That same audience, parenthetically, is a potential force for box office support, if only producers can find for its members the right kind of personalties. Its standards are peculiar, strangely low. One patron of *Holly Golightly,* thoroughly pleased by the show, bewildered because of its closing, inquired of a reviewer: "Does a show have to be sensible? I liked *Holly Golightly.* The costumes were pretty, and I enjoyed the songs, and Mary Tyler Moore is very sweet."

Bostonians of the regular downtown theaters also had a chance to see some turkeys, whose gobble was recognized by pretty nearly everyone. Some, like A. E. Hotchner's *The Hemingway Hero* and *Two Weeks Somewhere Else,* opened and closed here, cancelling other bookings. Some, such as *Agatha Sue, I love you* and *My Sweet Charlie* got as far as Broadway; so did *The Loves of Cass McGuire,* which was no turkey, but didn't quite work.

In addition to the tryouts, there were, of course, a number of touring shows of various quality: *A Delicate Balance,* an admirable play by Edward Albee, the best American work of the season, acted with distinction by most of the Broadway cast—also *Man of La Mancha* with José Ferrer; *Half a Sixpence,* badly done, and *The Odd Couple,* with Phil Foster and George Gobel.

Meanwhile, back in their little theaters, the performers of the Charles Playhouse and the Theater Company of Boston, Inc. were doing their best with dramas of the kind the commercial theaters wouldn't or hadn't produced, and, by and large, doing them rather well. For these two "regional theaters," this was not a season of dazzling brilliance, but it was generally interesting and there were some commendable productions.

Since this was the tenth season for the Charles, the managers made special efforts to break new ground and to lift their performances onto a higher level than that on which they have sometimes tended to rest. They had some success. The Theater Company of Boston managed to put on some provocative shows in the small playhouse which their members had made from a ballroom of the old Hotel Touraine and were able to cling to this property, to utilize it, though the hotel itself was closed down, leaving them in a cold grim first floor room from which they will probably be expelled. (This makes the second place which has been sold out from under them; they began three years ago in the Hotel Bostonian, which was taken over by a school.)

Getting back to the Charles Playhouse: their most ambitious production of the year was *Hamlet,* which they had not previously dared to do; now, they decided, was the time, and Edward Zang, who had been with the company and had served faithfully since it was founded in a hall over a fish market on Charles Street by Boston University students, would have the great leading role. (The Charles Playhouse is now located in a former night club on Warrenton Street, directly behind the Shubert Theater.)

The idea was good and, on paper at least, justifiable. It was time for the company to undertake a great play, time to present it to the considerable audience which the Charles Playhouse has painstakingly created and probably time, too, to reward a faithful player.

Unfortunately, Mr. Zang was not able to give a performance of any depth or distinction; his was a superficial Hamlet, all words and speeches and solemn attitudes, signifying very little.

Watching and listening carefully—and sympathetically—it occurred to one viewer that if this young actor had played the part five years ago when he knew much less about the techniques of acting—and the tricks—he might well have been erratic, but he would probably have got some life, some truth, some deep feeling and consequently some real excitement into it.

He has acquired in the course of the years a certain facility. He knows how to speak the lines rapidly enough to suggest that they are his own; and with emphasis on key words or phrases, and with knowing looks. At an early age, he is a master of the knowing look, which suggests that what is being said is most definitely significant. The old stock actors knew tricks like that; they had to learn them in self-defense, in order to be able to get through so many different roles in a short period of time. "Regional theater" actors are beginning to pick them up, too.

The Charles also undertook *Mother Courage and Her Children* in a production which was creditable. Probably this Brecht chronicle requires a really great actress to make it as moving as some Europeans have found it. Or perhaps, just perhaps, it is not really a great play at all, but a somewhat tedious one.

The Charles bestowed the title role on another veteran who has given much to the company down through the years and who, like Edward Zang, was a founding member. Olympia Dukakis was not spectacular as the pedlar woman of the Thirty Years War, not brilliant, not stirring; but she did make the Brechtian heroine seem strong enough, "earthy" enough, practical enough to keep that wagon rolling down through the difficult, tedious years and the adversities, the molehills and the mountains of her life.

Miss Dukakis had another prime role at the Charles and carried it off well. As Madama Irma in *The Balcony,* she was toughly realistic, yet reasonably human, if less than humane, in a production that suffered from some faulty acting but which got a good deal of what Jean Genet was driving at and did it boldly enough to drive a good many Bostonians out of the theater in protest. We no longer have censorship of drama in Boston, but we still have some theatergoers, who, when they feel that common decency has been violated, have enough spirit to get up and walk out. (Later in the season, some of them walked out of Jules Feiffer's *Little Murders,* a Broadway tryout at the Wilbur, and at least a few announced they would cancel their Theater Guild membership because of Mr. Feiffer's fondness for using and repeating short, ugly words.)

The Charles season also included a generally entertaining production of *Oh What a Lovely War,* staged by Eric House, a spottily funny *Luv* for *Love* and, at the end of the year, as a bonus for subscribers, John Osborne's *Inadmissible Evidence.*

The Theater Company of Boston, Inc., whose level of performance generally tends to be higher than that of the Charles, and which usually confines itself to plays of the avant garde, gave Bostonians their first look at Albee's *Tiny Alice* and at Peter Weiss' *Marat/Sade,* introduced John Arden's *Armstrong's Last Goodnight* and, as in past years, presented some new plays by Americans.

Tiny Alice was pretty well done, with Ralph Waite as Brother Julian. Mr. Waite is a younger actor than Sir John Gielgud, who originated the role, and his youthfulness gave the play another dimension, and a new sense of warmth.

There was much sense and some power in the *Marat/Sade,* too. Director David Wheeler, surprisingly, was able to get a good deal of the awesome background of the play, the groping, cringing, puling inmates of the asylum, and to fit all the pieces into a strong, if strange—and empty!—pattern of theatricality. But he was handicapped by a mistake in casting: the actor who played the elegantly evil Marquis de Sade sounded like a Down East storekeeper. (That a Down East storekeeper might be a Sadist is not impossible, but in the context of the play, it is a little incongruous.)

There were followers and friends of the Theater Company of Boston who considered *Armstrong's Last Goodnight* the best of their season. Certainly, they staged and acted this dynamic drama of a fiercely primitive Scottish chieftain's lust for freedom with clean power; but the Scottish dialect is impenetrable, and they kept it so.

They were effective in John Hawkes' *The Undertaker* and in *Candaules, Commissioner,* by Daniel C. Gerould, both new one-act plays of merit; and they gave an interesting performance of Geoffrey Brush's inconclusive new work, *A Memorial Service for William Jennings Bryan.*

At the end of the season, they presented O'Neill's *Desire Under the Elms,* which had been frowned out of town back in the 1920s by that extinct ogre, The Censor, ending an active year which was reasonably successful and active despite physical handicaps.

In nearby Waltham, meantime, Brandeis University was completing its second season with a professional acting company on campus. Howard Bay, as chairman of the Brandeis Theater Arts department, and Morris Carnovsky, as Adjunct Professor of Theater Arts, were among those heading a program that included classics like *The Seagull* and *The Tempest,* an interesting but imperfect new play, *Does a Tiger Wear a Necktie?* by Don Peterson, financed by a $25,000 grant from the National Foundation on the Arts, and a spottily amusing revue, *Only When I Laugh,* by Jules Feiffer.

Brandeis has three playhouses in the handsome new Spingold Theater, an enthusiastic administration, competent people and easy access to Boston, whose playgoers have profited by its adventures in drama enacted by casts that include a nucleus of Equity actors with "graduate interns" and some undergraduates.

HOUSTON and DALLAS

By Gynter Quill

Drama critic, Waco *Tribune-Herald*

IN HOUSTON, what was probably the next-to-last season in its old, inadequate home has been one of the best for the Alley Theater. At least it has been one of the most memorable because of one production, Chekhov's *The Seagull,* the only play which Nina Vance herself directed.

The season leaned a bit toward plays of Russian origin and was entirely Russian or Central European in locale, but it was well balanced as to type and contained more than the usual amount of classical material in which Miss Vance has been particularly at home. The productions were of a respectable calibre that any resident-theater public could appreciate. Houstonians showed that by keeping the Alley full to an average of 97 per cent of capacity, 99.8 per cent for Duerrenmatt's *The Physicists.*

If, in retrospect, that comedy-shocker *The World of Sholom Aleichem,* a very stylish mounting of Ostrovsky's *The Diary of a Scoundrel,* and *The Great Sebastians* seem a little less than great theater, it is in comparison with a *Seagull* that is one of most scintillating things Miss Vance has done in the Alley's twenty years. Incidentally, also among her very best was Chekhov's *Three Sisters* of three seasons ago. Her large cast was drilled to project the spiritual unrest that marked both Chekhov and turn-of-the-century Russia, and if her players were not of uniform excellence they acted and reacted beautifully together as an ensemble.

Particularly striking were Dale Helward and Lillian Evans as the young lovers, Konstantine (who like Chekhov was so desperate to give the world new theatrical ideas) and Nina (the girl next door, the seagull, whose heart is set on being both a great actress and the lover of the novelist Trigorin); Bella Jarrett as the flamboyant, avaricious actress-mother, Madame Arkadina; and Claude Woolman as the novelist and Tom Toner as the old doctor who voices, in this first of Chekhov's four great plays, his dream of a literature that can take life on its highest level.

It was a season that, in a sense, had no great problems other than meeting a large budget in a 231-seat house. But juggling two theaters, even if one will not be ready for yet another season, is not a carefree occupation.

A principal concern during this season has been selecting actors and staff with whom to augment the present company next year. (Of the *Seagull* cast, three were "jobbed"—including Woolman and Miss Jarrett, though the latter has been with the company before—to test both their capability and their compatibility.)

The new theater in the downtown heart of Houston, costing $3.4 million of which Ford Foundation contributed two-thirds, is running ahead of construction schedule. It will be ready for occupancy in June 1968, and will open that fall, perhaps with a new play for the occasion. As the time nears, Miss Vance will be increasingly occupied with selection, installation and testing of equipment and planning the initial season, and so she does not plan to direct any plays in the old Alley's last season. *The Seagull* was a fitting valedictory.

THE DALLAS Theater Center was again one of the nation's busiest theaters, seldom dark except for a brief layoff in the summer, with one or both of its two stages occupied for more than eleven months. And Paul Baker remained probably the nation's busiest managing director, playing split weeks in San Antonio, where he heads Trinity University's drama department and its new Ruth Taylor Theater.

The Center had its heaviest bill of modern plays in its seven years, and also its greatest attendance, which reflects approval and continued annual growth.

Of its ten new productions, all but four, plus two of the five returned in repertory, were contemporary; and three of the other four were of this era if not of this decade, of Feydeau-Coward-Brecht vintage.

The 450-seat Kalita Humphreys Theater opened with a recent but nevertheless creaky *Absence of a Cello*. It had better luck with a more pulsating *A Flea in Her Ear* (or *Bug* in the translation by the Center's Barnett Shaw), directed with Gallic spontaneity by Jean-Pierre Granval and dominated by Randy Moore in the dual husband-porter role and David Pursley as the fellow with a speech defect. This was followed by a completely winning *Blithe Spirit* for which honors were shared equally by Ryland Merkey as the husband, Martha Bumpas Gaylord (a Dallas actress but not of the Center) as his second wife, Kaki Dowling as a spritely ghost of wife No. 1, and Ella-Mae Brainard as the medium.

The turn-of-the-century *You Never Can Tell* is second-division Shaw, and not even the staging by Anna Paul Rogers which drew all the wit from his moralizing sallies, and a good cast headed by Mona Pursley, perhaps the Center's best comedienne, as the crusading mother, could improve its standing. The season in the main theater ended with the merry lampoon of *Luv* and a biting Brecht's *The Caucasian Chalk Circle*.

The tiny basement Down Center Stage had a brilliant *The Subject Was Roses* with Mary Sue Fridge Jones as the frustrated, ineffectual mother, a cramped but compelling *Tiny Alice,* an affecting if over-awed view of *The*

World of Carl Sandburg, and a thoughtful, compassionate look at some seamy misfits via *A Taste of Honey.*

There was nothing from the classics except in repertory, but these included some of the Center's best productions: last year's *The Tempest,* whose lavish scene and costume design is by Bjorn Winblad of Denmark; *Julius Caesar,* given for the sixth year with almost the same cast of principals; *Journey to Jefferson,* the dramatization of Faulkner's *As I Lay Dying* which won the jury prize in Paris's Théâtre des Nations competition three years ago; the musical *Little Mary Sunshine,* for which Miriam Gulager returned to sing and play the title role, and, downstairs, *The Amorous Flea,* the musical adapted from Molière's *The School for Wives.*

The Dallas Summer Musicals grossed $30,000 more than in 1965 and, in spite of two dismal box office failures, managed to keep head above water. Two road shows occupied terminal posts on the calendar and at the box office, *An Hour and Sixty Minutes with Jack Benny,* first in both, and the national company of *Half a Sixpense,* last. So you might say that Benny saved the season or that *Sixpence,* for all its being the best production of the season, almost sank it, though that would be letting an unresponsive public off lightly. That dubious distinction should belong to the mid-season home-produced *Gentlemen Prefer Blondes,* which had neither quality nor support. In short, Carroll Baker, the blonde bombshell, bombed out, was so inept as Lorelei that not even her blatant sex appealed to buyers.

And so the load fell on the other two-thirds of the season. With none of the other four even approaching all-time records, it was evenly distributed. Rivaling the Benny show for top honors was the perdurable favorite, *Oklahoma!,* starring Allen Case, who had, in addition to style, presence and solid vocal resources, the advantage of being a hometown boy.

Close on the heels of *Oklahoma!* were two other shows that can't miss if done even passably well. There was a Chinese approach to *Flower Drum Song* by director John Bishop and designer Peter Wolf that gave it a fey, whimsical character to soften the Rodgers and Hammerstein social theme, and a unit set that speeded the many scene changes and gave it a more congenial pace. And it had, as its Linda Low, a winning Pat Suzuki in a beguiling combination of comedy, charm and big brassy voice. *West Side Story* had humor, heart and pathos, plus the tall apartment sets of Peter Wolf and, for the choreography of Alan Johnson which followed that of his master Jerome Robbins and the ingratiating music of Leonard Bernstein, a chorus that surpassed the leads, Larry Ellis and Lee Berry.

LOS ANGELES

By Celeste Holm

Stage and screen star who appeared last season in productions of *Captain Brassbound's Conversion* and *Affairs of State* at the Pasadena Playhouse

THE THEATER season of 1966-67 for us in Los Angeles has been challenging, exhilarating, confusing and saddening, but still hopeful. Before I came to California I had been warned by my theater friends in New York that to the motion picture industry the theater was considered an irritatingly talented poor relative. To me, entertainment has always been one enormous community: a clown in the Paris circus moves you and makes you laugh in the same human terms as an actor in India who interprets and reveals the mysteries of life to a spellbound audience. The theater has long been the source of much of the best motion picture talent (and vice versa) in writing and directing as well as acting, so any insularity is ridiculous.

How deep this prejudice lay, however, was brought home to me in 1947 when I was asked by Benno Schneider to do three distinguished one-act plays in a small off-Yucca theater. I told the studio to which I was under contract that I would be doing this, as I was not currently filming, and was promptly forbidden any such "fol-de-rol." They could not take a chance with one of their properties (me) coming out badly, although I felt the chance they asked me to take in several of their films was a far greater risk.

Since then there has been an enormous burgeoning of theatrical activity in Los Angeles. Anything is being used as a theater—in the round, square, flat or three-quarters. But the wonderful intimacy of the little theaters is completely contrasted by the huge in-the-round theaters that have mushroomed in Anaheim, Woodland Hills (now defunct) and West Covina. Before we opened *The King and I* at Melodyland, during the helter-skelter of rehearsal, I was dismayed to hear a theater man say that he would do better business if David McCallum and Robert Vaughn, stars of TV's *The Man From Uncle*, would just stand there for twenty minutes. He felt that the creation of illusion was of little interest to his audience. I do not share his opinion.

When my good friend George Keathley asked us to open the 50th season of the Pasadena Playhouse with Shaw's *Captain Brassbound's Conversion*, Wesley Addy and I were playing at the Ivanhoe Theater in Chicago in Hugh and Margaret Williams' comedy *Not Even in Spring* to SRO business. When asked what classic I would like to play were the opportunity to present itself, that very Shaw play was the one I often named. The circumstances of this production were further clarified by the receipt of several front-page newspaper clippings telling us of the padlocking of the Pasadena Playhouse for non-payment of taxes. Further clippings then arrived (but not from the front pages) telling of the eager rallying-round of the Playhouse alumni, both great and small, who gave money. There was a large benefit organized by Albert McCleery, who, 30 years ago, hoped that one day he would be the Playhouse's executive producer (which he now indeed is). $11,000 was raised, enabling the Playhouse to open its doors both to students and to the audience.

At first we rehearsed with just the principals. I kept asking George Keathley where the required large cast of Arabs and sailors was going to come from. Then, in the course of each day, a few youths would wander in saying, "The office sent me for an Arab." One by one, we would absorb these youngsters into the cast. We opened on Wednesday, September 28, 1966, having homogenized our last Arab on Sunday the 25th.

Our reviews could not have been better. Cecil Smith's headline in the Los Angeles *Times* read "Brassbound Unlocks the Playhouse With Gusto." The review went on: ". . . . . radiant, glowing, the Playhouse is brought back to robust and throbbing life. How that play lit that stage as it has not been lighted in years. It was skyrockets again, the kind of theater that made the Playhouse famous."

For two weeks our business was very good indeed, but I was dismayed to discover that Hollywood and Beverly Hills—i.e., "Movieland"—was much farther away from Pasadena than the mere 20 miles via the Freeways. I suspect the prejudice against theater is almost as strong as ever. Of course, Shaw is also suspect to a large segment. Some were delighted with our notices, but I think fought making the trip for fear of finding themselves out of their depth intellectually. Many of those who came looked so startled when they said how surprised they were at what a good time they'd had.

It was fun to work with these youngsters, students who had come from all over the country to study the theater at the Playhouse. I think considerably fewer came this year because the news of its reopening had gotten so much less publicity than its closing. They came for many reasons; some for the dream of immediate fame and fortune promised by the proximity of Movieland, as well as the hope that the theater would, by means of some magic wand, change them from the uncertain youngsters they felt themselves to be into creatures of conviction and stature. I don't think from what I observed that any of them had any clue as to the amount of constant and perceptive work necessary to produce even a minimum of magic. We had to keep a tight rein on all of those sailors and Arabs after the third performance. It is hard to find that it takes as much concentration to be a part of a background as to be a leading character. But we found it a stimulating experience, and the board of directors made us promise to come back to the Playhouse next season.

Shortly after we opened in *Brassbound,* we were invited to attend a sort of forum conducted by the Hollywood Press Club entitled "How Legit Is L.A.?" at a restaurant in the Valley. We were dismayed to find ourselves on the dais, which seemed to indicate some position of knowledge and authority. I was asked the opening question from the floor: "What is the future of the Pasadena Playhouse?" I was hardly in a position to answer, as we were only scheduled to appear there for that one play and, after one week of performances, could hardly be expected to foretell its future. My answer was that if the Playhouse puts on good plays, beautifully done and critically acclaimed, audiences will come; but trust does not come overnight. It must be built by a continued standard of excellence.

The dialogue continued strangely. Each theater manager, from James A. Doolittle of the Greek Theater Association through Danny Dare of Melodyland and Isobel Lennart of the Stage Society to Gordon Davidson of the Mark Taper Forum gave an opinion of the state of his (or her) theater. They all shared the same complaint voiced in varying tones. No matter how good the notices, business was not good enough—and each pointed to his immediate rival as having, in some way, a better break. It would have been funny if it hadn't been so sad. They all felt that ABC ads in the papers would help. Gordon Davidson was the exception. He alone sounded a positive note that only good performances would bring in a constant audience. Most felt that he, at this moment, is in the strongest position, having the newest and most publicized theater in the new Music Center and bringing with him a shining reputation from UCLA as well as a large subscription.

Wesley Addy next appeared as Chamberlain in *The Right Honourable Gentleman,* a complete about-face from Captain Brassbound. Dan O'Herlihy and Eileen Herlie, once associated at the Abby Theater, were reunited in this play at the Huntington Hartford. The play was far better received than it had been in New York. With its well-bred atmosphere and venal implications, it titillated the public, and it did very nicely for its three scheduled weeks. I wonder if it would have continued to be a solid success had it run longer. It was not successful in New York—is Los Angeles therefore a different audience, or was the overall performance more interesting here?

It was only after I had agreed to appear in the National Company of *Mame* for eighteen months that I realized I would not be available next season. So, Mr. McCleery arranged to have me close this one in *Affairs of State.* It seemed an excellent choice for the spring, a romantic comedy which has always delighted audiences. Our cast was assembled in half an hour, and what an excellent one it was! We were enormously fortunate in being able to get Reginald Owen, who had played with me in the original production on Broadway. With his rare and contagious gift for twinkling humor, he was gloriously appreciated. The script needed political updating, which came out remarkably well. The trick was to sound current, but not so urgent that the lines would have to be changed every day.

The Pasadena Playhouse could afford no advertising, so no matter how marvelous our notices were, only the people who saw them the day they came out knew we were there. We had to depend completely on word of mouth, and all things considered we did very well. In the past few years, until recently, there has been no one to keep the Pasadena Playhouse's standards high, and depressing and inept productions have left its audience somewhat disillusioned. Only a constant standard of excellence will bring audiences back. Any really good performance anywhere is an incentive to an audience to go to the theater again.

Much continuously good work must be done to make Los Angeles a "theater town." For the responsibility *does* lie with the theater, with all those of us who participate in bringing it to an audience. The hope lies only in well written, stimulating scripts, fine direction and strong and sensitive performances, with an awareness of the humanity and value of the people who make up that audience. These can make the theater into what Shaw said it could be: a factory of thought, a prompter of conscience, an elucidator of social conduct, an armory against despair and dullness and a temple to the ascent of man.

Highlights of the Season in Los Angeles

By Dale Olson

TWO NEW major legitimate theaters—the Howard Ahmanson (2,200 seats) and the Mark Taper Forum (750 seats)—opened this season as part of Los Angeles' Music Center complex. (And there is the promise of a third important legitimate theater if the planned Cole Porter Auditorium will ever be finished.) The immediate public interest in these new theaters—the Ahmanson opening with *Man of La Mancha,* and the Taper opening with the newly-formed Center Theater Group's *The Devils*—has been rewarding. *The Devils* stimulated considerable controversy, but it woke up a sleepy theatrical community. It was staged well by Gordon Davidson and indicated the seriousness of purpose of Center Theater Group, an outgrowth of the earlier successful Theater Group housed at UCLA.

A major newspaper, the Los Angeles *Times,* has assigned Cecil Smith as a theater critic, a post formerly integrated in film coverage. The city itself is showing interest, in the sponsorship by Councilman James B. Potter Jr., of a new organization entitled The Council For the Extension of Professional Theater in Los Angeles. Renewed interest is currently developing in free professional Shakespeare in the park, a project initiated a year ago by the Junior Chamber of Commerce and continued this season under the sponsorship of several bodies.

There have been 132 professional theater productions staged in Los Angeles during the past season. The significant ones are listed below. Of these, the larger number (33) were theater-in-the-round productions. One cannot forget Frank Gorshin's superb performance in *What Makes Sammy Run?* or the revival of *Call Me Madam* with Ethel Merman and Russell Nype repeating their original roles. One of the three roundhouses, the Valley Music Theater, has closed (sadly, the one that had been most inventive in its programming). It is important to note that 16 full, major productions were mounted locally during the year to considerable individual success, along with seven important, if critically unsuccessful, attempts at new plays. Little-theater product has lessened, seemingly because the audience is requiring expanded material and facilities as their fare. So, too, have invitational productions (that group of material in which professional performers are presented in a showcase ostensibly for film or television work) decreased to 28 during the season.

All listings below are professional product (amateur or community productions are not included). Still, in this category, a mention might be made of the Burbank Little Theater, which has done increasingly good work, and the South Coast Repertory Company, which maintains a healthy standard of excellence. In this area, Robert Baker's set for *Look Homeward, Angel* in Burbank was outstanding.

OUTSTANDING PERFORMANCES

ANTHONY ZERBE
as Prince Henry de Conde
in *The Devils*

JOHN HARDING
as Bill Maitland in
Inadmissible Evidence

TOM TROUPE
as The Clerk in
The Diary of a Madman

EILEEN HERLIE
as Lila Rossiter in
*The Right Honourable
Gentleman*

NINA FOCH
as various characters in
The Honourable Estate

CELESTE HOLM
as Irene Elliott in
Affairs of State

JOYCE EBERT
as Sister Jeanne in
The Devils

FRANK GORSHIN
as Sammy Glick in
What Makes Sammy Run?

MALA POWERS
as Kate Stanton in
Hogan's Goat

LEON AMES
as Father in
Life With Father

LURENE TUTTLE
as Vinnie in
Life With Father

BEAH RICHARDS
as Sister Margaret in
The Amen Corner

PAT CARROLL
as Mrs. Banks in
Barefoot in the Park

TOM HATTEN
as Miles Pringle in
Drink to Me Only

OUTSTANDING DIRECTORS

GORDON DAVIDSON
Candide, The Devils

MALCOLM BLACK
Poor Bitos

ROBERT ELLENSTEIN
The Great God Brown

OUTSTANDING SCENE DESIGNERS

PETER WEXLER
The Devils

MICHAEL DEVINE
Poor Bitos

DON ROBERTS
Barefoot in the Park

OUTSTANDING NEW PLAYS

PEOPLE NEED PEOPLE by Henry F. Greenberg. Psychodrama involving case histories of mental patients. Directed by Alan Jay Factor. With Rudi Solari, Mike Mac-Ready, David Mauro, Ed Barth, Arthur Eisner. Actors Theater, Inc.

ALWAYS WITH LOVE by Tom Harris. Wacky fable of a gentle murderer. Directed by Mary Greene. With Isabelle Cooley, Don Marshall, Mark Dymally, William Wintersole, Sandra Rogers, Hal Torrey. Pasadena Playhouse.

LATE BLOOMING FLOWERS by Tim Kelly. Rambling story, adapted from a Chekhov novel, of the ruin of a once-proud family. Directed by Thomas B. Markus. With Susan

French, Kathleen Fitzgerald, Joe Jenekens, William Albert, Paul Vincent, Judson Morgan, Lea Marmer, Betty Harford. Ivar Theater.

THE DECENT THING by Jay and Connie Romer. Directed by Albert McCleery. Marital comedy with several humorous predicaments. With Jane Wyatt, John Lupton, Karen Black, Brett Parker. Pasadena Playhouse.

BALLAD OF ROBERT BURNS by Joy Parnes. A lyrical delineation of the poet and his work. Directed by Karl Swenson. With Marvin Miller, Salli Terri, Ken Remo, Joan Tompkins, Anne Marie Biggs. Beverly Hills High School.

THE HONOURABLE ESTATE adapted and directed by John Houseman. Collection of material about the human predicament. With Nina Foch, Norma Crane, Betty Harford, Joanne Linville, Theodore Marcuse, John Drury. Beckman Auditorium.

THE LOUDEST NOISE IN THE WORLD by Vincent Williams. Modern allegory concerning civil rights, racial problems, and people of today. Directed by Frank Silvera. With Stephenson Phillips, Frank Silvera, Whitman B. Mayo. Theater of Being.

LOVE AND WILLIAM SHAKESPEARE devised and directed by John Houlton. Compilation of Shakespearean love stories, with bridging material. With Lola Fisher, Michael

Forest, Robert Cornthwaite, Barbara Morrison, Katherine Henryk, Joan Tompkins, John McMurtry, Penelope Chandler. Beverly Hills Playhouse.

THE SHORT AND TURBULENT REIGN OF ROGER GINZBURG musical with book by David Colloff and Ronald Sossi; music by John Rubenstein; lyrics by David Colloff. An interesting, but ragged, review. With Gary Gardner, Martin Schmidt, Jan Schmidt, Flora Plumb, Melody Santangelo.

DASH POINT by George Savage and George Savage Jr. Story of the depression and its politics. Directed by Richard T. Johnson. With Joanna Dorian, John Drury, Chester Michaels. Curtain Call Theater.

OUTSTANDING NEW LOCAL PRODUCTIONS

(Not including the productions of Center Theater Group—formerly Theater Group-UCLA—which appear in the Directory of Professional Regional Theater at the end of this section)

THE RIGHT HONOURABLE GENTLEMAN by Michael Dyne. Directed by George Keathley. With Daniel O'Herlihy, Eileen Herlie, Carol Booth, Wesley Addy, Cay Forester. Huntington Hartford Theater.

INADMISSIBLE EVIDENCE by John Osborne. Directed by Mitchell Erickson. With John Harding, Brett Parker, Helena Nash, Lois Battle, Elizabeth Rogers, Sandra Hudson. Stage Society Theater.

THE ZULU AND THE ZAYDA by Howard Da Silva and Felix Leon. Directed by Jeb Schary. With Yaphet Kotto, Ned Glass. Warner Playhouse.

THE ROYAL HUNT OF THE SUN by Peter Shaffer. Directed by John Dexter. With Robert Burr, John Heffernan, Alan Mixon. Greek Theater.

LUV by Murray Schisgal. Directed by King Donovan. With Marvin Kaplan, Arlene Golonka, Martin Brooks. Warner Playhouse.

THE SECRET LIFE OF WALTER MITTY by Joe Manchester, Earl Shamon, Leon Carr. Directed by Gerald Gordon. With Ruth Warrick, Marc London, Anne Johnson. Las Palmas Theater.

HOGAN'S GOAT by William Alfred. Directed by Tom Palmer. With Mala Powers, Robert Hogan, Stuart Lancaster, James McCallion, Barbara Perry, Jeanne Arnold, Mark Gardner. Stage Society.

THREE ACTS OF LOVE: *The Music Cure* by George Bernard Shaw; *Literature* by Arthur Schnitzler; *Bedtime Story* by Sean O'Casey. Directed by Peter Nelson. With Tom Palmer, Peter Nelson, Christine Burke. Beckman Auditorium.

OUTSTANDING REVIVALS

THE STUDENT PRINCE musical with book and lyrics by Dorothy Donnelly; music by Sigmund Romberg. Directed by Edward M. Greenberg. With Frank Porretta, Eileen Christy, Hans Conried, Irra Petina, Murray Matheson. Dorothy Chandler Pavilion.

AH, WILDERNESS! by Eugene O'Neill. Directed by Lenore Shanewise. With Kent Smith, Edith Atwater, Jack Bailey, Alice Frost, Michael Margotta, Sally Anne Struthers, James O'Reare, Robert Legionaire, Bobby Ross, John Bangert. Pasadena Playhouse.

THE GLASS MENAGERIE by Tennessee Williams. Directed by George Keathley. With Ann Sothern, Piper Laurie, Ben Piazza, James Olson. Huntington Hartford Theater.

CAPTAIN BRASSBOUND'S CONVERSION by George Bernard Shaw. Directed by George Keathley. With Celeste Holm, Wesley Addy, Vaughn Taylor. Pasadena Playhouse.

BAREFOOT IN THE PARK by Neil Simon. Directed by Rod Amateau. With Margaret O'Brien, Dwayne Hickman, Pat Carroll, Alan Reed, Sid Melton, Sherwood Keith.

THE AMEN CORNER by James Baldwin. Directed by Frank Silvera. With Beah Richards, Gertrude Jeanette, Isabell Sanford, James Cameron, Alvin Childress. Theater of Being.

AFFAIRS OF STATE by Louis Verneuil. Directed by Celeste Holm. With Celeste Holm, Wesley Addy, Reginald Owen, Nelson Welch, Karen Norris, Harry Holcomb.

LADY IN THE DARK musical with book by Moss Hart; lyrics by Ira Gershwin; music by Kurt Weill. Directed by Albert McCleery, musical direction by Ernest Gold. With Marni Nixon, Audrey Christie, Don Matheson, Don Baggi, Monty Landis, Eric Brotherson, John Strong, Sara Dillon. Pasadena Playhouse.

LIFE WITH FATHER by Howard Lindsay and Russel Crouse. Directed by Mary Greene.

With Leon Ames, Lurene Tuttle. Pasadena Playhouse.

LOST IN THE STARS musical with book and lyrics by Maxwell Anderson; music by Kurt Weill. Directed by Leslie Abbott. With Chester Washington, Juanita Moore, Morris Erby, Gene Boland, DeMaris Gordon, Rene Robin, Jordan A. Morris, Edward Parrish, Joseph Ryan, Louis Silas, Johnny Williamson, Robert Garner. Ebony Showcase Theater.

THE RIVALRY by Norman Corwin. Directed by Robert Nichols. With John Anderson, Steven Gravers, Adrienne Marden. California Arts Commission touring company.

PURLIE VICTORIOUS by Ossie Davis. Directed by John E. Blankenship. With Morris Erby, Liz Van Dyke, Juanita Moore, Napoleon Whiting, Gar Campbell. Ebony Showcase.

OUTSTANDING INVITATIONAL PRODUCTIONS

THE PUBLIC EYE by Peter Shaffer and THE ZOO STORY by Edward Albee. Directed by Loel Minardi and Miles Dickson. With Mark Herron, Douglas Dick, Inger Stratton, Winston DeLugo, John Erwin.

SQUAT BETTY and THE SPONGE ROOM by Keith Waterhouse and Willis Hall. Directed by Charles Rome Smith. With Laurance Haddon, Richard Bull, Barbara Collentine, Paul Kent, Jacquelyne Hyde.

THE GREAT GOD BROWN by Eugene O'Neill. Directed by Robert Ellenstein. With

James Orr, Anthony Call, Elizabeth Perry, Anna Hagan, Betty Keeney, Robert Ellenstein, Victor Izay.

MISS JULIE by August Strindberg. Directed by Donald H. Molin. With John Milford, Adele Bellroth, Mary Dell Roberts.

DRINK TO ME ONLY by Abram S. Ginnes and Ira Wallach. Directed by William Woodson. With Tom Hatten, Ken Lynch, Pitt Herbert, Dennis Safren, Karen Dolin, Vinton Hayworth.

PHILADELPHIA and PITTSBURGH

By Ernest Schier

Drama critic, *The Bulletin*

BLACK COMEDY overflowed from the stages into the internal affairs of Pennsylvania's two major regional theaters. Before the 1966-67 season had come to a natural conclusion the artistic directors at Philadelphia's Theater of the Living Arts and Pittsburgh's thirty-three-year-old Playhouse had resigned and/or been fired.

It would be a mistake to interpret the twin upheavals which took place at opposite ends of the state as symptomatic of a basic conflict between young artistic directors, champing at the bit to create revolutionary theater, and backwards boards of directors who only want bland box-office hits. At Pittsburgh, the failure was the audience's. Young director John Hancock had produced a program that ranged from Brecht through Arthur Miller. The most talked about play of his season was an unconventional treatment of *A Midsummer Night's Dream* that mocked rather than supported the conventional romanticism of the play. But any season that also includes *Two for the Seesaw* can hardly be regarded as being dedicated to radicalism in the theater. Pittsburgh did not respond sufficiently to the plays at its Playhouse, and a majority of the board of directors, perhaps expressing a wish for instant success, blamed Hancock.

He could not, however, be blamed for a $380,000 deficit piled up over a seven-year-period, nor for the inflated $700,000 budget for the season he directed. A dramatic appeal to the public to save the Playhouse produced the needed $300,000 (including a $25,000 grant from the National Council on the Arts and a three-year, $450,000 contribution from the A. W. Mellon Educational and Charitable Trust) to continue the season. But the badly shaken board of directors found itself split over ways and means to run the Pittsburgh Playhouse, and before the differences could be ironed out, Hancock had been dismissed. Pittsburgh's record is further sullied by the fact that last year it vanquished William Ball, who is now the hero of San Francisco, the city to which he took his American Conservatory Theater.

At Philadelphia's Theater of the Living Arts, artistic director Andre Gregory's departure came as a surprise, to Gregory himself as well as to the board which fired him. Gregory's talent and value to Living Arts was admired and appreciated. The board knew full well that Gregory was the theater's artistic fountainhead and had brought to it a sense of excitement and distinction. But Gregory, miffed over the earlier firing of managing director David Lunney, engaged in the dangerous game of brinksmanship. He challenged the board's authority to make financial decisions. An intelligent and reasonable man most of the time, Gregory used language in challenging the board that was much, much too strong if he wished to remain. He claimed artistic interference but never got around to substantiating his claims.

Gregory, too, had produced a black comedy. Rochelle Owens' *Beclch* was a mildly controversial psycho-sexual-symbolic drama of violent relationships in an imaginary place—an "Africa of the mind," Gregory called it. The Living Arts board fussed nervously before the production but gave its consent. The actors were not hauled off to jail as some thought might happen, nor did the audience rise up to throw stones at the stage. The experience was a strengthening one for the theater.

But then, after *Beclch*, Gregory publicly disclaimed confidence in the artistic integrity and leadership of the board. In effect, he asked them to choose between him and Thomas T. Fleming, president of Living Arts. If Gregory wanted to stay on, his position was too uncompromising because he gave the board little choice. Hyperbole flew through the air, insults were exchanged and people said things they couldn't take back. Gregory's departure became inevitable.

Ironically, Living Arts has advanced plans to join with Academy of Music interests to construct a new culture complex on a centrally located site on Broad Street.

What this tale of two cities proves is that regional theater is costing a good deal more than anyone had anticipated both in dollars and in talent. Fiscal responsibility is the major area of authority for the boards of directors, but it does not eliminate the need for artistic leadership to be reasonable about money matters. And artistic policy, once agreed upon, should be entirely the province of the artistic director.

In Philadelphia, as in Pittsburgh, too much tinkering on both sides in the other's area of authority produced violent upheavals that were unquestionably setbacks for the regional theater movement. But in the long run—if there is to be a long run—the experiences can be beneficial if they clarify what each community wants for itself in the way of theater, what it needs and what it is willing to pay for.

Broadway's contributions to the Philadelphia season thinned almost to a trickle. Brian Friel's *The Loves of Cass McGuire* and David Westheimer's *My Sweet Charlie* were the only serious endeavors, both grossly inadequate. Musicals included *Illya Darling,* with Melina Mercouri, and *Sherry!,* the musical version of *The Man Who Came to Dinner,* which found Clive Revill replacing George Sanders in mid-engagement.

This year it was Alexander H. Cohen who blasted Philadelphia audiences for their lightweight tastes. The producer, like the others before him, failed to consider whether it might not be a case of the theater failing the audience.

SAN FRANCISCO

By Paine Knickerbocker

Drama critic, San Francisco *Chronicle*

BY FAR the most exciting and significant event of the season in San Francisco was the coming of the American Conservatory Theater to the city. Opening in January, 1967 with a schedule of sixteen productions to be staged in two theaters within twenty-two weeks, ACT offered a theatrical program of stunning proportions; one which the city must face with a new vigor if the company is to succeed.

Whatever their excellence (at this writing the complete repertory has not been performed) William Ball and his almost unbelievably energetic company of some 140 persons would not have been invited to San Francisco had it not been for two important departures during the last two years.

The first, of course, was that of Jules Irving, Herbert Blau, and a good portion of the Actor's Workshop who went to the Lincoln Center Repertory Company to open the Vivian Beaumont in the season of 1965-66. Not until they left did the community become interested in a capable resident theatrical company. On their leaving, sharp cries of grief and betrayal were heard.

Then Ken Kitch reorganized those of the company who remained behind and, with the assistance of John Hancock who was engaged as artistic director of the new Actor's Workshop, another season was mounted. While not entirely successful, it achieved several distinguished productions and attracted far greater attention from the community than had their predecessors.

Then, very suddenly, Hancock was invited to head the Pittsburgh Playhouse at an irresistible salary and a comparatively large budget. No similar counter-offers were made by San Francisco, and again the Actor's Workshop departed, this time causing the end of the company which had been founded in 1952. (Hancock and company unfortunately encountered unexpected resistance to their spirit in Pittsburgh, and Hancock's contract was not renewed after one year. Blau resigned from Lincoln Center in January, 1967.)

The second departure caused even more of a stir than the first, for by that time the San Francisco Chamber of Commerce, headed by Cyril Magnin, taking a far greater interest in a professional resident company as a cultural asset of the city, felt that something should be done. This same Chamber had, with happy results, taken over the administration of the San Francisco International Film Festival in 1965.

Coinciding with Hancock's resignation and farewell was the arrival of Ball and ACT in the San Francisco Bay Area. The timing was fortuitous.

With a nucleus of members who had studied at Carnegie Tech, ACT had been formed in the summer of 1965 under Ball's direction. His company was engaged to present a season at the Pittsburgh Playhouse where, after several months, a disagreement led to the relationship being terminated. (This was a year before Hancock's experience there.) Virtually homeless, although a large company with many assets such as costumes, lights, sets, training programs and talent, ACT was invited to participate in the Summer Festival at Stanford University, less than an hour's drive south of San Francisco.

The original plan was for a modest number of performances, but at that time Ball's vitality was unrecognized. He asked that the stay of his company be extended, that it be permitted to stage more productions at Stanford than were initially scheduled, and ACT performed at the University of California in Berkeley, and at other neighboring campuses. This visit was of immediate and considerable impact. Those civic leaders who expressed interest in San Francisco having a resident company were wooed by Ball and his staff. Members of ACT liked the Bay Area, and a cordial relationship ripened from the start.

Ball, who had in 1961 directed an Actor's Workshop production of *The Devil's Disciple* and who had scored a hit with his *Tartuffe* starring Michael O'Sullivan (a Workshop veteran) with the Lincoln Center Repertory Company, entered the discussions with audacity and tact. He was representing a large company, not negotiating as an individual.

He demonstrated that a city the size of San Francisco could become surfeited with as busy a company as ACT if it remained throughout the year. Furthermore, Chicago appeared equally interested in having ACT as its resident company. And since ACT has no intention of being self-sustaining, its conservatory aspect with training and educational programs being too costly for that, Ball was aware that assistance from two cities would be helpful.

During the early fall of 1966, Ball and representatives of both San Francisco and Chicago worked out an unusual, tentative plan. Chicago was not prepared to receive the company in the first half of 1967, and San Francisco was eager to have ACT as soon as possible. Eventually, ACT agreed to present its quite staggering repertory at San Francisco's Geary Theater which seats 1400 and has in the past been used by national touring companies, and at the Marines, seating 650, where the Workshop had staged its major productions. This first season of 283 performances, which opened on January 21 with an immediately acclaimed production of *Tartuffe,* was to last through the middle of June.

Then, because it was decided that San Francisco—if the plan works out—will regularly have ACT in the fall, and Chicago in the spring, San Francisco would have the second season as well, a schedule of about twenty-two weeks beginning in September 1967. But later, these arrangements became less definite. The two Chicago theaters are an unworkable three miles apart, and so it is possible that during the spring of 1968, ACT may make a national tour.

Well aware that a theatrical company can squander its creative energy endeavoring to raise money in order to survive, Ball and the civic leaders agreed on another essential point. A California Theater Foundation was formed, and this group of prominent citizens promised to raise some $450,000 for ACT. On the strength of that show of community support, which the Workshop had never achieved, the Ford Foundation extended a grant of $250,000 to the company.

O'Sullivan had scored a personal triumph in *Tartuffe* in New York and had played in *Six Characters in Search of an Author* in New York and London under Ball's direction. That he was in the cast of *neither* of these plays in San Francisco is an indication of the adventurous, refreshing spirit of ACT. *Tartuffe,* which many questioned as a suitable play to open the season, was an electrifying success. Immediately San Francisco recognized that this still youthful company is most unusual. Ball refers to *Tartuffe* as ACT's *La Boheme;* for like that popular, sure-fire opera by Puccini, *Tartuffe* has consistently been a sellout. Rene Auberjonois, in the title role, was immediately acclaimed. *Man and Superman,* a subsequent smash hit, also featured Auberjonois, who likewise starred in *Charley's Aunt* and directed *Beyond the Fringe.* Playing Hamm in *Endgame* at Stanford, and Clov in that play this season, he, Richard A. Dysart, O'Sullivan, DeAnn Mears, Ray Reinhardt, and Ken Ruta are among the most versatile players in the company.

Dear Liar, directed by its author, Jerome Kilty (he is a member of ACT and occasionally acts in it), was the second production. O'Sullivan played the Shaw role and Sada Thompson that of Mrs. Patrick Campbell. This too was enthusiastically received, becoming a popular production for the company to present in various communities and on many campuses in its "Out Rep" program.

Although this is being written before the season is complete—and indeed, before too is the fund-raising campaign—ACT appears established. With O'Sullivan as the Cardinal, and Miss Mears as Miss Alice, *Tiny Alice* has been a surprise hit with young audiences, as has *Endgame. Six Characters* was popular, and *Man and Superman,* a new production, proved surprisingly appealing to subscribers even before it opened. Directed by Kilty, it proved theatrically exciting and very entertaining. The *Don Juan in Hell* sequence was included. A typical ACT touch is that the rehearsal early in *Six Characters* was of *Charley's Aunt.*

Generally, however, ACT productions are neither startling nor dependent on gimmicks. Because many men direct, a welcome liveliness exists in the concepts of the plays. Faults are often corrected if the director wishes. When presented at Stanford, *Tiny Alice* was excessively homosexual. Ball changed this, toning down the approach when he redirected the play for San Francisco, and improving it considerably.

The Torch-Bearers, directed by Edward Payson Call, received indifferent reviews and attention and was dropped from the schedule, the weakest offering to date, despite a splendid contribution by Ruth Kobart, and several funny characterizations by local players who have joined the company. For including such a play, Ball has an explanation. He wants his actors to be trained in various kinds of comedy, to learn the timing that farce requires. Thus, such a selection as *Arsenic and Old Lace* in the repertory.

Also included were *Under Milk Wood, Long Day's Journey Into Night, Death of a Salesman,* and *Our Town.* The company has no intention of attempting an original play until its repertory, its audience, and the company itself are well-established, but Kilty is working on another letter-play, this based on Chekhov's correspondence with six individuals, which ACT will probably present informally to its subscribers.

Repertory is only a part of ACT. Almost more surprising is its training program. Under the supervision of Mark Zeller, who also teaches voice, are classes in a building across the street from the Geary. The Marines is only a block away. Robert Weede instructs in advanced voice; Frank Ottiwell in the Alexander method of body movements and control; Harold Lang in movement and dancing, and Shela Xoregos in vaudeville routines and tap dancing. Costumers, designers and musicians also teach, all under one roof; all programs coordinated. Ball wishes ACT to extend its influence and skills to other organizations in San Francisco—to assist opera singers to learn more about acting, for instance. The program resembles that of the old guilds, with veterans assisting apprentices or those less experienced.

At press time, the future of ACT is not assured. It appears that there is sufficient support to anticipate the next season with confidence, but for such success those who live in the Bay Area must attend the theater more frequently than they have in the past. Owing to the haste required to get the first schedule in production, there was insufficient time to work satisfactorily on subscriptions. Some 10,000 were sold; the goal was 15,000. (The Civic Light Opera sells 90,000 annually). But at a time when traveling companies are becoming fewer, and when the Theater Guild's programs are necessarily less predictable, it is expected that community interest in ACT will increase, unless the fall season makes excessive demands. At last, at least, San Francisco has a resident company which can afford to advertise adequately, something the Workshop was never permitted.

Although ACT received most attention locally this year, other companies have grown stronger. The group of actors and improvisers known as The Committee, still headed by Alan Myerson, is now operating in two theaters. Its original home, where improvisational theater continues, houses a young company, while the seasoned veterans, who founded the group in 1963, having now wearied of improvisations, are presenting plays. The first was Larry Hankin's *The Fool's Play* which opened the new Committee Theater, also a cabaret where food and drink are served. This was, however, an incoherent, ineffective piece, and like the production of *MacBird!* which followed a week later, was coolly received. Perhaps too long an association with improvisational theater led director Myerson to forget the advantages of bold, crisp, and imaginative staging.

In addition to its program of professional theater in the summer, Stanford has inaugurated the Stanford Repertory Theater, made up of professional actors and directors who present several plays during the year. These men and women teach and work with the students. Occasionally a student plays a small role, but not usually. Mel Shapiro staged a deft and sensitive *The Cherry Orchard* with Gerald Hiken and Paul E. Richards being particularly effective.

The Festival Theater, some fifteen miles north of San Francisco in San Anselmo, became professional, presenting a very successful and moving *Oh What a Lovely War,* and a less persuasive *Overkill and Megalove,* an original by Norman Corwin.

Two organizations folded in the East Bay. Ben Kapen's Melodyland, the first of the large theaters in this area to present familiar musicals with top stars and local supporting players for short runs, went into bankruptcy during a lightly lauded production of *The Boy Friend* starring an entrancing Leslie Uggams. Rachmael ben Avram, who founded the Oakland National Repertory Company, presented Mildred Dunnock in *The Glass Menagerie* with John Saxon, and Sylvia Sidney in *The Importance of Being Earnest,* but the supporting casts were weak and he resigned in midseason, his presentations, which he directed, having failed at the box office.

In San Francisco, Irma Kay's Opera Ring discontinued when she could not compete for the rights to popular musicals. Drama Ring, a company launched by faculty members at San Francisco State College in the same theater, staged an eloquent, intimate production of *Look Back in Anger* before becoming dormant.

Still operating in San Francisco are two resident unprofessional theaters: the Interplayers, headed by A. J. Esta and The Playhouse by Henry Stein. Their theaters are small but adequate, and their productions, while often uneven, of interest. *The Physicists* at the Playhouse was commendable, while the Interplayers' *Lysistrata* was marked by a discernible uneasiness at its ancient and Attic candor. And the San Francisco Mime Troupe maintains its impudent and contentious ways, often performing without charge in the city's parks during the summer months, in addition to its regular theatrical appearances.

WASHINGTON

By Leo Brady

Professor, Dept. of Speech and Drama, Catholic University

AS IF LIFE in the nation's capital isn't confusing enough, the two most striking theatrical exhibits this season were not "legitimate" presentations at all, but operas. The Washington Opera Society, after an otherwise routine season, unveiled a new work, *Bomarzo,* which it had commissioned Argentinian Alberto Ginastera to compose, and the Washington Cathedral sponsored the performance of a British piece called *The Judas Tree,* by Thomas Blackburn and Peter Dickinson. Both are pertinent to this discussion because in each case the music played second fiddle to the dramatic idea and each was given a rousing production. The stress on theatricality was the work of the respective directors: Tito Capobianco and Jack Cole for *Bomarzo,* and James D. Waring for *The Judas Tree.* There is some doubt in my non-musical mind that you would want to listen to either on records, but on stage they were greatly effective.

Show biz was given widespread sanctuary in the Episcopal Cathedral. The vast Gothic structure, architecturally way behind the times, is otherwise the swingingest place in town; at any time, pilgrims are liable to run into guitarist Charlie Byrd, or dancer Jose Limon or the Pro Musica group—all of whom performed there this year—or even a covey of mini-skirted dancers. And this is not the only local integration of church and stage. A group calling itself the Garrick Players performs in Grace Episcopal Church near the banks of the Potomac in the industrial part of Georgetown. The Players' final production of the season was a home-made revue called *Garrick's Follies* (a juxtaposition that might give both David and Flo a turn) and felt prosperous enough to convert themselves into an Equity company. They have gained some local notice by presenting Samuel Beckett's *Act Without Words* to elementary school children on a series of local junkets into classrooms and getting a knowledgeable response from the small fry.

The Washington Theater Club (which is next door to a Baptist church) continued to blossom: it announced virtual sell-outs for its season of eight avant-garde plays—and promptly made an Establishment advance by raising its prices. *The Waters of Babylon* by John Arden was characteristic of its offerings: able direction by Clifford V. Ammon, burlap-and-orange-crate settings, enthusiasm, intimacy, and a general air of seedy but mild rebellion. This company, which has both the awkwardness and abandon of youth, is enjoying the kind of fashionable attention given to Arena Stage in its toddling phase.

Arena, for its part, appeared to be grappling with the problems of middle age: affluence, uncertainty, the criticism of friends, and a degree of myopia. Tom Donnelly of the *News* thought its final production, of Saul Levitt's *The Andersonville Trial,* its best, and drew the general conclusion that the company was at home in melodrama. Its *Macbeth* provided startling scenic effects but little coherence; the witches appeared in a satisfying cloud of demonic smoke but in general the production gave little evidence of fire. Osborne's *Look Back in Anger* met a torpid reception, proving, perhaps, that yesterday's rebel is today's soporific. A revival of Pinero's *The Magistrate* pleased the large (and still growing) subscription audience but the reviewers were not enchanted. What Zelda Fichandler and her experienced staff have to do to make a dent in the op-pop-psychedelic world of the happening is not easy to say, but it might be—as the sports writers are always telling the second-division Senators—that standing pat isn't the answer. Mrs. Fichandler responded to this philosophy by importing three directors this season—Milton Katselas, Hy Kalus, and David William—to supplement the work of resident Edwin Sherin. Maybe regional theaters should go a step farther and exchange productions as well as performers the way symphony orchestras do, though the logistics of such shifting around might well defeat even the Ford Foundation.

The National Theater, Washington's "road" house, had its biggest moments with musicals. *Man of La Mancha,* with José Ferrer, was unquestionably the artistic high point of the regular season, and one can't help but be struck here with the part played, once again, by a happy union of music and drama in an unconventional mold. *I Do! I Do!* was popular also, but for more obviously conventional reasons, not the least of which was audience admiration for the way its energetic stars got through such a punishing evening, a feat that seemed more rigorous than a lifetime of marriage.

At American University, F. Cowles Strickland proved he could sing along with everybody else by capping his season for the second consecutive year with an opera, this time *The Secret Marriage.* The University of Maryland brought back graduate Robert Milli, who had played Horatio to Burton's *Hamlet,* to do the Dane with a campus cast. Catholic University grabbed extra-curricular headlines when the roof of its theater gave way under a snowstorm. The homeless drama students made scenes on campus for awhile in an effort to nudge along an un-culture-conscious administration but were finally forced to do their annual musical (*The Day the Senate Fell in Love*) at a local high school (with disappointing results).

The faith of local producers in the Washington audience never falters. The owners of the Shady Grove Music Tent in suburban Gaithersburg collapsed their canvas and went to work in the spring of 1967 to build a permanent theater which will operate in winter as well as summer. Arena, which once performed for four weeks, now goes for six (with a few previews at the beginning to cushion opening night). Olney Theater extended its run from three to four weeks and opened its 1967 season—with Lester Rawlins in *Richard III*—in the middle of May. Highly successful productions in 1966 of Hugh Leonard's *Stephen D* (with George Grizzard) and William Alfred's *Hogan's Goat* (with John Colicos) encouraged the expansion.

Just to make sure the audience doesn't stray, a group of organizations—Arena Stage, The National Symphony, the National Ballet, The Opera Society, the Washington Performing Arts Society, and the Washington Theater Club—banded together as the United Performing Arts of Washington in a subscription drive. They took joint ads in local papers, exchanged mailing lists, and made appearances at club meetings and other gatherings. The venture looked to be successful and will probably be repeated next year.

Clearly, the Washington season is best viewed against a musical background. At the Carter Barron Amphitheater, the Feld Brothers book in pop singers, ballet and opera, to large public response. The American Light Opera Company goes blithely along doing non-professional revivals of old and new Broadway musicals. Maybe more and more drama with music is on the horizon. As one of Shaw's characters reminds us Beaumarchais said: what's too silly to be said can be sung.

A DIRECTORY OF
PROFESSIONAL REGIONAL THEATER

Professional 1966-67 programs and repertory productions by leading resident companies around the United States (excluding Broadway, off Broadway, touring New York shows, summer theaters and festivals) are listed in alphabetical order of their locations. This directory was compiled by the American National Theater and Academy (ANTA) for *The Best Plays of 1966-67*. Figures in parentheses following titles give number of performances. Date given is opening date.

ABINGDON, VA.

Barter Theater

THE CAVE DWELLERS (9). By William Saroyan. June 7, 1966. Director, Peter W. Culman; scenery, William James Wall; lighting, Albin Aukerlund; costumes, Karin Bacon. With Robert Summers, Nancy Reardon, Jane Lowry, James Cahill.

YOU CAN'T TAKE IT WITH YOU (9). By Moss Hart and George S. Kaufman. June 14, 1966. Director, Ira Zuckerman; scenery, William James Wall; lighting, Albin Aukerlund; costumes, Karin Bacon. With James Cahill, Doris Gregory, Bert Houle, David Lynn Selby.

THE BAT (18). By Mary Roberts Rinehart and Avery Hopwood. June 21, 1966. Director, William Woodman; scenery, William James Wall; lighting, Albin Aukerlund; costumes, Karin Bacon. With Libby Lyman, Bert Houle, Cassandra Morgan, Dempster Leech.

THE MADWOMAN OF CHAILLOT (13). By Jean Giraudoux; adapted by Maurice Valency. July 26, 1966. Director, Peter W. Culman; scenery, William James Wall; lighting, Albin Aukerlund; costumes, Karin Bacon. With Nancy Reardon, Jane Lowry, Doris Gregory, Libby Lyman.

TWELFTH NIGHT (5). By William Shakespeare. August 6, 1966. Director, Ira Zuckerman; scenery, Lynn Pecktal; lighting, Albin Aukerlund; costumes, Karin Bacon. With David Birney, Robert Summers, David Sabin, Jane Lowry, Nancy Reardon.

THE DEVIL'S ADVOCATE (18). By Dore Schary; based on the novel by Morris L. West. August 23, 1966. Director, Peter W. Culman; scenery, William James Wall; lighting, Albin Aukerlund; costumes, Karin Bacon. With James Cahill, Nancy Reardon, Bert Houle, Libby Lyman.

ANY WEDNESDAY (18). By Muriel Resnik. September 20, 1966. Director, Peter W. Culman; scenery, William James Wall; lighting, Albin Aukerlund. With John Milligan, Nancy Reardon, Robert Summers, Betty Hellman.

HAMLET (19). By William Shakespeare. April 21, 1967. Director, Larry Gates; scenery, Ralph Swanson; lighting, John Baker; costumes, St. Clair Williams. With Saylor Creswell, Melissa Loving, Frederic Warriner, Carole Griffith, Anthony Palmer.

CHARLEY'S AUNT (16). By Brandon Thomas. May 12, 1967. Director, Ned Beatty; scenery, Ralph Swanson; lighting, John Baker; costumes, Judith Baker. With Tom Martin, Melissa Loving, Frederic Warriner, Margo McElroy.

ANN ARBOR, MICH. (See article on its season)

Association of Producing Artists (APA-Phoenix) Repertory (in University of Michigan Professional Theater Program)

THE SCHOOL FOR SCANDAL (8). By Richard Brinsley Sheridan. September 20, 1966. Director, Ellis Rabb; scenery, James Tilton; lighting, Gilbert V. Hemsley Jr.; costumes, Nancy Potts. With Ellis Rabb, Rosemary Harris, Helen Hayes, Sydney Walker, Keene Curtis, Clayton Corzatte.

THE CAT AND THE MOON by W.B. Yeats; director, Donald Moffat; SWEET OF YOU TO SAY SO by Page Johnson; director, Keene Curtis; ESCURIAL by Michel de Ghelderode; directors, Hal George and John Houseman (16). September 27, 1966. Scenery, James Tilton; lighting, Gilbert V. Hemsley Jr.; costumes, T. Pazik. With James Greene, Nat Simons, George Pentecost, Dee Victor, Paulette Waters, Ellis Rabb, Nicholas Martin, Joseph Bird, Alan Fudge.

RIGHT YOU ARE (8). By Luigi Pirandello. October 11, 1966. Director, Stephen Porter; scenery, James Tilton; lighting, Gilbert V. Hemsley Jr.; costumes, Nancy Potts. With Helen Hayes, Donald Moffat, Dee Victor,

Jennifer Harmon, Patricia Conolly, Sydney Walker, Betty Miller.

WE COMRADES THREE (8). By Richard Baldridge; arranged from works by Walt Whitman. October 18, 1966. Director, Ellis Rabb and Hal George; scenery, James Tilton; ligthting, Gilbert V. Hemsley Jr.; costumes, Nancy Potts. With Marco St. John, Sydney Walker, Will Geer, Helen Hayes, Patricia Conolly.

THE FLIES (16). By Jean-Paul Sartre. October 25, 1966. Director, Vinnette Carroll; scenery, James Tilton; lighting, Gilbert V. Hemsley Jr.; costumes, Nancy Potts. With Olivia Cole, Lawrence Luckenbill, David J. Stewart, Anne Francine.

ATLANTA, GA.

Pocket Theater

THE MERRY WIDOW (12). Musical by Franz Lehar. October 13, 1966. Director, Mitzi Hyman; scenery, Luis Maza; musical director, Byron Warner; choreography, Peggy Williams. With Barbara Somerset, David Johnson, Naomi Haag, William Chapman.

A DOLL'S HOUSE (16). By Henrik Ibsen; translated by William Archer. November 17, 1966. Director, Richard C. Munroe; scenery and costumes, Luis Maza; lighting, Ric Nardin. With Mitzi Hyman, John McDorman, Justine Gianetti, Bennett Baxley.

YOU CAN'T TAKE IT WITH YOU (16). By Moss Hart and George S. Kaufman. January 5, 1967. Director, Mitzi Hyman; scenery and costumes, Luis Maza. With Ann Simmons, Doris Bucher, Ed Bucher, Richard Bowden, Judith Van Buren.

THE GLASS MENAGERIE (16). By Tennessee Williams. February 9, 1967. Directors, Mitzi Hyman and Richard Bowden; scenery and costumes, Luis Maza. With Richard Bowden, Mitzi Hyman, Judith Van Buren, Bill Poulos.

THE CHERRY ORCHARD (16). By Anton Chekhov; translated by Stark Young. March 23, 1967. Director, Richard C. Munroe; scenery and costumes, Luis Maza. With Mitzi Hyman, Judith Van Buren, Pat Smith, Harold Hall, Jonathan Phelps, Meg Brush.

THE SKIN OF OUR TEETH (16). By Thornton Wilder. April 27, 1967. Director, Mitzi Hyman; scenery and costumes, Luis Maza; lighting, Ken Chapman. With Doris Bucher, Ann Simmons, George Humphries.

BALTIMORE

Center Stage

THE MISER (42). By Molière. September 22, 1966. Director, Rod Alexander; scenery and lighting, Stephen Hendrickson; costumes, James Edmund Brady. With Douglas Seale, Donald Symington, Elen Darrell Tovatt.

THE DEATH OF BESSIE SMITH by Edward Albee; director, Richard Gillespie and BENITO CERENO by Robert Lowell; director, Patrick Tovatt (42). October 27, 1966. Scenery, Whitney LeBlanc; lighting, David Ruecker; costumes, James Edmund Brady. With Richard Richardson, John Schuck, Jane Sanford, Graham Brown, David Rounds, Andre Womble.

LADY AUDLEY'S SECRET (42). Book by

Douglas Seale, from the novel by Mary Elizabeth Braddon; music, George Goehring; lyrics, John Kuntz. December 1, 1966. Director, Douglas Seale; scenery and lighting, Joan Larkey; costumes, James Edmund Brady; choreography, Zenaide Trigg; musical director, Thomas Conlin. With Gloria Maddox, William McKereghan, Donna Curtis, Ed Preble.

THE BALCONY (42). By Jean Genet; translated by Bernard Frechtman. January 5, 1967. Director, Brooks Jones; scenery, Niel Jampolis; lighting, Joseph Pacitti; costumes, James Edmund Brady. With Julie Bovasso, Marjorie Hirsh, John Braden.

BOSTON (See article on its season)

Charles Playhouse

LOVE FOR LOVE (47). By William Congreve. September 22, 1966. Director, Michael Murray; scenery and costumes, William D. Roberts; lighting, Hugh E. Lester. With Eric House, Gerald E. McGonagill, Edward Zang, Charles Keating, Barry Michlin, Lynn Milgrim, Lucy Martin.

THE BALCONY (47). By Jean Genet. November 3, 1966. Director, Ben Shaktman; scenery and costumes, William D. Roberts; lighting, Hugh E. Lester. With Olympia Dukakis, Gwyllum Evans, Gerald E. McGonagill, Louis Zorich, Barbara Tabor.

HAMLET (47). By William Shakespeare. December 15, 1966. Director, Michael Murray; scenery and costumes, William D. Roberts; lighting, Hugh E. Lester. With Edward Zang, Olympia Dukakis, Lynn Milgrim, Gerald E. McGonagill, Louis Zorich.

MOTHER COURAGE AND HER CHILDREN (47). By Bertolt Brecht; English version by Eric Bentley. January 26, 1967. Director, Michael Murray; scenery and costumes, William D. Roberts; lighting, Hugh E. Lester. With Olympia Dukakis, Lynn Milgrim, Charles Keating, Louis Zorich, Terence Currier.

OH WHAT A LOVELY WAR (47). Musical revue by Joan Littlewood and Ted Allan. March 9, 1967. Director, Eric House; scenery and costumes, William D. Roberts; lighting, Hugh E. Lester; choreography, Joseph Gifford. With Barbara Alleyn, Lee Caldwell, Jill Clayburgh, Jack Gianino.

INADMISSIBLE EVIDENCE (47). By John Osborne. April 20, 1967. Director, Michael Murray; scenery, William D. Roberts; lighting, Hugh E. Lester; costumes, Cecelia Eller. With Eric House, Gwyllum Evans, Charles Keating, Lynn Milgrim, Myra Carter, Pamela Blafer.

Theater Company of Boston, Inc.

WAITING FOR GODOT (16). By Samuel Beckett. October 3, 1966. Director, David Wheeler; scenery, Alexander Pertzoff; lighting, David Shaver; costumes, Leslie Shaver. With Paul Benedict, John Coe, Larry Bryggman, Joseph Hindy, Matthew Shaver.

MARAT/SADE (38). By Peter Weiss; English version by Geoffrey Skelton; verse adaptation by Adrian Mitchell. October 20, 1966. Director, David Wheeler; scenery and lighting, John Havens Thornton; costumes, Catherine M. King and Leslie Shaver. With Clinton Kimbrough, Bronia Stefan, Lisa Richards, F.M. Kimball.

ARMSTRONG'S LAST GOODNIGHT (22). By John Arden (American premiere). December 1, 1966. Director, David Wheeler; scenery, Alexander Pertzoff; lighting, Stephen Barnett; costumes, Leslie Shaver. With Ted Kazanoff, Larry Bryggman, Naomi Thornton.

TINY ALICE (38). By Edward Albee. January 3, 1967. Director, David Wheeler; scenery, Robert Allen; lighting, Gary Field; costumes, Leslie Shaver. With Ralph Waite, Olive Deering, Paul Benedict.

THE CAUCASIAN CHALK CIRCLE (31). By Bertolt Brecht; English version by Eric Bentley. February 8, 1967. Director, David Wheeler; scenery, Robert Allen; lighting, Lance Crocker; costumes, Leslie Shaver. With Penelope Allen, Morrie Peirce, Naomi Thornton, Ralph Waite.

A MEMORIAL SERVICE FOR WILLIAM JENNINGS BRYAN by Geoffrey Brush, director, David Wheeler; and CANDAULES, COMMISSIONER by Daniel C. Gerould (premiere), director, Ralph Waite (14). March 9, 1967. Scenery and lighting, Lance Crocker; costumes, Leslie Shaver. With Hector Elizondo, Arthur Merrow, Ralph Waite, Larry Bryggman, Anita Sangiolo.

THE UNDERTAKER by John Hawkes (premiere), and KRAPP'S LAST TAPE by Samuel Beckett (14). March 28, 1967. Director, David Wheeler; scenery and lighting, Lance Crocker; costumes, Leslie Shaver. With Hector Elizondo, Larry Bryggman.

DESIRE UNDER THE ELMS (22). By Eugene O'Neill. April 13, 1967. Director, David Wheeler; scenery, Robert Allen; lighting, Lance Crocker; costumes, Leslie Shaver. With Larry Bryggman, Ralph Waite, Bronia Stefan.

BUFFALO, N.Y.

Studio Arena Theater

CYRANO DE BERGERAC (27). By Edmond Rostand. October 6, 1966. Directors, Cyril Simon and Rocco Bufano; scenery, John Boyt; costumes, Colin Ferguson; lighting, David Zierk. With George Grizzard, Roy R. Scheider, Ned Wertimer, Aina Niemela.

THE MAN WHO CAME TO DINNER (27). By Moss Hart and George S. Kaufman. November 3, 1966. Director, Jon Jory; scenery, Myles Smith; lighting, David Zierk; costumes, Colin Ferguson. With Robert Eckles, Linda Selman, Elaine Kerr.

THE MIKADO (27). Operetta by Gilbert & Sullivan. December 8, 1966. Director, Allan Leicht; musical director, William Cox; scenery, Stephen Hendrickson; costumes, Carrie Fishbein; lighting, David Zierk. With Alan Zampese, Lee Stanleigh, Kenneth McMillan, Nan Withers, Jean Hebborn.

AFTER THE FALL (27). By Arthur Miller. January 5, 1967. Director, Tom Gruenewald; scenery, Mike English; lighting, David Zierk; costumes, Duane Andersen. With Gerald Richards, Linda Selman, Sally Rubin, Max Gulack, Jean Hebborn.

MARAT/SADE (27). By Peter Weiss; English version by Geoffrey Skelton; verse adaptation by Adrian Mitchell. February 2, 1967. Director, Jon Jory; scenery, Karl Eigsti; lighting, David Zierk; costumes, Melly Eigsti. With Max Gulack, John Schuck, Linda Selman, Elaine Kerr.

THE IMPORTANCE OF BEING EARNEST (27). By Oscar Wilde. March 2, 1967. Director, Tom Gruenewald; scenery, Clarke Dunham; lighting, David Zierk; costumes, Jeanne Button. With John Schuck, Alan Zampese, Jean Hebborn, Elaine Kerr, Aina Niemela.

THE LESSON by Eugene Ionesco and ANTIGONE by Jean Anouilh (27). March 30, 1967. Director, Allan Leicht; scenery, Douglas Higgins; lighting, David Zierk; costumes, Carrie Fishbein. With Nancy Kochery, Renee Leicht, Max Gulack, John Schuck, Linda Selman, Jean Hebborn, Elaine Kerr, Gerald Richards.

OH, KAY! (31). Musical with book by Guy Bolton and P.G. Wodehouse; music and lyrics by George and Ira Gershwin. April 27, 1967. Director, Allan Leicht; scenery, Robert Blackman; lighting, David Zierk; costumes, Jean Blanchette; musical director, Frank Renzulli; choreographer, Paul Hangauer. With Michael Bradshaw, John Schuck, Renee Leicht, Kenneth McMillan, Elaine Kerr.

CHICAGO

Goodman Memorial Theater

MARAT/SADE (25). By Peter Weiss; English version by Geoffrey Skelton; verse adaptation by Adrian Mitchell. October 21, 1966. Director, Charles McGaw; scenery, James Maronek; lighting, G. E. Naselius; costumes, D. Hudson Sheffield; choreography, Frances Allis. With Jerome Kilty, James Ray.

TARTUFFE (26). By Molière; translated by Richard Wilbur. December 21, 1966. Director, John Reich; scenery, George Pettit; lighting, G.E. Naselius; costumes, Uta Olson. With Jerome Kilty, Edgar Daniels, Sue Ann Park.

THE ECCENTRICITIES OF A NIGHTINGALE (23). By Tennessee Williams. February 5, 1967. Director, Bella Itkin; scenery, Marc Cohen; lighting, G. E. Naselius; costumes, Marna King. With Dolores Sutton, Lee Richardson, Beverly Younger.

MUCH ADO ABOUT NOTHING (23). By William Shakespeare; textual revisions by Robert Graves. February 17, 1967. Director, Joseph Slowik; scenery, George Pettit; lighting, Jerrold Gorrell. With Carrie Nye, James Ray, Vincent Park.

A DREAM PLAY (26). By August Strindberg; translated by Evert Sprinchorn; verse scenes by Lisel Mueller. March 31, 1967. Director, John Reich; scenery, James Maronek; lighting, G. E. Naselius; costumes, Marna King. With Gloria Foster, Frank Savino.

OH WHAT A LOVELY WAR (23). Musical revue by Joan Littlewood and Ted Allan. May 5, 1967. Director, Patrick Henry; scenery, Marc Cohen; lighting, G. E. Naselius; costumes, D. Hudson Sheffield; musical director, John Cina. With Terry Lomax, Susan Breeze, Dolores Kenan, Carrie Snodgress, John Christ, Richard Ooms, John Towey.

FRIEDMAN-ABELES

The entire cast of Harold Pinter's *The Homecoming* was a standout, as a group and as individual performers. Foreground, Vivien Merchant as Ruth; background, Paul Rogers as Max, Terence Rigby as Joey, John Normington as Sam, Michael Craig as Teddy and Ian Holm as Lenny.

Hume Cronyn as Tobias and Jessica Tandy (FAR RIGHT) as Agnes in *A Delicate Balance*

Martin Balsam as Richard Pawling in *You Know I Can't Hear You When the Water's Running* (FAR LEFT)

Barbara Harris as Eve *The Apple Tree*

Robert Preston as Michael and Mary Martin (FAR RIGHT) as Agnes in *I Do! I Do!*

Stacy Keach as MacBird in *MacBird!* (FAR LEFT)

Robert Salvio as Private Arthur Hamp in *Hamp*

el Grey as Master of
eremonies in *Cabaret*

osemary Harris (APA
pertory) as Lady
azle in *The School
r Scandal* (FAR RIGHT)

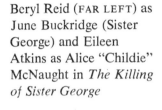

Beryl Reid (FAR LEFT) as
June Buckridge (Sister
George) and Eileen
Atkins as Alice "Childie"
McNaught in *The Killing
of Sister George*

nn Redgrave as Carol
elkett in *Black
omedy*

chard Benjamin as
orman Cornell in *The
ar-Spangled Girl*
AR RIGHT)

Norman Wisdom as Will
Mossop in *Walking
Happy* (FAR LEFT)

Reva Rose as Lucy in
*You're a Good Man
Charlie Brown*

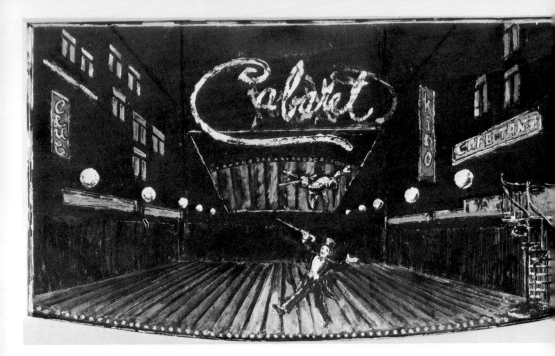

CABARET DESIGNS—*Above,* Boris Aronson's drawing of one of his settings, which won him the Tony Award for the year's best musical design. *Below,* two of Patricia Zipprodt's costume sketches for Sally Bowles (*left*), and Fraulein Schneider, likewise the Tony winner.

Hume Cronyn and Jessica Tandy, husband and wife offstage, played a married couple in Edward Albee's Pulitzer Prize-winning play *A Delicate Balance. Above* is the opening scene.

In Peter Shaffer's *Black Comedy* (*right*) the
characters were in pitch darkness. Lynn Redgrave (*center*) tries to hand a drink to Peter
Bull as her father (*left*), while Donald Madden (*right*) tries to catch Michael Crawford
sneaking out with a lamp.

Martin Balsam played an actor trying to get a job (*far left*) in *The Shock of Recognition;* a middle-aged husband (*above, center*) with a difficult wife (Eileen Heckart) in *I'll Be Home for Christmas;* and a middle-aged husband (*above, right*) with a young admirer (Melinda Dillon) in *The Footsteps of Doves*—all in Robert Anderson's program of one-acters entitled *You Know I Can't Hear You When the Water's Running.*

June Buckridge (Beryl Reid), soap opera actress who plays "Sister George," watches her pouting roommate (Eileen Atkins) being comforted by a lady executive (Lally Bowers) from the BBC, in Frank Marcus's *The Killing of Sister George*.

SETTINGS BY JO MIELZINER: *Above*, Mielziner's sketch of the Manhattan playground scene in Frank D. Gilroy's *That Summer—That Fall; at lower left*, his sketch of the Gulf Coast cottage for David Westheimer's *My Sweet Charlie*, on stilts, showing the fugitive climbing into what he thinks is an empty summer dwelling. *Below*, a scene from *My Sweet Charlie*, with Louis Gossett as a lawyer who has killed a man in a civil rights brawl and Bonnie Bedelia as a pregnant girl trying to have her baby in secret.

Above, Anthony Perkins, Richard Benjamin and Connie Stevens in Neil Simon's *The Star-Spangled Girl.* *Below,* Ferdi Hoffman speaks as one of the accused in Peter Weiss's *The Investigation*

PORTRAITS OF THE SEASON

Below, James Bolam, Peter Bayliss and Patricia Routle in *How's the World Treating You?,* British comedy Roger Milner

MISS ALIX JEFFRY

Above, Maureen Stapleton recreates her original role of Serafina in revival of *The Rose Tattoo,* with Harry Guardino

Above, Anthony Roberts, Anita Gillette and Lou Jacobi in Woody Allen's comedy *Don't Drink the Water*

FRIEDMAN-ABELES

Right, Mindy Carson, Walter Pidgeon, Arlene Francis and Daniel Keyes in revival of *Dinner at Eight*

MUSICALS

Left, Barbara Harris in the title role of the *Passionella* segment of *The Apple Tree*

Below, costume possibilities for Passionella in *The Apple Tree,* as sketched by Tony Walton. Top row, third from left, is the costume used in the show

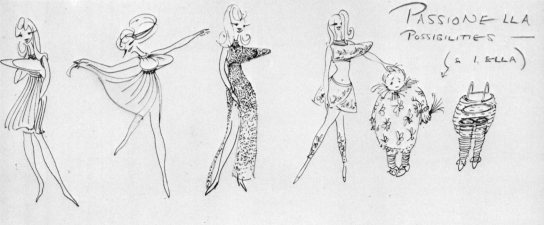

Above, the Clog Dance in *Walking Happy,* part of Danny Daniels' choreography for that show. Daniels also did the dances for the Music Theater of Lincoln Center revival of Irving Berlin's *Annie Get Your Gun* (*below*), starring Ethel Merman as Annie Oakley (*center,* singing "I Got the Sun in the Morning")

Above, Melina Mercouri in *Illya Darling*, musical version of *Never on Sunday*

Below, Robert Preston and Mary Martin as the husband and wife of *I Do! I Do!*

Right, Constance Towers and Bob Wright in the City Center revival of *The Sound of Music*

Below, Leslie Uggams (*center*) with dancers in *Hallelujah, Baby!*

MISS ALIX JEFFRY

FRIEDMAN-ABELES

John Raitt (*right*) and The Motley Crew in *A Joyful Noise*

FRIEDMAN-ABELES

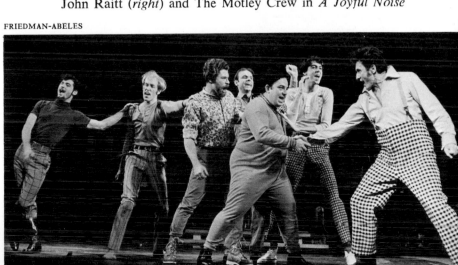

LINCOLN CENTER REPERTORY

Left, George Voskovec and Nancy Marchand in *The Alchemist*

Below, Anthony Quayle as bearded Galileo shows Sagredo (Philip Bosco) the stars in *Galileo*

LINCOLN CENTER DESIGNS—*Above*, David Hays setting and James Hart
Stearns costumes for *Yerma*, with the laundry scene in progress. *Below*, Stearns
costume sketches for *The Alchemist* (*left*) and *Galileo*

VISITORS

APA-PHOENIX — In repertory, (*right*) Sydney Walker, Helen Hayes and Donald Moffat in *Right You Are*; (*below*) Donald Moffat, Christine Pickles, Sydney Walker and Rosemary Harris in *War and Peace*

BRITISH ENSEMBLES—*Above*, The D'Oyly Carte Opera Company in *The Mikado*; *below*, Bristol Old Vic in *Measure for Measure*

The Man and Woman dolls in the *Motel* segment of Jean-Claude van Itallie's *America Hurrah*. The third character in the playlet, the Motel Keeper doll, is partly visible in left portion of photo

The Interviewers and Applicants (*above*) in the *Interview* segment of *America Hurrah* were played by Conard Fowkes, Bill Macy, Henry Calvert, James Barbosa, Cynthia Harris, Ronnie Gilbert, Brenda Smiley and Joyce Aaron

Right, Rip Torn and
Hugh Marlowe
(reclining) in
Norman Mailer's *The
Deer Park*

Leslie Barrett as Padre, Robert Salvio as Pvt. Hamp and Michael Lipton as Lt. Hargreaves in John Wilson's British drama of World War I, *Hamp*

Left, Jeanne Button's sketch for MacBird's costume. *Right*, in Barbara Garson's *MacBird!*, "Robert Ken O'Dunc" (William Devane) and "MacBird" (Stacy Keach) come to grips in the final scene

Right, Reid Shelton and Alice Cannon in the musical *Man With a Load of Mischief*

MISS ALIX JEFFRY

Below, Alan Kimmel's sketch of the setting for *You're a Good Man Charlie Brown*

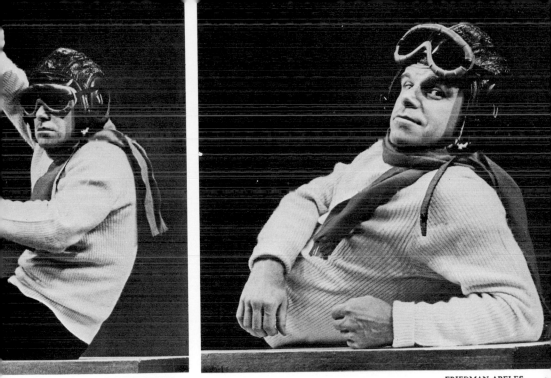

SNOOPY VS. THE RED BARON—In the musical *You're a Good Man Charlie Brown,* as in the comic strip "Peanuts," the dog Snoopy (Bill Hinnant) sits atop his doghouse and dreams that he is a World War I flying ace attacking (*above, far left*) the Red Baron, outfought and retreating (*center*) and living to fight the Red Baron another day (*right*)

Terry Kiser, Vic Arnold, Robert Christian and Bill Moor as cellmates in *Fortune and Men's Eyes*

A scene from *Viet Rock*

CINCINNATI — U.S. premiere of *Eh?* (*left*), later produced off Broadway, took place at Playhouse in the Park, with Edward Zang (back to camera) and Sam Waterston

IVOR PROTHEROE

LOS ANGELES—*Above,* Theater Group-UCLA production of
Next Time I'll Sing to You. Right,
Joyce Ebert and David Opatoshu
in *The Devils* produced by the
same company, renamed Center
Theater Group, at new Mark Taper Forum.

ERIC SKIPSEY

HOUSTON — Alley Theater's *Th Diary of a Scoundrel* (*below*), wit Bettye Fitzpatrick

SAN FRANCISCO—The American Conservatory Theater production of *Under Milk Wood* (*above*), with Rene Auberjonois

NEW HAVEN—Long Wharf Theater's *The Tavern* (*below*), with Bruce Weitz, Robert Milli, Jan Farrand and William Swetland

BLISS

EVELAND and MIN-
APOLIS—Mr. Antrobus
mes home carrying a
eel, which he has just in-
ated, in this scene from
e *Skin of Our Teeth* as
duced (*above*) by the
eveland Play House and
ght) by Minneapolis' Ty-
he Guthrie Theater

BOSTON—Edward Zang
(*right*) as Hamlet at the
Charles Playhouse

WASHINGTON—Arena Stage production of *The Inspector-General*

SEATTLE—*The Crucible* in Seattle Repertory, with Jonathan Farwell and Elizabeth MacDonald

LOUISVILLE—The Actors Theater production of *All My Sons,* with Max Howard and Grant Sheehan

HARTFORD—Charles Cioffi and David Birney in Hartford Stage Company's *Endgame*

NEW ORLEANS—Rex Thompson and Gretchen Corbett as Romeo and Juliet in repertory

STANFORD — Gilbert Green, Jane Hoffman and Jerome Raphel in *A Slight Ache (right)* at Stanford Repertory's Little Theater

MILWAUKEE —
Repertory production of *Electra*

YPSILANTI—Summer season at Greek Theater presented Bert Lahr (*left*) in *The Birds* and Judith Anderson (*below*) in *The Eumenides*

CINCINNATI

Playhouse In The Park

BENITO CERENO by Robert Lowell, and THE AMERICAN DREAM by Edward Albee (23). April 28, 1966. Director, Brooks Jones; scenery, Douglas W. Schmidt; lighting, Joe Pacitti; costumes, Caley Summers. With Ann Whiteside, Ralph Drischell, Margaretta Warwick, David Hooks, Andrew Robinson, Lawrence Luckenbill, Roscoe Lee Browne.

SODOM AND GOMORRAH (23). By Jean Giraudoux; translated by Herma Briffault. May 25, 1966. Director, Stephen Porter; scenery and lighting, Joe Pacitti; costumes, Caley Summers. With Roscoe Lee Browne, Charles Cioffi, Neil Vipond, Pauline Elliott, Paddy Edwards.

CHARLEY'S AUNT (23). By Brandon Thomas. June 16, 1966. Director, David Hooks; scenery, Douglas W. Schmidt; lighting, Joe Pacitti; costumes, Caley Summers. With Neil Vipond, Andrew Robinson, Mariclare Costello, Pauline Elliott.

EH? (23). By Henry Livings (American premiere). July 13, 1966. Director, Melvin Bernhardt; scenery, Douglas W. Schmidt; lighting, Joe Pacitti; costumes, Caley Summers. With Charles Cioffi, Edward Zang, Paddy Edwards, Sam Waterston, David Hooks, Linda Segal.

THE SKIN OF OUR TEETH (23). By Thornton Wilder. August 4, 1966. Director, Brooks Jones; scenery, Douglas W. Schmidt; lighting, Joe Pacitti; costumes, Caley Summers. With Paddy Edwards, Barbara Cason, David Hooks, Alice Cannon, Ty McConnell.

THE FANTASTICKS (23). Musical with book and lyrics by Tom Jones; music by Harvey Schmidt; based on Les Romantiques by Edmond Rostand. August 31, 1966. Directors, Brooks Jones and Ty McConnell; musical director, Frederic Gahr. With Charles Cioffi, Alice Cannon, Ty McConnell, David Hooks, Donald Ewer, John Coe. Re-produced for 13 performances beginning March 30, 1967.

THE IMPORTANCE OF BEING EARNEST (28). By Oscar Wilde. April 13, 1967. Director, David Hooks; scenery, Douglas W. Schmidt; lighting, Joe Pacitti; costumes, Caley Summers. With Edward Zang, Charles Cioffi, Margaret Bannerman, Charlotte Moore, Alice Cannon.

CLEVELAND

Cleveland Play House: Euclid-77th Theater

ABSENCE OF A CELLO (7). By Ira Wallach. September 13, 1966. Director, Kirk Willis; scenery, Paul Rodgers. With Edith Owen, William Paterson, Susan Sullivan, Vaughn McBride.

A PROFILE OF BENJAMIN FRANKLIN (7). By William Paterson. September 20, 1966. With William Paterson.

A PROFILE OF HOLMES (12). By William Paterson. September 21, 1966. With William Paterson.

THE MISER (30). By Molière; adapted by Miles Malleson. September 28, 1966. Director, William Woodman; scenery and lighting, Paul Rodgers; costumes, Doris J. Ramsey. With Ronald B. Parady, Mary Shelley, David Snell, Richard Halverson, June Gibbons, Sally St. John.

THE SKIN OF OUR TEETH (29). By Thornton Wilder. November 2, 1966. Director, William Woodman; scenery, Paul Rodgers; costumes, Doris J. Ramsey. With Adale O'Brien, Betsy Thurman, Richard Oberlin, Catherine Heiser, David Snell.

A CASE OF LIBEL (41). By Henry Denker; based on My Life in Court by Louis Nizer. December 7, 1966. Director, Tom Brennan; scenery, Paul Rodgers; costumes, Doris J. Ramsey. With Richard Oberlin, David Snell, Edith Owen, Vivienne Stotter, Allen Leatherman.

BLITHE SPIRIT (35). By Noel Coward. January 25, 1967. Director, William Paterson; scenery, Paul Rodgers; costumes, Doris J. Ramsey. With Margaret Hamilton, Richard Halverson, Jeanne Vanderbilt, Judith Adams.

ANY WEDNESDAY (42). By Muriel Resnik. March 8, 1967. Director, Raphael Kelly; scenery, Mary McGinness. With Susan Sullivan, William Paterson, Susan Sadler, David Snell.

THE TEMPEST (13). By William Shake-speare. April 4, 1967. Director, Robert Snook; scenery, Paul Rodgers; costumes, Doris J. Ramsey. With Robert Allman, Ronald B. Parady, John Howard, Norman Parker, Heidi Murray, Mary Shelley.

Cleveland Play House: Francis E. Drury Theater

THE SUBJECT WAS ROSES (24). By Frank D. Gilroy. October 12, 1966. Director, Kirk Willis; scenery, Paul Rodgers. With Robert Allman, Edith Owen, William Howey.

U.S.A. (19). By Paul Shyre and John Dos Passos; based on the novel by John Dos Passos. November 16, 1966. Director, Stuart Levin; scenery, Barbara Leatherman; costumes, Doris J. Ramsey. With David Selby, Robert Allman, David Frazier, Mary Shelley, Marjorie Johnson, Jeanne Vanderbilt.

LIFE WITH FATHER (39). By Howard Lindsay and Russel Crouse. December 21, 1966. Director, Stuart Levin; scenery, Paul Rodgers; costumes, Doris J. Ramsey. With William Paterson, Mary Hopkins, David Heppard, Dorothy Quinn, Catherine Heizer.

THE HOSTAGE (35). By Brendan Behan. February 8, 1967. Director, Richard Oberlin; scenery, Paul Rodgers; costumes, Doris J. Ramsey; music director, Keith Mackey; choreography, Sarah May. With June Gibbons, Robert Allman, Edith Owen, Susan McArthur, Bob Moak.

BAREFOOT IN THE PARK (36). By Neil Simon. March 29, 1967. Director, Richard Oberlin; scenery, Paul Rodgers. With Sandra Kane, William Howey, Dorothy Paxton, Richard Oberlin.

Cleveland Play House: Brooks Theater

BRECHT ON BRECHT (22). By George Tabori. December 27, 1966. Director, Robert Snook. With Robert Allman, Jan E. Bruml, Philip Kerr, Edith Owen, David Selby, Mary Shelley, Bertolt Brecht's recorded voice.

DALLAS (See article on its season)

Dallas Theater Center: Down Center Stage

MY BROTHER'S KEEPER by John Logan; director, Cecile Guidote; THE DANCE by Claudette Gardner; director, Howard A. Karlsberg; ONE DEAD INDIAN by Randy Ford; director, Leonard T. Wagner (6). (American premieres) June 16, 1966. Scenery, Kathleen Benke, Lorenzo Nelson, Edward K. Herrmann; lighting, Duk Hyung Yoo; costumes, Janice Rabinovitz. With Johnny McBee, Jon Stephen Crane, Sue Sellors Finley, Synthia Rogers, Mike Dendy, Marilyn Markley, Janice Rabinovitz, Preston Jones, Art Greenhaw, Bob Baca, Dale Blair.

TINY ALICE (24). By Edward Albee. October 13, 1966. Director, Louise Mosley; scenery, Charlote Cole; lighting, Duk Hyung Yoo; costumes, Kathleen Benke. With John Figlmiller, Ken Latimer, Gene Leggett, Campbell Thomas, Judith Davis.

A TASTE OF HONEY (32). By Shelagh Delaney. February 2, 1967. Director, David Pursley; scenery, Anne Butler; costumes, David Pursley; lighting, Pat Baca. With Roberta Rude, Jacque Thomas, John Shepherd, James Nelson Harrell, Clyde Evans.

THE SUBJECT WAS ROSES (32). By Frank D. Gilroy. July 26, 1966. Director, George Webby; scenery, Nancy Levinson; lighting, Sally Netzel; costumes, Ryland Merkey. With Preston Jones, Mary Sue Fridge Jones, Randolph Tallman.

THE AMOROUS FLEA (12). Musical with book by Jerry Devine; music and lyrics by Bruce Montgomery; based on Molière's The School for Wives. November 24, 1966. Director, Anna Paul Rogers; scenery and costumes, David Pursley; lighting, Matt Tracy; musical director, Beatrice Gaspar; choreography, Anna Paul Rogers. With David Pursley, Linda Giese, Penny Metropulos, Richard Jenkins.

THE WORLD OF CARL SANDBURG (27). By Norman Corwin; adapted from the works of Carl Sandburg. May 11, 1967. Director, Mike Dendy; scenery and costumes, Ella-Mae Brainard; lighting, Bob Baca. With Lynn Trammell, Thomas Nichols, Randolph Tallman.

Dallas Theater Center: Kalita Humphreys Theater

YOU CAN'T TAKE IT WITH YOU (14). By Moss Hart and George S. Kaufman. June 15, 1966. Director, Ken Latimer; scenery and costumes, Charlote Cole; lighting, Ruthanne Boyles. With Sandra Moore, Anna Gonyaw, Ryland Merkey, James Nelson Harrell, Mary Sue Fridge Jones.

LITTLE MARY SUNSHINE (31). Musical by Rick Besoyan. July 5, 1966. Director, Ivan Rider; musical director, Raymond Allen; scenery, Richard Slocum; lighting, Bill Enix. With Ryland Merkey, Ronald Wilcox, Miriam Gulager, Louise Mosley.

ABSENCE OF A CELLO (23). By Ira Wallach. August 18, 1966. Director, John Figlmiller; scenery and costumes, Richard Slocum; lighting, Bob Baca. With Betty June Lary, James Nelson Harrell, Pat Baca, Gene Leggett.

A BUG IN HER EAR (24). By Georges Feydeau; translated by Barnett Shaw. October 20, 1966. Director, Jean-Pierre Granval (Théâtre de France); scenery and costumes, David Pursley; lighting, Kathleen Benke. With David Pursley, Mike Dendy, Kaki Dowling, Randy Moore.

BLITHE SPIRIT (18). By Noel Coward. November 25, 1966. Director, Paul Baker; scenery and costumes, Nancy Levinson; lighting, Randy Moore. With Martha Bumpas Gaylord, Ryland Merkey, Ella-Mae Brainard, Kaki Dowling.

ALICE IN WONDERLAND (17). Musical based on the book by Lewis Carroll, adapted by Sally Netzel; music, Beatrice Gaspar; lyrics, Sally Netzel and Beatrice Gaspar. December 22, 1966. Director, Louise Mosley; scenery and costumes, Thomas Nichols; lighting, Robyn Baker Flatt; choreography, Colibri Wegerer. With Nancy Collins, Jacque Thomas, Mona Pursely, Victor Fichtner, Judith Davis.

JOURNEY TO JEFFERSON (14). By Robert L. Flynn; adapted from the novel As I Lay Dying by William Faulkner. January 12, 1967. Director, Paul Baker; scenery, Virgil Beavers; lighting, Robyn Baker Flatt and Randy Moore; costumes, Mary Sue Fridge Jones. With James Nelson Harrell, Mary Sue Fridge Jones, Drexel H. Riley, Ken Latimer, Robert Frost, Robyn Baker Flatt, Buddy Smith.

YOU NEVER CAN TELL (24). By George Bernard Shaw. February 9, 1967. Director, Anna Paul Rogers; scenery and costumes, Charlote Cole; lighting, Matt Tracy. With Mona Pursley, Edward K. Herrmann, Campbell Thomas, Barbara Gilstrap.

THE TEMPEST (8). By William Shakespeare. March 14, 1967. Director, Paul Baker in association with Ken Latimer; scenery, Bjorn Winblad; lighting, Bob Baca; costumes, Charlote Cole. With Mike Dendy, Randolph Tallman, Preston Jones, Penny Metropulos.

JULIUS CAESAR (14). By William Shakespeare. March 28, 1967. Director, Randy Moore; scenery and costumes, Mary Sue Fridge Jones; lighting, Sally Netzel. With Preston Jones, Randy Moore, Campbell Thomas, Mike Dendy, Sally Netzel, Pat Baca.

THE CAUCASIAN CHALK CIRCLE (25). By Bertolt Brecht; English version by Eric Bentley. May 9, 1967. Director, Harry Buckwitz; scenery and costumes, Mary Sue Fridge Jones. With Ryland Merkey, Judith Davis and Kaki Dowling.

HARRISBURG, PA.

Arena House Theater

MY WIFE AND I (15). Musical with book, lyrics, and music by Bill Mahoney (premiere). September 21, 1966. Director-designer, Tom Ross Prather. With Helon Blount, Robert R. Wait, Ed Penn.

ANY WEDNESDAY (28). By Muriel Resnik. October 6, 1966. Director-designer, Howard Crampton-Smith. With Mary E. Small, Robert Baines, Barney Hodges, Gloria Hermes.

THE HOSTAGE (28). By Brendan Behan. November 3, 1966. Director-designer, Tom Ross Prather. With Steven Meyer, Gloria Hermes, Curt Williams.

THE OWL AND THE PUSSYCAT (21). By Bill Manhoff. November 30, 1966. Director-designer, Tom Ross Prather. With Steven Meyer, Cherry Davis.

THE KNACK (17). By Ann Jellicoe. December 31, 1966. Director-designer, Tom Ross Prather. With Stuart Howard, Lowell Christy, Michael Sander, Elizabeth Swain.

THE ROPE (13). By Patrick Hamilton. January 18, 1967. Director-designer, Tom Ross Prather. With Michael Sander, Lowell Christy, Robert R. Wait.

HARVEY (15). By Mary Chase. February 1, 1967. Director-designer, Tom Ross Prather. With Robert R. Wait, Elizabeth Kerr.

ABSENCE OF A CELLO (20). By Ira Wallach. February 16, 1967. Director-designer, Tom Ross Prather. With Bruce Hall, Gloria Hermes, Robert R. Wait.

THE ROSE TATTOO (27). By Tennessee

Williams. March 8, 1967. Director-designer, Tom Ross Prather. With Mary Tahmin, Jamil Zakkai.

COME BLOW YOUR HORN (20). By Neil Simon. April 1, 1967. Director-designer, Tom Ross Prather. With Gil Brandsen, Elizabeth Kerr, Bruce Hall.

IRMA LA DOUCE (23). Musical with book and lyrics by Alexandre Breffort; music, Marguerite Monnot; English translation, book and lyrics by Julian More, David Heneker and Monty Norman. Director-designer, Tom Ross Prather; lighting, William A. Meinecke; musical director, James Reed Lawler; choreography, Darwin Knight. With Gene Bira, Johanna Lawrence, Robert R. Wait.

HARTFORD, CONN.

Hartford Stage Co.

POOR BITOS (34). By Jean Anouilh; translated by Lucienne Hill. October 7, 1966. Director, Jacques Cartier; scenery, Neil Jampolis; lighting, Peter Hunt; costumes, Caley Summers. With Robert Gaus, Ted D'Arms, Gene Gross, David Birney, Susan Sullivan.

ENDGAME and ACT WITHOUT WORDS (34). By Samuel Beckett. November 11, 1966. Directors, Paul Weidener and Jacques Cartier; scenery and lighting, Neil Jampolis; costumes, Caley Summers. With John Bottoms and alternating casts for Endgame, Gene Gross, Charles Cioffi, Ted D'Arms, David Birney, Henry Thomas, K. Lipe O'Dell, Vivian Reis, Robert Gaus.

THREE SISTERS (34). By Anton Chekhov. December 16, 1966. Director, Jacques Cartier; scenery and lighting, Neil Jampolis; costumes, Caley Summers. With Charlotte Moore, Vivian Reis, Lisa Richards, Ted D'Arms, Ann Whiteside, Paul Weidener, Osceola Archer.

UNDER THE GASLIGHT (34). By Augustin Daley. January 20, 1967. Director, Gordon Hunt; scenery, Neil Jampolis; lighting, Peter

Hunt. With David Birney, John Bottoms, Marilyn Chris, Robert Gaus, Gene Gross.

ENRICO IV (34). By Luigi Pirandello; translated by John Reich. February 24, 1967. Director, Jacques Cartier; scenery, John Conklin; lighting, Peter Hunt; costumes, Caley Summers. With Charles Cioffi, Barbara Beckley, Gene Gross, Eve Collyer.

THE SERVANT OF TWO MASTERS (34). By Carlo Goldoni; translated by Paul Weidener. March 31, 1967. Director, Paul Weidener; scenery, John Conklin; lighting, Peter Hunt; costumes, Caley Summers. With Henry Thomas, Jacqueline Coslow, Gene Gross, Eve Collyer, Robert Gaus.

THE FANTASTICKS (34). Musical with book and lyrics by Tom Jones; music by Harvey Schmidt; based on Edmond Rostand's Les Romantiques. May 5, 1967. Director and lighting, Peter Hunt; scenery and costumes, John Conklin. With Judith McCauley, Gary Krawford, Tom Urich, Robert Gaus, Gene Gross.

HOUSTON (See article on its season)

Alley Theater

THE WORLD OF SHOLOM ALEICHEM (45). By Arnold Perl. October 19, 1966. Director, John Wylie; scenery, Paul Owen. With Tom Toner, Alice Drummond, Joseph Ruskin, Virginia Payne, J. Robert Dietz, Jerry Hardin.

THE DIARY OF A SCOUNDREL (45). By Alexander Ostrovsky; adapted by Rodney Ackland. November 30, 1966. Director, Joseph Ruskin; scenery, Paul Owen. With Dale Helward, Jerome Ballew, Jerry Hardin, Trent Jenkins, Bettye Fitzpatrick, Jeannette Clift.

THE PHYSICISTS (45). By Friedrich Duerrenmatt; translated by James Kirkup. January 11, 1967. Director, Louis Criss; scenery, Paul Owen. With Lillian Evans, Virginia Payne, J. Robert Dietz, Dale Helward.

THE SEAGULL (47). By Anton Chekhov; adapted by Nina Vance. February 22, 1967. Director, Nina Vance; scenery and costumes, Paul Owen; lighting, Florine Pulley. With Alexandra Berlin, John Wylie, Bella Jarrett, Claude Woolman, Dale Helward, Lillian Evans, Tom Toner.

THE GREAT SEBASTIANS (45). By Howard Lindsay and Russel Crouse. April 5, 1967. Director, William Hardy; scenery and costumes, Paul Owen. With Jeannette Clift, John Wylie, Tom Toner, Bettye Fitzpatrick, Jerry Hardin, Dale Helward.

OH WHAT A LOVELY WAR (40). Musical revue by Joan Littlewood and Ted Allan. June 2, 1967. Director, Edward Parone; scenery, Robin Wagner; lighting, William Eggleston; costumes, Marjorie Plaimin; musical director, George Manos. With the resident company and Alexandra Berlin, Sue Driesen, April Shawhan.

KANSAS CITY

Kansas Circle Theater

OH WHAT A LOVELY WAR (26). Musical revue by Joan Littlewood and Ted Allan. November 9, 1967. Director, George Wasko; scenery and lighting, Dennis Rexroad; costumes, Dick Donahue and Dennis Rexroad; musical director, Robert Parke; choreography, Tom Steinhoff. With Dick Donahue, Jane Fopeano, Arne Gundersen, Barbara Kaiser, Ann Poindexter.

THE PLAYBOY OF THE WESTERN WORLD (26). By John Millington Synge. December 7, 1966. Director, Robert Ennis Turoff; scenery, Bill Peterson; lighting, Dennis Rexroad. With John Armstrong, John Swearingen, Mary Sullivan, Bernard Taylor.

SWEET BIRD OF YOUTH (26). By Tennessee Williams. January 4, 1967. Director, George Wasko; scenery and lighting, Dennis Rexroad; costumes, Kathleen Harrington. With George Reinhalt, Lois Daniel, John Armstrong.

HARVEY (26). By Mary Chase. February 1, 1967. Director, Richard France; scenery and lighting, Dennis Rexroad; costumes, Dick Donahue. With Rudy Tronto, Velma Royton, John Armstrong.

AN ENEMY OF THE PEOPLE (26). By Henrik Ibsen; translated by Eva Le Gallienne. March 1, 1967. Director, Charles Maryan; scenery and lighting, Dennis Rexroad; costumes, Kathleen Harrington. With Ronnie Wallman, George Wasko, William Brydon, John Ferguson, Mary Sullivan, John Armstrong.

PAL JOEY (26). Musical with book by John O'Hara; music by Richard Rodgers; lyrics by Lorenz Hart. March 29, 1967. Director and choreography, Richard France; musical director, Robert Parke; scenery and lighting, Dennis Rexroad; costumes, Kathleen Harrington. With Bryan David Scott, Jane Fopeano, Guen Omeron.

TINY ALICE (26). By Edward Albee. April 26, 1967. Director, Lois Daniel; scenery and costumes, Kent Broadhurst; lighting, Dennis Rexroad. With Signe Hasso, Bernard Taylor, Rudy Tronto.

THE KNACK (26). By Ann Jellicoe. May 24, 1967. Director, George Wasko; scenery, William Patterson; lighting, Dennis Rexroad. With Dick Donahue, Bernard Taylor, John Swearingen, Jane Fopeano.

LOS ANGELES (See article on its season)

Center Theater Group (formerly Theater Group UCLA)

NEXT TIME I'LL SING TO YOU (29). By James Saunders. June 1, 1966. Director, Malcolm Black; scenery, Sydney Rushakoff; lighting, Myles Harmon; costumes, Diana Palsky. With Christopher Cary, Patrick Horgan, Carol Booth, James B. Douglas, Robert Casper.

CANDIDE (11). Musical with book by Lillian Hellman; music by Leonard Bernstein; lyrics by Richard Wilbur; based on the satire by Voltaire. July 12, 1966. Director, Gordon Davidson; musical director, Maurice Peress; scenery, costumes, and lighting, Peter Wexler; choreography, John Wilson. With Carroll O'Connor, David Watson, Mary Grover, Nina Dova, Andre Philippe.

THE BIRTHDAY PARTY (29). By Harold Pinter. July 26, 1966. Director, Mel Shapiro; scenery and costumes, Michael Devine; lighting, Gilbert V. Hemsley Jr. With Mary Jackson, Gilbert Green, Gerald Hiken, Kelly Jean Peters, Paul E. Richards, Harold Gould.

POOR BITOS (30). By Jean Anouilh; translated by Lucienne Hill. September 7, 1966. Director, Malcolm Black; scenery and costumes, Michael Devine; lighting, Myles Har-

mon. With James A. Douglas, Patrick Horgan, Barbara Babcock.

THE DEVILS (48). By John Whiting; based on a story by Aldous Huxley. April 14, 1967. Director, Gordon Davidson; scenery, lighting and costumes, Peter Wexler. With Frank Langella, Joyce Ebert, Mark Lenard, David Opatoshu, Anthony Zerbe.

LOUISVILLE, KY.

Actors Theater of Louisville

ALL MY SONS (27). By Arthur Miller. September 22, 1966. Director, Richard Block; scenery, Bette Kaelin; lighting, Richard Mix; costumes, Lucile Paris. With Ned Beatty, Max Howard, Jo Deodato.

CHARLEY'S AUNT (28). By Brandon Thomas. October 20, 1966. Director, Jock Ferguson; scenery, Bette Kaelin; lighting, Richard Mix; costumes, Lucile Paris. With Max Leonard, Lenny Baker, Jane Singer, Melody Greer.

MISS JULIE (27). By August Strindberg. November 17, 1966. Director, Richard Block; scenery, Bette Kaelin; lighting, Richard Mix; costumes, Lucile Paris. With Jane Singer, Grant Sheehan.

THE KNACK (25). By Ann Jellicoe. December 15, 1966. Director, Richard Block; scenery, Bette Kaelin; lighting, Richard Mix; costumes, Lucile Paris. With Andre Womble, Lenny Baker, Max Howard, Melody Greer.

IN WHITE AMERICA (28). By Martin B.

Duberman. January 12, 1967. Director, Jordon Hott; scenery, Brooke Karzen; lighting, Richard Mix; costumes, Lucile Paris. With Gloria James, William Redden, Grant Sheehan, Jane Singer, Paul Watson, Andre Womble.

SLOW DANCE ON THE KILLING GROUND (27). By William Hanley. February 9, 1967. Director, Richard Block; scenery, Brooke Karzen; lighting, Richard Mix; costumes, Lucile Paris. With Grant Sheehan, Andre Womble, Jane Singer.

NATHAN WEINSTEIN'S DAUGHTER (27). By David Rayfiel. March 9, 1967. Director, Gennaro Montanino; scenery, Brooke Karzen; lighting, Richard Mix; costumes, Lucile Paris. With Bryan C. Clark, Jane Singer, Lenny Baker, Jo Deodato.

A STREETCAR NAMED DESIRE (27). By Tennessee Williams. April 6, 1967. Director, Philip Minor; scenery, Brooke Karzen; lighting, Richard Mix; costumes, Lucile Paris. With Jane Welch, Grant Sheehan, Jane Singer, James Carruthers.

MEMPHIS

Front Street Theater

A FUNNY THING HAPPENED ON THE WAY TO THE FORUM (26). Musical with book by Burt Shevelove and Larry Gelbart; music and lyrics by Stephen Sondheim. September 29, 1966. Director, George Touliatos; scenery, Grady Larkins; choreography, Errol Strider; costumes, Kurt Wilhelm; musical director, Douglas Finney; lighting, Lynn LePelley. With Robert Levine, Doris Karnes, Tom Carson, Allen Hamilton, Duane Campbell.

THE LITTLE FOXES (26). By Lillian Hellman. October 27, 1966. Director, Curt Reis; scenery, Grady Larkins; costumes, Kurt Wilhelm; lighting, Curt Reis. With Nancy Cole, Cassandra Morgon, Tom Carson, Leon Russom, Myra Carter.

YOU NEVER CAN TELL (26). By George Bernard Shaw. November 24, 1966. Director, Louis Criss; scenery, Grady Larkins; costumes, Kurt Wilhelm; lighting, Lynn LePelley. With Joseph Valentine, Nancy Baker, Myra Carter.

A STREETCAR NAMED DESIRE (24). By Tennessee Williams. December 22, 1966. Scenery, Grady Larkins; costumes, Kurt Wilhelm, lighting, Lynn LePelley. With Dawn Greenleigh, Karen Grassle, Anthony Hamilton.

MACBETH (26). By William Shakespeare. January 19, 1967. Director, Curt Reis; scenery, Grady Larkins; costumes, Kurt Wilhelm. With Roland Hewgill, Macon McCalman, Patricia Elliott.

THE MISER (26). By Molière. February 16, 1967. Director, Carl Neber; scenery, Grady Larkins; costumes, Kurt Wilhelm; lighting, Lynn LePelley; original music, William Bolcom. With Al Corbin, Leon Russom, Karen Grassle.

SIX CHARACTERS IN SEARCH OF AN AUTHOR (26). By Luigi Pirandello. Translated by Paul Avila Mayer. March 16, 1967. Director, George Touliatos; scenery, Grady Larkins; costumes, Kurt Wilhelm; lighting, Lynn LePelley. With Robert Karns, Nancy Baker.

GYPSY (25). Musical with book by Arthur Laurents; lyrics by Stephen Sondheim; music by Jule Styne. April 13, 1967. Director, George Touliatos; scenery, Grady Larkins; costumes, Kurt Wilhelm; lighting, Lynn LePelley; choreography, Barry Fuller, Otis Smith. With Chris Colbert, Mary Shelton, Nancy Baker.

MILWAUKEE

Milwaukee Repertory Theater

ELECTRA (33). By Sophocles. October 20, 1966. Director, Tunc Yalman; scenery and costumes, William James Wall; lighting, James W. Hook. With Gregory Abels, Nicholas Stamos, Erika Slezak, Eleanor Wilson, Charles Kimbrough.

THE PHYSICISTS (26). By Friedrich Duerrenmatt; translated by James Kirkup. November 24, 1966. Director, Hy Kalus; scenery, William James Wall; lighting, N. Wersel Hook; costumes, Gail Singer. With Roger Hamilton, Rhoda B. Carrol, Gregory Abels, Charles Kimbrough, Eleanor Wilson, Tom Tarpey.

DESIGN FOR LIVING (26). By Noel Coward. December 29, 1966. Director, Tunc Yalman; scenery and costumes, William James Wall; lighting, Merry Tigar. With Erika Slezak, Charles Kimbrough, Michael Fairman.

THE MERCHANT OF VENICE (41). By William Shakespeare. January 26, 1967. Director, Eugene Lesser; scenery and costumes, William James Wall; lighting, William Mintzer. With Boris Tumarin, Janet Kaprol, Charles Kimbrough.

THE MISER (26). By Molière; translater-adapter, Kirk Denmark. March 9, 1967. Director, Louis Criss; scenery and costumes, William James Wall; lighting, William Mintzer. With Charles Kimbrough, Rebecca Lombard, Gregory Abels, Eleanor Wilson.

PUNTILA AND HIS SERVANT (26). By Bertolt Brecht; translated by Gerhard Nelhaus. April 6, 1967. Director, Robert Kalfin; scenery, William James Wall; lighting, William Mintzer; costumes, Gail Singer. With Roger Hamilton, Mary Jones Kimbrough, Michael Fairman.

HEDDA GABLER (27). By Henrik Ibsen; translated by Eva Le Gallienne. May 4, 1967. Director, Tunc Yalman; scenery and costumes, William James Wall; lighting, William Mintzer. With Erika Slezak, Charles Kimbrough, Gregory Abels, Janet Kaprol.

THE INVESTIGATION and HOT BUTTERED ROLL (11). By Rosalyn Drexler. October 25, 1966. Director, Thomas Bissinger; scenery and costumes, William James Wall. With Rhoda B. Carrol, Michael Fairman, Rebecca Lombard, Nicholas Stamos, Tom Tarpey.

THE SUDDEN AND ACCIDENTAL RE-EDUCATION OF HORSE JOHNSON (9). By Douglas Taylor. February 28, 1967. Director, Robert Benedetti; scenery, Robert Benedetti; lighting, William Mintzer; costumes, Gail Singer. With Michael Fairman, Tom Tarpey, Mary Jane Kimbrough, Gregory Abels.

MINNEAPOLIS

Tyrone Guthrie Theater

THE SKIN OF OUR TEETH (50). By Thornton Wilder. May 31, 1966. Director, Douglas Campbell; scenery, lighting, costumes, Tanya Moiseiwitsch and Carolyn Parker. With Lee Richardson, Ruth Nelson, Nancy Wickwire.

THE DANCE OF DEATH (30). By August Strindberg; translated by Norman Ginsbury. June 1, 1966. Director, Douglas Campbell; scenery, lighting, costumes, Lewis Brown. With Robert Pastene, Nancy Wickwire, Patricia Elliott, Paul Ballantyne.

AS YOU LIKE IT (51). By William Shakespeare. June 2, 1966. Director, Edward Payson Call; scenery, costumes, lighting, Tanya Moiseiwitsch. With Len Cariou, Robert Pastene, Ed Flanders, Patricia Elliott, Ellen Geer, Paul Ballantyne, Ken Ruta.

THE DOCTOR'S DILEMMA (47). By George Bernard Shaw. September 6, 1966. Director, Douglas Campbell; scenery, Dahl Delu;

costumes, Lewis Brown. With Lee Richardson, Nancy Wickwire, Ed Flanders, Sandy McCallum.

S.S. GLENCAIRN (45). By Eugene O'Neill. September 7, 1966. Directors, Douglas Campbell and Edward Payson Call; scenery, Dahl Delu; costumes, Lewis Brown. With the company.

MORRISTOWN, N.J.

Morris Theater

THE MISER (35). By Molière. November 4, 1966. Director, Michael Sisk; scenery and costumes, Henry Heymann; lighting, Harold Warren.

U.S.A. (25). By Paul Shyre and John Dos Passos; based on the novel by John Dos Passos. November 6, 1966. Director, Michael Sisk; scenery, Dennis Keith; lighting, Harold Warren; costumes, Neil Fischer and Laura Matz. With Enid Edelman, I.M. Hobson, Margaret Sandilands, Beth Bowden, Robert Drean, Dennis Keith.

UNDER MILK WOOD (20). By Dylan Thomas. November 25, 1966. Director-designer, Michael Sisk; lighting, Vincent Piacentini. With Dennis Keith, Ken Hill, Sid Borov, Beth Bowden, Enid Edelman, I.M. Hobson, Margaret Sandilands, Robert Drean, Robert Willis.

LOST IN THE STARS (30). Musical with book and lyrics by Maxwell Anderson; music by Kurt Weill; based on the novel by Alan Paton. December 9, 1966. Director, Michael

Sisk; musical director, Robert Bruyr; lighting, Vincent Piacentini; costumes, Elizabeth A. Cassidy and Linda J. Goebel. With Margaret Sandilands, Robert Keja-Hill, Victor Raider-Wexler, Bill Bowden, Michael Del Medico, Thomas Cassidy.

THE WAKEFIELD MYSTERY PLAYS (10). Director, Michael Sisk; scenery and costumes, Henry Heymann; lighting, Ray Barron; music, John Corrigliano. With Michael Del Medico, Robert Drean, Dennis Keith, Margaret Sandilands, Beth Bowden.

KING LEAR (25). By William Shakespeare. January 27, 1967. Director-Designer, Michael Sisk; lighting, Neil Jampolis. With Michael Del Medico, Thea Ruth, Enid Edelman, Beth Bowden, Dennis Keith, Richard Novello.

THE CHERRY ORCHARD (10). By Anton Chekhov. March 3, 1967. Director, Michael Del Medico; scenery and costumes, Michael Sisk; lighting, Harrold Warren. With Margaret Sandilands, Thea Ruth, Richard Coate, Rod Nash.

NEW HAVEN, CONN.

Long Wharf Theater

THE LOON HUNT and I'M NOBODY (14). By David Kranes (American premiere). June 27, 1966. Director, Jon Jory; scenery, David Hager; lighting, Ron Wallace; costumes, Rosemary Ingham. With David Byrd, Susan McArthur, Margaret Cowles, Nicholas Kepros.

THE GREEN LUTE (14). By J. Gladden Schrock (American premiere). July 11, 1966. Director, Jon Jory; scenery, David Hager; lighting, Ron Wallace; costumes, Rosemary Ingham. With James Cromwell, Kate Wilkinson, Leslie Cass, Abe Vigoda.

THUMBY (14). By Jerry Blatt (American premiere). July 25, 1966. Director, Jon Jory; scenery, Karl Eigsti; lighting, Ron Wallace; costumes, Rosemary Ingham; choreography, Noel Schwartz. With Jennifer Darling, John Fink, Robert Gaus.

THE HAPPY HAVEN (14). By John Arden (American premiere). August 8, 1966. Director, Douglas Seale; scenery, David Hager; lighting, Ron Wallace; costumes, Rosemary Ingham. With Nicholas Kepros, Marcie Hubert, Robert Gaus, David Byrd.

OH WHAT A LOVELY WAR (31). Musical revue by Joan Littlewood and Ted Allan. September 30, 1966. Director, Jon Jory; musical director, Paul Alan Levi; scenery, David Hager; lighting, Ron Wallace; costumes, Rosemary Ingham; choreography, Sally Noble. With Leslie Cass, Jennifer Darling, Dalton Dearborn, Stacy Keach, William Swetland.

THREE SISTERS (31). By Anton Chekhov; translated by Tyrone Guthrie and Leonid Kipnis. November 4, 1966. Director, Arvin Brown; scenery, David Hager; lighting, Ron Wallace; costumes, Margaret Mahoney. With Anna Lindig, Denise Fergusson, Laurie Hutchinson, Stacy Keach, David Spielberg, Leslie Cass.

THE MAN WHO CAME TO DINNER (31). By George S. Kaufman and Moss Hart. December 9, 1966. Director, Jon Jory; scenery, David Hager; lighting, Ron Wallace; costumes, Alec Sutherland. With Sally Noble, William Swetland, Leslie Cass, Anna Lindig.

MISALLIANCE (31). By George Bernard Shaw. January 13, 1967. Director, Arvin Brown; scenery, David Hager; lighting, Ron Wallace; costumes, Alec Sutherland. With Michael Levin, Robert Moberly, Joyce Ebert, Jan Farrand, Albert M. Ottenheimer, William Swetland.

MOTHER COURAGE AND HER CHILDREN (31). By Bertolt Brecht; English version by Eric Bentley. February 17, 1967. Director, Michael Youngfellow; costumes, Rosemary Ingham; lighting, Ron Wallace. With Evie McElroy, Denise Fergusson, Michael Levin, Robert Milli, Joyce Ebert, Jan Farrand.

THE TAVERN (31). By George M. Cohan. March 24, 1967. Director, Jon Jory; scenery, David Hager; lighting, Ron Wallace; costumes, Rosemary Ingham, Alec Sutherland. With Bruce Weitz, William Swetland, Jan Farrand, Raymond Allen, Leslie Cass.

NIGHT OF THE IGUANA (31). By Tennessee Williams. April 28, 1967. Director, Jon Jory; scenery, David Hager; lighting, Ron Wallace; costumes, Rosemary Ingham. With Leslie Cass, Michael McGuire, Jan Farrand, Raymond Allen.

NEW ORLEANS

Repertory Theater

CHARLEY'S AUNT (24). By Brandon Thomas. November 17, 1966. Director, Stuart Vaughan; scenery and costumes, Gordon Micunis; lighting Chuck Hover. With R. Scott Thomas, Rex Thompson, Anne Thompson, Gretchen Corbett.

ROMEO AND JULIET (21). By William Shakespeare. January 5, 1967. Director, Stuart Vaughan; scenery and costumes, Gordon Micunis; lighting, R. Patrick Mitchell. With Tessie O'Shea, Rex Thompson, Gretchen Corbett, Humbert Allen Astredo, Peter Stuart.

OUR TOWN (18). By Thornton Wilder. February 23, 1967. Director, Stuart Vaughan; scenery and costumes, Gordon Micunis; lighting, R. Patrick Mitchell. With Parker Fennelly, Michael Goodwin, Anne Thompson, Nina Polan, Herbert Nelson, Eugenia Rawls.

THE RIVALS (18). By Richard Brinsley Sheridan. April 6, 1967. Director, Stuart Vaughan; scenery and costumes, Gordon Micunis; lighting, Thomas P. Struthers. With June Havoc, Anne Thompson, Herbert Nelson, R. Scott Thomas, Don Perkins.

PHILADELPHIA (See article on its season)

Theater of the Living Arts

A DREAM OF LOVE (44). By William Carlos Williams. September 13, 1966. Director, Lawrence Kornfeld; scenery and lighting, Eugene Lee; costumes, Pearl Somner. With Lois Smith, George Bartenieff, Sam Schacht, Dimitra Steris.

ROOM SERVICE (44). By John Murray and Allan Boretz. November 1, 1966. Director, Harold Stone; scenery and lighting, D. Atwood Jenkins; costumes, Pearl Somner. With David Hurst, Ron Leibman, Crystal Field, Tom Brannum.

BECLCH (44). By Rochelle Owens. December 20, 1966 (premiere). Director, Andre Gregory; scenery, John Conklin; lighting, Richard Nelson; costumes, Eugene Lee; music, Teiji Ito. With Sharon Gans, Jerome Dempsey, Miriam Phillips.

THE TIME OF YOUR LIFE (44). By William Saroyan. February 7, 1967. Director, Harold Stone; scenery and lighting, D. Atwood Jenkins; costumes, Leigh Rand. With Jerome Dempsey, Merwin Goldsmith, Tom Brannum, Sharon Gans.

U.S.A. (44). By Paul Shyre and John Dos Passos; based on a novel by John Dos Passos. March 28, 1967. Director, Harold Stone; scenery and costumes, John Conklin; lighting, Richard Nelson. With George Bartenieff, Marilyn Coleman, Tom Brannum, Joan Darling.

PHAEDRA (44). By Robert Lowell; based on the play by Racine. May 16, 1967. Director, Stephen Porter; scenery and lighting, Robin Wagner; costumes, John Conklin. With Diana Sands, Jerome Dempsey, Miriam Phillips, Andrew Robinson.

PHOENIX, ARIZ.

Arizona Repertory Theater

NUDE WITH VIOLIN (12). By Noel Coward. March 28, 1967. Director, Paul Sobol; scenery and lighting, John Retseck; costumes, Dianne Richard. With Robert L. Aden, Dolores Clark, Sandy Gibbons, Leah Munson, Sarah Jane Miller.

THE LOWER DEPTHS (12). By Maxim Gorki; translated by Jenny Covan. April 11, 1967. Director, Robert L. Aden; scenery and lighting, John Retseck; costumes, Dianne Richard. With Barbara Le Cocq, Helen C. Begam, Daniel Witt, Joe Jenckes, William Edmonson.

THE TYPISTS and THE TIGER (12). By

Murray Schisgal. April 25, 1967. Director, Robert L. Aden; scenery and lighting, John Retseck; costumes, Dianne Richard. With Joe Jenckes, Sarah Jane Miller.

THE BEAUTIFUL PEOPLE (12). By William Saroyan. May 9, 1967. Director, Robert L. Aden; scenery and lighting, John Retseck; costumes, Dianne Richard. With Mitch Stone, Leah Munson, Terry Callahan, Daniel Witt.

THE MISER (12). By Molière; adapted by Miles Malleson. May 23, 1967. Director, Robert L. Aden; scenery and lighting, John Retseck; costumes, Dianne Richard. With Robert L. Aden, Joseph Jenckes, Terry Callahan.

PITTSBURGH (See article on its season)

Pittsburgh Playhouse: Hamlet Street Theater

A STREETCAR NAMED DESIRE (44). By Tennessee Williams. October 21, 1966. Director, Marc Estrin; scenery, Leon Ericksen; lighting, Jane Reisman; costumes, Alicia Finkel. With Winifred Mann, Barton Heyman, Carolee Campbell, John M. Simpson III.

THE ENTERTAINER (30). By John Osborne. December 16, 1966. Director, Stephen

Aaron; scenery, lighting, costumes, Eldon Elder. With Charles Durning, Winifred Mann, Carolee Campbell, William Hansen, Hugh Alexander.

TWO FOR THE SEESAW (26). By William Gibson. February 3, 1967. Director, Hugh Alexander; scenery, Holly Haas; lighting, Pat Simmons; costumes, Alicia Finkel. With Baron Heyman, Carolee Campbell.

Pittsburgh Playhouse: Craft Avenue Theater

A MAN'S MAN (31). By Bertolt Brecht; adapted by Eric Bentley. November 13, 1966. Director, John Hancock; scenery, Robert LaVigne; lighting, Jane Reisman; costumes,

Alicia Finkel, Patricia Zipprodt. With Rhoda Gemignani, Charles Durning, Harvey Solin, Alfred Leberfeld, Alan Manson, Gretchen Oehler.

A MIDSUMMER NIGHT'S DREAM (35). By William Shakespeare. November 25, 1966. Director, John Hancock; scenery, Jim Dine, Robert LaVigne; lighting, Al Jutzi; costumes, Jim Dine, Robert LaVigne, Alicia Finkel; choreography, Cecil Kitcat. With William Hansen, Gretchen Oehler, Robert Benson, Leonardo Cimino, Alfred Leberfeld, Anne Gerety.

PROFESSIONAL REGIONAL THEATER   95

A MEMORY OF TWO MONDAYS and A VIEW FROM THE BRIDGE (34). By Arthur Miller. January 20, 1967. Director, K. K. Kitch; scenery, Holly Haas; lighting, Jane Reisman; costumes, Alicia Finkel. With William Pappas, Gretchen Oehler, Leonardo Cimino, Alfred Leberfeld, Alan Manson, Laura Julian, Catherine Gabrielson, Edd K. Gasper.

THREE SISTERS (23). By Anton Chekhov; translated by Tyrone Guthrie and Leonid Kipnis. March 10, 1967. Director, Thomas Hill; scenery, Holly Haas; lighting, Pat Simmons;

costumes, Alicia Finkel. With Winifred Mann, Anne Gerety, Carolee Campbell, Leonardo Cimino, William Hansen, Charles Durning, Gretchen Oehler.

THE FANTASTICKS (52). Musical with book and lyrics by Tom Jones; music by Harvey Schmidt; based on Edmond Rostand's Les Romantiques. April 8, 1967. Director, Word Baker; scenery, Holly Haas; lighting, E. Allen Kent; costumes, Alicia Finkel. With Baker Salsbury, Ann Sachs, Jeff Chandler, Robert Benson, Marshall Efron.

Pittsburgh Playhouse: The Playhouse

BAREFOOT IN THE PARK (37). By Neil Simon. April 22, 1967. Director, Robert Baker; scenery, Mary Ellen Kennedy; lighting,

Jane Reisman; costumes, Alicia Finkel. With Pamela Grey, Edd K. Gasper, Don Fenwick, Ruth Gregory.

PRINCETON, N.J.

McCarter Theater

WAITING FOR GODOT (6). By Samuel Beckett. February 3, 1967. Director, Michael Schultz; scenery, Clyde Blakeley; lighting, Marshall Williams, costumes, Charles D. Tomlinson. With George Hearn, Marc Alaimo, Toby Savage.

THE BRAGGART WARRIOR (6). By Plautus. February 10, 1967. Director, Gordon Phillips; scenery, John Lithgow; lighting, Marshall Williams; costumes, Lyn Carroll. With Gordon Fearing, Jake Dengel, Rick Johnson, Lauren Jones.

THE TEMPEST (6). By William Shakespeare. February 24, 1967. Director, Anthony Stimac; designer, Charles D. Tomlinson; lighting, Clyde Blakeley. With Susan Babel, George Hearn, Michael Shultz, Lauren Jones, Peter Bailey Britton.

HAMLET (2). By William Shakespeare. February 26, 1967. Director, Arthur W. Lithgow; designer, Charles D. Tomlinson; scenery and lighting, Clyde Blakeley. With George Hearn, Peter Bailey Britton, Tamara Daniel, Gordon Phillips, Susan Babel.

THE EMPEROR JONES (6). By Eugene O'Neill. March 10, 1967. Director, Michael Schultz; lighting, Clyde Blakeley and Marshall Williams; costumes, Charles D. Tomlinson. With Clayton Corbin, Marc Alaimo.

THE SERVANT OF TWO MASTERS (5). By Carlo Goldoni. March 31, 1967. Director, Frederic O'Brady; scenery, Henri Pennec; lighting, Marshall Williams; costumes, Lyn Carroll. With John Genke, Susan Babel, Eve Johnson, George Hearn.

PROVIDENCE, R.I.

Trinity Square Playhouse

SAINT JOAN (16). By George Bernard Shaw. October 11, 1966. Director, Adrian Hall; scenery, Lynn Pecktal; lighting, Roger Morgan; costumes, John Lehmeyer. With Clinton Anderson, William Cain, Mary Doyle, Stefan Gierasch, Skip Hinnant, Richard Kneeland.

A STREETCAR NAMED DESIRE (29). By Tennessee Williams. November 8, 1966. Di-

rector, Adrian Hall; scenery, Lynn Pecktal; lighting, Roger Morgan; costumes, John Lehmeyer. With Katherine Helmond, Donald Gantry, Pamela Payton-Wright, James Gallery.

THE GRASS HARP (17). Musical with book and lyrics by Kenward Elmslie; music by Claibe Richardson; based on the novel by Truman Capote (premiere). December 27, 1966. Director, Adrian Hall; musical director,

Theodore Saidenberg; scenery, Lynn Pecktal, lighting, Roger Morgan; costumes, John Lehmeyer; choreography, Zoya Leporska. With Barbara Baxley, Louis Beachner, Carol Brice, Carol Bruce, Elaine Stritch, Skip Hinnant, David Hooks.

AH, WILDERNESS! (16). By Eugene O'Neill. January 17, 1967. Director, Rocco Bufano; scenery, Lynn Pecktal; costumes, John Lehmeyer; lighting; Roger Morgan. With Clinton Anderson, Peter Gerety, Stefan Gierasch, Pamela Payton-Wright, Joanna Roos.

A MIDSUMMER NIGHT'S DREAM (10). By William Shakespeare. February 7, 1967. Director, Louis Beachner; scenery, Lynn Pecktal; lighting, Roger Morgan; costumes, John Lehmeyer. With Donald Gantry, Dennis Longwell, Virginia Blue, Blythe Danner, Ed Hall, Katherine Helmond, Schorling Schneider.

THE QUESTIONS by John Hawkes, and

DUTCHMAN by LeRoi Jones (10). February 14, 1967. Director, Adrian Hall; scenery, Lynn Pecktal; lighting, Roger Morgan; costumes, John Lehmeyer. With Richard Kneeland, Pamela Payton-Wright, Ed Hall, Katherine Helmond.

THE BIRTHDAY PARTY (24). By Harold Pinter. March 14, 1967. Director, Adrian Hall; scenery, Lynn Pecktal; lighting, Roger Morgan; costumes, John Lehmeyer. With Louis Beachner, Marguerite Lenert, Richard Kneeland, Pamela Payton-Wright, Clinton Anderson, William Cain.

THREE SISTERS (14). By Anton Chekhov; translated by Robert Corrigan. April 26, 1967. Director, Adrian Hall; scenery, Lynn Pecktal; lighting, Roger Morgan; costumes, John Lehmeyer. With Katherine Helmond, Blythe Danner, Pamela Payton-Wright, Clinton Anderson, Donald Gantry, Barbara Orson.

RICHMOND, VA.

Virginia Museum Theater

THE SUBJECT WAS ROSES (17). By Frank D. Gilroy. October 12, 1966. Director, James Dyas; scenery and lighting, John H. Doepp; costumes, Andre Bruce Ward. With Bruce Hall, Lloyd Shockley, Dorothy Lee Tompkins.

ROCHESTER, MICH.

John Fernald Company

THE CAUCASIAN CHALK CIRCLE (31). By Bertolt Brecht; English version by Eric Bentley. January 4, 1967. Director, John Fernald; scenery and costumes, Tom A. Aston; lighting, James Gaine Jr. With Lorna Lewis, Eric Berry, Angela Wood, Terence Scammell.

LOVE'S LABOUR'S LOST (31). By William Shakespeare. February 1, 1967. Director, John Fernald; scenery, Tom A. Aston; lighting, James Gaine Jr. With Terence Scammell, Eric Berry, Barbara Caruso.

YOU NEVER CAN TELL (31). By George Bernard Shaw. March 1, 1967. Director, Robin Ray; scenery, Tom A. Aston; lighting, James Gaine Jr. With Susan Stranks, Terence Scammell, Curt Dawson, Jenny Laird, Roni Dengel, Eric Berry.

THE IMPERIAL NIGHTINGALE (8). By Nicholas Stuart Gray. March 28, 1967. Director, Robin Ray; scenery and costumes, Tom A. Aston; lighting, James Gaine Jr. With Curt Dawson, Paulene Reynolds, Terence Scammell, Eric Berry.

THE WALTZ OF THE TOREADORS (31). By Jean Anouilh. April 5, 1967. Director, Robin Ray; scenery, Tom A. Aston; lighting, James Gaine Jr. With Angela Wood, Robert Donley, Barbara Caruso.

THREE SISTERS (31). By Anton Chekhov; translated by J.P. Davis. Director, John Fernald; scenery, Frank Masi; lighting, Pat Simmons; costumes, Elizabeth Penn. With Lorna Lewis, Barbara Caruso, Angela Wood, Paulene Reynolds, Eric Berry, Joshua Bryant.

ROCHESTER, N.Y.

Theater East

LONG DAY'S JOURNEY INTO NIGHT (17). By Eugene O'Neill. November 10, 1966. Director, Dorothy Chernuck; scenery, lighting, costumes, Charles G. Stockton. With Fred Miller, Constance Dix, Robert Blackburn, DeVeren Bookwalter, Martha Miller.

LIFE WITH FATHER (18). By Howard Lindsay and Russel Crouse. December 1, 1966. Director, Dorothy Chernuck; scenery, lighting, costumes, Charles G. Stockton. With Robert Blackburn, Constance Dix, DeVeren Bookwalter.

SHE LOVES ME (18). Musical with book by Joe Masteroff; music by Jerry Bock; lyrics by Sheldon Harnick. December 22, 1966. Director, Clint Atkinson; scenery, lighting, costumes, Charles G. Stockton; choreography, Tom Cahill; musical director, Byron Tinsley. With Carolyn Chrisman, DeVeren Bookwalter, Fred Miller, Myra Mailloux.

HAY FEVER (18). By Noel Coward. January 12, 1967. Director, Dorothy Chernuck; scenery, lighting, costumes, Charles G. Stockton. With Constance Dix, Robert Blackburn, Myra Mailloux, Jerry Grasse.

TWELFTH NIGHT (11). By William Shakespeare. February 2, 1967. Director, Robert Blackburn; scenery, lighting, costumes, Charles G. Stockton. With Myra Mailloux, Jerry Grasse, Richard Kuss, Bernie McInerney, Thomas Barbour.

MAJOR BARBARA (11). By George Bernard Shaw. February 16, 1967. Director, Dorothy Chernuck; scenery, lighting, costumes, Charles G. Stockton. With Lydia Bruce, Robert Blackburn, Thomas Barbour.

THE BIRTHDAY PARTY (11). By Harold Pinter. March 2, 1967. Director, Robert Blackburn; designer, Charles G. Stockton. With Bernie McInerney, Ann Driscoll, DeVeren Bookwalter, Thomas Barbour.

UNDER THE YUM-YUM TREE (11). By Lawrence Roman. March 16, 1967. Director, Dorothy Chernuck; designer, Charles G. Stockton. With Ann Driscoll, Myra Mailloux, Bernie McInerney, Robert Blackburn.

THE GLASS MENAGERIE (12). By Tennessee Williams. March 30, 1967. Director, Dorothy Chernuck; designer, Charles G. Stockton. With Ann Driscoll, Bernie McInerney, Myra Mailloux, Robert Blackburn.

ST. LOUIS

Repertory Theater of Loretto-Hilton Center

THE PRIVATE EAR and THE PUBLIC EYE (31). By Peter Shaffer. July 1, 1966. Director, Michael Flanagan; scenery, Lewis Crickard. With Robert Murch, Peter Coffeen, Barbara Caruso, Bernie Passeltiner, Marilyn Chris, Lawrence Linville.

WAITING FOR GODOT (13). By Samuel Beckett. July 19, 1966. Director, Wayne Loui; scenery and costumes, Lewis Crickard; lighting, Peter Sargent. With Thomas Kampman, Bernie Passeltiner.

THE SCHOOL FOR WIVES (20). By Molière; translated by Sarah Sanders. August 2, 1966. Director, Sarah Sanders; scenery, Lewis Crickard. With Michael Flanagan, David Sabin, Barbara Caruso, Marilyn Chris.

THE CAGE (9). By Mario Fratti. August 16, 1966. Director, Charles Maryan; scenery, Lewis Crickard; lighting, Peter Sargent; costumes, Vita. With David Huffman.

A MIDSUMMER NIGHT'S DREAM (38). By William Shakespeare. September 13, 1966. Director, J. Robert Dietz; scenery, John Wright Stevens; lighting, Peter Sargent; costumes, Lewis Crickard. With David Huffman, Marilyn Chris, Peter Coffeen, Robert Murch, David Sabin.

OH WHAT A LOVELY WAR (30). Musical revue by Joan Littlewood and Ted Allan. October 12, 1966. Director, James Bernardi; musical director, Dwight Jack; scenery, Lewis Crickard; lighting, Peter Sargent; choreography, Michael Simms. With Barbara Caruso, Kate Geer, Bernie Passeltiner, David Sabin, Gerald Simon.

TWELFTH NIGHT (35). By William Shakespeare. November 16, 1966. Director, Philip Minor; scenery, John Wright Stevens; lighting, Peter Sargent; costumes, Lewis Crickard. With Grace DiGia, Robert Murch, David Sabin, Marian Mercer, David Huffman.

SAN FRANCISCO (See article on its season)

American Conservatory Theater

NOTE: The ACT season of repertory in San Francisco opened January 21, 1966 with *Tartuffe*. Owing to the many changes in program and schedule after that date, no accurate record of opening dates and number of performances was available as of press time.

TARTUFFE. By Molière; English version by Richard Wilbur. Director, William Ball; scenery, Stuart Wurtzel; lighting, John McLain; costumes, Jane Greenwood. With Rene Auberjonois, Ruth Kobart, Ramon Bieri, Sada Thompson.

TINY ALICE. By Edward Albee. Director, William Ball; scenery, Stuart Wurtzel; lighting, John McLain. With Michael O'Sullivan, Ray Reinhardt, Paul Shenar, Al Alu, DeAnn Mears.

THE TORCH-BEARERS. By George Kelly. Director, Edward Payson Call; scenery, Stuart Wurtzel; lighting, John McLain; costumes, Ann Roth. With Richard A. Dysart, Ruth Kobart, Austin Pendleton, Lynne Arden.

DEAR LIAR. By Jerome Kilty. Director, Jerome Kilty; scenery, Stuart Wurtzel; lighting, John McLain; costumes, Walter Watson. With Sada Thompson, Michael O'Sullivan.

BEYOND THE FRINGE. By Alan Bennett, Peter Cook, Jonathan Miller, Dudley Moore. Director, Rene Auberjonois; scenery, Stuart Wurtzel; lighting, John McLain. With Rene Auberjonois, David Grimm, Scott Hylands, Austin Pendleton.

ENDGAME. By Samuel Beckett. Director, Edward Payson Call; scenery, Stuart Wurtzel; lighting, John McLain; costumes, David Toser. With Rene Auberjonois, Ken Ruta, Jay Doyle, Josephine Nichols.

SIX CHARACTERS IN SEARCH OF AN

AUTHOR. By Luigi Pirandello; English adaptation by Paul Avila Mayer. Directors, William Ball and Byron Ringland; scenery, Stuart Wurtzel; lighting, John McLain; costumes, Walter Watson. With Richard A. Dysart, Josephine Nichols, Barbara Colby, Scott Hylands.

MAN AND SUPERMAN. By George Bernard Shaw. Director, Jerome Kilty; scenery, Stuart Wurtzel; lighting, John McLain; costumes, Marianna Elliott. With Paul Shenar, Ray Reinhardt, Rene Auberjonois, DeAnn Mears, Ruth Kobart.

THE SEAGULL. By Anton Chekhov. Director, Edward Payson Call; scenery, Stuart Wurtzel; lighting, John McLain; costumes, Ann Roth. With Angela Paton, Austin Pendleton, Ellen Geer, Ramon Bieri.

CHARLEY'S AUNT. By Brandon Thomas. Director, Edward Hastings; scenery, Stuart Wurtzel; lighting, Allan Melad; costumes, William French. With Al Alu, David Grimm, Rene Auberjonois, Charlene Polite, Ellen Geer.

DEATH OF A SALESMAN. By Arthur Miller. Director, James Way; scenery, Stuart Wurtzel; lighting, John McLain; costumes, David Toser. With Richard A. Dysart, Carol Teitel, Patrick Tovatt, Scott Hylands.

UNDER MILK WOOD. By Dylan Thomas. Director, Byron Ringland; scenery, Stuart Wurtzel; lighting, John McLain; costumes, David Toser. With Ray Reinhardt, Paul Shenar, Richard A. Dysart, Ken Ruta, Carol Teitel, Barbara Colby.

SEATTLE

Seattle Repertory Theater

THE CRUCIBLE (31). By Arthur Miller. November 2, 1966. Director, Allen Fletcher; scenery, Alan Kimmel; lighting, Barbara Nollman; costumes, Allan Granstrom. With Jonathan Farwell, Pauline Flanagan, John Gilbert, Patrick Hines, Elizabeth MacDonald.

THE HOSTAGE (30). By Brendan Behan. November 9, 1966. Director, Pirie MacDonald; scenery, Alan Kimmel; lighting, Barbara Nollman; costumes, Allan Granstrom. With

Marjorie Nelson, Patrick Hines, Archie Smith, Sheila Larkin, Thomas Heaton, Richard Kavanaugh.

BLITHE SPIRIT (30). By Noel Coward. December 14, 1966. Director, Allen Fletcher; scenery, Alan Kimmel; lighting, Barbara Nollman; costumes, Sandee Strand. With Pauline Flanagan, Jonathan Farwell, Margaret Hamilton, Kay Doubleday.

TARTUFFE (29). By Molière; adapted by Richard Wilbur. January 25, 1967. Director, Allen Fletcher; scenery, Robert Darling; lighting, Barbara Nollman; costumes, Allan Granstrom. With George Vogel, Josef Sommer, Richard Kavanaugh, Marjorie Nelson, Kay Doubleday.

THE VISIT (30). By Friedrich Duerrenmatt; adapted by Maurice Valency. February 8, 1967. Director, Pirie MacDonald; scenery, Robert Darling; lighting, Barbara Nollman; costumes, Allan Granstrom. With Archie Smith, Pauline Flanagan, George Vogel, Marjorie Nelson, Patrick Hines.

THE NIGHT OF THE IGUANA (29). By Tennessee Williams. March 15, 1967. Director, Allen Fletcher; scenery, Robert Darling; lighting, Barbara Nollman; costumes, Allan Granstrom. With Kay Doubleday, Frank Converse, Pauline Flanagan, Archie Smith.

STANFORD, CALIF.

Stanford Repertory

ANTONY AND CLEOPATRA (15). By William Shakespeare. October 19, 1966. Director, Erik Vos; scenery, Richard L. Hay; lighting, Paul Landry and Stephan A. Maze; costumes, Jean Schultz Davidson. With Morgan Sterne, Loretta Leversee.

THE BEGGAR'S OPERA (15). By John Gay. January 18, 1967. Director, John Wright; scenery, Dwight Richard Odle; lighting, Paul Landry; costumes, Carolyn Parker. With Paul E. Winfield, Paul E. Richards, Jane Hoffman, Carol Androsky.

THE CHERRY ORCHARD (15). By Anton Chekhov. March 1, 1967. Director, Mel Shapiro; scenery, Richard L. Hay; lighting, Paul Landry; costumes, Dwight Richard Odle. With Jane Hoffman, Gerald Hiken, Paul E. Richards, Loretta Leversee, Astrid Willsrud, Paul E. Winfield, Ruth Silvera, Morgan Sterne, Carol Androsky, Glenn Cannon.

INADMISSIBLE EVIDENCE (12). By John Osborne. April 5, 1967. Director, Robert Loper, scenery, Jerome Marcel; lighting, Paul Landry and Larry Davidson; costumes, Dwight Richard Odle. With Gerald Hiken, Carol Androsky, Jerome Raphel, James G. Medales, Jennifer Haefele.

Little Theater

A SLIGHT ACHE by Harold Pinter and OUT AT SEA by Slawomir Mrozek (12). November 30, 1966. Director, Erik Vos; scenery, Richard L. Hay; lighting, Paul Landry; costumes, Dwight Richard Odle. With Jane Hoffman, Siebert Green, Jerome Raphel, Paul E. Winfield, Paul E. Richards.

SYRACUSE, N.Y.

Syracuse Repertory Theater

LOVE'S LABOUR'S LOST (11). By William Shakespeare. January 26, 1967. Director, Rod Alexander; scenery and costumes, Jack Martin Lindsay; lighting, Ken Moses. With Michael McGuire, Adale O'Brien, Laura MacFarlane, Don Phelps, David C. Jones, Sandy McCallum.

TIGER AT THE GATES (10). By Jean Giraudoux; translated by Christopher Fry. February 1, 1967. Director, Rex Henriot; scenery and costumes, James R. Crider; lighting, Ken Moses. With Chet London, Adale O'Brien, Zoaunne Henriot, Earl Warren Hindman, Don Phelps.

THE DEVIL'S DISCIPLE (10). By George Bernard Shaw. February 16, 1967. Director, G.F. Reidenbaugh; scenery, Daniel S. Krempel; lighting, Ken Moses. With Michael McGuire, Brendan Fay, David C. Jones, Shirley Ann Fenner, Zoaunne Henriot, Adale O'Brien.

SLOW DANCE ON THE KILLING GROUND (10). By William Hanley. March 8, 1967. Director, Rex Henriot; scenery, James C. Mitchell; lighting, Ken Moses. With Roger Robinson, Gary Gage, Zoaunne Henriot.

WASHINGTON, D.C. (See article on its season)

Washington Theater Club

THE KNACK (30). By Ann Jellicoe. October 13, 1966. Director, Davey Marlin-Jones; scenery and costumes, James Parker; lighting, Ralph Strait. With Christopher Carrick, Sue Lawless, Haig Chobanian, Bob Spencer.

THE LOVER by Harold Pinter, directed by Clifford V. Ammon, and HUGHIE by Eugene O'Neill, directed by Davey Marlin-Jones (30). November 10, 1966. Scenery and costumes, James Parker; lighting, Ralph Strait. With John Hillerman, Sue Lawless, Haig Chobanian, Ralph Strait, Bob Spencer.

THE FANTASTICKS (46). Musical with book and lyrics by Tom Jones; music by Harvey Schmidt; based on Edmond Rostand's *Les Romantiques*. December 8, 1966. Director, Davey Marlin-Jones; scenery and costumes, James Parker; lighting, Ralph Strait. With Haig Chobanian, Susan Hufford, Joneal Joplin, Bob Spencer, Ralph Strait.

TINY ALICE (30). By Edward Albee. January 19, 1967. Director, Davey Marlin-Jones; scenery, James Parker; lighting, Ralph Strait; costumes, Robin Alexander. With John Hillerman, Scottie Mac Gregor, Bob Spencer.

THE MARRIAGE OF MR. MISSISSIPPI (30). By Friedrich Duerrenmatt; translated by Michael Bullock. February 16, 1967. Director, Davey Marlin-Jones; scenery and costumes, James Parker; lighting, John C. Jackson. With Clifford V. Ammon, Haig Chobanian, John Hillerman, Scottie Mac Gregor, Bob Spencer, Ralph Strait.

THE KILLER (30). By Eugene Ionesco. March 16, 1967. Director, Davey Marlin-Jones; scenery and costumes, James Parker; lighting, Peter R. Jacoby. With Haig Chobanian, Suzanne Granfield, Colin Hamilton, John Hillerman.

THE WATERS OF BABYLON (30). Musical with book by John Arden; music by William Goldstein. April 13, 1967. Director, Clifford V. Ammon; scenery and costumes, James Parker; lighting, Peter R. Jacoby. With Haig Chobanian, Cliff Frazier, Suzanne Granfield, Colin Hamilton, John Hillerman, Christopher Lloyd, Bob Spencer.

SON OF SPREAD EAGLE (30). Edited by Herb Sufrin. May 11, 1967. Director, Davey Marlin-Jones; scenery and costumes, James Parker; lighting, Peter R. Jacoby; musical director, Richard Sleigh. With John Hillerman, Colin Hamilton, Ralph Strait, Bob Spencer, Sue Lawless, Marsha Wood.

Arena Stage

MACBETH (40). By William Shakespeare. October 25, 1966. Director, Edwin Sherin; scenery, Robin Wagner; lighting, Jules Fisher; costumes, Judith Haugan. With Michael Higgins, Nan Martin, Richard Venture, Jane Alexander.

THE MAGISTRATE (40). By Arthur Wing Pinero. December 6, 1966. Director, David William; scenery, Robin Wagner; lighting, William Eggleston; costumes, Nancy Potts. With Phyllida Law, James Kenny, George Ebeling, Jane Alexander.

THE CRUCIBLE (40). By Arthur Miller. January 17, 1967. Director, Milton Katselas; scenery, Ming Cho Lee; lighting, William Eggleston; costumes, Nancy Potts. With Melissa Loving, Michael Higgins, Douglas Rain.

THE INSPECTOR-GENERAL (48). By Nicolai Gogol. February 23, 1967. Director, Edwin Sherin; scenery, Robin Wagner; lighting, William Eggleston; costumes, Domingo A. Rodriquez. With Paul Mann, George Ebeling, Conrad Bromberg, William Larson.

LOOK BACK IN ANGER (40). By John Osborne. April 11, 1967. Director, Hy Kalus; scenery and costumes, Judith Haugan; lighting, William Eggleston. With Douglas Rain, Martha Henry, Robert Foxworth, Jane Alexander, James Kenny.

THE ANDERSONVILLE TRIAL (50). By Saul Levitt. May 23, 1967. Director, Edwin Sherin; scenery, Robin Wagner; lighting, William Eggleston; costumes, Marjorie Slaiman. With William Larson, Ted D'Arms, Richard Venture, Eugene Wood.

O
O
O

THE SHAKESPEARE FESTIVALS

and Other Summer Repertory

O
O
O

INTRODUCTION

By Peter Raby

Dramaturge of The Stratford Shakespearean
Festival Foundation of Canada

WHEN THE Shakespeare festival at Stratford, Ontario was launched in a tent theater in 1953 under the direction of Tyrone Guthrie, two plays were presented during a six-week season. The coming fifteenth season (summer 1967) extends for 18 weeks: on the Festival Theater's open stage *Antony and Cleopatra, Richard III, The Merry Wives of Windsor* and Gogol's *The Government Inspector* will be produced, as well as an extensive series of concerts; while *Cosi fan tutte, Albert Herring,* and a new work by the Ontario writer James Reaney will be shown at the proscenium-arch Avon Theater, a refurbished vaudeville house. The annual attendance at the plays alone is now over 250,000.

The focus for this steady expansion has always been the high quality of the Shakespeare productions on the open stage conceived and designed by Guthrie and Tanya Moiseiwitsch. Despite gloomy prognostications, people filled the theater night after night and have continued to come in increasing numbers ever since. Perhaps, as some suggest, a certain social cachet or cultural snobbery prompted part of the initial response, but this can scarcely be true today. Stratford draws on a wide area—a quarter of the attendance comes from the United States—but the bulk of the audience is from Ontario and returns year after year. Fortunately, the season is also attracting a new generation of theatergoers: the school matinees, which now run for five weeks in the fall, undoubtedly introduce many to an experience which becomes a habit.

The development of the Stratford audience is by no means an automatic and purely numerical process. The comparatively unenthusiastic 1966 box-office response to *Henry V* and the John Barton adaptation of *Henry VI*—unenthusiastic beside a 90 per cent 1965 attendance—indicated a surfeit of history. The cycle had begun in 1964, and it was planned to complete it in 1967 with *Edward IV* and *Richard III*. In contrast to the American notices, both Canadian press comment and individual reactions suggested a certain dis-

101

enchantment with the sweeping political themes, the clash of office and personality, of the great design. Of course, the cycle's continuitv is threatened even at the rate of two histories a year; and *Henry VI* especially, whether presented in its original three parts or the adapted two, needs to be seen as an entity. Two histories out of a year's offering of three Shakespeare plays is a demanding proportion. It was decided to forego another history-dominated season and to skip through to *Richard III*.

By the end of 1967, only *Cymbeline, Titus Andronicus, Pericles,* and the rest of *Henry VI* will remain to be seen for the first time at Stratford, and seven of Shakespeare's plays will have been shown twice. No field offers better scope for nostalgia than the theater, and comparisons are inevitable. Michael Langham's 1956 production of *Henry V,* making telling use of French-Canadian actors, ended on a note of reconciliation with yards of fleurs de lys and lions couchants fluttering in consort. His 1966 production brought out the muddy realism of a play which is almost half prose. In a strong cerebral performance, Douglas Rain revealed the ruthlessness demanded of a king towards his friends, his countrymen, and his defeated enemies. We saw the brutality, as well as the glory, of a war of conquest, labeled by some as anti-war and anti-French. Others felt that the understanding both of the ecstasy of success and the price paid for it were nicely counterpoised.

John Hirsch's production of *Henry VI,* continuing the cycle historically and yet cast in so different a form, made a fascinating companion piece. The mildest tampering with Shakespeare requires caution, and John Barton's adaptation is radical in places. But while valuable elements are inevitably omitted, the tightened structure can only add to appreciation of this fierce, mediaeval work which has such a contemporary ring. The metallic, heraldic mood was reflected by an emblazoned floor the designer, Desmond Heeley, had thrown over the stage; and over it moved the chess pieces of power politics. Among them was Tony van Bridge's Gloucester, who emerged as a sympathetic figure to the same degree as the King himself. As in *Henry V,* most of the French characters were played by French Canadians, and their distinctive style added a further dimension.

Twelfth Night, directed by David William, proved the most popular play of the 1966 season and was an excellent contrast to the starker world of the histories. This is not to say that the production neglected the more substantial elements in the comedy. It brought out the exaggerated introspection of the courtly lovers and tempered the febrile gusto of the lighter people with the darker moods introduced by Malvolio and Feste. Through it all Martha Henry as Viola maintained an integrity of emotion that was the fixed point round which the play turned.

Since 1960, the current Shakespeare productions have served as a catalyst for a Shakespeare Seminar organized for the Universities of Canada by the Department of Extension of McMaster University. There are now two weekly programs, each attended by more than a hundred from all over Canada and the United States, who see each production and attend a series of lectures, symposia, and discussions. Over the years such scholars as Professors Harbage, Northrop Frye and L.C. Knights have lectured at Stratford; but the seminars are by no means exclusively academic, since the organizers make a point of including addresses by critics, directors and actors. The actual membership of the seminars ranges from those with some professional interest in Shakespeare, such as teachers and librarians, to pure theater-lovers. While this cross-section of an audience may not be wholly typical, the fortnight provides an excellent opportunity for those who produce Shakespeare, study Shakespeare, teach Shakespeare, and pay to see and hear Shakespeare, to exchange ideas, opinions and even creative insults in the most agreeable of company and conditions. In a more informal way, the practise after each school matinee for one of the cast to talk to the audience and answer questions provides a similar and essential bridge between those who create and those they create for.

From what is said at these discussions, as well as from the night-by-night response of the audience, there is obviously no need to labor Shakespeare's relevance to the contemporary world. For each theme and word that has become obsolete, there are scores more in every play than any production can take into full account. Inevitably, either by transportations of time and place, or by spotlighting themes of particularly current significance, allusions will be made to the world of today. An existentialist *Lear*, an Italian *Shrew*, a patriotic or anti-war *Henry V*—such connections will be made by someone, whatever a director's intentions, and it is for the individual to decide whether Shakespeare is illuminated or clouded. What must be avoided is a museum theater, where Shakespeare is removed with reverence from the icebox, displayed soggily and meaninglessly for an interval, and then thrust back into cold storage. Shakespeare is only worth performing today if he speaks to the people who form our 20th century culture. As he has so much to say, it is pointless to worship at his shrine as though he and his works were dead.

Nor can one exist productively on an exclusive diet of Shakespeare. Once the Stratford Festival had become established, it was logical from everyone's point of view to expand the repertory. As early as 1954 Guthrie produced Sophocles' *Oedipus Rex;* and the last few years have seen *Cyrano, The Country Wife, Le Bourgeois Gentilhomme, The Cherry Orchard,* and plays by contemporary and Canadian authors. It is, in fact, a proof of Shakespeare's stature that work on his plays should stimulate directors and actors to explore the classical writers of other periods and cultures as well as the output of their own society.

As the season and repertory extends, so the actors who come each summer to Stratford begin to form a more or less permanent company. In October 1966, the cast of *Henry V* moved to Toronto to recreate for television the production they had worked on through the summer. In January 1967, rehearsals started for a six-week cross-Canada tour, for which a partly recast *Twelfth Night* was redirected for the proscenium arch, and a new production of *The Government Inspector* was launched which will be restaged for the Festival Theater in June 1967. In October 1967, *Antony* and another play will be shown in Montreal. This experience of different types of audiences and theater and media, the cross-fertilization that comes from exploring Shakespeare in repertory with other writers, are essential if a primarily Shakespeare festival and company are to retain their vitality.

Fortunately, the development of Stratford has coincided with a growing interest in theater across Canada and, even more important, the practical expression of that interest in repertory companies of increasing quality. The more opportunities for actors, and the more competition for Stratford, the better. When Michael Langham hands over the artistic directorship at the end of next season, he will be succeeded by Jean Gascon (who has been largely responsible for the international reputation won by the Théâtre du Nouveau Monde in Montreal) and John Hirsch, founding Artistic Director of the flourishing Manitoba Theater Center in Winnipeg. The Canadian actor Christopher Plummer, who made his name at Stratford, Ontario before achieving wider recognition in London and New York, returns in 1967 to play Antony. Cleopatra will be the Australian actress Zoe Caldwell, Octavius the young Canadian actor Ken Welsh. The music is by the Greek composer Manos Hadjidakis. Michael Langham, the director, leaves Stratford to start a theater in close collaboration with the university at La Jolla, Calif. Tanya Moiseiwitsch, after designing Antony, goes to Minneapolis and then the National Theater in London. Passports mean little in themselves, but the blend of national and international experience and freshness that they indicate is an essential ingredient for Stratford's continuing success.

The Shakespeare plays have from the start been complemented by the other arts. A resident orchestra now serves the opera company and also holds a series of concerts, supplemented by visiting artists, and conducts a music workshop. Members of the opera chorus appeared in the 1966 production of Michael Bawtree's The Last of the Tsars. Duke Ellington, a regular visitor, composed the music for Timon of Athens. Creative barrier-breaking is continually suggested by the atmosphere of this sort of festival. Other offshoots include a series of exhibitions ranging from the Sidney Fisher Collection of Rare Books and Shakespeareana to "A Hundred Years of Theater in Canada"; the establishment of a Stratford Seminar on Civic Design; and the opening of the Rothmans Art Gallery this year.

The Shakespeare industry is one of the largest in the world. Happily, chocolate replicas of Ann Hathaway's Cottage and terra-cotta busts of the Bard form only a minute proportion of the innumerable activities he inspires. By making the products of his imagination the center of a Stratford season which embraces a widening range of experience, the Festival has so far ensured that neither it nor Shakespeare is allowed to petrify.

The Stratford Shakespearean Festival Foundation of Canada. Repertory of three plays by William Shakespeare, one by Michael Bawtree and one by August Strindberg. **Henry V** (52). Opened June 6, 1966; directed by Michael Langham; designed by Desmond Heeley; music, John Cook. **Henry VI** (40). Condensation by John Barton. Opened June 7, 1966; directed by John Hirsch; designed by Desmond Heeley; music, John Cook. **Twelfth Night** (51). Opened June 8, 1966; directed by David William; designed by Brian Jackson; music, Louis Applebaum.

The Last of the Tsars (11). By Michael Bawtree. Opened July 12, 1966; directed by Michael Langham; designed by Leslie Hurry; music and effects, Louis Applebaum. **The Dance of Death** (8). By August Strindberg. Opened July 19, 1966; directed by Jean Gascon; designed by Mark Negin. Produced by The Stratford Shakespearean Festival; Shakespeare plays at the Festival Theater, Bawtree and Strindberg plays at the Avon Theater, Stratford, Ontario, Canada. (Repertory closed October 8, 1966).

PERFORMER	"HENRY V"	"HENRY VI"	"TWELFTH NIGHT"	"THE LAST OF THE TSARS"
Bernard Behrens	Fluellen	Somerset		Kerensky; Diplomat
Mervyn Blake	Macmorris; Bates	Lord Talbot		Frederieksz
Barbara Bryne		Margery Jourdain	Maria	
John Byron	Gower	Mortimer		Milyukov; Diplomat
Eric Christmas	Bardolph		Feste	
Leo Ciceri	(Charles VI)	de la Pole	Malvolio	
Eric Donkin	York; Ely	Bolingbroke; Legate	Antonio	
Thomas Donohue	Grandpré		Valentine	
Colin Fox		2d Murderer		Officer
Jacques Galipeau	Orleans	Orleans		
Jean Gascon	(Charles VI)			
Lewis Gordon	Nym	Lawyer; Simpcox		Sergei Mikov
Amelia Hall	Hostess Quickly	Simpcox's Wife		Tsarina
Max Helpmann	Westmoreland	Bedford; 1st Citizen		Benckendorff
Martha Henry		Joan	Viola	
William Hutt	Chorus	Warwick		Grand Duke
Frances Hyland		Margaret		Ania; Mother Mikov
Joel Kenyon				Nicholas II
Al Kozlik	Alexander Court	Basset; 3d Citizen		Ivan
Gaëtan Labréche	Dauphin	Dauphin		
Heath Lamberts	Boy	Messenger	Fabian	
Diana LeBlanc	Katharine			Maria Golovina
Guy L'Ecuyer	Governor; Lefer	Alençon	Priest	
Barry MacGregor	Michael Williams	Plantagenet		Johnson
Roberta Maxwell			Olivia	
Richard Monette	Montjoy		Sebastian	
William Needles	Jamy Gloucester	Exeter		Voykov; Baron
Christopher Newton		Hume	Orsino	
Michael O'Regan	Lancaster		Curio	
Denise Pelletier	Isabel	Eleanor		
Briain Petchey	Canterbury	Henry VI	Sir Andrew Aguecheek	
Kenneth Pogue	Cambridge; Erpingham	Vernon; 2d Citizen		Commander-in-Chief; Diplomat
Leon Pownall	Scroop	John Talbot; Townsman		Britnov
Douglas Rain	Henry V	Prologue Voice	Sir Toby Belch	
Jean-Louis Roux	Burgundy	Burgundy		
Marcel Sabourin	Constable	Reignier		

PERFORMER	"HENRY V"	"HENRY VI"	"TWELFTH NIGHT"	"THE LAST OF THE TSARS"
Powys Thomas	Pistol	Beaufort		Rasputin
Tony van Bridge	Exeter	Gloucester		Samoilov
Kenneth Welsh	Grey	1st Murderer; Capt. to Talbot		
Kim Yaroshevskaya	Alice			Natalie

(Parentheses indicate role in which the actor alternated)

THE DANCE OF DEATH

Edgar .... Jean Gascon
Alice .... Denise Pelletier
Kurt .... Jean-Louis Roux
Jenny .... Marilyn Gardner
An Old Woman .... Elsie Sawchuck
A Sentry .... Raymond L'Heureux

Others in all productions: Ernest Atkinson, Larry Aubrey, Dominique Briand, Bruce Buxton, Mary Carr, Leatham Carroll, Beth Anne Cole, Patrick Crean, Carrol Anne Curry, Neil Dainard, Richard Davidson, Sarah Davies, Angela Fusco, David Geary, Paul Gummow, Doninic Hogan, Krysia Jarmicki, Peter Jobin, Mona Kelly, Karen Malone, Evan McGowan, Jimmy McGorman, Tom Murray, Blaine Parker, Irene Poujol, Oskar Raulfs, Herman Rombouts, Roxolana Roslak, Arthur Sclater, John Smythe, Danny Tait, Joy Tepperman, Jerome Tiberghien, Hans Werner Tolle, Paul Trepanier, John Turner.

NOTE: Other programs produced by the Stratford Shakespeare Festival at the Avon Theater were *Don Giovanni* (in English), July 8-September 3; and *The Royal Winnipeg Ballet*, August 16-September 3.

New York Shakespeare Festival. Season of three plays by William Shakespeare. **All's Well That Ends Well** (16). Opened June 15, 1966 (Closed July 2, 1966); directed by Joseph Papp; music, David Amram. **Measure for Measure** (17). Opened July 12, 1966 (Closed July 30, 1966); directed by Michael Kahn; music, David Amram. **Richard III** (17). Opened August 9, 1966 (Closed August 27, 1966); directed by Gerald Freedman; music, John Morris; fights, James J. Sloyan. All plays: scenery, Ming Cho Lee; costumes, Theoni V. Aldredge; lighting, Martin Aronstein. Produced by Joseph Papp in cooperation with the City of New York at the Delacorte Theater, Central Park, New York City.

ALL'S WELL THAT ENDS WELL

Countess of Rossillion .... Joanna Roos
Bertram .... Richard Jordan
Lafew .... Staats Cotsworth
Helena .... Barbara Barrie
Parolles .... J. D. Cannon
King of France .... George Bartenieff
Charles Dumaine .... Al Freeman, Jr.
Jacques Dumaine .... Paul Hecht
Rinaldo .... Robert Ronan
Lavatch .... Charles Durning
Duke of Florence .... Maury Cooper
Widow Capilet .... Jane Rose
Diana .... Marian Hailey
Mariana .... Bette Henritze
A Soldier Interpreter .... Christopher Carrick
A French Gentleman .... Wayne Wilson

Others: Einar Berg, Georg Stanford Brown, Rod Browning, John Campbell, William H. Cox, Mervyn Haines, Jr., Anna Lindig, Pedro Santaliz, Anthony Sciabona, Thurman Scott, J. Walter Smith, John Starr, John Valentine, Ralph Wainwright, Marlene Warfield, Fama Wilson.

MEASURE FOR MEASURE

The Duke .... Shepperd Strudwick
Escalus .... Bill Moor
Angelo .... Tom Aldredge
Lucio .... Al Freeman, Jr.
First Gentleman .... Stan Dworkin
Second Gentleman .... Joseph Palmieri
Mistress Overdone .... Jane Rose
Pompey .... Charles Durning
Claudio .... Christopher Walken
Provost .... Moses Gunn
Friar Peter .... Paul Hecht
Isabel .... Barbara Baxley
Francisca .... Trescott Ripley
Elbow .... David Margulies
Froth .... Robert Frink
A Justice .... Silas Pickering II
Attendant to Angelo .... Ian Jenkins
Juliet .... Amy Taubin
Boy .... John Pleshette
Mariana .... Bette Henritze
Abhorson .... Gregory Sierra
Barnadine .... Warren Wade
Varrius .... Wayne Wilson
Mistress Kate Keep Down .. Phyllis Schneider

Others: Fay Chaiken, Cheryl Kilgren, Anna Lindig, Suzanne Pred, Fama Wilson, Einar Berg, Georg Stanford Brown, Rod Browning, John Campbell, Christopher Carrick, William Cox, Mervyn Haines, Jr., Pedro Santaliz, Anthony Sciabona, Thurman Scott, J. Walter Smith, John Starr, John Valentine, Ralph Wainwright.

RICHARD III

Richard, Duke of Gloucester	Joseph Bova
Duke of Clarence	Paul Hecht
Sir Robert Brakenbury	John Campbell
Lord Hastings	Harris Yulin
Lady Anne	Penny Fuller
Tressel	Patrick Gorman
Berkeley	Thurman Scott
Anthony Woodeville	Ian Jenkins
Lord Grey	John Valentine
Marquess of Dorset	John Pleshette
Elizabeth	Nan Martin
Duke of Buckingham	Philip Bosco
Earl of Derby	Stan Dworkin
Sir William Catesby	George Hearn
1st Murderer	Charles Durning
2d Murderer;	
2d Citizen	Tom Aldredge

Edward IV	John Devlin
Lady Margaret Plantagenet	Laura Michaels
Edward Plantagenet	Richard Lee
Duchess of York	Jane Rose
1st Citizen	Rod Browning
Scrivener	Frank Groseclose
Archbishop of York	Robert Ronan
Richard, Duke of York	Richard Thomas
Edward, Prince of Wales	Peter Reznikoff
Lord Mayor of London	George E. McGonagill
Sir Richard Ratcliffe	Brian Turkington
Sir Thomas Vaughn	John Starr
Bishop of Ely	Wayne Wilson
Lord Lovel	Rod Browning
George Stanley	Peter Jacobs
Sir James Tyrrel	Einar Berg
Henry, Earl of Richmond	Charles Siebert
Duke of Norfolk	William H. Cox
Earl of Surrey	Ted Nils Hoen
Sir William Brandon	Mervyn Haines, Jr.
Earl of Oxford	John Starr
Sir Walter Herbert	Anthony Sciabona
Sir William Blunt	J. Walter Smith

Others: Georg Stanford Brown, Christopher Carrick, Walter Hadler, Anna Lindig, Pedro Santaliz, Ralph Wainwright, Angela Wood.

New York Shakespeare Festival Mobile Theater. Mobile productions of a play by William Shakespeare. **Macbeth** (47). Opened June 28, 1966 (Closed August 20, 1966); directed by Gladys Vaughan; music, David Amram. **Macbeth** (in the Spanish language) (9). Translation by Leon Felipe. Opened August 26, 1966 (Closed September 4, 1966); directed by Osvaldo Riofrancos; music, Gary William Friedman. Both plays: scenery, David Mitchell; costumes, Jose Varona; lighting, Lawrence Metzler; press, Merle Debuskey. Produced by Joseph Papp on tours of the five boroughs of New York City.

ROLE	"MACBETH" (English version)	"MACBETH" (Spanish version)
1st Witch	Gabrielle Strasun	Violeta Landek
2d Witch	Lynn Hamilton	Ann Collins
3d Witch	Jacqueline Britton	Vala Cliffton
Duncan, King of Scotland	Leonard Hicks	Osvaldo Riofrancos
Malcolm	Tom K. Slater	Lorenzo Weisman
Wounded Sergeant	John McCurry	Cesar Castro
Lennox	Martin Shakar	Frank Ramirez
Ross	Joseph Mascolo	Alfonso Manosalves
Macbeth		Ignacio Lopez Tarso
(Macbeth)	James Earl Jones	
(Macbeth)	Michael McGuire	
Banquo	Ed Setrakian	Gonzalo Madurga
Angus	Rod Griffis	Francisco Prado
Lady Macbeth	Ellen Holly	Maria Brenes
Seyton	Fred Pinkard	Ernesto Colon
Fleance	John FitzGibbon	Pilo Gonzales
Porter	Albert Quinton	Edmond Faccini
Macduff		Raul Julia
(Macduff)	Michael McGuire	
(Macduff)	James Earl Jones	

ROLE	"MACBETH" (English version)	"MACBETH" (Spanish version)
Donalbain	Mark Jenkins	Mario Cueto
Old Man	Fred Pinkard	Michael Coquat
1st Murderer	Madison Arnold	Antonio Flores
2d Murderer	Ray Stubbs	Cesar Castro; Felix Fernandez
Hecate	Lucille Saint-Peter	Francisco Prado
Lady Macduff	Monica Lovett	Marta Lucia
Boy	Robert Benson Ross Burr	Hermes Franqui
Girl		Dillian Martinez
Doctor	Seymour Penzner	Gregory Sierra
Gentlewoman	Gabrielle Strasun	Norma Pagan
Menteith	Leonard Hicks	Gonzalo Madurga
Caithness	Albert Quinton	Julio Lucia
Siward	Lee Wallace	Paul Delgado
Young Siward	John Perry McDonald	Felix Fernandez

(Parentheses indicate roles in which the actor alternated)

Others (English): Lawrence Cook, Michael Coquat, Laura Hicks, Cleavon Little, George McGrath, Anthony McKay, James J. Sloyan, Hertha Trenkle. (Spanish): Eddie Alvarez, Jaime Castro, Ali Colon, Chan Daniels, Hernando Gonzales, Charles Lutz.

The American Shakespeare Festival. Repertory of three plays by William Shakespeare and one by T.S. Eliot. Falstaff (29). Shakespeare's Henry IV, Part 2. Opened June 18, 1966; directed by Joseph Anthony; scenery, Ed Wittstein; lighting, Tharon Musser; costumes, Domingo A. Rodriguez; music and songs and musical director, John Duffy. Murder in the Cathedral (31). By T.S. Eliot. Opened June 19, 1966; directed by John Houseman in collaboration with Pearl Lang; scenery, David Hays; lighting, Tharon Musser; costumes, Jane Greenwood; musical director, John Duffy. Twelfth Night (29). Opened June 21, 1966; directed by Frank Hauser, scenery, Will Steven Armstrong; lighting, Tharon Musser; costumes, Jane Greenwood; music and songs, Conrad Susa; musical director, John Duffy. Julius Caesar (29). Opened June 22, 1966; scenery and costumes, Will Steven Armstrong; lighting, Tharon Musser; music and songs, Conrad Susa; musical director, John Duffy; duels, Christopher Tanner. Produced by The American Shakespeare Festival Theater and Academy at the Festival Theater, Stratford, Conn. (Repertory closed September 11, 1966.

NOTE: A season of special preview performances for school children opened on February 28, 1966 and ran through June 7, 1966. The performance schedule was Julius Caesar 49, Twelfth Night 46 and Falstaff 18.

PERFORMER	"FALSTAFF"	"MURDER IN THE CATHEDRAL"	"TWELFTH NIGHT"	"JULIUS CAESAR"
Peter Bosche	Feeble	3d Priest		Cicero; Cinna the Poet
Adolph Caesar	Rumor; Bullcalf	2d Priest	Priest	Cobbler
Mary Carter		Woman of Canterbury		
Alexander Clark	Chief Justice	3d Tempter		
Barbara Colby		Woman of Canterbury		Portia
John Cunningham	Prince Hal	Brito	Orsino	
Joan Darling		Woman of Canterbury	Viola	Girl
Olive Deering		Woman of Canterbury		

PERFORMER	"FALSTAFF"	"MURDER IN THE CATHEDRAL"	"TWELFTH NIGHT"	"JULIUS CAESAR"
Todd Drexel	Mowbray	2d Tempter		Soothsayer; Pindarus
Alix Elias	Doll Tearsheet			
Patrick Hines	Silence	de Traci	Sir Toby Belch	Casca
Alan Howard	Falstaff's Page			Lucius
Dennis Jones	Travers; Fang; Shadow		Valentine	Trebonius; Strato
Stephen Joyce	Archbishop	1st Tempter		Marcus Antonius
Jerome Kilty	Falstaff			
David Little	Prince John	4th Priest	Curio	Varro; Octavius' Servant
Nancy Marchand		Woman of Canterbury		
Richard Mathews	Poins; Wart	Messenger	Feste	Octavius
Edith Meiser		Woman of Canterbury		
Julian Miller	Morton; Davy		Fabian	
Jan Miner	Mistress Quickley	Woman of Canterbury		
Garry Mitchell	Durham			Lucilius; Antony's Servant
Michael Parish	Gloucester; Francis		2d Officer	Metellus Cimber; Drunken Soldier
Elizabeth Parrish			Maria	Calpurnia
Patricia Peardon			Lady Olivia	
Stephen Pearlman	Northumberland; Mouldy		Antonio	Popilius Lena; Messala
Edward Rudney	Westmorland		1st Officer	Spokesman; Young Cato; Marullus
Roger Serbagi	Bardolph		Sea Captain	Lepidus
Paul Sparer	Shallow	Fitz Urse		Cassius
Michael Stein	Justice's Servant	1st Priest		Titinius
Josef Sommer	Henry IV	4th Tempter	Malvolio	Caesar
Peter Stuart	Clarence; Frail		Sebastian	China, Claudius
R. Scott Thomas	Hastings			Bully; Volumnius; Flavius
James Valentine	Warwick		Sir Andrew Aguecheek	Decius Brutus
Douglas Watson	Pistol	de Morville		Marcus Brutus
Joseph Wiseman		Thomas Becket		

Others: Richard Abbott, John Bakos, Peter Bernuth, Harriet Bigus, Sidney Borov, Yusef Bulos, Brandwell Czar, Grace DiGia, Robert Drean, Joseph Dunnea, Leticia Ferrer, John Genke, Arne Gundersen, Ken Kliban, Anthony Mainionis, Philip Mancuso, Dan McNally, Ward Morehouse, Richard Novello, Chris Pennock, Charles Pfluger, Alan Rachins, John Hamburg, Margaret Mauran.

Murder in the Cathedral Gregorian Choir: Daniel Hannafin, Warren Galjour, Frank Bouley, Bruce Peyton, Glenn Kezer, Thomas A. Head, George McWhorter, Robert Neukum; chants edited and conducted by John Duffy.

Great Lakes Shakespeare Festival. Repertory of three plays by William Shakespeare, one by Oscar Wilde and one by Oliver Goldsmith. **Twelfth Night** (19). Opened July 8, 1966. **She Stoops to Conquer** (19). By Oliver Goldsmith. Opened July 12, 1966. **King Lear** (17). Opened July 26, 1966. **The Importance of Being**

Earnest (9). By Oscar Wilde. Opened August 9, 1966. **The Winter's Tale** (8). Opened August 23, 1966. All plays: Directed by Lawrence Carra; scenery, Milton Howarth; costumes, Joseph F. Bella; lighting, William Nelson (first two plays), Merry Tigar. Produced by Great Lakes Shakespeare Festival, Lakewood, Ohio. (Repertory closed September 30, 1966).

PERFORMER	"TWELFTH NIGHT"	"SHE STOOPS TO CONQUER"	"KING LEAR"	"THE WINTER'S TALE"
Hugh Alexander	Orsino		Edmund	Autolycus
Emery Battis			King Lear	Camillo
Peter Blaxill	Fabian	Tony Lumpkin	Edgar	Clown
Richard Bowden	Sebastian	Diggory	Oswald	Florizel
Charles Butler		Roger	Tenant to Gloucester	
Maury Cooper	Antonio	Sir Charles	Gloucester	Polixenes
Peggie Eichhorn	Page	Pimple		Lady; Servant to Old Shepherd
Edward Epstein				Cleomenes
Clarence Felder	Sir Toby Belch	Mr. Hardcastle	Fool	Old Shepherd
Gregg Heschong		Thomas	British Captain	
Brett Joseph				(Mamillius)
Norma Joseph		Miss Hardcastle	Cordelia	Perdita
Robin Joseph				(Mamillius)
Albert Katz	Captain; Priest	Jeremy	Burgundy; Doctor	
Gerald Kline	Valentine		Knight	Lord; Officer
Betty Low	Viola	Miss Neville	Regan	
Margret O'Neill	Olivia		Goneril	Hermione
Michael Paul	Curio		Captain to Edmund	Dion
Victor Raider-Wexler	Malvolio	Stingo	Albany	Antigonus
Joan Shafran	Duenna			Emilia
Mario Siletti	Feste	Mr. Hastings	Kent	Leontes
George Vafiadis	Sir Andrew Aguecheek	Mr. Marlow	Cornwall	
Pat Van Dyke		Bridget		Mopsa
Susan Willis	Maria	Mrs. Hardcastle		Paulina
Greer Woodward				Dorcas

(Parentheses indicates role in which the actor alternated)

THE IMPORTANCE OF BEING EARNEST
John Worthing, J.P. ....George Vafiadis
Algernon Moncrieff ....Hugh Alexander
Rev. Canon Chasuble, D.D. ....Emery Battis
Merriman, butler ....Richard Bowden
Lane, manservant ....John Sucke
Lady Bracknell ....Margret O'Neill

Hon. Gwendolen Fairfax ....Betty Low
Cecily Cardew ....Norma Joseph
Miss Prism, governess ....Susan Willis

Others in all plays: Diane Dalton, Lynn Henry, Margaret Hlinka, Mark Krieger, John Schambach, Dean Tait, Robert Stager.

The Ypsilanti Greek Theater. Repertory of three plays by Aeschylus and one by Aristophanes. **The Oresteia** (40). Aeschylus' *Agamemnon, The Libation Bearers* and *The Eumenides,* translated by Richmond Lattimore. Opened June 28, 1966; production conceived and directed and costumes by Alexis Solomos; choreography, Helen McGehee; music, Iannis Xenakis. **The Birds** (40). Aristophanes' play, translated by William Arrowsmith. Opened June 29, 1966; production conceived and directed by Alexis Solomos; costumes, Eldon Elder; choreography, Gemze de Lappe; music, Herman Chessid; orchestration and dance music, John Carisi. Both plays: scenery, Eldon Elder; lighting, Gilbert V. Hemsley Jr.; music director, Konstantin Simonovic; festival stage designed by Eldon Elder. Produced by The Ypsi-

JUDITH ANDERSON, JACQUELINE BROOKES (WITH SPEAR), DONALD DAVIS, RUTH VOLNER, JOHN MICHAEL KING, FREDERIC WARRINER, KAREN LUDWIG AND RUBY DEE PERFORM IN THREE PLAYS BY AESCHYLUS AT THE YPSILANTI GREEK THEATER. JACK FLETCHER AND BERT LAHR (UPPER RIGHT) APPEAR IN "THE BIRDS" BY ARISTOPHANES.

lanti Greek Theater, Ypsilanti, Mich., Alexis Solomos artistic director, Richard Kirschner executive director. (Repertory closed September 4, 1966).

PERFORMER	"AGAMEMNON"	"THE LIBATION BEARERS"	"THE EUMENIDES"	"THE BIRDS"
David-Rhys Anderson		(Manservant)		Legislator
Judith Anderson	Clytemnestra	Clytemnestra		
Jacqueline Brookes			Ghost of Clytemnestra	
John Buck Jr.		Pylades	Athene	
Tamara Daniel				Flamingo
Donald Davis	Agamemnon		Apollo	Hoopoe
Ruby Dee	Cassandra			Iris
Julia de Lacy				Town Crier's Asst.
Jeff Delson			Hermes	
Richard Esckilsen				Sentry
Jack Fletcher				Euelpides
Melissa Foster				Nightingale

Michael Harrah			Sandpiper
Lloyd Harris	Watchman		Guzzle-guzzle;
			Town Crier
			Bird
William Herter			Little Hoopoe;
			Delinquent;
			Triballos
John Michael King		Orestes	Orestes
Bert Lahr			Pisthetairos
Karen Ludwig		Electra	
Richard Mangoode	Herald		
Donald Marlatt		(Manservant)	Inspector
Gene Nye			Messenger Bird
Dina Paisner		Priestess	
Nelson Phillips			Priest; Herakles
Phillip Piro			Poet; Kinesias
Peter Shebaya			Prophet;
			Prometheus
David Thompson		(Manservant)	Meton
Ruth Volner		Nurse	Informer
Frederic Warriner	Aegisthus	Aegisthus	Poseidon
David Zirlin			Persian Bird;
			Herald

(Parentheses indicates role in which the actor alternated)

Choruses and others: Paul Bengston, Leonard Peters, Don Leach, William Cross, Connie Barron, Marilyn Black, Margaret Cicierska, Anna Carparelli, Alice Condodina, Martha Craven, Jeanette Dabish, Diane Gray, Loi Leabo, Tonia Shimin, Cinda Siler, Joan Tyson, Richard Ball, Ken Brown, Don C. DiLella, Harry Dittenbar, Frank Helle, James C. McCullough, Michael A. Moore, Ira Neil Shor, Chuck Webster, Richard P. Worswick.

Asolo Theater Festival. Repertory of five plays, one each by William Shakespeare, Molière, Robert Bolt, Sophocles and Eugene Ionesco. **Much Ado About Nothing** (18). Opened July 7, 1966; directed by Robert Strane; settings, Jack Montgomery; music, Stephen Smith. **The Miser** (18). By Molière. Opened July 9, 1966; directed by Robert Strane; scenery and costumes, David M. Martin. **A Man for All Seasons** (18). By Robert Bolt. Opened July 12, 1966; directed by Richard G. Fallon. **Oedipus Rex** (18). By Sophocles. Opened July 14, 1966; directed by Eberle Thomas; costumes, Joy Breckenridge. **The Bald Soprano** (18). By Eugene Ionesco; translated by Donald M. Allen. Opened July 14, 1966; directed by Eberle Thomas; costumes, Joy Breckenridge; music, Stephen Smith. Produced by Asolo Theater Festival at the Asolo Theater, Sarasota, Florida. (Repertory closed August 27, 1966).

PERFORMER	"MUCH ADO ABOUT NOTHING"	"THE MISER"	"A MAN FOR ALL SEASONS"	"OEDIPUS REX"
Paul Bressoud	Antonio	Commissioner	Wolsey	
Robert Britton		La Fleche	Cromwell	Creon
Trina Ciuffo	Hero	Elise		
C. David Colson	Claudio	Valere		Messenger
Annette Hannon			Lady Margaret	
Donald C. Hoepner	Dogberry	Jacques	Richard Rich	
Polly Holliday	Beatrice		Woman	
Margaret Kaler	Ursula			
Michael Keenan	Leonato		Canterbury	Man from Corinth

PERFORMER	"MUCH ADO ABOUT NOTHING"	"THE MISER"	"A MAN FOR ALL SEASONS"	"OEDIPUS REX"
Sammy Kilman	Son of Antonio; Watchman		Roper	
Grant Kilpatrick	Balthasar; Friar Francis	Anselme	Common Man	
Gretchen Kirch				Ismene
John F. Krich	Don Pedro		Henry VIII	Oedipus
Macon McCalman	Don John		Norfolk	Priest
Charlotte Moore	Margaret	Mariane		
Batchelor Owen	Sexton	Simon		
Peter Saputo	Conrade		Chapuys	
Albert L. Smelko	Borachio	Cleante	Thomas More	
Robert Strane				Tiresias
Gail Strickland				Nurse
Eberle Thomas	Benedick			
Isa Thomas		Jacques	Lady Alice	Jocasta
Janet Van Pelt		Dame Claude		
Pamela Vorce				Antigone
Paul Weidner	Verges	Harpagon		Shepherd

THE BALD SOPRANO

Mr. Smith .... Paul Weidner
Mrs. Smith .... Polly Holliday
Mr. Martin .... John F. Krich
Mrs. Martin .... Isa Thomas
Mary, the maid .... Charlotte Moore
The Fire Chief .... C. David Colson

Others in all plays: O. David Dye, Jane Frutig, Jennifer Pierson, Marc Vorce, William Gammon, Bill Gwynn, Douglas Morrison, Frederic H. Jones, Nelson M. Carpenter, Henry A. Polic, Alan Harris, Ragnar Bergstrom, Dan Parr.

NOTE: Asolo Festival's 1967 season, March 11-September 10, includes repertory productions of *As You Like It, Major Barbara, The Fan* and *The Cherry Orchard.*

The Southern Shakespeare Repertory Theater. Repertory of four plays by William Shakespeare. **A Midsummer Night's Dream** (6). Opened July 12, 1966; directed by Hank Diers; costumes, Roberta Baker and Ann Whitlock. **Macbeth** (6). Opened July 13, 1966; directed by Robert Lowery; costumes, Roberta Baker. **The Winter's Tale** (6). Opened July 14, 1966; directed by William Lang; costumes, Ben Gutierrez-Soto. **Coriolanus** (6). Opened July 15, 1966; directed by Delmar E. Solem; costumes, Lillian Winkler. All plays: scenery, Kenneth Kurtz. Produced by the Faculty of the Drama Department, the College of Arts and Sciences and the Division of Continuing Education, University of Miami, Miami, Florida. (Repertory closed August 7, 1966).

PERFORMER	"A MIDSUMMER NIGHT'S DREAM"	"MACBETH"	"THE WINTER'S TALE"	"CORIOLANUS"
Joey Argenio		Attendant; Siward		Menenius
John Sterling Arnold	Bottom	Macbeth	Old Shepherd	Messenger; Aedile
Samuel Assaid	Flute	Murderer	Clown	Citizen
Lana Beidelman	Hermia	Macduff's Son	Mopsa	
Parris Buckner			Archidamus	Aedile
Dalton Cathey	Lysander	Malcolm	Gaoler	Roman Senator
Donna Cellini	Hippolyta	Lady Macbeth	Lady	Citizen
Paula Winters Cline	Helena	Lady Macduff	Paulina	

Donna Jean Coe	Peaseblossom	Lady	Dorcas	
Terence Daugherty	Robin	Donalbain; Doctor	Florizel	Volscian Soldier
Dino DeFilippi	Puck	Lennox	Antigonus	Junius Brutus
Debby Diers	Cobweb			
Charlotte Edmonds	2d Fairy	Lady		Virgilia
Naomi Fink				Volumnia
Richard Greene		Banquo	Leontes	Roman Senator
Helen Grossman			Time	Valeria
Ben Gutierrez-Soto			Autolycus	
Donald Hayes	Demetrius	Macduff	Camillo	Tullus Aufidius
Stuart Martin Joseph	Attendant	Fleance		
Ingrid Christel Macaulay	Mustardseed		Hermione	Citizen
Mina E. Mina		Porter	Polixenes	Cominius
Robert Parsons	Egeus	Duncan		Coriolanus
Lois Pearlman	Moth	Gentlewoman	Perdita	Gentlewoman
Christopher Renaud	Snug	Captain	Cleomenes	Titus Lartius
Michael Routenberg		Seton	Mariner	Nicanor
John Schewel	Tom Snout		Dion	Citizen
Douglas Wallace	Quince	Angus	Sicilia Lord	Sicinius Velutus
Barry Wasman	Theseus	Ross	Sicilia Lord	Volscian Soldier

San Diego National Shakespeare Festival. Repertory of three plays by William Shakespeare. **Romeo and Juliet** (41). Opened June 14, 1966; directed by Mel Shapiro; costumes, Peggy Kellner; fights and duels, Raymond St. Jacque. **The Tempest** (39). Opened June 22, 1966; directed and designed by Hal George. **The Two Gentlemen of Verona** (31). Opened July 14, 1966; directed by Allen Fletcher; costumes, Peggy Kellner. All plays: scenery, Peggy Kellner; lighting, Parker Young; music and songs, Conrad Susa. Produced by the Seventeenth San Diego National Shakespeare Festival at the Old Globe Theater, San Diego, Calif. (Repertory closed September 11, 1966).

PERFORMER	"ROMEO AND JULIET"	"THE TEMPEST"	"THE TWO GENTLE-MEN OF VERONA"
J. Phillip Babb	Balthasar	Adrian	Servant
Rand Bridges	Apothecary	Alonso	Outlaw
Kristina Callahan		Miranda	Silvia
Victor Eschbach	Tybalt	Boatswain	Outlaw
Jonathan Frid	Capulet	Caliban	Duke of Milan
James Gallery	Escalus	Stephano	Antonio
Will Geer	Friar Lawrence	Prospero	
Richard Lupino		Gonzalo	Proteus
John McMurtry	Peter	Trinculo	Eglamour
Priscilla Morrill	Nurse	Iris	Lucetta
Terrence O'Connor	Lady Capulet	Attendant	Attendant to Silvia
Halcyon Oldham	Lady Montague		
John Oldham	Montague	Mariner	
Don Perkins	Benvolio	Sebastian	Launce
Lauri Peters	Juliet		Julia
Alan Stambusky	Gregory		Outlaw
Robert Teuscher	Paris	Master of the Ship	Speed
Gil Turner	Ballad Singer	Ferdinand	Host; Panthino
Jon Voight	Romeo	Ariel	Thurio
Anthony Zerbe	Mercutio	Antonio	Valentine

Others: Tom Aycock, Mary Carle, Donna Couchman, Dawn Daniel, Alan Donovan, Jim Eggleston, Ron Gold, Nathan Haas, Merrill A. Harrington, Kiel Mueller, Jack Phippin, Ron Ray, Harold Robinson, J. Michael Ross, Izetta Jewell Smith, Robert Sterling, Christie Virtue, Marilyn Walk, Adrienne Webb. Musicians in *The Two Gentlemen of Verona:* Harry Davis, Pat Myers, William E. Copeland, Conrad Susa, Bill Lindley, Claudine Miller, Bill Matthews, Frank Myers.

Oregon Shakespeare Festival. Repertory of four plays by William Shakespeare and one by John Gay. **A Midsummer Night's Dream** (13). Opened July 23, 1966; directed by Hugh C. Evans. **Othello** (13). Opened July 24, 1966; directed by Richard Risso. **The Two Gentlemen of Verona** (13). Opened July 25, 1966; directed by Nagle Jackson. **Henry VI, Part 3** (12). Opened July 26, 1966; directed by Jerry Turner. **The Beggar's Opera** (8). By John Gay. Opened August 16, 1966; directed by Carl Ritchie. All plays: producing director, Angus L. Bowmer; scenery, Robert Kern McFarland; costumes, Jack A. Byers (Shakespeare plays), Jean Schultz Davidson; lighting, Robert Brand (Shakespeare plays), Robert D. Swanson; choreographer, Shirlee Dodge; music director, W. Bernard Windt. Produced by The Oregon Shakespearean Festival Association, Ashland, Oregon (Repertory closed September 11, 1966).

PERFORMER	"A MIDSUMMER NIGHT'S DREAM"	"OTHELLO"	"THE TWO GENTLEMEN OF VERONA"	"HENRY VI, PART 3"
Suzanne Anderson	1st Fairy			
Jim Baker	Bottom	Gratiano	Thurio	Earl of March
Harold Berninghausen	Mustardseed			
Karen Boettcher	Hermia			Bona
Angus L. Bowmer	Peter Quince			
Gretchen Corbett		Desdemona		Lady
Carol Davis			Ursula	Lady
Louis Del Grande			Valentine	Admiral; Mayor
Tom Donaldson	Oberon	Othello		Plantagenet
Weldon Durham		Duke of Venice	Outlaw	Westmoreland; A Father That Has Killed His Son
Rick Hamilton		Montano		Richmond
Nagle Jackson	Demetrius			Lewis XI
David H. Jones		2d Senator	Panthino; Spy	Rivers
Zoe Kamitses	Hippolyta	Emilia	Julia	
Enid Kent	Helena			Lady Grey
Vincent Landro	Egeus		Speed	Montague
Robert Lawson	Lysander	Sailor		Somerset; Son That Has Killed His Father
Richard Lincoln	Flute	Gentleman		Prince of Wales
Larry Martin		Roderigo	Launce	Clarence
Rhys McKay				Rutland
William Oyler	Snout	Iago		Clifford
Pat Patton	Starveling	Gentleman	Antonio	
Ray Keith Pond	Theseus	Cassio	Eglamour	Oxford
Karen Reiss	Cobweb			
Richard Risso				Gloucester
Bob Robinson		1st Senator	Outlaw	Exeter
Baker Salsbury		Lodovico	Duke of Milan	Warwick
Cindy Skerry	Moth			
Mara Manly Stahl		Bianca	Silvia	Lady
Emily Tracy	Titania			

PERFORMER	"A MIDSUMMER NIGHT'S DREAM"	"OTHELLO"	"THE TWO GENTLEMEN OF VERONA"	"HENRY VI, PART 3"
Jerry Turner	Philostrate			
Peter Vogt	Snug	Brabantio	Outlaw	Hastings; Tutor
Victor Walston	Peaseblossom			
Claudia Wilkens			Lucetta	Margaret
Laird Williamson	Puck		Proteus	Henry VI

THE BEGGAR'S OPERA

Captain Macheath ....Richard Lincoln
Peachum ....Angus L. Bowmer
Lockit ....Pat Patton
The Beggar ....Peter Vogt
The Player ....David H. Jones
The Jailor ....Dan Hays
The Drawer ....Jack Sine
Polly Peachum ....Emily Tracy
Lucy Lockit ....Karen Boettcher
Mrs. Peachum ....Claudia Wilkens
Diana Trapes . .Zoe Kamitses; Nina M. Lowry

Macheath's Gang: Rick Hamilton, Sidney McLain, David H. Jones, David Sampels, Perry W. Langenstein, Bob Robinson, Weldon Durham, Larry Martin, Richard Ponton, Robert Black. Women of the Town: Enid Kent, Betsy Lee Sacks, Mary Young, Carol Davis, Suzanne Anderson, Mary F. Elliott, Marsha Price, Jacqueline Ames, Maureen McKovich.

Others in all plays: Frank Asta, Bruce Calvin Boatwright, David Lane, Pat Rucker, Dennis Sparks, Maureen McKovich, Byron DeWitt Daugherty, Josh Fredricks, Russell A. Murphy.

The Royal Shakespeare Theater. Repertory of five plays by William Shakespeare and one by Cyril Tourneur. **Henry IV, Part 1** (61) and **Henry IV, Part 2** (44). Opened April 6, 1966; directed by John Barton with Clifford Williams and Trevor Nunn; design, John Bury. **Hamlet** (68). Opened April 28, 1966; directed by Peter Hall; design, John Bury. **Twelfth Night** (56). Opened June 16, 1966; directed by Clifford Williams; design, Sally Jacobs. **Henry V** (21). Opened August 11, 1966; directed by John Barton and Trevor Nunn; design, John Bury. **The Revenger's Tragedy** (8). By Cyril Tourneur. Opened October 5, 1966; directed by Trevor Nunn; design, Christopher Morley. All plays: music by Guy Woolfenden. Produced by The Royal Shakespeare Company at Stratford-on-Avon, England. (Repertory closed November 12, 1966).

PERFORMER	"HENRY IV, PART 1"	"HENRY IV, PART 2"	"HENRY V"	"HAMLET"
Sheila Allen	Lady Percy	Lady Percy		
John Bell		Gloucester; Travers	Gloucester; Governor	Rosencrantz
Christopher Bidmead		Prince John		Fortinbras
Donald Burton		Chief Justice	Constable	Horatio
Patsy Byrne		Doll Tearsheet		
John Corvin	Douglas	Peto; Bullcalf	Bates	Capt. to Fortinbras
Tony Church	Henry IV	Henry IV	Canterbury	Polonius
Jeffery Dench	York; Sheriff	York	Charles VI	Marcellus; Ambassador
Peter Geddis	Gadshill	Mouldy	Nym	Barnardo
Robert Grange	Mortimer	Doctor		
Terrence Hardiman	Vernon; Carrier	Lord Bardolph	Montjoy	Priest
Davyd Harries	Hastings	Hastings	Gower	Reynaldo; Prologue
Ian Holm	Prince Hal	Prince Hal	Henry V	
Sarah Hyde			Katharine	
Stanley Illsley	Colville	Colville; Servant	Ely	
Michael Jayston	Exeter	Exeter	Exeter	Laertes

PERFORMER	"HENRY IV, PART 1"	"HENRY IV, PART 2"	"HENRY V"	"HAMLET"
John Kane	Francis	Francis	Francis	Francisco
Estelle Kohler	Lady Mortimer			Ophelia
Brewster Mason				Claudius; Ghost
Richard Moore	Carrier	Morton	Pistol	Guildenstern
Daniel Moynihan	Poins	Poins	Orleans	
John Normington	Glendower	Shallow		Osric; Player Queen
Godfrey Quigley	Northumberland	Davy; Northumberland	Williams	
Ian Richardson			Chorus	
Norman Rodway	Hotspur	Pistol		
Paul Rogers	Falstaff	Falstaff		
Elizabeth Spriggs	Mistress Quickly	Mistress Quickly	Hostess Quickly	Gertrude
Patrick Stewart	Blunt	Mowbray	Dauphin	1st Player
Madoline Thomas		Lady Northumberland	Isabel	
David Waller	Worcester	Silence	Fluellen	Gravedigger; Voltemand
David Warner				Hamlet
Tim Wylton	Bardolph	Bardolph	Bardolph; Lefeu	

TWELFTH NIGHT

Orsino .... Alan Howard
Viola .... Diana Rigg
Olivia .... Estelle Kohler
Maria .... Patsy Byrne
Malvolio .... Ian Holm
Feste .... Norman Rodway
Sir Toby Belch .... Brewster Mason
Sir Andrew Aguecheek .... David Warner
Antonio .... Godfrey Quigley
Sebastian .... Christopher Bidmead
Fabian .... Tim Wylton

THE REVENGER'S TRAGEDY

The Duke .... David Waller
The Duchess .... Brenda Bruce
Lussurioso .... Alan Howard
Spurio .... Norman Rodway
Ambitioso .... Terrence Hardiman
Supervacuo .... John Kane
Junior .... Christopher Bidmead

Vendice .... Ian Richardson
Hippolito .... Patrick Stewart
Gratiana .... Patience Collier
Castiza .... Lynn Farleigh
Antonio .... Jeffery Dench
Piero .... Davyd Harries
1st Gentleman .... Ted Valentine
2d Gentleman .... Robert Davis

Others in the 1966 Stratford Company: Dallas Adams, David Ashford, Christopher Bond, Ray Callaghan, John Challis, Bruce Condell, Timothy Darwen, Frances de la Tour, Robert East, Christopher Fagan, Tom Georgeson, Terence Greenidge, John Gulliver, Brian Gwaspari, Phillip Hinton, Andrew Jack, Ian McDonald, Malcolm McDowell, Ann McPartland, Peter Mair, Chris Malcolm, Seymour Matthews, Patricia Maynard, Phillippe Monnet, Clifford Norgate, Peter Rocca, Louis Selwyn, Derek Steen.

THE SEASON IN LONDON

By Frank Marcus

Author of *The Killing of Sister George* (a Best Play in this volume) and
drama critic for *The London Magazine* and *Plays and Players*

A SLUGGISH beginning; an exciting finish. Once again, the theatrical land-
scape was dominated by the twin peaks of the National Theater and the Royal
Shakespeare Company. The most far-reaching development, in my view, was
the clarification of the function of these two worthy and essential institutions.
The sense of rivalry between them seems to have abated. The National Theater is catholic in its aims: the training and maintenance of a group of versatile
players, capable of interpreting anything from Greek tragedy to French farce,
from Congreve to O'Casey. Using eminent foreign guest directors like Franco
Zeffirelli, Jacques Charon and, it is hoped, Jerome Robbins, the talented ensemble should soon be the most malleable putty in the world. Significantly,
their resident director, John Dexter, has resigned, but the coming season will
mark the return of the two prodigal knights, Guthrie and Gielgud. The National is not a director's theater; the repertory selected bears the imprint not
so much of Sir Laurence Olivier as of his fiendishly astute literary manager,
Kenneth Tynan.

Having said this, it must be admitted that until February of this year their
sole contribution, Ostrovsky's *The Storm,* proved a dud. Then things began
to happen. Strindberg's *The Dance of Death* was a revelation. Acknowledged
as a genius but rarely performed, Strindberg emerged here as the founder of
the Theater of Cruelty, as well as the Theater of the Absurd, to name but
two. And Olivier, as the Captain, gave (to my mind) his greatest performance.
The ferocious power of this man has surely been unequalled since Kean, as
Richard III, caused spectators to faint. Geraldine McEwen and Robert Stephens were fine in trembling support. Then came the National's greatest gam-
ble: the first production in London of a play by an unknown author. *Rosencrantz and Guildenstern Are Dead* was seen briefly in a student production at
last year's Edinburgh Festival. Snapped up and brightly polished, this "existential footnote to *Hamlet*" left the critics gasping for superlatives. The two
shadowy lords, waiting and whiling away their time, uncertain of their fate
and uncomprehending of their destiny, becoming enmeshed in the relentless
action of the play, foredoomed, puzzled, and innocent, struck a profound
chord. Pirandello and Beckett were invoked, and the young author was hailed
as the discovery of the decade. Having started at the top, we must now keep
our fingers crossed for Tom Stoppard, and wish him well. Whatever happens
to him, the National Theater has vindicated its judgment; from now on they
can confidently look to the future, as well as to the past.

The Royal Shakespeare Company has set itself a different task: the evolution of a style of presentation that is relevant to, and expressive of, contemporary feeling. With nods in the direction of Antonin Artaud and Jan Kott, theirs is a more intense, committed theater. The pragmatic Peter Hall and the dazzling but erratic Peter Brook are great gatherers of international avant-garde techniques. The result is sometimes insufficiently digested and unduly ephemeral—but that is the essence of theater. Their productions are characterized by moral seriousness. Their season was given up to a program of new plays, foreign and English, using small casts (the consequence of insufficient subsidies). They opened with *Tango,* a modern morality play by the Pole Slawomir Mrozek. This showed a young man, traditionally decent, confronting a family comprising a father who walks about in pyjamas and organizes "happenings", a mother who carries on an open affair with the lodger, a lesbian grandmother, an uncle in boy scout shorts, and a fiancee who cheerfully offers her body only to be told by her young man that he wants marriage, not sex. This witty parable was played with elephantine clumsiness and hardly raised a smile. *Days in the Trees* by Marguerite Duras was a subtle essay about a voracious mother who returns to her gigolo son—a son made useless (which means free, according to Mme. Duras) by her indulgence of him when a child. Clumsily constructed and often perversely mysterious, this play provided Peggy Ashcroft with opportunities for bravura acting, culminating in a drunk scene in a tawdry cafe. Duerrenmatt's metaphysical joke on the subject of death, *The Meteor,* shone but briefly and left no afterglow.

Then Peter Brook displayed his box of tricks in *US,* a revue on the contentious subject of Vietnam, devised by a group of artists under his direction. This was hotly debated. The first half, a vivid historical pageant using mime, songs, and *tableaux vivants,* was brilliant theater. The second half, dealing with self-immolation and the search for solutions, ultimately turned on the audience, accusing them of smugness and indifference. It ended with actors representing the maimed invading the stalls, moaning heartrendingly, their heads covered in paper bags, while the rest of the company lined up on the stage, accusingly out-staring the departing patrons.

David Mercer's new play, *Belcher's Luck,* was a sad disappointment: a heavily symbolic melodrama concerning a crumbling estate (England), owned by a doddering general (the upper class), his randy old batman (the working class), and the latter's illegitimate and impotent son (the young generation). It all ended gorily, with the general being kicked to death by a mare-in-foal (fertility symbol), which was then shot by the batman. Lastly came the RSC's greatest success, *The Staircase* by Charles Dyer, a dialogue between two shabby, aging, homosexual hairdressers They were played by Patrick Magee and the indispensable Paul Scofield. The latter's much admired virtuosity seemed to me to defeat the character's credibility; I preferred Magee. The fact that I didn't really like any of their offerings—at least not wholeheartedly—should not be taken as disapproval of their policy. Their importance, and that of their sister company at Stratford-on-Avon, is incalculable. As the season closes they are presenting the annual World Theater Season, organized by Peter Daubeny, at which companies from all parts of the globe present traditional as well as experimental work. In one way or another, the RSC shoulders a tremendous cultural burden.

US gave rise to the label of the year: Theater of Fact. This means a dramatization of a political or historical event, based on documentary sources. We had examples in *The Silence of Lee Harvey Oswald* and *In the Matter of J. Robert Oppenheimer.* These painstaking accounts of well-known causes celebres were of doubtful value. The basic assumption appears to be that some happenings, e.g. the concentration camps, can only be treated in the most direct factual way. This overlooks the fact that playwrights reflect their time indirectly in many subtle ways. Theater of Fact seems designed for the ill-informed and the unimaginative. We are promised treatments of the Cuban missile crisis (National Theater) and the Russian Revolution (RSC). Funny that none of them deal with English themes.

And what of the home of The New Drama, the Royal Court Theater? A checkered season. Director William Gaskill has given his theater a schizophrenic, Jekyll-and-Hyde personality. On the one hand, devoted—even austere—revivals and exhumations (Arnold Wesker's *Roots* and D.H. Lawrence's *The Daughter-in-Law*), and honest, though not particulary exciting new plays (Wesker's rather dated Utopian mammoth *Their Very Own and Golden City,* David Cregan's promising *Three Men for Colverton* and Wole Soyinka's charming Nigerian comedy of manners *The Lion and the Jewel*); on the other, quirky gimmicks. Sir Alec Guinness was unable to redeem a Brechtian, brightly-lit *Macbeth* which appeared to be set in a sandpit, and boasted three Negroes as the Witches and a sometimes unintelligible French Lady Macbeth (Simone Signoret). The critics gasped with horror; Gaskill retaliated fiercely. Following so soon on Osborne's open declaration of war (a consequence of the critical reception of *A Bond Honoured*), the critics protested their innocence and good faith. The crisis was resolved by a melancholy television confrontation, with Gaskill and Wesker in one corner, and a pair of drama critics in the other. The critics were righteously indignant and hurt: apparently—God help us!—they want to be loved, as well as feared. It all ended amicably, with pats on the back all round. So there's every prospect that playwrights and directors will go on making mistakes, and critics will continue to be hated. Anyway, Gaskill's latest gimmick—the casting of a pop singer, Marianne Faithfull, as Irina in *Three Sisters*—came off. The girl can act. Sighs of relief.

The Royal Court, as well as the Hampstead Theater Club and the Jeannetta Cochrane, continued to feed exciting new material into the West End, unfortunately with poor commercial results. From the Royal Court came *When Did You Last See My Mother?* by Christopher Hampton, written at the age of eighteen. This was a delicate, compassionate study of two friends, caught in the limbo between leaving school and entering university. One of them has an affair (his first) with the other's mother, with disastrous results. The remarkable thing about this play was its tone. Cool, humourous, entirely free of breast-beating self-pity, this bore the heretical message that teenage is a stage of development not to be wallowed in, but to be overcome. It was beautifully played by Victor Henry and Gwen Watford. A heartening experience.

From Hampstead came John Bowen's adaptation of his novel, *After the Rain.* An uncommonly intelligent and witty parable play, this took the form of a demonstration-lecture, delivered 200 years hence, on the Great Flood of 1967, describing the fate of a handful of survivors whose leader—a chartered accountant named Arthur—gradually assumes the role of God. Alec Mc-Cowen, as this pinched fanatic, gave an outstanding performance.

The little Jeannetta Cochrane Theater sent, first, *The Bellow Plays,* which gave Miriam Karlin the opportunity of playing three very funny ladies, and, later, Joe Orton's award-winning *Loot.* Orton is a unique stylist. In his outrageous farces he blends plots of extreme sordidness, bordering on depravity, with dialogue of the most polished formality and epigrammatic Wildean elegance. The pivot of *Loot* is the corpse of Mrs. McLeavy, murdered by her nurse, whose delinquent son requires the coffin for stowing away the proceeds of a bank robbery. Michael Bates, as an over-zealous, totally unimaginative detective investigating this cesspool, gave the funniest performance of the year. Orton, like oysters, is an acquired taste.

Lastly, the Mermaid launched *Let's Get a Divorce!,* a successful period farce—by Sardou, of all people!—which exploited the talents of the feline Fenella Fielding. Otherwise, they had a poor season: some enjoyable evenings of short plays by Shaw and O'Casey, but little else. Robert Lowell's *Benito Cereno* was thought well-intentioned but boring.

The commercial theater trailed a long way behind. An early and abiding pleasure was *The Prime of Miss Jean Brodie,* a dramatization by Jay Presson Allen of Muriel Spark's novel. Here was a gorgeously unfamiliar setting—an Edinburgh girls' school in the 1930s—and a most extraordinary central character. Poor dotty Miss Brodie, hooked on fascism and early Italian paintings, entangled with two crushed members of the staff, and exerting influence of a somewhat unconventional kind on a group of favorite pupils (the Brodie Set)—the "creme de la creme", as she put it—was a superb stage character. This spectacular part was spectacularly played by Vanessa Redgrave and, later, in a more quiet key, by Anna Massey. As the leader of the Set, Vickery Turner began as a sharp and rather ugly 13-year-old and matured before our very eyes in a way which would have warmed the heart of Humbert Humbert. The acting and direction (by Peter Wood) was impeccable.

The H.M. Tennent management was again unadventurous, playing safe with costume revivals with big stars, in this case *The Rivals,* with Sir Ralph Richardson, and *Lady Windermere's Fan,* opulently over-decorated by Cecil Beaton, with an incisive performance by Isobel Jeans, and a sensitive one from Ronald Lewis. Their only successful incursion into modern drama was *The Odd Couple,* amusingly embodied by Jack Klugman and Victor Spinetti, although we're beginning to get a little tired of seeing the American Male in the guise of overgrown schoolboy.

Other American imports (non-musical) fared worse. *The Impossible Years,* clumsily transposed, sank in mid-Atlantic; *Cactus Flower* had, well . . . Margaret Leighton. *World War 2½*, by Roger O. Hirson, raised a few smiles.

The entire middle-brow terrain was covered with meticulous thoroughness by Peter Bridge. Bridge is not so much a manager as a quantity surveyor: at one point he had no fewer than nine plays in the West End. Equity ought to give him a medal. His output ranged from *Come, Spy with Me*—a shoddy farce serving as a vehicle for the skilful female impersonator Danny La Rue—to a competent thriller, *Wait Until Dark;* from a period piece, *On Approval,* with the popular husband-and-wife team Michael Denison and Dulcie Gray, to the Oxford Playhouse production of Jonson's *Volpone.* There were also some curiosities: Arbuzov's *The Promise,* a modern Russian play, tracing the lives of a girl (Judi Dench) and two boys (Ian McShane and Ian McKellen) from their meeting in a derelict room during the siege of Leningrad, to marriage (to the wrong man), and a belated new start with the right one. Charmingly old-fashioned and chastely sentimental, this play gave a lot of pleasure. Another creditable presentation—brief, alas—was Giles Cooper's macabre comedy, *Happy Family.* Here a young woman was deliberately kept in a state of retardation, in a world of childhood fantasy, shared by her brother and sister. The play showed the impact of an outsider—the sister's fiance—on the deluded family. Cooper, a master of suburban menace better known for his radio and television plays, died tragically last year in a train accident. A sad loss. Bridge's latest offerings were a light comedy, *Relatively Speaking,* by a new and stylish young author, Alan Ayckbourn, with Celia Johnson and Michael Hordern in a mix-up of identities, and Shaw's *Getting Married,* stuffed to bursting point with ten stars (most of them film favorites of twenty years ago). Thus last year's much-vaunted Shaw revival is petering out; we must hope that his plays will now find a regular, less hysterical place in the repertory, treated as classics.

His influence was discernible in *Public and Confidential,* which marked the welcome return of Benn W. Levy. His play—about a womanizing politician, and the resultant scandal—was neatly constructed and intelligently written, but did not survive very long. Constance Cummings was memorable as an alcoholic secretary. She is currently on view (with Joan Greenwood) in a revival of Coward's *Fallen Angels.* Another Shavian essay, *The Burglar,* was contributed by the novelist Brigid Brophy. This was a static and dry discussion of middle-class morality. It didn't succeed, but I hope she'll try again.

John Mortimer's new play, *The Judge,* was more Ibsenite than Shavian. The subjects under discussion were Guilt and Retribution. A harsh old judge (Patrick Wymark) on the brink of retirement re-visits the town where he grew up—and where he corrupted a young girl. The girl, now a fey old antique dealer and brothel keeper, punctures his recollection. Robbed of his punishment (his raison d'etre), the judge goes mad. Strong meat, unfortunately dissipated by a fussy production and an excessively broad canvas (a cast of sixteen!). Still, there were gripping moments and some fine writing.

Once again, we had a sizeable crop of one-man entertainments: Max Adrian as G.B.S., Roy Dotrice as the diarist John Aubrey (author of *Brief Lives*), Malcolm Muggeridge, the Sage of Television, reading gems of literature (assisted by friends) and chatting amiably, and—at about the time Sir Francis Chichester rounded Cape Horn—Nicol Williamson tackling Gogol's *The Diary of a Madman:* another feat calling for stamina and endurance. The English haven't changed since Oliver Goldsmith's day— they'd still travel miles to see an exhibition of paintings, provided the artist held the brush between his toes!

So much for the legitimate stage. It was a bad year for British musicals. What could be more desperate than the revival, only six months after closure (following a six years' run) of Lionel Bart's *Oliver? Strike a Light,* yet another musical treatment of the famous Matchgirls' Strike of 1888, (the second in less than a year) lacked originality; *Jorrocks,* based on the famous chronicle of a fox hunting enthusiast by Surtees, did not convey much to swinging London; *Joey Joey,* Ron Moody's devoted treatment of the life of the first clown, Grimaldi, had charm but a cliche-ridden libretto; and, lastly, *Houdini, Man of Magic* was technically ingenious, but never developed the promising suggestion that Houdini, alias Harry Weiss, suspended himself upside down in a straitjacket from Brooklyn Bridge as a symbolic gesture of escape from an over-possessive mother. The latter uttered my favourite line of the year. Mrs. Weiss (after witnessing one of her son's most sensational exploits): "What a way to make a living!"

Predictably, all these musicals were put in the shade—and this includes *110 in the Shade*—by the arrival of *Fiddler on the Roof.* This opened triumphantly. The hitherto unknown Israeli actor Topol became a star overnight; queues stretched down the Haymarket, booking seats for next year.

There were no revues worth mentioning. The comedian Frankie Howerd had a deserved success in the show *Way Out in Piccadilly;* the Palladium remained true to its brash identity. There's a season of popular farces, under the experienced management of Brian Rix, at the Garrick Theater; *There's a Girl in My Soup*—a most successful sex comedy—in Shaftesbury Avenue.

Last, but by no means least, the irreplaceable Joan Littlewood returned to her theater in Stratford East after a four years' absence. She opened with a dismally emasculated version of *MacBird!,* but that's nothing to go by. She's back, and her very presence radiates hope.

Among the more amusing sideshows was the spectacle of Mr. Harold Hobson, senior drama critic of *The Sunday Times,* being so shocked by the sight of an exposed male behind (in a phantasmagoria called *The Ballad of the False Barman*) that he demanded increased powers for the Lord Chamberlain, at a time when a parliamentary inquiry deliberated on how to modify or abolish the iniquitous stage censorship. Typically, the Lord Chamberlain himself is anxious to shed his burden. Maybe he could be succeeded by Mr. Hobson?

A lively season, then, taking the rough with the smooth. The big guns were silent, but instead of new plays by Pinter, Osborne, and Arden we saw the debuts of three new writers under the age of thirty (Stoppard, Hampton, Ayckbourn), a great performance from Olivier, a strengthening of the subsidized companies, a lot of promise and some solid achievement, and Joan's return. Not bad to be getting on with.

Highlights of the London Season

Selected and compiled by Ossia Trilling

OUTSTANDING LONDON PERFORMANCES

ROBERT STEPHENS as Leonido in *A Bond Honoured*	PEGGY ASHCROFT as The Mother in *Days in the Trees*	ALEC GUINNESS as Macbeth in *Macbeth*
ANNA MASSEY as Jean Brodie in *The Prime of Miss Jean Brodie*	DANNY LA RUE as Danny Rhodes in *Come, Spy with Me*	RALPH RICHARDSON as Sir Anthony Absolute in *The Rivals*
PAUL SCOFIELD as Charles Dyer in *The Staircase*	PATRICK MAGEE as Harry Leeds in *The Staircase*	NICOL WILLIAMSON as Proprichtchine in *The Diary of a Madman*
DAVID WALLER as Harry Belcher in *Belcher's Luck*	LAURENCE OLIVIER as Edgar in *The Dance of Death*	MARGARET LEIGHTON as Stephanie in *Cactus Flower*
TOPOL as Tevye in *Fiddler on the Roof*	GLENDA JACKSON as Masha in *Three Sisters*	JACK MACGOWRAN as Seumas Shields in *The Shadow of a Gunman*

OUTSTANDING DIRECTORS

PETER BROOK *US*	GLEN BYAM SHAW *The Dance of Death*	DEREK GOLDBY *Rosencrantz and Guildenstern Are Dead*

OUTSTANDING SCENE DESIGNERS

JOSEF SVOBODA *The Storm*	CECIL BEATON *Lady Windermere's Fan*	ALAN TAGG *Belcher's Luck*

OUTSTANDING NEW ENGLISH PLAYS

(D)—Playwright's London debut. Figure in parentheses is number of performances; plus sign (+) indicates play was still running on June 1, 1967.

A BOND HONOURED by John Osborne. Long one-act version of Lope de Vega's *La Fianza Satisfecha,* though with repentant sinner turned impenitent blasphemer. With Robert Stephens, Maggie Smith. (30+in repertory)

WHEN DID YOU LAST SEE MY MOTHER? by Christopher Hampton. (D) A well-meaning mother brings disaster to a pair of adolescent friends. With Victor Henry, Gwen Watford. (26)

BREAD AND BUTTER by Cecil P. Taylor. Glasgow Jewish couple's Odyssey from 1930 to 1966. With Bernard Goldman, David Graham. (27)

LOOT by Joe Orton. Unwanted corpse and burglarious loot get mixed up. With Michael Bates, Sheila Ballantine. (275+)

AFTER THE RAIN by John Bowen. Philosophical science-fiction psychodrama. With Alec McCowen, Anthony Oliver, Valerie White. (46)

US by Denis Cannan, Adrian Mitchell, Peter Brook and others. Agit-prop drama about Vietnam. With Glenda Jackson, Ian Hogg, Henry Woolf. (49)

THE BALLAD OF THE FALSE BARMAN by Colin Spender and Clifton Parker. Joycean musical about sex and power relations. With Caroline Blakiston, Robert Bernal. (19)

THE SILENCE OF LEE HARVEY OS-
WALD by Michael Hastings. Semi-documen-
tary view of the mind of an alleged tyranni-
cide. With Alan Dobie, Sarah Miles, Bessie
Love. (20)

THE JUDGE by John Mortimer. Guilt-rid-
den British judge's clumsy effort to invite
retribution. With Patrick Wymark, Patience
Collier, Michael Pennington. (104+)

THE DAUGHTER-IN-LAW by D.H. Lawrence. First performance of forty-year-old
drama set in North of England mining-town.

With Victor Henry, Mike Pratt, Judy Parfitt.
(25)

STUDIES OF THE NUDE by Frank Marcus. Two pornographers and a model see
their illusions shattered. With Anna Middle-
ton, John Stratton, Barry Warren. (28)

ROSENCRANTZ AND GUILDENSTERN
ARE DEAD by Tom Stoppard. (D) Illusion-
ist view of the destiny of two shadowy Shakespearean characters. With John Stride, Edward
Petherbridge, Graham Crowden. (16+in repertory)

LIMITED RUNS OF INTERESTING NEW BRITISH PLAYS

PRIDE AND PREJUDICE by James Liggatt
and Robert Sheaf. New adaptation of Jane
Austen book. With Petra Davies, Terence
Longdon, Jack Allen. (18)

EARLY ONE MORNING by Glyn Jones.
Sex-starved dominie meets good-time society
girl. With Trevor Bannister, Jill Browne. (27)

THE RUFFIAN ON THE STAIR by Joe
Orton. One-act black comedy involving a murder. With Sheila Ballantine, Bernard Galla-
gher, Kenneth Granham. (1)

PICTURES IN THE HALLWAY by Paul
Shyre. Dramatization of second volume of
Sean O'Casey's autobiography. With Annette
Crosbie, Denys Hawthorne. (17)

THREE MEN FOR COLVERTON by David
Cregan. A religious satire on evangelism gone
wrong. With Sylvia Coleridge, Margery Mason,
Leonard Sachs, Malcolm Tierney. (25)

BELCHER'S LUCK by David Mercer. Impotence of crumbling ruling class versus inadequacy of aspiring lower orders. With Sebastian Shaw, David Waller, John Hurd,
Sheila Allen. (22)

JOEY, JOEY by Keith Waterhouse, Willis
Hall and Ron Moody. Musical based on Grimaldi's life. With Ron Moody, Vivienne Martin. (14)

HUTCH-BUILDER TO HER MAJESTY by
Leo Aylen. (D) The story of Jonah through
modern eyes, set to music. With Annette
Batam, Philip Anthony. (6)

THE LION AND THE JEWEL by Wole
Soyinka. Nigerian's study of sexual and social
tussles in a Nigerian village. With Hannah
Bright-Taylor, Femi Euba, Lionel Ngankane.
(32)

PINKUS by Cecil P. Taylor and Monty Norman. Musical based on Jewish "Helm" anec-
dotes. With Bernard Bresslaw, Nancy Nevin-
son. (41)

THE HOMECOMING by Harold Pinter. Revival prior to New York tour. With New
York cast. (4)

JOHN AUBREY'S BRIEF LIVES by Patrick
Garland. One-man show based on the 17th-
century biographer's works. With Roy Dotrice. (21)

THE EXPERIMENT by David Halliwell and
David Calderisi. Actors rehearse a documen-
tary about President Garfield's assassination.
With Tom Kempinski, the authors. (28)

WILL SOMEBODY PLEASE SAY SOME-
THING? by David Baxter. Actorish stream-
of-consciousness duologue about life. With
David Baxter, Stephen Moore, Susan Baxter.
(19)

THE BURGLAR by Brigid Brophy. (D)
Near-Shavian sex thriller. With Sian Phillips,
Jim Dale. (21)

HOWARD'S END by Lance Sieveking and
Richard Cottrell. Adaptation of E. M. For-
ster's novel. With Gwen Watford, Gemma
Jones, Joyce Carey, Andrew Ray, Marda
Vanne. (38)

HAPPY FAMILY by Giles Cooper. Revival
of last year's tryout of sinister drama of re-
tarded adulthood. With Michael Denison, Dulcie Gray, Robert Flemyng. (30)

NEIGHBOURS by James Saunders. British
one-act view of color prejudice. With Calvin
Lockhart, Toby Robins. (20)

POPULAR ATTRACTIONS

THE PRIME OF MISS JEAN BRODIE by Jay Presson Allen. Stage version of Muriel Spark's novel, originally featuring Vanessa Redgrave, later re-cast. With Anna Massey (later Elizabeth Sellars), Vickery Turner (later Sally Jane Spencer). (416+)

THE DOCTOR'S DILEMMA by George Bernard Shaw. Revival of famous Shavian comedy. With Barry Justice, Eleanor Bron, Griffith Jones, Max Adrian. (36)

THERE'S A GIRL IN MY SOUP by Terence Frisby. Middle-aged TV-personality meets disturbed teenager. With Donald Sinden, Barbara Ferris (later Belinda Carroll), Jon Pertwee. (302+)

WAIT UNTIL DARK by Frederick Knott. Blind girl outsmarts small time crooks. With Honor Blackman (later Barbara Murray). (278+)

HE WAS GONE WHEN WE GOT THERE by Bill Naughton. Science-fiction comedy in a computerized world. With Bernard Miles. (43)

THE THUNDERBOLT by Arthur Wing Pinero. Adapted revival of famous 1908 farce. With Brian Oulton, Peggy Thorpe-Bates. (25)

PRIVATE AND CONFIDENTIAL by Benn W. Levy. Sexual hanky-panky in the corridors of political power. With Constance Cummings, John Gregson, Peter Copley. (71)

MAN OF DESTINY, and O'FLAHERTY V.C. by George Bernard Shaw. Shavian double-bill debunks false patriotism. With Ian McKellen, Sian Phillips, Marie Kean. (47)

FOUR DEGREES OVER by four Oxford graduates from Edinburgh Festival fringe. With John Gould, Bob Scott, Adele Weston, David Wood. (68)

JORROCKS by Beverley Cross and David Heneker. Musical of R.S. Surtees' famous fox-hunting book. With Joss Ackland, Thelma Ruby, Heather Chasen. (180)

THE RIVALS by Richard Brinsley Sheridan. Opulent all-star-cast revival of Restoration comedy. With Ralph Richardson, Margaret Rutherford, Daniel Massey, Keith Baxter. (261+)

LADY WINDERMERE'S FAN by Oscar Wilde. Opulent all-star-cast revival of Wildean comedy. With Isobel Jeans, Ronald Lewis, Coral Browne, Juliet Mills. (146)

THE BIG BAD MOUSE by Philip King and Falkland Cary. Two top comedians on the rampage. With Jimmy Edwards, Eric Sykes. (259+)

THE BED-SITTING ROOM by Spike Milligan and John Antrobus. Revised edition of notorious crazy comedy. With Spike Milligan, Valentine Dyall. (179+)

MACBETH by William Shakespeare. With Alec Guinness (later Maurice Roeves), Simone Signoret (later Suzanne Engel). (46)

THE STAIRCASE by Charles Dyer. Vicissitudes of a homosexual couple. With Paul Scofield, Patrick Magee. (70)

WAY OUT IN PICCADILLY by Ray Galton, Alan Simpson and Eric Sykes. Lavish revue offers Frankie Howerd endless opportunities to shine. With Frankie Howerd, Cilla Black. (268+)

HOUDINI, MAN OF MAGIC by John Morley, Aubrey Lack and Wilfred Wylam. A life of Houdini. With Stuart Damon, Doris Hare. (102)

JUSTICE IS A WOMAN by Jack Roffey and Ronald Kinnoch. Scottish woman Q.C. defends English boy on murder charge. With Constance Cummings, Naunton Wayne. (61)

ON APPROVAL by Frederick Lonsdale. Revival of 1927 smash-hit comedy of ill manners. With Michael Denison, Dulcie Gray, Robert Flemyng, Polly Adams. (142)

THE THWARTING OF BARON BOLLIGREW by Robert Bolt. Revival of popular Christmas attraction. With Roy Kinnear. (20)

THE SOLDIER'S FORTUNE by Thomas Otway. Revival of Restoration romp. With Sheila Hancock, Wallas Eaton. (39)

VOLPONE by Ben Jonson. With Leo McKern, Alan Dobie. (46)

TRIFLES AND TOMFOOLERIES (Augustus Does His Bit, Press Cuttings and Passion, Poison and Petrifaction) by George Bernard Shaw. The Irish wit knocks down some favourite Aunt Sallies. With Moira Redmond, Hazel Hughes, Murray Melvin, Peter Bayliss. (49)

THE SACRED FLAME by W. Somerset Maugham. Revival of play that Gladys Cooper produced in 1929. With Gladys Cooper, Leo Genn, Wendy Hiller. (52)

RELATIVELY SPEAKING by Alan Ayckbourn. (D) The tangled web woven by a womanising husband and his marriageable mistress. With Celia Johnson, Michael Hordern, Jennifer Hilary, Richard Driero. (72+)

FALLEN ANGELS by Noel Coward. Revised version of Coward's broadside against middle-class values of the 1920's. With Constance Cummings, Joan Greenwood. (65+)

THE SHADOW OF A GUNMAN, and A POUND ON DEMAND by Sean O'Casey. Revival of two of O'Casey's celebrated anti-Irish explosions. With Jack MacGowran. (47)

GETTING MARRIED by George Bernard Shaw. Opulent revival of famous Shavian tract on marriage. With Googie Withers, Ian Carmichael, Alec Clunes, Moira Lister, Margaret Rawlings, Raymond Huntley, Esmond Knight, Perlita Neilson, Hugh Williams. (48+)

UPROAR IN THE HOUSE by Anthony Marriott and Alastair Foot. High jinks in the real estate business. With Brian Rix, Elsbet Gray. (16+) In alternate weekly repertory with Stand By Your Bedouin.

STAND BY YOUR BEDOUIN by Ray Cooney and Tony Hilton. Fun and games in an army-ridden foreign outpost. With Brian Rix, Leo Franklyn, Alan Tilvern, Anna Dawson. (48+) In alternate weekly repertory with Uproar in the House.

IN AT THE DEATH by Duncan Greenwood and Robert King. The multiple deceptions of a thriller writer. With Jean Kent, Terence Alexander, Julian Holloway. (43)

HORIZONTAL HOLD by Stanley Price. (D) A female TV pundit's marital trials. With Yvonne Mitchell, Derek Godfrey, Richard Leech, Moira Redmond. (10+)

NATIONAL THEATER AT THE OLD VIC. Continuing schedule of repertory. Othello, by William Shakespeare (20+). Juno and the Paycock, by Sean O'Casey (23+). Trelawney of the "Wells" by Arthur Wing Pinero (25+). Love for Love by William Congreve (51+). The Royal Hunt of the Sun by Peter Shaffer (54+). Much Ado About Nothing by William Shakespeare. (68+)

SOME AMERICAN PLAYS PRODUCED IN LONDON

DO NOT PASS GO by Charles Nolte. With Derren Nesbitt, Wilfrid Brambell. (21)

THE BELLOW PLAYS three one-act plays by Saul Bellow. With Miriam Karlin, Harry Towb. (105)

THE KING'S MARE by Anita Loos; adapted from a play by Jean Canolle. With Keith Michell, Glynis Johns. (164)

LETTERS FROM AN EASTERN FRONT adapted by James Roose Evans from an American play by David Nemiroff. (D) With Robert Bernal, Geoffrey Whitehead, Richard Gale. (21)

THE ODD COUPLE by Neil Simon. With Jack Klugman, Victor Spinetti. (263+)

THE IMPOSSIBLE YEARS by Bob Fisher and Arthur Marx. With David Tomlinson, Sandra Fair. (84)

110 IN THE SHADE (musical) book by N. Richard Nash, music by Harvey Schmidt, lyrics by Tom Jones. With Inga Swenson, Stephen Douglass. (53)

FIDDLER ON THE ROOF (musical) book by Joseph Stein, music by Jerry Bock, lyrics by Sheldon Harnick. With Topol, Miriam Karlin, Jonathan Lynn. (120+)

CACTUS FLOWER by Abe Burrows. With Margaret Leighton, Tony Britton. (75+)

BENITO CERENO by Robert Lowell. With Alan Dobie, Peter Eyre. (47)

FREEZE and STAMP two one-act plays by Ed.B. (D) Surrealist inquiry into life's meaning. With Kathleen Moffat, Hayne Ryan. (6)

WORLD WAR 2½ by Roger O. Hirson. (D) With Sarah Miles, Roy Dotrice. (57+)

MACBIRD! adapted by Joan Littlewood from the American play by Barbara Garson. With Ed Bishop, Bob Grant, Howard Goorney, Stephen Lewis. (43)

DUTCHMAN by LeRoi Jones. With Calvin Lockhart, Toby Robins. (21)

THE DESERT SONG (musical) book and lyrics by Otto Harbach, Oscar Hammerstein II and Frank Mandel, music by Sigmund Romberg. With John Hanson, Patricia Michael. (21+)

SOME FOREIGN PLAYS PRODUCED IN LONDON

TANGO by Slawomir Mrozek. With Michael Williams replacing Trevor Nunn. (37)

LET'S GET A DIVORCE! by Victorien Sardou (free version of *Divorçons!*). With Fenella Fielding (later Barbara Young), Hugh Paddick. (388)

DAYS IN THE TREES by Marguerite Duras. With Peggy Ashcroft, George Baker, Frances Cuka. (62)

THE METEOR by Friedrich Duerrenmatt. With Patrick Magee, Robert Eddison, Charles Kay. (36)

THE SQUARE, and LA MUSICA by Marguerite Duras. With Amanda Reiss, Paul Gillard, Sandor Eles, Joanna Dunham. (18)

JENUSIA by René de Obaldia. With Paul Hardwick, Harriette Johns. (10)

THE STORM by Alexander Ostrovsky, adapted by Doris Lessing. With Jill Bennett, Beatrix Lehmann, Frank Finlay, John Stride. (25)

NEVER SAY DIE by Armand Salacrou (*L'Archipel Lenoir*). With Richard Goolden, Mary Hignett. (1)

IN THE MATTER OF J. ROBERT OPPENHEIMER by Heinar Kipphardt. With Robert Harris, Robert Eddison, Steve Plytas. (76)

THE FIGHTING COCK by Jean Anouilh (*L'Hurluberlu*). With John Clements, Zena Walker, John Standing. (118)

THE GENERALS' TEA-PARTY by Boris Vian. With Richard Murdoch, Gwen Nelson. (11)

THE PROMISE by Aleksei Arbuzov, adapted by Ariadne Nicolaieff from *My Poor Marat*. With Judi Dench, Ian McKellen, Ian McShane. (135+)

THE INSIDERS by Stuart Gilman. (D)

First performance of Canadian play about youth's search for identity. With Hayne Ryan, Sandy Macdonald. (18)

THE DANCE OF DEATH by August Strindberg. With Laurence Olivier, Geraldine McEwen, Robert Stephens. (30+)

OH! by Sandro Key-Aberg. With Vyvyan Denzey, John Junkin, Richard Mayes, Stanley Meadows. (10)

THE DIARY OF A MADMAN by Nikolai Gogol, adapted by Walter Eysselinck. With Nicol Williamson. (33)

WORLD THEATER SEASON, with Polish National Theater in *The Glorious Resurrection of Our Lord* (8), Comédie Française in *Le Cid* (4) and *Le Jeu de l'Amour et du Hasard* with *Feu la Mère de Madame* (4), Japanese Noh Theater in two mixed programs (8 each), Bremen City Theater in *Spring Awakening* (4) and *The Ill-Advised* (4), Israel Cameri Theater in *King Solomon and the Cobbler* (8), Greek Art Theater in *The Frogs* (6) *The Birds* (6), and *The Persians* (4), Milan Piccolo Theater in *The Servant of Two Masters* (8), and Czech Balustrade Theater in *The Trial* (5) and *The Fools* (3).

ARCHITRUC and HYPOTHESIS by Robert Pinget. With Robert Eddison. (19)

THE DEADLY GAME by James Yaffe, adapted from a story by Friedrich Duerrenmatt. With Leslie Stephens, Stephen Murray, Ernest Milton. (41+)

THE DETOUR by Martin Walser. With Geoffrey Chater. (12)

THE TROJAN WARS (*Iphigenia & Hecuba, and Electra & Orestes,* played in repertory as two double bills) by Euripides, translated by Jack Lindsay. With Beatrix Lehmann, Michele Dotrice, Lisa Daniely, Christopher Guinee. (17+) and (3+).

THE SEASON ELSEWHERE IN EUROPE

By Ossia Trilling

One of the most striking features of the theatrical season on the continent of Europe was the wholesale invasion of English plays long before the burning question of British entry into the Common Market hit the world headlines. Sometimes, as in the case of Peter Ustinov's *Halfway in the Tree,* which Boleslaw Barlog staged with comic felicity at the Berlin Schlosspark Theater, but with no unusually resounding comic echoes resulting from this world premiere, this might have been due less to the assiduity of the agents in the export-market and more to the reluctance of producers in the homemarket. But mostly, the plays in question had already made their mark in London or some important provincial center, and the world premiere of John Mortimer's *The Judge* at the Hamburg Deutsches Schauspielhaus (starring Werner Hinz) only came first because the British production, with Patrick Wymark, had to be postponed by a few weeks.

In Germany, Peter Zadek set the ball rolling at the Bremen City Theater with John Osborne's *A Patriot for Me,* translated by the actor who had created the leading role in London (Maximilien Schell). The outspokenness of John Arden's *Live Like Pigs,* brilliantly staged by Peter Palitzsch in Stuttgart, caused a furore and a walk-out on the part of the Burgomaster that gave the play some useful if unintended publicity. Arnold Wesker and Arden were to be seen in many theaters, both in the West and, for the first time, in the East. Edward Bond's sensational study of juvenile delinquency, *Saved*—banned, like Osborne's play, from public performance in London, and, like it, staged before club audiences there—was to be seen (after a Viennese tryout in local dialect at the 1966 Festival) in Bavarian dialect in Munich, adapted by a team of translators headed by the Bavarian actor-playwright Martin Sperr. It was well received by the press and caused no untoward ripples in the smooth surface of the German bourgeois playgoer's habitual impassiveness.

The British names that cropped up unfailingly on playbills were Harold Pinter *(The Homecoming)* and Frank Marcus *(The Killing of Sister George).* The latter play, if it did nothing else, helped many a theater manager solve the problem of how to employ some of the less easily usable middle-aged actresses on his payroll. So that this generalization does not work too unfairly, a special tribute is due to Maria Becker's excruciatingly realistic and totally

129

convincing title role in the Zurich production. Although the Germans still tend to consider Shakespeare a home-made product, he should, properly speaking, be considered in the British category. Two productions that I saw deserve mention. The first was the two-night synthesis of the three parts of *Henry VI* made by Jörg Wehmeier and Peter Palitzsch and staged in Stuttgart in Wilfried Minks' typically neo-Brechtian decors, using sliding panels in an effort to achieve something corresponding to the technique of the "wipe" in the cinema for continuity. The second was Erich Fried's new translation of *Hamlet,* his ninth play by the poet, and his fifth to be staged in Heidelberg: it probably came closer to the original in feeling than any other existing German version.

It is worth noting that, for all the artistic and technical pre-eminence of the German theater, established native dramatists are not apparently following up the promise of the first half of the present decade. The emphasis has shifted slightly from the intelligentsia to the craftsman author, as exemplified by Martin Sperr and Hartmut Lange. Sperr's *Hunting-Scenes from Lower Bavaria* is a remarkable dramatic document from the pen of a 22-year-old actor. Tried out in Bremen, it reappeared in an improved form at the progressively-minded Schaubuhne am Halleschen Ufer in West Berlin, with the author himself playing the weak-minded country lad who provokes a twofold tragedy behind which lurk incorrigible Nazi habits of thought and behavior. Lange, self-exiled from eastern Germany, had two plays of Brechtian intent and Schillerian stamp to his credit. *Marski,* staged with the bovine Hans-Dieter Zeidler in Frankfurt, and in Minks' eye-catching Lucullan settings at the West Berlin Free People's Theater, carried echoes of Brecht's *Puntila* in its contemporary East German setting. *The Deliverance of the Wise Man Ch'ien Wan-hsüan* is a laudable attempt to improve on an earlier piece of ironic chinoiserie (staged by the Berliner Ensemble) in which the symbolical sage of the title is spurned by all and sundry, framed, and finally saved from the noose by a benevolent ruler. Lange has proved himself to be a more than competent director as well.

Mere competence, however, will not suffice where taste is lacking, and this is the sad reflection to be made about Ernst Schröder's monumentally ill-judged attempt to translate Part 2 of Goethe's unplayable *Faust* to the stage of Berlin's Schiller Theater, with himself as Mefisto in one of two alternating casts. If only he had had the sensibility of the 75-year-old veteran director, Fritz Kortner, impenitent *enfant terrible* as always yet gaining in authority over the years, most outstandingly with his *Othello* at Vienna's Burgtheater and his *The Father* (by Strindberg) at Hamburg's Schauspielhaus (with Werner Hinz and Maria Wimmer impersonating folly and wisdom by turns in the roles of the Captain and his devouring wife, Laura). *The Father* proved the outstanding directorial achievement of the past twenty years. Two notable firsts in Vienna were Curt Jurgens as Galileo in Brecht's debut at the otherwise conservatively-orientated Burgtheater and Maximilien Schell's prestigious double-act in Goldoni's *The Venetian Twins.* Brecht's juvenilia, now coming to light, included *The Catch,* at Heidelberg (a one-acter portraying infidelity and tippling in a fisherman's hovel) and the uncompleted anticapitalist agit-prop drama *The Breadshop,* which was superseded by *Saint Joan of the Stockyards,* but which the Berliner Ensemble completed from contemporary material and world premiered with their accustomed bravura. Manfred Karge and Matthias Langhoff, who staged it, and Uta Birnbaum, responsible for a disturbingly hilarious first performance of *Man Is Man* (starring Hilmar Thate), are three directors of the younger generation of whom Brecht would not have felt ashamed.

Still, it is Benno Besson who continues to steal the directorial thunder in East Berlin. His approach to Sophocles' *Oedipus Tyrannus* (starring Fred Düren) at the Deutsches Theater resulted in a hypnotic, awe-inspiring, ritualistic performance in masks and African musical rhythms. Frankfurt, ever Western champion of Brecht, offered two memorable items on neighboring stages, *Puntila and His Servant Matti* (starring Hans-Dieter Zeidler) and *The Rise and Fall of the City of Mahagonny* (with the American soubrette Olive Moorefield as an entrancing Jenny), both directed with *savoir-faire* by Harry Buckwitz, prematurely retiring on account of reduced civic subsidies. Cologne's *Celestina,* by Rojas, in Karl Paryla's sumptuous production and starring Grete Wurm, rightly earned an invitation to the annual parade of German theater in Berlin. Among several new playhouses built during the year were those at Wuppertal, unveiled with the late Else Lasker-Schüler's early symbolist *The Wupper* (for which Teo Otto, born not a stone's-throw from the scene, did some apt designs), and at Bochum, which Hans Schalla inaugurated with Maximilien Schell's *Herostratus,* a didactic drama, his first, that regrettably misfired. Zurich offered its staid patrons a revised version of Duerrenmatt's first play *(As It Is Written)* entitled *The Anabaptists.* Stunningly directed by Werner Düggelin in Otto's decors, this pseudo-historical epic drama revealed the writer's maturity in tackling a theme dear to his heart—man's incapacity to order his affairs on earth—and the explosively winning talents of Ernst Schröder, and the regular crew of Zurich worthies, Gustav Knuth and Mathias Wieman among them.

The end of the season saw a rash of German plays by authors both new and old. Apart from Jochen Zeim's *The Invitation,* they dealt with death and violence, an obsessional theme with German writers today. Even Zeim's first play did not avoid aspects of either. At the Berlin Schlosspark Theater it had the benefit of Hans Schweikart's skilled handling as director, though its treatment of a burning contemporary theme shirked the main issue, that of the moral gulf dividing Western and Eastern Germans, both, in the author's jaundiced view, unlovely products of petty-bourgeois prejudice. The Hitlerian blood bath served as a source of inspiration for Michael Ende's *The Killjoys* as well as for Heinar Kipphardt's *The Night on Which the Boss Was Bumped Off.* The former, at Frankfurt, took an allegorically dismal view of the human race and of its future. The latter, at Stuttgart, departed from the author's recent documentary line (e.g. the Oppenheimer and Joel Brand dramas) and took the form of a dream-play horror-comic. Director Peter Palitzsch and guest-designer Wilfried Minks staged it in an intriguing op and pop art decor that filled out some of its thinness. An ordinarily peaceable bank clerk lives out his

bloodthirsty fantasies in neo-Kafkaesque nightmares in which his barbarian instincts are given full play. This piece of guignolesque tomfoolery pilloried the
Germans for displaying the failings of middle-class morality.

Murder most foul was the theme of Tankred Dorst's *Wittek on the Prowl,*
at Dusseldorf, a typical German guignol drama set in Napoleonic times that
show how easily people are led to condone mass murder and profit by it. That
the parable made its mark may be assumed from the demonstrative walk-out
on opening night of the Burgomaster. In a category of its own was the 15-
year-old dramatization of the medieval *People's Book of Duke Ernst* by Peter
Hacks of Eastern Germany. This was a picaresque drama that aims to ex-
plode traditional heroic cliches. Sumptuously staged in Mannheim, in the
West, by Jean-Pierre Ponnelle from France, it also served to show how hard
it is for certain kinds of social criticism to win the imprimatur of the East
German authorities.

I see that I have as usual given a great deal of space to the German-speak-
ing theater. This is unavoidable, so long as it remains, by quantity and quality,
the dominant creative theatrical furnace and melting-pot of all Europe. How
France pales by comparison! Georges Wilson's slapdash production of *Mahagonny* at the Théâtre National Populaire in Paris is a case in point, despite
the brilliant decors by Jacques Le Marquet. Not that there were no comparatively dazzling highlights, too: such as Roger Planchon's own play in Villeur-
banne about the way in which revolution either devours or spares its children
(called *The Libertines*); the young Greek-born newcomer Jean Tasso's dynamic handling of *Marat/Sade* at the Sarah-Bernhardt, from which A. M.
Julien, after running a successful season, at one time producing as many as
17 performances of four different plays in repertory in a single week, and
after years in the saddle, was shamefully ousted by an ungrateful municipal-
ity; Laurent Terzieff's forceful twofold role as director and leading actor in
Mrozek's *Tango* at the Lutèce; the Théâtre de l'Est Parisien's startlingly realistic production of *Live Like Pigs,* that won them critical encomiums at the
Florence Festival; the three real-life sisters in Andre Barsacq's production of
Chekhov's play of that name; or the sensational virtuosity of writing and performance of Arrabal's scabrously melodramatic *The Architect and the Emperor of Assyria.* The English invasion of France was further represented
by Pinter (with John Bury's original decor for *The Homecoming*), Saunders
(two one-acters at the Lutèce, and *Next Time I'll Sing to You* at the Antoine,
where the producer had this Pirandellian drama alternate in repertory with
Pirandello's own *Trovarsi*), Ann Jellicoe's *The Knack,* Osborne's *Inadmissible Evidence* (in which Michel Bouquet grew to new histrionic heights),
Kops' *The Hamlet of Stepney Green,* C. P. Taylor, David Halliwell, Roger
Milner, and, above all, Arnold Wesker, whose *The Kitchen* was staged in a
circus-tent in the round to packed houses for weeks on end. Romain Wien-
garten, author of *Summer,* at the little Poche Montparnasse, was the one true
discovery of the year, delicately revealing the world in all its complex facets
as seen through the eyes of two youngsters and their two pet cats which take

on human shape and talk in human accents, a delightful poetic drama of immense imagination and conspicuous promise.

The Boulevard had little to be proud of, unless it be Françoise Sagan's trivially novelletish *The Horse That Fainted,* in which unconvincing upper-middle-class English people and equally cardboard French middle-class social climbers meet in the never-never-land of the dramatist's fictional imagination. Still, it got rave notices and sold out throughout the year, so it evidently answered some sort of need somewhere. At the establishment theaters, Jean-Louis Barrault and Wilson opened new ancillary stages at the Théâtre de France and the Palais de Chaillot respectively, a much-needed innovation, though the 105-seater in the former was too tiny to be taken seriously. On the larger stages, each made an attempt to merge stage and auditorium to achieve Shakespearean continuity: *Henry VI* (all three parts in a single evening) at the former, and *King Lear,* on a circular projecting stage, at the latter. Jean-Pierre Granval (Madeleine Renaud's son) showed a nice taste for boisterous stylishness in a new production of *The Barber of Seville* at Barrault's theater, where later Maurice Béjart made his directorial debut with a Flaubert epic that served his extreme conception of total theater to perfection. The T.N.P. brought Julius Hay's forty-year-old political drama about moral expediency *(God, Emperor and Peasant)* to the capital from the 1966 Avignon Festival. The casting of A.M. Julien's son, François Maistre, first as the 15th-century unacknowledged Pope John XXIII and then as Emperor Sigismund of Hungary (where the author was born 67 years ago and still lives) revealed as much of the director's indecision as of the actor's versatility. It was a good year for the Comédie Française: one success after another (despite the inadequacy of *Krechinsky's Wedding* for the direction and the design of which Nicolai Akimov was brought all the way from Leningrad) culminated in the outrageously unorthodox *Dom Juan* with décor by an abstract sculptor, that also marked the debut of Antoine Bourseiller at France's oldest of five national theaters. A quaint performance, if only because of antiquarian interest, was their discovery of Marivaux's long-lost *La Commère,* in which the titular matchmaker was endearingly acted by Françoise Seigner. A sort of off-off-boulevard theater, supplying the needs of young theatrical rebels, came into being in the shape so-called of "cafe-theaters," and one bold venturer (Bernard da Costa) even hired a river-going boat moored in the Seine to accommodate his fans in an 80-seater perspex-enclosed auditorium. Otherwise much of theatrical value was to be seen in the suburban playhouses that are supplanting or supplementing the central Parisian venues artistically. Here Weiss's *The Investigation* rubbed shoulders with foreign and classical dramas and even sturdy centralists like A.M. Julien turned up (in Aubervilliers) as a leading actor in a strangely glacial production by Gabriel Garran of *The Iceman Cometh.*

The Investigation in the Milan Piccolo's version, directed by Virginio Puecher, toured twenty Italian cities, playing in churches and arenas; it opened in the Santa Maria in Vado Basilica in Ferrara (built in 1475) before 1,000 awestruck spectators. Arden and Wesker also made their mark in Italy (notably with *Chips With Everything* at the Piccolo). The Piccolo also paid its centenary tribute to Pirandello in the shape of Strehler's highly-appreciated revival of *The Giants of the Mountain*. So did other companies including the Anna Proclemer—Giorgio Albertazzi group (with *As You Desire Me*). The group headed by Giorgio De Lullo scored two bull's-eyes with a new version of the salacious 16th-century farce *La Calandria*, by Cardinal Bibbiena, and Giuseppe Patroni Griffi's latest stream-of-consciousness drama of illicit passion entitled *Imagine, One Evening at Supper* starring the incomparable Rossella Falk and with Pier Luigi Pizi's Mondrian-like decor. The Turin City Theater spread its wings throughout the peninsula with, at one time, four simultaneous ensembles, in new plays by Moravia and Ginsburg, and Paolo Levi's *Is This a Man?*, an autobiographical documentary poem set in Auschwitz, in a harrowingly realistic production by Gianfranco De Bosio.

Scandinavia held several surprises, one of which was Ingmar Bergman's defection from the theater after staging his first foreign production (of Pirandello's *Six Characters* in Oslo, with his latest film discovery, Liv Ullman, as the daughter-in-law). It would be a pity, if he meant it; his idiosyncratic handling of Molière's double-bill *The School for Wives* and *Critique of The School for Wives,* with their stylistic echoes of a previous season's *Hedda Gabler,* supported this view. Another surprise was the departure for Oslo of Vivica Bandler from Helsinki, after creating and running the Little Theater there for 12 years, and yet another that of Ralf Langbacka, the white hope of the Swedish National Theater there, who failed to get on with his colleagues and succumbed to the invitations that every major Swedish theater heaped on him from across the Gulf of Bothnia. In Copenhagen, too, there were changes, most striking of them being the appointment of Meir Feigenberg, a grandson of Sholom Aleichem, the Russo-Jewish author, to the direction of the New Theater, while at the new municipal theater down the road (The New Scala), a well-turned production of *Fiddler on the Roof,* with which he was in no way connected, played for months on end. Ernst Bruun Olsen and Finn Savery, authors of *Teenager Love,* almost repeated their earlier success with a social satire, with music, based on Olsen's youthful experiences and post-war disillusionment in the "bourgeoisification," as he called it, of the labor movement, entitled *The Country Ball*. Musical satire was all the rage throughout the North, pride of place going to Peter Weiss's *The Song of the Lusitanian Bogeyman,* an oblique criticism in verse and rhythmic prose of 20th-century colonialism, which had its world premier in Swedish translation at the Scala Theater in Stockholm, with a versatile cast of seven and a jazz combo.

Several East European artists came west, not in a permanent sense, but as guests, such as Kazimierz Dejmek from Warsaw, Alfred Radok and Josef Svoboda from Prague, and Nicolai Akimov (already mentioned). The center of avant-garde activity was firmly established in Prague, partly through Svoboda's highly original scenic designs and lighting techniques (and those of other Czech artists working on similar lines), and partly through the increased activity of the state-subsidised "private theaters," that is, theaters run not as state or city enterprises but as arts or studio theaters. The work of Ladislav

Smocek, whose playlets and productions impressed the Swedes during the Scandinavian Theater Congress, and that of Otomar Krejca, assisted by Josef Topol, at the Theater Behind the Gate, and of Jan Grossman, at the Theater on the Balustrade, continued to expand and deepen. *Three Sisters,* at the former, designed by Svoboda in a neutrally stylised non-realistic setting, was pioneering effort of tremendous potential. Here, too, Topol made a promising directorial debut with his *Nightingale for Supper,* a typically Kafkaesque study of violence and death. Kafka's *The Trial* in Grossman's allegorical version, and starring Jan Preucil, at the latter, was the most important single contribution of the Czechs to the European theater (it was later seen in London, and was due for the Paris and Venice Festivals). A sad note on which to end this year's East European comment: the sacking of the brilliant young director, Anatoli Efros, from the direction of the Lenin Komsomol Theater in Moscow, for refusing to heed official criticism of his repertorial policy.

Highlights of the Paris Season

Selected and compiled by Ossia Trilling

OUTSTANDING PERFORMANCES

MICHEL BOUQUET as Bill Crawford* in *Inadmissible Evidence*	DANIELLE DARRIEUX as Laurette in *Laurette*	PAUL-EMILE DEIBER as King Ferrante in *The Dead Queen*
EMMANUÈLE RIVA as Ruth in *The Homecoming*	JEAN-PAUL ROUSSILLON as Raspluyev in *Krechinsky's Wedding*	PHILIPPE NOIRET as David** in *The Odd Couple*
DELPHINE SEYRIG as Donata Genzi in *She Wanted to Find Herself*	MICHEL HERBAULT as Jacques Roux in *Marat/Sade*	ROBERT DHÉRY as Charley** in *The Odd Couple*
PIERRE BERTIN as Bartholo in *The Barber of Seville*	LAURENT TERZIEFF as Arthur in *Tango*	RAYMOND GÉROME as the Emperor in *The Architect and the Emperor of Assyria*
JEAN-LOUIS BARRAULT as St. Anthony in *The Temptation of St. Anthony*	JACQUES CHARON as Sganarelle in *Dom Juan*	RENÉE FAURE as Madame Arkadina in *The Seagull*

* In the French version of *Inadmissible Evidence* the name of the protagonist was changed from Bill Maitland to Bill Crawford.

** In the French version of *The Odd Couple* the names of the leading characters Oscar and Felix were changed to David and Charley.

OUTSTANDING DIRECTORS

JEAN-LOUIS BARRAULT *Henry VI*	ANTOINE BOURSEILLER *Dom Juan*	MAURICE BÉJART *The Temptation of St. Anthony*

OUTSTANDING DESIGNERS

ANDRE ACQUART *Marat/Sade*	JACQUES LE MARQUET *The Rise and Fall of the City of Mahagonny*	OSCAR GUSTIN *Dom Juan*

OUTSTANDING NEW FRENCH PLAYS

(D)—Playwright's Paris debut

L'ÉTÉ (Summer) by Romain Weingarten. Two children and two country cats make some ironic discoveries. With Nicolas Bataille, Dominique Labourier, Richard Leduc, the author.

LA FÊTE NOIRE (The Black Feast) by Jacques Audiberti. Posthumous drama on the legend of the Beast of Gevaudan. With Catherine Rouvel, Claude Titre, Monique Delaroche.

LA CONVENTION BELZÉBIR (The Belzebir Convention) by Marcel Aymé. The consequences of legalizing murder. With Yves Robert, Christiane Minazzoli, Catherine Allegret, René Dupuy.

L'AIR AU LARGE (Out in the Open) by René de Obaldia. A strange couple's solution of the housing shortage. With Marie-José Nat (later Evelyne Dandry), Bernard Noël.

LE SILENCE and LE MENSONGE (Silence and The Lie) by Nathalie Sarraute. (D) A silent guest and a lying guest upset a party in two one-acters. With Madeleine Renaud, Gabriel Cattand.

LES ANCÊTRES REDOUBLENT DE FÉROCITÉ (The Ancestors Double Their Violence) by Kateb Yacine. Two Algerians strug-gle and die for an ideal. With Med Hondo, Armand Meffre, Laurence Bourail.

SPECTACLE MADELEINE ROBINSON (The Madeleine Robinson Show), triple bill included A La Nuit, La Nuit (Nighttime at Night) by François Billetdoux. A tragic duologue for an incompatible couple. With Madeleine Robinson.

LE LABYRINTHE (The Labyrinth) by Francisco Arrabal. The nightmare resistance of a man condemned to die. With Jacques Coutureau.

L'ARCHITECTE ET L'EMPEREUR D'ASSYRIE (The Architect and the Emperor of Assyria) by Francisco Arrabal. Two shipwrecked marathon talkers re-enact their sexual and other fantasies. With Raymond Gérome, Jean-Pierre Joris.

L'AGRESSION (Aggression) by Georges Michel. Dead-end kids of the 1960's. With Robert Sireygeol, Michel Lebret.

LA COMMÈRE (The Gossip) by Marivaux. Long-lost classic rediscovered in the Comédie Française library. With Françoise Seigner.

CRIPURE by Louis Guilloux. (D) Ill-fated daydreams of a 1917 Breton schoolmaster. With Marcel Maréchal, Tatiana Moukine.

LIMITED RUNS OF INTERESTING NEW FRENCH PLAYS

A MEMPHIS IL Y A UN HOMME D'UNE FORCE PRODIGIEUSE (There's a Real He-Man in Memphis) by Jean Audureau. (D) Ma Barker lives to rue the day she brought up her four sons to be gangsters. With Marcelle Ranson, Maria D'Apparecida.

LA COMMUNIANTE ET LA PRINCESSE (The Communicant and the Princess) by Francisco Arrabal. An adolescent kicks against the pinpricks of formal sexual teaching. With Claude Génia, Claire Duhamel, Marc Dudicourt. Coupled with three short pieces— Leçons de Français pour Américains (French Lessons for Americans), La Jeune Fille à Marier (The Marriageable Daughter) and Au Pied de Mur (At the Foot of the Wall)— send-ups, respectively, of linguistics, bourgeois ideals and tourist cliches, by Eugene Ionesco, with the same cast.

LA VENGEANCE D'UNE ORPHELINE RUSSE (A Russian Orphan Girl's Vengeance) by Henri Rousseau. Hitherto unperformed play by the famous Douanier Rousseau about a wronged girl in Tsarist Russia. With Elisabeth Wiener.

LE POINT H (H Marks the Spot) by Yves Jamiaque. Abortive meeting between enemy atom-bomb scientists. With Pierre Dux, Michel Lonsdale.

L'ÉVÈNEMENT (The Event), L'ARTHRITE (Arthritis) and EN REGARDANT TOMBER LES MURS (See How the Walls Tumble), triple-bill by Guy Foissy. Satirical view of truth that is stranger than fiction. Anne-Marie Nat, Christian Bouillette, Maurice Travail, Hervé Denis.

COMÉDIE (Play) and VA ET VIENT (Come and Go) by Samuel Beckett; LA LACUNE (The Omission) and DÉLIRE À DEUX (Bedlam for Two) by Eugene Ionesco; HYPOTHÈSE (Hypothesis) by Robert Pinguet. A mixed bill of French premieres. The first two give views of life in the hereafter;

the next two discuss (a) the fatal gap in an Academician's career and (b) the sex war that overshadows real war; the last sends up academic gobbledygook.

LADY GODIVA by Jean Canolle. A naked lady's ride through Coventry. With Cyrille Fontaine.

L'OBJET AIMÉ (The Loved One) and PAR LA TAILLE (By the Waist) by Alfred Jarry. Two hitherto unperformed Jarryesque farces about love. With Hillia d'Aubeterre, Georges Tournaire, Jérôme Savary.

MÊLÉES ET DÉMÊLÉES (Mixed and Unmixed) by Eugene Ionesco. Pot-pourri of nine sketches and one new playlet about marriage. With Claude Génia, Michel Galabru, J.-M. Serreau.

LADY JANE by Jean Mogin. Historical drama about Lady Jane Grey by a Belgian author. With Tania Torrès, Pierre Didier, Yvon Sarret.

LA TRUITE DE SCHUBERT (Schubert's Trout) by Bernard Da Costa. Absurdist view of the eternal triangle. With Celita, Maria Laborit, Michel Gonzales.

LA VIE SENTIMENTALE (Living and Loving) by Louis Velle. The road to four blissful days in Venice paved with bad intentions. With Jacqueline Gauthier, Ida Lonati, the author.

MORT D'UNE BALEINE (Death of a Whale) by Jacque Jaquine. (D) The vengeance a feeble victim wreaks on the bully he envies succeeds beyond expectation. With Raymond Hermantier, Gerard Darrieu.

LA MACHINE À SOUS (The Slot-Machine) by David Guerdon. A scheming female's murderous plan succeeds. With Agnès Capri, Geneviève Thénier, Gérard Croce, Raymond Jourdan.

CAVALIER SEUL (Knight-Errant Solo) by Jacques Audiberti. Posthumous picaresque drama about a crusader. With the Loïc Voland—Jacques Rosny company.

LA TRIBU (The Tribe) by Jean Hubert Sibnay. (D) Clash of old and new in an emergent country. With Gabriel Glissant, Claude Chazel, Hilarion.

COEUR À CUIRE (Stout-Heart) by Jacques Audiberti. Posthumous drama based on the life of Charles VII's steward Jacques Coeur. With Gabriel Monnet, Françoise Bertin.

POPULAR ATTRACTIONS

LA PERRUCHE ET LE POULET (The Budgerigar and the Cop) by Robert Thomas. Adaptation of Jack Popplewell's thriller, to French milieu, about a cop and a telephonist joining forces. With Jane Sourza, Raymond Souplex.

LE GUICHET (The Ticket-Office) by Jean Tardieu, with LE BEL INDIFFÉRENT (The Uncaring Beau) by Jean Cocteau, and a Pirandello, made up a long-running triplebill. The first portrays the tyranny of bureaucracy, the second of unrequited love. With Arlette Thomas, Jacques Thébault, Pierre Peyrau.

L'ÉCHARDE and LE CHEVAL ÉVANOUI (The Thorn and The Horse That Fainted), double bill by Françoise Sagan. A faded actress's nostalgic day-dreams. An unscrupulous French couple ruffle the surface calm of an Englishman's castle. With Jacques François, Nicole Courcel, Hélène Duc.

LES MONSTRES SACRÉS (The Holy Terrors) by Jean Cocteau. Revival of the 20-year-old backstage drama of an aging actress on the defensive. With Arletty, Huguette Hue, Yves Vincent.

KNOCK by Jules Romains. Revival of famous comedy of a medico's intrigues. With Henri Virlojeux.

LA REINE MORTE (The Dead Queen) by Henry de Montherlant. Revival of 24-year-old Comédie Française hit. With Paul-Emile Deiber, Christine Fersen, François Chaumette, Geneviève Casile, Jacques Toja.

LE NEZ EN TROMPETTE (Snub-Nose) by Michel Fermaud. A girl and a traffic-jam cause a heap of trouble. With Bernard Lavalette, Raymond Buissière, Evelyne Valentino.

L'HOTEL RACINE by Michèle Perrin. (D) An adolescent girl refuses to grow up. With Nicole Garcia, Claire Nadeau.

L'OBSÉDÉ (Obsession) by France Roche. Adaptation of John Fowles' The Collector about an abductor. With Robert Hossein, Annie Sinigalia.

LAURETTE by Marcelle Maurette and Marc-Gilbert Sauvajon. The adventures of a notorious lady-crook. With Danielle Darrieux, Lucien Raimbourg, Michel Roux.

BECKET by Jean Anouilh. Revival of popular pseudo-historical drama. With Daniel Ivernel (later Claude Brosset), Paul Guers.

DEMANDEZ VICKY! (Call Vicky!) by Marc-Gilbert Sauvajon. Adapted from an English farce about a lonely girl who sends out assignations by balloon. With Dany Robin, Armontel.

LE ROI SE MEURT (Exit the King) by Eugene Ionesco. Revival of famous allegory of life and death. With Jacques Mauclair, Tsilla Chelton, René Dupuy.

MARC AURÈLE A DISPARU (Marcus Aurelius Has Vanished) by Jean Le Marois. A straying dog changes a misogynist's heart. With Sylvie Pelayo, Jean-Paul Coquelin, Jacques Provin.

LA LOCOMOTIVE (The Locomotive) by André Roussin. A sentimental Russian refugee pays for the error of living on her memories. With Elvire Popesco, Fernand Ledoux, Henri Crémieux.

LA BOUTEILLE À L'ENCRE (The Inkpot) by Albert Husson. The pitfalls that await the author of indiscreet memoirs. With Claude Dauphin, Anne Vernon, Renaud-Mary, Monique Mélinand.

OPÉRATION LAGRELÈCHE by and with Jean Poiret and Michel Serrault. A Frenchman is unexpectedly shot into the strange new world of American movie-makers. Also with Jacqueline Jefford, Jacques Jouanneau, Roger Carel.

MÉDOR by Charles Vildrac (billed with L'AIR AU LARGE by René de Obaldia). An estranged couple's reconciliation. With Marie-José Nat, Bernard Noël.

TÊTE-BÊCHE (Topside Down) by Guy Bedos and Jean-Loup Dabadie. Twenty-one comic sketches and five songs. With Sophie Daumier, Guy Bedos.

LE VOYAGE DE MONSIEUR PERRICHON (Mr. Perrichon's Journey) by Eugène Labiche and Edouard Martin. And LE COMMISSAIRE EST BON ENFANT (The Police Inspector Is a Good Lad) by Georges Courteline and Jules Levy. The first is a Comédie Française revival of a farcical story of a trip to the Swiss Alps. The second is about wrong arrests and marital misunderstandings. With Louis Seigner, Jacques Charon, Jean-Paul Roussillon, Paul Noelle.

LA BONNE ADRESSE (The Right Address) by Marc Camoletti. Vicissitudes of a foursome who answer an ad. With Jean-Pierre Darras, René Havard, Guy Grosso, Patrick Réjean.

DÉCIBEL by Julien Bartet. (D) Conflicting loyalties of sex and industrial strife. With Jacques Duby, Philippine Pascal, Marie Daëms, Jacques Dufilho.

LA PARISIENNE by Henri Becque and LE CAROSSE DU S. SACREMENT (The Carriage of The Holy Sacrament) by Prosper Mérimée. Revival of two famous classics in a double bill. With A. M. Julien, Jacqueline Danno, Dominique Blanchar.

LA COURTE PAILLE (The Short Straw) by Jean Meyer. Boy and girl romance almost ruined by disclosures. With Simone Simon, Christian Alers, Denise Benoit, the author.

UN JOUR J'AI RENCONTRÉ LA VÉRITÉ (One Day I Found the Truth) by Félicien Marceau. How a born liar undeceives himself. With François Périer, Geneviève Brunet, Odile Mallet.

COMME AU THÉÂTRE (As in the Theater) by Frédérick Renaud (alias Françoise Dorin). Deceptions in a Paris apartment, but truth will out. With Michel Roux, Renaud-Mary, Martine Sarcey.

DOM JUAN (Don Juan) by Molière. Controversial Comédie Française revival. With Georges Descrières, Jacques Charon.

XAVIER by Jacques Deval. A young widow covets her late husband's sequestered fortune. With Lise Delamare, Annie Sinigalia, Michel Creton, Jacques Dynam.

LES CAISSES, QU'EST-CE? (What's What's-It?) by and with Jean Bouchaud. A series of sketches and gags. Also with Danièle Girard, Pierre Richard, Claude Everard.

MOI AUSSI, J'EXISTE (I, Too, Am Alive) by Georges Neveux. Adapted from Dostoyevsky's The Gambler and Letters from the Underground: a lonely man faces his phantoms. With André Reybaz, Hélène Sauvaneix, Maria Mériko.

LA FAMILLE ÉCARLATE (The Scarletts) by Jean-Loup Dabadie. (D) A family conspires to do away with an autocratic grandfather. With Rosy Varte, Françoise Rosay, Christian Alers, Gérard Lartigau, Pierre Brasseur, Jean Leuvrais.

LA TENTATION DE S. ANTOINE (The Temptation of St. Anthony) by Gustave Flaubert, adapted by Maurice Béjart. A classic novel turned into total theater. With Jean-Louis Barrault, Simone Valère, Anne Carrère, Jean Desailly, Madeleine Renaud.

LE DUEL by André Barsacq. Adapted from a Chekhov story about a prig and a ne'er-do-well. With Pierre Vaneck, Alain Mottet, Etienne Bierry.

SACRÉE FAMILLE! (Dreadful Family!) by Eugène Labiche, adapted by Jacques d'Aubrac. Musical revival of famous 19th-century vaudeville. With Micheline Bourday, the adaptor.

MARIUS by Marcel Pagnol. Revival of 30-year-old first part of Marseille trilogy. With Rellys, Fernand Sardou, René Sarvil.

LA POLKA DES LAPINS (The Rabbit Polka) by Tristan Bernard. Revival of farcical comedy of human foibles. With Michel de Ré, Jean Parédès, Isabelle Ehni, Nicole Anouilh.

L'ERREUR EST JUSTE (Wrong But Right) by Jean Paxet. Typical vaudeville in which professionals of both sexes get across one another. With Jacques Meyran, Suzanne Grey.

PETITAPON (Rubadubdub) by Jacques Martin and Francis Veber. Musical about a pop singer and his molls. With Jacques Martin, Emma Vetty.

MAMAN, J'AI PEUR! (Ma, I'm Scared!) by Brigitte Fontaine, Jacques Higelin, and Rufus. (D) Satirical revue transferred from La Vielle Grille Café-Théâtre. With the authors.

LORSQUE L'ENFANT PARAIT (The Blessed Event) by André Roussin. Revival of popular pregnancy comedy. With André Luguet, Gisèle Casadesus.

LES LETTRES DE MON MOULIN (Letters From My Mill) by Alphonse Daudet. Three short stories adapted into a play by Gil Beladou. With the company of the Comédie de Provence.

LES JUSTES (The Righteous) by Albert Camus. Revival of famous conspiracy thriller. With Nadine Basile, Marcel Bozzufi.

JEAN DE LA LUNE by Marcel Achard. Revival of famous sentimental comedy of romantic loyalty of 1929. With Dany Robin, Pierre Mondy, Jean Le Poulain, Daniel Ceccaldi.

LE NOUVEAU TESTAMENT (The New Testament) by Sacha Guitry. Revival of Molièresque comedy about a suspicious legator. With Fernand Gravey, Mony Dalmès, Michèle André.

SOME AMERICAN PLAYS PRODUCED IN PARIS

ANY WEDNESDAY by Muriel Resnik. With Fernand Gravey, Mony Dalmès, Maria Daëms, Bernard Woringer.

THE ODD COUPLE by Neil Simon. With Robert Dhéry, Philippe Noiret.

MOUCHE (Carnival) musical with book by Michael Stewart, music and lyrics by Bob Merrill. With Christine Delaroche, Jean-Claude Drouot, Magali Noël.

ERIS by Lee Falk. With Michel Galabru, Max Vialle (With Ionesco's Mêlées et Démêlées).

BABY HAMILTON. By Anita Loos and Maurice Braddell. With Robert Murzeau, Claude Rollet.

SLOW DANCE ON THE KILLING GROUND by William Hanley. With Maurice Teynac, Med Hondo, Marlene Jòbert.

SOME OTHER FOREIGN PLAYS PRODUCED IN PARIS

THEATER OF THE NATIONS SEASON included, in 1966, the Living Theater's productions of The Brig and of Mysteries and Smaller Pieces; in 1967, the Dusseldorf Schauspielhaus's of Mrozek's Tango and the Circle in the Square's of Trumpets of the Lord.

THE CARD-INDEX by Tadeusz Rozewicz. With Philippe Drancy, Christian Bouillcttc.

THE LOVERS by Goldoni. With Jacques Aveline, Simone Couderc, Roger Crouzet.

THE NEIGHBOURS and ALAS, POOR FRED! by James Saunders. With Pascale de Boysson, Gordon Heath, Daniel Emilforck.

NEXT TIME I'LL SING TO YOU by James Saunders. With Delphine Seyrig, Jean Rochefort, Claude Piéplu.

THE KNACK by Ann Jellicoe. With Monique Tarbès, Bernard Fresson.

MARAT/SADE by Peter Weiss. With Jean Servais, Michel Vitold, Françoise Brion, Michel Herbault, Pierre Tabard.

INADMISSIBLE EVIDENCE by John Osborne. With Michel Bouquet, Catherine Lecouey.

THE ORDEAL, OR LITTLE CATHERINE OF HEILBRONN by Kleist, adapted by Jean Anouilh. With Caroline Cellier, Jacques Dacqmine, Jean Davy.

RAIN BEFORE SEVEN by Marc Brandel. With Philippe Mareuil, Jacques Meyran.

THE HOMECOMING by Harold Pinter. With Pierre Brasseur, Emmanuèle Riva, Claude Rich, Jean Topart.

THE LOWER DEPTHS by Maxim Gorki. With Sacha Pitoëff, Harry Max, André Oumansky.

LIVE LIKE PIGS by John Arden. With Rosy Varte, Etienne Bierry.

WAIT UNTIL DARK by Frederick Knott. With Annie Girardot, Dalio.

WOYZECK by Georg Büchner. With Wolfram Mehring, Rosita Fernandez.

THREE SISTERS by Anton Chekhov. With Hélène Vallier, Odile Versois, Marina Vlady.

OH WHAT A LOVELY WAR by Charles Chilton and Joan Littlewood. With Dany Dauberson.

KRECHINSKY'S WEDDING by A. V. Sukhovo-Kabylin. With René Arrieu, Jacques Eyser, Jean-Paul Roussillon, Catherine Hubeau.

THE RISE AND FALL OF THE CITY OF MAHAGONNY by Bertolt Brecht and Kurt Weill. With Danielle Grima, Pia Colombo, William Pirie.

RUZZANTE, BACK FROM THE WARS by Ruzzante. With André Weber, Anne Carrère.

HENRI VI by William Shakespeare (in a single evening), adapted by and with Jean-Louis Barrault. Also with Maria Casarès, Jean Desailly.

DEIRDRE OF THE SORROWS by J. M. Synge. With the company of the Grenier de Vilbert.

SJT. DOWER MUST DIE by Terence John Feely. With René Dary, Roxane Flaviau.

SHE WANTED TO FIND HERSELF by Luigi Pirandello. With Delphine Seyrig, Jean-Pierre Marielle, Sami Frey.

GOD, EMPEROR AND PEASANT by Julius Hay. With François Maistre, Georges Wilson, Georges Riquier.

THE FATHER by August Strindberg. With the Darie-Rouvray company.

FROM MORN TO MIDNIGHT by Georg Kaiser. With Jacques Cisel, Rosita Fernandez.

THE HAMLET OF STEPNEY GREEN by Bernard Kops. With Pascal Sainvic, Christian Van Cau.

LITTLE MALCOLM AND HIS STRUGGLE AGAINST THE EUNUCHS by David Halliwell. With José-Maria Fletats, Ulysse Renaud, Anick Jarry.

ABUSE AT THE GREAT WALL by Tankred Dorst. With Eléonore Hirt, Jean-Marie Bory.

HOW'S THE WORLD TREATING YOU? by Roger Milner. With Sacha Pitoëff, Marthe Mercadier, Lucia Garcia-Ville, Pierre Doris.

TANGO by Slawomir Mrozek. With Laurent Terzieff, Pascale de Boysson.

COLD AND HOT by Fernand Crommelynck. With Danièle Delorme, René Clermont, Henri Virlojeux, Caroline Cellier.

THE SEAGULL by Anton Chekhov. With Renée Faure, Lucia Garcia-Ville, Danielle Ajoret, Sacha Pitoëff, Denis Manuel, Olivier Hussenot.

ALLERGY by Cecil P. Taylor and THE LUNCH HOUR by John Mortimer. With Jacques Plancy, Anne Rochant, Dominique Mareux.

THE SILVER TASSIE by Sean O'Casey. With Arlette Téphany, Serge Lannes.

MEDEA by Seneca, adapted by Jean Vauthier. With Pierre Vaneck, Françoise Brion.

THE KITCHEN by Arnold Wesker. With the company of the Théâtre du Soleil.

LA CELESTINA by Fernando Rojas. With Maria Mériko.

THE BROTHERS KARAMAZOV, by Feodor Dostoyevsky, adapted by Jean-Pierre Laruy. With Martine Leclerc, Claire Deluca, Jacques Coasquen.

KING LEAR by Shakespeare. With Georges Wilson, Charles Denner, Judith Magre, François Maistre.

THE CHILDISH LOVERS by Fernand Crommelynck. With Marie Diaz, Helene Salignac, Michel Hermon.

THE GIANTS OF THE MOUNTAIN by Luigi Pirandello. With Pierre Dux, Eléonore Hirt.

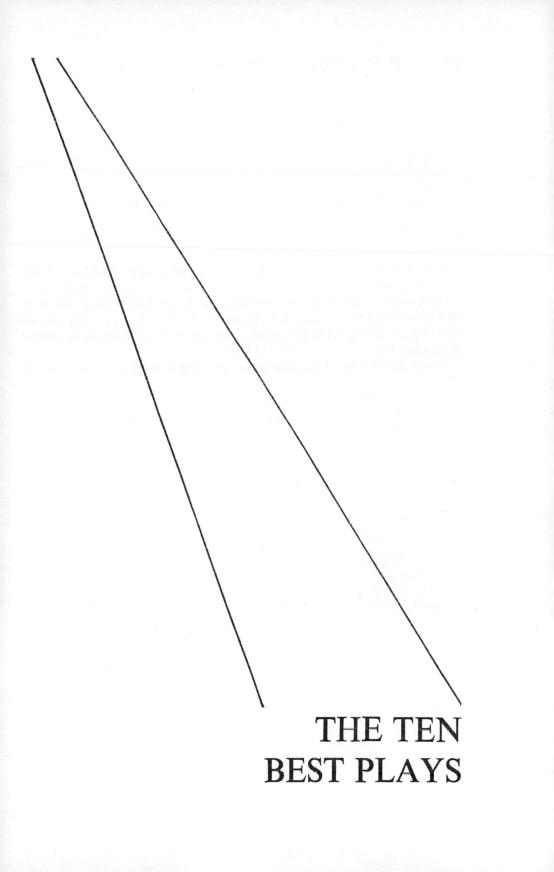

THE TEN
BEST PLAYS

In the following synopses of 1966-67's Best Plays, scenes and lines of dialogue, stage direction and description quoted from the scripts appear *exactly* as in the stage version of the play unless (as in a very few instances, for technical reasons) an abridgement is indicated by five dots (. . . . .). The appearance of three dots (. . .) is the script's own punctuation to denote the timing of a spoken line.

Description of major dance numbers is included in the synopses of musicals.

A DELICATE BALANCE

A Play in Three Acts

BY EDWARD ALBEE

Cast and credits appear on page 357

EDWARD ALBEE was born on March 12, 1928, in Washington, D.C. Two weeks after his birth he was adopted by a branch of the Keith-Albee theater family. He attended several schools including Rye Country Day, Lawrenceville, Valley Forge Military Academy and Choate, and he spent a year and a half at Trinity College. In 1958 he wrote The Zoo Story *which was produced in German in West Berlin in 1959; then by the Actors Studio before its off-Broadway presentation in 1960. Other Albee plays produced off Broadway were* The Sandbox *(1960),* Fam and Yam *(1960),* The American Dream *(1961),* Bartleby *(a one-act opera in collaboration with James Hinton Jr. and William Flanagan, based on a Herman Melville story) and* The Death of Bessie Smith *(1961).*

Albee made his Broadway debut with Who's Afraid of Virginia Woolf? *(1962), a Best Play of its season and the winner of the Drama Critics Award, and in 1966 a successful movie. His* Tiny Alice *(1964) was named a Best Play of its year. Albee has also been represented on Broadway by two adaptations:* The Ballad of the Sad Cafe *(1963) from the novella by Carson McCullers and* Malcolm *(1966) from the novel by James Purdy. His new work,* A Delicate Balance, *has won the Pulitzer Prize. Albee is a bachelor and lives in New York City.*

Time: Now

*Place: The living room of a large and well-appointed
suburban house*

ACT I

SYNOPSIS: The spacious library-living room gives an impression of comfort,
stability, status. The room itself is furnished smartly but not ostentatiously,
with sofa and chairs in the center. At left are a fireplace, a sideboard serving
as a bar and a door leading to dining room and kitchen. Upstage, through a
wide archway is a large, airy front hall with the front door upstage center and
stairs leading off left. To the right, up one step, is a glass-domed solarium full
of plants, furnished with a small game table and two chairs.

Agnes *("a handsome woman in her late 50s")* is seated, while her husband
Tobias *("a few years older")* examines the bottles at the sideboard. Agnes's
taste in clothes is exemplified by the simple, very expensive dress ornamented
merely by the double string of pearls round her neck. Her clothes are always
entirely suitable for the occasion, and she will have various changes of costume during the play.

Agnes and Tobias are in the after-dinner phase of a quiet Friday evening
at home. Agnes muses out loud on one of her favorite subjects.

AGNES *(speaks usually softly, with a tiny hint of a smile on her face; not
sardonic, not sad . . . wistful, maybe):* What I find most astonishing—aside
from that belief of mine, which never ceases to surprise me by the very fact
of its surprising lack of unpleasantness, the belief that I might very easily—
as they say—lose my mind one day, not that I suspect I am about to, or am
even . . . nearby . . .

TOBIAS *(he speaks somewhat the same way):* There is no saner woman on
earth, Agnes.

Putters at the bottles.

AGNES: . . . for I'm not that sort; merely that it is not beyond . . . happening: some gentle loosening of the moorings sending the balloon adrift—and
I think that is the only outweighing thing: adrift; the . . . becoming a stranger
in . . . the world, quite . . . uninvolved, for I never see it as violent, only a
drifting—what are you looking for, Tobias?

TOBIAS: We will all go mad before you. The anisette.

AGNES *(a small happy laugh):* Thank you, darling. But I could never do
it—go adrift—for what would become of you? Still, what I find most astonishing, aside, as I said, from that speculation—and I wonder, too, sometimes,
if I am the only one of you to admit to it: not that *I* may go mad, but that
each of you wonders if each of *you* might not—why on earth do you want
anisette?

TOBIAS (*considers*): I thought it might be nice.

AGNES (*wrinkles her nose*): Sticky. I will do cognac. It is supposed to be healthy—the speculation, or the assumption, I suppose, that if it occurs to you that you might be, then you are not; but I've never been much comforted by it; it follows, to my mind, that since I speculate I might, some day, or early evening I think more likely—some autumn dusk—go quite mad, then I very well might. (*Bright laugh.*) Some autumn dusk: Tobias at his desk, looks up from all those awful bills, and sees his Agnes, mad as a hatter, chewing the ribbons on her dress.

TOBIAS (*pouring*): Cognac?

The cordials poured, Tobias sits by Agnes in cozy intimacy. But Agnes drifts onto the subject of her own difficult sister, Claire, and for some reason this causes Tobias to rise, in sudden tension, and move away.

AGNES: If I were to list the mountain of my burdens—if I had a thick pad and a month to spare—that bending my shoulders *most*, with the possible exception of Julia's trouble with marriage, would be your—it must be instinctive, I think, or *reflex*, that's more like it—your reflex defense of everything that Claire . . .

TOBIAS (*very nice, but there is steel underneath*): Stop it, Agnes.

AGNES (*a little laugh*): Are you going to throw something at me? Your glass? My goodness, I hope not . . . that awful anisette all over everything.

TOBIAS (*patient*): No.

AGNES (*quietly daring him*): What then?

TOBIAS (*looking at his hand*): I shall sit very quietly . . .

AGNES: . . . as always . . .

TOBIAS: . . . yes, and I shall will you to apologize to your sister for what I must in truth tell you I thought a most . . .

AGNES: Apologize! To her? To Claire? I have spent my adult life apologizing *for* her; I will not double my humiliation by apologizing *to* her.

Agnes brings the subject back to her own madness; if it ever happened it would be a level form of madness, as she is a level kind of person.

AGNES: . . . . . There are no mountains in my life . . . nor chasms. It is a rolling, pleasant land . . . verdant, my darling, thank you.

TOBIAS (*cutting a cigar*): We do what we can.

AGNES (*little laugh*): Our motto. If we should ever go downhill, have a crest made, join things, we must have that put in Latin—We do what we can—on your blazers, over the mantel; maybe we could do it on the linen as well . . .

Should they do something about Claire now? Tobias wonders. Should they go to her room to see how she is? Agnes advises against it, dips once again into the subject of madness. Her goal would be permanent peace of mind, not mere temporary relief such as one could find with drugs.

Tobias thought that Claire acted better this evening and shouldn't have received the "going-over" which Agnes gave her. Agnes, submitting her glass for another cognac, decides that she will *not* go mad, after all.

Claire *("Agnes' sister, several years younger.")* enters and apologizes stiffly to Agnes almost before they notice she has come into the room.

CLAIRE: I apologize that my nature is such to bring out in you the full force of your brutality.

TOBIAS *(to placate):* Look, now, I think we can do without any of this sort of . . .

AGNES *(rises from her chair, proceeds toward exiting):* If you come to the dinner table unsteady, *if* when you try to say good evening and weren't the autumn colors lovely today you are nothing but vowels, and *if* one smells the vodka on you from across the room—and *don't* tell me again, *either* of you! that vodka leaves nothing on the breath: if you are expecting it, if you are sadly and wearily expecting it, it *does*—if these conditions exist . . . *persist* . . . then the reaction of one who is burdened by her love is not brutality—though it would be excused, believe me!—not brutality at all, but the souring side of love. If I scold, it is because I wish I needn't. If I am sharp, it is because I am neither less nor more than human, and if I am to be accused once again of making too much of things, let me remind you that it is my manner and not the matter. I apologize for being articulate. Tobias, I am going to call Julia, I think. Is it one or two hours difference? . . . I can never recall.

Agnes exits to phone her daughter Julia, who may be having another divorce. Conspiratorially, Tobias offers Claire a large balloon of brandy, at the same time affectionately calling her "a great damn fool."

Claire wonders why Tobias doesn't grab a gun and shoot them all (or maybe only Agnes). Tobias considers this slapstick suggestion and decides he couldn't do it in cold blood, it would have to be an act of passion. Tobias's feelings are hurt when Claire hints he is not the passionate type.

Tobias angers Claire with a hint about Alcoholics Anonymous; then he soothes her by pouring her a second large brandy. Claire lies on the floor, balancing the glass, taunting Tobias. She has nothing in common with the AA group, just as Tobias has nothing in common, really, with his so-called friends; not even with his *very* best friend Harry.

CLAIRE: What do you really have in common with your very best friend . . . 'cept the coincidence of having cheated on your wives in the same summer with the same woman . . . girl . . . woman? What except that? And hardly a distinction. I believe she was upended that whole July.

TOBIAS *(rather tight-mouthed):* If you'll forgive me, Claire, common practise is hardly . . .

CLAIRE: Poor girl, poor whatever-she-was that hot and very *wet* July. *(Hard.)* The distinction would have been to have not: to have been the one or two of the very, very many and oh, God, similar who did not upend the poor . . . unfamiliar thing that dry and oh, so wet July.

TOBIAS: Please! Agnes!

CLAIRE *(quieter):* Of course, you had the wanton only once, while Harry! Good friend Harry, I have it from the horse's mouth, was on top for good and keeps twice, with a third try not so hot in the gardener's shed, with the mulch, or whatever it is, and the orange pots . . .

TOBIAS *(quietly):* Shut your mouth.

CLAIRE *(stands, faces Tobias; softly):* All right. *(Down again.)* What was her name?

TOBIAS *(a little sad):* I don't remember.

CLAIRE *(shrugs):* No matter; she's gone. *(Brighter.)* Would you give friend Harry the shirt off your back, as they say?

TOBIAS *(relieved to be on something else):* I *suppose* I would. He *is* my best friend.

CLAIRE *(nicely):* How sad does that make you?

TOBIAS *(looks at her for a moment, then):* Not much; some; not much.

CLAIRE: No one to listen to Bruckner with you; no one to tell you're sick of golf; no one to admit to that—now and then—you're suddenly frightened and you don't know why?

TOBIAS *(mild surprise):* Frightened? No.

Tobias lights Claire's cigarette; from her position on the floor she holds out her arms to him in an invitation which he refuses. Claire decides to tell Tobias why she doesn't like AA.

There was one spring when Claire was drinking so heavily that Agnes moved her out to an apartment near the railroad station, where she lived in alcoholic misery and squalor. She began going to AA meetings with a friend (but "I'm not an alcoholic now and never was," Claire insists to Tobias).

When it became Claire's turn to confess herself to the AA gathering, she had one martini in a test of self-control. Then, when she rose to speak, she felt a wave of pity and resorted to babytalk to say "My name is Claire and I am a alcoholic"—just like that, *a* alcoholic. Encouraged by this small act of faith (but remaining a doubter), Claire devoted herself to AA and its principles until she decided that she alone of all the group was *not* an alcoholic, but merely a drunk. ". . . . . They were sick and I was merely . . . willful." She had little in common with them.

Agnes has entered, unobserved; she makes an icy comment on the drink in Claire's hand. Lamely, Tobias suggests that Claire "can drink . . . a little," and this infuriates Agnes. Agnes cries out in controlled anger at those who want to kill themselves but do it slowly, lingeringly.

CLAIRE *(little-child statement, but not babytalk):* I am not a alcoholic!

AGNES: We think that's very nice. We shall all rest easier to know that it is willful; that the vomit and the tears, the muddy mind, the falls and the absences, the cigarettes out on the tabletops, the calls from the club to come and get you please . . . that they are all . . . willful, that it *can* be helped. *(Scathing, but softly.)* If you are not an alcoholic, you are beyond forgiveness.

As long as Claire is living in this house—and as long as Tobias does not contradict Agnes—if Agnes says Claire is an alcoholic, then Claire *is* an alcoholic.

Agnes turns away from Claire, ignoring her (and the comments she makes while Agnes is talking to Tobias) in order to tell Tobias the latest news of their daughter Julia. Julia is leaving her fourth husband, Douglas (Claire comments "Right on schedule, once every three years") and is coming home. Her place is here, even though Agnes would greatly prefer to enjoy life with Tobias with *nobody* else in the house. Tobias promises to talk to Douglas and to Julia, too. But he has no great conviction that he can get through to either of them.

Claire becomes so vocally irritating that Agnes is forced to reprimand her. Claire retaliates fiercely, wishing Agnes dead.

Tobias, musing by himself, remembers a cat he once owned; an indifferent animal who liked only Tobias. Then, when the cat grew old, there came a day when Tobias realized the cat didn't like him any more. He tried to force the cat's affection.

TOBIAS: I'd close her in a room with me; I'd pick her up, and I'd *make* her sit in my lap; I'd make her stay there when she didn't want to. But it didn't work; she'd abide it, but she'd get down when she could, go away.

CLAIRE: Maybe she was ill.

TOBIAS: No, she wasn't; I had her to the vet. She didn't like me any more. One night—I was *fixed* on it now—I had her in the room with me, and on my lap for the . . . the what, the fifth time the same evening, and she lay there, with her back to me, and she wouldn't purr, and I *knew:* I knew she was just waiting till she could get down, and I said, "Damn you, you like me; God damn it, you stop this! I haven't *done* anything to you!" And I shook her; I had my hands around her shoulders, and I shook her . . . and she bit me; hard; and she hissed at me. And so I hit her. With my open hand, I hit her, smack, right across the head. I . . . I *hated* her!

Tobias hated the cat because "there was no *reason*" for its betrayal of him. He had the cat killed—Agnes tries to substitute the expression "put to sleep," but Tobias insists on "killed." If only he had tried harder, loved the cat more —but Claire argues that love is not enough.

The sound is heard of a car pulling up the driveway and stopping. It is Tobias's best friend Harry and his wife Edna *("very much like Agnes and Tobias")* who enter through the front door in a surprise visit *("they seem somewhat ill at ease for such close friends")*. They have timed their drop-in a bit awkwardly, but Agnes and Tobias try very hard to make them feel welcome. Claire, on the other hand, pokes and prods to find the meaning behind this unusual visit.

They try small talk: Harry is having his shortness of breath again, Agnes has taken the summer slip covers off the living room furniture. But pushed by Claire, they keep returning to the subject of the visit itself. Harry and Edna have *not* just dropped by on the way home from the club. They have *not* come to a party on the wrong night. They were just sitting home . . . Harry leaves it at that, but Claire demands to know what happened. Claire reassures embarrassed Agnes that Harry *wants* to get it off his chest by telling about it.

Harry begins: they were just sitting home, alone. Harry had been tired all week, and he and Edna had decided on spending a restful evening together. Agnes tries to put in a word of comfort and understanding, but Claire shushes her.

HARRY: So we were sitting, and Edna was doing that—that panel she works on . . .

EDNA *(wistful, some loss)*: My needlepoint.

HARRY: . . . and I was reading my French; I've got it pretty good now— not the accent, but the . . . the words.
    A brief silence.

CLAIRE *(quietly)*: And then?

HARRY *(looks over to her, a little dreamlike, as if he didn't know where he was)*: Hmmm?

CLAIRE *(nicely)*: And then?

HARRY *(looks at Edna)*: I . . . I don't know quite what happened then; we . . . we were . . . it was all very quiet, and we were all alone . . .
    Edna begins to weep, quietly; Agnes notices, the others do not; Agnes does nothing.
. . . and then . . . nothing happened, but . . .
    Edna is crying more openly now.
. . . nothing at all happened, but . . .

EDNA *(open weeping; loud)*: WE WERE . . . FRIGHTENED.
    Open sobbing. No one moves.

HARRY *(quiet wonder, confusion)*: We got scared.

EDNA *(through her sobbing)*: WE WERE . . . FRIGHTENED.

HARRY: There was nothing . . . but we were very scared.
    Agnes comforts Edna, who is in free sobbing anguish. Claire lies slowly back on the floor.

EDNA: We . . . were . . . terrified.

HARRY: We were scared.
    Silence; Agnes comforting Edna. Harry stock still. Quite innocent, almost childlike.
It was like being lost: very young again, with the dark, and lost. There was no . . . thing . . . to be . . . frightened of, but . . .

EDNA *(tears, quiet hysteria)*: WE WERE FRIGHTENED . . . AND THERE WAS NOTHING.
    Silence in the room.

HARRY *(matter-of-fact, but a hint of daring under it)*: We couldn't stay there, and so we came here. You're our very best friends.

EDNA *(crying softly now):* In the whole world.

AGNES *(comforting, arms around her):* Now, now, Edna.

HARRY *(apologizing some):* We couldn't go anywhere else, so we came here.

AGNES *(a deep breath, control):* Well, we'll . . . you did the right thing . . . of course.

TOBIAS: Sure.

EDNA: Can I go to bed now? Please?

AGNES *(pause; then, not quite understanding):* Bed?

HARRY: We can't go back there.

EDNA: Please?

AGNES *(distant):* Bed?

EDNA: I'm so . . . tired.

HARRY: You're our best friends in the world. Tobias?

TOBIAS *(a little bewilderment; rote):* Of course we are, Harry.

EDNA *(on her feet, moving):* Please? *(Cries a little again.)*

AGNES *(a million things going through her head, seeping through management):* Of . . . of course you can. There's . . . there's Julia's room, and . . .
Arm around Edna.
Come with me, dear.
Reaches doorway; turns to Tobias; a question that has no answer
Tobias?

HARRY *(rises, begins to follow Edna, rather automaton-like):* Edna?

TOBIAS *(confused):* Harry?

HARRY *(shaking his head):* There was no one else we could go to.
Exits after Agnes and Edna. Claire sits up, watches Tobias as he stands for a moment, looking at the floor; silence.

CLAIRE *(a small, sad chuckle):* I was wondering when it would begin . . . when it would start.

TOBIAS *(hearing her only after a moment):* Start? *(Louder.)* START? *(Pause.)* WHAT?!

CLAIRE *(raises her glass to him):* Don't you know yet? *(Small chuckle.)* You will.
Curtain.

ACT II

Scene 1

Early the next evening, Saturday, before dinner, Agnes sits and watches Julia *("Agnes' and Tobias' daughter, 36, angular")* pacing irritably. Julia has come home to take refuge from her unhappy marriage, only to find the house full of people. Julia finds it hard to believe that Harry and Edna are truly frightened and need sanctuary. They have remained in their room—which happens to be Julia's room—all day. Agnes agrees to move them to Tobias' room.

Agnes, feeling the annoyances and responsibilities of motherhood and wife-hood, wonders half-longingly if she would be better off as a man. Julia wants to confide in Agnes and is annoyed by her gentle joking about changing sex.

AGNES: I shall try to hear you out, but if I feel my voice changing, in the middle of your . . . rant, you will have to forgive my male perogative, if I become uncomfortable, look at my watch, or jiggle the change in my pocket . . .
        Sees Julia marching toward the archway as Tobias enters.
. . . where do you think you're going?
JULIA *(head down, muttered):* . . . you go straight to hell . . .
TOBIAS *(attempt at cheer):* Now, now, what's going on here?
JULIA *(right in front of him; force):* Will you shut her up?
TOBIAS *(overwhelmed):* Will I . . . what?
AGNES *(marching toward the archway herself):* Well, there you are, Julia; your father may safely leave the room now, I think.
        Kisses Tobias on the cheek.
Hello, my darling. *(Back to Julia.)* Your mother has arrived. Talk to *him!* *(To Tobias.)* Your daughter is in need of consolation or a great cuffing around the ears. I don't know which to recommend.

Agnes confirms that Harry and Edna haven't yet come downstairs, and she exits. Tobias tells Julia her being home is a "joy" to him. He doesn't want to discuss Harry and Edna, he does not want to be pressed by Julia and her problems, either.

JULIA *(exploding; but anger, not hysteria):* Great Christ! What the hell did I come home to? And why? Both of you? Snotty, mean . . .
TOBIAS: LOOK! *(Silence; softer, but no nonsense.)* There are some . . . times, when it all gathers up . . . too much.
JULIA *(nervously):* Sure, sure.
TOBIAS *(not put off):* Some *times* when it's going to be Agnes and Tobias, and not just Mother and Dad. Right? Some *times* when the allowances aren't going to be made. What are you doing, biting off your fingernails now?
JULIA *(not giving in):* It broke off.
TOBIAS: There are some *times* when it's all . . . too much. *I* don't know what the hell Harry and Edna are doing sitting up in that bedroom! Claire is drinking, she and Agnes are at each other like a couple of . . . of . . .
JULIA *(softly):* Sisters?
TOBIAS: What? The goddamn government's at me over some deductions, and you!
JULIA *(head high, defiant):* And me? Yes?
TOBIAS: This isn't the first time, you know. This isn't the first time you've come back with one of your goddamned marriages on the rocks. Four! Count 'em!
JULIA *(rage):* I know how many marriages I've gotten myself into, you . . .
TOBIAS: Four! You expect to come back here, nestle in to being fifteen and

misunderstood each time! You are thirty-six years old, for God's sake! . . .

JULIA: And you are one hundred! Easily!

TOBIAS: Thirty-six! Each time! Dragging your . . . your—I was going to say pride—your marriage with you like some Raggedy Ann doll, by the foot. You, you fill this house with your whining . . .

JULIA (rage): I DON'T ASK TO COME BACK HERE!

TOBIAS: YOU BELONG HERE!

After glaring at one another, Tobias and Julia begin to chuckle at themselves, and Tobias suggests a martini. As Tobias mixes the cocktails, Julia remembers her childhood; a little brother of whom she was jealous, and who died; her father growing old and ineffectual, a "gray non-eminence"; and now her father starting to roar all over again.

Tobias is willing to speak to Julia's husband, Doug, but Julia doesn't think it would do any good. Once again, Julia has made a poor choice of husbands. Her previous three were a gambler, a homosexual (who looked something like Julia's dead brother Teddy) and a lecher. Tobias comments, "Your brother would not have grown up to be a fag."

Claire comes in and embraces Julia, persuades Tobias against his better judgment to fix her a martini. Claire tells an amusing story about trying to buy a topless bathing suit from a spinsterish saleswoman at the department store. Claire dreams that maybe Tobias will whisk them all away to a far-off isle; but no, Tobias cannot because "It's . . . it's too late, or something."

Claire comments on the irony of Julia "home from the wars, four purple hearts," when Claire can't even find one man to call her own. Claire insinuates that Julia is very quick to run home, and she has almost started a fight with Julia when Agnes's entrance calms them all down.

Agnes asks for a martini before dinner; reports that Harry and Edna are all right behind their closed door. Earlier in the day, when the family was all out, Edna came downstairs and ordered sandwiches brought up. Agnes takes the view that it is right for Harry and Edna to be here; right for Julia to have come home.

Julia insists on telling them all what went wrong with her marriage, refusing to wait for a more opportune moment. Doug is *against* everything—government, children, marriage—and everybody including Tobias. Julia will have no more of him.

At this moment, Harry and Edna come to the archway, carrying their coats. They greet Julia affectionately.

AGNES (on her feet): There's just time for a drink before dinner, if my husband will hurry some . . .

HARRY: No, we're . . . going home now.

AGNES (relief peeking through the surprise): Oh? Yes?

EDNA: Yes.

        Pause

AGNES: Well. (Pause.) If we were any help at all, we . . .

HARRY: To . . . uh, to get our things. *(Silence.)* Our clothes and things.
EDNA: Yes.
HARRY: We'll be back in . . . well, after dinner, so don't . . .
EDNA: An hour or two. It'll take us a while.
   Silence
HARRY: We'll let ourselves . . . don't bother.
   They start out, tentatively, see that the others are merely staring at them. Exit. Silence.
JULIA *(controlled, but near tears):* I want my room back! I want my room!
AGNES *(composed, chilly, standing in the archway):* I believe that dinner is served . . .
TOBIAS *(vacant):* Yes?
AGNES: If any of you have the stomach for it.
   Curtain.

Scene 2

After dinner that same evening, Julia accuses her mother of behaving like a nanny, or like a drill sergeant, directing their conversation and behavior all through dinner. Agnes declares her determination to keep this family "in shape"; to maintain and hold it together, and to shout if necessary in order to be heard.

AGNES: If I am a stickler on certain points *(Just as Julia's mouth opens to speak.)*—a martinet, as Julia would have it, would you not, sweet? in fact, were you not about to?—if I am a stickler on points of manners, timing, tact —the graces, I almost blush to call them—it is simply that I am the one member of this . . . reasonably happy family blessed and burdened with the ability to view a situation objectively while I am in it.
JULIA *(not really caring):* What time is it?
AGNES *(a little harder now):* The double position of seeing not only facts but their implications . . .
TOBIAS: Nearly ten.
AGNES *(some irritation toward both of them):* . . . the longer view as well as the shorter. There *is* a balance to be maintained, after all, though the rest of you teeter, unconcerned, or uncaring, *assuming* you're on level ground . . . by divine right, I gather, though that is hardly so. And if I must be the fulcrum . . . *(Sees neither of them is really listening, says in the same tone.)* . . . I think I shall have a divorce. *(Smiles to see that her words have had no effect.)*
TOBIAS *(it sinks in):* Have what? A *what?*
AGNES: No fear; merely testing. Everything is taken for granted and no one listens.
TOBIAS *(wrinkling his nose):* Have a divorce?
AGNES: No, no; Julia has them for all of us. Not even separation; that is taken care of, and in life: the gradual . . . demise of intensity, the private preoccupations, the substitutions. We become allegorical, my darling Tobias,

as we grow older. The individuality we hold so dearly sinks into crotchet; we see ourselves repeated by those we bring into it all, either by mirror or rejection, honor or fault. *(To herself, really.)* I'm not a fool; I'm really not.

Tobias agrees: really not. Julia wonders what Claire is up to, still worries at the subject of her room. Agnes, angry, suggests that Julia go up and barricade herself in the room.

Claire enters, wearing an accordion whose bursting chords irritate Agnes into anger at Claire, into memory that Claire even as a young girl was always emancipated, "very . . . advanced." Claire retaliates with vulgarity, telling Julia "Your mommy got her pudenda scuffed a couple times herself 'fore she met old Toby, you know."

Agnes rides out the vulgarity; Claire removes the accordion after a couple more bursts of sound. Through the window, Tobias sees Harry and Edna returning, and Julia's impulse is to take physical possession of her room at once. But Agnes warns Julia the room is Harry and Edna's for the time being. Julia tries to attract attention to herself, to no avail. Agnes and Toby exit to cope with Harry and Edna.

Julia turns to Claire.

JULIA: . . . . . Harry and Edna: what do they want?
CLAIRE: Succor.
JULIA *(tiny pause):* Pardon?
CLAIRE *(brief smile):* Comfort. *(Sees Julia doesn't understand.)* Warmth. A special room with a night light, or the door ajar so you can look down the hall from the bed and see that Mommy's door is open.
JULIA *(no anger; loss):* But that's my room.
CLAIRE: It's . . . the *room.* Happens you were in it. You're a visitor as much as anyone, now.
   We hear mumbled conversation from the hallway.
JULIA *(small whine):* But I *know* that room.
CLAIRE *(pointed, but kind):* Are you home for good now?
   Julia stares at her.
Are you home forever, back from the world? To the sadness *and* reassurance of your parents? Have you come to take my place?
JULIA *(quiet despair):* This is my home!
CLAIRE: This . . . ramble? Yes? *(Surprised delight.)* You're laying claim to the cave! Well, I don't know how they'll take to that. We're not a communal nation, dear. . . . .

Edna comes in and reports that Harry, Agnes and Tobias are coping with the bags. Edna insists on behaving as though she belonged here, which infuriates Julia. Edna goes to the point of deciding that one of the chairs needs to be recovered. She even administers a gentle rebuke to Julia about her marriage failure and homecoming.

Julia's tension mounts. She loses first her temper, then her manners, then her self-control. Edna wants a drink, and Harry enters also in search of a drink. Julia, succumbing to hysteria, spreads herself across the bar area to "protect" it from Harry and Edna. Julia is *curiously disturbed and frightened by something.* Julia shouts for her mother; she cries for her mother and father. Agnes comes into the living room.

AGNES *(pained):* Julia? You're shouting?

JULIA: Mother!

AGNES *(quite conscious of the others):* What *is* it, dear?

JULIA *(quite beside herself, seeing no sympathy):* THEY! THEY WANT!

EDNA: Forget it, Julia.

HARRY *(a tiny, condescending laugh):* Yes, for God's sake, forget it.

JULIA: THEY WANT!

AGNES *(kindly, but a little patronizing):* Perhaps you *had* better go upstairs.

JULIA *(still semi-hysterical):* Yes? Where!? What room?

AGNES *(patient):* Go up to my room, lie down.

JULIA *(an ugly laugh):* Your room!

EDNA *(calm):* You may lie down in *our* room, if you prefer.

JULIA *(a trapped woman, surrounded):* Your room! *(To Agnes.)* Your room? MINE!!

      Looks from one to another, sees only waiting faces.

MINE!!

HARRY *(makes a move toward the sideboard):* God.

JULIA: Don't you go near *that!*

AGNES: Julia . . .

JULIA: I *want!*

CLAIRE *(sad smile):* What do you want, Julia?

JULIA: I . . .

HARRY: Jesus.

JULIA: I WANT . . . WHAT IS *MINE!!*

AGNES *(seemingly dispassionate; after a pause):* Well then, my dear, you will have to decide what that is, will you not.

Julia runs from the room calling "Daddy" as she hasn't done since she used to skin her knee—since the summer her brother Teddy died; that strange summer when, Agnes feels, Tobias may have been a little out of love with her.

AGNES: . . . . . I think I thought Tobias was unfaithful to me then. Was he, Harry?

EDNA: Oh, Agnes.

HARRY *(unsubtle):* Come on, Agnes! Of course not! No!

AGNES *(faint amusement):* Was he, Claire? That hot summer, with Julia's knees all bloody and Teddy dead? Did my husband . . . cheat on me?

CLAIRE *(looks at her steadily, toasts her; then):* Ya got me, sis.

AGNES *(an amen):* And that will have to do.

Harry hands Edna a drink and starts to make one for Agnes. Agnes has a moment of hostility to Harry and Edna; she would like to know what they *want*. Edna, suddenly mettlesome, protects Harry from Agnes's sharpness and cries "Don't you make fun of us!" Agnes, contrite, apologizes.

Claire shoulders the accordion and Tobias appears. Tobias wants to know why his daughter rushed upstairs in hysterics, why she is "pressed against a corner of the upstairs hall, arms wide, palms back? Eyes darting? Wide?"; why she has pulled the clothes from the closet in Harry and Edna's room; why she is weeping on the bed in Agnes's room.

Edna describes what happened: Julia's defense of the bar-sideboard "like a princess in the movies, hiding her lover in the closet from the king." Tobias thinks Agnes should go upstairs and cope, but Agnes refuses on the grounds that she doesn't have time for a four-hour soothing talk about all the sadnesses in Julia's past. It makes Agnes feel her own age every time she has to do this.

Harry offers to make Tobias a drink, confusing him momentarily as to whose house this really is. Edna criticizes Agnes' and Claire's edginess toward each other; it creates an environment which is "not all that it might be."

AGNES *(to Edna):* . . . . . Is that for you to say?

EDNA *(to Agnes; calm, steady):* We must be helpful when we can, my dear; that is the . . . responsibility, the double demand of friendship . . . is it not?

AGNES *(slightly schoolteacherish):* But, when we are *asked*.

EDNA *(shakes her head, smiles gently):* No. Not only. *(This heard by all.)* It seemed to me, to us, that since we were living *here* . . .

Silence, Agnes and Tobias look from Edna to Harry.

CLAIRE: *That's my cue!*

A chord, then begins to yodel, to an ump-pah bass. Julia appears in the archway, unseen by the others; her hair is wild, her face is tear-streaked; she carries Tobias' pistol, but not pointed; awkwardly and facing down.

JULIA *(solemnly and tearfully):* Get them out of here, Daddy, getthemoutofheregetthemoutofheregetthemoutofheregetthemoutofheregetthemoutofhere . . .

They all see Julia and the gun simultaneously; Edna gasps but does not panic; Harry retreats a little; Tobias moves slowly toward Julia.

Tobias coaxes the pistol out of Julia's hand; Julia urges him to use it to evict Edna and Harry. Agnes is furious at Julia for embarrassing her—Julia "ought to be horsewhipped."

Once again Edna and Harry affirm their intention to stay—their *right* to stay here—and Edna scolds Julia in Agnes's voice, as though she shared Agnes's very personality and family position as well as her home. It is Julia who is the intruder—and with a gun, too.

EDNA: *We* belong here, do we not?

JULIA *(triumphant distaste):* FOREVER!!

Small silence.

HAVE YOU COME TO STAY FOREVER??

    Small silence.

EDNA *(walks over to her, calmly slaps her):* If need be. *(To Tobias and Agnes, calmly.)* Sorry; a godmother's duty. *(This next calm, almost daring, addressed at, rather than to the others.)* If we come to the point . . . *if* we are at home one evening and the . . . terror comes . . . descends . . . if all at once we . . . NEED . . . we come where we are wanted, where we know we are expected, not only where we want; we come where the table has been laid for us in such an event . . . where the bed is turned down . . . and warmed . . . and has been ready should we need it. We are not . . . transients . . . like some.

    JULIA: NO!

EDNA *(to Julia):* You must . . . what is the word? . . . coexist, my dear. *(To the others.)* Must she not?

    Silence; calm.

Must she not. This is what you have meant by friendship . . . is it not?

    AGNES *(pause; finally, calmly):* You have come to live with us, then.

    EDNA *(after a pause; calm):* Why, yes; we have.

AGNES *(dead calm; a sigh):* Well, then. *(Pause.)* Perhaps it is time for bed, Julia? Come upstairs with me.

    JULIA *(a confused child):* M-mother?

    AGNES: Ah-ah; let me comb your hair, and rub your back.

    Arm over Julia's shoulder, leads her out. Exiting.

And we shall soothe . . . and solve . . . and fall to sleep. Tobias?

    Exits with Julia. Silence.

    EDNA: Well, I think it's time for bed.

    TOBIAS *(vague, preoccupied):* Well, yes; yes, of course.

    EDNA *(she and Harry have risen; a small smile):* We know the way.

    Pauses as she and Harry near the archway.

Friendship *is* something like a marriage, is it not, Tobias? For better and for worse?

    TOBIAS *(vague, preoccupied):* Sure.

EDNA *(something of a demand here):* We *haven't* come to the wrong place, have we?

    HARRY *(pause; shy):* Have we, Toby?

    TOBIAS *(pause; gentle, sad):* No. *(Sad smile.)* No, of course you haven't.

    EDNA: Good night, dear Tobias. Good night, Claire.

    CLAIRE *(a half smile):* Good night, you two.

    HARRY *(a gentle pat at Tobias as he passes):* Good night, old man.

    TOBIAS *(watches as the two exit):* Good . . . good night, you two.

    Claire and Tobias alone; Tobias still holds the pistol.

CLAIRE *(after an interval):* Full house, Tobias, every bed and every cupboard.

    TOBIAS *(not moving):* Good night, Claire.

CLAIRE *(rising, leaving her accordion):* Are you going to stay up, Tobias? Sort of a nightwatch, guarding? *I've done it.* The breathing, as you stand in the quiet halls, slow and heavy? And the special . . . warmth, and . . . permeation . . . of a house . . . asleep? When the house is sleeping? When the people *are* asleep?

TOBIAS: Good night, Claire.

CLAIRE *(near the archway):* And the difference? The different breathing and the cold, when every bed is awake . . . all night . . . very still, eyes open, staring into the dark? Do you know that one?

TOBIAS: Good night, Claire.

CLAIRE *(a little sad):* Good night, Tobias.
    Exit as the curtain falls.

ACT III

At 7:30 next morning, Sunday, Tobias sits alone in his pajamas, robe and slippers. Agnes joins him in her dressing gown. During the night (Agnes remembers) a "stranger" came to her room—Tobias, dispossessed from his own room by Julia and forced to spend the night in his wife's bed. It was the first time in a long time, and Agnes enjoyed his company.

Both Agnes and Tobias stayed awake in the night, silently. Then at 3 or 4 a.m. Tobias left—not to "go to Claire" as Agnes suggests ("I never go to Claire" Tobias insists). He came downstairs and sat alone with a drink or two, calmly reviewing events of the evening before.

Did Tobias make a decision? No, but he must, and he asks Agnes' help. But Agnes refuses.

AGNES: No, I don't *think* so.

TOBIAS *(some surprise):* No?

AGNES: No. I thought a little last night too: while you were seeing everything so clearly here. I lay in the dark, and I . . . revisited—our life, the years and years. There are many things a woman does: she bears the children—if there *is* that blessing. Blessing? Yes, I suppose, even with the sadness. She runs the house, for what that's worth: makes sure there's food, and not just anything, and decent linen; looks well; assumes whatever duties are demanded—if she is in love, or loves; and plans.

TOBIAS *(mumbled; a little embarrassed):* I know, I know . . .

AGNES: And plans. Right to the end of it; expects to be alone one day, abandoned by a heart attack or the cancer, *prepares* for that. And prepares earlier, for the children to become *adult* strangers instead of growing ones, for that loss, and for the body chemistry, the end of what the Bible tells us is our usefulness. The reins we hold! It's a team of twenty horses, and we sit there, and we watch the road and check the leather . . . if our . . . man is so disposed. But there are things we do not do.

TOBIAS *(slightly edgy challenge):* Yes?

AGNES: Yes. *(Harder)* We don't decide the route.

Angrily, Tobias accuses Agnes of "copping out." She has never been merely a follower on moral issues. But Agnes sticks to her position that it is Tobias's duty to judge and decide, not hers.

Tobias's anger and frustration are expressed in a voice loud enough to rouse the house. Julia enters in her dressing gown. She has regained her self-control; she is sorry for her behavior last night; she will go to make some coffee. But her parting shot at Tobias, as she exits, is: "Aren't you sorry for embarrassing me, too?"

Julia is a problem—Tobias's problem, Agnes reminds him to his irritation. She always has been his problem.

AGNES: Each time that Julia comes, each clockwork time . . . do you send her back? Do you tell her, "Julia, go home to your husband, try it again"? Do you? No, you let it . . . slip. It's your decision, sir.

TOBIAS: It is not! I . . .

AGNES: And I must live with it, resign myself one marriage more, and wait, and hope that Julia's motherhood will come . . . one day, one marriage. *(Tiny laugh.)* I am almost too old to be a grandmother as I'd hoped . . . too young to be one. Oh, I had wanted that: the *youngest* older woman in the block. *Julia* is almost too old to have a child properly, *will* be if she ever does . . . if she marries again. *You* could have pushed her back . . . if you'd wanted to.

TOBIAS *(bewildered incredulity):* It's very early yet: that must be it. I've never heard such . . .

AGNES: Or Teddy! No? No stammering here? You'll let this pass?

TOBIAS *(quiet embarrassment):* Please.

AGNES *(remorseless):* When Teddy died? *(Pause.)* We *could* have had another son; we could have tried. But no . . . those months—or was it a year—?

TOBIAS: No more of this!

AGNES: . . . I think it was a year, when you spilled yourself on my belly, sir? "Please? Please, Tobias?" No, you wouldn't even say it out: I don't want another child, another loss. "Please? Please, Tobias?" And guiding you, *trying* to hold you in?

TOBIAS *(tortured):* Oh, Agnes! Please!

AGNES: "Don't leave me then, like that. Not again, Tobias. Please? *I* can take care of it: we *won't* have another child, but please don't . . . leave me like that." Such . . . silent . . . sad, disgusted . . . love.

Finally, Agnes reminds him, Tobias took to his own room, racked with guilt for which Agnes had to suffer too. Agnes lived with his decision, and she will live with whatever he decides now.

Claire joins them, also in a dressing gown; she is sent to assist Julia with the coffee. Again, Agnes insinuates to Tobias: "Claire is a comfort in the early hours . . . I have been told." Again, Tobias ignores the insinuation and tries to make Agnes help him decide: shall he throw out Harry and Edna,

Julia and Claire? Agnes refuses to concern herself with the choices Tobias *has,* only with the choice he will finally *make.*

Claire and Julia come in with orange juice and coffee. Julia calls Tobias "Pop," to his surprise, and takes charge of picking up last night's debris and serving the coffee.

Claire, serving the orange juice, offers Julia a glass, but Julia is preoccupied with the cups of coffee. Claire notices that Julia is "playing early-morning hostess." Julia, nettled, retorts (to Agnes's delight) that Claire might like a shot of vodka in her coffee. Thus challenged, Claire pours herself some vodka, arguing that each person must keep to his own pattern: "The drunks stay drunk; the Catholics go to Mass, the bounders bound. We can't have changes —throws the balance off."

The hostility between Claire and Julia reaches its climax as Julia rudely suggests that Claire pick up her own coffee cup, and Claire pours Julia's orange juice out on the rug.

Tobias jumps to his feet and shushes them all. He wants their attention; something happened in this house last night, and he has been thinking about it. Harry and Edna have asked for help—but Tobias is interrupted by Julia who tenses up when this subject is raised. Once again Julia brands Harry and Edna as intruders. Julia threatens to resign from the family if Harry and Edna stay.

Agnes also has an observation to make: Harry and Edna are carriers of a disease called terror.

JULIA *(furious):* TERROR!?

AGNES *(unperturbed):* Yes: the terror. Or the plague—they're both the same. Edna and Harry have come to us—dear friends, our very best, though there's a judgment to be made about that, I think—have come to us and brought the plague. Now, poor Tobias has sat up all night and wrestled with the moral problem.

TOBIAS *(frustration; anger):* I've not been . . . *wrestling* with some . . . abstract problem! These are *people!* Harry and Edna! These are our friends, God damn it!

AGNES: Yes, but they've brought the plague with them, and that's another matter. Let me tell you something about disease . . . mortal illness; you either are immune to it . . . or you fight it. If you are immune, you wade right in, you treat the patient until he either lives, or dies of it. But if you are *not* immune, you risk infection. Ten centuries ago—and even less—the treatment was quite simple . . . burn them. Burn their bodies, burn their houses, burn their clothes—and move to another town, if you were enlightened. But now, with modern medicine, we merely isolate; we quarantine, we ostracize—if we are not immune ourselves, or unless we are saints. So, your night-long vigil, darling, your reasoning in the cold, pure hours, has been over the patient, and not the illness. It is not Edna and Harry who have come to us—our friends— it is a disease.

TOBIAS *(quiet anguish, mixed with impatience):* Oh, for God's sake, Agnes!

It is our friends! What am I supposed to do? Say: "Look, you can't stay here, you two, you've got trouble. You're friends and all, but you come in here *clean*." Well, I can't do that. No. Agnes, for God's sake, if . . . if that's all Harry and Edna mean to us, then . . . then, what about *us*? When we talk to each other . . . what have we meant? Anything? When we touch, when we promise, and say . . . yes, or please . . . with our*selves*? have we meant, yes, but only if . . . if there's any condition, Agnes! Then it's . . . all been empty.

AGNES *(noncommittal):* Perhaps. But blood binds us. Blood holds us together when we've no more . . . deep affection for ourselves than others. I am *not* asking you to choose between your family and . . . our friends . . .

TOBIAS: Yes you are!

AGNES *(eyes closed):* I am merely saying that there is *disease* here! And I ask you: who in this family is immune?

Claire believes she has had the disease of terror and is immune. Agnes agrees. She is waiting for Tobias's decision, and she is prepared to catch Harry and Edna's disease and die of it, if Tobias decides to take them in.

Harry and Edna appear in the archway; they are dressed. Harry wants to talk to Tobias alone, so the women leave. The two men decide this is an occasion for a drink before breakfast. Harry confides to Tobias that he crawled into bed with Edna last night; Edna not only permitted him to do this, but seemed to enjoy his presence.

After a pause, Harry and Tobias start to talk at once; each is saying to the other that he has been thinking the situation over. Tobias continues: he thinks he'll be able to work out Harry and Edna's continued presence in the house. But Harry in his own turn has come to a decision: "No . . . we're . . . we're going, Tobias." Tobias can hardly believe it; there is no joy, no relief in his reaction; he is simply bewildered.

TOBIAS: You *came* here.

HARRY: Do you *want* us here?

TOBIAS: You *came! Here!*

HARRY *(too clearly enunciated):* Do you want us here? *(Subdued, almost apologetic.)* Edna and I . . . there's . . . so much . . . over the dam, so many . . . disappointments, evasions, I guess, lies maybe . . . so much we remember we wanted, once . . . so little that we've settled for . . . we talk, sometimes, but mostly . . . no. We don't . . . "like." Oh, sure, we *like* . . . but I've always been a little shy—gruff, you know, and . . . shy. And Edna isn't . . . happy—I suppose that's it. We . . . we like you and . . . and Agnes, and . . . well Claire, and Julia, too, I guess I mean . . . *I* like you, and you like me, I think, and . . . you're our best friends, but . . . I told Edna upstairs, I said: Edna, what if they'd come to us? And she didn't say anything. And I said: Edna, if they'd come to us like this, and even though we don't have . . . Julia, and all of that, I . . . Edna, I wouldn't take them in.

Brief silence.

I wouldn't take them in, Edna; they don't . . . they don't have any right. And she said: yes, I know; they wouldn't have the right.
  Brief silence.
Toby, I wouldn't let *you* stay. *(Shy, embarrassed.)* You . . . you don't *want* us, do you Toby? You don't want us here.
      This next is an aria. It must have in its performance all the horror and exuberance of a man who has kept his emotions under control too long. Tobias will be carried to the edge of hysteria, and he will find himself laughing, sometimes, while he cries from sheer release. All in all it is genuine and bravura at the same time, one prolonging the other. I shall try to notate it somewhat.
   TOBIAS *(softly, as though the word were unfamiliar):* Want? *(Same.)* What? Do I what? *(Abrupt laugh; joyous.)* DO I WANT? *(More laughter; also a sob.)* DO I WANT YOU HERE! *(Hardly able to speak from the laughter.)* You come in here, you come in here with your . . . wife, and with your . . . terror! And you ask me if I want you here! *(Great breathing sounds.)* YES! OF COURSE! I WANT YOU HERE! I HAVE BUILT THIS HOUSE! I WANT YOU IN IT! I WANT YOUR PLAGUE! YOU'VE GOT SOME TERROR WITH YOU? BRING IT IN! *(Pause, then, even louder.)* BRING IT IN!! YOU'VE GOT THE ENTREE, BUDDY, YOU DON'T NEED A KEY! YOU'VE GOT THE ENTREE, BUDDY! FORTY YEARS! *(Soft, now; soft and fast, almost a monotone.)* You don't need to ask me, Harry, you don't need to ask a thing; you're our friends, our very best friends in the world, and you don't have to ask. *(A shout.)* WANT? ASK? *(Soft, as before.)* You come for dinner don't you come for cocktails see us at the club on Saturdays and talk and lie and laugh with us and pat old Agnes on the hand and say you don't know what old Toby'd do without her and we've known you all these years and we love each other don't we? *(Shout.)* DON'T WE?! DON'T WE LOVE EACH OTHER? *(Soft again, laughter and tears in it.)* Doesn't friendship grow to that? To love? Doesn't forty years amount to anything? We've cast our lot together, boy, we're friends, we've been through lots of thick OR thin together. Which is it, boy? *(Shout.)* WHICH IS IT, BOY?! THICK?! THIN?! WELL, WHATEVER IT IS, WE'VE BEEN THROUGH IT, BOY! *(Soft.)* And you don't have to ask. I like you, Harry, yes, I really do, I don't like Edna, but that's not half the point, I like you fine; I find my liking you has limits . . . *(Loud.)* BUT THOSE ARE MY LIMITS! NOT YOURS! *(Soft.)* The fact I like you well enough, but not enough . . . that best friend in the world should be something else—more—well, that's my poverty. So, bring your wife, and bring your terror, bring your plague. *(Loud.)* BRING YOUR PLAGUE!
      The four women appear in the archway, coffee cups in hand, stand, watch.
I DON'T WANT YOU HERE! YOU ASKED?! NO! I DON'T *(LOUD.)* BUT BY CHRIST YOU'RE GOING TO STAY HERE! YOU'VE GOT THE RIGHT! THE RIGHT! DO YOU KNOW THE WORD? THE RIGHT! *(Soft.)* You've put nearly forty years in it, baby; so have I, and if

it's nothing, I don't give a damn, you've got the right to be here, you've earned it *(Loud.)* AND BY GOD YOU'RE GOING TO TAKE IT! DO YOU HEAR ME?! YOU BRING YOUR TERROR AND YOU COME IN HERE AND YOU LIVE WITH US! YOU BRING YOUR PLAGUE! YOU STAY WITH US! I DON'T WANT YOU HERE! I DON'T LOVE YOU! BUT BY GOD . . . YOU STAY!! *(Pause.)* STAY! *(Softer.)* Stay! *(Soft, tears.)* Stay. Please? Stay? *(Pause.)* Stay? Please? Stay?

> *A silence in the room. Harry, numb, rises; the women come into the room, slowly, stand. The play is quiet and subdued from now until the end.*

EDNA *(calm):* Harry, will you bring our bags down? Maybe Tobias will help you. Will you ask him?

HARRY *(gentle):* Sure.

> *Goes to Tobias, who is quietly wiping tears from his face, takes him gently by the shoulder.*

Tobias? Will you help me? Get the bags upstairs?

> *Tobias nods, puts his arm around Harry. The two men exit. Silence.*

Quietly, Edna tells the others of the night before; how Harry joined her in bed and how they talked of whether they would let Tobias and Agnes stay under reversed circumstances. It is sad, Edna declares, to come near the end and "still not have learned . . . the boundaries, what we may not do . . . not ask, for fear of looking in a mirror."

Agnes deplores the futile passage of time; then she deplores the bad coffee. Claire offers them all a drink, and Julia decides to accept.

Tobias and Harry appear with the bags. The parting words among the two couples sound almost ordinary: routine thanks, and a gentle admonition from Edna to Claire to be good, to Julia to reflect, and a date made with Agnes to go to town Thursday. Their goodbys are perfunctory, except for one last plaintive "Please? Stay?" from Tobias, parried by Harry with "See you at the club."

After Harry and Edna depart, Agnes puts her arm around Tobias, who looks for his unfinished drink.

AGNES: Well, I would seem to have *three* early-morning drinkers now. I hope it won't become a club. We'd have to get a license, would we not?

TOBIAS: Just think of it as very late at night.

AGNES: All right, I will.

> *Silence.*

TOBIAS: I tried. *(Pause.)* I was honest.

> *Silence.*

Didn't I? *(Pause.)* Wasn't I?

JULIA *(pause):* You were very honest, father. And you tried.

TOBIAS: Didn't I try, Claire? Wasn't I honest?

CLAIRE *(comfort; rue):* Sure you were. You tried.

TOBIAS: I'm sorry. I apologize.

AGNES *(to fill a silence):* What I find most astonishing—aside from my belief that I will, one day . . . lose my mind—but when? Never, I begin to think, as the years go by, or that I'll not *know* if it happens, or maybe even *has*— what I find most astonishing, I think, is the wonder of daylight, of the sun. All the centuries, millenniums—all the history—I wonder if that's why we sleep at night, because the darkness still . . . frightens us? They say we sleep to let the demons out—to let the mind go raving mad, our dreams and nightmares all our logic gone awry, the dark side of our reason. And when the daylight comes again . . . comes order with it. *(Sad chuckle.)* Poor Edna and Harry. *(Sigh.)* Well, they're safely gone . . . and we'll all forget . . . quite soon. *(Pause.)* Come now; we can begin the day.
    Curtain.

○○○
○○○
○○○
○○○ # THE KILLING
○○○
○○○ # OF SISTER GEORGE
○○○

A comedy in three acts

BY FRANK MARCUS

Cast and credits appear on page 360

FRANK MARCUS was born in Germany in 1928 and with his parents and sister managed to emigrate to England in 1939. Other members of his family were murdered at Auschwitz during the war years. Following his regular schooling, Marcus studied at St. Martin's School of Art and then formed an experimental company, the International Theater Group, in which he acted, designed and directed productions in little theaters around Notting Hill Gate. Marcus's stage works include the pantomime Les Trois Perruques *for his close friend Marcel Marceau; translations of* La Ronde, Liebelei *and one other Schnitzler work, and three original TV plays. His first West End playscript was* The Formation Dancers *at the Arts Theater Club and then at the Globe in the season of 1964-65. Marcus's* The Killing of Sister George *was cited by London theater critics and others as the best play of London's 1965-66 season.*

Marcus has spent much of his time assisting in the family business, an antique silver shop. He also holds the post of drama critic for The London Magazine *and* Plays and Players, *and as an essayist he has written a chapter on "The Season in London" for this volume of* Best Plays. *He is married, with three children, and lives in London near the Marble Arch.*

INTRODUCTION BY THE PLAYWRIGHT *

If you were to walk down a typical South London street, with its endless rows of identical semi-detached houses and neat front gardens, and listened unobtrusively at the doors, you would be aware of a strange phenomenon. Punctually every morning at 11:15 a.m. (except Saturdays and Sundays) there is a break in the household chores: washing machines cease their gurgling, steaming tea kettles are hurriedly switched off, the hoovering stops. In millions of homes all over England housewives settle down to listen to a radio serial, *Mrs. Dale's Diary.*

For twenty years, for fifteen minutes every day, this chronicle of a small-town doctor's wife and her everyday problems and experiences has held the attention of listeners. Mrs. Dale is a busy, well-meaning, socially aware lady of impeccable conventional character, coping successfully with people and events. Very little has changed over the years. Her mother, a crusty old battleaxe, has not noticeably aged in twenty years; a recent rumor that she was about to die brought such a flood of protests from listeners that an official denial was issued by the B.B.C., disclaiming any such bloodthirsty intentions.

Vying with *Mrs. Dale* for popular favor—or possibly complementing it— is another radio serial, *The Archers.* As old as *Mrs. Dale,* and of the same length, *The Archers* panders to rural nostalgia. Its heroes, a farmer and his family, are as sterotyped and unchanging as the Dales. As the countryside recedes and urban settlements encroach hungrily on the few remaining areas of unspoilt nature, the Archers, with their soft burring accents, are a comforting reminder of old ideals and help to assuage our urban guilt as we push this "green and pleasant land" into the sea.

Death is a rare visitor to these soap operas of the air. When a character is killed off, in the interest of "realism," millions of listeners lose a close friend and daily companion. The housewives and old age pensioners, who lives are lived daily at one remove from reality, are suddenly made aware of their own mortality: an intolerable reminder, to be chased from consciousness by the comforting sounds of domestic gadgets. The washing machines gurgle, the kettle screams for tea, and the hoover brings the reassuring and necessary proof of continuing life. And the radio, too, brings back memories with the old songs and voices, and then, when evening comes and the husband is back from work, there's the television.

Applehurst, in *The Killing of Sister George,* is a radio serial like *Mrs. Dale* and *The Archers.* Those of us who are truly alive can laugh at it.

FRANK MARCUS

* These remarks, reprinted from the New York *World Journal Tribune,* appeared as an author's note in *Playbill,* as part of the theater program for *The Killing of Sister George.*

Time: The present

Place: The living room of June Buckridge's flat in Devonshire Street, London

ACT I

SYNOPSIS: The "Applehurst Theme," a happy folk tune, is heard as the house lights dim; then the music fades and the curtain rises on June Buckridge's London flat on a Tuesday afternoon in late September.

The furniture is mixed antique and modern, and there is a lot of it. A sofa with attendant chairs and tables holds the center of the stage. At stage left is a table with chairs near the door to the kitchen, also reached through a serving hatch. On the upstage wall are, at left, a couple of broad stairs leading to the bedroom and bathroom hall and, center, a window with window seat looking onto the roofs of the city. Left of the window is a console radio. Bookcases to the right of the window adjoin an electric fireplace in the right wall, and downstage right is the door to the hall, furnished with a small table and umbrella stand.

> *When the curtain rises . . . . . the room is empty. The front door is heard to slam off right. June Buckridge enters from the hall. She is a rotund, middle-aged woman, wearing a belted white mackintosh. She carries a leather brief case and string gloves. She is very agitated.*

ALICE *(off in the kitchen, calling):* George? George, is that you?

> *June shows exasperation at the sound of Alice's voice, throws her gloves and brief case onto the sofa and goes to the table behind it. She opens a cigar box on the table, finds it empty and throws it violently to the floor, then moves to the fireplace.*
>
> *Alice "Childie" McNaught, in the kitchen, opens the hatch and looks into the room. She is a girl-woman in her thirties, looking deceptively young. She conveys an impression of pallor: her hair, eyes and complexion are all very light. She is wearing a sweater and jeans, with a plastic apron and orange rubber gloves.*

ALICE *(surprised):* George, what on earth . . . ?

> *June takes a cheroot from a box on the mantelpiece, reaches for a lighter, finds a doll in long clothes in the way and throws it into the fender.*

George! What are you doing at home at this time of the afternoon?

> *June lights her cheroot.*

JUNE *(after a pause):* They are going to murder me.

ALICE: What . . . ?

JUNE: I've suspected it for some time.

Alice, who shares this flat with June, closes the hatch and enters the living room. June paces. June explains: during tea break she received a nasty hint from a bitchy colleague. They are plotting to "kill" June. Despite June's six years' seniority as an actress in a radio serial program called *Applehurst,* they're planning to kill off her character of Sister George in a future episode of the story.

June was upset enough to walk out of rehearsal and come home, even though she knows that the authorities at the B.B.C. frown on tantrums from contract artists. June pours herself a drink from the gin bottle.

> *Alice picks up a doll from the pouffe then sits on the pouffe and hugs the doll.*

ALICE: Nobody wants to write you out. It's unthinkable. *Applehurst* couldn't survive without you.

JUNE *(sitting):* Don't you be too sure. Applehurst is more than a village, you know—it's a community, it's a way of life. It doesn't depend on individuals. *(In a country accent.)* There's many a stone in that churchyard . . .

ALICE: You talk as if it was real.

JUNE *(leans forward and raises her voice; in her own voice):* It is real to millions. It stands for the traditional values to English life—common sense—tenacity—our rural heritage . . .

ALICE: Oh, belt up!

JUNE: You're getting above yourself, missy.

ALICE: You *are* the serial. It would be nothing without you.

JUNE: Stranger things have happened. Only the other day Ronnie said to me: "There'll have to be some changes, you know."

ALICE: He probably meant the story line.

JUNE: No—no—it's the axe again. We're losing listeners, and they're looking for a scapegoat. It's over a year since old Mrs. Prescott was kicked by a horse.

June downs a swig of gin and Alice hems her doll's skirt as the two discuss events on the *Applehurst* program (often it's hard to tell which they mean, the characters or the actors). Sister George, the District Nurse, is still the most popular character—by a narrow margin over Ginger Hopkins the pub keeper. And Sister George lost four percentage points the past week. Rosie is pregnant—a character, not an actress—and Applehurst hasn't been told who the father is. In the next installment, Rosie will come to Sister George to try to get rid of the baby.

JUNE *(sighs):* . . . . . Don't know what the younger generation's coming to.

ALICE: What do you tell her?

JUNE: What *don't* I tell her. *(Puts out her cheroot in the ash tray.)* I give her a dressing-down she won't forget in a hurry. *(Rises and speaks in her country accent.)* Where is he? Mr. Clever Lad? Show me where he is so's I can tear some strips off him, the fine young fellow. Just don't you aggravate yourself, my dear—leave it to me. Just you tell me who it was, my dear. Just you tell me who it was.

ALICE: And does she tell you?

JUNE. No. *(She pauses, then crosses to table at left and sits.)* But I'll wheedle it out of her, never fear. Just give me three installments, that's all. *(She picks up her drink.)*

June insists that Applehurst *needs* her; the town needs its District Nurse. Alice surmises that maybe the colleague's remark was innocent, and not hinting at all. June rises in exasperation.

JUNE: Oh, shut up! Silly bitch! *(She moves to the table behind the sofa, puts down her glass, picks up a framed certificate and reads.)* "And in recognition of your devoted work and care for the old and sick, we name the Geriatric Ward the Sister George Ward." *(She replaces the certificate.)*
   Alice applauds slowly and ironically.
Take care, Childie, you're trailing your coat . . .

ALICE *(giggling):* You're the bull. *(She moves to the pouffe, kneels on it with one knee and puts the doll's clothes straight.)*

JUNE *(dangerously):* We're very cocky all of a sudden.

June wonders why Alice is home from work. Alice says Mr. Katz, her boss, gave her the day off because this is a Jewish holiday. June suggests that Mr. Katz has been "having a go" at Alice; last time it happened he tore her blouse. June becomes angry, and Alice takes refuge in the bathroom. June demands that she come out, but Alice refuses.

   June turns, picks up Emmeline the doll from the table behind the sofa and calls toward the bathroom.
JUNE: Can you hear me, Childie? I've got Emmeline here, your favorite doll. *(Softly but clearly.)* And if you don't come out of the bathroom *at once* —I'm going to pull Emmeline's head off.
   Alice, tear-stained, rushes in, tears the doll out of June's hand and hugs it.
ALICE: Monster!

JUNE: There, that's better. *(She pauses.)* And now: apologize.

ALICE: What for?

JUNE: For causing me unnecessary aggravation.

ALICE: I'm sorry.

JUNE: You don't sound it.

ALICE: Look, George, I know that you're worried and everything, but that's no reason . . .

JUNE: Don't answer back. Don't be cheeky.

ALICE: Look, George . . .

JUNE: Has Mr. Katz "had a go" at you?

ALICE *(screaming):* No!

JUNE: Don't screech at me. Apologize this instant, or there'll be severe chastisement.

ALICE: I'm sorry.

JUNE: That's better. Now, down on your knees.

ALICE: Must I?

JUNE: Yes. Come on.

Alice, still hugging the doll, goes on her knees.

Show your contrition.

ALICE: How?

JUNE: You must eat the butt of my cigar.

ALICE: I couldn't; it would make me sick.

JUNE *(standing over Alice):* Are you arguing with me?

ALICE: O.K. Hand it over.

June crosses to the table, picks up the ash tray and holds it out to Alice, who takes the cigar butt.

JUNE: Good girl. Now eat it.

ALICE: Can I take the ash off?

JUNE: You may take the ash off, but you must eat the paper.

Alice, with an expression of extreme distaste, eats the butt.

ALICE: Ooh, it tastes vile.

JUNE: Good.

The telephone rings.

That'll teach you to be rude.

Alice answers the phone, then passes it to June. It is Mrs. Mercy Croft, an Assistant Head at the B.B.C. who conducts a weekly radio program giving advice. She has something to tell June, so June invites her to come to the apartment instead of meeting at the office.

After she hangs up, June confesses to Alice that she fears the worst. June directs Alice to get tea organized; to make a good impression on Mrs. Mercy Croft. Alice, in her turn, urges June to calm down—June tends to become aggressive when she's nervous.

While Alice goes to the kitchen to prepare tea, June places her many citations and awards around the room so that no visitor could overlook them. One of her prized possessions—a stag's head symbolizing nomination as "Honorary Stag"—is missing. Alice enters and is forced to admit she hated it, she threw it away. June is furious, but the buzzer rings; Mrs. Mercy Croft has arrived. After the time it would take to walk upstairs the doorbell rings and June goes to usher in her guest.

Mrs. Mercy Croft enters through the arch at right. She is a well-groomed lady of indeterminate age, gracious of manner and freezingly polite. She is wearing a navy blue two-piece suit, matching hat and accessories, and a discreet double string of pearls round her neck. She carries a brief case.

After an awkward introduction, Alice is sent to the kitchen to finish tea. June is left alone with Mercy.

MERCY (*she looks around*): To be perfectly honest, I imagined your home to be—different.

JUNE: Really?

MERCY (*Indicating the ornaments on the book case*): This charming Victoriana—the dolls—somehow . . .

JUNE (*slightly embarrassed*): They're Miss McNaught's.

MERCY: Oh, of course, that would explain it. They just weren't *you*. I didn't know . . .

JUNE (*rather sheepishly*): Yes, I have a flat-mate.

MERCY (*sympathetically*): How nice. It's so important to have—companionship—especially when one's an artist.

JUNE (*indicating the brasses on the wall*): These are mine—I collect horse brasses.

MERCY: How useful. . . . .

Mercy goes to the window, shouts with the delight of recognizing Broadcasting House—"that reassuring presence"—in the view from June's window.

As the two women talk, Mercy puts her brief case, bag and gloves on the table behind the sofa. June has a habit of lapsing into the country speech of her Sister George character, but Mercy doesn't mind: ". . . . . you *are* Sister George far more than Miss June Buckridge to all of us at B.H."

The two women sit (June in the armchair with knees apart) and enter into small talk. June was in a tough outfit during the war; she doesn't scare easy. Mercy approaches the subject of her visit.

MERCY: As you know, I hold a monthly "surgery" in my office, when I welcome people to come to me with their problems. I've always made it a rule to be approachable. But in certain cases, involving matters of special importance, I prefer to visit the subjects in their own homes, so that we can talk more easily, without any duress. That's why I'm here today.

JUNE (*in her country accent*): Ah, well, a farmer's footsteps are the best manure. (*She laughs.*)

MERCY: Quite. But there is rather a serious matter I wish to discuss with you.

JUNE: I see.

Alice comes in with the tea. Mercy is slightly annoyed by the interruption. But she is determined to have tea first, *then* talk, even though June urges her to speak freely in front of Alice.

Alice serves Scotch scones and Dundee cake. Alice and Mercy begin to chat about the recipe for scones as June becomes increasingly impatient.

ALICE: I use half a level teaspoon of bicarbonate of soda—

MERCY: Now you're giving away trade secrets.

ALICE: —and one level teaspoonful of cream of tartar—

JUNE: Shut up!

There is a moment's silence.

ALICE: —eight ounces of flour—

JUNE *(exploding):* Shut up!

ALICE *(softly but firmly):* —and one egg.

JUNE: Shut up!

She picks up the lump of Dundee cake and hurls it at Alice. Alice ducks. The cake flies to pieces against the sideboard. There is a pause during which Mercy continues to eat unperturbed.

MERCY: Now then, girls!

ALICE *(after a pause):* She hates me to talk about food. *(Confidentially.)* She's a wee bit overwrought.

JUNE *(rising):* Overwrought my arse! *(She stumps over to the fireplace, takes a cheroot from the box on the mantelpiece, and lights it.)*

Still, Mercy is unperturbed at this display of temperament. Alice confesses that she once wrote a poem about June's raging temper; June makes a rude noise about the poem while Mercy continues to consume her tea in a ladylike manner. The row reminds Mercy of school, and June recalls that she was captain of the hockey team—and heaven help any teammate who got out of line.

They return to the subject of Sister George. It is part of her character to drive around on a motor bicycle (a Moped) singing hymns as she goes—and whenever June happens to hum the wrong kind of tune, say a pop number, hundreds of listeners write in, objecting.

Mercy observes: "We must constantly examine criticism, and if it's constructive, we must act on it. Ruthlessly." This brings her to the reason for her visit—but first she would like to visit the "little girls' room." Alice shows her the way.

While Mercy is out of the room, June opens Mercy's brief case, finds the envelope marked "Sister George. Confidential," hides it in the sofa and replaces the brief case before Mercy returns.

When Mercy comes back into the room, Alice goes into the kitchen so that the two colleagues can talk. Mercy has come to administer "a severe reprimand." She had hoped that June would have learned to behave herself after the incident about a year ago in which June poured a glass of beer over the Assistant Head of Talks. But apparently not. The Director of Religious Broadcasting has received a complaint. Mercy hands the memo to June.

June reads the memo, calls it a lie, calls Alice in to bear witness, but Alice wasn't with June on the evening cited in the complaint, so she cannot give June an alibi.

JUNE: . . . . . All right; I possibly was drinking at The Bells on the night in question, having a few pints with the boys. There's no crime in that, is there?

MERCY: Miss Buckridge, according to this letter—*(She refers to the second paper on her clip board.)* from the Mother Superior of the Convent of the Sacred Heart of Jesus, you boarded a taxi which had stopped at the traffic lights at Langham Place . . .

JUNE: I thought it was empty.

MERCY *(reading):* "A taxi bearing as passengers two novitiate nuns from Ireland who had just arrived at King's Cross Station."

JUNE: How was I to know?

MERCY: You boarded this taxi in a state of advanced inebriation—*(She looks at June.)* and—*(She consults the paper.)* proceeded to assault the two nuns, subjecting them to actual physical violence.

ALICE: You didn't really!

JUNE: No, no, no, of course not. I'd had few pints—I saw this cab, got in—and there were those two black things—screaming blue murder.

MERCY: Why didn't you get out again?

JUNE: Well, I'd had a very nasty shock myself. What with their screaming and flapping about—I thought they were bats, vampire bats. It was they who attacked me. I remember getting all entangled in their skirts and petticoats and things—the taxi driver had to pull me free.

MERCY: A deplorable anecdote. *(She refers to the paper.)* According to the Mother Superior, one of the nuns required medical treatment for shock, and is still under sedation. *(She pauses.)* She thought it was the devil. *(She moves toward the sofa, sits on it and replaces the clip board in her brief case.)*

Alice is distressed. June condemns the Mother Superior for reporting the incident.

MERCY: The Mother Superior is responsible for the nuns in her charge.

JUNE: Then she should jolly well teach them how to behave in public. I got the fright of my life, in there. Those nuns were like *mice*—albino mice—with teeny little white faces and weeny little red eyes. And they were vicious, too. They scratched and they bit. *(She bares her arm.)* Look—you can still see the tooth marks—do you see that? I've a good mind to make a counter-complaint to the Mother Superior. They deserve to be scourged in their cells.

MERCY *(wearily):* I can hardly put through a report to the Controller, informing him of your allegation that you were bitten by two nuns.

JUNE: No, well, you could say . . .

MERCY: Let's be practical, Sister George—we're concerned with retaining the trust and respect of the public. Now people are perfectly well aware that artists frequently work under great emotional stress. We do all we can to gloss over minor disciplinary offences, but we simply cannot tolerate this sort of behavior. It's things like this which make people resent paying more for their wireless licenses. Thousands of pounds spent on public relations—*(She rises.)* and you jeopardize it all with your reckless and foolish behavior. Really, Sister George, we have every reason to be very, very angry with you.

June, beaten, sits wearily.

June's penance will be a written apology to the Mother Superior, with a copy and covering letter to the Director of Religious Broadcasting. June must humble herself—and Alice assures Mercy that she will keep June out of trouble from now on.

MERCY *(to June):* . . . . . I'll leave you in Miss McNaught's expert charge.
JUNE: What about *Applehurst?*
MERCY *(non-committally):* That's another, rather more complex problem.
JUNE *(rising):* But—has anything been decided about the future?
MERCY: I'm afraid I can't say anything about that at the moment.
JUNE: It comes as a bit of a shock to me, you know, all this.
MERCY: It comes as a bit of a shock to me, too, I assure you, particularly as I understand that you often open church bazaars.

Conspiratorially, Alice assures Mercy that between the two of them they'll be able to keep June out of trouble. Mercy departs after a final, friendly caution to June: no more walking out on rehearsals.
Alice finds it hard to forgive June the nuns.

ALICE: It's the sort of thing you used to do when I first knew you. In that club in Notting Hill Gate. I remember how you used to go clomping about, without a bra, hitting girls over the head. *(She picks up the tray and puts it through the hatch.)*
JUNE: Kindly keep your foul-mouthed recollections to yourself.
    Alice returns to the table.
In my young days . . .
ALICE *(collecting the jam and plates):* Your young days were spent in a cul-de-sac in Aldershot, with the Band of Hope on one side and the Foot Clinic on the other. You told me so yourself. *(She puts the jam and plates through the hatch.)*
JUNE *(angrily):* How dare you! *(She moves to the sofa and sits.)* This is a respectable house—and I'll thank you to remember who's paying the rent.
ALICE *(folding the tablecloth):* Not much longer, perhaps.

June is indeed worried about her future. She asks Alice to go fetch Madame Xenia, the fortune-teller who lives in the flat downstairs. Alice is reluctant to go because Madame Xenia suspects Alice of making a play for her lodger. After a caustic remark or two June sends Alice off to get Madame Xenia anyhow. June reads one of her framed testimonials ". . . in recognition of your devoted work and care for the old and sick." Then she tries to open the stolen envelope but dares not and returns it to its hiding place. Alice comes in with Madame Xenia.

> *Madame Xenia enters through the arch. She is a hawk-faced, elderly woman of foreign origin, hennaed and hung with beads. She carries a little evening bag with a pack of playing cards in it.*

Alice has interrupted Madame Xenia in the middle of a session with a client, but Madame Xenia realizes that her friend June really needs her help. June draws the curtains, sits facing east, gives Madame Xenia a handkerchief to represent one of her personal possessions. They sit at a table and June cuts the cards.

Madame Xenia predicts trouble with a woman in black (the Mother Superior?) a large social gathering (the drag ball at Richmond?), a broken romantic association and a bad cold, a red-headed man (Ginger the Applehurst publican?) and a letter. At the mention of a letter, Alice retrieves the stolen envelope and hands it to June, who gives it to Madame Xenia.

> *Xenia steps mysteriously downstage center and holds the envelope to her cheek.*

JUNE: Do you—do you get any—vibrations?

XENIA *(carefully):* Mmm. It's difficult to say. It could mean one of two things.

JUNE *(squaring her shoulders):* Give it to me. I'm going to open it. *(She takes the envelope from Xenia and opens it.)* What must be, must be. *(She glances at the contents and collapses onto a chair.)* Oh, my God! *(She drops the letter to the floor.)*

> *Alice rushes and kneels by June. Xenia kneels and picks up the letter.*

ALICE: George! What's the matter? George!

> *June remains impassive. Xenia reads the letter. Alice speaks to Xenia.*

What does it say?

XENIA *(reading):* "Memo from Audience Research. Latest Popularity Ratings." *(She rises slowly.)* "Sister George sixty-four point five per cent. Ginger Hopkins sixty-eight."

> *Alice collapses, sitting back on her heels.*

JUNE: That's the weapon they've been waiting for. *(She rises.)* Now they'll kill me.

> *June rushes toward the bedroom door as the curtain quickly falls.*

ACT II

Scene 1

A week later, at 4 a.m. the sun is just coming up and June is sitting with a bottle of gin and her scrap book of press notices. The alarm clock goes off in the bedroom. Alice enters clad in black brassiere and pants and carrying a bundle of clothing. She pinches and punches June playfully, then begins to dress.

Alice is getting ready to stand in line, starting at 5 a.m., with the ballet regulars, who will queue up now for queue tickets for the box office line at the Royal Ballet.

Alice asks June to come with her, but June doesn't like the ballet crowd. Alice wants June to stop drinking, relax; June has been "impossible ever since that day Mrs. Mercy came to tea."

June ran into Mercy—literally, with a hard bump—rounding a corner of a corridor at Broadcasting House. June makes Alice act out this little incident of collision in the corridor, then describes how Mercy greeted her with ominous sympathy, oversolicitously.

ALICE: You're imagining things again.

JUNE: She's been avoiding me, I tell you, and I know why.

ALICE: She was probably in a hurry to get somewhere. A committee meeting or something.

JUNE: They've had that. And I found out what happened.

ALICE (alarmed): What?

JUNE (sitting): I'm to be written out of next Tuesday's episode.

ALICE: What?

JUNE: Are you deaf? I said . . .

ALICE: I heard. So what? It's happened before. Every time you go on holiday.

JUNE: But I'm not going on holiday, am I?

Alice is silent.

Sister George is confined to bed with a bad cold.

ALICE: Oh, now, that in itself . . .

JUNE (rises, moves above the arch and turns away): That in itself could mean a dress rehearsal for my extinction.

ALICE (sitting on the pouffe): Nothing of the sort.

JUNE: They want to see what it sounds like without me. If I am expendable.

ALICE: What about the following episodes?

JUNE (grimly): We shall know soon. The new scripts are due in the post this morning. I can see what is going to happen. (She moves downstage right and wraps her dressing gown tightly around her.) That cold's going to get worse—I can feel it in my bones. It'll turn to bronchitis, then pneumonia, and before I know where I am I shall be out like a light.

And June has another worry—she heard Alice talk in her sleep, saying, "Take me, Isidore." Alice denies she is having an affair, accuses June of thinking the worst of every little event.

Alice brews some coffee as she complains that June isn't as much fun as she used to be. June promises to enjoy the fancy dress ball they are planning to attend that evening—it'll be Alice who will fade. This reminds Alice to take her iron pill (June suggests that it may really be a birth pill). Alice chides June for her fits of jealousy (once, June phoned Alice's boss Mr. Katz pretending to be Mrs. Katz and gave him a good fright).

As Alice takes long socks from a knapsack and draws them on, June comments on her white legs: "luminous white, loooo-minous white." June remembers how they met; they lived in the same rooming house and every morning June would watch Alice hurry to work.

Alice picks up her shoes, scarf and woollen cap and puts the scarf and cap in the knapsack.

ALICE: I had no idea you were watching me. *(She sits in the armchair.)*

JUNE: One night I went into the bathroom just after you'd had a bath. The mirror was all steamed up, and the bath mat was moist and glistening where you'd stood on it. There was a smell of talcum powder and bath crystals—it was like an enchanted wood. I stood quite still on that mat—in your footsteps—and I saw that you'd left your comb behind. It was a small pink plastic comb, and it had your hairs in it. I kept that comb as souvenir. And all this time I'd never spoken a word to you.

ALICE *(after a pause):* You soon made up for it. *(She puts on her shoes.)*

JUNE: That night your boy friend saw you home, I knew I'd have to strike quickly.

ALICE *(rises, picks up the knapsack, puts it on the pouffe, then kneels on the floor above the pouffe):* That was Roger. He wanted to marry me.

JUNE *(bitterly):* That's what they all said—and you fell for it, silly goose.

Alice puts on the knitted cap, which ties under her chin like a baby's, and urges June to go to bed. But June is on edge. Alice adjusts June's dressing gown while June clutches the gin bottle and frets about the future.

Alice begs leave to depart. But June requires obeisance; half-drunkenly, she orders complacent Alice to kiss the hem of her garment and repeat an oath never to allow Mr. Katz or anyone else "gratification of his fleshly instincts" with Alice, now or ever.

Alice obeys but still cannot leave; June has hold of her scarf. June notices the scarf and wonders where Alice got it. It carries a name tape reading "J.V.S. Partridge" and Alice can't joke June out of wanting to know who Partridge is. He is Madame Xenia's lodger. Alice assures June that there is nothing between them, she stole the scarf—but June's jealousy still seethes.

JUNE: . . . . . I forbid you to speak to him.

ALICE: You must be raving mad. He's a neighbor, there's no harm in being friendly.

JUNE *(shouting):* I forbid you to speak to him, do you hear?

ALICE: I'll flipping well speak to him if I want to—why shouldn't I?

JUNE *(venomously):* You fancy him, don't you? *(She shouts.)* Don't you?

ALICE: He seems perfectly agreeable.

June's face is contorted with suspicion.

Yes, I do fancy him—he's a dish.

June steps threateningly towards Alice. She shrinks back against the sideboard.

Don't you touch me—you've no right to . . .

JUNE: I've got every right.

ALICE: I'm not married to you, you know.
> *There is a long pause, then June hands the scarf to Alice, who speaks in a low voice.*

I'm sorry, George, but you asked for it.

JUNE: You'd better get along, you'll be late.

ALICE *(picks up the knapsack but doesn't put it on):* Look after yourself. Don't forget the party tonight.

> *Alice makes a kissing motion to June, but June has turned away and does not see it. Alice exits through the arch. June wanders upstage, turns and surveys the room for a few moments, swaying slightly. She moves to a chair with her arms out.*

JUNE *(in her country accent):* Ah, there's my beautiful bike. *(She pats the back of the chair.)* 'Morning, old friend. We'll have you started up in no time. *(She turns the chair and places it with the back to the audience, stands left of it, looks after Alice for a moment, then makes a starting movement with her foot, and a purring noise to indicate the start of the engine.)* Prrrrm! Prrrrrrrrrrrr! *(She sits astride the chair and grasps the back as handlebars.)* Prrrr! Prrrr! 'Bye, Jean, 'bye, Rosie. Tell your dad to mind his gammy leg. *(She sways the chair from side to side.)* Prrrr! Prrrrr! Prrrrr! *(She sings.)* "Oh God, our help in ages past—" Prrr—prrr—prrr— "our hope for years to come." Prrr—prrr! 'Morning, Ginger, 'morning, Vicar, my word you're up early. Prrr—prrr! Yes, first call old Mrs. Hinch. Prrrr—prrrr! *(She sings.)* "Be Thou our guard while troubles last—" Prrr—prrrr! "And our eternal—" —prrr— "home . . ."

> *The curtain quickly falls.*

Scene 2

In late afternoon of the same day, the sun is setting. Laughter can be heard coming from the bedroom; then the sound of Laurel and Hardy's signature tune played on a penny whistle. June and Alice enter from the bedroom costumed as Laurel (Alice) and Hardy (June) for the fancy dress ball. They practice their routine, including a little dance. Alice jabs June a bit too hard, and June retaliates. Alice borrows June's hat.

> *Alice bends over the bowler and spits into it slowly, then puts the hat on June's head again, giving it a little tap. June makes no protest while this is going on, but watches coldly.*

JUNE *(as herself):* What was that supposed to be?

ALICE *(as herself):* I don't know. Just an idea. Horseplay, you know. We're celebrating because you're back in the series, aren't we?

JUNE *(with an evil glint in her eye):* Just because the script writers have cured my cold, there's no need to go raving bloody mad, you know.

ALICE: I thought it was funny.

JUNE: You thought it was funny?

ALICE: Yes, I thought it was funny.

JUNE: You thought it was funny. *(As Hardy.)* Stan.

ALICE *(as Laurel):* Yes, Olly?

JUNE: Give me your hat.

ALICE: What for, Olly?

JUNE: I just want to look at something.

> *Alice gives June her hat. June points up right.*

Look up there, Stan.

> *Alice obediently looks up. June goes to the table, squirts soda water from a siphon into Alice's hat.*

ALICE *(staring upwards):* There's nothing up there, Olly.

JUNE: Try this, then, Stan.

> *She empties the water over Alice as she puts the hat on Alice's head.*

ALICE *(as herself):* Oh! You fool—now you've spoilt my costume.

> *She hits June.*

Alice menaces June with water in a vase of flowers. June, laughing, prepares to take her punishment, but Alice can't bring herself to soak June. They are both laughing as the door bell rings. They think it is Madame Xenia. Alice answers the door—it is Mrs. Mercy Croft.

Alice and June explain their odd appearance to Mercy, who has come right over from a meeting. Mercy's first news is good: all is forgiven by the Mother Superior (though June must not forget that she promised to send a donation). But then Mercy proceeds to the main business of her visit.

MERCY: . . . . . Well, now, Miss Buckridge, I'm afraid I have some bad news for you.

> *The lights dim a little for dusk effect.*

JUNE: Bad news?

MERCY: You're the first to be told. It's only just been decided; or, rather, it's only just received the official stamp of approval.

ALICE *(terrified):* You can't mean . . .

JUNE: Be quiet, Childie.

MERCY: Yes. I'm sorry, Miss Buckridge: it's the end of Sister George.

> *There is a stunned pause. June sinks into a chair.*

ALICE *(suddenly shouting):* But why? Why?

MERCY: Believe me, dear Miss Buckridge, the decision is no reflection on your ability as an actress. You created a character that has become a nation-wide favorite.

ALICE *(still incredulous):* But why kill her?

MERCY: Why do some of our nearest and dearest have to die? Because that's life.

> *Alice moves slowly to the pouffe and sits on it.*

In *Applehurst* we try to recreate the flavor of life, as it is lived in hundreds of English villages.

ALICE: But she's the most popular character in it.

MERCY *(slightly uncomfortable):* I know. The B.B.C. took that into consideration. They felt—and I must say I concurred—that only some dramatic event, something that would get into the news headlines, could save *Applehurst.* We felt that in their grief, robbed of one of their greatest favorites, listeners would return again to *Applehurst* with a new loyalty, with a . . .

JUNE *(interrupting dully):* How?

MERCY *(quietly):* It's not for another fortnight. It's scheduled for the twelfth.

June insists on knowing how Sister George will die. Mercy tells her: on an ordinary Applehurst morning, in full character and full career on her motor bike, in an accident with a ten-ton truck. It will coincide with Road Safety Week.

June fears that her audience will judge Sister George a reckless driver, but Mercy reassures her that it will be obviously the truck driver's fault. Still, June would prefer that Sister George die in line of duty, perhaps from a disease, and she threatens to go over Mercy's head to have the script changed. Mercy indicates that the B.B.C. will want to keep June on in some other capacity, and this mollifies June somewhat. But how about the funeral?

MERCY *(moving to the pouffe and sitting on it; cheerfully):* Oh, it'll be done in style. Don't you worry your head about that. There's some talk of a special memorial broadcast, with contributions from all sorts of famous people— but I shouldn't really be talking about that, as everything's still in the planning stage.

JUNE: Would I be in it? In the memorial broadcast, I mean?

MERCY: Naturally. There will be lots of recorded extracts of Sister George.

JUNE: No, I meant: would I be able to tell the people how the character developed?

MERCY: Oh, no! That would spoil the illusion.

JUNE: But you said the B.B.C. wanted to use me again.

MERCY: Yes, but not as Sister George.

JUNE *(on the brink of hysteria):* What's wrong with Sister George?

MERCY: Nothing, dear Miss Buckridge. She'll be dead, that's all.

> *There is a pause. June's head droops. Alice gently helps June to her feet.*

June is beginning to accept the inevitability of her loss; she moves with slow dignity, like one bereaved; she does not feel like discussing ideas for new series at this time. She goes into the bedroom to be alone with her grief and bolts the door, leaving Alice alone with Mercy.

Alice asks Mercy to stay, and the two sit down. Alice takes off her bowler hat and unburdens herself to Mercy's willing ear: life with June has been hell, June drinks too much and takes out her troubles on Alice. Mercy observes that Alice shouldn't put up with June: ". . . . . surely there must be lots of openings for a girl with your qualifications." But Alice has been with June for seven years of time-monopolizing association.

Gently and subtly, Mercy exploits this opportunity to divide and, perhaps, to conquer. She refers to Alice's hidden literary ability; she invites Alice to try radio writing, to come to see her about it in her B.B.C. office.

Alice takes the cue and flatters Mercy; then exaggerates her own difficulties with June. June (Alice declares) tends to get violent and beats Alice often. Alice is afraid (she suggests in an obvious play for Mercy's sympathy), perhaps even for her life.

MERCY *(with sudden sharpness):* But why do you put up with it?

ALICE *(after a pause):* I have nowhere else to go.

MERCY: Surely there's somewhere . . .

ALICE: I couldn't face living alone. Not any more.

MERCY *(overcome):* My poor child. This is terrible. *(She rises, glances at the bedroom door then moves above the table and leans over to Alice.)* Look, if there's any more trouble—with George, I mean, don't hesitate to give me a ring. Please regard me as your friend.

ALICE *(seizing Mercy's hand):* Oh, you are kind, Mrs. Mercy.

MERCY: And we must find somewhere for you to go.

ALICE *(gratefully):* Would you? Would you really?

MERCY *(patting Alice's hand):* Leave it to me.

Mercy picks up Alice's doll Emmeline and babies it; then she puts it down and moves to depart.

MERCY: . . . . . Now remember what I told you: if there's any more trouble, get straight on the telephone to me.
    Alice picks up her bowler hat from the sofa and puts it on.
That's the spirit.

ALICE *(in a Laurel voice):* Gee, I'm frightened.

MERCY: Don't let her bully you.

ALICE *(in a Laurel voice):* She's a devil when roused.

MERCY: Goodbye, dear. Must run. Have fun. *(Exits through the arch.)*

ALICE *(mechanically):* Must run—have fun. *(She looks towards the bedroom, undecided, picks up the whistle from the table and goes to the bedroom door, playing the Laurel and Hardy signature tune. She calls.)* George. *(She knocks on the door and tries the handle but the door is bolted. She calls.)* George, are you all right? *(She taps on the door with the whistle and chants.)* Geor-orge. *(She suddenly angrily kicks the door and shouts.)* George! *(She pauses, then runs to the table, slams down the whistle and throws the bowler hat onto the sofa. Rapidly and intensely.)* What am I going to do?
    The curtain quickly falls.

INTERLUDE

Following the intermission, the house lights dim, but the curtain does not rise. Instead, the following recording is heard:

> *There is the sound of Sister George's Moped, a background of country noises, the twittering of birds, mooing and neighing, etc.*

SISTER GEORGE *(sings):*

Oh God, our help in ages past,
Our hope for years to come,
Our shelter from the stormy blast
And our eternal home.

> *The singing fades out. The monotonous sound is heard of the engine of a heavy lorry.*

BILL *(in a thick North Country accent):* You awake, Fred?

FRED *(grunting something unintelligible):* Oh, ay . . .

BILL: Won't do to fall asleep now. We're nearly there.

FRED *(in a thick North Country accent):* I'm not up to it any more—this all-night driving.

BILL: There's the turning coming up now—don't miss it.

SISTER GEORGE *(approaching, singing):*

Oh God, our help in ages past . . .

> *There is the sound of acceleration and changing of gears from the lorry.*

FRED: Let's get there fast—I'm hungry.

BILL *(shouting):* Look out.

> *There is a screeching of brakes, followed by an explosion. Bill is near hysteria.*

We hit her! Fred, we hit her!

> *The lorry cab door is heard to slam.*

FRED: It weren't my fault. I braked . . .

BILL: Is she . . . ? My God, she looks bad. *(He calls.)* Hey, there!

> *The sound of heavy footsteps is heard, coming nearer.*

FARMER BROMLEY *(in a country accent):* What happened?

BILL: Bike came round the corner, oh—fast.

FRED: I tried to brake. It weren't my fault.

FARMER BROMLEY *(panting):* I always did say it's a dangerous crossing. Is she—is she badly . . . ? Holy Saints! It's—it's Sister George!

FRED: It *were.*

> *The "Applehurst Theme" swells up and plays cheerfully.*

ACT III

On a sunny October morning, two weeks later, the room is filled with flowers and wreaths, and there are piles of telegrams. Madame Xenia is seated alone, listening to a tape-recorder replay the demise of Sister George. This comes to an end as the phone rings. Madame Xenia, acting as June's "temporary secretary," answers it and brushes off still another admirer offering condolences.

Alice enters from the bedroom dressed in baby doll pajamas, yawning. She and Xenia are both worried about June, who has wandered off somewhere by herself. Perhaps June shouldn't have listened to the "accident" on the radio; or perhaps she can't stand to remain in the flat with all those flowers and messages.

Alice pokes through the telegrams, arranged into three piles: personal, official and doubtful. Today is the day of the "funeral," the official B.B.C. ceremonies marking Sister George's passing (the private farewell party took place the night before). Alice, her nerves on edge, quarrels with Madame Xenia and nearly forces her to leave; but they are interrupted by the rattling of the front door handle. June is coming home.

XENIA: Look cheerful—she must see happy faces.
> The sound is heard of a door closing offstage right. Xenia moves to the fireplace.

ALICE (rushing towards the kitchen door): She'll kill me if she sees me walking about like this.

JUNE (offstage, shouting): Open the windows and let the sunshine in.
> Alice realizes it is too late to escape, grabs the cross of yellow roses by the sideboard and tries to hide behind it.

XENIA (apprehensively): We are here, my darling.
> June sails in through the arch wearing an extravagant orange chiffon hat with her tweed suit and carrying a picnic basket.

JUNE (as she enters): It's glorious out. (Turns to Xenia.) Darling—how sweet of you to hold the fort—I do hope you weren't pestered too much.
> Alice's wreath rustles. June turns and sees her.

Oh God, down in the forest something stirred. (She puts the basket on the table.)

XENIA: George, we were so worried—where have you been?

JUNE (opening the basket): Shopping. I picked up this marvellous Christmas Gift hamper packed full of goodies. And two bottles of Veuve Cliquot 'fifty-three. (She takes two bottles from the basket and puts them on the table.)

XENIA: But—what for?

JUNE: I've decided to skip the funeral and have a celebration.

XENIA: Celebration?

JUNE: Yes, more a coming-out party, really.

XENIA: But who is coming out?
JUNE: *I* am.

Madame Xenia likes June's hat; Alice sniggers behind her floral tribute when Xenia tells June it makes her look younger. Cheerfully, June orders Alice to get dressed and make them some tea. Alice almost forces June to become angry by calling June's hat a "mistake"; but even then, June keeps her good humor. Alice goes off to the kitchen.

XENIA *(picking up the red and pink wreath):* Would you like to go through the latest tributes?
JUNE: If it's absolutely necessary.
XENIA: Look at this—from the patients and staff of the Sister George Geriatrics Ward. In that hospital your name will never die.
JUNE *(firmly): Her* name.
XENIA: Her name, your name: it's the same thing.
JUNE: No, it's not. George and I have parted company. And do you know, I'm glad to be free of the silly bitch.
XENIA: What?
JUNE: Honestly.
XENIA: George, what are you saying?
JUNE: I'm saying that my name is *June.* June Buckridge. I'm endeavoring to memorize it.
XENIA *(laughing):* You are incredible.

Xenia replaces the wreath and Alice enters with a tea tray. One of the plates holds a crumpled telegram. June reads it; it is from someone named Liz who was formerly a very close friend of June's. Alice, asking for trouble, hums a bar of "Auld Lang Syne" meaningfully. When, inevitably, June reminisces about Liz, remembering her as a thoroughbred, "nervy, stringy, temperamental. I remember I used to tease her because her hair grew down her neck, like a thin mane, between her shoulder blades," Alice stalks off to the bedroom in a huff.

June tells Xenia she has been dissatisfied with Alice's behavior lately; perhaps she will complain to Alice's ultra-refined mother in Glasgow.

June and Xenia prepare to celebrate, but the door bell rings. Xenia goes to answer it. Just as June is popping the cork on a bottle of champagne, Mrs. Mercy Croft enters—dressed in mourning and carrying a sheaf of lilies.

Mercy hands the flowers to June in tribute from the B.B.C. June introduces Mercy to Madame Xenia, who throws her arms around Mercy in a close embrace; Xenia is a great fan of Mercy's weekly radio program of advice to people with problems. Magnanimously, Xenia gives a startled Mercy some free advice about the future, then goes to put the lilies in water.

MERCY *(inspecting the flowers):* What beautiful tributes. May I read some? I *adore* inscriptions.

JUNE: There's a whole lot more in the bathroom. As soon as Childie's dressed she can take them all and dump them on the Cenotaph.

MERCY: But you can't do that. They're for *you*. *(Seriously.)* Do you know the entire *Applehurst* company turned up for the recording today in black? It was quite spontaneous.

JUNE *(annoyed):* They must be bonkers. . . . .

Now, after six years in the role, June wants to forget. Madame Xenia sails through the room, dropping off the lilies, on the way down to her own flat.

Mercy hints that June may be lonely now; June reminds her that she has Miss McNaught for companionship. And June doesn't intend to listen to future *Applehurst* broadcasts. Mercy describes what is going to happen next: a community getting over the shock of losing its most beloved member.

MERCY: . . . . . But eventually the gap must be filled; new leaders will arise.

JUNE: Leaders? What new leaders? Who?

MERCY *(confidentially):* Well, it's not really ready for release yet, but between you and me—I believe Ginger . . .

JUNE *(rising; horrified):* Ginger? *(In her country accent.)* He couldn't lead a cow down Buttercup Hill, couldn't Ginger. He's weak. Weak as the rotten apples that fall off a tree.

MERCY: Ginger will be our new anti-hero.

JUNE *(turning to face Mercy):* An anti-hero in *Applehurst?*

MERCY: Contemporary appeal, Sister George. *Applehurst* is facing up to the fact that the old values become outdated.

There is to be wholesale slaughter in the coming episodes. Old Mrs. Hinch will die of bronchitis; Mr. Burns is due for a stroke next Friday.

JUNE: Who's going to look after the—survivors?

MERCY: Nurse Lawrence.

JUNE: *What!*

MERCY: Yes, she arrives from the District Hospital tomorrow to take over from you.

JUNE: But she's a probationer. She couldn't put a dressing on a—salad. They won't stand for that, you know.

MERCY: On the contrary, Nurse Lawrence wins the trust and affection of the village, and becomes known, rather charmingly, I think, as "Sister Larry."

JUNE: *Sister Larry!* You're going to make this ill-bred, uneducated little slut . . .

MERCY *(shouting):* Contemporary appeal, Sister George. People like that *do* exist—and in positions of power and influence: flawed, credible characters like Ginger, Nurse Lawrence, Rosie . . .

Rosie, the pregnant one, is going to marry her boy friend—not the father of her child from the Army camp.

Alice enters in a gaily-colored dress. June tells her the news about "Nurse Lawrence" as Alice prepares to make tea for Mercy. Alice is unconcerned, but momentarily June feels that the results of her life's work are being demolished.

Alice pours a gin for June, then goes to the kitchen as Mercy discusses June's future. To celebrate the "funeral" there is to be a party at Broadcast House. One of the guests will be Mrs. Coote, in charge of the program *Toddler Time* which is slipping badly in the ratings.

MERCY: The script writers are running around in circles—one of them's had a nervous breakdown: the one who wrote the series about Tiddlywink, the Cockerel, which, as you know, was withdrawn after only three installments. Anyway, to cut a long story short, there's been some agonizing reappraisal over *Toddler Time*. A completely new approach has been decided on.

JUNE: Don't tell me—marauding gollywogs, drunk teddy bears and pregnant bunnies.

> *Alice enters from the kitchen with a tray of tea for one which she puts on the table.*

MERCY *(smiling enigmatically)*: Not quite, dear.

> *Alice sits left of the table.*

But we're preparing an absolutely super new adventure series, in which we've all got loads of confidence, which will combine exciting narrative with a modern outlook—and you're being considered for the title role.

JUNE: What's it called?

MERCY: *The World of Clarabelle Cow.*

> *There is a pause. June rises.*

JUNE: Am I to understand that this—this character is a cow?

MERCY: A very human one, I assure you: full of little foibles and prejudices.

JUNE *(slowly)*: A—flawed—credible—cow?

MERCY: Credible in human terms, certainly. Otherwise the children wouldn't believe in her. Children are very discerning.

ALICE: Ought to be fun.

JUNE: I don't think I could have understood you correctly. I don't believe I really grasped the meaning of your words.

MERCY: I thought I made myself perfectly clear.

ALICE: Oh, don't be dense, George.

JUNE *(to Alice)*: Shut up! *(She turns to Mercy.)* Am I to take it that you have come here today—the day of the funeral of Sister George—to offer me the part of a cow?

MERCY: We must be practical, dear. None of us can afford to be out of work for too long.

JUNE: Pour me out another gin, Childie, will you?

Alice refills June's glass as Mercy tells June the B.B.C. cow offer is no joke. "I'm going mad!" June shouts as Xenia enters with a cross of white chrysanthemums from old Mrs. Hinch. This reminds June that they're planning to "murder" old Mrs. Hinch, too. June, frantic, shouts at Mercy: "Is your blood lust sated? How many other victims are you going to claim?"

June manages to regain her self-control. With great dignity, June makes it clear: "I am not playing the part of a cow!" The buzzer sounds and Xenia answers it; it is two nuns coming to pay their respects. June rushes off in dismay to the bathroom, as Xenia refuses admittance to the nuns.

Alice goes to see if June is all right; June is running a bath and chooses to be left alone. Xenia departs, leaving Mercy and Alice together.

Mercy sympathizes with Alice, having to cope with June's violent nature, and Alice plays upon this sympathy as heavily as she can. Mercy's offer of sanctuary still stands, and Alice has almost made up her mind to accept it.

ALICE: . . . . . But she's so possessive. I'm never allowed anywhere near the B.B.C. I'm kept a guilty secret.

MERCY: She's shackled you to her. (She sits.) Anyway, you wouldn't be working for the B.B.C. You'd be working for me as my own private secretary, in my London flat.

ALICE (rising): It sounds absolutely super. I'm sorry I'm being so slow about making up my mind.

MERCY: A thought has just occurred to me: if you're in any kind of trouble—you know, with George—you can always camp down at the flat. There's a divan.

ALICE: Oh, that'd be wonderful.

The flat will be an escape for both of them—if Alice can manage to escape, to break the habit of living with George. Alice clutches her doll Emmeline and kneels by Mercy's chair, grasping Mercy's knees, begging her help.

ALICE: Please don't leave me. I'm terrified of what she will do.

MERCY: Calm yourself, Alice. No one's going to hurt you. Here, put your head on my shoulder.

Alice lays her head on Mercy's shoulder.

Close your eyes. Relax. My goodness, you're trembling like a leaf. (She strokes Alice's hair.)

ALICE (with her eyes shut): That's nice.

MERCY: You're my little girl. You're going to be—my little girl.

June enters. She is wearing her bath robe.

JUNE: What a touching sight.

ALICE: George!

Panic-stricken, Alice rises, runs right and shrinks against the armchair. June crosses to Alice, snatches the doll from her and turns to Mercy.

JUNE: I always did say she had nice hair. I always said that for her.

ALICE: George, you don't understand.

JUNE *(to the doll):* Did you hear what your mummy said, Emmeline? She said I don't understand. Did you see what your mummy was doing with that strange lady?

MERCY: She was overwrought, Miss Buckridge. *(She rises.)* I tried to comfort her.

JUNE: How absolutely sweet of you. And how well you have succeeded.

With Mercy protesting, June grabs Alice and sets a punishment: Alice must take a drink of June's bath water. Alice cries "No, no, *no!*" against this revolting suggestion. Mercy, shocked, advises Alice to leave June at once. At last Alice makes up her mind: she is leaving June, she begs June to hand Emmeline back to her. Alice bursts into tears.

MERCY *(crossing quickly to Alice):* Can't you see you're upsetting the child. *(She puts her arm protectively around Alice.)*

JUNE *(shouting):* The child? The child is a woman—she's thirty-four.

      Alice sobs loudly.

She's old enough to have a grandchild.

MERCY: Oh, really, now you're exaggerating.

JUNE *(to Alice):* Am I? *Am* I?

ALICE *(whimpering):* Don't George—don't.

JUNE *(with disgust):* Look at you: whimpering and pleading. Have you no backbone, can't you stand up like a man?

ALICE *(sobbing):* I can't—help it.

JUNE *(imitating her savagely):* "I can't help it." She'll never be any different—feckless, self-indulgent. *(She throws the doll onto the sofa.)*

ALICE *(jumping up and running towards the bedroom door):* I'm going. I'm packing my bag.

      June intercepts Alice, grabs her by the arm and drags her to center stage.

JUNE: Come back here.

MERCY: Let her go. Let her go.

JUNE *(to Mercy):* You've got yourself a prize packet there, and no mistake.

ALICE *(screaming):* Let me go! *(She wrenches herself free and collapses on the floor, weeping.)*

JUNE *(after a pause; looking down at Alice):* She had an illegitimate child when she was eighteen.

      Alice weakly covers her ears.

She gave it away—to strangers. She's got a daughter of sixteen.

      Alice sobs.

Do what you like—you make me sick.

June sits, takes another drink of gin. She remains sitting and not looking at the other two. Mercy takes command: she orders Alice to stop crying and go pack her things, which Alice does.

Mercy apologizes to June, who indicates "no hard feelings" with a shake of her head. Mercy switches on the radio as she gives June a parting piece of advice.

MERCY: . . . . . Remember: Sister George was killed, not because she was hated, but because she was loved.
> *Alice enters from the bedroom. She carries a mackintosh and a small suitcase.*

If you study anthropology, you'll discover that in primitive societies it was always the best-loved member of the community who was selected as the sacrificial victim. They felt that by killing him the goodness and strength of the victim would pass into them. It was both a purge and a rededication. What are you about to hear is the purge and—
> *The slow tolling of a bell sounds softly from the radio.*

—rededication of *Applehurst.* Goodbye, Sister George.
> *Mercy crosses to the arch and looks back. Alice picks up the doll Emmeline, hesitates and looks back at June.*

ALICE: I think she's right in what she said, George—Mrs. Mercy, I mean. I love you, too, that's why I've got to leave you. You do understand, don't you? I mean . . . *(She weeps and looks almost impatiently at Mercy.)* All right, Mrs. Mercy, I'm coming.
> *Mercy exits through the arch.*

Goodbye, George, and—you know—thanks for everything.
> *Alice exits through the arch. June, who has not looked up, remains sitting. An Announcer's voice is heard from the radio, backed up by the tolling bell.*

ANNOUNCER: *Applehurst,* a chronicle of an English village. This is a sad day for Applehurst. The church bell is tolling for the funeral of Sister George, the well-beloved District Nurse, whose forthright, practical, no-nonsense manner had endeared her to the community, but death—
> *Very soft music, a slow and minor variation on the "Applehurst Theme" is heard over the Announcer's voice and continues softly to the end of the scene.*

—comes to the best of us, and the picturesque village of Applehurst is today swathed in mourning.

JUNE *(a very plaintive sound):* Moo! *(Louder.)* Moo! Moo! *(A heart-rending sound)*
> *The music increases in volume as the curtain falls.*

O O O
O O O
O O O
O O O
O O O
O O O

HAMP

A Play in Three Acts

BY JOHN WILSON

Based on an episode from the novel Return to the Wood
by J.L. Hodson

Cast and credits appear on page 416

JOHN WILSON was born in 1921 in Hamilton, Scotland. He spent most of his working life in Scotland, though he now lives in London. He is a novelist, short story writer (for magazines on both sides of the Atlantic), radio, television and screen play writer and now a playwright with a Best Play to his credit in his debut. The story of Hamp *was based on an episode of the novel* Return to the Wood *by J.L. Hodson. It made its first dramatized appearance in screen play form in the movie* King *and* Country, *directed by Joseph Losey and shown in America during the 1963-64 season. Wilson then turned his screen play into a stage play which was produced in Edinburgh and London and now in New York.*

190

INTRODUCTION BY THE PLAYWRIGHT *

This story is about a group of men who, required to implement a law they believe to be in principle necessary and just, experience its workings in practise as horrifyingly wrong.

It is the law which defines their Army's right to punish desertion by death. They believe that the circumstances of their war, in particular the possibility of mass desertions from their Army, justify its assumption of this right. Yet they find that the death of their own deserter, Hamp, even while they are preparing for it in the ceremony of a court-martial, is unimaginable to them. It is quite unthinkable—yet it must happen. When it does happen, they know they are taking part in an act of ritual murder.

They know that in terms of their law Hamp has been justly proved guilty beyond any doubt; but for the rest of their lives they will not be able to forget his innocence.

JOHN WILSON

Time: 1917 during the Battle of Passchendaele

Place: The Western Front near Passchendaele

ACT I

SYNOPSIS: A small barn is serving as a British Army prison near the fighting front in World War I. The entrance to the barn is at right. Some of the walled barnyard is visible upstage center. A Corporal, who is also a jailer, sits writing a report. The prisoner, Hamp, is hidden behind a bale of straw, but he can be heard playing the harmonica.

Hamp stops playing and pokes his head above the straw; he is young, ingenuous, a bit rumpled in appearance. He wonders aloud what "they" intend doing with him. The Corporal, a little too sharply, remarks that "they" can hardly afford to let Hamp off scot-free after what he did.

Lieutenant Hargreaves arrives just outside the door with a Guard Private, and the Corporal joins them (as Hamp rises to eavesdrop on their conversation). Hargreaves is capable, articulate, experienced—an intellect and a personality to be reckoned with.

HARGREAVES: How is he behaving?
CORPORAL: He's—oh yes, he's all right, sir.

* These comments were made as an introduction to the published version of *Hamp* and were designated by the author to introduce his play here.

HARGREAVES: No trouble?

CORPORAL: No, sir.

GUARD: He's not like that, sir.

CORPORAL: Only, he doesn't know how it could turn out. He doesn't give no sign of knowing, sir, if you see what I mean.

GUARD: That's true, sir. You can't help remarkin' on it. It's like he's not much bothered most of the time.

Hamp loses interest in their talk, rummages in the straw for eggs, finds a few. Hargreaves warns the Corporal and the Guard Private not to relax the rules with Hamp; treat him by the book. Hargreaves enters the prison part of the barn. When Hamp sees the officer he jumps to his feet, but it is too late to present a soldierly appearance (Hargreaves warns Hamp he should keep up a smart soldierly appearance, even in prison).

Hamp knows Hargreaves; has seen him in battle (though Hargreaves doesn't remember Hamp). Hargreaves is a solicitor by profession. Hamp accepts him readily as defense counsel for the coming court-martial. Hargreaves begins to take notes on Hamp. Age? 23. Occupation (before joining the Army in 1914)?

HAMP: I had a trade, sir. I were what they call a Little Piecer. It's a trade in t'mills. Cotton, like.

HARGREAVES: Yes—I've heard of it.

HAMP: Lamton I come from.

HARGREAVES: Yes, I have a note of that. Now—

HAMP: D'you know it, like, sir?

HARGREAVES: Mm?

HAMP: Lamton. I were wondering if you—

HARGREAVES: Yes, I do know it as a matter of fact. My home's not far from there.

HAMP: I were just wondering.

HARGREAVES: Had you always worked in the mill?

HAMP: Well, like, since I left t'school, sir.

HARGREAVES: When was that?

HAMP: Long while now, sir.

HARGREAVES: Yes, but I mean, how old were you?

HAMP: Twelve, sir.

HARGREAVES: And this was your only job from then until the time when you joined up?

HAMP: Weren't much else in Lamton, sir, were there? You would know. Same as—(Pause.)

HARGREAVES: Yes?

HAMP: No—I were only going to say, same as my father and grandad afore. My grandad did sixteen hours a day in his time.

Hargreaves continues to draw information from Hamp. Hamp is married, has one child, a boy. Hamp and his wife always lived with her mother. Hamp's platoon commander—Lieutenant Webb, whom Hamp likes—has told Hargreaves that there is something wrong at home in Hamp's case. Yes—Hamp got a letter telling him his wife had taken up with another man.

Hargreaves points out that this is a mitigating morale factor—an excuse, possibly. But Hamp didn't keep the letter, and the only person he mentioned it to, an acquaintance named Willie, has been killed.

Hargreaves prompts Hamp to say that his wife's infidelity preyed on his mind. Hamp agrees to so testify if Hargreaves wants—but all Hargreaves wants from Hamp (he insists) is the truth. Hamp isn't sure exactly what the truth is.

HAMP: . . . . . D'you think it'll come out all right, sir?

HARGREAVES: What d'you mean—all right? It can't be all right. Don't you realize, man, this is—

HAMP: What I mean is, sir—like, they could make this into a shooting job, according to rights. According to the book, like.

HARGREAVES *(gravely):* So you are aware of that?

HAMP: But I expect it'll come out all right.

HARGREAVES *(after a baffled pause):* Tell me, Hamp—why did you enlist?

HAMP: Same as everybody else I reckon, sir.

HARGREAVES: No, that won't do. Think back.

HAMP *(trying it out, because he has to say something):* Well, king and country, sir.

HARGREAVES: That does you credit, if it's true.

HAMP: They egged me on as well.

HARGREAVES: You mean they dared you to join up?

HAMP: Aye, sir, it were more that than—

HARGREAVES: Who did?

HAMP *(trying to be crafty):* Well, like, the wife, sir.

HARGREAVES *(hopefully):* Is that true?

HAMP: Well, I could say it, if—

HARGREAVES: Now, Hamp, I warned you!

HAMP: She never said anything against it—and that's not telling a lie.

HARGREAVES: Did anyone—dare you?

HAMP: Well, it were her mother, mostly. They never thought I would go, but I did.

And he had no way of knowing how horrible it was going to be (the same for everybody, Hargreaves reminds him). Hamp was among the first to come out—with Kitchener's army. Hamp volunteered for this duty because he didn't know any better. (As to that last comment, Hargreaves warns Hamp, he must learn to guard his tongue, he will need sympathy at the trial). Now Hamp is the last one left from his original unit. He has been through many battles, and he has been wounded lightly.

Now Hamp has Hargreaves to speak for him—and Hargreaves can say it all so much better than Hamp can.

Hargreaves wants Hamp to tell him exactly what happened the day he ran away. Hamp begins his story but soon breaks off and rings the bell for the guard. He must go to the latrine at once.

Lieutenant Webb, Hamp's platoon commander, arrives to see Hargreaves, who asks the Corporal to show Webb in and hold Hamp in the guard room until they are through consulting. Hargreaves rolls and lights a cigarette as Webb enters.

WEBB: Hello, Bill. Are you going to get this gormless little bastard off, d'you think?

HARGREAVES: What's the matter with you?

WEBB: All this bloody pomp and circumstance about—that.

HARGREAVES: What would you do? Just shoot him?

WEBB: It's going to happen anyway, isn't it?

HARGREAVES: Not necessarily. In fact, not if I can help it.

WEBB: By God, you mean it don't you?

HARGREAVES: You can't do this job without thinking a bit about it.

WEBB: Dangerous game, Bill.

HARGREAVES: Why the hell do they allow anything like that out here?

WEBB: He's quite cheerful, I hear. Probably thinks his troubles are over now.

Webb grudgingly admits Hamp's record has been pretty good up till now. Webb will testify to this effect, if Hargreaves so wishes. What Webb resents is, they'll all waste so much effort going through the motions with this little nonentity.

Would they *really* shoot Hamp? Hargreaves wonders. They would, Webb says, and furthermore he guesses that he would be picked to command the firing squad. So he has good reason for not wanting Hamp shot—but he would execute Hamp if ordered to do it, because obeying orders is what he's here for.

Webb gets away before Hamp comes in to resume his account of *why*. "I couldn't stand it no more, sir" he tells Hargreaves. He nearly ran away before.

HARGREAVES: But you're a soldier, man. You've got to stand it. You stood it all the other times.

HAMP: I'm not saying there were sense in it, sir, but—

HARGREAVES: Suppose your comrades had ever run away and left *you* to it—say, at Loos, or Trones Wood—you'd have been in a fine mess, wouldn't you?

HAMP (*after thinking about this*): I don't think it could have been much worse nor it were, sir—and that's the God's truth.

Hargreaves is momentarily silenced by this.

HARGREAVES: All right. Now, from the beginning, tell me what happened.

HAMP: Well, I were in that attack, sir. It were very bad.

HARGREAVES: Yes, I know.

HAMP: Didn't get wounded—but the time when this came into my head were—I got blown into a shell-hole. It were a deep one, deepest muck ever I saw. I thought I were done for, sure—getting sucked down into t'muck. Only just when I were going right under two of the lads saw it. They gave me butt-end of a rifle and they pulled me out. It's not sense, sir, but that were worse nor anything else that ever came on me afore. It were same as I couldn't get over it, like. I couldn't stand it no more—after.

But Hamp got out of that attack all right, and his battalion was sent back for a rest. Ten days later, from the rest area, not from the front, Hamp deserted: "Same as I said, sir. I couldn't stand it no more." From the shell-hole incident on, he was "different in himself." He couldn't stand the sound of guns any more. Webb understood, and gave Hamp extra rum to tide him over.

Hamp "knew all the time I were going to do what I did"—not that he actually planned desertion, but he knew he could not go back up the line. He doesn't know why he waited ten days to run away. Hargreaves suggests maybe Hamp was trying to find his strength again, and Hamp agrees that it's possible.

Hamp went to see the Medical Officer at one point (Hargreaves regards this as important). He told the doctor—Captain O'Sullivan—that he couldn't sleep more than ten minutes at a time and couldn't stop shaking. Hamp was telling the doctor the *truth*. The doctor merely gave Hamp a pill for his bowels. Hamp didn't take it; it was the last thing he needed. He wanted medicine for his nerves—he had read about such stuff—but the doctor merely accused him of having cold feet. This incident did not (as Hargreaves prompts) make Hamp feel any more desperate than before, but it certainly didn't do him any good.

In any case "I knew all the time I weren't going to go back up the line."

HARGREAVES: So you *had* made up your mind to desert?

HAMP: No, sir. It's the God's truth I were wanting to stop myself, but it's same as I couldn't help it.

HARGREAVES: You knew before you went that the battalion was going to be sent back into the line?

HAMP: Yes, sir.

HARGREAVES: Was that what finally decided you?

HAMP: No, sir.

HARGREAVES: Is that true?

HAMP: Yes, sir.

HARGREAVES: What did decide you, then?

HAMP: There weren't nothing special, sir. Only, it were same as this night were the time for it. This night, soon as it got dark, like, I put on a bandolier, took me gas helmet and rifle—let on I had to go on a message—and I just started walking.

HARGREAVES: Did you know where you were making for?

HAMP: I were walking away from it, sir, that were the most of it.

It happened that no one stopped Hamp. He walked away from the guns, and soon he had an idea he was making for Lamton. He got onto a train when it stopped for a crossing in the middle of the night, and when he woke up the sun was shining and there was no sound of guns. When Hamp got off the train he was arrested. He pretended to be on leave, but he had no papers.

For a moment, Hamp is worried about the punishment. He has been out longer than anybody; he doesn't see how they can shoot him.

HAMP: . . . . . I don't reckon to get off, but—I dunna think they'll bother shooting the like o' me.

HARGREAVES: I tell you again—military law lays it down quite clearly that —Unless we can convince the Court that you were acting under extraordinary and intolerable strain at the time when you committed this crime you will almost certainly be sentenced to death. Don't you understand that?

HAMP: If you tell me, sir. But—

HARGREAVES: Yes?

HAMP: I mean, this were the first time—

HARGREAVES: For the crime of cowardice in battle once is enough. . . . .

Any history of mental illness in Hamp's family? No, nor in Hamp's own case. Of course, none of them realized what they were getting into when they came out with the Army. The same for everybody, Hargreaves repeats, and he asks Hamp again if anything special was preying on his mind.

Hamp thinks perhaps the death of his friend Willie—well, perhaps not a friend, but someone who lived up the street in Lamton—was and is on his mind. It was a quick death.

HAMP: . . . . . Couldn't tell you what kind of shell it were. I were nobbut five-six yards away, like, and I were only bleeding—scratches—five-six yards from him—but Willie weren't nowhere—only all over me. Bits. Red and yellow. You know what it's like without me telling you. They had to give me a new uniform.

Pause.

Same as I were saying, sir—couldn't tell you what were special about it, but it's the God's truth it's in my mind, like, if that's what you want to know. Not as bad as it was for a while, but—

HARGREAVES: Yes. Yes, I understand.

HAMP: I'm still seeing it, like, sir, that's what I mean. True, sir.

HARGREAVES: Yes. I know.

Silence as he packs up his notes, etc.

Now listen, there's one more thing I want to ask you—perhaps the most important thing of all. It's about something I'll want to say in court—perhaps ask you there too. Could you be relied on, if the Court were lenient enough to send you to prison, could you be relied upon to do your duty when you came out?

HAMP: I would try my best, sir.

HARGREAVES: I mean, could you be relied on to go up the line and stay up? I mean exactly that—nothing less. Do you understand me? Do you?

HAMP: Yes, sir.

HARGREAVES: Well?

HAMP: Sir?

HARGREAVES: Yes?

HAMP: Is there nobbut else for it, sir? Do I have to tell them that?

HARGREAVES: Yes. Could you? Could you be relied on?

HAMP: I'll say it if you can tell me, sir.

HARGREAVES: If I can tell you what?

HAMP: If you know any way of being sure, sir.

HARGREAVES: Who the hell d'you think I am, man? God Almighty?
Exit. Curtain.

ACT II

Hamp's court martial is convened in one of the war-damaged rooms of a nearby chateau. Sitting in judgment (at right) are a brigadier-general (the President of the Court), a captain and two lieutenants. Captain Prescott, a lawyer, sits with them to advise them on legal matters.

The prosecuting officer, Captain Midgley, sits near the Court at right. Hamp and Hargreaves are positioned at left. Witnesses stand facing the audience upstage center. The Corporal is serving as Court Usher.

Under Hargreaves's direct examination, the Padre testifies that judging from his knowledge of the prisoner, Hamp shouldn't be found guilty of desertion. But under cross-examination the Padre admits he didn't know Hamp, personally, before the incident. The Padre is basing his belief on his subsequent knowledge of Hamp's innocent and honest nature.

PADRE: I don't believe he can be blamed to the extent that the charge states, or to the appalling extent of the penalty it implies.

MIDGLEY: I must put it to you, Padre, that the sentence of the Court, if he is found guilty, is no concern of yours.

PADRE: Can any of us help being concerned?

Midgley gets the Padre to admit that there are *no* circumstances under which he would approve of a sentence of death for cowardice. So the Padre's opinion is valueless. His Christianity is a prejudice.

Midgley states his position: he is not here to demand Hamp's death; he is merely doing his duty as prosecuting officer, under the law.

Hargreaves postulates the facts of the desertion but argues that because of the state of Hamp's mental health he could not be held responsible for his actions.

Webb takes the stand and testifies that after the shell-hole incident Hamp's nerve was gone. Under questioning by the President of the Court, Webb admits that others were in a bad way too. Webb is only guessing that Hamp was worse off than the others, because of what Hamp did.

HARGREAVES: Was Private Hamp well liked in the platoon?

WEBB: Yes. Always whacked out anything he had. And of course he's the nearest we've got now to a founder member. He had a name for brewing a good cup of tea too.

HARGREAVES: What sort of soldier would you say he was before this happened?

WEBB: About average, near enough. Nothing special one way or the other. Not particularly bright. But one thing about him—he was never a grouser.

HARGREAVES: From all your experience of him you regarded him as a reasonable average?

WEBB: Yes. He's not a born soldier, but not many of us are.

HARGREAVES: Were you surprised when you heard he'd gone absent?

WEBB: Yes, I was.

HARGREAVES: Can you tell us why?

WEBB: It just wasn't like him. He—

HARGREAVES: Yes?

WEBB (looking at Hamp): Well, to tell you the truth, I wouldn't have said he had enough gumption to do anything of the kind.

Webb thinks it was a sign that Hamp must have been "seriously out of balance." Hamp must have been mentally ill.

Under cross-examination, Webb testifies that he didn't actually detect Hamp's mental illness, but it must have been present. Hamp had had a bad time, over a long period of time, longer than most.

MIDGLEY: Perhaps longer than the others in your platoon, yes, but surely there are plenty of men in the company whose service is as long as his and longer?

WEBB: I don't know about plenty, but there are some. Anyhow, length of service isn't the only thing that counts. We're not all built the same way. As they say, every man has his own war.

MIDGLEY: Yes, I've heard the phrase too, but—

WEBB: You know very well it's only one soldier in a thousand who never gets windy.

MIDGLEY: Yes, that's exactly what I'm suggesting. Every man, as you say, has his own war, against his own fear. Wouldn't you agree that's what the phrase means?

WEBB: That's not what I was getting at.

MIDGLEY: Nevertheless, isn't it true? And isn't it true that, however much we may regret it, and however much we may sympathize, isn't it true that this man simply allowed his own fear to become his master, instead of mastering it as his duty required him to do?

WEBB: There's a lot more in it than that.

Midgley finishes with Webb, who steps down. Hamp raises his hand—he has to go to the latrine, and the Corporal escorts him. The President asks Hargreaves about his case and is told there is only one more witness, Captain O'Sullivan, the Chief Medical Officer.

PRESIDENT: About when do you expect to have your case completed?

HARGREAVES: I can't really be sure, it depends on—

PRESIDENT: By lunch-time, d'you think?

HARGREAVES: By when, sir?

PRESIDENT: Lunch-time.

HARGREAVES: I may have, but I don't know. *(Then sharply, slightly losing control.)* A man's life is at stake, sir.

PRESIDENT *(after a pause):* I don't think any of us is unaware of that, Mr. Hargreaves.

> *Then, after an accusing silence from Hargreaves, he is forced to go on.*

I think perhaps we might have another window open. Getting a bit stuffy.

> *Lieutenant moves to open window.*

HARGREAVES: I'm sorry, sir, if I—

PRESIDENT *(to Lieutenant as he comes back):* Thank you. You will of course be given all the time you require, Mr. Hargreaves.

> *Hargreaves acknowledges with a slight bow of head.*

Hamp returns with the corporal. The medical officer—Captain O'Sullivan —is called in to testify (he is *"tired-looking and capless"*). His medical records show that Hamp came to him with a common complaint: "nerves" (he didn't record Hamp's specific symptoms, like the inability to sleep, and the trembling). Captain O'Sullivan didn't believe Hamp.

HARGREAVES: . . . . . If you didn't believe this man, you must have decided that he was lying.

O'SULLIVAN: I didn't believe he had any right to expect from me—what he obviously did expect.

HARGREAVES: I must again repeat the question. Did this man tell you any lies, and if so, what were they?

O'SULLIVAN: He obviously expected me to relieve him from front-line duty —send him down the line.

HARGREAVES: Captain O'Sullivan, did he say so?

O'SULLIVAN: Did he what?

HARGREAVES: Did he ask you to relieve him from battle-duty?

O'SULLIVAN: I didn't need him to tell me what he was after. He wasn't the first one.

HARGREAVES: Would it be fair to say that you may now have reconsidered your statement that he lied to you?

O'SULLIVAN: I didn't say he lied.

HARGREAVES: I put it to you, again, that you said a moment ago you didn't believe this man's story, and you quite clearly conveyed the impression that he lied to you. Will you now either withdraw that allegation or tell us specifically what the lie or lies consisted of?

O'SULLIVAN: I think he exaggerated his symptoms.

O'Sullivan did nothing further to investigate Hamp's case; he merely assumed that it resembled all the other examples of goldbricking in his experience. O'Sullivan recalls that he had a talk with Hamp; gently; man-to-man. In Hargreaves' words, O'Sullivan "gave him a laxative, talked to him for a few minutes, then told him to go away and pull himself together."

O'SULLIVAN: It's not my job to supply a man with guts if he hasn't got enough of his own.

HARGREAVES: Did you consider the possibility that his nervous and mental stability might be seriously disturbed, and that he should be sent down the line for diagnosis by a specialist in that kind of illness?

O'SULLIVAN: I did not. Suppose I did think of such a thing, every time a man comes complaining of "nerves", suppose I did think of sending him down the line for psychological treatment, what d'you think the state and strength of this battalion would be? You can ask me clever questions till you're blue in the face, but I know that illness and lack of guts are two different things. I'm here to fight illness—they have to fight the other thing for themselves. We all have.

Hargreaves cites the illness known as "shell-shock." O'Sullivan admits this is an illness but insists Hamp was not suffering from shell-shock. Hargreaves' questions suggest that the doctor wouldn't have been able to recognize the exact point at which shell-shock set in, before it became advanced enough to be obvious. The doctor evades these questions and is reprimanded by Hargreaves, who in turn receives a reprimand from the President.

O'Sullivan insists he was sure there was no shell-shock in Hamp's case. True, it was a short examination, but he cannot be expected to let wounded men wait while he wastes time on psychological problems. And if he did— "—suppose I did admit this sort of thing as a proper reason for a man going sick, what d'you think it would do to the morale of the company? (Then he loses his temper suddenly.) I'll tell you this. I not only disagree in my own mind with the line you're taking—I consider I have a duty to resist it! I believe this whole rigmarole of yours here is a ridiculous waste of time—all this damned debating over one miserable—little—when thousands of men are being—"

The President admonishes the Captain. Hargreaves points out that Hamp behaved so stupidly in his manner of deserting that he couldn't have been in possession of his senses.

CAPTAIN: Are you suggesting, Mr. Hargreaves, that desertion—or absence from duty—are you suggesting that we should regard such an action merely as a symptom of illness?

HARGREAVES: No, sir. But—

PRESIDENT: You seem to have come very near to it, I must say.

HARGREAVES: I'm trying, sir, to—because it's my duty here, I'm trying to bring all of us as near as we can get to the truth.

PRESIDENT: We must none of us forget why we are here, Mr. Hargreaves. We are not here primarily to examine the individual character of this man, or even to consider the predicament he finds himself in—now or in the past— however much sympathy we may feel for him. I can understand your obvious concern for the individual man in this soldier's uniform—and remember our law is so concerned for him too—that's why we're here, spared by the Army from its war up there. But the law must also be concerned with him as a sol- dier—*and* concerned for his comrades. I can understand why you have ap- pealed to our sympathy for the man who is here within our sight, but it is our duty to resist your appeal and reach a just verdict not only about this man, but about this soldier and about what this soldier has done. Have you any more questions for Captain O'Sullivan?

HARGREAVES: No, sir.

Midgley cross-examines briefly. The doctor insists that Hamp was fit for duty, provided he could be discouraged from malingering.

Then Hamp takes the stand. He tells the court about the mud in the shell hole (he felt as though devils were after him). The President asks Hamp whether the devils stayed with him, but Hamp isn't sure that they did. Then why did he run away? "I don't rightly know, sir, not rightly. I couldn't stand it no more, I can't rightly say it. Mr. Hargreaves can tell you better." Hamp, it seems, has trouble answering clearly when anyone other than Hargreaves is questioning him.

Under Hargreaves' questioning Hamp testifies—rather mechanically—that he didn't know what he was doing when he ran away—his wife's infidelity was preying on his mind—he ran away without thinking, he had made no plan.

HARGREAVES *(more hopefully):* Had you any idea where you were going?

HAMP: I were only wantin' to get left alone for a bit, sir, that's all.

HARGREAVES: Did you—?

PRESIDENT: You say you wanted to be left alone "for a bit." Does that mean you intended to go back to the battalion?

HAMP *(after looking helplessly at Hargreaves):* I don't know, sir.

PRESIDENT: This is a very important question, Private Hamp. I can't em- phasize too much how important it is. Did you intend to return to the bat- talion?

HAMP *(in great difficulty):* Honest to God, sir, I—I can't say.

HARGREAVES *(sudden outburst):* My God, can't you see it's because he didn't know what he was doing. He doesn't know how to lie to you.

Then he turns to Hamp and asks, very gently.

Wasn't it simply because you can't clearly remember?

HAMP: That's right, sir.

Hamp can't remember why he ran away. He had no plan, but he couldn't stop himself. He tells Hargreaves: "Same as you told me to say, sir, I couldn't help it." But he wishes Hargreaves would do *all* the talking for him, Hargreaves says it all so much better.

Midgely cross-examines: did Hamp know he was doing wrong? Hamp didn't think much about that. He just couldn't stop himself, he might have stayed if there had been someone to stop him.

MIDGLEY: Let me put it to you quite simply. Did you know what you were doing?

HAMP: Yes, sir. But I couldn't help myself.

MIDGLEY: And you knew your comrades were staying at their posts, prepared to do their duty while you were deserting them? Didn't you? Didn't you?

HAMP *(after a pause—beaten):* I never did the like of this before, sir, never. This were the very first time.

MIDGLEY *(to President):* That's all, sir.

Hargreaves sums up the defense: as the Battle of Passchendaele continues within their hearing, they are concerned with one of its mentally wounded; with "a question of responsibility. I believe it is something about which we are only now beginning to learn a little wisdom—I mean the extent to which a man may be blamed, or should be punished, for such things as Captain O'Sullivan calls 'lack of guts.' "

This may be a dangerous question, Hargreaves continues, but it must be faced. Obviously, Hamp is not a liar, is not cunning—Hargreaves could have wished he were a little quicker with his answers, in fact. Hamp did what he did because he had been maimed by war, "maimed in many battles, the question of yes or no, courage or cowardice, had gone beyond his responsibility, and, I believe, beyond our right to make a sacrifice of him. If we do, I believe it will be on our consciences for the rest of our lives."

Midgley makes no closing statement. Prescott—the legal advisor to this Court—explains that Hamp is innocent unless proved guilty beyond a reasonable doubt. He maximizes the doctor's testimony and minimizes "the eloquence of the Defending Officer." He explains other points of law and evidence.

Hamp exits under guard, in drill fashion, and the Court retires to consider its verdict. Webb enters and talks over the case with Hargreaves. They won't know the verdict for several days, until after the Commander in Chief has given it his O.K. But Hargreaves has a tip: if the Court finds the prisoner guilty they will ask to see his conduct sheet; if not, not.

If Webb had his way he would "send the poor sod up the line and hope he gets a packet."

HARGREAVES: You think O'Sullivan was quite right then?

WEBB: Listen, why don't we just admit when there's nobody listening—friend Hamp was no more off his head than you or me? He'll tell you himself—he hasn't the bloody sense to go off his head.

HARGREAVES: So he was just a plain coward?

WEBB: Christ, I don't know if he has the sense to be that either.

HARGREAVES: That's the real trouble, isn't it? You can't call him any names. He's just bloody Hamp. He can't help it. Never pretended to be anything else.

WEBB: Well, if you want an argument, the Army can't help being the Army.

Hamp had one false pretense, Hargreaves admits—he pretended to be a soldier. But the Army is entitled to shoot Hamp, Webb asserts, because his stupidity—his cowardice—is infectious. Webb helped Hamp for the reason stated: "Top of the list for the bloody executioner if it's on."

Hamp asks to see Hargreaves and is brought in. He only wants to apologize for his poor performance and to thank Hargreaves—in case he is sent to prison and doesn't see Hargreaves soon again.

HARGREAVES: This isn't a bloody game, you know.

HAMP: It's not same as I haven't thought about it, sir. I have—honest. I know the way it could turn out. I'm only hopin'—that's what I mean. And Lieutenant Hargreaves—he made the best of it—I were only wantin' to tell him he's been very good to me. Wouldn't have no chance if it wasn't for him. But I were only tryin' to look on the cheery side—no sense doin' anythin' else.

HARGREAVES: All right. And thank you. Now you'd better go back if there's nothing more. We'll see you later.

HAMP: Yes, sir. *(Then, as he is about to be taken away.)* In case I forget, sir, Corporal here got a message from them in there.

CORPORAL: It's nothing important, sir. I would have told you.

HAMP: Well, I were thinking maybe it's—like, quite a good sign—them wanting to see what's been put down about me before. I mean, same as you said to them, there's not been much against me.

HARGREAVES: What was the message?

HAMP: Well, Corporal says they want to see my conduct sheet, like, sir.
Curtain.

ACT III

Scene 1

Two weeks later, Hamp is in the barn-prison as before, playing the harmonica. The Corporal comes in to tell Hamp (whom he calls "Arthur") that his outfit is back from a bad time up the line, and that the Guard has saved up some rum for a song-fest tonight.

But the Corporal is interrupted by the Guard Private, who takes him aside and tells him that Hamp is to be executed tomorrow morning. Poor Hamp had been hoping for the best. They decide not to tell him. Instead, they take him to the guard room, where it's warm, for a drink.

Hargreaves, Webb and the Padre come in. It has been decided that Hamp's guilt is clear-cut, his sentence is death. Webb has been assigned the duty, as he feared. In this ritual it is the Orderly Officer's duty to tell Hamp (the song-fest offstage can now be heard). Webb insists it must be done at once—"He still won't believe in it anyway, you wait. God knows he's been told definitely enough already—it was only a question of when, but he still managed to expect it would be all right."

Hargreaves and the Padre have a bitter taste in their mouths. The Padre will stay with Hamp all night. Webb, too, has made arrangements to help Hamp: rum and morphia. Hargreaves pulls the bell to summon the guard (and the singing dies). The Padre comments, "Apparently there's no objection if the prisoner makes himself insensible beforehand."

Hargreaves sends the Corporal for Hamp—time Hamp was told. The Medical Officer has given the Padre the green light to render any assistance he thinks Hamp requires. Webb announces his intention of administering the morphia himself. Everything is set to go like clockwork. Everything has been arranged, nothing forgotten—"Only mercy," the Padre comments.

A Sergeant Major and Orderly Officer enter, soon followed by the Corporal and Hamp. Webb slips away.

HAMP (to Hargreaves): Is it—word, like, sir?
SERGEANT MAJOR: Prisoner—shun!
ORDERLY OFFICER: Private A. Hamp, Number 873426, it is my duty to inform you that the General Officer Commanding in Chief has decided that the sentence passed on you by a Field General Court Martial to suffer death by being shot for desertion is to be carried out on Thursday, September 16th at 05:30 hours.
HAMP (after a silence, to Hargreaves): When's that, sir?
HARGREAVES: Tomorrow.
PADRE: Tomorrow morning.
HAMP: Are they goin' to do it, then?
HARGREAVES: It's been ordered. There's nothing else for it.

Hamp is silent. The Sergeant Major, Corporal and Orderly Officer go out. Hargreaves pours Hamp a drink. The Padre tries to comfort Hamp: God will see and understand. Plenty of his comrades are dying right now in battle, they will keep him company. Jesus loves him. Hamp need not fear death.

Hamp cannot get out anything but "Yes, sir" and he tolds out his cup to Hargreaves for another drink. But immediately Hamp finds he must give the signal for the latrine, and he goes out with the Corporal. What can the Padre say to Hamp, how can he help him? Hargreaves comments bitterly that at least now Hamp finally understands he is going to be shot, that in itself is something.

Webb comes in with bottles of rum, a mug and a medical syringe, which he acquired from Captain O'Sullivan.

WEBB: . . . . . He didn't like the idea, but he liked it a lot better than doing it himself. There's enough here and more to put a man out for twenty-four hours. Saw the Sergeant Pioneer too, by the way—arranged for rope and a chair to lash him on to. Might as well do that before we take him out. He'll have to be carried out anyhow—and he'll have to be lashed onto something upright for the shooting. At least, that's if—what d'you think, Padre?

PADRE: Yes, I think you're right about the morphia. I shouldn't say it, but I can't see any other way. But will you let me try to give him Communion first?

WEBB: That's your department. But I think after that the sooner the better.

PADRE: Yes. There isn't any right way.

WEBB (to Hargreaves): What the hell are you looking at me like that for?

HARGREAVES: Do you believe it's going to happen? Do you believe you're going to do it?

WEBB: All right, I'll tell you. Once. This is the worst bloody thing ever, but I can't see any difference between doing it and watching it. Maybe better get it to do—make sure nobody else makes a muck of it—I like things practical, all right? There are different ways of trying to help him, you know.

The Padre lays out an altar cloth, arranging a Communion table. Hargreaves pours a drink for Webb, as Hamp comes back with the Corporal. Hamp has been sick but feels better now. He accepts another rum and takes a long pull of it.

HAMP (to Hargreaves): Did you think you'd got me off, sir?

HARGREAVES: I tried to tell you there wasn't much hope that the verdict would be changed.

HAMP: I were sure you would manage it, sir. I were sweating on it. I don't mind telling you I never thought they would go to the bother of this (Another pull.) I reckon it'll be quick, sir?

HARGREAVES: Yes.

HAMP: D'you reckon it's fair?

HARGREAVES (after a silence): I don't know. It's not for me to say.

HAMP: I could've been still working at home. Same as you said to them— I weren't made to come here.

Hargreaves offers to write letters home for Hamp. Hamp wonders what Hargreaves will tell Hamp's family when Hargreaves writes—after.

HARGREAVES: I'll say you died like a soldier.

HAMP: It's not true, sir.
HARGREAVES: It could be.
HAMP: I'll try my best *(Another pull.)* I will.

Hamp accepts the Padre's invitation to Communion. Hamp kneels at the Communion table and the Padre begins the service. Hamp's head sinks lower until it is resting on the table; he is insensible. The Padre takes Communion on Hamp's behalf. Then Webb and Hargreaves ease Hamp into a prone position in the straw. They send the Corporal out—then Webb administers the morphine. Hamp will know no more.

Hargreaves wonders where the soul is now that Hamp is drugged; the Padre tells him it is still in the body: "I know. And so do you. If not, why are you concerned?" The Padre will remain with Hamp through the night.

PADRE: This is where my work is.
WEBB: I promise you he's out.
PADRE: Yes.
WEBB: So why not be practical? Remember we've all got to be on our best behavior in the morning—C.O.'s ordered the smartest possible turn-out.
PADRE: Go and get some rest—please.
WEBB: There's nothing here. All that's here is a few hours of bloody nothing.
HARGREAVES *(looking back at Hamp, as they go out):* He took it very well, you know.
WEBB: I suppose you were right about him. I suppose he was a likeable little bastard, wasn't he? God damn him and blast him.

Scene 2

Next morning, at early dawn, Hargreaves and the Padre are watching the Corporal and the Guard Private, supervised by Webb, preparing to lift Hamp, who is still unconscious and is now lashed to a chair. Beyond the wall can be heard the sounds of the battalion assembling—shouted drill orders, etc.

They carry Hamp out. Hargreaves has been excused from this parade. He remains with the Padre. Hargreaves tries to write a letter, but cannot. He is slightly drunk. The Padre prays, and Hargreaves takes a swig of whisky. The Padre, too, takes an offered drink: "This makes a kind of ceremony of it. . . . . ."

Hargreaves confesses that he has been drinking all night, and so has Tom Webb, but maybe Webb is able to hold it better.

HARGREAVES: . . . . . Maybe the more ceremony the better. If we surround it with words from your book and a few toasts to old comrades and the full-dress ritual out there we may not even notice it happening at all.
C.O. *(off):* Battalion! Battalion—shun!
        Massive drill movement in response.
PADRE *(meanwhile in rapid prayer):* Almighty God, teach us who survive,

in this and other daily spectacles of mortality, to see how frail and uncertain our own condition is—

C.O. *(off):* Slope—hup!

Drill sounds again.

PADRE: O Saviour of the world, who by Thy cross and precious blood has redeemed us, save us and help us we humbly beseech Thee, O Lord.

WEBB *(off):* Squad! Firing position—hup!

PADRE: Lord, have mercy on us.

WEBB *(off):* One round each man—take aim!

PADRE: Christ, have mercy on us.

WEBB *(off):* Fire!

Sound of ragged firing, two ricochets, startled calls and wingbeats of rooks, frightened neighing from the horses, then silence. Hargreaves during this, having taken another swig from the flask, has gone out of the door to a position from which he can obviously see what is happening and is standing almost involuntarily in a formal "attention" position.

PADRE *(meanwhile):* O Lord God most holy, O Lord most mighty, O holy and most merciful Saviour, deliver him not into the bitter pains of eternal death. For that it has pleased Thee to—

HARGREAVES *(trying to be calm):* Not yet. It may not be finished yet. I don't think it is.

Some crowd reaction, and shouts of "Keep silence."

God knows it must have been atrociously bad shooting. Even worse than he expected.

Sudden single shot, with sound reaction as before.

PADRE: Oh my God—*no.*

HARGREAVES *(walking back):* He was quite prepared to do it. Part of the job if there's any doubt. All part of the ritual.

PADRE: Almighty God, with whom the souls of the faithful after they are delivered from the burden of the flesh are in joy and felicity—for that it pleaseth Thee—

Webb appears in the doorway, putting revolver back in holster, Corporal behind him.

—to deliver this our brother out of the miseries of this sinful world—we give Thee hearty thanks.

WEBB: Waiting for you, Padre. I'm told he's allowed a funeral.

PADRE: There will be no service yet, if that's what they expect.

WEBB: C.O. said he'd leave it to you to decide when. *(To Corporal.)* Tell him no service now, Corporal.

CORPORAL: Sir! *(Exit.)*

WEBB: Means another parade, that's the trouble. Not much time before we move up again. Still, it's your job.

PADRE: I hope I shall do what I have to do at the right time. And I hope I shall not be ashamed of it.

WEBB: None of my business. But are you open to advice, Padre?

PADRE: I hope so, yes.

WEBB: Why not just let me finish the job now? Why not let us bury him and say no more about it? Too many bloody words, all along. Are you ready, Bill?

HARGREAVES *(moving to go):* Yes. *(Then, looking back to Padre.)* It's done now, why not leave it alone? It's a fact.

WEBB: I can vouch for that. And I'll tell you something else—I feel a hell of a lot better for it.

PADRE *(shout):* No!

HARGREAVES *(savagely):* Leave him alone. Leave us all alone to get on with our bloody war.

> *Webb and Hargreaves go out. Padre kneels in prayer, silently, with the sounds of the departing battalion in the background. Curtain.*

CABARET

A Musical Comedy in Two Acts

BOOK BY JOE MASTEROFF

MUSIC BY JOHN KANDER

LYRICS BY FRED EBB

Based on the play I Am a Camera *by John van Druten and stories by Christopher Isherwood*

Cast and credits appear on page 370

JOE MASTEROFF (book) was born in Philadelphia in 1919 and graduated from Temple in 1940. During World War II he served for four years in the Air Force. Pursuing a theater career, he finally made it to Broadway as Howard Lindsay's assistant, and as one of the actors, in The Prescott Proposals *(1954). This was Masteroff's first and last Broadway acting role. In 1956 the Theater Club, a women's organization, cited him as "most promising unproduced playwright" He was finally produced on Broadway on October 20, 1959 when his play* The Warm Peninsula, *starring Julie Harris, opened and ran for 86 performances.*

Masteroff's first musical book was She Loves Me *(1963), with music by Jerry Bock and lyrics by Sheldon Harnick, a Best Play of its season. Now, with* Cabaret, *he has again come up with a Best Play which also won the New York Drama Critics Circle award for best musical—and, what's more, was cited as the best play of the year by that same Theater Club, which, a decade ago, named him "most promising."*

Masteroff now lives in New York City. He is president of the New Dramatists Committee and is its active member of longest standing.

JOHN KANDER (music) is a native of Kansas City (March 18, 1927). He received his B.A. at Oberlin (1951) and his M.A. at Columbia (1953). He gained experience conducting stock productions, and he did the dance arrange-

209

ments for Gypsy *and* Irma La Douce. *He collaborated on the Broadway musical* A Family Affair *(1962) and wrote the incidental music for* Never Too Late *the same year.*

Kander's first collaboration with his Cabaret *lyricist, Fred Ebb, was on the song "My Coloring Book," followed by "I Don't Care Much," a Barbra Streisand hit. In 1965 Kander and Ebb wrote the music and lyrics for the Broadway production* Flora, the Red Menace, *which starred Liza Minnelli.*

FRED EBB (lyrics) is a New Yorker born on April 8, 1932 and educated at New York University and Columbia. He wrote both book and lyrics for the Phoenix Theater production of Morning Sun *(1963). He has contributed lyrics to revues including* Put It in Writing *and* From A to Z *and sketches to the TV show* That Was The Week That Was. *He has collaborated with his* Cabaret *composer, John Kander, on the works listed in Kander's biographical sketch above, and also on several leading night club acts including those of Liza Minnelli, Kaye Ballard, Chita Rivera, Juliette Prowse and Carol Channing.*

Our method of synopsizing Cabaret *in these pages differs from that used for the other nine Best Plays.* Cabaret's *story is told mostly in pictures, to present the total "look" of a popular Broadway musical attraction in the 1966-67 season.*

The photographs depict the succession of scenes as produced and directed by Harold Prince, at the opening November 20, 1966 at the Broadhurst Theater, with dances and cabaret numbers by Ronald Field, scenery by Boris Aronson and costumes by Patricia Zipprodt. Our special thanks are enthusiastically tendered to Mr. Prince and his press representative, Mary Bryant, for help in obtaining the excellent photographs by Friedman-Abeles, plus three by Van Williams.

INTRODUCTION BY THE LYRICIST

Because *Cabaret,* the musical for which I supplied the lyrics, has won many awards, I might be considered a suitable subject by an interviewer. At last! And the interview, as some performers are fond of saying before they go into their next number, might go something like this . . .

Q: Whose idea was *Cabaret?*

A: I honestly don't know. It seems to me that Hal Prince was first attracted to the idea. Or was it Joe Masteroff? Anyway, Joe became the librettist. They worked together for some time before bringing a treatment to John Kander and me.

Q: Do you mean the idea of *Cabaret* or the idea of *I Am a Camera?*

A: Originally we spoke of *I Am a Camera. Cabaret* as it now stands represents many months of development and change in which we all took part.

Q: Why were you attracted to the material?

A: I wasn't.

Q: You weren't?

A: I wasn't. I thought it was entirely too unmusical at first. But Hal was wildly enthusiastic, and I am wildly enthusiastic about Hal. Also, John and I had just written a failure called *Flora, the Red Menace*. I doubt that anyone but Hal would have hired me.

Q: When were you won over?

A: At about the third meeting. I began to realize what Hal and Joe were talking about. The decadence, vulgarity and indifference of Berlin in the early 1930s began to "sing" to me. I think John was hooked at about the same time.

Q: Did any of you think of it as a commercial musical?

A: We never discussed that. After awhile it hardly seemed to matter. The main thing was getting it up there and doing it well.

Q: Will you explain that, please?

A: I don't believe it's practical to sit down and think of writing a "hit" musical. I don't believe you can sit down to write a "hit" song either. The public, to say nothing of the critic, is far too capricious for that. With *Cabaret* I hoped for a hit, naturally. But I wanted it to look right and sound right and come across as we intended. Being commercial with a subject as inflammatory as the emergence of Nazism in Germany seemed a ludicrous consideration.

Q: At what point did *I Am a Camera* become *Cabaret*?

A: Very early on we decided that we would use practically nothing of *I Am a Camera* except the essence of Sally Bowles, who interested and intrigued us. We began to turn more and more to Isherwood's *Berlin Stories* for character and color. But the real form of *Cabaret* came when we hit on the idea of a Master of Ceremonies. This character was a totally original creation, and he personified for us the underlying point of the material. By turning his back on the reality of the story being told upstage, and by dedicating himself solely to his own pleasure, he stood as an indictment of his time and the peculiar morality prevalent then. Originally he was meant to be used in only one or two places. But as the material took shape we found him more and more useful.

Q: What would you say *Cabaret* is about?

A: Commitment. The act of being committed. Its contemporary application is obvious. In November 1966, the very month we opened in New York City, the Neo-Nazi Party won 7.9 percent of the vote in the Hessian State elections. In Bavaria, they won 7.4 percent electing a total of twenty-three persons to the State Parliaments. In Manhattan, the Civilian Review Board was defeated. In California, Watts stood as a grotesque reminder that America could be a cauldron of bitterness and violence. Everywhere one looked it seemed there was unrest and the promise of something more sinister to come. And the worst sin is apathy. Four of the five leading characters in *Cabaret* reject the truth in one way or the other. Sally doesn't believe that politics has anything to do with her ("After all, it's only politics and what has that to do with us?"). Herr Schultz thinks it will all blow over ("Governments come. Governments go."). Fraulein Schneider thinks there is no other way ("What other choice have I?"). And the M.C., of course, chooses to disregard it ("We have no troubles here. Here life is beautiful."). Only Clifford Bradshaw, the writer living with Sally, recognizes the terror of the situation and refuses to remain in the middle of it.

Q: Do you think *Cabaret* is an important musical?

A: Honestly, I don't know. The French say *"Qui vivra verra."* I know it was important to me. And to Hal and John and Joe. And to Boris Aronson who designed it and Pat Zipprodt who clothed it and Ron Field who choreographed it. As for history, who can say? I do know one thing though. A few short years ago it would have been impossible for a musical with this kind of subject matter to succeed. I think the same is true of *West Side Story* and *Fiddler on the Roof.* All of these musicals have been supported by the public. Maybe there are fewer "verboten" topics now. Maybe the musical theater can experiment on a large scale for the first time. And still be "commercial." I think *that's* important, don't you?

FRED EBB

Time: 1929–30, before the start of the Third Reich
Place: Berlin

ACT I

Scene 1: The Master of Ceremonies (Joel Grey, above) appears in a spotlight to greet the audience with the song "Willkommen." "Leave your troubles outside," he urges. "In here life is beautiful." He is joined by an all-girl orchestra and by the Cabaret Girls ("Each and every one a virgin. . . . . Outside it is winter. But here it is so hot—every night we have a battle to keep the girls from taking off all their clothing. So don't go away. Who knows? Tonight we may lose the battle!") Finally the Emcee is joined by waiters, busboys, entertainers, all the Kit Kat Klub folk reflected in a huge tilted mirror upstage, and singing . . .

ALL:
Willkommen, bienvenue, welcome
Fremde, étranger, stranger
Glucklich zu sehen
Je suis enchanté
Happy to see you
Bliebe, reste, stay
Willkommen, bienvenue, welcome
Im cabaret, au cabaret, to cabaret!

Scene 2: On a train to Berlin, Clifford Bradshaw (Bert Convy, below left), an American writer and teacher, helps Ernst Ludwig (Edward Winter, below right) through an awkward moment with the customs. Ernst, a young German whose smuggling may not be entirely harmless, is grateful and promises to open all Berlin doors for Cliff and to become his first pupil in learning English.

Scene 3: In Berlin, Ernst directs Cliff to Fraulein Schneider (Lotte Lenya, above center) who rents him a room. Herr Schultz (Jack Gilford, above left), another tenant, comes in with a bottle of schnapps. Fraulein Schneider sings her feelings about life: "So What?"

FRAULEIN SCHNEIDER:
  So once I was rich and now all my
    fortune is gone,
  So what?
  And love disappeared and only the
    memory lives on,
  So what? . . . . .
  For the sun will rise and the moon will
    set
  And you learn how to settle for what
    you get
  It'll all go on if we're here or not
  So who cares . . . so what?
  So who cares . . . so what?
  So who cares? Who cares? Who cares?
  So what?

Scene 4: Cliff visits the Kit Kat Klub where Sally Bowles (Jill Haworth, below on dais) and Cabaret Girls sing "Don't Tell Mama":

SALLY:
   Mama thinks I'm living in a convent
   A secluded little convent
   In the southern part of France.
   Mama doesn't even have an inkling
   That I'm working in a night club
   In a pair of lacy pants . . . . .

GIRLS:
   So let's trust one another

Keep this from my mother
Though I'm still as pure as mountain
   snow.

SALLY:
   You can tell my uncle, here and now
   'Cause he's my agent anyhow.

GIRLS:
   But don't tell mama what you know.

Sally notices Cliff, brazenly calls him on a table phone. Soon she has joined him and made friends (she is English, lives with a German). Patrons exchange phone calls in "Telephone Song," which becomes a dance number and turns into *Scene 5.*

Scene 6: Sally surprises Cliff by showing up at his room (Fraulein Schneider makes only a token protest). Ernst has been offering Cliff big money for a few little smuggling trips to Paris (but his activities are politically motivated). Cliff is reading *Mein Kampf.*

Sally sings that it would be "Perfectly Marvelous" if she moved in with Cliff, who agrees, just as her baggage arrives.

CLIFF:
  I met this truly remarkable girl
  In this really incredible town,
  And she's skillfully managed to talk
    her way into my room . . . . .
  I have a terrible feeling I've said a
    dumb thing
  Besides, I've only got one narrow
    bed.
SALLY:
  We'll think of something.
CLIFF:
  And now this wild, unpredictable girl
SALLY:
  And this perfectly beautiful man
CLIFF:
  Will be living together and having a
    marvelous time.

Scene 7:
The Emcee and two Cabaret Girls sing
of "Two Ladies" . . .

EMCEE:
      . . . . . We switch partners daily
    To play as we please
LADIES:
    Twosie beats onesie
EMCEE:
    But nothing beats threes.
    I sleep in the middle
1st LADY:
    I'm left
2d LADY:
    And I'm right
EMCEE:
    But there's room on the bottom if
      you drop in some night.
LADIES:
    Beedle-dee-deedle-dee-dee

EMCEE:
    Two ladies
    Beedle-dee-deedle-dee-ee
LADIES:
    Two ladies
    Beedle-dee-deedle-dee-dee
    And he's the only man, ja
ALL:
    Beedle-dee-deedle-dee-dee
EMCEE:
    I like it
ALL:
    Beedle-dee-deedle-dee-dee
EMCEE:
    We like it
ALL:
    Beedle-dee-deedle-dee-dee
    This two for one
    Beedle-dee-deedle-dee-deedle-dee-
      deedle-dee-dee.

Scene 8: In her living room, Fraulein Schneider berates a tenant, Fraulein Kost (Peg Murray), for inviting sailors into her room. But Fraulein Schneider has an affair of her own brewing. Herr Schultz has brought her a pineapple . . .

FRAULEIN SCHNEIDER:
 If you brought me diamonds
 If you brought me pearls
 If you brought me roses like some
  other gents
 Might bring to other girls
 It couldn't please me more
 Than the gift I see

A pineapple for me.
 . . . . . I can hear Hawaiian breezes
  blow
SCHULTZ:
 It's from California.
FRAULEIN SCHNEIDER:
 Even so,
 How am I to thank you?

Flustered, Fraulein Schneider flees to her room. But when Herr Schultz knocks, she opens the door to him. He enters, the door is closed behind him.

Scene 9: An interlude (not shown in photos). Waiters and Emcee warn in song, "Tomorrow Belongs to Me": tomorrow the world will belong to the Fatherland.

Scene 10: In Cliff's Room, Sally sings of contentment:

SALLY:
Why should I wake up?
This dream is going so well.
When you're enchanted
Why break the spell?
Drifting in this euphoric state
Morning can wait
Let it come late
Why should I wake up
Why waste a drop of the wine?
Don't I adore you
And aren't you mine?
Maybe some day I'll be lonely
    again
But why should I wake up till
    then?

Casually (above) Sally lets Cliff know she's going to have a baby. Cliff is happy—but aware that now he *must* make some money. Ernst (left) arrives and tells them the little errand in Paris is urgently necessary. Ernst will pay well. Cliff accepts the mission.

Ernst steps forward and warns Fraulein Schneider: ". . . . . think what you are doing. This marriage is not advisable. I cannot put it too strongly. For your own welfare . . . . . He (Schultz) is not a German. Good evening." But before Ernst can leave, Fraulein Kost sings him a song.

FRAULEIN KOST:
  The sun in the meadow is summery warm
  The stag in the forest runs free
  But gather together to greet the storm
  Tomorrow belongs to me
  The branch of the linden is leafy and green
  The Rhine gives its gold to the sea.

But somewhere a glory awaits unseen
Tomorrow belongs to me.

FRAULEIN KOST, ERNST, GUESTS:
  Oh Fatherland, Fatherland, show us the sign
  Your children have waited to see
  The morning will come when the world is mine
  Tomorrow belongs to me.

The guests applaud, then freeze as the Emcee crosses the stage like a symbol of doom; the scenery disappears. *Curtain.*

ACT II

Scene 1: An interlude (not shown in photos). Emcee joins the chorus line dressed as a girl. The dance breaks up into a goose-step to the sound of martial drums.

Scene 2: At the shop (above), Fraulein Schneider tells Herr Schultz that she cannot run the risk of marrying a Jew. If the Nazis come to power, she might lose her rooming-house license. He reassures her: nothing will happen. But a brick is thrown through the shop window. She "understands."

Scene 3: An interlude (not shown in photos). Emcee sings "If You Could See Her" and waltzes with a gorilla dressed as a girl.

Scene 4: In Cliff and Sally's room (left), Fraulein Schneider returns a present. She isn't getting married after all.

FRAULEIN SCHNEIDER:
Alone like me
And this is the only world I know
Some rooms to let
The sum of a lifetime even so
I'll take your advice
What would you do?
Would you pay the price?
What would you do?
. . . . . With a storm in the wind
What would you do?

Scene 5: Sally returns to the Kit Kat Klub against Cliff's wishes—he had decided they should go to America. The party's over "And what is Berlin doing *now?* Vomiting in the street." At the cabaret, Cliff breaks with Ernst, punchcs him, but is beaten up by bodyguards. Sally sits in the spotlight to sing "Cabaret."

SALLY:

What good is sitting alone in your
   room?
Come hear the music play
Life is a cabaret, old chum
Come to the cabaret.
Put down the knitting, the book and
   the broom
Time for a holiday
Life is a cabaret, old chum
Come to the cabaret.

Come taste the wine,
Come hear the band,
Come blow a horn, start celebrating,
Right this way, your table's waiting.

No use permitting some prophet of
   doom
To wipe every smile away
Life is a cabaret, old chum
Come to the cabaret.

Scene 6: In Cliff's room, Sally confesses to Cliff that he will not be a father, just yet; she's been to the doctor and left her fur coat in payment. Cliff slaps her, then tries to induce her to give up Berlin and the cabaret and come to Paris. But Sally chooses to remain in Berlin in the life she loves. As Cliff leaves, her goodbye is farewell.

Scene 7: On the Berlin-Paris Express, Cliff writes: "There was a cabaret and there was a Master of Ceremonies and there was a city called Berlin in a country called Germany and it was the end of the world and I was dancing with Sally Bowles—and we were both fast asleep . . ." As Cliff writes, his memory-figures come alive. the Emcee goes into "Willkommen"; the orchestra, dancers, characters appear.

As in the opening scene, the Emcee assures the throng that "We have no troubles here" in the cabaret. But somehow the mood is harsher, the music dissonant, the atmosphere dream-like instead of bright.

SALLY: It'll all work out. It's only politics, and what's that got to do with us?
SCHULTZ: After all, what am I? A German.
FRAULEIN SCHNEIDER: I must be sensible. If the Nazis come, what other choice have I? I know I'm right.

Sally is lifted in a chair to sing one more chorus of "Cabaret"; then Sally and the cabaret folk disappear.

The Emcee is left alone onstage for the last word: "Auf wiedersehn! À bientot." He signals goodbye. The stage darkens. *Curtain.*

THE APPLE TREE

A Musical in Three Acts

BOOK BY SHELDON HARNICK
AND JERRY BOCK

ADDITIONAL BOOK MATERIAL BY
JEROME COOPERSMITH

MUSIC BY JERRY BOCK

LYRICS BY SHELDON HARNICK

*Based on stories by Mark Twain, Frank R. Stockton and Jules
Feiffer*

Cast and credits appear on page 364

*JERRY BOCK (music and co-author of book) was born in New Haven,
Conn., in 1928. He attended Flushing High School and the University of Wis-
consin and received early, intensive training in writing music while working
on ten musical shows a year at Camp Tamiment in the Poconos. He wrote
much of the music for the Max Liebman TV productions entitled* Your Show
of Shows, *starring Sid Caesar and Imogene Coca. He wrote three songs (with
Larry Holofcener as lyricist) for the revue* Catch a Star *(1955) and contributed to an edition of* The Ziegfeld Follies. *His first full Broadway score was*
Mr. Wonderful *(1956). He teamed up with Sheldon Harnick, lyricist, for* The
Body Beautiful *(1958),* Fiorello *(1959; New York Drama Critics Award,
Pulitzer Prize and a Best Play of its year),* Tenderloin *(1960);* She Loves Me
(1963; a Best Play) and Fiddler on the Roof *(1964; a Best Play and Critics
Award winner).*

With The Apple Tree, *the highly successful Bock-Harnick collaboration*

213

enters a new phase, as this time they also functioned as co-authors of the book. Bock supplied the incidental music for last season's comedy Generation. *He is married to Margery Gray, who is an actress.*

SHELDON HARNICK (lyrics and co-author of book) was born in Chicago in 1924. Following the example of his mother, who liked to commemorate all occasions in verse, he wrote verses while he was still at grammar school. After graduation from high school in 1943 he went into the Army. He wrote songs and performed them in between violin solos at USO shows. He returned to Chicago in 1946 and enrolled in Northwestern University, where he wrote for the student musical and doubled on the fiddle.

After graduation from Northwestern, Harnick worked as a violinist for Xavier Cugat's orchestra and as a member of the Compass, a group which specialized in improvising and which advanced the careers of Shelley Berman, Mike Nichols (director of The Apple Tree), *Elaine May, Alan Arkin, Barbara Harris* (The Apple Tree's *leading lady), the* Second City *troupe and others. He contributed "The Boston Beguine" to the revue* New Faces of 1952. *Other reviews of the 1950s which included his work were* Two's Company, John Murray Anderson's Almanac, Take Five, Kaleidoscope *and* The Littlest Revue. *In 1958 he teamed up as lyricist with Jerry Bock, and their collaborations are listed above in Bock's biographical note. In addition, Harnick did the lyrics for the off-Broadway musical* Smiling the Boy Fell Dead *(1961). He is married to Margery Gray, who is an actress.*

JEROME COOPERSMITH (additional book material) was born in New York City and his first job in the theater was as an office boy for Shubert Theatrical Company. He completed his formal education at New York University, following Army service; then he began writing for TV and contributed many scripts to Armstrong Circle Theater. *His* I Was Accused *won the Robert E. Sherwood Award for TV plays in 1956, and he contributed to all the leading hour-long anthology programs on TV. His documentary training film* Prescription Hypnosis *is still in use by doctors. His only previous major Broadway credit was the book for* Baker Street *(1965), the Sherlock Holmes musical.*

INTRODUCTION BY THE LYRICIST-LIBRETTIST *

Once, in an interview, my partner Jerry Bock and I were asked the inevitable question: "Which comes first, the words or the music?" Jerry's unexpected answer was, "The book." As far as Jerry and I are concerned the book is of primary importance and always comes first. It's true that we have occasionally written second-act songs while the librettist was still carving out the first act, but we were able to do this only because all of us were working from

* These comments appeared in the *Dramatists Guild Quarterly* and were designated by Mr. Harnick to introduce his play here.

the same source material and we had agreed beforehand that certain scenes and material would of necessity appear in the final script. Even then we were running the risk that the "tone" of the songs we wrote would not match the "tone" of the dialogue that the librettist was evolving.

I have heard of situations in which a whole score was written and then a librettist hired to weave a book around the score. For all I know, some successful shows may have been written this way, but it would be difficult for me to believe that they were the "homogeneous" kind of shows that I admire myself.

Jerry and I prefer to have a draft of the libretto first, so that we can write the type of song that (in addition to being entertaining) attempts to continue the flow of the story, to provide insight into character, to heighten climactic moments, or to enrich the feeling of time and place. This means working very closely with the librettist, and working out problems together.

One of the first things that occurs to me regarding any close collaboration is the matter of generosity. And let me state right here that Jerry and I have been blessed with librettists of singular generosity. (Maybe *all* librettists are generous and noble, but we haven't worked with all of them yet.) Each of our four librettists has been extremely modest about suggesting where songs should fall within scenes. Another variety of generosity, and I would guess a much more difficult thing for a librettist to tolerate, is the expropriation of ideas, jokes, lines of dialogue, and occasionally entire scenes by the lyricist and composer. A ready example springs immediately to mind.

One of Jerome Weidman's early drafts of *Fiorello* contained a scene in which a number of ward-heelers were playing poker when they should have been attending to the business of choosing a candidate to run for Congress from their district. As written, it was an amusing scene which seemed certain to play well. When I read it I had an instant vision of an effective song which could incorporate much of the scene and to which I felt I could contribute a great deal. I asked him if he would mind if Jerry and I tried to "musicalize" his scene. Generously, he told us to go ahead and feel free to use anything in the scene which we felt would be valuable. (I am sorely tempted to say that this was the origin of our sentimental waltz "Till Tomorrow," but no.) I then proceeded to construct the lyric for "Politics and Poker," rephrasing what I felt were the most valuable aspects of the scene, and adding to them my own notions. When we played the song for Mr. Weidman, he was genuinely delighted, which must have taken great generosity of spirit indeed, for he must have seen that he would get no credit for a number of funny notions in the song, including the notion for the punch line—"You idiot, that's me!"

I have lately been brooding about styles of songs and, by implication, styles of musicals. The source of this brooding may very well come from a mystery I've never solved to my own satisfaction with regard to *The Apple Tree*.

Originally, Jerry and I started out to write three one-act musicals with librettist Jerome Coopersmith. The first musical, by common agreement and enthusiasm, was to be based on Mark Twain's short story *The Diary of Adam and Eve*. Since Mr. Coopersmith is an experienced librettist, we had a minimum of preliminary talks on this material; he felt he knew how to treat it, and he went ahead and wrote several drafts. Part of the mystery was this: Mr. Coopersmith created a libretto that we all found amusing, charming, and that seemed theatrically sound, but Jerry and I couldn't find the songs in it. We came up with a few, but it took an astonishing length of time, and the rest of the songs proved stubbornly elusive. I'm not speaking of good songs or bad songs but of *any* songs.

Finally, Stuart Ostrow, our producer, suggested that the problem might lie in the one-act form itself. He suggested that in so short a form (shorter even than a first act of an average musical) the librettist and lyricist might be getting in each other's way. Eventually, on the supposition that Mr. Ostrow was right, Mr. Coopersmith graciously stepped aside after it had been decided that I was to attempt a libretto using his as a basis. I had never attempted one before, except for a few long musical sketches. The rest of the mystery (to me) lies in the fact that I don't feel I've changed Mr. Coopersmith's libretto that much, and yet by making what I consider to be minor changes, cuts, additions, and transpositions, suddenly the hitherto elusive score materialized.

After thinking about this for many, many months I'm *still* not sure why the songs were so elusive in Mr. Coopersmith's version and why they came so easily in mine. Because, as I say, I feel that with all the changes I made, the end product was still *essentially* his libretto. Possibly Mr. Ostrow's surmise was right. And possibly, underlying that surmise was some very subtle difference in the way we each "saw" the Twain material, a difference so subtle as to remain hidden from me still.

SHELDON HARNICK

PART I—THE DIARY OF ADAM AND EVE

Time: Saturday, June 1st

Place: Eden

SYNOPSIS: Adam is asleep on the ground in the Garden of Eden, which is symbolized sparingly on the stage with a tree at right, a mound of flowers at left and an Apple Tree in the misty distance (behind a scrim). Adam is an average physical specimen dressed in brown trousers and shirt. Eve in her turn will be dressed in a beige sheath.

A Voice commands sleepy Adam to awake and take possession of his garden and name its creatures and eat its fruits—except for that of the Apple Tree on the other side of the hill.

ADAM *(yawning and mumbling):* —well, I might as well get it over with. *(Rises.)* I, Adam, by virtue of the authority vested in me do hereby name all you creatures flying around in the sky—flyers.
> *Music chord.*

And you things crawling on the ground I name—crawlers.
> *Chord.*

And you things swimming around down there are swimmers, and you're growlers, and you're hoppers. . . . .

Just as Adam comes to realize he's the only man among all these creatures, he feels a sharp pain in his ribs.

ADAM: Ahh. Now what?
> *A mound rolls on from left with Eve asleep on it. Adam turns and crosses to it, circling it in curiosity.*

I'll name it later.
> *He exits and the music swells. The lights slowly change and Eve wakes, instinctively reaching out for a companion. She sits up and is struck with bewilderment and wonder.*

EVE *(staring out in front—sitting up):* Sunlight? Hummingbirds? Lions? Where am I? I? What am I? *(The music fades as she looks down and is startled by the sight of herself.)* Oh!! *(She studies herself carefully, running her fingers over her face and hair.)* Whatever I am, I'm certainly a beautiful one.

She is an experiment, Eve guesses—but probably only a part of it, not all of it. She begins to look around her and make notes about Eden.

EVE *(sings):*
> So many creatures
> So many things
> Each wonderous object is beautiful and striking
> And I see nothing that isn't to my liking
> Here in Eden.
>
> There's plums and peaches
> And pears and grapes
> So ripe and juicy and utterly inviting
> I find the apples especially exciting
> Here in Eden. . . . .
>
> It's all so perfect
> And so ideal
> And yet I do have one tiny reservation
> There's nothing handy for making conversation
> Here in Eden. . . . .

Nevertheless, Eve sings, she expects to be perfectly happy here.
Adam enters carrying a fish. After they stare at each other for a moment,

Eve orders Adam sharply to put the fish back in the water. Eve reaches for a rock as Adam, startled, jumps into his tree for safety.

Eve threatens to throw the rock at Adam unless he hands over the creature he calls a "swimmer" and she a "pickerel." Adam throws the fish down to her. Eve fondles the fish, calls Adam a bully and departs, dragging her mound.

Adam comes out of the tree and in his turn picks up rocks for throwing at Eve, but he can't bring himself to do it.

On the second day, Adam thinks he has hidden himself so cleverly in his tree that Eve will think he's left the Garden. Eve enters, ignores his concealment and tells him to come down out of the tree, she has something very important to discuss.

Adam, sensing that he is the stronger of the two and thus perfectly safe on the ground with Eve, comes down from the tree. Eve explains that they are an "us," a part of the same experiment. She knows this must be so because, for one thing, she and Adam are the only two creatures who are able to talk.

ADAM *(backing off):* That's how much you know! So can—so can— *(Looking around for the illustration.)* so can that flyer up there.

EVE: Where?

ADAM: In that tree.

EVE *(staring hard):* You mean that parrot? I didn't know parrots could talk!

ADAM: Well, they can. Why do you call it a parrot?

EVE: Because it looks like a parrot.

ADAM: Well, not to me it doesn't. It looks like a loud-mouthed fat-beak.

EVE *(laughing condescendingly):* Nevertheless, it's a parrot.

ADAM: What makes you so positive?

EVE: I just happen to have this talent. The minute I set eyes on an animal, I know what it is. I don't have to think. The right name comes out by inspiration. So far, you're the only exception.

Under Adam's questioning, she rattles off the names of many animals, thereby injuring Adam's ego.

EVE: . . . . . I'm so sorry.

ADAM: Well, don't be, because you're wrong. Anyway, I can't waste any more time here. I have to go empty the four-pronged white-squirter.

EVE: You mean the cow?

ADAM: Thank you very much! *(Exits.)*

EVE: Somehow we got off on the wrong foot. I seem to aggravate it. I think it's a reptile. But I do wonder what it's for. I never see it do anything. Nothing seems to interest it—except resting. It's a man! If it *is* a man, then, it isn't an *it,* is it? No. It should be: Nominative: He. Dative: Him. Possessive: His'n. I think that's right. It gets harder and harder to concentrate ever since I met the reptile. Just thinking about him, gives me the most distracting sensations: *(Sings.)*

Feelings are tumbling over feelings
Feelings I do not understand
And I am more than slightly worried
That they are getting out of hand.

Sometimes they happen in my stomach
Sometimes they happen on my skin
What is the name of this condition
That I am in? . . . . .

By June 4 Eve has found something which she hopes will interest Adam: fire. But after trying to name it "pink dust" and burning his fingers, Adam pretends to ignore it and her. Eve continues to wonder, in song, how she will ever attract Adam's attention and esteem.

EVE *(sings):*
     . . . . . Is there some tid-bit that will please him?
What should I wear?
What is the source of this congestion
That I must learn to rise above?
Is there a name for this condition?
Yes, there's a name. . .
And it is hell!

On the sixth day, Adam's tree is gone and Adam is building a primitive shelter out of some planks. As he constructs his "dry-top" tripod-style, he complains to himself that Eve is officiously naming everything whatever it looks like to her. And she makes him feel "hampered" and "anxious" by coming too close to him.

Eve enters, eating an apple. Adam grabs it, then finds to his relief that it isn't from the forbidden tree over the hills; he tells Eve about the forbidden tree.

Eve tells Adam her name, explains that she's a "she," praises him for inventing the word "superfluous" (though he applies it to her). Adam sits under his planks carving a bowl and trying to ignore her. When it begins to rain Eve wants to take shelter, too. She starts to cry, which Adam cannot bear. He makes room for her in the tiny hut.

EVE: What's your name?
ADAM: What do I look like? Wait. My name is Adam.
EVE: Adam . . . Adam . . . that sound is pleasanter in my ears than any I have heard so far. *(She looks at the walls of the hut.)* Adam?
ADAM: What?
EVE: What made you pick brown?
ADAM: Because wood is brown.
EVE *(she rises. The end of this speech will be drowned out by a rising swell*

of musical "rain".): But berries are red. We could squeeze some berries against the wood and make it nice and colorful . . . not all over, just from here to here. We'll leave a border on top and bottom . . . and on that wall, some shells I think. Have you thought of hanging grass in the doorway?

The lights fade out and then come up on the refurbished hut. By Sunday, June 9 (Adam complains in song) Eve has taken over.

ADAM *(sings):*
  She keeps filling up the hut with rubbish
  Like flowers
  And plants
  And not only is it overcrowded
  It's loaded
  With ants
  She is definitely too intrusive
  A nuisance
  And yet . . .
  She's an interesting creature
  This Eve. . . . .

As Adam continues his song he searches for and finds the right word to describe Eve: beautiful.

ADAM *(sings):*
  . . . . . There are animals around this Garden
  More soothing
  Than she
  But there's nothing in the whole of Eden
  More pleasant
  To see.
  If she'd only learn to keep her mouth shut
  One minute at a time
  Why, I believe
  I could possibly enjoy
  Just watching
  This curiously interesting creature—
  Called Eve.

As Adam thumps melons to test their ripeness, Eve enters wearing a hat made of flowers. Adam considers flowers "rubbish" and Eve calls them "the smile of God." Adam counters Eve's accusation of narrowness with the boast that he has just invented something brand new: humor.

EVE: Humor?
ADAM: Does that word puzzle you? I thought it might. I'll be happy to ex-

plain. Yesterday, I was sitting beside the path that leads to the cornfield and I happened to notice this yellow clucker. . .

EVE: Chicken.

ADAM: All right!

EVE: It looks like. . .

ADAM: All right! Have it your way! I happened to notice this chicken. For a long time it walked slowly back and forth, hesitating, and then suddenly it zipped across the path. And I thought to myself, "Why did that chicken cross that path?" And then I thought, "To get to the other side!" *(He is hysterical and falls about—finally reaching up to her.)* That's the world's first joke. And I made it up. Don't you see the humor of it?

> *Eve has been growing increasingly puzzled by this whole thing. She obliges Adam with a smile but shrugs apologetically.*

I guess you had to be there . . . and I'm going there.

Adam moves to exit, but Eve insists on telling him what's on her mind: they are different from other creatures, so the grass around their home should be different—it should be shorter. Maybe Adam should cut it.

By June 10, Adam is complaining about Sunday chores. Eve is still a puzzle to him, but at least she is not around all the time; she has taken up with a Snake and is spending a lot of time down by the pond.

> *Lights fade on Adam, who exits, and come up on Eve, looking at herself in the pond and making up her face with petals.*

EVE *(sings):*
Look at you
Look at me
How much more alike could
Two girls be
Here we stand
Sisters and
Friends.

The lights fade and then come up on Adam, who is sitting on a tub. He's laughing at the memory of Eve falling into her pond the day before. Eve nearly strangled; she found the water so cold and uncomfortable that she gathered as many fish as she could and brought them home to get them warm.

Eve enters, and Adam persuades her that the fish aren't happy out of water; Eve agrees to put them back. Adam picks up his tub and starts toward his favorite activity: going over Eden's waterfall. It's cool, and he likes the plunge at the end. Eve warns Adam that it's dangerous, making him angry; after all, she complained about his going over the falls in a barrel and so he made the tub, and now she's complaining again. Adam walks off in a huff, telling Eve "I hate flowers!" after she asks him to bring back some hollyhocks. Hurt and petulant, Eve returns to her pond and her song to her reflection in the water.

EVE *(sings):*
> And on days when he withdraws
> I'm less lonely now because
> If
> I should need sympathy
> You would never turn your
> Back on me
> I have you
> Who needs two
> Friends.

>> *The Snake—in tuxedo, smoking a pipe—enters behind Eve. He*
>> *throws a pipe cleaner into the pond, making the reflection shatter.*

EVE: Wait! Don't go away!

SNAKE: There's no one there, Eve.

EVE *(whirls, startled):* What? Oh, hello, Snake.

The Snake explains that there's no one in the pond, it's just a reflection; he tells Eve about light rays. Realizing she's friendless except for Adam, Eve feels that if she knew a lot, like the Snake, Adam might like her better. The Snake offers her knowledge, if she will eat an apple. Forbidden? Nonsense, the Snake tells Eve, the forbidden fruit in *this* Garden is chestnuts—and when he says "chestnuts" he means mouldy humor.

SNAKE *(sings):*
> Listen closely. Let me fill you in
> About the rich ripe round red
> Rosy apples they call forbidden fruit
> What I'm about to say is
> Confidential so promise you'll be mute.
> Because if every creature in the garden knows
> They'll come 'round like hungry buffalos
> And in no time there'll be none of those
> Precious apples left for you and me.
>
> Now, in the average apple
> You're accustomed to skin, seeds, flesh and core
> But you will find that these are
> Special apples that give you something more
> Why, every seed contains some information you
> Need to speed your education, the
> Seeds, indeed, of all creation are here
> Why be foolish, my dear
> Come with me
> To that tree.

Eve resists weakly—Adam wouldn't like her to disobey—but the Snake sings on. With knowledge, she can be Adam's inspiration. She can teach him "plumbing and philosophy." Adam will be "overjoyed."

SNAKE *(sings):*
      . . . . . And he will say
          Holding her in his arms.
      "Oh, Eve, you're
      Indispensable! Please don't leave my side!"
      And with your nifty, new-found education, he'll
      Relish every conversation, why
          Crossing around her.
      You'll be Adam's inspiration this way!
      Just an apple a day
      Wait and see
      Come with me
      To that tree!
      Now!

The Snake pulls Eve offstage as the lights come up on Adam sitting on his tub and drying himself with a towel.

ADAM *(sings):*
      I see animals and birds and flowers
      Every color, every shape and size
      Moss and pebbles and a host of wonders
      Gleaming everywhere I aim my eyes
      So if ever I'm attacked by boredom
      I'll just open up my eyes and see
      This diversified, curious, fascinating, bountiful
      Beautiful, beautiful world,
      I love.
          He laughs and suddenly freezes, calls out in alarm.
      ADAM: Hey—hey—you there, growler—I mean, Lion. Leave that lamb alone. Don't do that, you'll hurt him. I said stop that! What do you think you're doing? Stop it! Stop it! *(He steps back in horror.)* Oh, my God! Oh, my God! *(He looks about in anguish as the stage darkens.)* Oh, my God!
          Thunder is heard rolling down ominously.

Eve enters, robed in flowers, concealing one of the forbidden apples. Adam is angry, sensing that she has eaten the forbidden fruit and brought Death to the Garden, but Eve denies that it's her fault. As the Snake explained, it's Adam's fault, Adam and his "chestnuts."

EVE: . . . . . Have you been making up jokes, Adam? Tell the truth.
ADAM: I did think of one . . .
          She reacts audibly and turns away.

. . . but I didn't say it out loud! Oh, my . . . I was standing here—just before it all happened—and I was thinking about the falls. And I thought, "How wonderful it is to see that vast body of water tumble down there." And then I thought, "Yes, but it would be a lot more wonderful to see it tumble up!"

EVE: That's it. That's what did it.

ADAM: Oh, my. Oh my, oh my . . . *(to heaven.)* . . . why was I born so witty?

EVE: We have to leave the garden, don't we?

ADAM: We broke the rule . . . *I* broke the rule. I'm sorry, Eve.

EVE: Oh . . . you didn't know.

They embrace. Adam suddenly notices Eve's costume.

ADAM: Eve, you know I can't stand to see you wearing that rubbish. Please take it off.

He makes a gesture toward helping her off with her robe. To his surprise she resists, with some embarrassment.

EVE: No, don't do that. You mustn't. Please, Adam. No, don't please!

ADAM: You're behaving like an idiot. If you want to make a silly spectacle of yourself, go right ahead. I know what I'm going to do. I haven't eaten all day.

EVE *(showing it to him)*: Would you like an apple?

ADAM: Oh, it's one of those.

EVE: They're not forbidden.

ADAM: I know, but somehow it still goes against my principles. *(Takes apple.)* It's certainly a fine looking specimen, isn't it? Considering the lateness of the season and all. I guess principles have no real force unless you're well fed. *(He takes a bite and chews it for a moment. He reaches down and picks up his towel.)* Turn your back. Don't you have any modesty at all? *(He wraps himself in the towel.)*

EVE: Sorry *(She turns her back.)* Adam?

ADAM: What?

EVE *(starting to cry)*: It looks like rain.

ADAM: I know. Come on. We'll have to build a new shelter somewhere.

They exit.

The stage setting for Eden disappears. It is replaced by a platform with a rail on one end and a bench. This is the porch of a place Eve calls "Tonawanda." Adam enters puffing on a corn cob pipe and whittling at a hickory twig; Eve enters and throws a rough wool sweater over his shoulders. Adam has invented fire and Eve has just baked him an apple.

Adam, now working on inventing the multiplication table while Eve tends the garden, notices that Eve is getting fat . . .

The lights fade and then come up again, as Adam has returned from a hunting trip to find Eve cherishing a new kind of creature.

ADAM *(sings)*:
Now I could swear

That it's a fish
Tho' it resembles us in every way but size

She gives it milk
And every night
She picks it up and pats and pets it when it cries

I always knew
She pitied fish
But it's ridiculous to make them household pets

She says it's not a fish
I say it is a fish

'Cause it surrounds itself with water
Almost every chance it gets.

Eve enters with the little creature bundled in her arms. Adam wants to experiment with it, to try it out in the water. But Eve is fiercely protective and carries her bundle back into the cabin.

Adam speculates, in song, that this new creature might be some sort of kangaroo. Eve brings the bundle out again when the coast is clear and sings it a lullaby.

EVE *(sings):*
Go to sleep, whatever you are,
Lay your head on my breast.

Close your eyes and open your paws
You need plenty of rest.

Doesn't faze me
If you grow up to be
Pony or poodle or sheep

You're my own, whatever you are
Sleep . . . sleep . . . sleep.

Eve goes back into the house. Adam returns, still singing about this creature.

ADAM *(sings):*
. . . . . I've searched the woods
I've baited traps
And yet I couldn't find its sister or its brother
And tho' I've hunted far and wide
While Eve has hardly stepped outside
I'll be damned if she didn't catch another!
Blackout.

Some time later, Eve is snapping beans in a wooden bowl and shouting for Cain and Abel (she knows now that the strange creatures are boys) to keep out of her garden. Adam, with plow and rake, worries about Cain's disposition; admits to himself that he now enjoys the sound of Eve's incessant voice.

The lights fade and come up again on Eve sewing a sweater. Cain has killed Abel and run away, and now the house seems empty. Adam and Eve discuss death; each would like to be the one to go first.

ADAM (changing the subject): Listen, listen—I've got a good one for you. Why do I always wear brown suspenders?

EVE (laughing heartily): That's my favorite. (Still laughing.)

ADAM (beginning to laugh): Oh, I forgot . . .

Adam leaves Eve alone to ponder why she loves him even though he is a mass of faults.

EVE (sings):

. . . . . He is a good man
Yet I would love him
If he abused me
Or used me ill.

And tho' he's handsome
I know inside me
Were he a plain man
I'd love him still.

What makes me love him
It's quite beyond me
It must be something
I can't define
Unless it's merely that he's masculine
And that he's mine.

> Eve slowly gathers the sweater up and the bowl of beans. Feeling the chill of the night she rises and exits into the house.

ADAM (entering bearing a great sadness): Eve died today. I knew she would, of course. Well, at least her prayer was answered—she went first. Now that she's gone, I realize something I didn't realize before. I used to think it was a terrible tragedy when Eve and I had to leave the Garden. Now I know it really didn't matter. Because, wheresoever she was, there was Eden.

> The lights pick up the flower bed area.

And now, I have to go water her flowers. She loved them, you know.

> The strains of "Here In Eden" are heard as Adam crosses, picks up the watering can and tends the flowers. After a bit, he wipes his brow and bends down and weeds. Curtain.

PART II—THE LADY OR THE TIGER?

Time: A long time ago

Place: A semi-barbaric kingdom

SYNOPSIS: At curtain rise, the actor who was the Snake in the previous episode is now a Balladeer, alone and spotlit, accompanying himself on a guitar.

BALLADEER *(sings):*
I'll tell you a truth
That's hard to swallow
I'll tell you a truth
Oh, listen well.
If you are in love
With a lover who's jealous
Then sooner or later
You're headed for hell

The Balladeer tells of an absolute monarch of a primitive kingdom, King Arik, and his arrogant daughter Barbara (pronounced Barbára with the same rhythm and sound as "barbarian," indicated in this text when necessary for scansion of lyrics). The lights come up and King Arik enters sumptuously dressed and grandly enthroned in procession, preceded by three King's Men snapping whips in savage manner. Four handmaidens in long, feathery trains announce the arrival of Princess Barbara, who is also drawn onstage enthroned.

MAIDENS *(sing):*
Make way!
She comes!
Her regal proudness!
Her flashing eye-ness!
Her self-indulgeness!
Her goddessness!
Make way!
She comes!
Princess Barbára!

A spotlight picks up the Balladeer who describes King Arik's savage form of justice. The center of the stage is lit as an arena.

BALLADEER: . . . . . In this arena there were two doors. They stood side by side and looked exactly alike.

A wall with two rather large, primitive doors appears upstage.

The prisoner had his choice.

The Prisoner is brought downstage center from the bleachers and looks apprehensively at the King.

He could open either door . . . but, he knew that behind one of them there was a ferocious, and ravenous . . . tiger!

The Guards hurl the Prisoner to the floor and return to their places on bleachers either side of the arena doors, where the court has taken places.

KING *(sings):*

Pris'ner
Choose!
It's your chance to prove
Your innocence or guilt!

ALL *(sing):*

Salute!
Yeh yeh manna!
Yeh yeh callu!
Yeh yeh manna callu!
Yeh yeh!

During the preceding chant, everyone gives the ritual salute. They point one arm heavenward and the other earthward, symbolizing the alternate outcomes of the two choices. Then they put a hand over each eye, symbolizing the blindness of chance. When this ceremony is over, the Prisoner makes an elaborate bow to the King and to the Princess. Then he faces upstage and goes to the two doors. He can't decide which to choose. The crowd reacts vocally as the Prisoner reaches for the door on their side of the arena. He is confused and turns front in abject confusion. Finally in desperation he chooses one door and opens it. The tiger leaps at his throat. He screams, he tries to run, he falls, kicks and finally lies quiet.

The chorus sings its terror ("But better him than me! Yeh!"). The Balladeer suggests that the wretch could have chosen the other door, and as he does so the scene on the stage is reversed and played backwards, like a movie film being run through the camera backwards, to the moment when the Prisoner makes his choice. This time he chooses the other door, and a beautiful Lady comes forth. She dances with the Prisoner downstage to the King, who marries the pair at once. The chorus sings its joy ("But better he than I! Yeh!").

Now (the Balladeer continues in a spotlight), there was also in this kingdom a brave soldier named Captain Sanjar, who has just returned from battle. Lights come up on the Palace setting: thrones and stairs leading through an arch. The King summons Sanjar to his presence.

Sanjar enters in primitive battle garb, helmet in hand. He is tired and tattered.

SANJAR *(kneels in salute at the top of the stairs):* We won!
> *The court cheers. Sanjar collapses and rolls down the stairs, unconscious.*

KING *(ignoring Sanjar, rises):* Victory is ours!

The King leads a victory procession offstage, leaving Princess Barbara and Nadjira, a lovely handmaiden of the Princess, alone with the unconscious Sanjar. Nadjira kneels by Sanjar and embraces him, but Princess Barbara orders her away. After Nadjira leaves, the Princess embraces Sanjar, who regains consciousness and embraces the Princess in his turn.

Sanjar and Princess Barbara declare their love for each other, a love which is of course forbidden.

SANJAR *(sings):*
> When battle had all but drained me
> One vision alone sustained me
> The thought of you
> And our forbidden love.

BARBARA:
> Whenever my days were harried
> And father would say "Get married"
> I thought of you
> And our forbidden love. . . . .

Their love scene is continually interrupted by passers-by, and they long to go away somewhere where they can be alone: Gaul.

SANJAR *(sings):*
> They tell me it's divided in three parts
> We'll pick the part that's closest to our hearts.
>
> In Gaul
> We'd live so simply
> No more feathers and fuss
> Just the children and us.
>
> In Gaul
> We'd have a garden
> On the outskirts of town
> And a house painted brown—

BARBARA: Why brown?

In each other's arms, they continue to dream musically of how great it would be "in Gaul." But they know this is not to be, that their "forbidden love" must remain concealed.

As they embrace, the King enters with two Guards. Seeing that Sanjar has dared to love the Princess, the King has him arrested for trial in the arena.

BARBARA *(left alone as the lights fade, leaving her in a spot, she faces front):*
A trial! The tiger! *(Sings.)*
    Those razor teeth
    Those iron claws
    His handsome throat
    Between those jaws
    Not my Sanjar . . .
    Lying there!
    Dying there!
    I'll stop that . . .
    If it's the last thing . . .

But how? she wonders; then, in another spotlight she sees the Balladeer wearing the hat of the Tigerkeeper and carrying his whip. Of course—the Tigerkeeper must know which door hides the beast at the trial.

The Balladeer-Tigerkeeper warns the Princess in song that "There are things it is better not to know." But Princess Barbara ignores this warning; she wants to know which door will conceal the tiger in Sanjar's trial. She strips herself of jewelry and gives it to the Tigerkeeper, who finally whispers the secret into her ear and then exits. Princess Barbara is delighted.

BARBARA *(sings):*
    I've got what you want
    I've got what you need
    I know how much you want it
    Yeh! Yeh! Sanjar.

    . . . . . If we don't share this secret
    You just might die
    So I will give it to you
    And when I give it to you
    You'll shout for joy
    And so will I!! . . . . .

As Barbara finishes her song, Nadjira is brought in glamorously enthroned. Nadjira is also singing "I've Got What You Want," because she has been chosen to be the lady at Sanjar's trial. Sanjar will either be eaten by the tiger —or married on the spot to lovely Nadjira.

Furiously jealous, Barbara tries to stop the procession, but it continues to the arena. The Balladeer-Tigerkeeper enters with the tiger in his cage, and Barbara sings to the beast.

BARBARA *(sings):*
    Tiger, tiger,
    Put on your napkin
    Someone is coming to dine
    Tiger, tiger
    You do the carving
    Your claws are sharper than mine.

The Tigerkeeper pushes the cage off. Barbara begins to regret her impulse
to throw Sanjar to the tiger.

BARBARA *(sings):*
    Sanjar, Sanjar,
    What am I saying?
    I'd have your blood on my hands!
    Your dying screams
    Haunting my dreams
    AI!!
    AI!!

    I don't want him dead
    Better dead than wed
    Nobody else, nobody else
    Gets you, Sanjar!
    How can I decide?
    Burial or bride?
    AI!! The lady or the tiger? . . . . .

Barbara exits in her quandary. The court comes to the arena, the King and
Barbara enthroned as before. Sanjar is led in by guards as the court hails the
King and Princess in song and ceremonial with Oriental dance gestures.
    Sanjar knows that Barbara knows which door is which—he looks to her
for a sign.

BARBARA *(facing front, sings):*
    Which door should I choose?
    Left? Right? Left? Right?
    Torment! Torture!
    The lady, the tiger?
    Sanjar! Sanjar!
    This choice is tearing me apart!
        She eats grapes. The spotlight picks up the King and the entire
        court as they join the song.
KING and CHORUS *(in canon):*
    Which door will he choose?
    Left? Right? Left? Right?

Dead man? Wed man?
The lady, the tiger?
This door? That door?
Which door will he choose?

> *The entire court does the ritual incantation, which includes a stylized clapping of hands.*

Yeh, yeh, manna,
Yeh, yeh, callu,
Yeh, yeh, manna callu
Yeh, yeh.

> *The lights black out. Spots remain on Barbara and Sanjar. Barbara's hands slowly uncover her eyes. With agonizing deliberateness she reaches a decision and finally points to a door. The music builds in suspense as Sanjar rises and after a long look at Barbara he reaches for a door. The entire action freezes.*

BALLADEER *(entering behind the King's throne; sings):*
Before we go on
Let's look at the problem:
The lady or tiger
Which will come out?
The deeper we probe
The heart of Barbára
The more we discover
The outcome's in doubt.

If you have loved
You understand
How love and hate can
Walk hand in hand
So place yourself
In Barbára's shoes:
The lady or the tiger
Which did she choose?

> *The Balladeer exits—the freeze picture remains as the curtain slowly falls, with only Barbara in a spotlight.*

PART III—PASSIONELLA

Time: Now

Place: Here

SYNOPSIS: The scene is a rooftop with the New York skyline in the distance. Sooty, raggedy Ella, a chimney sweep, is plying her trade among the chimney-pots of a big office building, as a Narrator at a podium at left tells Ella's story. While Ella works, she dreams.

ELLA *(sings):*
> Chimneys are cozy
> Chimneys are warm
> I think of chimneys
> As ports in a storm
> But warm and cozy, or not,
> I would give up the lot
> If I could only be a movie star.
>
> . . . . . A movie star
> Oh, to be a movie star
> A beautiful, glamorous, radiant, ravishing movie star!

Ella pantomimes her life as the Narrator (who was also the Snake and the Balladeer in previous episodes) explains it: every night Ella goes home after work and watches her beloved TV right through the Late-Late Show to "The Star Spangled Banner," dreaming of being a movie star.

That's how Ella spends her days—working and dreaming, working and dreaming—until the sad day when her employer visits her rooftop to tell her that her job is being replaced by automation.

Now Ella wanders the streets, jobless, hungry and cold. Her piggy bank is empty. She fears (as she sings through a severe head cold) that she will starve to death before she can become a "mooo-vie star."

On the night of the full moon, Ella returns home only to find that something is amiss with her last comfort, the TV set.

ELLA *(pounding the set in panic):* No picture! No picture! No picture! No picture!

NARRATOR: No picture. Stunned, disbelieving, she stood before the TV. Her eyes searched the screen for a trace of an image.

She is crouching low, glaring into the set.
Then, Ella heard a voice.
Electronic blips are heard as the TV glows weirdly.
Hello, out there! This is your friendly neighborhood Godmother! The pro-
gram usually scheduled for this hour will not be seen. Instead, I have the
pleasure to bring you the answer to your most cherished dream. Plink!
Flashes go off.
Plank!
The lights black out.
Plunk!

*More flashes. There is a blinding flash from the TV set. The music
hits a dramatic climax. When the stage is visible again, Ella has
been transformed into Passionella.*

Gone is soot-stained, shapeless Ella. In her place is Passionella, a glittering
blonde sculptured in a gold evening dress, with a bosom like two open bureau
drawers. Passionella is delighted with herself.

PASSIONELLA *(sings):*
    Look at me! I am . . .
    Gorgeous!

    I am absolutely gorgeous
    Here's this avalanche of beauty
    In one woman and I'm it.
    Look at the way all of the parts fit together!
    Stunning!
    See the way my nose stopped running!
    I was positive this creature was there
    Inside the old me
    All bottled up waiting to get free. . . . .

Now every studio will be after her, Passionella sings joyfully. But her Godmother, in the voice of the Narrator, adds a word of warning.

NARRATOR: Your friendly neighborhood Godmother has power only from
Huntley-Brinkley to the Late-Late Show. During those hours you shall be
ravishing. You shall be Passionella. But only during those hours.
PASSIONELLA: And the rest of the day?
NARRATOR: The rest of the day, my dear, you shall be your usual sooty
self. This is your friendly neighborhood Godmother returning you to your
local network.
The music stops.
ELLA: I have not a moment to lose!
NARRATOR: Said Ella. And off she ran to El Morocco.

Ella's room rolls offstage, and a group of dowdy folk packed together as straphangers in a crowded subway car (which this is) enter. The "car" stops for Ella. She gets on, and the passengers are agog.

ALL *(sing):*
..... But who can she be?
Do you know?
Do you?
PASSENGER:
No!
ALL:
Then who, who, who, who
Is she
And where's she off to tonight?
You'd think a chauffeur would drive
Her there in her
Private car!
Unless of course she's an
Underground movie star! .....

The "car" stops and Ella gets off. The "car" continues offstage as Ella is ushered by the doorman into El Morocco. The subway riders, now elegantly dressed, come on as dancing couples. Still they wonder who Ella can be.

A movie producer approaches Ella and offers a lifetime contract. A screen is lowered and on it a movie depicts Ella's rise to stardom. She is pictured in glamor poses, as a magazine cover girl; she is photographed with various well-known escorts including George Hamilton and Robert Kennedy; her name is seen flashing on marquees in lights and colors, with the letters growing ever larger.

NARRATOR: A legend grew around her. Strange stories circulated. Stories of how she would only allow her films to be shot between the hours of Huntley-Brinkley and the Late-Late Show, and how at 4 a.m. she would hop into her sports car and vanish. And, as the mystery grew, so did her popularity. Her pictures set new attendance records, she was in demand everywhere. And when there were no pictures to make, life became a ceaseless round of cocktail parties, premieres and public appearances marked by frenzied adoration. Yes, Passionella had arrived!
      Passionella bursts through a large photo of herself.
PASSIONELLA *(sings):*
Look at me! I'm a
Movie star!
Every inch a movie star!
A beautiful, glamorous . . .

Five men come on and interrupt Ella. They sing their devotion to her while a succession of glamorous closeups appears on the screen. The men are adoring fans; they worship her as a goddess.

ALL *(sing):*
    Let me touch your sacred body
    Oh!! . . . . .
    Beautiful
    Incredible
    Extraordinary
    Passionella!!!
NARRATOR: But—was Passionella happy? Now that she had wealth, fame, fans, success, glamor and excitement—was she truly content? Let us hear the answer in her own words.
PASSIONELLA: Isn't this what I wanted? Isn't this what we all want?

The chorus goes out, and Passionella is left alone to sing her thoughts, while the key words of her song are cartooned in color on the screen behind her. She has wealth, fame, fans and success. Toward the end of her song, the word "Life" on the screen falls apart; the "e" drops off the end.

PASSIONELLA *(sings):*
    . . . . . Glamor and excitement
    Lucky me, a movie star
    I was made for caviar
    And that's what I've got.

    My life
    Is exactly what I wished for
    So of course
    I must be truly content
    But I'm not.
        The lights black out and the screen flies out. Then the lights restore.
What does it all mean if I cannot have love? Oh, how hollow is all this beauty without the right man to share it with.
NARRATOR: And then one day Passionella met the right man. She met him on Hollywood's famed Sunset Strip at the opening of a new . . .
        A statue is brought on, covered with a large cloth.
. . . psychedelic drug store. This man, a celebrated recording star who combined the outspoken fervor of Patrick Henry, the barbaric yawp of Walt Whitman, the crackerbarrel irreverence of Will Rogers, the flamboyant symbolism of Dylan Thomas, the swashbuckling elegance of Errol Flynn, the skeptical toughness of Bogart, the rugged earthiness of Brando, the sulky masculinity of Presley, the simple humanity of Roy Rogers, the zany vitality of the Beatles, the compassionate arrogance of Bob Dylan, and the hair style of Eleanor Roosevelt, had spoken to the hearts of discontented Americans everywhere. In short, he was the idol of millions: Flip, the Prince Charming.

The statue's covering is taken off, revealing Flip. He is a long-haired, broad-shouldered rocker dressed for cycling in a black leather jacket. The mob screams, and Passionella falls in love at first sight as Flip speaks to her.

FLIP: You dig Allen Ginsberg, man?
PASSIONELLA: Who?
NARRATOR: Beauty did not interest Flip.
FLIP: You dig Timothy Leary?
PASSIONELLA: Who? Who?
NARRATOR: Glamor did not interest Flip.
FLIP: You dig Harley-Davidson?
PASSIONELLA (looking around in confusion): Who? Who? Who?
NARRATOR: Only one thing interested Flip.
FLIP: Reality, man. Truth. Soul. No woman is gonna crack my soul without she is real. Somewhere, she waits, down there, close to the soil among the real people. Real!

Passionella pleads that she is real, but Flip draws her a musical picture of herself. Flip sings into a microphone he happens to have handy, while a chorus of motorcyclists poses around him.

FLIP (sings):
    The newspapers call you
    The goddess of sex
    If you are a goddess
    I'm Oedipus Rex
    Neither goddess nor woman
    You're something apart
    With a Cinerama body
    And a celluloid heart.
    Instead of a soul
    You got a sign, sayin'
    Decor by Helena Rubinstein.
        He crosses behind her and the chorus closes in and surrounds her.
ALL:
    How does it feel
    To be the world's ideal
    When you know an' I know
    That you are not real—real—real
    You are not real. . . . .

They continue to sing at Passionella. The girl of Flip's dreams must be a slob; Passionella is too glamorous, too unreal. Convinced that they are right, Ella the next day tells her studio chief that she's "tired of being a cardboard figure on a tinsel background." She wants to play one of the real people—a chimney sweep. Otherwise she'll quit the movies.

The studio head is forced to accede to her wishes. Passionella the glamor girl will sweep all her own chimneys in a *daytime* shooting schedule. The first day of shooting, Passionella arrives at the set in her gold car. When she throws off her cloak the many technicians and spectators gasp to see how Passionella looks the part of a sooty, humble chimney sweep; how realistically she acts it.

PRODUCER *(weeping):* Marvelous! Not since Paul Muni!
NARRATOR: Cried the Producer.
DIRECTOR *(weeping):* This is sheer folk art.
NARRATOR: Cried the Director.
REPORTER *(weeping):* At last, movies have come of age!
NARRATOR: Cried a reporter from the *Saturday Review.*

The scene changes to the Academy Award ceremony, with a huge replica of Oscar. A starlet enters, hands Flip a statuette and an envelope and then exits. Flip announces the winner: Passionella, who comes down the theater aisle to tumultuous cheering.

A teary Passionella accepts the award, thanking everyone. Flip proposes to her on the spot, and she accepts. The lights black out.

Dreamy eyed—the Narrator explains—the lovers went home and "passed the night making tender love in front of the television set." The lights come up on Passionella's Bel-Air home with a huge TV screen on which Greta Garbo and Robert Taylor are playing the final scene of *Camille.* A sofa faces upstage towards this screen. Passionella and Flip jump up from this sofa as the movie ends and the Late-Late Show begins its 4 a.m. signoff. Plink! Plank! Plunk!

> *The lights black out and there is a huge flash. The lights restore and the stage is empty.*

ELLA *(appearing behind the couch and dressed as she was in the beginning):* Flip? Flip? Flip?

> *She is shyly looking about. Flip appears as a mousy, shy man (narrow-shouldered, his hair plastered down) from behind the other end of the couch. They see each other and cry out in surprise. They laugh and giggle. Flip points to the TV set and pantomimes if that was her before watching with him. She agrees. The music begins.*

FLIP: Were you . . . ? *(He pantomimes the large bosom.)*

ELLA *(nods "Yes"):* Were you . . . ? *(She pantomimes the huge head of hair.)*

FLIP *(nods "Yes"):* Imagine that . . .

ELLA: I never would have guessed . . .

FLIP: I know. I know. *(Sings)*

   Here we are

ELLA:

   The star

FLIP:

And the star.

ELLA:

Well, it just goes to show

FLIP:

We were some pair
Me with my crazy hair

ELLA:

Me with my solid gold gown.

FLIP:

What's your name?

ELLA: Ella. What's yours?

FLIP *(sings):*

George L. Brown.

ELLA: Oh, I love brown!!

They slowly and shyly move to each other. They embrace.

NARRATOR: And they lived happily ever after.

The National Anthem is heard—the screen showing the flag flying in bright colors. The Narrator rises and salutes as the curtain falls.

AMERICA HURRAH

A Program of Three One-Act Plays

BY JEAN-CLAUDE VAN ITALLIE

Cast and credits appear on pages 405-406

JEAN-CLAUDE van ITALLIE is an American playwright who was born in Brussels in 1936 but came to the United States with his family at the age of 4. He is a Harvard graduate (1958). He writes for television and has actively pursued a career of writing for the stage over a broad area of experimental production. His works have been produced "off off Broadway" at Cafe La Mama, the Caffe Cino and by the Albarwild (Albee, Barr and Wilder) Playwrights Unit, and he is a playwright member of Joseph Chaikin's Open Theater. Van Itallie's plays have been produced in Copenhagen, Paris and Zagreb, and one of them—Dis Is De Queen—was produced by Firehouse Theater in Minneapolis under a grant from the Rockefeller Foundation.

Van Itallie's first professional production was the one-acter War, *produced last season off Broadway for 16 performances as part of the program 6 From La Mama.* America Hurrah, *his second, is a program of three one-act plays. The first,* Interview, *was performed under the title* Pavane *at the Academy Theater in Atlanta, Ga., in 1965 and received subsequent stagings by the Open Theater, the Sheridan Square Playhouse, the Cafe La Mama, the La Mama's Europe troupe and National Educational TV. The second, entitled* TV, *had its world premiere in this production. The third,* Motel, *was staged at the Cafe La Mama in 1965 under the title* America Hurrah. *Van Itallie is a bachelor and lives in New York City.*

INTERVIEW

Time: The present

Place: An employment agency

SYNOPSIS: The stage is set with eight gray blocks. Subway steps are at the back of the stage, and there are entrances stage right and left.

The action will spread out over many city scenes, but it begins in an employment agency, where the Interviewers wear translucent plastic masks. At times in the play there is singing, whistling and humming onstage, a rhythmic expression to harpsichord accompaniment, mostly familiar tunes. *("The successful transition from one setting to the next depends on the actors' ability to play together as a company and to drop character instantaneously and completely in order to assume another character, or for a group effect.")*

The First Interviewer, a young woman, enters and sits. The First Applicant, a housepainter, comes in.

FIRST INTERVIEWER *(standing):* How do you do?

FIRST APPLICANT *(sitting):* Thank you, I said, not knowing where to sit.
    The characters will often include the audience in what they say;
    as if the characters were being interviewed by the audience.

FIRST INTERVIEWER *(pointedly):* Won't you sit down?

FIRST APPLICANT *(standing again quickly, afraid to displease):* I'm sorry.

FIRST INTERVIEWER *(busy with imaginary papers, pointing to a particular seat):* There. Name please?

FIRST APPLICANT: Jack Smith.

FIRST INTERVIEWER: Jack What Smith?

FIRST APPLICANT: Beg pardon?

FIRST INTERVIEWER: Fill in the blank space, please. Jack blank space Smith.

FIRST APPLICANT: I don't have any.

FIRST INTERVIEWER: I asked you to sit down. *(Pointing.)* There.

FIRST APPLICANT *(sitting):* I'm sorry.

Having no middle name is a problem—but before it can be solved, in comes Second Applicant, a floorwasher. First Interviewer fires the same questions. The floorwasher's name is Jane *Ellen* Smith. As the questions continue rapidly ("What job are you applying for?" "What experience have you had?") *both* applicants supply answers.

The Third Applicant, a banker, appears. He is Richard F. Smith. (In reanswering the questions, First Applicant solves his problem by calling himself

Jack None Smith). The Fourth Applicant enters this question-and-answer fugue. She is a lady's maid named Mary Victoria Smith.

The Second Interviewer appears. He looks over the Applicants and asks much the same questions ("Have you any children?" "Have you ever earned more than that?"). Then the Third Interviewer, a woman, enters. With each new Interviewer the speed of the questions increases. A Fourth Interviewer enters right after the third.

Interviewers do the next four speeches in a round.

FIRST INTERVIEWER: Will you be so kind as to tell me a little about yourself?

SECOND INTERVIEWER: Can you fill me in on something about your background please?

THIRD INTERVIEWER: It'd be a help to our employers if you'd give me a little for our files.

FOURTH INTERVIEWER: Now what would you say, say, to a prospective employer about yourself?

Applicants address parts of the following four speeches, in particular, directly to the audience.

FIRST APPLICANT: I've been a union member twenty years, I said to them, if that's the kind of thing you want to know. Good health, I said. Veteran of two wars. Three kids. Wife's dead. Wife's sister, she takes care of them. I don't know why I'm telling you this, I said, smiling. *(Sits.)*

SECOND APPLICANT *(standing):* So what do you want to know, I told the guy. I've been washin' floors for twenty years. Nobody's ever complained. I don't loiter after hours, I said to him. just because my boy's been in trouble is no reason, I said, no reason—I go right home, I said to him. Right home. *(Sits.)*

THIRD APPLICANT *(standing):* I said that I was a Republican and we could start right there. And then I said that I spend most of my free time watching television or playing in the garden of my four-bedroom house with our lovely daughters, aged nine and eleven. I mentioned that my wife plays with us, too, and that her name is Katherine, although, I said, casually, her good friends call her Kitty. I wasn't at all nervous. *(Sits.)*

FOURTH APPLICANT *(standing):* Just because I'm here, sir, I told him, is no reason for you to patronize me. I've been a lady's maid, I said, in houses you would not be allowed into. My father was a gentleman of leisure, *and* what's more, I said, my references are unimpeachable.

FIRST INTERVIEWER: I see.

SECOND INTERVIEWER: Alright.

THIRD INTERVIEWER: That's fine.

FOURTH INTERVIEWER: Of course.

Applicants do the following four speeches simultaneously.

FIRST APPLICANT: Just you call anybody at the Union and ask them. They'll hand me a clean bill of health.

SECOND APPLICANT: I haven't been to jail if that's what you mean. Not me. I'm clean.

THIRD APPLICANT: My record is impeccable. There's not a stain on it.

FOURTH APPLICANT: My references would permit me to be a governess, that's what.

The interview continues in this fugue-like form. Where did the Applicants work last? (The Interviewers inspect the Applicants closely, checking teeth, checking under arms.) Were they ever in trouble for dishonesty? This question makes the Applicants indignant. They perform a type of square dance as they deny vigorously any wrongdoing, threatening the Interviewers with reprisals—after all, these Applicants are not without influence in high places. The would-be lady's maid warns: "Miss Thumblebottom married into the Twiths and if you start insulting me, young man, you'll have to start in insulting the Twiths as well. . . . ."

The interview goes on more calmly. Will they smoke? No. The Applicants sneeze, the Interviewers bless them. The Applicants sit.

> *Interviewers stand on their seats and say the following as if one person were speaking.*

FIRST INTERVIEWER: Do you

SECOND INTERVIEWER: speak any

THIRD INTERVIEWER: foreign

FOURTH INTERVIEWER: languages?

FIRST INTERVIEWER: Have you

SECOND INTERVIEWER: got a

THIRD INTERVIEWER: college

FOURTH INTERVIEWER: education? . . . . .

The Applicants state their special skills: Italian, Gaelic, Spanish, the ability to sew a straight seam.

As they arrive at the closing amenities of the interview, the Interviewers bow to the Applicants in turn. The Applicants jump onto the Interviewers' backs, explain that they need jobs in a hurry, then jump off.

The Interviewers bow and remain in the bowing pose. The Applicants leap-frog and then the Interviewers leap-frog, as they exchange a chorus of one-line courtesies like "I'm sorry" and "Excuse *me*."

> *The leap-frogging continues. . . . . Then the Interviewers confer in a huddle and come out of it.*

FIRST INTERVIEWER: Do you enjoy your work?

FIRST APPLICANT: Sure, I said, I'm proud. Why not? Sure I know I'm no Rembrandt, I said, but I'm proud of my work, I said to him.

SECOND APPLICANT: I told him it stinks. But what am I supposed to do, sit home and rot?

THIRD APPLICANT: Do I like my work, he asked me. Well, I said, to gain time, do I like my work? Well, I said, I don't know.

FOURTH APPLICANT: I told him right straight out: for a sensible person, a lady's maid is the *only possible* way of life.

SECOND INTERVIEWER: Do you think you're irreplaceable?

ALL APPLICANTS: Oh, yes indeed.

ALL INTERVIEWERS: Irreplaceable?

ALL APPLICANTS: Yes, yes indeed.

THIRD INTERVIEWER: Do you like me?

FIRST APPLICANT: You're a nice man.

SECOND APPLICANT: Huh?

THIRD APPLICANT: Why do you ask?

FOURTH APPLICANT: It's not a question of "like."

FIRST INTERVIEWER: Well, we'll be in touch with you.

> *This is the beginning of leaving the agency. Soft music under. Applicants and Interviewers push their seats into two masses of four boxes on either side of the stage. Applicants leave first, joining hands to form a revolving door.*

All disappear into the two subway entrances, chattering. The Fourth Interviewer makes a siren sound which persists, above crowd noises. The Fourth Interviewer comes back onstage, still making his siren noise, closely followed by the Fourth Applicant.

FOURTH APPLICANT *(speaking directly to the audience):* Can you direct me to Fourteenth Street, please, I said. I seem to have lost my—I started to say, and then I was nearly run down.

> *The remaining actors return to the stage to play various people on Fourteenth Street—ladies shopping, a panhandler, a man in a sandwich board, a peddler of "franks and orange," a snooty German couple, a lecher, a pair of sighing lovers, and so on.*

The Fourth Applicant continues to express her bewilderment, even hysteria, to the audience as she wanders up one aisle and down the other. She was going shopping for a bargain on Fourteenth Street; but she has lost her wallet, she is confused by the big city.

FOURTH APPLICANT: . . . . . So I asked the most respectable looking man I could find, I asked him, please can you direct me to Fourteenth Street. He wouldn't answer. Just wouldn't. I'm lost, I said to myself. The paper said— the television said—they said, I couldn't remember what they said. I turned for help: "Jesus Saves," the sign said, and a man was carrying it, both sides of his body, staring straight ahead. "Jesus Saves," the sign said.

> *The passers-by jostle her more and more.*

I couldn't remember where I was going. "Come and be saved," it said, so I asked the man with sign, please, sir, won't you tell me how to, dear lord, I thought, anywhere, please sir, won't you tell me how to—can you direct me to Fourteenth Street, *please!*

> *The passers-by have covered the Fourth Applicant. All the actors mill about until they reach designated positions on the stage where they face the audience, a line of women and a line of men, students in a gym class; the Second Interviewer has stayed coolly out of the crowd during this last; now he is the Gym Instructor.*

The Gym Instructor is training his students to look like the glamorous people in ads and in the movies. He is dying for a cigarette as he tells his class: sell, sell all the time, keep selling and smiling but don't smile too broadly.

The gym class's movements become the movements of passengers on a shaking subway (a couple of the "passengers" pretend to be subway advertisements). Another "passenger" soliloquizes to herself about her life: she has grown old and her lover has died. The actors are hissing subway noises; then their sound changes to the whistling of a telephone circuit. They join hands in two "circuits" around the pile of boxes at left.

Meanwhile, Third Interviewer becomes a Telephone Operator speaking in two voices: her official voice and her personal voice on another line as she tells her troubles to a friend named Roberta. The other actors change the patterns of their "circuits" as the Operator coolly voices the routine telephone phrases—"Hang up and dial again please" or "Thank you for giving us the area code"—while at the same time she is confessing to Roberta that she is in fierce pain.

The Telephone Operator falls to the floor in pain, and the whistling becomes a siren as she is carried left to the boxes, which become an operating table. Some actors express the motion of doctors and nurses. Others imitate the Operator's breathing, which accelerates and then stops. Immediately, the scene becomes a cocktail party.

> *The actors find a position and remain there, playing various aspects of a party in slow motion and muted tones. They completely ignore the First Interviewer who, as a Girl at the Party, goes from person to person as if she were in a garden of living statues.*

GIRL AT THE PARTY: And then after the ambulance took off I went up in the elevator and into the party. Did you see the accident, I asked, and they said they did, and what did he look like, and I said he wore a brown coat and had straight brown hair. He stepped off the curb right in front of me. We had been walking up the same block, he a few feet ahead of me, this block right here, I said, but she wasn't listening. Hi, my name is Jill, I said to somebody sitting down and they looked at me and smiled so I said his arm was torn out of its socket and his face was on the pavement gasping but I didn't touch him and she smiled and walked away and I said after her, you aren't supposed to touch someone before—I *wanted* to help, I said, but she wasn't listening. When a man came up and said, was it someone you knew and I said, yes, it was someone I knew slightly, someone I knew, yes, and he offered me a drink and I said no thanks, I didn't want one, and he said well how well did I know him, and I said I knew him well, yes, I knew him very well. You were coming together to the party, he said. Yes, I said, excuse me. Hi, my name is Jill, did you hear a siren, and they said, oh you're the one who saw it, was he killed?

She has been speaking rapidly and excitedly, but now she begins to resign to the fact that no one is listening.

And I said, yes I was, excuse me, and went back across the room but couldn't find another face to talk to until I deliberately bumped into somebody because I had to tell them one of us couldn't come because of the accident. It was Jill. Jill couldn't come. I'm awfully sorry, I said, because of the accident. She had straight brown hair, I said, and was wearing a brown coat, and two or three people looked at me strangely and moved off. I'm sorry I said to a man, and I laughed and moved off. I'm dead I said to several people and started to push them over, I'm dead, thank you, I said, thank you, please, I said, I'm dead, until two or three of them got hold of my arms and hustled me out. I'm sorry, I said, I couldn't come because of the accident. I'm sorry. Excuse me.

The Girl at the Party is lowered to the floor by two of the men and then all fall down except the actor who played the Fourth Interviewer. He remains seated as the Psychiatrist. The Third Applicant, on the floor, props his head up on his elbow and speaks to the audience.

THIRD APPLICANT: Can you help me, Doctor, I asked him.

The Third Applicant was watching television, when suddenly he became ill. The earth seemed to slip out from under him; now all he can do is sit and stare at the wall. The Psychiatrist makes his comment.

PSYCHIATRIST:
    Blah, blah, blah, blah, blah, blah, *hostile.*
    Blah, blah, blah, blah, blah, blah, *penis.*
    Blah, blah, blah, blah, blah, blah, *mother.*
    Holding out his hand.
    Blah, blah, blah, blah, blah, blah, *money.*

The Third Applicant gets up, taking the Psychiatrist's hand. All the actors rise, join hands, do a grand right and left while voicing the Psychiatrist's chant. They form couples and move in a smaller circle. This becomes a church procession, with the women, heads bowed, chanting "Kyrie Eleison" in counterpoint with the now slower-paced blah, blah chant.

The First Applicant confesses to the Fourth Interviewer (now a Priest) his dreams and his dissatisfaction with life. There is too much white paint in life —he would like to paint a barn door red. But the Priest says nothing.

Confessor and confessed join the others for a rock Virginia Reel, while reciting phrases of apology and distress. They form a revolving door, then the Second Interviewer becomes a Square Dance Caller shilling for a candidate for Governor. The actors form a pressing crowd, and the Fourth Interviewer becomes a Politician offering cliche answers to their questions, agreeing with all of them, wishing them good luck. Various characters already established— the Girl at the Party, the Telephone Operator, a pair of lovers from Fourteenth Street—approach the Politician and receive his cheery evasions.

But when the Politician mentions war, the crowd turns sullen.

POLITICIAN: Of course, I said frowning, we must all support the President, I said as I turned concernedly to the next one.
> *Crowd makes a very angry sound, then freezes.*
I'm sorry about the war, I said. Nobody could be sorrier than I am, I said sorrowfully. But I'm afraid, I said gravely, that there are no easy answers. *(Smiles, pleased with himself.)* Good luck to you too, I said cheerfully, and turned my smile to the next one.
> *The Politician topples from his box, beginning his speech all over again. Simultaneously, all the other characters lurch about the stage, speaking again in character—the Shopper on Fourteenth Street, the Gym Instructor, the Subway Rider, the Telephone Operator, the Girl at the Party, the Psychiatrist and the Housepainter. Simultaneously, they all stop and freeze, continue again, freeze again, then continue with music under. The Second Interviewer, acting as policeman, begins to line them up in a diagonal line, like marching dolls, one behind the other. As they are put into line they begin to move their mouths without sound, like fish in a tank. The music stops. When all are in line the Second Interviewer joins them.*

SECOND INTERVIEWER: My
FOURTH APPLICANT: fault.
SECOND APPLICANT: Excuse
FOURTH INTERVIEWER: me.
FIRST INTERVIEWER: Can you
SECOND APPLICANT: help
FIRST APPLICANT: ME?
FOURTH INTERVIEWER: Next.
> *All continue marching in line, moving their mouths, and shouting their lines as the lights come slowly down.*

SECOND INTERVIEWER: My
FOURTH APPLICANT: fault.
SECOND APPLICANT: Excuse
FOURTH INTERVIEWER: me.
FIRST INTERVIEWER: Can you
SECOND APPLICANT: help
FIRST APPLICANT: me?
FOURTH INTERVIEWER: Next.
> *Curtain.*

TV

Time: The present

Place: Viewing room of a television rating company

SYNOPSIS: A control console with screen above it (on which the logo of a TV station is projected from the rear) faces the audience downstage right. A bulletin board is near it. Two doors at right lead to the rest rooms and the hall. At left is a water cooler, a closet and a telephone; upstage center is a table with a coffee maker.

> *Hal and Susan are seated at the console. Susan sits in the middle chair. They are both in their twenties. Hal is playing, as he often will, with his penknife; whittling pencils, paring his nails, or throwing it at the bulletin board. Susan is involved with the papers on the console, with sharpening pencils, and so forth. At the back of the stage, on the left, are the five actors who will portray what will appear on television. For the moment they have no light on them and their backs are to the audience.*

Hal has asked Susan to take in a movie after work, but Susan wants to go home to fix up her apartment—and she can't do it later, she needs at least eight hours' sleep a night. George comes in *("he is older than Hal and Susan and is in charge of the viewing room")*. George comments on Susan's new dress, then changes into a cardigan.

George tells Hal to keep a running total of check marks as he monitors the TV programs—"If you don't make at least a hundred marks, they'll dock you." This group hasn't been asked to make a report in weeks, and Hal wonders whether they've been forgotten. George reassures him. Susan keeps on talking about how she looks, while George warns them not to upset him—his stomach is queasy.

The three sit down and prepare for the day's work, as two of the People on Television get ready to perform their roles.

> *All of the People on Television are dressed in shades of gray. They make no costume changes and use no real props. Their faces are made up with thin horizontal black lines to suggest the way they might appear to a viewer. They are playing television images. Their style of acting is cool, not pushy. As television characters, they have only a few facial masks, such as "cute," "charming," or "serious," which they use infallibly, like signals, in the course of each*

*television segment. After each television segment, the people in-
volved in it will freeze where they are until it is time for them to
become another character. As the play progresses, the People on
Television will use more and more of the stage. The impression
should be that of a slow invasion of the viewing room. . . . .*

In the course of the action, events occur simultaneously "in the viewing
room" and "on television" (with slides on the console screen). To indicate
the timing and juxtaposition of these events, the script segments quoted in
this synopsis are divided into two columns (as they were in the playscript).
Events concerning Hal, Susan and George in the viewing room are expressed
in the left-hand column. Events in television programs are expressed in the
right-hand column.

Susan has *still* been going on about her appearance, and Hal has just suggested that she let herself go. If nature intended her to be a fat slob, then *be*
a fat slob.

	Slide on screen: Wonderboy's face. Helen and Harry Fargis are at home. Helen is baking cookies.
HAL: Why try to look like some-body else?	HELEN: Harry, what are you working on in the garage?
SUSAN: I'm trying to look like myself, thin. Very thin.	
	HARRY: If I succeed in my experiments, nobody in the world will be hungry for love. Ever again.
HAL (*offering him one*): Want a cigarette, George?	
GEORGE: No, thanks.	
	HELEN: Hungry for love? Harry, you make me nervous.
HAL: Just one?	HELEN: You really do.
GEORGE: No.	HARRY: Men will put down their arms.
SUSAN: Hal, why don't you try to help George instead of being so cruel?	HELEN: You haven't been to work for a week now. You'll lose your job.
George has tried to give up ciga-rettes, and Hal is deliberately tan-talizing him. George can't help him-self—he takes a cigarette.	Harry's experiment goes awry. He turns into a monster and comes through the wall at Helen.
Susan tells Hal the president of their company has an Eames chair—a friend showed it to her.	Wonderboy abandons his home-work and comes to Helen's rescue. He saves her from Harry.

Slide: the Vice President.

FIRST NEWS ANNOUNCER: In Washington, D.C., as he left John Foster Dulles Airport, as President Johnson's favorite . . .

Slide: second view of the Vice President.

FIRST NEWS ANNOUNCER: . . . representative, the Vice President, said he was bursting with confidence.

Slide: first view of Viet Namese mourners.

SECOND NEWS ANNOUNCER: U.S. spokesmen in Saigon said families would be given adequate shelter and compensation. Our planes are under strict orders not to return to base with any bombs. The United States regrets that a friendly village was hit. The native toll was estimated at sixty.

HAL: Did you sit in it?

SUSAN: I didn't dare. What would I have said if he'd come in?
George goes to the rest room.

Hal jokes with Susan about her wanting to see the president's chair.

Hal and Susan continue joking. Hal goes into the hall after cokes and George returns from the rest room.

George turns off the sound of a cigarette commercial and tries to date Susan that evening—but she already has a date. George proposes a late date starting at 1 a.m.

Having nothing better to do, George and Susan stare straight ahead as though watching TV, until Hal returns with the cokes.

George phones his wife to tell her that after dinner George must go out again for the midnight-to-3 a.m. shift.

The three discuss the matter of overtime (after George once again turns the sound off). George suspects Hal may be angling for a better job elsewhere, but Hal swears he loves his work.

Susan tells a silly joke, as Hal turns the volume up. Susan cannot stop laughing at her own joke. George rises to fetch Susan a glass of water,

After another report of U.S. callousness, a cigarette commercial begins.

A Western unfolds. The hero says goodby to the heroine.

The villain enters and tells the heroine that the hero is dead.

The heroine slaps the villain as he tries to embrace her, and they struggle.

The hero comes in—he is only wounded. Hero and villain fight. Hero is losing, so heroine shoots villain. The happy couple rides off in the dusk.

Slides are seen of the President and

so that Susan can take a tranquilizer. Hal, impatient to watch TV, slaps Susan to end the distraction.

George returns—apparently these laughing fits of Susan's are a daily annoyance. She is a hysteric, according to her analyst, who has been seeing her for a year. She has two or three more years of treatments in view.

GEORGE: Can you feel the tranquilizer working?

SUSAN: A little bit. I think so.

GEORGE: Maybe I should have one too.

SUSAN (turning volume off): Are you upset?

GEORGE: I can feel my stomach.

Susan gives George a pill, then dashes out to get lunch for the group. George wonders about Susan in her absence: is she too odd for an organization like this? What does Hal (who has thrown his penknife into the bulletin board) think of her—and has he been to bed with her?

Hal counters with a question: how

his family. The President makes a speech against aggression.

The President promises that U.S. towns and cities will remain safe, regardless of what happens abroad. He and his family are cheered by a corps of cadets.

A Spanish-language teacher offers instruction.

Researchers parade on the screen in a commercial for a company which makes many kinds of products.

Slide: a civil rights demonstration.

FIRST NEWS ANNOUNCER: Three men were critically injured during a civil rights demonstration in Montgomery, Alabama today.

Slide: the Vice President.

FIRST NEWS ANNOUNCER: This afternoon the Vice President arrived in Honolulu. As he stepped off the plane he told newsmen things are looking up.

Slide: a map of China.

FIRST NEWS ANNOUNCER: The Defense Department today conceded that United States aircraft may have mistakenly flown over Chinese territory last month. It regrets the incident.

Slide: a rock and roll group is seen singing and playing.

old is George? 43? Hal doesn't intend to live that long. (He turns up the volume.)

George and Hal talk politics.

George confesses he's a Republican (Hal has friends who won't speak to Republicans. George decides he'd rather not talk politics on an upset stomach.

There's a special knock on the door. George calls "One minute." Hal is mystified.

George turns off the sound, then turns out the lights in the room. Susan comes through the door with a cake decorated with lighted candles. Susan and George sing "Happy Birthday" to Hal, who blows out his candles.

Susan and George have presents for Hal. George's is a necktie.

George bites into his egg salad sandwich (he is getting it all over the dials). He turns up the volume.

Susan goes to make coffee. Hal and George are hypnotized by Lily.

George needs another tranquilizer, the first didn't work.

Hal turns the sound off and opens his present from Susan—an art book. Now all Hal needs is an apartment to put it in (he hands George a piece of cake. Susan has the coffee things all ready). He wants one room under a hundred dollars, anywhere, even the Village.

George feels the Village is too crowded with too many bums. This

The rock and roll group takes a bow, and a group of peace marchers appears. They march and sing "We Shall Overcome."

The First News Announcer tells of a girl whose message is: "burn yourselves, not your draft cards." She is a cheerleader and a supporter of the American Nazi Party.

Slide: A jar of K-F soap-cream.

A famous TV personality comes onto the screen and delivers a plug for a cleaning agent.

The Lily Heaven show begins. Lily comes on strong.

LILY *(sings):*
    When I fall in love . . .
    It will be completely . . .
    Or I'll never—

Another slide of Lily Heaven.

Lily Heaven begins signing off. This is a long procedure, using every cliche there is before finally saying goodby.

The Weather Announcer comes on and starts giving the weather.

Without sound, a woman is shown before and after taking headache pills.

A Lady Announcer comes on. There is a view of a bank.

controversial subject makes him feel sick—and he shouldn't be eating cake.

George snaps the volume on.

Susan's been listening to Norman Thomas and feels she's been drifting to the left.

George has to go to the men's room. Susan feels for him, but Hal is interested only in whether or not he has a date for the movies with Susan that evening.

Susan can't quite make up her mind. She really wants to work on her apartment.

Susan wants to put off her decision, but Hal is losing interest.

Susan decides to go to the movies with Hal.

The Lady Announcer is conducting a luncheon interview program sponsored by a bank and a dog food packager.

Her guest is an American soldier, a much-decorated "Green Beret" who quit the war in Vietnam because he feels that "Whoever in Hanoi or Peking or Washington is sending men out to be killed, *they're* doing something wrong.

But when the soldier gets down to a description of exactly what the war is like, the Lady Announcer cuts him off and signs off brightly, with a dog food commercial.

Slide: Billion Dollar Movie. A very English man and a very English woman appear in the movie.

HE: Sarah.

SHE: Yes, Richard.

HE: Our old apartment.

SHE: Yes, Richard. It's still here.

HE: It seems very small to me.

SHE: It does to me, too.

HE: Do you think we can live in it again?

SHE: Not in the old way.

HE: In a better way.

SHE: You've changed too, Richard, for the better.

HE: So have you, darling, for the better.

SHE: I've learned a lot.

HE: Maybe that's what war is for. *The People on Television hum "White Cliffs of Dover."*

The movie comes to and end with He and She hoping there is no more war, and the others singing.

Susan offers Hal sugar for his coffee, and this reminds Hal of his grandmother.

HAL: "Hal," she used to say to me, my grandmother, "You're going to be a big man. Everybody's going to love you." She used to sing that song to me: "Poppa's gonna buy you a dog named Rover, and if that dog don't bark, Poppa's gonna buy you a looking glass, and if that looking glass should break, you're still the sweetest little boy in town."

SUSAN: That's nice.

George enters and goes directly to the telephone.
GEORGE: Hello, darling? Listen, I've gotten out of it. Isn't that good news? The midnight shift.

GEORGE: I'm looking forward to being home nice and comfy with you.

GEORGE: You know my stomach is killing me. . . . .

But George's wife has some errands for him to do. She gives him a list of things to bring home.

His wife suggests George has been drinking. George says goodby and hangs up. Susan offers him a cup of coffee. George accepts a cup, with sugar, and starts on a chicken sandwich.

Hal plays with his penknife; Susan has another piece of cake, while

The First News Announcer begins an obituary of Greg Pironelli, a baseball player.

Slide: a baseball game.
FIRST NEWS ANNOUNCER: In 1963, the year he was elected to baseball's hall of fame in Cooperstown, New York, Pironelli suffered his first stroke. Pironelli owned a Florida-wide chain of laundries.

Slide: "Johnny Holland Show".
JOHNNY: We're back.
Slide: Johnny and Luci.
JOHNNY: That's a very pretty dress you've got on, Luci.
LUCI: Thank you, Johnny.

JOHNNY: How does it feel living in Austin after all the excitement of the big wedding?
LUCI: It feels fine.

JOHNNY: Do you miss your father?
LUCI: Oh sure, I miss him.

Luci loves her father, and when she wants something "I just march right in, cuddle up in his lap and give him a great big kiss."
Luci amuses Johnny by referring to "nervous nellies" interfering with "daddy's war."
The interview with Luci comes to an end and is replaced by an Evangelist with a choir singing "Onward Christian Soldiers."
The Evangelist defends wealth:

George consumes the chicken sandwich.

George starts to cough. Susan fears it may be a fit. Hal claps George on the back. George manages to gasp out that it is chicken; he has a bone stuck in his throat; Hal looks into George's throat and sees it, shows it to Susan.

George falls to the floor as Hal and Susan argue whether water or bread would help George. George is choking to death during their argument—but finally he coughs up the bone himself.

George is gasping. Susan tries to mother him, but he shouts a four-letter obscenity, pushes her away and staggers toward the bathroom, accidentally turning up the volume as he passes.

Hal changes channels. He and Susan sit down and half-heartedly mention their movie date; vaguely they decide that George's trouble is none of their business.

George comes back, asks to go to the movies with Hal and Susan.

GEORGE: I'd be pleased as punch.

SUSAN: Hal, say something.

HAL (to George): You look bushed to me, George.
GEORGE: Who's bushed?

EVANGELIST: . . . . . Money, the Bible says, is the root of evil, not evil itself. I have seen a roomful of men and women, powerful Hollywood celebrities at 4 o'clock a.m. in the morning, listening to me with tears streaming down their faces crying out to me that they had lost touch with God. "In God We Trust" is on our coins, ladies and gentlemen.
Slide: a second view of the Evangelist. The Evangelist's choir sings "Onward Christian Soldiers."

"Onward Christian Soldiers" is louder than ever.

Mother, Father and Daughter appear in "My Favorite Teenager." As they speak inanities about Daughter's social life, the remaining People on Television make the sound of canned laughter. Daughter doesn't want to go to the prom with Harold Sternpepper, so Father offers to take her.

FATHER: I'd be pleased as punch.
DAUGHTER (aside to mother): Help.
Canned laughter.
MOTHER (to Father): Now, dear, don't you think for your age—
Canned laughter.

FATHER: My age?
Canned laughter.
FATHER (standing and doing a two-step): I'd like to see anybody laugh at my two-step.

George sits in his chair.

Hal, Susan and George are completely mesmerized by the television show.

Now they all speak like situation-comedy characters.

HAL: What movie shall we go to?

GEORGE: Let's talk about it over dinner.

HAL: Who said anything about dinner?

SUSAN: Isn't anybody going to ask me what I want to do?

GEORGE: Sure, what do you want, Susan?

HAL: It's up to you.

SUSAN: Well, have I got a surprise for you two. *I'm* going home to fix up my apartment and you two can have dinner to-*gether.*

Canned laughter.

DAUGHTER *(in despair):* Oh, daddy. Mother, *do* something.

Canned laughter.

MOTHER *(putting her arm around George's shoulder):* I think it's a very nice idea. And maybe I'll go with Harold Sternpepper.

Canned laughter.

DAUGHTER *(loudly, sitting on Hal's knee):* Oh, mother, oh, daddy, oh no!

The canned laughter mounts and the "My Favorite Teenager" sign and music come on. All of the people on Television do canned laughter now. They are crowded around the control console.

Canned laughter.

Slide: Hal, Susan and George with the same facial expressions they now have on the stage.

Hal, Susan and George join in the canned laughter. Then, lights off. Slide off. Curtain call: all are in the same position, silent, their faces frozen into laughing masks. Curtain.

MOTEL

Time: The present

Place: A motel room

SYNOPSIS: Lights, which will grow in intensity as the play progresses, come up on a Motel-Keeper doll. Like the other two dolls in this play, she is larger than human life-size, an impression which is heightened by the size of her head, about three times what it should be in proportion to her body.

The Motel-Keeper doll is worked by an actor inside, on platform shoes. The entire body of the doll can be moved about the stage, but only the arms can be moved separately.

> *She is all gray. She has a large full skirt which reaches to the floor. She has squarish breasts. The hair curlers on her head suggest electronic receivers. The Motel-Keeper doll has eye glasses which are mirrors. It doesn't matter what these mirrors reflect at any given moment. The audience may occasionally catch a glimpse of itself, or be bothered by reflections of light in the mirrors. It doesn't matter; the sensory nerves of the audience are not to be spared.*

The motel room is modern, in violent color combinations of oranges, pinks and reds. There is a neon sign blinking outside.

The Motel-Keeper doll's voice will be heard in a continuous monologue. The voice will change with the light from soft to hard: *"hard finally, and patronizing and petty."*

> *As the voice begins, the arms move, and then the Motel-Keeper doll fusses about the room in little circles.*

MOTEL-KEEPER'S VOICE: I am old, I am an old idea: the walls; that from which it springs forth. I enclose the nothing, making then a place in which it happens. I am the room: a Roman theater where cheers break loose the lion; a railroad carriage in the forest at Compiegne, in 1918, and in 1941. I have been rooms of marble and rooms of cork, all letting forth an avalanche. Rooms of mud and rooms of silk. This room will be slashed too, as if by a scimitar, its contents spewed and yawned out. That is what happens. It is almost happening, in fact. I am this room.

Doors at the back of the room open, and the Man and Woman dolls are seen passing in front of automobile headlights. The Motel-Keeper continues:

this motel room is up to date, with a touch of home—an antimacassar from her mother's house in Boise.

> *The Woman doll enters. Her shoulders are thrown way back, like a girl posing for a calendar. Her breasts are particularly large and perfect. She has a cherry-lipstick smile, blonde hair and a garish patterned dress.*

The Man and Woman dolls are the same size as the Motel-Keeper and also have proportionately large heads. But they can move much more freely. The Woman doll enters, inspects the room; undresses down to lace panties and bra.

The Motel-Keeper's voice continues, but she never speaks to the other two dolls, nor are her words responsive to their actions or influence. She boasts of the newness of her facilities: "The toilet flushes of its own accord. All you've got to do is get off." Everything for the weary traveler, including a touch of home.

The Woman doll goes into the bathroom. The Motel-Keeper's voice is addressing an imaginary client who has arrived, without children, to rent the last available room at $12 a night.

> *The Man doll enters carrying a suitcase. He has a cigar and a loud Florida shirt. He closes the door, inspects the room, and takes off his clothes, except for his loudly patterned shorts.*

MOTEL-KEEPER'S VOICE: There now. What I say doesn't matter. You can see. It speaks for itself. The room speaks for itself. You can see it's a perfect 1966 room. But a taste of home. I've seen to that. A taste of home. Comfy, cozy, nice, but a taste of newness. That's what. You can see it. The best stop on route six sixty-six. Well, there might be others like it, but this is the best stop. You've arrived at the right place. This place. And a hooked rug. I don't care what, but I've said no room *is* without a hooked rug.

> *Sound of the toilet flushing.*

Reasonable rates, too, the Motel-Keeper says, as the toilet is heard flushing again. The Man doll tests the bed, pulls at the bedspread. The Woman doll comes in to fetch her negligee, then returns to the bathroom.

> *The Man doll pulls the bedspread, blankets and sheets off the bed, tearing them apart. He jumps hard on the bed.*

MOTEL-KEEPER'S VOICE: Any motel you might have come to on six sixty-six. Any motel. On that vast network of roads. Whizzing by, whizzing by. Trucks too. And cars from everywhere. Full up with folks, all sitting in the very palm of God. I can tell proper folks when I get a look at them. All folks.

> *The Man doll rummages through the suitcase, throwing clothes about the room.*

MOTEL-KEEPER'S VOICE: Country roads, state roads, United States roads. It's a big world and here you are. I noticed you got a license plate. I've not been to there myself. I've not been to anywhere myself, excepting town for supplies, and Boise. Boise, Idaho.

> *Toilet articles and bathroom fixtures, including toilet paper and the toilet seat, are thrown out of the bathroom. The Man doll casually tears pages out of the Bible.*

The Motel-Keeper points out the plastic flowers, which were made in Japan. Everything in here was ordered from the catalogue, she says, and she begins to name various objects. She names object after object; soon her list has no longer any reference to the room, but becomes a nonsense catechism of materialism: ". . . . . catnip, club feet, canisters, bannisters, holy books, tattooed toilet articles. . . . ."

Meanwhile, objects keep flying in from the bathroom. The Man drags down the curtains. The Woman doll comes in, with negligee over panties and bra. She opens her negligee, the Man doll pulls off her bra and then hugs and kisses her.

The Woman doll rings her bare nipples with lipstick, while the Man doll finds loud rock and roll music on TV (and the Motel-Keeper continues her catalogue listing).

The Man doll writes simple, men's-room-type obscenities on the wall in large, legible letters; the Woman doll does the same with her lipstick. Finally she is inspired to say it in a large lipstick drawing: an obscene caricature of the male sex organ, with all the details traditional in men's-room art.

Next year, the Motel-Keeper boasts, she will offer the complete security of a bomb shelter-motel with all rooms underground. The Man and Woman dolls dance, as the music gets louder and a Civil Defense siren begins its wail.

The Man and Woman dolls move deliberately to a crescendo of vandalism. They smash the TV set, the windows and finally they tear the arms out of the Motel-Keeper doll, who has returned to her catalogue listing:

MOTEL-KEEPER'S VOICE: . . . . . fish-tackles, bug bombs, toasted terra-cottaed Tanganyikan switch blades, ochre closets, ping pong balls, didies, capricorn and cancer prognostics, crackers, total uppers, stick pins, basting tacks . . .

> *The Motel-Keeper's voice is drowned out by the other sounds— siren and music—which have built to a deafening pitch and come from all parts of the theater. The door opens again and headlights shine into the eyes of the audience.*
>
> *The actor inside the Motel-Keeper doll has slipped out of it. The Man and Woman dolls tear off the head of the Motel-Keeper doll, then throw her body aside.*
>
> *Then, one by one, the Man and Woman dolls leave the motel room and walk down the aisle. Fans blow air through the debacle on stage onto the audience.*
>
> *After an instant more of excruciatingly loud noise: blackout and silence. Curtain.*

THE HOMECOMING

A Play in Two Acts

BY HAROLD PINTER

Cast and credits appear on page 380

HAROLD PINTER was born in London October 10, 1930. He spent his childhood in Hackney, where his father had a ladies' tailor shop, and where Pinter attended grammar school. He entered the Royal Academy of Dramatic Art but left after three months to begin his theater career as an actor in Anew McMaster's company in Ireland; thence to Donald Wolfit's company in England. In 1957 he wrote his first short play, The Room. *He soon completed two other short plays,* The Dumbwaiter *and* The Birthday Party, *which latter was Pinter's first London production.*

The first Pinter play produced on Broadway was the full-length The Caretaker *(1961), a Best Play of its season. His off-Broadway productions have taken place as follows:* The Dumbwaiter *and* The Collection *(originally written for TV, a Best Play of its season), 1962;* The Lover *(originally written for TV), 1964;* The Room *and* A Slight Ache, *1964; and* The Caretaker *(in revival), 1964.*

Pinter has also written a number of screen plays including The Servant, The Quiller Memorandum *and* Accident. *He is married to Vivien Merchant, the actress who played the feminine role in* The Homecoming. *They live in a Regents Park house in London.*

260

INTRODUCTION BY THE PLAYWRIGHT *

As far as I'm concerned my play *The Homecoming* means exactly what it says; exactly what it does; exactly what happens on the stage. Any play is an object created between curtain going up and curtain coming down. If the characters are rounded and properly embodied, its meaning is continual, forward to the end and back to the beginning. In general I feel audiences should pay more attention to *exactly* what happens, *exactly* what is said on the stage. Any other search for meaning behind everything is a little wasteful of the energies of the people who participate in it.

There's a scene in *The Homecoming* in which the father knocks the athletic son down and the son gets up and crosses the stage. On the very first night in New York, as the son walked very slowly toward the father, and one didn't know whether he was going to hit him or what was going to happen, an extraordinarily deep sound filled the theater. Everyone thought it a cunning Royal Shakespeare Company theatrical effect. I was asked about its meaning and purpose a number of times.

In fact, it was the Queen Mary, or something, in New York harbor.

HAROLD PINTER

Time: The present, summer

Place: An old house in North London

ACT I

SYNOPSIS: A large gray living room extends the width of the stage; it has all the cozy charm of a warehouse. Once, there may have been a door in its rear wall. Now that door has been knocked out, along with some of the wall, to leave a square archway exposing the hall and much of the stairway leading off left to the bedroom floor. In the hall is a coat stand, and the living room furniture includes two armchairs in the center, a sofa at left and a large sideboard upstage right. There is a mirror above the sideboard and a record player and a bowl of apples on it, and to its right is the room's only visible window.

---

* These comments were made during an interview on "The Pinter Puzzle," a television program produced by WNDT, Channel 13, the Public Television Station in New York City, and were designated by the author to introduce his play here.

Lenny, in his early thirties—a tense young man in a dark suit—is seated on the sofa, marking horses in the newspaper. Max, aged 70, the head of this household, comes in from the direction of the kitchen down the hall at right. Max is wearing an old cardigan and cloth cap. He rummages in the sideboard, then asks Lenny where the scissors are.

LENNY *(looking up, quietly):* Why don't you shut up, you daft prat?

MAX *(lifts his stick and points it at him):* Don't you talk to me like that. I'm warning you. *(He sits in a large armchair.)* There's an advertisement in the paper about flannel vests. Cut price. Navy surplus. I could do with a few of them.

Pause.

I think I'll have a fag. Give me a fag.

Pause.

I just asked you to give me a cigarette.

Pause.

Look what I'm lumbered with. *(He takes a crumpled cigarette from his pocket.)* I'm getting old, my word of honor. *(He lights it.)* You think I wasn't a tearaway? I could have taken care of you, twice over. I'm still strong. You ask your Uncle Sam what I was. But at the same time I always had a kind heart. Always.

Pause.

I used to knock about with a man called MacGregor. I called him Mac. You remember Mac? Eh?

Pause.

Huhh! We were two of the worst hated men in the West End of London. I tell you, I still got the scars. We'd walk into a place, the whole room'd stand up, they'd make way to let us pass. You never heard such silence. Mind you, he was a big man, he was over six foot tall. His family were all MacGregors, they came all the way from Aberdeen, but he was the only one they called Mac.

Pause.

He was very fond of your mother, Mac was. Very fond. He always had a good word for her.

Pause.

Mind you, she wasn't such a bad woman. Even though it made me sick just to look at her rotten stinking face, she wasn't such a bad bitch. I gave her the best bleeding years of my life, anyway.

LENNY: Plug it will you, you stupid sod, I'm trying to read the paper.

MAX: Listen! I'll chop your spine off, you talk to me like that! You understand? Talking to your lousy filthy father like that!

LENNY: You know what, you're getting demented.

Their hostility is a ritual. Lenny sneers as though he could dominate his father; Max bullies as though he could recapture his youthful vigor, but neither effort is successful.

Talking of race horses, Max remembers that he once had a way with horses, "a gift." Lenny changes the subject, criticizes Max's cooking.

LENNY: . . . . . Why don't you buy a dog? You're a dog cook. Honest. You think you're cooking for a lot of dogs.

MAX: If you don't like it, get out.

LENNY: I am going out. I'm going out to buy myself a proper dinner.

MAX: Well, get out! What are you waiting for?

LENNY *(looks at him):* What did you say?

MAX: I said shove off out of it, that's what I said.

LENNY: You'll go before me, Dad, if you talk to me in that tone of voice.

MAX: Will I, you bitch? *(Max grips his stick.)*

LENNY: Oh, Daddy, you're not going to use your stick on me, are you? Eh? Don't use your stick on me, Daddy. No, please. It wasn't my fault, it was one of the others. I haven't done anything wrong, Dad, honest. Don't clout me with that stick, Dad.

> *Silence. Max sits hunched. Lenny reads the paper.*

Sam, Max's brother, about 63, enters left from the front-door end of the hall. He is wearing a chauffeur's uniform. He hangs up his hat, takes a seat and sighs wearily. Sam talks to Lenny as though Max wasn't there, describing his day: he chauffeured an American all day, finally dropping him at the airport. The American gave Sam a box of cigars.

Sam offers Max a cigar. They both light up and pronounce the cigars first-rate. Sam boasts of his expert chauffering. He is the best in the firm because "(a) I'm the best driver, and because . . . (b) I don't take liberties." He doesn't force himself on the passengers in his Humber Super Snipe but can pass the time of day pleasantly, when required.

Lenny goes out, as Max taunts Sam for never having married.

SAM: There's still time.

MAX: Is there?

> *Pause.*

SAM: You'd be surprised.

MAX: What you been doing, banging away at your lady customers, have you?

SAM: Not me.

MAX: In the back of the Snipe? Been having a few crafty reefs in a layby, have you?

SAM: Not me.

MAX: On the back seat: What about the armrest, was it up or down?

SAM: I've never done that kind of thing in my car.

MAX: Above all that kind of thing, are you, Sam?

SAM: Too true.

MAX: Above having a good bang on the back seat, are you?

SAM: Yes, I leave that to others.

MAX: You leave it to others? What others? You paralyzed prat!

SAM: I don't mess up my car! Or my . . . my boss's car! Like other people.

MAX: Other people? What other people?

Pause.

What other people?

Pause.

SAM: Other people.

Pause.

MAX: When you find the right girl, Sam, let your family know, don't forget, we'll give you a number one send-off, I promise you. You can bring her to live here, she can keep us all happy. We'd take it in turns to give her a walk round the park.

SAM: I wouldn't bring her here.

Sam rises and takes an apple from the sideboard; then goes to the window and looks out, while reminiscing about Max's dead wife, Jessie, the mother of Max's sons. Sam used to love to drive Jessie around, to stop and buy her a cup of coffee.

Joey enters; he is Max's youngest son, in his middle twenties; he throws his jacket onto a chair and announces that he is hungry. Joey is husky, a would-be boxer, and he has just been training at the gym.

Lenny comes in, deprecates Max's cooking and then goes out again, as Max deprecates Joey's boxing prowess. Joey picks up his jacket and goes upstairs.

Sam returns to the subject of Jessie. Sam is proud that Max trusted him to take care of Jessie on occasions—he would not even have trusted his close friend MacGregor.

Max turns on Sam and warns him that when Sam gets too old to pay his way, Max will throw him out of the house. Sam claims that the house is his as much as Max's, it was their mother's house. Max reminisces about their father; how he used to dandle Max affectionately. Following Max's memories, the stage lights black out to denote the end of the scene.

> *Lights up. Night. Teddy and Ruth stand at the threshold of the room. They are both well dressed in light summer suits and light raincoats. Two suitcases are by their side. They look at the room. Teddy tosses the key in his hand, smiles.*

TEDDY: Well, the key worked.

Pause.

They haven't changed the lock.

Pause.

RUTH: No one's here.

TEDDY *(looking up):* They're asleep.

Teddy, Max's oldest son, is a college professor in his middle thirties, a PhD who lives and teaches in America. His wife Ruth is in her early thirties. They have left their children back home during their summer trip to Europe, which is coming to an end with this surprise visit to Teddy's family, in the house where Teddy was born.

Ruth is tired but does not sit down. Teddy runs upstairs and then down again; his room is still there, and the bed is empty. Teddy tells Ruth how they knocked the door out of the wall and made an archway to open up the living area.

TEDDY: . . . . . The structure wasn't affected, you see. My mother was dead.
          Ruth sits.
Tired?
RUTH: Just a little.
TEDDY: We can go to bed if you like. No point in waking anyone up now. Just go to bed. See them all in the morning . . . see my father in the morning . . .
          Pause.
RUTH: Do you want to stay?
TEDDY: Stay?
          Pause.
We've come to stay. We're bound to stay . . . for a few days.

Ruth suggests the children may be missing them—but Teddy's attention is on his surroundings, his remembered home. He suggests that Ruth go to bed, but she doesn't want to. Teddy reassures Ruth that she need not be nervous, his family aren't ogres, and besides, he's here to protect her.

As soon as Teddy decides it's time for bed, Ruth decides she wants to go out for a breath of air. Teddy insists on waiting up for her and gives her the key. Ruth departs, and Teddy goes to the living room window to watch her. Teddy chews his knuckles as Lenny enters from the left in his pajamas and stands watching Teddy.

Teddy turns and sees Lenny. Their greeting is most casual; Lenny complains of a ticking in his room that is keeping him awake, in the kind of conversation he might hold with Teddy if they saw each other every day. Teddy suggests the disturbance is probably caused by Lenny's clock, and Lenny agrees.

Teddy asks after the family, then decides to go to bed. Lenny offers him a glass of water, but Teddy declines. Teddy picks up the suitcases and goes upstairs. The light in the upper landing goes out.

Lenny stands at the window, watching; when he turns away he is holding a small clock which he places on the table. He sits down and lights a cigarette.

          *Ruth comes in the front door. She stands still. Lenny turns his head,
          smiles. She walks slowly into the room.*
LENNY: Good evening.
RUTH: Morning, I think.

LENNY: You're right there.
> *Pause.*

My name's Lenny. What's yours?
RUTH: Ruth. *(She sits, puts her coat collar around her.)*
LENNY: Cold?
RUTH: No.
LENNY: It's been a wonderful summer, hasn't it? Remarkable.

Lenny offers her an aperitif. Ruth refuses—luckily, as Lenny explains, because they haven't anything in the house.

Lenny deduces that Ruth must be Teddy's companion, and he places his problem before her: all sorts of commonplace objects begin ticking during the night, objects which are silent during the day. "So . . . all things being equal . . . this question of me saying it was the clock that woke me up, well, that could very easily prove something of a false hypothesis."

Lenny goes to the sideboard, pours Ruth a glass of water from a pitcher and hands it to her. She sips it and puts it on the table. Lenny questions her about her life with Teddy, and for the second time Ruth informs him that she is Teddy's *wife.* They have been to Italy—Venice—and are now on their way home to America. Lenny has a feeling that he might have gone through Venice in the Italian campaign in World War II, if he hadn't been too young to serve in the army at that time.

Lenny wants to hold Ruth's hand—and he tells her a sordid story of an encounter down by the docks, in which he beat up a woman who had accosted him and who, he judged, was diseased. He thought of killing her but decided against it at the last moment.

Lenny tells Ruth that Teddy, to whom she has been married for six years now, has always been Lenny's favorite brother. Teddy is a PhD, and Lenny envies him his sensitivity. "I'm very sensitive to atmosphere," Lenny explains, "but I tend to get desensitized, if you know what I mean, when people make unreasonable demands on me."

Lenny launches into a rambling story about an episode in which he took a job clearing snow and found himself trying to help an old lady move a heavy mangle. Lenny strained to move it but could not, while the old lady looked on.

LENNY: . . . . . So after a few minutes I said to her, now look here, why don't you stuff this iron mangle up your arse? Anyway, I said, they're out of date, you want to get a spin drier. I had a good mind to give her a workover there and then, but as I was feeling jubilant with the snow-clearing I just gave her a short-arm jab to the belly and jumped on a bus outside. Excuse me, shall I take this ash tray out of your way?
RUTH: It's not in my way.
LENNY: It seems to be in the way of your glass. The glass was about to fall. Or the ash tray. I'm rather worried about the carpet. It's not me, it's my father. He's obsessed with order and clarity. He doesn't like mess. So, as I don't believe you're smoking at the moment, I'm sure you won't object if I

move the ash tray. *(He does so.)* And now perhaps I'll relieve you of your glass.

RUTH: I haven't quite finished.

LENNY: You've consumed quite enough, in my opinion.

RUTH: No, I haven't.

LENNY: Quite sufficient, in my own opinion.

RUTH: Not in mine, Leonard.

> *Pause.*

LENNY: Don't call me that, please.

RUTH: Why not?

LENNY: That's the name my mother gave me.

> *Pause.*

Just give me the glass.

RUTH: No.

> *Pause.*

LENNY: I'll take it, then.

RUTH: If you take the glass . . . I'll take you.

> *Pause.*

LENNY: How about me taking the glass without you taking me?

RUTH: Why don't I just take you?

> *Pause.*

LENNY: You're joking.

> *Pause.*

You're in love, anyway, with another man. You've had a secret liaison with another man. His family didn't even know. Then you come here without a word of warning and start to make trouble.

> *She picks up the glass and lifts it towards him.*

RUTH: Have a sip. Go on. Have a sip from my glass.

> *He is still.*

Sit on my lap. Take a long cool sip.

> *She pats her lap. Pause. She stands, moves to him with the glass.*

Put your head back and open your mouth.

LENNY: Take that glass away from me.

RUTH: Lie on the floor. Go on. I'll pour it down your throat.

LENNY: What are you doing, making me some kind of proposal?

RUTH *(laughs shortly, drains the glass):* Oh, I was thirsty.

> *She smiles at him, puts the glass down, goes into the hall and up the stairs. He follows into the hall and shouts up the stairs.*

LENNY: What was that supposed to be? Some kind of proposal?

> *Silence. He comes back into the room, goes to his own glass, drains it.*

Lenny's shouting has wakened Max, who comes downstairs in pajamas and cap. Max has heard conversation, too, and thinks Lenny has someone hidden. Lenny takes this opportunity to ask his father what it was like on the night

Lenny was conceived. Max spits at him, infuriated, and goes back upstairs. Blackout.

When the lights come up again, it is morning. Max and Joey, dressed, are downstairs, with Joey practising exercises in front of a mirror. Max hates this room, would prefer his tea in the kitchen. Max invites Joey to attend a football game with him, but Joey is training that afternoon.

Sam comes in, and Max accuses him of resenting his chore of making the breakfast. Max pleads that he has never given Sam cause for resentment. On the contrary, he has obeyed their father's dying instruction: "Max, look after your brothers." Max boasts that he honored his father, he "commemorated his name in blood," he took over the butcher shop and begat three sons of his own—in contrast to Sam, who has done nothing. Sam hands Max the washing-up cloth, as though it were some contested symbol of authority or privilege.

Teddy and Ruth come downstairs in their dressing gowns for their surprise appearance. At first, Max is resentful, feeling that he is a laughing-stock, he ought to have been told they were in the house. Max looks Ruth over and calls her a tart.

MAX: We've had a smelly scrubber in my house all night. We've had a stinking pox-ridden slut in my house all night.

TEDDY: Stop it! What are you talking about?

MAX: I haven't seen the bitch for six years, he comes home without a word, he brings a filthy scrubber off the street, he shacks up in my house!

TEDDY: She's my wife! We're married!

Pause.

MAX: I've never had a whore under this roof before. Ever since your mother died. My word of honor. *(To Joey.)* Have you ever had a whore here? Has Lenny ever had a whore here? They come back from America, they bring the slopbucket with them. They bring the bedpan with them. *(To Teddy.)* Take that disease away from me. Get her away from me.

TEDDY: She's my wife.

MAX *(to Joey):* Chuck them out.

Pause.

A Doctor of Philosophy. Sam, you want to meet a Doctor of Philosophy? *(To Joey.)* I said chuck them out.

Pause.

What's the matter? You deaf?

JOEY: You're an old man. *(To Teddy.)* He's an old man.

Lenny walks into the room, in a dressing-gown. He stops. They all look round. Max turns back, hits Joey in the stomach with all his might. Joey contorts, staggers across the stage. Max, with the exertion of the blow, begins to collapse. His kness buckle. He clutches his stick. Sam moves forward to help him. Max hits him across the head with his stick. Sam sits, head in hands. Joey, hands pressed to his stomach, sinks down at the feet of Ruth. She looks down at him. Lenny and Teddy are still. Joey slowly stands. He is close to Ruth. He turns from Ruth, looks round at Max. Sam clutches his head. Max breathes heavily, very slowly gets to his feet. Joey moves to him. They look at each other. Silence. Max moves past Joey, walks toward Ruth. He gestures with his stick.

MAX: Miss.

RUTH *(walks toward him):* Yes?

MAX *(looks at her):* You a mother?

RUTH: Yes.

MAX: How many you got?

RUTH: Three.

MAX *(turns to Teddy):* All yours, Ted?

Pause.

Teddy, why don't we have a nice cuddle and kiss, eh? Like the old days? What about a nice cuddle and kiss, eh?

TEDDY: Come on, then.

Pause.

MAX: You want to kiss your old father? Want a cuddle with your old father?

TEDDY: Come on, then. *(Moves a step toward him.)* Come on.

Pause.

MAX: You still love your old Dad, eh?

They face each other.

TEDDY: Come on, Dad. I'm ready for the cuddle.

Max begins to chuckle, gurgling. He turns to the family and addresses them.

MAX: He still loves his father!

Curtain.

ACT II

It is afternoon, just after lunch, the same day. Max, Teddy, Lenny and Sam are lighting cigars; Joey comes in with the coffee tray, and Ruth passes the cups around.

Ruth compliments Max on his cooking. Max feels a glow in this family gathering; remembers Jessie, how she would have loved her grandchildren, how she taught her boys "all the morality they know." Max remembers one intimate evening when he gave the boys a bath, then sat with his wife Jessie, the boys at their feet, with a drop of cherry brandy, discussing what they would buy when their ship came in.

Abruptly, Max's mood changes, as he asks Sam about his job.

MAX: You've got a job on this afternoon, haven't you?

SAM: Yes, I know.

MAX: What do you mean, you know? You'll be late. You'll lose your job? What are you trying to do, humiliate me?

SAM: Don't worry about me.

MAX: It makes the bile come up in my mouth. The bile—you understand? *(To Ruth.)* I worked as a butcher all my life, using the chopper and the slab, the slab, you know what I mean, the chopper and the slab! To keep my family in luxury. Two families! My mother was bedridden, my brothers were all invalids. I had to earn the money for the leading psychiatrists. I had to read books! I had to study the disease, so that I could cope with an emergency at every stage. A crippled family, three bastard sons, a slutbitch of a wife—don't talk to me about the pain of childbirth—I suffered the pain, I've still got the pangs—when I give a little cough my back collapses—and here I've got a lazy idle bugger of a brother won't even get to work on time. The best chauffeur in the world. All his life he's sat in the front seat giving lovely hand signals. You call that work? This man doesn't know his gearbox from his arse!

SAM: You go and ask my customers! I'm the only one they ever ask for.

MAX: What do the other drivers do, sleep all day?

SAM: I can only drive one car. They can't all have me at the same time.

MAX: Anyone could have you at the same time. You'd bend over for half a dollar on Blackfriars Bridge.

SAM: Me!

MAX: For two bob and a toffee apple.

Sam shakes hands with Ruth and leaves. Abruptly, Max's mood softens as he catches up on Teddy's news. Max is sorry that Teddy and Ruth got married the day they left England for America, without telling anyone, because Max would have given them a wedding with all the trimmings. Max is proud that Teddy is a PhD. He gives them his blessing.

RUTH: I'm sure Teddy's very happy . . . to know that you're pleased with me.
>*Pause.*

I think he wondered whether you would be pleased with me.

MAX: But you're a charming woman.
>*Pause.*

RUTH: I was . . .

MAX: What?
>*Pause.*

What she say?
>*They all look at her.*

RUTH: I was . . . different . . . when I met Teddy . . . first.

TEDDY: No you weren't. You were the same.

RUTH: I wasn't.

MAX: Who cares? Listen, live in the present, what are you worrying about? I mean, don't forget the earth's about five thousand million years old, at least. Who can afford to live in the past?
>*Pause.*

TEDDY: She's a great help to me over there. She's a wonderful wife and mother. She's a very popular woman. She's got lots of friends. It's a great life, at the University . . . you know . . . it's a very good life. We've got a lovely house . . . we've got all . . . we've got everything we want. It's a very stimulating environment.

> *Pause.*

My department . . . is highly successful.

> *Pause.*

We've got three boys, you know.

MAX: All boys? Isn't that funny, eh? You've got three, I've got three. . . . .

Ruth hears of Joey's boxing ambitions; then she receives a compliment from Max, who is warming to her.

Lenny tries to engage Teddy in a philosophic discussion about the nature of reverence (that's not in Teddy's province), then the nature of an everyday piece of furniture like a table.

LENNY: . . . . . All right, I say, *take* it, *take* a table, but once you've taken it, what you going to do with it? Once you've got hold of it, where you going to take it?

MAX: You'd probably sell it.

LENNY: You wouldn't get much for it.

JOEY: Chop it up for firewood.

> *Lenny looks at him and laughs.*

RUTH: Don't be too sure though. You've forgotten something. Look at me. I . . . move my leg. That's all it is. But I wear . . . underwear . . . which moves with me . . . it . . . captures your attention. Perhaps you misinterpret. The action is simple. It's a leg . . . moving. My lips move. Why don't you restrict . . . your observations to that? Perhaps the fact that they move is more significant . . . than the words which come through them. You must bear that . . . possibility . . . in mind.

> *Silence. Teddy stands.*

I was born quite near here.

> *Pause.*

Then . . . six years ago, I went to America.

> *Pause.*

It's all rock. And sand. It stretches . . . so far . . . everywhere you look. And there's lots of insects there.

> *Pause.*

And there's lots of insects there.

> *Silence. She is still. . . . .*

Max takes Joey and Lenny out, leaving Teddy and Ruth alone. Teddy suggests they cut short their visit; he is thinking of the boys, and of the "clean" way of life back home, the swimming. Ruth is noncommittal about going home, but Teddy goes to pack.

Lenny comes in, and Lenny and Ruth talk of clothes—women's clothes.

Ruth, it seems, was "a photographic model for the body" before she married. Dreamily, Ruth remembers a country place past a big white tower near a lake where she would occasionally do some of her modeling. Before she went to America, Ruth paid the place a goodbye visit: "I walked up the drive. There were lights on . . . I stood in the drive . . . the house was very light."

Teddy comes downstairs with the suitcases. Lenny puts a slow jazz record on the record player and asks Ruth for one last dance before she leaves.

> *Ruth stands. They dance, slowly. Teddy stands, with Ruth's coat. Max and Joey come in the front door and into the room. They stand. Lenny kisses Ruth. They stand, kissing.*

JOEY: Christ, she's wide open. Dad, look at that.
> *Pause.*

She's a tart.
> *Pause.*

Old Lenny's got a tart in here.
> *Joey goes to them. He takes Ruth's arm. He smiles at Lenny. He sits with Ruth on the sofa, embraces and kisses her. He looks up at Lenny.*

Just up my street.
> *He leans her back until she lies beneath him. He kisses her. He looks up at Teddy and Max.*

It's better than a rubdown, this.
> *Lenny sits on the arm of the sofa. He caresses Ruth's hair as Joey embraces her.*

Max, seeing the suitcases, wishes that Teddy didn't have to leave so soon (neither Max nor Teddy are disturbed by, or hardly even aware of, the scene on the sofa). Max is "broadminded" enough to have enjoyed meeting Teddy's wife, even if Teddy did marry beneath him. Max stares at Ruth's face, under Joey on the sofa, and comments: "Mind you, she's a lovely girl. A beautiful woman. And a mother too. A mother of three. You've made a happy woman out of her. It's something to be proud of. I mean, we're talking about a woman of quality. We're talking about a woman of feeling."

At this point Joey and Ruth, still locked in their embrace, roll off the sofa onto the floor. Lenny touches Ruth with his foot; Ruth pushes Joey away and they both stand up. Suddenly Ruth is hungry and thirsty; and suddenly she is giving orders about what glass she wishes to drink out of, and how she wants her drink fixed. Lenny obeys her and Joey hovers, as though anxious to please her.

RUTH *(to Teddy):* Have your family read your critical works?

MAX: That's one thing I've never done. I've never read one of his critical works.

TEDDY: You wouldn't understand them.
> *Lenny hands drinks all round.*

JOEY: What sort of food do you want? I'm not the cook, anyway.

LENNY: Soda, Ted? Or as it comes?

TEDDY: You wouldn't understand my works. You wouldn't have the faintest idea of what they were about. You wouldn't appreciate the points of reference. You're way behind. All of you. There's no point in my sending you my works. You'd be lost. It's nothing to do with the question of intelligence. It's a way of being able to look at the world. It's a question of how far you can operate on things and not in things. I mean it's a question of your capacity to ally the two, to relate the two, to balance the two. To see, to be able to *see!* I'm the one who can see. That's why I can write my critical works. Might do you good . . . have a look at them . . . see how certain people can view . . . things . . . how certain people can maintain . . . intellectual equilibrium. Intellectual equilibrium. You're just objects. You just . . . move about. I can observe it. I can see what you do. It's the same as I do. But you're lost in it. You won't get me being . . . I won't be lost in it.

    Blackout.

When the lights come up, it is evening. Teddy is sitting in his coat, by the suitcases, talking to Sam, who confides to Teddy that he was always his mother's favorite.

Lenny comes in, complains that someone has taken his cheese roll. Teddy admits he took it deliberately, and ate it, and he defies Lenny to do anything about it. Lenny complains at length that Teddy, living as he does in his comfortable American campus, should be more gracious than he is. The family misses him when he is away; they look up to him, they feel he is part of the family unit. "And so," Lenny concludes, "when you at last return to us, we do expect a bit of grace, a bit of *je ne sais quoi,* a bit of generosity of mind, a bit of liberality of spirit, to reassure us. . . . ."

Joey comes downstairs carrying a newspaper. Joey has been upstairs with Ruth for two hours and, he confesses, "I didn't get all the way." Yet Joey has a way with women; supposedly, he is irresistible. Lenny and Joey tell Teddy of a recent adventure in which they picked up two girls after driving away their escorts.

LENNY: . . . . . So you can't say old Joey isn't a bit of a knockout when he gets going, can you? And here he is upstairs with your wife for two hours and he hasn't even been the whole hog. Well, your wife sounds like a bit of a tease to me, Ted. What do you make of it, Joey? You satisfied? Don't tell me you're satisfied without going the whole hog?

    Pause.

JOEY: I've been the whole hog plenty of times. Sometimes . . . you can be happy . . . and not go the whole hog. Now and again . . . you can be happy . . . without going any hog.

    Lenny stares at him. Max and Sam come in the front door and into the room.

MAX: Where's the whore? Still in bed? She'll make us all animals.

LENNY: The girl's a tease.

MAX: What?

LENNY: She's had Joey on a string.

MAX: What do you mean?

TEDDY: He had her up there for two hours and he didn't go the whole hog.

Ruth never teases Teddy in this way, he "gets the gravy," as Lenny puts it, infuriating frustrated Joey.

MAX: . . . . . You know something? Perhaps it's not a bad idea to have a woman in the house. Perhaps it's a good thing. Who knows? Maybe we should keep her.

Pause.

Maybe we'll ask her if she wants to stay.

Pause.

TEDDY: I'm afraid not, Dad. She's not well, and we've got to get home to the children.

Sam accuses Max of talking rubbish. Teddy treats Max's suggestion as an ordinary invitation for Ruth to stay on in an extended visit with the family; he refuses it in her name, but not so emphatically that he couldn't be talked into changing his mind.

Max persists: if Ruth is so keen on children, she can have more, right here. They will have to pay her for her services, of course; they can all chip in. Joey offers to pay for her clothes. Lenny warns that her tastes may be expensive.

MAX: . . . . . Listen, we're bound to treat her in something approximating, at least, to the manner in which she's accustomed. After all, she's not someone off the street, she's my daughter-in-law!

JOEY: That's right.

MAX: There you are, you see. Joey'll donate. Sam'll donate.

Sam looks at him.

I'll put in a few bob out of my pension, Lenny'll cough up. We're laughing. What about you, Ted? How much you going to put in the kitty?

TEDDY: I'm not putting anything in the kitty.

MAX: What? You won't even help to support your own wife? I thought he was a son of mine. You lousy stinkpig. Your mother would drop dead if she heard you take that attitude.

LENNY: Eh, Dad. *(Walks forward)* I've got a better idea.

MAX: What?

LENNY: There's no need for us to go to all this expense. I know these women. Once they get started they ruin your budget. I've got a better idea. Why don't I take her up with me to Greek Street?

Pause.

MAX: You mean put her on the game?

Pause.

We'll put her on the game. That's a stroke of genius, that's a marvellous idea. You mean she can earn the money herself—on her back?

LENNY: Yes.

MAX: Wonderful. The only thing is, it'll have to be short hours. We don't want her out of the house all night.

LENNY: I can limit the hours.

MAX: How many?

LENNY: Four hours a night.

MAX *(dubiously):* Is that enough?

LENNY: She'll bring in a good sum for four hours a night.

MAX: Well, you should know. After all, it's true, the last thing we want to do is wear the girl out. She's going to have her obligations this end as well. Where you going to put her in Greek Street?

LENNY: It doesn't have to be right in Greek Street, Dad. I've got a number of flats all around that area.

MAX: You have? Well, what about me? Why don't you give me one?

LENNY: You're sexless.

Max asks Teddy how he feels about Ruth paying her own way, but Teddy doesn't reply. Joey is reluctant to share Ruth with anyone, but Max tells him he must, otherwise Ruth will be sent straight back to America.

Max is worried that Ruth may be just a tease, but Teddy reassures him; so does Lenny, who gives his "professional opinion" that Ruth is not. Lenny suggests that Teddy might distribute cards to potential customers in America. They'll give Ruth a professional name like Spanish Jacky . . . or Gillian. Teddy would be a good salesman. Teddy would know all about Ruth, about how far she would be prepared to go to satisfy the customers' "little whims and fancies."

TEDDY: She'd get old . . . very quickly.

MAX: No . . . not in this day and age! With the health service? Old! How could she get old? She'll have the time of her life.
> *Ruth comes down the stairs, dressed. She comes into the room. She smiles at the gathering, and sits. Silence.*

TEDDY: Ruth . . . the family have invited you to stay, for a little while longer. As a . . . as a kind of guest. If you like the idea I don't mind. We can manage very easily at home . . . until you come back.

RUTH: How very nice of them.
> *Pause.*

MAX: It's an offer from our heart.

RUTH: It's very sweet of you.

MAX: Listen . . . it would be our pleasure.

There hasn't been a woman in the house since his wife Jessie died, Max tells Ruth, because any other woman would have been an insult to Jessie's memory. But not Ruth. ". . . . . you're kin. You're kith. You belong here."

Ruth is "very touched." Teddy and Max continue to explain: Ruth will be expected to pull her own weight, financially, until Joey makes it as a boxer. They tell Ruth they'll provide her with a little flat in London which she would visit each night.

RUTH: A flat?
LENNY: Yes.
RUTH: Where?
LENNY: In town.
    Pause.
But you'd live here, with us.
MAX: Of course you would. This would be your home. In the bosom of the family.
LENNY: You'd just pop up to the flat a couple of hours a night, that's all.
MAX: Just a couple of hours, that's all. That's all.
LENNY: And you make enough money to keep you going here.
    Pause.
RUTH: How many rooms would this flat have?
LENNY: Not many.
RUTH: I would want at least three rooms and a bathroom.

Ruth insists on this, and she makes other conditions. She must have a personal maid. They must set her up in business, pay for her wardrobe.

RUTH: I would naturally want to draw up an inventory of everything I would need, which would require your signatures in the presence of witnesses.
LENNY: Naturally.
RUTH: All aspects of the agreement and conditions of employment would have to be clarified to our mutual satisfaction before we finalized the contract.
LENNY: Of course.
    Pause.
RUTH: Well, it might prove a workable arrangement.
LENNY: I think so.
MAX: And you'd have the whole of your daytime free, of course. You could do a bit of cooking here if you wanted to.
LENNY: Make the beds.
MAX: Scrub the place out a bit.
TEDDY: Keep everyone company.
    Sam comes forward.
SAM *(in one breath):* MacGregor had Jessie in the back of my cab as I drove them along.
    He croaks and collapses. He lies still. They look at him.

At first they think Sam is dead, but find that he is not. Max, obsessed with neatness and order, demands to have the corpse removed from his floor. He judges that Sam has a "diseased imagination."

Ruth decides that the family offer is acceptable. They will shake hands on it later. Now, Teddy is leaving, picking up his suitcase, starting for the underground, because now Sam cannot drive him to the airport.

Max and Teddy exchange conventional father-and-son goodbyes; Max gives Teddy a photo of himself to show the grandchildren. Teddy's goodbyes to Lenny and Joey are brief; to Ruth nonexistent until he reaches the front door, at which point Ruth calls to him, "Don't become a stranger."

> *Teddy goes, shuts the front door. Silence. The three men stand. Ruth sits relaxed in her chair. Sam lies still. Joey walks slowly across the room. He kneels at her chair. She touches his head, lightly. He puts his head in her lap. Max begins to move above them, backwards and forwards. Lenny stands still. Max turns to Lenny.*

MAX: I'm too old, I suppose. She thinks I'm an old man.

> *Pause.*

I'm not such an old man.

> *Pause.*

(To Ruth.) You think I'm too old for you?

> *Pause.*

Listen. You think you're just going to get that big slag all the time? You think you're just going to have him . . . you're going to just have him all the time? You're going to have to work! You'll have to take them on, you understand?

> *Pause.*

Does she realize that?

> *Pause.*

Lenny, do you think she understands . . . *(He begins to stammer.)* What . . . what . . . what . . . we're getting at? What . . . we've got in mind? Do you think she's got it clear?

> *Pause.*

I don't think she's got it clear.

> *Pause.*

You understand what I mean? Listen, I've got a funny idea she'll do the dirty on us, you want to bet? She'll use us, she'll make use of us, I can tell you! I can smell it! You want to bet?

> *Pause.*

She won't . . . be adaptable!

> *He falls to his knees, whimpers, begins to moan and sob. He stops sobbing, crawls past Sam's body round her chair, to the other side of her.*

I'm not an old man. *(He looks up at her.)* Do you hear me? *(He raises his face to her.)* Kiss me.

> *She continues to touch Joey's head, lightly. Lenny stands, watching.*
> *Curtain.*

BLACK COMEDY

A Play in One Act

BY PETER SHAFFER

Cast and credits appear on pages 381-382

PETER SHAFFER was born in England, at Liverpool, in 1926. He attended St. Paul's School in London and spent three years at Trinity College, Cambridge (and three years working in English coal mines). In 1951, aged 25, he came to the United States where for still another three years he worked in New York City at Doubleday's Book Shop and the Acquisitions Department of the New York Public Library while pursuing a writing career. He returned to England for the production of his The Salt Land, The Prodigal Father *and* Balance of Terror *on British television. In 1958 his play* Five Finger Exercise *was a success in London. In December, 1959, it was presented at the Music Box and was named a Best Play of its season and was the New York Drama Critics choice for Best Foreign Play.*

A pair of Shaffer one-acters, The Private Ear *and* The Public Eye, *were produced in 1963 at the Morosco after a London production that ran eighteen months. Shaffer's* The Royal Hunt of the Sun *was the first work by a contemporary playwright to be done by England's National Theater, under the directorship of Laurence Olivier; it played 269 performances on Broadway last season and was named a Best Play.* Black Comedy *was commissioned by the National Theater and was produced in London last season. In New York,* Black Comedy *was presented on a double bill with the new Shaffer one-acter* White Lies, *written especially for this production.*

278

Time: 9:30 on a Sunday Night

*Place: Brindsley Miller's apartment in South Kensington,
London*

SYNOPSIS: The curtain rises and the play begins in complete darkness. In the blackness, two voices are heard onstage chatting as though their world were bathed in light. They are the voices of Brindsley Miller *("A young sculptor, late twenties, intelligent and attractive, but nervous and uncertain of himself")* and Carol Melkett *("His fiancee. A young debutante; very pretty, very spoilt; very silly. Her sound is that unmistakable, terrifying deb quack").* Brindsley and Carol are in Brindsley's flat, preparing for important visitors.

> *They must give the impression of two people walking round a room with absolute confidence, as if in the light. We hear sounds as of furniture being moved. A chair is dumped down.*

BRINDSLEY: There! How do you think the room looks?

CAROL *(quacking):* Fabulous! I wish you could always have it like this. That lamp looks divine there. And those chairs are just the right color. I told you green would look well in here.

BRINDSLEY: Suppose Harold comes back?

CAROL: He is not coming back till tomorrow morning.

BRINDSLEY *(paces nervously):* I know. But suppose he comes tonight? He's mad about his antiques. What do you think he'll say if he goes into his room and finds out we've stolen them?

CAROL: Don't dramatize. We haven't stolen all his furniture. Just three chairs, the sofa, that table, the lamp, the bowl and the vase of flowers, that's all.

BRINDSLEY: And the Buddha. That's more valuable than anything.

CAROL: Oh, do stop worrying, darling.

BRINDSLEY: Well, you don't know Harold. He won't even let anyone touch his antiques.

Georg Bamberger, a multi-millionaire art collector, is coming to look over Brindsley's sculpture. But the furniture has been borrowed, not to impress him, but to impress Carol's father, who has also been invited in hope that he will witness Bamberger's approval of Brindsley's work and so be persuaded to give his own approval to Brindsley as a son-in-law.

Glass clinks against glass as Carol mixes Brindsley a drink. Carol's father is a military man, and Brindsley is afraid of him. Carol urges her "sweetipegs" not to be bullied: "Faint heart never won fair ladypegs."

Carol and Brindsley sit on the sofa and embrace. Carol is jealous of Brindsley's other girls, particularly the one named Clea.

CAROL: What was she like?

BRINDSLEY: She was a painter. Very honest. Very clever. And just about as cozy as a steel razor blade.

CAROL: When was the last time you saw her?

BRINDSLEY (evasively): I told you . . . two years ago.

CAROL: Well, why did you still have her photo in your bedroom drawer?

BRINDSLEY: It was just there. That's all. Give me a kiss . . . No one in the world kisses like you.

CAROL (murmuring): Tell me something . . . did you like it better with her—or me?

BRINDSLEY: Like what?

CAROL: Sexipegs.

BRINDSLEY: Look, people will be here in a minute. Put a record on. . . . .

They select "The Band of the Coldstream Guards" to please Carol's father. Carol puts the record on the player while Brindsley worries out loud.

BRINDSLEY: . . . . . Oh God, let this evening go all right! Let Mr. Bamberger like my sculpture and buy some! Let Carol's monster father like me! And let my neighbor Harold Gorringe never find out that we borrowed his precious furniture behind his back! Amen.

A Sousa march; loud. Hardly has it begun, however, when it runs down—as if there is a failure of electricity.

Brilliant light floods the stage. The rest of the play, save for the times when matches are struck or for the scene with Schuppanzigh, is acted in this light, but as if in pitch darkness. (On the few occasions when a lighter is lit, matches are struck or a torch is put on, the light on stage merely gets dimmer. When these objects are extinguished, the stage immediately grows brighter.)

They freeze: Carol by the end of the sofa; Brindsley by the drinks table. The girl's dress is a silk flag of chic wrapped around her greyhound's body. The boy's look is equally cool: narrow, contained and sexy. Throughout the evening, as things slide into disaster for him, his crisp, detached shape degenerates progressively into sweat and rumple—just as the elegance of his room gives way relentlessly to its usual near-slum appearance. For the place, as for its owner, the evening is a progress through disintegration.

Blast! A fuse!

Brindsley's room is on the ground floor opposite Harold Gorringe's, so that Gorringe's door is visible across the hall when Brindsley's door, upstage left, is open. Upstage center is a curtain screening off Brindsley's studio, where his current work awaits Bamberger's perusal. Steep stairs at right lead to a bedroom visible on the floor above. A trap door downstage right gives access to the cellar. *"It is a gay room when we finally see it, full of color and space and new shapes;"* that is, except for Harold Gorringe's furniture now dominating the center of the room.

> *This consists of three elegant Regency chairs in gold leaf; a Regency chaise-longue to match; a small Queen Anne table bearing a fine opaline lamp, with a silk shade; a Wedgewood bowl in black basalt; a good Coalport vase containing summer flowers, and a fine porcelain Buddha.*

By contrast, Brindsley's own furniture is shabby, except for the artistic creations around the room. Two of them are Brindsley's: an iron sculpture with two long metal prongs and, at right on a dais, an assembly of metal pieces which jangle when touched.

Finding themselves in total "darkness" which in the play's reversal appears fully lighted to audience's eye, Carol and Brindsley stumble about; Brindsley flicks the light switch to no avail. They grope for matches.

> *The telephone rings.*

BRINDSLEY: Would you believe it?

> *He blunders his way toward the sound of the bell. Just in time he remembers the central table—and stops himself colliding into it with a smile of self-congratulation.*

All right! I'm coming!

> *Instead he trips over the dais, and goes sprawling—knocking the phone onto the floor. He has to grope for it on his knees, hauling the receiver back to him by the wire.*

Brindsley hears the voice on the phone, then sends Carol upstairs on a pretext. With Carol safely out of earshot, Brindsley returns to the phone. It is Clea, who was supposed to be in Finland. She wants to come over at once. Brindsley, *"beginning to be fussed,"* begs her not to come and struggles to hang up the phone just as Carol edges her way downstairs.

Miss Furnival from the flat on the next floor can be heard making her way down the hall. She is *"a middle-aged spinster. Prissy; and refined. Clad in the blouse and sack skirt of her gentility, her hair in a bun, her voice in a bun. . . . ."* Miss Furnival calls Brindsley's name.

> *She gropes her way in. Brindsley crosses to find her, but narrowly misses her.*

MISS FURNIVAL: Oh, thank God, you're there; I'm so frightened! . . .

BRINDSLEY: Why? Have your lights gone too?

MISS FURNIVAL: Yes.

BRINDSLEY: It must be a power cut.

> *He finds her hand and leads her to the chair downstage left.*

MISS FURNIVAL: I don't think so. The street lights are on in the front. I saw them from the landing.

BRINDSLEY: Then it must be the mains switch of the house.

CAROL: Where is that?

Miss Furnival gasps at the strange voice.

BRINDSLEY: Down in the cellar. It's all sealed up. No one's allowed to touch it but the electricity people.

CAROL: What are we going to do?

BRINDSLEY: Get them—quick!

Brindsley accidentally touches Miss Furnival's breasts. She gives a little scream.

Brindsley remembers to introduce Carol to Miss Furnival as he gropes toward the phone. He tries to reach the London Electricity Board (after a delay explaining to the operator that he is in the dark and cannot dial them himself). He is holding the phone when Miss Furnival suggests that Harold, across the hall, might have some candles. Brindsley hands the phone to Carol and feels his way to Harold's apartment.

Carol finally reaches the Electricity Board, reports the power failure and their urgent need for a repairman. She offers Miss Furnival a drink, but Miss Furnival is a teetotaler.

Someone is heard stumbling among the milk bottles offstage. It is Carol's father, Colonel Melkett *("brisk, barky, yet given to sudden vocal calms which suggest a deep and alarming instability"),* arriving as per invitation.

COLONEL *(barking):* Is there anybody there?

CAROL *(calling):* In here, daddypegs!

COLONEL: Can't you put the light on, dammit? I've almost knocked myself out on a damned milk bottle.

CAROL: We've got a fuse. Nothing's working.

Col. Melkett appears, holding a lighter which evidently is working —we can see the flame, and of course, the lights go down a little.

MISS FURNIVAL: Oh what a relief! A light!

Miss Furnival is introduced to Colonel Melkett and follows his light around the room, until the Colonel turns and glares at her, driving her back to the sofa.

COLONEL *(getting his first sight of Brindsley's sculpture):* What the hell's that?

CAROL: Some of Brindsley's work.

COLONEL: Is it, by Jove? And how much does that cost?

CAROL: I think he's asking fifty pounds for it.

COLONEL: My God!

CAROL *(nervously):* Do you like the flat, Daddy? He's furnished it very well, hasn't he? I mean it's rich, but not gaudipegs.

COLONEL *(seeing the Buddha):* Very elegant—good: I can see he's got excellent taste. Now that's what I understand by a real work of art—you can see what it's meant to be.

MISS FURNIVAL: Good heavens!

CAROL: What is it?

MISS FURNIVAL: Nothing . . . It's just that Buddha—it so closely resembles the one Harold Gorringe has.

Judging from the valuable Buddha, displayed on a low stool downstage, the Colonel guesses Brindsley must be quite well off. But Miss Furnival has noticed the Buddha and now examines and recognizes the sofa on which she is sitting. Carol, panicky, sends her father to the studio (the lights get brighter as he carries his lighter out of the room), tells Miss Furnival what is going on and begs her not to tattle. Miss Furnival will keep their secret, provided they replace the furniture when the party is over. Carol offers her a bitter lemon and she accepts.

The Colonel comes back into the room, judging that Brindsley's sculptures would make "good garden implements." He snaps off his lighter to save fuel.

Brindsley comes back. He hasn't been able to find any candles, so they are still in "pitch darkness"—and, of course, he can't see that the Colonel has arrived.

BRINDSLEY: . . . . . What a lookout! Not a bloody candle in the house. A millionaire to show sculpture to—and your monster father to keep happy. Lovely!

COLONEL (grimly lighting his lighter): Good evenin'.

    Brindsley jumps.

CAROL: Brin, this *is* my father—Colonel Melkett.

BRINDSLEY (wildly embarrassed): Well, well, well, well, well! . . . (Panic.) Good evening, sir. Fancy you being there all the time! I—I'm expecting some dreadful neighbors, some neighbor monsters, monster neighbors, you know . . . They rang up and said they might look round . . . Well, well, well . . .

COLONEL (darkly): Well, well.

MISS FURNIVAL (nervously): Well, well.

CAROL (brightly): Well!

    The Colonel rises and advances on Brindsley who retreats before
    him across the room.

COLONEL: You seem to be in a spot of trouble.

Brindsley is highly nervous now, and characteristically he gives a wild braying laugh. The Colonel points out Brindsley's lack of "basic efficiency"—no matches, no candles. "By basic efficiency, young man," the Colonel snorts, "I mean the simple state of being At Attention in life rather than At Ease."

The Colonel analizes the situation as though it were a military problem. They have no matches, no candles, so what they need is a flashlight. Brindsley starts for the pub to borrow one, when Harold Gorringe is heard offstage coming down the hall. ("The camp owner of an antique china shop. . . . .

Harold comes from the North of England. His friendship is highly conditional and possessive: sooner or later, payment for it will be asked. A specialist in emotional blackmail, he can become hysterical when slighted, or—as inevitably happens—rejected. He is older than Brindsley by several years.")

Harold, in a raincoat and with his hair falling over his brow, allows himself to be led into the room by Brindsley. Miss Furnival announces her presence to Harold, who is then introduced to Carol and a hostile Colonel by the light of the Colonel's flickering lighter.

BRINDSLEY: Here, let me take your raincoat, Harold.
    Harold is wearing a tight grey suit and a brilliant strawberry shirt.
HAROLD *(taking it off and handing it to Brindsley):* Be careful, it's sopping wet.
    Adroitly, Brindsley drops the coat over the Wedgewood bowl on the table.
COLONEL: You got no candles, I suppose?
HAROLD: Would you believe it, Colonel, but I haven't? Silly me!
    Brindsley crosses and blows out the Colonel's lighter, just as Harold begins to look round the room. The stage brightens.
COLONEL: What the devil did you do that for?
BRINDSLEY: I'm saving your wick, Colonel. You may need it later and it's failing fast.
    The Colonel gives him a suspicious look. Brindsley moves quickly back, takes up the coat and drops it over the right end of the sofa, to conceal as much of it as possible.
HAROLD: It's all right. I've got some matches.
CAROL *(alarmed):* Matches!
HAROLD: Here we are! I hope I've got the right end.
    He strikes one, Brindsley immediately blows it out from behind, then moves swiftly to hide the Wedgewood bowl under the table, and drop the tablecloth over the remaining end of the sofa. Miss Furnival sits serenely unknowing between the two covers.
Hey, what was that?
BRINDSLEY *(babbling):* A draught. No match stays alight in this room. It's impossible. Cross-currents, you know. Old houses are full of them. They're almost a permanent feature in this house. . . . .

Again, Harold lights a match and again Brindsley blows it out. This makes Harold suspicious that they are hiding "a dead body or something." Another match and another blow-out *("All these strikings and blowings are of course accompanied by swift and violent alterations of the light").*

Suddenly Brindsley gets an idea: he tells them all that the fuse box and gas meter are side by side, so it's dangerous to light a naked flame when there is electrical trouble. Grudgingly, they accept this circumstance, and Carol goes to make drinks for everyone, offering them "Winnie Whiskey, Vera Vodka, or dear old standby Ginette."

It occurs to Harold that he ought to go to his apartment for a few minutes to wash up, to unpack, but Brindsley manages to talk him out of this for the time being. Brindsley excuses himself and leads Carol upstairs where they hold a whispered council of war.

Meanwhile, the Colonel is interrogating Harold about Brindsley.

COLONEL: Is that boy touched or somethin'?
HAROLD: Touched? He's an absolute poppet.
COLONEL: A what?
HAROLD: A duck. I've known him for years, ever since he came here. There's not many secrets we keep from each other, I can tell you.
COLONEL *(frostily):* Really?
HAROLD: Yes, really. He's a very sweet boy.

But upstairs, Brindsley and Carol's guilty secret is weighing too heavily; with Harold here, there's too much risk; they must replace all Harold's furniture, at once. Brindsley orders Carol: "Look, you hold the fort. Serve them drinks. Just keep things going in the dark. Leave it all to me. I'll try and put everything back."

As Brindsley and Carol return, Brindsley tumbles down the stairs in his eagerness to get started. Brindsley pretends to be off and away to the pub once more to borrow a flashlight.

> *He reaches the door, opens it, then slams it loudly, remaining on the inside. Then he stealthily opens it again, stands dead still for a moment center, silently indicating to himself the position of the chairs he has to move—then he finds his way to the first of the Regency chairs, downstage left, which he lifts noiselessly.*

CAROL *(with bright desperation):* Well, now, drinks! What's everyone going to have? . . . It's Ginette for Mr. Gorringe and I suppose Winnie for Daddy.
COLONEL: And how on earth are you going to do that in the dark?
CAROL: I remember the exact way I put out the bottles.
Brindsley bumps into her with the chair and retreats.
It's very simple.
HAROLD: Oh look, luv, let me strike a match. I'm sure it's not that dangerous, just for a minute. *(He strikes a match.)*
CAROL: Oh no! . . .
Brindsley ducks down, chair in hand, and blows out the match.
Do you want to blow us all up, Mr. Gorringe? . . . All poor Mr. Bamberger would find would be teensy weensy bits of us. Very messypegs.
> *Brindsley steals out, Felix-the-cat-like, with the chair as Carol fumblingly starts to mix drinks. He sets it down, opens Harold's door and disappears inside it with the chair.*
HAROLD: Bamberger? Is that who's coming? Georg Bamberger?
MISS FURNIVAL: Yes. To see Mr. Miller's work. Isn't it exciting?

HAROLD: Well, I never. I read an article about him last week in the Sunday Pic. He's known as the mystery millionaire. He's almost completely deaf —deaf as a post, and spends most of his time indoors alone with his collection. He hardly ever goes out, except to a gallery or a private studio. That's the life! If I had money that's what I'd do. Just collect all the china and porcelain I wanted.

> *Brindsley returns with a poor, broken-down chair of his own and sets it down in the same position as the one he has taken out. The second chair is harder. It sits right across the room, upstage right. Delicately he moves toward it—but then he has difficulty finding it. We watch him walk round and round it in desperately narrowing circles till he touches it, and with relief picks it up.*

Brindsley carries on with his ghostly chore while the others make conversation in the "dark." Brindsley struggles out with the second Regency chair, while Miss Furnival discourses on softness of skin as a sign of gentility.

Brindsley comes back into the room with his own broken-down rocking chair and moves toward the Colonel's position, just as the Colonel volunteers to help with the drinks.

CAROL: You can take this bitter lemon to Miss Furnival if you want.
> *Brindsley sets down the rocker immediately next to the Colonel's chair.*

COLONEL: Very well.
> *He rises just as Brindsley's hand pulls it from beneath him. With his other hand Brindsley pulls the rocker into the identical position. The Colonel moves slowly across the room, arms outstretched for the bitter lemon. Unknowingly, Brindsley follows him carrying the third chair. The Colonel collides gently with the table. At the same moment Brindsley reaches it upstage of him and searches for the Wedgewood bowl. Their hands narrowly miss. Then the young man remembers the bowl is under the table. Deftly he reaches down and retrieves it—and carrying it in one hand and the chair in the other, triumphantly leaves the room through the arch unconsciously provided by the outstretched arms of Carol and the Colonel, giving and receiving a glass of Scotch—which they think is lemonade.*

CAROL: Here you are, Daddy. Bitter lemon for Miss Furnival.
COLONEL: Right you are, dumpling.

Harold sits down beside Miss Furnival to tell her a story about a customer's rudeness in his shop. Guided by his voice, the wandering Colonel delivers the drink and then reaches his own chair, which has now become a rocker.

Brindsley re-enters, mistakenly carrying one of the Regency chairs he already took out.

The Colonel, not expecting a rocking chair, sits down heavily and falls over backwards, cursing.

Harold rises and leans against the center table, still telling his story about a rude customer. Brindsley lifts the end of the sofa by mistake, frightening Miss Furnival. Then Brindsley collides with the sculpture, jangling it, and Carol covers up for him, pretending that she made the noise.

Brindsley finds the lamp on the table downstage, but as he starts out with it the cord catches around the Colonel's rocker. Brindsley tugs and the rocker is pulled forward until the Colonel falls out of the chair again. Brindsley follows the lamp's wire and pulls out the plug, but in the meantime he has become tangled in the wire and has lost the lampshade.

Harold finishes his story as he tells the rude customer never to cross his shop's threshold again. Carol delivers two drinks: Harold's gin-and-lime (which is really the bitter lemon) and the Colonel's Scotch (which is really gin-and-lime).

While Brindsley searches frantically along the floor for the lampshade, the Colonel mentions the Buddha statue he saw when he first came in, arousing Harold's curiosity and Carol's and Brindsley's horror.

All raise their glass in a toast and drink. They realize they have the wrong drinks (Miss Furnival is vocally appalled that she has the Scotch, but she takes another large gulp in the dark before surrendering the glass). As Brindsley finds the lampshade, they drink bottoms up. This time Miss Furnival has the gin and the Colonel has the bitter lemon, which he spits out all over Brindsley.

The Colonel, exasperated, lights his lighter and sees Brindsley kneeling at his feet, tangled in the lamp cord. Brindsley tries to pretend he's been to the pub and back (as he immediately blows out the lighter and moves to the table downstage right).

> *Quickly he lifts the table, and steals out of the room with it and the wrecked lamp.*

COLONEL (*who thinks Brindsley is still kneeling at his feet*): Now look here: there's somethin' very peculiar goin' on in this room. I may not know about art, Miller, but I know men. I know a liar in the light, and I know one in the dark.

CAROL: Daddy!

COLONEL: I don't want to doubt your word, sir. All the same, I'd like your oath you went out to the public house. Well?

CAROL (*realizing Brindsley isn't there, raising her voice*): Brin, Daddy's talking to you!

COLONEL: What are you shoutin' for?

BRINDSLEY (*rushing back from Harold's room, still entangled in the lamp*): Of course. I know. He's absolutely right. I was—just thinking it over for a moment.

Brindsley tries flattery, but it doesn't work. The Colonel refuses to permit his daughter to marry a born liar. This mention of Brindsley's and Carol's engagement is news to Harold, and it infuriates him because the engagement has been kept a secret from him. He thought he and Brindsley were close enough to deserve each other's confidences. Huffily, Harold concludes: "There's no need to say anything! It'll just teach me in future not to bank too much on friendship. It's Silly Me again! Silly, stupid, trusting me!"

Miss Furnival makes her way toward the bar.

MISS FURNIVAL *(groping about on the drinks table):* My father always used to say, "To err is human: to forgive divine."

CAROL: I thought that was somebody else.

MISS FURNIVAL *(blithely):* So many people copied him. *(She finds the open bottle of gin, lifts it and sniffs it.)*

CAROL: May I help you, Miss Furnival?

MISS FURNIVAL: No, thank you, Miss Melkett. I'm just getting myself another bitter lemon. *(She boldly drinks from bottle.)* That is—if I may, Mr. Miller.

BRINDSLEY: Of course. Help yourself.

MISS FURNIVAL: Thank you, most kind! *(She pours more gin into her glass and returns slowly to sit upstage. . . . .)*

The Colonel is softening and agrees to overlook Brindsley's odd behavior and give his consent to the marriage, if Brindsley can offer some indication that he can take care of Carol.

CAROL: Of course he can look after me, daddy. His works are going to be world-famous. In five years I'll feel just like Mrs. Michelangelo.

HAROLD *(loftily):* There wasn't a Mrs. Michelangelo, actually.

CAROL *(irritated):* Wasn't there?

HAROLD: No. He had passionate feelings of a rather different nature.

CAROL: Really, Mr. Gorringe. I didn't know that. *(She puts out her tongue at him.)*

Brindsley is smoothing Harold's ruffled feathers, when Clea enters, wearing a raincoat and carrying an airlines bag. Clea *("Brindsley's ex-mistress: late twenties; dazzling, emotional, bright and mischievous")* stands there in the inexplicable dark—no one realizes she has arrived—trying to grasp the situation.

Harold, mollified by Brindsley and Carol, agrees to have another drink, as Clea moves toward the sofa. So do Harold and Brindsley. The three converge on the sofa and sit down in unison—Clea in the middle, with Harold and Brindsley thinking they are sitting next to each other.

Carol brings up the subject of Clea, calling her "pretty stunning in a blowsy sort of way." Brindsley has to be tactful in talking of Clea to Carol; he even needs to lie, and he and Harold keep nudging each other in warning—although, of course it is Clea they are really nudging.

Harold calls Clea ugly. Brindsley disagrees as firmly as the present circum-

stances will permit. Miss Furnival and Carol join in the chorus of denounce-
ment of Clea, as Clea, outraged, rises from the sofa.

HAROLD: Just a ruddy show-off, if you ask me.
CAROL: You mean she was as pretentious as her name?
    *Clea, who has been reacting to this last exchange of comments
    about her like a spectator at a tennis match, now reacts to Carol
    open-mouthed.*
I bet she was. That photograph I found showed her in a dirndl and a sort of
sultry peasant blouse. She looked like *The Bartered Bride* done by Lloyd's
Bank.
    *They laugh, Brindsley hardest of all. Guided by the noise, Clea
    aims her hand and slaps his face.*
BRINDSLEY: Ahh!
CAROL: What's wrong?
MISS FURNIVAL: What is it, Mr. Miller?
BRINDSLEY *(furious):* That's not very funny, Harold. What the hell's the
matter with you?
    Clea makes her escape.
HAROLD *(indignant):* With me?
BRINDSLEY: Well, I'm sure it wasn't the Colonel.
COLONEL: What wasn't, sir?
    *Brindsley, groping about, catches Clea by the bottom, and instantly
    recognizes her.*
BRINDSLEY: Clea! . . . (In horror.) Clea!

Clea evades Brindsley's grasp, as Brindsley gives an excuse for thus suddenly calling out Clea's name. Now Brindsley is frantically telling the others
how beautiful and attractive Clea really is. Carol reminds Brindsley that he
described Clea as "cosy as a steel razor blade."
  Brindsley, braying his helpless laugh, has to admit that he did call Clea that.
Meanwhile, Clea has gone to the bar and picked up the bottle of vodka. As
she crosses the room she bumps into Brindsley, who is making a gesture with
outstretched arms. Instantly, Brindsley and Clea are locked in an embrace.

BRINDSLEY *(sotto voce, into Clea's ear as they stand just behind Harold):*
I can explain. Go up to the bedroom. Wait for me there.
HAROLD *(in amazement, thinking he is being addressed):* Now? Do you
think this is quite the moment?
BRINDSLEY: Oh God! . . . I wasn't talking to you.
CAROL: What did you say?
HAROLD *(to Carol):* I think he wants *you* upstairs. *(Slyly.)* For what pur-
pose, I can't imagine.
COLONEL: They're going to do some more of that plotting, I daresay.

The three climb the stairs to the bedroom—Clea first with Brindsley's hands on her hips, Carol with her hands on Brindsley's. As they reach the top of the stairs, Brindsley tells Carol he has transported everything but the sofa, then sends her back downstairs and goes into the bedroom with Clea, on the pretext of looking for a flashlight.

Brindsley tells Clea what is going on, as downstairs the others grope for another round of drinks. Brindsley begs Clea to leave without making a fuss, but somehow they wind up stretched out on the bed, in an embrace.

Downstairs, Harold thinks he might go to his apartment in search of a taper, but Carol decoys him into the studio.

Upstairs, Clea agrees to get undressed and get into bed, waiting for Brindsley to rid himself of the others and join her.

Clea goes off to get undressed, carrying her vodka. Brindsley closes the bedroom door and sits on the stairs. Carol and Harold come back from the studio having found no candles there. Carol is getting discouraged: the "boring little millionaire" is now half an hour late and is obviously not coming.

HAROLD: Oh, that's nothing. Millionaires are always late. It's their thing. *(Sits on the sofa.)*

MISS FURNIVAL: I'm sure you're right, Mr. Gorringe. That's how I imagine them. Hands like silk and always two hours late.

COLONEL *(calling to Carol who has bumped into the table):* Watch out how you go, dumpling. Be careful of that Buddha.

Brindsley shoots up in alarm.

HAROLD: Buddha?

BRINDSLEY: Buddha . . . W-w-w-w-what d'you mean, Buddha?

COLONEL: Your Buddha, sir! The one I saw when I came in. Very fine.

HAROLD *(suspiciously):* Buddha?

BRINDSLEY *(creeping downstairs):* You must have made a mistake, Colonel. There's no Buddha here. I wouldn't have a Buddha in my house. I'm a Confucian.

He gingerly lifts the raincoat from the end of the sofa and steals down to the Buddha, wraps the statue in it, places it on the table.

There is no Buddha here, Brindsley insists, confusing the Colonel, who gropes for the porcelain figure on its stool and finds it gone. Harold is suspicious. Brindsley covers the end of the sofa with a dust sheet, still arguing that perhaps Colonel Melkett is "kinky for Buddhas."

At this moment, Schuppanzigh ("a middle-class German refugee, chubby, cultivated and effervescent") enters carrying a tool bag and wearing the overcoat and peaked cap which are standard uniform for the repairmen of the London Electricity Board.

SCHUPPANZIGH *(German accent):* 'Allo, please?

All rise, startled out of their wits.

Mr. Miller? Mr. Miller? I have come as was arranged.

BRINDSLEY: My God, it's Bamberger! He's arrived! . . .

CAROL: Bamberger!
BRINDSLEY: Yes!

They think Schuppanzigh is the millionaire art collector they are expecting; they defer to him, they shout at him (because he is supposed to be stone deaf).

Schuppanzigh takes out his flashlight and lights it (as the stage lights dim). He puts his tool bag, coat and cap on the Regency chair, concealing it (a stroke of luck for Brindsley).

Brindsley introduces Schuppanzigh to the others in the room. Schuppanzigh is astonished to be offered a drink but orders a vodka. Miss Furnival takes his hand and exclaims that like all millionaires' hands it is much softer than the hands of ordinary people.

Carol cannot find the vodka bottle—it seems to have disappeared. On the bedroom level, above, Clea appears dressed in Brindsley's pajama top. Clea gets into bed, taking the vodka bottle and a tooth glass with her.

Schuppanzigh is in a hurry to get down to business (which the others assume is inspecting the sculpture). So they point out the two-pronged figure, which Schuppanzigh examines by the light of his flashlight. Brindsley describes it as "the two needles of man's unrest. Self Love and Self Hate." Schuppanzigh calls it "fascinating."

COLONEL: You mean to say you like it?
SCHUPPANZIGH: Very much. Very much indeed. Don't you?
COLONEL: Oh . . . Yes—splendid! Splendid, of course.
SCHUPPANZIGH: Simple, but not simple minded. Ingenious but not ingenuous. Above all, they have real moral force. Of how many modern works can one say that?
MISS FURNIVAL (drunkenly): Oh none, really. None . . . !
SCHUPPANZIGH: I do not wish to exaggerate, but these are, in my view, entirely Shakespearean.
HAROLD: Shakespearean?
SCHUPPANZIGH: Certainly. I will christen them for you. (Touching the spikes.) Malvolio—Hamlet! Malvolio, as you know, was sick of self-love. Hamlet of self-hate. He could not love others because he could not love himself. This is an old disease, diagnosed long ago by St. Augustine. But you obviously know that.
Brindsley makes modest gurgles.
I hope I do not lecture. It is a fault with me.

Schuppanzigh insists that Brindsley is a genius, suggests that he charge "immense sums" for his work. Carol tells him that Brindsley does—five hundred guineas. Schuppanzigh protests that this is not half enough. Carol seizes this obvious opportunity to offer Brindsley's creation for sale.

They eagerly await the "millionaire's" reply, which is: he would love to have the sculpture but can't afford it. All believe at first that this is a rich man's little joke, but finally Schuppanzigh makes them realize that he is really an electricity repairman who can't afford thousand-guinea works of art. The Colonel takes his flashlight, shines it on him as he berates him. All are angry at Schuppanzigh, no one more so than Miss Furnival.

MISS FURNIVAL: . . . . . My father always warned me: Kill the middle class and you murder the idea of public service. How right he was. Now all the responsible jobs are held by layabouts and foreigners.
She staggers away, not quite in control.
BRINDSLEY: Miss Furnival, please.
CAROL: Well, all the same, Daddy's right, Brin. It was pretty impertipegs.
SCHUPPANZIGH: You are quite right. I take it back. *(To Brindsley.)* You are not a genius.
COLONEL *(handing the flashlight to Brindsley):* Miller, will you kindly show this feller his work?
BRINDSLEY: The mains are in the cellar. You can go down through here. There's a trap door. *(Indicating.)* Do you mind?
SCHUPPANZIGH *(snatching the flashlight furiously):* Why should I mind? It's why I came, after all.
He takes his coat, cap and bag off Harold's Regency chair. Seeing it.
Now there is a really beautiful chair!
Brindsley stares at the chair aghast—and in a twinkling seats himself in it to conceal it.

Brindsley cannot get up, so Carol struggles with the trap door, as the Colonel looks askance at Brindsley for his lack of gallantry. Harold helps Carol get the trap open.
Schuppanzigh descends, and Harold lets the trap slam shut (as the lights take on their former full brightness and the characters are once more in the pitch black dark). Clea, aroused by the sharp sound of the trap, gets out of bed and comes to the head of the stairs. Miss Furnival is flapping around the room, singing a Baptist hymn.
Carol tries to cheer Brindsley up, telling him how Bamberger, when he arrives, will like Brindsley's work.

CAROL: . . . . . we can buy a super Georgian house and live what's laughingly known as happily ever after. I want to leave this place just as soon as we're married.
Clea hears this. Her mouth opens wide.
BRINDSLEY *(nervously):* Sssh!
CAROL: Why? I don't want to live in a slum for our first couple of years— like other newlyweds.
BRINDSLEY: Sssh! Ssssh! . . .
CAROL: What's the matter with you?
BRINDSLEY: The gods listen, darling. They've given me a terrible night so far. They may do worse.

CAROL (cooling): I know, darling, You've had a filthy evening. Poor baby-kins. But I'll fight them with you. I don't care a fig for those naughty old Goddipegs. (Looking up.) Do you hear? Not a single little fig!
> Clea aims at the voice and sends a jet of vodka splashing over Carol.

Ahh ! ! !

Clea broadcasts vodka more widely. Miss Furnival screams and the Colonel exclaims. Brindsley pretends it must be the water mains breaking, but Clea drops the tooth mug, and the clatter startles them all.

Now they know that someone else is on the scene, and Brindsley pretends, desperately, that it is his cleaning woman, Mrs. Punnet, arriving conscientiously at 11 p.m. to straighten up the flat. He suggests: "Why don't we just leave her to potter around upstairs with her duster?"

COLONEL (roaring): MRS. PUNNET!
CLEO (startled into speaking): 'Allo! Yes?
BRINDSLEY: It is.
> Clea stands trapped, her hand over her mouth, but it is too late.
Good heavens, Mrs. Punnet, what on earth are you doing up there?
> A tiny pause.
CLEA (deciding on a Cockney voice of great antiquity): I'm just giving the bedroom a bit of a tidy, sir.
BRINDSLEY: At this time of night?
> The mischief in Clea begins to take over.
CLEA: Better late than never, sir, as they say. I know how you like your bedroom to be nice and inviting when you're giving one of your parties.

To Brindsley's embarrassment, Clea pretends she believes they are all in the dark because Brindsley is playing one of his "kinky games." Brindsley tries to shut her up, but she comes down into the room "describing" one of Brindsley's usual parties: underwear in the sink, bottles all over the place. When Brindsley tries to silence her, Clea bites his hand.

The Colonel warns "Mrs. Punnet" to watch what she says, because Brindsley's fiancee is present. "Mrs. Punnet" pretends to be pleased about this marriage on everyone's behalf, including the Colonel's.

COLONEL: Thank you.
CLEA: You must be Miss Clea's father.
COLONEL: Miss Clea? I don't understand.
> Triumphantly, Clea sticks out her tongue at Brindsley, who collapses his length on the floor, face down, in a gesture of total surrender. For him it is the end. The evening can hold no further disasters for him.
CLEA (to Carol): Well, I never! So you've got him at last! Well done, Miss Clea! I never thought you would—not after four years. . . . .

As "Mrs. Punnet", Clea continues her needling. It's high time Brindsley married Clea, she declares, because the "little bun in the oven" is beginning to show. She quotes Brindsley on the subject of Carol: ". . . . she's just a bit of Knightsbridge candyfloss. A couple of licks and you've 'ad 'er."

All are flabbergasted at "Mrs. Punnet's" revelations until Harold, recognizing Clea's voice, guesses her identity and exposes her presence to the others.

Instead of shrinking, Clea launches an all-out offensive. Against Brindsley: "Oh you coward, you bloody coward! Just because you didn't want to marry me, did you have to settle for this lot?" Against Harold: "All those years of living with your porcelain—you've turned into a Crown Derby and Joan." Against Miss Furnival: "The words say 'bitter lemon' but the voice squeals 'gin'." Against Carol: "Miss Laughingly-Known-As and her Daddipegs!"

The Colonel, trying to comfort Carol, takes Clea's hand by mistake; Clea sneers at them all for their lack of perception and challenges them to guess each other's hands in the dark. Clea puts Carol's hand in Harold's. Carol thinks the hand is Brindsley's, and when she discovers her mistake she over-reacts, in a state of near-hysteria.

Clea puts Harold's hand into Brindsley's. Harold guesses Brindsley's hand correctly, without hesitation.

CAROL: How does he know that? How does he know your hand and I don't?

BRINDSLEY: Calm down, Carol.

CAROL: Answer me! I want to know!

BRINDSLEY: Stop it!

CAROL: I won't!

BRINDSLEY: You're getting hysterical!

CAROL: Leave me alone! I want to go home.

And suddenly Miss Furnival gives a sharp short scream.

MISS FURNIVAL: Prams! Prams! Prams—in the supermarket! . . .

They all freeze. She is evidently out of control in a world of her own fears. She speaks quickly and strangely.

All those hideous wire prams full of babies and bottles—cornflakes over there, is all they say—and then they leave you to yourself. Biscuits over there—cat food over there—fish cakes over there—Harpic over there. Pink stamps, green stamps, free balloons—television dinners—pay as you go out—oh, Daddy, it's awful! . . . And then the black men. Black men grinning at you—I've seen them waiting behind the tins of soup—white eyes rolling behind the piles of Heinz tomato. The government allows it, of course. It's shameless! The government allows it! Keep off! Keep off! It's shameless! *(She pulls them off with her hands.)* Keep off! Keep off! . . . Keep—

Brindsley strikes a match. Silence.

HAROLD: Come on, Ferny, I think it's time we went home.

MISS FURNIVAL *(pulling herself together)*: Yes. You're quite right . . . *(With an attempt at grandeur.)* I'm sorry I can't stay any longer, Mr. Miller: but your millionaire is unpardonably late. So typical of modern manners . . . Express my regrets, if you please.

BRINDSLEY: Certainly,

> *Leaning heavily on Harold's arm, she leaves the room. Brindsley's match goes out.*

Brindsley joins Clea in sitting on the low stool, and they play out a lover's quarrel as though there were no one else in the room.

BRINDSLEY: . . . . . Pick-pick-pick away! Why is *that*, Clea? Have you ever thought why you need to do it? Well?

CLEA: Perhaps because I care about you.

BRINDSLEY: Perhaps there's nothing to care about. Just a fake artist.

CLEA: Stop pitying yourself. It's always your vice. I told you when I met you: you could either be a good artist, or a chic fake. You didn't like it, because I refused just to give you applause.

BRINDSLEY: God knows, you certainly did that!

CLEA: Is that what *she* gives you? Twenty hours of ego-massage every day.

BRINDSLEY: At least our life together isn't the replica of the Holy Inquisition you made of ours. I didn't have an affair with you: it was just four years of nooky with Torquemada!

They protest to each other how relieved and happy they felt when they finally broke up, but they fail to convince each other or themselves. Clea quotes her own "Mrs. Punnet" dialogue to prove Brindsley still loves her, and they both laugh at this. Clea puts her head on Brindsley's shoulder, as the Colonel begins to make the noises of an irate father whose daughter has been trifled with.

Carol tears off her engagement ring and throws it at Brindsley but hits her father in the eye. The Colonel gropes in the dark for Brindsley, intending to thrash him and describing how, in the old days, he would have horsewhipped Brindsley.

COLONEL: You'd have raised your guttersnipe voice in a piteous scream for mercy and forgiveness!

> *A terrible scream is heard from the hall. They freeze, listening as it comes nearer and nearer, then the door is flung open and Harold plunges into the room. He is wild-eyed with rage: a lit and bent taper shakes in his furious hand.*

HAROLD: Ooooh! . . . Ooooh! . . . Ooooooh! You villain!

BRINDSLEY: Harold—

HAROLD: You skunky, conniving little villain!

BRINDSLEY: What's the matter?

HAROLD (*raging*): Have you seen the state of my room? My room? My lovely room, the most elegant and cared for in this entire district—one chair turned absolutely upside down, one chair on top of another like a Portobello junkshop! And that's not all, is it Brindsley? Oh no, that's not the worst by a long chalk, is it Brindsley?

To Harold, the worst of it is that, after years of friendship, Brindsley would not confide in Harold, but would walk in and steal Harold's beloved furniture just to impress a girl—without letting Harold in on the secret. The worst of it is, Harold was the last to know.

Harold rattles off the inventory of objects he wants returned to him, at once: one Regency chair, one Regency sofa, one Coalport vase, which Brindsley hands to Harold.

HAROLD: Ooooh! You've even taken the flowers! I'll come back for the chair and sofa in a minute. *(Drawing himself up with all the offended dignity of which a Harold Gorringe is capable.)* This is the end of our relationship, Brindsley. We won't be speaking again, I don't think.

> *He twitches his raincoat off the table. Inside it, of course, is the Buddha, which falls on the floor and smashes beyond repair. There is a terrible silence.*

(Trying to keep his voice under control.) Do you know what that statue was worth? Do you? More money than you'll ever see in your whole life, even if you sell every piece of that nasty, rusty rubbish. *(With the quietness of the mad.)* I think I'm going to have to smash you, Brindsley.

BRINDSLEY *(nervously):* Now steady on, Harold . . . don't be rash . . .

HAROLD: Yes, I'm very much afraid I'll have to smash you . . . Smash for smash—that's fair do's.

> *He pulls one of the long metal prongs out of the sculpture.*

Smash for smash. Smash for *smash!*

> *Insanely he advances on Brindsley holding the prong like a sword, the taper burning in his other hand.*

BRINDSLEY *(retreating):* Stop it, Harold. You've gone mad!

COLONEL: Well done, sir. I think it's time for the reckoning.

> *The Colonel grabs the other prong and also advances.*

Brindsley retreats before the onslaught. Carol horrifies Brindsley by urging on his attackers. In contrast, Clea comes to Brindsley's rescue and blows out Harold's taper, takes Brindsley's hand and pulls him out of danger. Brindsley and Clea get up onto the table, silently, while the Colonel and Harold stalk them, listening for sounds of breathing.

Schuppanzigh opens the trap, then goes back down into the cellar, as some one trips over the milk bottles in the hall.

> *Enter Georg Bamberger. He is quite evidently a millionaire. Dressed in the Gulbenkian manner, he wears a beard, an eye-glass, a frock-coat, a top-hat and an orchid. He carries a large deaf-aid. Bewildered, he advances into the room.*

Harold and the Colonel stalk Bamberger, but as soon as the millionaire speaks they take him for Schuppanzigh (the two German-accented voices sound very much alike). To make matters worse, Schuppanzigh comes up from the cellar and, hearing Bamberger, believes that someone in the room is making fun of his way of speaking, imitating it.

Bamberger explains who he is, and at last the others understand that their long-awaited millionaire has arrived. Bamberger moves in the direction of the open trap door, as Brindsley tries to explain to the deaf man why the lights are out.

BRINDSLEY (shouting): Don't worry, Mr. Bamberger! We've had a fuse, but it's all right now! . . .
> Standing on the table, he clasps Clea happily. Bamberger misses the trap by inches.

Oh, Clea, that's true. Everything's all right now! Just in the nick of time!
> But as he says this Bamberger turns and falls into the open trap door. Schuppanzigh slams it to with his foot.

SCHUPPANZIGH: So! Here's now an end to your troubles! Like Jehovah in the Sacred Testament, I give you the most miraculous gift of the Creation! Light!

CLEA: Light!

BRINDSLEY: Oh, thank God. *Thank God!*
> Schuppanzigh goes to the switch.

HAROLD (grimly): I wouldn't thank Him too soon, Brindsley, if I were you!

COLONEL: Nor would I, Brindsley, if I were you!

SCHUPPANZIGH (grandly): Then thank *me.* For I shall play God for this second. (Clapping his hands.) Attend, all of you. God said: "Let there be light!" And there was, good people, suddenly! —astoundingly!—instantaneously! — inconceivably! — inexhaustibly! — inextinguishably and eternally— LIGHT!
> Schuppanzigh, with a great flourish, flicks the light. Instant darkness. The turntable of the gramophone begins moving, and with a great crescendo wheeze the Sousa march starts up again and blazes away in the blackness. Curtain.

YOU'RE A GOOD MAN CHARLIE BROWN

A Musical Comedy in Two Acts

BOOK, MUSIC AND LYRICS BY CLARK GESNER

Based on the comic strip "Peanuts" by Charles M. Schulz

Cast and credits appear on page 415

CLARK GESNER, 28, was born in Massachusetts, the son of a Unitarian minister. He graduated from Princeton in 1960. He has pursued a writing career with contributions to Julius Monk and Leonard Sillman revues, to various magazines and TV shows including That Was The Week That Was *and* Captain Kangaroo.

Gesner first put together You're a Good Man Charlie Brown *as a demo record. It so delighted Charles M. Schulz, creator of Charlie Brown's comic strip "Peanuts", and others that it was soon made into a children's record by King Leo (MGM) with Orson Bean as Charlie Brown and Barbara Minkus as Lucy. The off-Broadway show was, in a sense, a spinoff from this record. And of course now there is still another record, the off-Broadway cast album (with Gary Burghoff as Charlie Brown and Reva Rose as Lucy).*

298

INTRODUCTION BY THE ARTIST

CHARLIE BROWN, LUCY AND SNOOPY AS THEY APPEAR IN A CHARLES M. SCHULZ
DRAWING MADE IN HONOR OF THE OFF-BROADWAY SHOW.

Time: An Average Day
Place: The Life of Charlie Brown

ACT I

SYNOPSIS: The house lights dim to the faint sound of a waltz. In the dark, the music builds to a crescendo; then voices are heard:

LINUS: I really don't think you have anything to worry about, Charlie Brown. After all, science has shown that a person's character isn't really established until he's at least five years old.

CHARLIE BROWN: But I *am* five. I'm more than five.

LINUS: Oh, well, that's the way it goes.

Several times the music peaks and voices come through. Only Linus has a good word to say about Charlie Brown. The others—Schroeder, Patty, Snoopy and Lucy—complain of his total ineptness. Lucy insists that Charlie Brown has a Failure Face: "It has failure written all over it."

> *Music moves on strongly, swells to a crescendo, then holds a single, high sustained note. For the first time, a light appears on the stage, illuminating Charlie Brown's face at center stage. He stares with wonder and peace out over the audience.*

CHARLIE BROWN: Some days I wake up early to watch the sunrise, and I think how beautiful it is, and how my life lies before me, and I get a very positive feeling about things. Like this morning for instance: the sky's so clear and the sun's so bright. How can anything go wrong on a day like this?

The lights come up. The others begin to mime the members of a band, against a white backdrop which serves as a canvas for changing colors and intensities of light throughout the play. The furnishings are varied geometrical shapes which can be moved about and combined like toy blocks to represent a bench, a desk, a rock, Snoopy's doghouse or anything else imagination requires.

The inhabitants of this special world are Charlie Brown himself (a born loser, sticking his neck out optimistically from his loose-hanging sweater), Linus (tender and ever-hopeful, hugging his blanket for security), Patty (blonde, one-track-minded), Schroeder (cool and musical), Lucy (Linus's big sister, the black-haired demon, merciless) and Snoopy (a dog; alternately self-centered and gregarious, depending on how close it is to supper time).

The early-morning euphoria of this group extends even to its members' opinion of Charlie Brown:

ALL *(except Charlie Brown; sing):*
  You're a good man, Charlie Brown
  You're the kind of reminder we need
  You have humility, nobility and a sense of honor
  That are very rare indeed. . . . .
            All dance around.
  You're a good man, Charlie Brown
  You're a prince and a prince could be king
  With a heart such as yours
  You could open any doors
  You could go out and do anything
  You could be king, Charlie Brown
  You could be king.

LUCY: If only you weren't so wishy-washy.

A school bell rings as all exit except Charlie Brown who is sitting holding a lunch bag.

CHARLIE BROWN: I think lunch time is about the worst time of the day for me. Always having to sit here alone. Of course sometimes mornings aren't so pleasant either—waking up and wondering if anyone would really miss me if I never got out of bed. Then there's the night, too—lying there and thinking about all the stupid things I've done during the day. And all those hours in between—when I do all those stupid things. Well, lunch time is *among* the worst times of the day for me. Well, I guess I'd better see what I've got.
      Opens bag, unwraps sandwich, looks inside.
Peanut butter. *(Bites and chews.)* Some psychiatrists say that people who eat peanut butter sandwiches are lonely. I guess they're right. And when you're really lonely the peanut butter sticks to the roof of your mouth.
      Eats. Fingers bench.
Boy, the PTA sure did a good job of painting these benches. *(Eats.)* There's that cute little red-headed girl eating her lunch over there. I wonder what she would do if I went over and asked her if I could sit and have lunch with her. She'd probably laugh right in my face. It's hard on a face when it gets laughed in. There's an empty place next to her on the bench. There's no reason why I couldn't just go over and sit there. I could do that right now. All I have to do is stand up. *(Stands.)* I'm standing up. *(Sits.)* I'm sitting down. I'm a coward. I'm so much of a coward she wouldn't even think of looking at me. She hardly ever *does* look at me. In fact, I can't remember her ever looking at me. Why shouldn't she look at me? Is there any reason in the world why she shouldn't look at me? Is she so great and I'm so small that she can't spare one little moment . . . *(He freezes.)* . . . She's looking at me. *(In terror he looks one way, then the other.)* She's looking at me.
            His head looks all around, trying frantically to find something else to notice. His teeth clench. Tension builds. Then with one motion he pops the paper bag over his head.

Lucy and Patty wander in and out, not deigning to notice Charlie Brown except to sketch a dress on the top of his paper bag. Charlie Brown begins to realize he's making a fool of himself. He takes off the bag and sees to his relief that the little redhead isn't looking his way—then again he wonders why she never looks at him.

"Oh, well," Charlie Brown concludes, "another lunch hour over with. Only 2,863 to go."

Events begin to happen in the life of Charlie Brown in rapid succession, as in the march of panels in a comic strip, with swiftly-changing characters and situations.

Lucy breaks Schrocder's concentration at the piano by asserting her intentions in song:

LUCY *(sings):*
  D'ya know something, Schroeder?
  I think the way you play the piano is nice.
  D'ya know something else?
  It's always been my dream
  That I'd marry a man who plays the piano.

Patty pledges allegiance to the flag.

Charlie Brown and Linus enter, praising newspapers. Lucy runs in and grabs Linus's blanket. Linus confuses Lucy by playing it cool, spouting jargon about the psychology of blanket-lovers. Then, when Lucy hesitates, Linus yanks the blanket back.

Snoopy wanders in and meets Patty who would like to kiss him but can't bring herself to do it. Snoopy lies down, commenting "The curse of a fuzzy face."

Patty and Linus are seated together.
LINUS: Happiness is a fleeting thing Patty, but I think that a man can really come closer to it by directing the forces of his life towards a single goal that he believes in, and I think that a man's personal search for happiness is not really a selfish thing either because by achieving happiness himself he can help others to find it. Does that make sense to you?
PATTY: We had spaghetti at our house three times this week.

Lucy drives Schroeder to the edge of his patience by suggesting that, some day, they might be so poor that they'd have to sell Schroeder's piano to buy saucepans.

Snoopy imagines himself a fierce jungle animal but his dream shatters when he finds that he's unable to make a ferocious noise.

Patty suddenly decides that jumping rope is futile.

Snoopy poses atop his doghouse and boasts: "I would have made a terrific trophy."

Lucy's birthday party has been cancelled owing to bad behavior. Linus suggests that Lucy apologize to their mother, but Lucy cannot even imagine herself feeling sorry for her actions.

Hearing Lucy shouting offstage, Schroeder envies Beethoven the peace and quiet of his life in the country.

Everyone pats and jollies Snoopy until he is moved to sing what starts out to be a song of happiness.

SNOOPY (sings):
. . . . . Faithful friends always near me,
Bring me bones, scratch my ear,
And little birds come to cheer me,
Ev'ry day sitting here,
On my stomach with their sharp little claws,
Which are usually cold, and occasionally painful,
And sometimes there's so many that I can hardly stand it . . .
Rats!
I feel ev'ry now and then that I gotta bite someone.
I know ev'ry now and then what I wanna be.
A fierce jungle animal crouched on the limb of a tree. . . . .

He'd pounce! Snoopy sings; but then he notices how far he is from the ground, there on the roof of his doghouse. He reverts to the happy version of his song.

Charlie Brown resolves to walk right up and speak to the little redhead— and to flap his arms and fly to the moon.

Snoopy deplores the situation in which he finds himself: he will always be a dog, with no chance of advancement.

Linus sings about his beloved blanket. He pretends that he could get along without it.

LINUS (sings):
. . . . . Yes I'll walk away and leave it
Though I know you won't believe it
I'll just walk away and leave it on the floor.
        *Hums and walks away from blanket. Tries to remain nonchalant
        but the independence is too much for him and he grabs his blanket
        back again. Sings:*
Got you back again.

It's foolish, I know it
I'll try to outgrow it
But meanwhile
It's my blanket and me.

Linus watches television, but Lucy comes in and makes him switch channels by waving a fist at him.

Lucy launches into a daydream about becoming a queen cheered by her admiring subjects. Gravely, Linus explains that Lucy can never be a queen because royalty is an inherited position.

LUCY: I know what I'll do. If I can't be a queen, then I'll be very rich. I'll work and work until I'm very rich and then I will buy myself a queendom.
LINUS: Good grief.
LUCY: Yes, I'll buy myself a queendom and then I'll kick out the old queen and take over the whole operation myself. I will be head queen. And then all the people . . . when I go out in my coach all the people will shout at me . . .
    She glances at the TV, becomes engrossed. Linus looks at her.
LINUS: What happened to your queendom?
LUCY: Huh?
LINUS: What happened to your queendom?
LUCY *(engrossed in TV):* Oh that, I've given it up. I've decided to devote my life to cultivating my natural beauty.

Charlie Brown enters and pantomimes a struggle to get his kite into the air. Other kids can do it, he sings to himself.

CHARLIE BROWN *(sings):*
    . . . . . Leave it to me to have the one fool kite
    Who likes to see a little kid cry.

    Little less talk, little more skill,
    Little less luck, little more will,
    Gotta face this fellow eye to eye.
    Now that I've seen you chasing moles,
    Climbing trees, digging holes,
    Catching your string on everything passing by
    Why not fly.

Suddenly Charlie sees the kite soar into the air and he has his moment of elation—"I'm not such a clumsy guy"—before the kite falls.

Patty complains that her incoming Valentine count has dropped off from last year's and blames this on the zip code.

Charlie Brown tries to give Lucy a Valentine but finds himself wishing her "Merry Christmas," by mistake.

A Valentine dropped by Patty has the initials CB on it, but it is meant for another boy in Patty's class. Charlie Brown gets "about as many Valentines as a dog"—many fewer, in fact, because Snoopy walks by with a batch of them.

Lucy is in her booth with the sign "The Doctor Is In." Charlie Brown consults her.

CHARLIE BROWN *(sings):*
    I'm not very handsome, or clever, or lucid,
    I've always been stupid at spelling and numbers.

I've never been much playing football, or baseball,
Or stickball, or checkers, or marbles, or ping-pong.
I'm us'ally awful at parties, and dances,
I stand like a stick or I cough, or I laugh,
Or I don't bring a present, or I spill the ice cream,
Or I get so depressed that I stand and I scream,
Oh, how could there possibly be
One small person as thoroughly, totally, utterly blah as me.

Lucy agrees with Charlie Brown, he is not much of a person, but she feels that yet there is hope.

LUCY *(sings):*
    For although you are no good at music, like Schroeder,
    Or happy like Snoopy, or lovely like me,
    You have the distinction to be
    No one else but the singular, remarkable, unique Charlie Brown.
CHARLIE BROWN:
    I'm me!
LUCY:
    Yes—it's amazingly true,
    For whatever it's worth, Charlie Brown,
    You're you.

Charlie is grateful for this comforting, friendly advice, for which Lucy demands her fee of five cents.

Snoopy has a moment of depression because he is always called something like "fuzzy face," never "sugarlips."

The whole class has been assigned to do a book report on "Peter Rabbit."

ALL: Homework. Yeough!
LUCY *(sings):*
    "Peter Rabbit" is this stupid book
    About this stupid rabbit who steals
    Vegetables from other peoples' gardens.
        Counts words 1-17.
Hm. 83 to go.
SCHROEDER *(sings):*
    The name of the book about which
    This book report is about, is
    "Peter Rabbit" which is about this . . .
    Rabbit.

    I found it very—
        Crosses out.
    I liked the part where—
        Crosses out.

It was a—
    Slash.
It reminded me of "Robin Hood."

And the part where Little John jumped from the rock
To the Sheriff of Nottingham's back.
And then Robin and everyone swung from the trees
In a sudden surprise attack.
And they captured the sheriff and all of his goods
And they carried him back to their camp in the woods
And the Sheriff was guest at their dinner and all
But he wriggled away and he sounded the call
And his men rushed in and the arrows flew—

Peter Rabbit did sort of that kind of thing too.
LUCY *(sings):*
    The other people's name
    Was MacGregor.
        Counts 18-23.
Hm.

LINUS: In examining a work such as "Peter Rabbit" it is important that the superficial characteristics of its deceptively simple plot should not be allowed to blind the reader to the more substantial fabric of its deeper motivations. In this report I plan to discuss the sociological implications of family pressures so great as to drive an otherwise moral rabbit to perform acts of thievery which he consciously knew were against the law. I also hope to explore the personality of Mr. MacGregor in his conflicting roles as farmer and humanitarian.
        Charlie Brown begins to sing.
Peter Rabbit is established from the start as a benevolent hero and it is only with the increase of social pressure that the seams in his moral fabric . . .
    CHARLIE BROWN *(sings):*
    If I start writing now
    When I'm not really rested
    It could upset my thinking
    Which is not good at all.
    I'll get a fresh start tomorrow
    And it's not due till Wednesday
    So I'll have all of Tuesday
    Unless something should happen.
    Why does this always happen,
    I should be outside playing
    Getting fresh air and sunshine,
    I work best under pressure,
    And there'll be lots of pressure
    If I wait till tomorrow,
    I should start writing now.

But if I start writing now
When I'm not really rested
It could upset my thinking
Which is not good at all.
LUCY:
The name of the rabbit
Was Peter
    Counts 24-30.
SCHROEDER:
Down came the staff on his head—smash!
And Robin fell like a sack full of lead—crash!
Sheriff laughed and he left him for dead—ha!
But he was wrong.
LUCY: Thirty-five, thirty-six, thirty-seven, thirty-eight, thirty-nine, forty.

That's the way it goes, singly, in counterpoint and in harmony, a book report on "Peter Rabbit," with Schroeder describing "Robin Hood," Lucy counting words, Linus psychoanalizing and Charlie Brown procrastinating. Finally:

LUCY *(sings):*
And they were very, very, very, very, very, very happy to be home.
SCHROEDER:
The end.
LUCY:
. . . Ninety-four, ninety-five. The very, very, very end.
LINUS:
A-men.
CHARLIE BROWN:
A book report on "Peter Rabbit."

The scene changes and Charlie Brown is alone, staring at a leaf on a tree.

CHARLIE BROWN: Y'know, I don't know if you'll understand this or not, but sometimes, even when I'm feeling very low, I'll see some little thing that will somehow renew my faith. Just something like that leaf, for instance— clinging to its tree in spite of wind and storm. Y'know that makes me think that courage and tenacity are the greatest values a man can have. Suddenly my old confidence is back and I know that things aren't half as bad as I make them out to be. Suddenly I know that with the strength of his convictions a man can move mountains, and I can proceed with full confidence in the basic goodness of my fellow man. I know that now. I know it.
    He exits with a new strength to his step. The stage is still for a moment, then, silently, the leaf drops off its tree and wiggles its way to the ground. The stage lights dim. Curtain.

ACT II

Snoopy is discovered on top of his doghouse.

SNOOPY: Here's the World War I flying ace high over France in his Sopwith Camel, searching for the infamous Red Baron! I must bring him down! Suddenly anti-aircraft fire, "archie" we call it, begins to burst beneath my plane. The Red Baron has spotted me. Nyahh, Nyahh, Nyahh! You can't hit me! (Actually tough flying aces don't say Nyahh, Nyahh) I just ah . . . Drat this fog! It's bad enough to have to fight the Red Baron without having to fly in weather like this. All right, Red Baron! Come on out! You can't hide from me forever! Ah, the sun has broken through . . . I can see the woods of Montsec below . . . and what's that? It's a Fokker triplane! Ha! I've got you! You can't escape me this time, Red Baron! Aaugh! He's diving down out of the sun! He's tricked me again! I've got to run! Come on, Sopwith Camel, let's go! Go, Camel, go! I can't shake him! He's riddling my plane with bullets! Curse you, Red Baron! Curse you and your kind! Curse the evil that causes this unhappiness!

> *Pause.*

Here's the World War I flying ace back at the airdrome in France, he is exhausted and yet he does not sleep, for one thought continues to throb in his brain . . .

> *Pause.*

Someday, someday I'll get you, Red Baron!

Patty comes in and summons unwilling Snoopy to chase rabbits. Patty insists, so Snoopy sniffs around and receives a pat on the head for his effort. But, he confesses, he wouldn't know a rabbit if he smelled one.

Charlie Brown, baseball manager, is giving a fight talk to his team: Lucy, Schroeder, Linus, Patty and Snoopy. They're discouraged because (as Lucy says) they have less than a million-to-one chance of winning. But Charlie Brown leads them into a cheer.

ALL *(sing):*
> There is no team like the best team
> Which is our team right here.
> We will show you we're the best team
> In the very little league this year.
> And in no time we'll be big time
> With the big league baseball stars.
> For all we have to do is win just one more game
> And the championship is ours.

After the game, Charlie Brown is writing to a pen pal, describing his team's performance:

CHARLIE BROWN *(sings):*

    Snoopy helped out by biting a runner and catching a ball in his teeth
    Linus caught flies from a third story window by holding his blanket be-
       neath
    Yes, we had fortitude, no one could argue with that.
    And one run would win us the game as I came up to bat. . . . .

    Two men were on with two outs and me with one strike to go.
    Then I saw her this cute little redheaded girl I know
    Firmly I vowed I would win it for her
    And I shouldered my bat and I swung . . .
    Dear pen pal, I'm told where you live is really quite far.
    Would you please send directions on how I can get where you are?
    Your friend, Charlie Brown.

Schroeder advises Lucy: know thyself. She is, Schroeder believes, "a very crabby person."

Lucy acquires a clip board and a pencil to take a poll on public opinion of herself. Her first samplings are taken from Snoopy and Charlie Brown, who rates her "forceful" and 51 points crabby on a scale of 100. Snoopy records his opinion of Lucy by turning thumbs down at her. Patty breezes by, rating Lucy 110 points crabby.

Linus is Lucy's next victim. When Lucy assures Linus that she expects him to be frank, Linus rates her 95 points crabby, so Lucy slugs him.

Now Lucy's survey is complete.

LUCY: . . . . . There, it's all done. Now, let's see what we've got.
        She begins to scan the page. A look of trouble skims over her face.
        She becomes more intense. Her eternal look of self-confidence has
        crumbled.

It's true. I'm a crabby person. I'm a very crabby person and everybody knows it. I've been spreading crabbiness everywhere I go. I'm a super crab. It's a wonder anyone will still talk to me. It's a wonder I have any friends at all— or even associates. I've done nothing but make life miserable for everyone. I've done nothing but breed unhappiness and resentment. Where did I go wrong? How could I be so selfish? How could . . .
        Linus, who overhears this, comes over to her and sits down beside
        her.

LINUS: What's wrong, Lucy?

LUCY: Don't talk to me, Linus. I don't deserve to be spoken to. I don't de- serve to breathe the air I breathe. I'm no good, Linus. I'm no good.

LINUS: That's not true, Lucy.

LUCY: Yes, it is. I'm no good, and there's no reason at all why I should go on living on the face of this earth.

LINUS: Yes there is.

LUCY: Name one. Just tell me one single reason why I should still deserve to go on living on this planet.

LINUS: Well, for one thing you have a little brother who loves you.
Lucy looks at him in dead silence and then breaks out in loud sobs.
Every now and then I say the right thing.
Lucy and Linus exit together.

Soon Lucy and Linus are heard fighting again, offstage; they enter quarreling. Linus has taken Lucy's pencil. Lucy wants it back at once, or she'll tell Patty something Linus said about her.

Schroeder is onstage trying to organize a glee club rehearsal. Charlie Brown and Snoopy run in, late. The quarrel between Linus and Lucy continues, while under Schroeder's direction they all sing "Home on the Range." Schroeder, wrapt, doesn't notice the disturbance taking place during the singing.

ALL *(sing):*
. . . . . And the skies are not cloudy all day.
PATTY *(sings):*
If you don't tell me what you told Lucy I'm just going to . . .
LUCY *(sings):*
Give me my pencil you . . .

ALL:	LUCY:	PATTY:
Home,	. . . Blockhead.	Scream.
Home on the range		

ALL:	LINUS:
Where the deer	No!
and the antelope play	Not until you promise
	Not to tell her.

LUCY:
What're you trying to do,
Stifle my freedom of speech?
ALL:
Where seldom is heard
LUCY:
Give me my pencil.
ALL:
A discouraging word,
LINUS:
No promise no pencil,
ALL:
And the skies are not cloudy all day.
PATTY:
What pencil?
LINUS *(looks at hands, sees he is no longer holding pencil):*
No!
Patty victoriously holds up pencil. Linus looks horrified at it.
ALL:
Oh, give me a land,

LINUS:
Give me that pencil.
He grabs it.

ALL:	PATTY:
Where the bright diamond sand	Linus, it just isn't fair.

SCHROEDER: Sing!

ALL *(with vigor):*
Flows leisurely down the stream.

They continue the song, but the irate singers peel off and exit one by one until only Snoopy is left. Snoopy blows a kiss to Schroeder at the end of the song.

Snoopy, alone, observes that just *once* he'd like to have his supper in the yellow dish and water in the red dish, instead of the opposite, to "live it up a little."

Linus has a feeling that Dr. Seuss is his family doctor.

Snoopy's teeth are tingling again: "I feel like I've just got to bite somebody before sundown or I'll go stark raving mad. And yet, I know that society frowns on such action. So what happens? I'm stuck with tingly teeth."

Lucy comes up behind Schroeder and shouts "Hooray for Irving Berlin!"

Snoopy confesses that he hates cats—and fears them.

Linus, the worm, turns on Lucy and Patty and scares them off the stage by pretending to be Count Dracula.

Snoopy admits that he might become a wandering adventurer—except that he is tied down by his supper dish.

Much to Charlie Brown's disgust, Lucy leads Linus around filling him with a vast store of misinformation.

LUCY *(sings):*
Do you see this tree?
It is a fir tree.
It is called a fir tree because it gives us fur,
For coats,
It also gives us wool in the wintertime. . . . .

And way up there, the little stars and planets,
Make the rain, that falls in showers.
And when it's cold and winter is upon us,
The snow comes up, just like the flowers.

CHARLIE BROWN: . . . . . Oh, good grief.

LINUS: Lucy, why is Charlie Brown banging his head against a tree?

LUCY: To loosen the bark so the tree will grow faster. Come along, Linus.

Snoopy's stomach clock goes off. He can hardly wait for Charlie Brown to bring his supper dish. When Charlie arrives with the "brimming bowl of meat and meal," Snoopy dances about and makes a very big fuss over it, in joyous anticipation.

SNOOPY *(sings):*
. . . . . Wintertime's nice with the ice and snow,
Summertime's nice with a place to go,
Bedtime, overtime, half-time too,
But they just can't hold a candle to
My suppertime. Oh, yeah.

Br-r-ing on the hamburg, bring on the bun,
Pappy's little puppy loves ev'ryone.
'Cause it's supper, supper, supper, supper,
Supper super pepper upper
Supper super duper duper
Dupa dupa dupa dupa dupa dipa dupa dupa

CHARLIE BROWN: Now wait a minute, Snoopy. Hey, get down, you're spilling it all over—NOW CUT THAT OUT! Why can't you eat your meal quietly and calmly like any normal dog?

SNOOPY *(very softly):* So what's wrong with making mealtime a joyous occasion? *(Sings, quietly)*
Doo doo doo doo-de doo-doo doo.

Lucy and Linus, Schroeder and Patty enter watching a bright, blinking star—or satellite—or airplane. Snoopy, having finished his supper, makes a coyote sound because that's what is needed among the sounds of the night.

Charlie Brown enters.

CHARLIE BROWN: I'm so happy. That little red-headed girl dropped her pencil. It has teeth marks all over it. She nibbles her pencil. She's human! It hasn't been such a bad day after all. *(Sings):*
Happiness is finding a pencil

SNOOPY:
Pizza with sausage

LINUS:
Telling the time

SCHROEDER:
Happiness is learning to whistle

LINUS:
Tying your shoe
For the very first time.

PATTY:
Happiness is playing the drum in your own school band. . . . .

Gradually the euphoria of their song creeps over them all, even Lucy.

LINUS (sings):
   Happiness is having a sister
LUCY:
   Sharing a sandwich
LUCY AND LINUS:
   Getting along.
ALL:
   Happiness is singing together when day is through.
   And happiness is those who sing with you.

   Happiness is morning and evening,
   Daytime and nighttime, too,
CHARLIE BROWN:
   For happiness is anyone and anything at all
   That's loved by you.
         Everyone moves to exit.
   LUCY (*to Charlie Brown, as she comes over to shake his hand*): You're a
good man, Charlie Brown!
         Curtain.

YOU KNOW I CAN'T HEAR YOU WHEN THE WATER'S RUNNING

A Program of Four One-Act Plays

BY ROBERT ANDERSON

Cast and credits appear on page 384

ROBERT ANDERSON is a native New Yorker born April 28, 1917. At Harvard (A.B. 1939, M.A. 1940, Ph.D. 1942) he wrote, acted in and directed plays, wrote drama criticism and taught drama and writing. In the Navy in World War II he won the National Theater Conference Award for the best play written by a service man overseas. After about 70 radio and television scripts, he made his Broadway debut as the author of Tea and Sympathy *September 30, 1953.* Tea and Sympathy *ran 712 performances, was named a Best Play of its season and appeared in a movie version for which Anderson wrote the screen play.*

Anderson became a member of the Playwrights Company, an association of playwrights which produced his next two Broadway scripts: All Summer Long *(1954) and* Silent Night, Lonely Night *(1959). Last season his new play* The Days Between *was chosen by the American Playwrights Theater circuit for production in college and community theaters around the country (Anderson's article describing this experience appears in "The Season Around the United States" section of this volume).*

Anderson's screen play credits include The Nun's Story *(nominated for an Academy Award),* Until They Sail *and* The Sand Pebbles. *Anderson initiated playwriting classes at the American Theater Wing and the Actors Studio. He was one of the first members of the New Dramatists, a professional association of aspiring playwrights, and he served for a time as its president. Anderson and his wife, Teresa Wright, live in Connecticut.*

I. THE SHOCK OF RECOGNITION

Time: The present

Place: A producer's office

SYNOPSIS: Jack Barnstable, a playwright—*"slight, intellectual"*—waits in the office of Herb Miller, a Broadway producer. The office contains a desk, chairs, the usual clutter; there are doors left and right. After a moment, Herb Miller —*"large, a rough diamond"*—enters right. Herb and Jack shake hands warmly. Herb is excited about producing Jack's play, and he tells his secretary not to disturb them while they discuss a small problem: the script says "Patrick, aged 43, enters from the bathroom naked." Does Jack mean literally, really naked? Jack does. Herb protests: this will outrage everybody, the law as well as the audience.

JACK: Damn it, Herb, it's about time our theater grew up . . . We got to let some air in here someplace . . . It's not as though I were trying to do something sexy. Far from it . . . Look, when Ibsen put a real life scene on the stage in 1889, the audience recognized their own lives and stood up and cheered.

HERB: Well, if you put a naked man on the stage, they're gonna stand up and go home.

JACK: I'm not asking you to show a couple making love on stage.

HERB: That'll come next.

JACK: I just want the audience to get that shock of recognition . . . to feel at home . . . to say, "My God, that's just like us." . . . Look, the wife's lying there in bed reading the morning newspapers . . .

Herb suddenly looks at the script frantically.
What's the matter.

HERB: I just thought I'd better check. Is she naked too?

JACK: No, Herb. For God's sake . . . she's lying there. She can be dressed six layers deep, as far as I'm concerned . . . and she's reading the papers and chattering away to her husband, who is in the bathroom . . . water running. Suddenly the water is turned off. Husband appears in the bedroom, with toothbrush in his hand, naked, and says, "Honey, you know I can't hear you when the water's running." He stands there a moment . . .

HERB: Just long enough for everyone to faint.

JACK: . . . goes back in, and the next time we see him, he has a robe on, and that's that.

What Jack wants is the momentary shock of recognition, as when running water was used onstage in *The Voice of the Turtle.* He wants to show man as he *is.*

JACK: . . . What Shakespeare called a poor forked radish . . . with no implications except of mortality and ridiculousness.

HERB: You find a naked man ridiculous?

JACK: Mostly, yes. And so do you. I think the males in the audience will howl with delight and recognition.

HERB: At seeing this guy flapping in the breeze?

JACK: Yeah. A real man, naked. And, of course, in the play he's quite a guy. He's our hero.

HERB *(looking in script):* You know you didn't say in the script that not only do you want a naked man . . . you want a ridiculous looking naked man.

JACK: That's the whole point. I don't want an Adonis on stage.

Jack has described the naked man as "touching" because that is the word his own wife applied to Jack's *rear* view (Herb's wife merely calls him Mr. Big-Ass. Herb's retort is, "Honey, you can't drive a spike with a tack-hammer.") Herb offers to allow the "touching" rear view in the play—after all they did it it *Marat/Sade* and got away with it.

HERB: I hesitate to ask you how your wife characterizes your . . . uh . . . your . . . Does she find that touching, too?

JACK: She finds it no work of art . . . nor does any woman, as I understand it, though I haven't done a house-to-house poll on it. It's the boys who find it a work of stunning magnificence . . . And I want to blast that. I want every man in the audience to want to reach out and shake my hand.

HERB: And every woman to reach out and pat your fanny . . .

Jack has brought pictures to help make his point: pictures of an idealized naked man and of a real, pathetic-looking guy—it's the latter quality he wants on the stage. Herb protests—no man thinks of his equipment as ridiculous; he thinks of it, rather, as a formidable weapon . . . the sight of a pathetic naked man on stage would antagonize all the men in the audience.

Jack suggests that "Hank" would be a good choice to act this part. Herb accuses Jack of a "compulsion to exhibit yourself via some poor actor bastard . . . before the admiring public." All right, says Jack, then they will cast an unknown. It would ruin the unknown's future, Herb suggests, people would continue to think of him naked, with a toothbrush in hand.

Jack is a well-known serious playwright, not some upstart sensation-monger. He claims the right to match his playscript to the daring of modern books and movie scenes.

HERB: Look, it's already hard enough putting on a serious play this day and age. People say, "I got enough troubles in my life. Why come to the theater to see the same thing?" Now, you'll have them saying, "Look, I see my poor pathetic, ridiculous husband walking around naked all the time. I don't want to come to the theater to see another ridiculous naked man I don't even know."

JACK *(vehement):* I want to say to that plain, ordinary man, her husband . . . I want to say to him in the audience . . . "Hello. We haven't forgotten you."

HERB: And he'll call back and say, "I wish the hell you would."

Jack threatens to withdraw the play, which Herb really likes, and Herb reasons with him: how about the casting problem if "Hank" won't do the part?

HERB: . . . . . I mean, actors are used to being turned down because they're too short or too tall. But to be turned down because their equipment is not ridiculous enough.

JACK: You're so damn prudish you won't even call it by its right name . . . all these euphemisms . . . Equipment . . . Thing . . .

HERB: What would you like me to call it?

JACK: The technical word . . . the correct word . . . is penis.

HERB: If you go around calling it that, I understand why you think of it as pathetic and ridiculous. It's a ridiculous and belittling name. . . . .

Besides—Herb confesses—there's something about Jack that forbids immodesty, that puts people on their best behavior in his presence, that gives them an impulse to excuse themselves for any lapses of decorum. The public, likewise, does not think of Jack as a daring writer. Jack is furious at this insult to his sophistication, but Herb insists: there is something about Jack that demands modesty.

Herb calls in his secretary, Dorothy, "a Bennington girl," impressed by Jack's celebrity as a playwright. Dorothy has read the play and she blushes and giggles when the naked scene is mentioned; yet she wants to pretend that she is *not* blushing. Would she pay $6.90 to see a naked man on the stage? She can't answer the question directly. Has she ever, in reality, seen a naked man?

DOROTHY: You certainly don't expect a person to answer that.

HERB: All right, go out and pull yourself together . . . I just wanted to demonstrate to our playwright here what even the idea of a naked man does to you.

DOROTHY: That's not fair.

HERB: There go your matinees . . .

JACK: Nonsense. I gave this to my grandmother to read, and her only comment was, "Let me know when it opens and I'll be there with my opera glasses." . . . Women are bored with this respectability which red-blooded but prudish men have forced on them . . . They want to be let in on the joke . . .

HERB: Dorothy, do you find a man's sexual equipment ridiculous and pathetic?

DOROTHY: Mr. Miller! *(She runs out gasping and in confusion.)*

HERB: Do you think she meant "yes" or "no"?

JACK: You're a cruel bastard. That's a cheap way of getting your kicks.

Herb was just trying to make a point (and having a little fun at the same time). He suggests that they can fake the scene with a strategically-placed piece of furniture to hide the man as he comes out of the bathroom. But Jack insists: this moment should be real, it is a moment which makes the whole play real. Jack is obsessed with certain aspects of reality: for example, he has made notes for a scene in some future play about a man trying to make a woman, and at the same time "running a race with his bladder . . . And he's finally got to go, and he's lost it." (This revolts Herb.) Life, Jack concludes, is "a tragedy played by comedians," and he wants to demonstrate this on the stage.

Herb insists that you can't shift *tone* in a play the way it shifts in real life—at least in Jack's real life (Herb doesn't walk around his house naked; Jack sometimes does).

Again in the spirit of experiment, Herb brings into the office an actor who happens to be in the outer office, to drop off some new photos of himself. The actor, Richard Pawling, is *"age 35. He is over-eager . . . self-explaining . . . anxious"*. Pawling hastens to tell them that he has his hair long for a Western and is wearing a mustache for a TV commercial, but all that can be changed. He once worked for Jack, as an understudy.

Herb tells Pawling that they are casting a lead part.

> *Jack is aghast and goes and sits at one side of the room. Pawling, worried that he is giving the wrong impression, follows Jack.*

PAWLING: I can be taller . . . I don't have my elevator shoes on . . . Or do you want someone shorter? . . . I mean . . . I can pretty well adapt . . . The hair is dark now, but you may remember, Mr. Miller, it was blond when I worked for you last.

HERB: Oh, yes.

PAWLING (*going on nervously*): I'm pretty well tanned up because of this Western . . . I told you . . . but if I stay away from the sunlamp for a couple of days . . . I . . . well . . . look more . . . intellectual, Mr. Barnstable . . . if that's what you're looking for . . . Also, I have my contact lenses in now, but I do have glasses if that's closer to the image.

> *He whips them out and puts them on . . . Thrown off balance at first by the double vision . . . then takes them off.*

And, of course, I do have other clothes . . . And my weight's variable . . . I mean, if you're looking for someone thinner . . .

HERB: Actually, we're looking for someone rather . . . well, someone who can look a little pathetic and ridiculous.

PAWLING (*without a moment's hesitation*): That's me . . . I mean, put me in the right clothes . . . a little big for me . . . and I look like a scarecrow . . . I can shrink inside my clothes.

Herb asks Jack to take over the final description of the role, but Jack protests that Pawling isn't the type. Pawling keeps trying; he acts younger, older, asks to read the script. Herb, noting that Jack does not intend to carry this any farther, describes the opening scene to Pawling, then notices Pawling smiling.

HERB: . . . . . Why are you smiling?

PAWLING: Well, I mean . . . that's a situation I know like the back of my hand. My wives . . . they could never get it through their heads that you can't hear when the water's running.

HERB: That's his first line. He turns off the water, and he comes out and says, "Honey, you know I can't hear you when the water's running."

PAWLING: Well, you've got every husband with you from then on . . . I didn't say "honey" . . . But I remember distinctly saying, "For Christ's sake, how many times do I have to tell you I can't hear you when the God damned water's running?"

Turns to Jack.

Excuse me, Mr. Barnstable.

JACK *(burning):* Why did you say "excuse me" . . . to me?

PAWLING: I don't know . . .

Shrugs "Did I do something wrong?"

Herb continues his explanation—gradually he makes Pawling understand that this character is brushing his teeth in the nude (Pawling can handle *that*, he's done it). The actor must do the scene, as Herb puts it, "bare-ass." Jack hastens to explain the intellectual value of this scene: "Like Nora slamming the door in *A Doll's House*."

But Pawling has only one thing on his mind—getting the part. He apologizes for a hole in a sock and starts to strip. As he does this, he shows them how average he is; no muscle, and he can shave the hair off his chest. He examines himself from the side view, planning how he ought to look.

HERB: But you see, Mr. Pawling, you don't come in from downstage. You come in from upstage. I believe that's Mr. Barnstable's idea.

Pawling stares out at the audience, full-face, gradually getting the idea of what this involves . . . Then, finally . . .

PAWLING: Well . . . *(Starts to take off his trousers.)*

JACK *(embarrassed):* I think that will be all, Mr. Pawling.

But Pawling persists. He takes off his trousers, stands there in his shorts commenting on his "ridiculous" legs. Herb insists that he must make certain —does the rest of Pawling look ridiculous enough?

PAWLING: Well, I . . . It's embarrassing discussing this sort of thing, but . . . Girls have sometimes . . . uh . . . laughed, or giggled . . . At first! . . . Of course, it's not the look that counts. I mean, we all know that.

They are all silent for a moment.
Well, I've been turned down for parts because I was too short or too tall . . .
too fat or too thin . . . too young or too old . . . *(He swings his arms in em-
barrassment . . . then)* What the hell!
He starts to unbutton his shorts.
JACK: Hold it, Mr. Pawling!
He gathers up Pawling's clothes.

Pawling is willing to show himself naked, but Jack can't go through with
it. Jack tries to usher Pawling out, then flees into the secretary's office at left.
Herb maneuvers Pawling off into the room at right, then calls Jack back into
the office.

Herb feels he has won his point: "Theory is theory . . . Life is life." Pawling comes back, still in his shorts, and offers to send some Polaroid pictures
of himself in a plain wrapper; then exits again.

Herb offers to show a naked woman on the stage in that scene and Jack,
disgusted, starts to leave. Herb gets down to business and tells Jack: "Hank"
has agreed to do the part. They can have $300,000 pre-production money
from Warner Brothers—only "Hank" won't do the scene naked. Jack wants
to know: did Herb ask "Hank" about that scene specifically? No, Herb is
just assuming that "Hank" will refuse.

JACK: Will you put it on, as written, if Hank'll play it that way?
HERB: Sure.
JACK: Okay . . . I gotta get out of here, but after lunch I'll call Hank . . .
Let *me* talk to him . . . let me give him the background of my thinking . . .
(Heads for door. Stops. Returns.) Of course, we still got a problem.
HERB: What now?
JACK: We haven't any idea what Hank looks like naked.
HERB: Well, before we sign the contract, we could invite him to the Y for
a swim.
*Jack thinks about this for a second, nods assent, and leaves. Herb
shakes his head, smiling . . . reaches for the phone and dials a number.*
Hello, Hank . . . Herb Miller here . . . Sorry to call you at home, but I wanted
to get to you fast . . . I'm going ahead with the play for sure this season . . .
Barnstable's crazy to have you do it . . . He just left here . . . And he may be
getting in touch with you, so I thought I ought to warn you about one thing
. . . and ask for your help . . . He's kind of a nut about that first scene. I don't
know if you read all the stage directions, but the guy is supposed to be standing there in the bedroom naked . . . Oh, you did read that? . . . Well, Barnstable's got the crazy idea he wants it played just like that . . . Naked . . .
What!? *(He rises.)* But good God, Hank. We can't do that! *(He continues to
listen . . . consternation on his face.)* The shock of recognition.
He nods dully. The right door bursts open.
PAWLING'S VOICE: Hey, Mr. Miller, look!

> *Pawling's right hand can be seen on the edge of the door. Herb*
> *dully motions Pawling to go away, and barely gives him a glance*
> *. . . Then suddenly realizes what he's seen . . . His head jerks up,*
> *straight front, then he does a slow turn to check out what he's*
> *seen . . .*

I told you . . . Ridiculous!

> *Herb's eyes close, shutting out the sight of what he has seen . . .*
> *and he is sinking to his chair . . . as the lights go out . . . Curtain.*

II. THE FOOTSTEPS OF DOVES

Time: The present

Place: A basement showroom of a bedding store

SYNOPSIS: There is a standard, 54-inch-wide double bed on display at right; twin beds at left. The Salesman *"a dried neuter of a man"*—enters down the stairs, upstage center, with George and Harriet.

> *George and Harriet are an attractive, successful couple in the late*
> *forties. She wears a very nice suit, conservative hat and white*
> *gloves . . . He wears a gray flannel suit, button-down blue shirt and*
> *brown felt hat. He has had one and one-third martinis.*

George and Harriet have come to shop for twin beds, and the Salesman goes into his spiel about foam rubber and dimple mattresses. George ignores the whole thing and lies down on "good old 54," the standard 54-inch-wide double bed, of the kind he and Harriet have been sleeping in for their twenty-five years of married life.

Harriet forces George to get up and lie down beside her on one of the twin beds, testing it for length.

GEORGE: Put sides and a lid on it and bury us.

HARRIET *(sitting up):* This is how wide?

SALESMAN: That's your thirty-six. They come thirty-nine, too. But of course, it's not meant to hold two people . . . except under special circumstances.

GEORGE *(gets up):* That's what I'm interested in. The special circumstances.

> *He moves to the 54-inch bed and sits down on it, patting it.*

This is the kind of bed George likes; that his mother and father slept in and died in; too small to stay apart in; a bed for the days when people were more loving, less detached from each other; sleeping all mixed up with each other, like cats . . .

GEORGE: . . . . . Or puppies, or bears. One stirs, the other stirs . . . kind of slow and easy accommodation to each other . . . but they stay in a lump. For reassurance, comfort. All day you bump up against hard facts, hard edges, cold bodies. Good old fifty-four throws you up against something warm and round and soft . . .

He looks to Harriet. She looks away.
(To Salesman.) Are you married?

SALESMAN: No.

GEORGE: Let me tell you about twin beds . . . The longest distance in the world is the distance between twin beds. I don't care if it's six inches or six feet. It's psychological distance . . . In an old fifty-four, you may get into bed. You don't know what you feel like . . . then you roll up together . . . and you know! . . . In twins, you got to make up your mind all by yourself, and then cross that damned gulf and find out if your twin feels like it . . . And then if you get there, and find out you were wrong about yourself, well, it's a lot of embarrassment retreating . . . Or if you find out she's not in the mood . . . it's a big rejection . . . But in good old fifty-four, you don't make a move until you're sure of yourself, and you can pretty well sense if she's in the mood . . . And if it still doesn't work out, what the hell, you just fall asleep, all wrapped around each other. No damage done.

HARRIET *(elaborately ignoring him):* The price is just for the mattress?

The Salesman continues his pitch. Harriet tells George she wants their old double bed taken away when they deliver the new twins, but George insists that it be stored in the attic They quarrel over this, and over whether to have a footboard. The Salesman leaves them alone to make up their minds, reassuring them: "People have been known to go mad down here."

George declares he is not drunk—he had only two martinis at lunch and Harriet drank most of the second deliberately, to keep it away from him. George insists: he has changed his mind. He fights to keep the double bed; he is fighting for their marriage. He quotes Nietzche: "The big crises in our lives do not come with the sound of thunder and lightning, but softly like the footsteps of doves."

George is 47, he reminds Harriet—a dangerous age; an age when the warm, arousing touch is important. The distance between twin beds can become "like the Persian Gulf" and the marriage comes to an end when the husband "finally decides he doesn't want to get his feet wet sloshing from bed to bed."

George and Harriet have discussed divorce without going through with it, and now—George argues—they shouldn't go through with this twin bed business, even though they've discussed it. Harriet claims that she needs a separate bed because of her ailing back, but George calls her doctor a quack.

They go over all the arguments: temporarily, Harriet feels she wants to be left alone, but soon, probably, she'll come back with "fierce desires." Harriet likes to read in bed, while George likes to go right to sleep; George is a morning person. There isn't room to compromise on a queen or king-size double bed ("Then let's sell the house," George offers).

Finally, Harriet suggests that maybe she'd prefer to have George make that extra effort of crossing the gulf. George insists that he's always been a good husband, always considerate of her, never selfish. But Harriet remains adamantly in favor of a change to twin beds.

GEORGE: What happens six months from now when you return to combat with fierce desires? But I'm over the hill from disuse. Muscles atrophy, you know.

HARRIET: People will hear you.

GEORGE: I want people to hear me. Specifically, you!

HARRIET: I hear you.

GEORGE: You hear me, but you're not listening.

HARRIET (low): We'll get the thirty-nine-inch width. If you insist, we'll start the nights wrapped around each other . . . and then when you've decided what's playing or *not* playing that night, you can either stay for a while, or go back to your own bed.

GEORGE: I get the cold bed.

HARRIET: *I'll* go to the other bed. My God!

GEORGE: How long do I get to make up my mind each night? Do we set an oven timer?

HARRIET: Now, I'm going to look at headboards. You decide on the firmnes you want for your mattress.

She moves towards another showroom.

GEORGE: I warn you, Harriet. We are at the Rubicon.

HARRIET: I thought it was the Persian Gulf.

GEORGE: I can hear the doves!

But she is gone.

George takes a few aimless steps around the showroom, then wanders off in an opposite direction from Harriet. Jill enters *("She is a swinging, charming and disarming young woman of 23 . . . dressed in a slack suit.")* Jill takes off her jacket and shoes and is lying on the double bed, trying it out, when George re-enters, sits on the single bed, sees Jill, jumps to his feet.

Jill practises various sleeping positions, pantomimes someone else in the bed beside her before, finally, she sees George. Easily, she strikes up a conversation with him as she sits up. Jill tells George: she has just been divorced.

JILL: We slept together in *two* single beds.

GEORGE: I see.

JILL: "So much better when either of you gets a cold." His mother said.

GEORGE: Do you get colds?

JILL: No. His mother got the colds. I got a divorce.

She didn't know her husband well enough before she married him (she had only a 30-inch twin bed) but next time things are going to be different. She wants a big double bed, brass, with a canopy, like the one she was born in.

George endorses the double bed, speaking as a man who has enjoyed one for twenty-five years of marriage. Jill compliments George on how young he looks, stresses the modern woman's responsibility to stay young-looking for her husband. Jill believes that men improve with age. She likes older men . . . and older environments. She lives in a brownstone and casually tells George the address.

Jill asks George's height and weight, which he gladly tells her; then she asks him to test the bed with her. They both lie on the double bed—George keeping a cautious eye out for Harriet. They sit up—he is greatly enjoying this very friendly experience with Jill—and he shows her the scar on his knee.

JILL: . . . . . Scars on a man are rather attractive. I noticed you have a small scar on your upper lip. The war?

GEORGE (looks at the girl a moment . . . then): No. My dog bit me.
        Jill lies down again.
(Still sitting up.) Of course, the proper technique in a fifty-four inch is not to lie like two mummies, but entwined.

JILL: Yes, all snuggled around each other. I'm an indiscriminate snuggler. Cats, dogs, dolls, stuffed animals, etcetera.

GEORGE: Are you a morning person or a night person?

It turns out that, like George, she's a morning person . . . but Jill must stop this day-dreaming. She can't afford to buy a double bed yet, and she must get back to work, typing manuscripts at home. George happens to remember that he started a novel in college—maybe this would be a good time to finish it, and he has Jill's address where he can have it typed. George tells Jill his name, and she wishes him goodbye and good luck with his novel.

> She smiles sweetly and leaves briskly. George remains at the foot
> of the stairs . . . wondering what has happened . . . a silly grin on
> his face.

HARRIET (coming in): George . . . I've picked the headboards . . . Very simple, clean lines.

GEORGE (out of his reverie): Okay.

For a moment, Harriet relents; she offers to "struggle on with the old bed for a while" if George really cares that much. George is touched, but now he has a new notion. He agrees to change to single beds ("He pats one of the singles . . . a little desperately.") He agrees with Harriet that they've had twenty-five good years, but they're older now. The pleasures of reading in bed beckon.

HARRIET: . . . . . George, if you want to keep the old bed up in the attic . . .

GEORGE: No. No. There's really no room for it. I'll just shove it in the station wagon, and give it to some charity.

HARRIET: You should be able to get something for the brass frame.

GEORGE: I'll dicker.

HARRIET (looking at 54-inch bed): I'm not denying I'll miss it. (She smiles.) If we get lonesome for it, we can sneak off to a motel like a couple of kids.

              They hug a moment. Harriet starts for the stairs.

GEORGE (a step towards the 54-inch bed): Goodbye, old friend. (He moves a step towards the stairs . . . turns . . .) Be seeing you.

              Harriet laughs, reaches out her hand, and they disappear up the stairs . . . The lights fade, but last of all on the 54-inch bed . . . Curtain.

III. I'LL BE HOME FOR CHRISTMAS

Time: The present

Place: An apartment living room and kitchen

SYNOPSIS: The stage is set for a living room area right and center with sofa, a small table, a record player; at left, for a kitchen area with a table, stool and a suggestion of fixtures and appliances.

In the living room, Chuck Berringer (*"about 45 . . . large and brawny"*) is stretched out on the sofa smoking, drinking beer, listening to old tunes played on records—and worrying. After a few moments his wife, Edith, enters.

              She is about 40. Her hair is up in curlers, covered by a scarf. She is wearing attractive blouse, sweater and slacks. She is carrying a small bag from the market . . . Her approach to things is direct, hearty, no nonsense . . . apparently somewhat insensitive . . . though this may only be her way of coping with things that frighten her to death.

Edith sees what Chuck is doing (it's not like Chuck to smoke, drink or play records). She comments that Chuck should not be home from the office this early; tells him that their daughter Clarice will entertain her boy friend Teddy here later; and tells him: "Go easy on the beer, huh? We got that thing for Crippled Children tonight." Chuck doesn't react to Edith's presence or words, so she goes to the kitchen and sets down her bundle. She phones a friend to find out whether any of the other husbands are home from work early (they are not). Meanwhile, Chuck gets up from the sofa, goes over and shuts the living room door, comes back and lies down again.

EDITH: . . . . . Probably just one of his moods. *(She mimics broadly.)* "What ever happened?" . . . "Where did it all go?" . . . He used to scare the Bejesus out of me when he started wondering about the meaning of it all . . . I just don't listen any more because I know that when he starts saying "What happened?" . . . He's really meaning, "You happened." . . . as though I were personally responsible for the high cost of living and the menopause . . . I tell you, kiddo, never marry a man at war with the inevitable . . . I'll let you know. 'Bye.

> *She hangs up. Her heartiness disappears . . . She comes back to the living room door . . . finds it shut . . . She hesitates a moment, then opens it . . . She comes in . . . looks at Chuck a moment . . . then . . .*

Did you see Clarice got a letter from Donny today?

> *She gestures toward the table in the hall where the mail is left.*

If we get a letter from that boy once a month . . . I know you won't hear of it, but I'd stop his allowance . . .

> *She moves an ash tray near him.*

Nothing happen at the office?

> *He nods "No." She turns away from him. While she turns away, he takes a letter from the breast pocket of his shirt and casually stuffs it in his trousers pocket . . . He doesn't make any big thing of it . . .*

Yes, (Chuck nods to Edith) he is going away on a business trip the next day. Edith tries to reach him with the grocery bill, but fails. Finally she makes a more serious effort: they have two family problems, one of which is all Chuck's responsibility. Wearily, Chuck stops the record player to listen to her.

CHUCK: Which thing is all my responsibility?
EDITH: I think Timmy is playing with himself.
> *Chuck takes cigar from his mouth.*

Playing with himself.
CHUCK: I hope to God he is. If he isn't, he's a freak.
EDITH: Well, I'm sure he is. He moons around. He's losing weight.
CHUCK: You think perhaps he's in imminent danger of going blind or getting epilepsy?
EDITH: I think *he* might think that. He goes around sheepish, and full of some kind of guilt. I think you should have a talk with him.

Edith's instinct is to attack this problem frontally; Chuck's instinct is to leave the boy alone. Edith feels that Chuck should help relieve the boy's guilt feelings by telling him the practise is not dirty, but normal for everyone including his own father when he was a boy. It might do Timmy good (Edith suggests) to have his father's image tarnished a bit.

Edith mentions a sign their son has tacked over his bed.

EDITH: A cardboard sign . . . about so big, and on it he'd printed in large letters the word . . . WILLPOWER.

CHUCK: And you figured out from this . . .

EDITH: Yes.

CHUCK: Maybe the best thing for me to do would be just to turn the cardboard over and write . . . ENJOY YOURSELF . . . How do you know this WILLPOWER doesn't apply to any number of other things? "Don't oversleep in the morning." . . . "Do your pushups." . . . "Love your parents." . . . You've got a dirty mind.

EDITH: That's exactly the point. I don't want him to look on it as dirty. I want him to look on it as a normal, healthy part of his life.

CHUCK: Edith he may, in spite of your desire and efforts to give it the Good Housekeeping seal of approval . . . He may just crave a corner of dirtiness in his life . . .

Edith is afraid that Timmy, as well as their son Donny in college, will marry the first girl they meet, all because Chuck never talks to them about the facts of life. Very well, she will send Timmy to the doctor, or give him a book . . . but Chuck objects; he wants "A little mystery. A little snicker left in sex . . . please." He'll speak to Timmy when and how he sees fit.

In Edith's opinion, Chuck is unnaturally reticent about sex—he should be more open, more "normal." Chuck defends himself: "A little laughter, a little levity . . . leavening. Life is not, dear Edith, a desperate struggle and straining for the technically perfect orgasm . . . It's a laugh now and then. . . . . I think sex is beautiful. . . . ."

Edith feels Chuck's humorous evasions about sex make the children feel it's dirty; Chuck believes Edith's so-called "naturalness" about it embarrasses the children—and embarrassed him, too, that time she was sick for such a long while after an operation and suggested that Chuck go in search of a substitute.

EDITH: Your son knows how you are about these matters . . . Did you know he came to me to buy him his first jock strap?

CHUCK: Oh, Lord, I have failed my own son because he went to his mother for his first jock strap! . . . As I remember, he came to me first, and I said he didn't need one yet.

EDITH: Well, I don't want to even begin to think what damage that did to him.

Chuck starts the record player (the tune is "I Should Care") to end the conversation, but Edith stops it again to discuss a second problem: their daughter Clarice. She has told Clarice everything about sex but wishes Chuck might enlighten Clarice from the man's point of view. Chuck puts his foot down: "I am not going to discuss with my daughter a man's . . . erogenous zones."

Edith argues that it might have been better if Edith had known of Chuck's "peculiar"—she changes the word to "special"—little likes before they got married. Chuck challenges Edith to talk to Donny about a *woman's* sexual responses. Edith boasts; she already has. Chuck protests: she's probably frightened him with her disclosures.

EDITH: Nature abhors a vacuum. And you have created a vacuum as far as the sex education of your children is concerned.

CHUCK *(serious):* Edith, for God's sake . . . I have told them all I think they want to hear from me. Can't you get it through your head that it's grotesque, us talking to them about sex. Sex to them is full of spring and beauty and something old people like you and me don't experience . . . It's absurd to them that we are capable of feeling the same thing they are feeling . . . And maybe we're not . . . They should feel something unique about love and sex . . . they should feel they're experiencing something unique and personal.

But Edith has another problem that won't wait. Clarice is going to college, where morals are notoriously lax. Chuck should take her to the doctor and arrange for a fitted contraceptive device. Chuck scoffs at her, believing that only 5 per cent of the youth are "out for everything they can get," the other 95 per cent are idealists who, with the girls they love, "sometimes hope they don't get it."

Chuck urges Edith to stop "understanding," to look at their daughter Clarice as an individual with the good sense and judgment they have instilled in her. Chuck believes the best example he and Edith could set their children would be to make a show of affection in front of them.

But Edith persists: if their own doctor is too stuffy to arrange this precaution, Chuck must take Edith to another doctor. Chuck has always understood that virgins can't be fitted with. . . . But Edith interrupts him with the news that Clarice is *not* a virgin, the doctor has told her.

Chuck hopes it wasn't Teddy, begins to act like an irate father—but Edith brings him back to the subject. Facing it head-on, Chuck pleads that a boy doesn't like to find that his girl is "prepared" at a passionate moment.

CHUCK: . . . . . He does not like to hear from the girl . . . no matter how modern he is, no matter how many books on the subject he's read . . . "Go ahead, honey. It's all right. I'm prepared." . . . If she said that, I'll tell you what goes through his head at that moment . . . "Does this mean she does this with all the boys? Does it mean she took me for granted? . . . Does it mean if I hadn't made a pass, she would have thought me a schmo?"

EDITH: What is your solution?

CHUCK: The man makes the arrangements . . . at least the first time.

EDITH: You mean they stop while he goes hunting for a corner drug store?

CHUCK: Well . . .

EDITH: Or does he just happen to have one . . . or an economy size dozen, in his pocket? . . . In which case, what does the girl think?

CHUCK: It's different. I can't explain why. But there's a nicety in it some-place . . .

EDITH: And what happens if they can't find a drug store open . . . as we couldn't . . . if you'll remember . . . and the moment is possibly lost. You weren't prepared.

CHUCK: I was.

EDITH: We drove all over the damn countryside looking for a drug store that was open . . .

CHUCK: I had something in my wallet. Only by the time we got to the point, I loved you so much . . . I didn't want you to think I was the kind of guy who carried them around in his pocket . . . just in case.

EDITH: Well, that's very touching. Nowadays I think the girl would think you were a fink not to be prepared, after getting her all worked up.

There's something sordid about a ready contraceptive, Chuck argues; bet-ter than the ridiculous search for a drug store, Edith counters. She wouldn't have been shocked, because she had the kind of father who prepared her; who told her about the needs of a man; who explained to Edith the reason for his own marital infidelities to Edith's mother.

Chuck thinks about this, deduces that Edith believes Chuck has been un-faithful to her on occasions and is enduring this knowledge stoically. He tells her: "I'm sorry as hell to disappoint you, but there have been no little mean-ingless sexual skirmishes . . . My life is full enough of meaninglessness not to go looking for it in outlying districts." He wishes Edith would stand up and howl, if she believes the contrary.

EDITH: Difficult as it is for you to grasp, your virginity was not a concern of mine before we were married, and your strict fidelity is not a concern of mine now. I am not your jailer, and I am not stupid. The subject is closed as far as I am concerned.

She starts for the door. Chuck heads her off and grabs her.

CHUCK: Jesus Christ, men are not all like your father. All men do not relish meaningless rolls in the hay, in their own beds or other beds.

EDITH *(moves away from him, back into the room)*: We were discussing the children.

CHUCK: I feel like clobbering you for assuming that I've laid every broad in every small town I've visited, all because your father gave you the low-down. Why didn't he let you find out for yourself what your man . . . your husband would do? . . . Because if it doesn't matter to you, it matters to me . . . It's hard as hell trying to keep any meaning going, but here, here in the most personal and private core of me, I insist that there be meaning, I want there to be meaning . . . I long for there to be meaning.

Clarice enters, her arms full of school books *("she is 18 and lovely")*. She is surprised to see her father home so early . . . she goes to the kitchen. When she is out of earshot Chuck puts his foot down: he will not intrude on her private emotional life and he forbids Edith to do so while he is off on a trip.

EDITH *(after a moment):* All right. But I wish to God you'd join the twentieth century.
She starts to open the door.
CHUCK: When Timmy comes in, send him to me, and I'll set his mind at rest about . . .
Edith opens the door, and leaves, closing the door after her . . . She stands for a moment in the shadows between the kitchen and living room. Chuck slowly returns to the couch and sits, saddened by the scene he has just had . . . then he shifts his mood slightly.
CHUCK: You see, Timmy . . . many good men and true do that . . . soldiers, sailors, men at war . . . men on long trips into the Arctic . . . and other places . . . And, Timmy, there's nothing wrong with it . . . except it's awfully lonely.
He has said this last very simply . . . He turns and lies down on the couch . . . starts the record . . . . . takes letter from his pocket and re-reads it . . .

In the kitchen, Clarice brings up the subject of "Donny's letter to dad." Donny sent Clarice a copy of this letter—but of course Edith knows nothing of it. Clarice reads to Edith from Donny's letter: Donny knows it's cowardly to write his father this way instead of facing him in person, but they've never been able to communicate.

College makes no sense to Donny. He is leaving it, in search of a useful life. His letter continues:

CLARICE *(reading Donny's letter):* ". . . . . I think you've been preparing me for the only kind of life you know. Your kind of life. I don't want to hurt you, dad, because you've always been a good Joe to me . . . but I could never take that kind of life. The life of your generation. You all fought a war. Nobody can take that away from you . . . But after that, what happened?
She is finding the letter more difficult and painful to read.
"Whatever it was, it scares me, and I don't want it to happen to me . . . Sometimes I don't know how you do it, dad . . . Sometimes . . .
She falters as her eye reads ahead . . . then:
"Sometimes I don't know how you have the courage to get up in the morning."
EDITH *(after a moment):* He wrote that to your father?
CLARICE *(saddened and disturbed by the letter):* I guess so.
Hands it over to Edith. Edith looks at it a moment.
EDITH *(more in sympathy with Chuck than anger at Donny):* Your father gets up in the morning . . . so that he can send your brother to a fine college so that he can write insulting letters like this . . .
She turns toward the living room, and moves into the shadows by

*the door . . . her concern for Chuck clearly showing on her face
. . . . Chuck has finished re-reading the letter.*
CHUCK *(suddenly starts to sing with the record . . .):*
I'll be home for Christmas
If only in my—
*His voice breaks . . . he closes his eyes . . . the record finishes . . .
the lights dim. Curtain.*

IV. I'M HERBERT

Time: The present

Place: A side porch

SYNOPSIS: It is summer. Herbert, a very old man, is seated in one of two rocking chairs on a porch, bird-watching through binoculars. He identifies a few birds, then sees one worth talking about.

HERBERT: A black-billed cuckoo.
He speaks louder, to someone off.
Grace, I saw a black-billed cuckoo.
Muriel, a very old woman dressed with faded elegance, comes on, carrying a rose.
MURIEL: My name is Muriel . . . foolish old man.
She sits in the other rocker.
HERBERT: I know your name is Muriel. That's what I called you.
MURIEL: You called me Grace. Grace was your first wife.
HERBERT: I called you Muriel. You're just hard of hearing and won't admit it . . . Grace . . . Grace . . . That's what I said!
MURIEL: There! You said it.
HERBERT: What?
MURIEL: Grace . . . You called me Grace.
HERBERT: Silly old woman. You call me Harry. But I call you Grace.
MURIEL: Can't you hear yourself?
HERBERT: What?
MURIEL: I said, "Can't you hear yourself?"
HERBERT: Of course I can hear myself. It's you that can't hear. I say you call me Harry. Sometimes. Your second husband . . . and sometimes George . . . Your first.
MURIEL: I never did. You're saying that because you call me Grace . . . and once in a while Mary.
HERBERT: You just don't hear.

MURIEL: What's my name?

HERBERT: Silly question . . . Muriel. You're Muriel . . . Grace was my first wife. Mary was . . . way long ago.

MURIEL: Mary was before Grace.

They try to straighten it out. They argue about who did what with whom.

MURIEL: You and I went to Europe.

HERBERT: We did not. Grace and I went to Europe on our honeymoon. That's when I had money, before women had taken it all.

MURIEL: I've been to Europe with you.

HERBERT: You and Harry went to Europe.

MURIEL: I went to Europe with George, too.

HERBERT: Yes. Well, I'm Herbert.

Now that that's settled, Muriel remembers the "scandalous good times" they had in Venice, but Herbert insists he's never been there, it must have been one of the two other husbands. This leads to another difference of opinion over who was Herbert's first wife.

MURIEL: Grace wasn't your first wife. Mary was.

HERBERT: Were you there? . . . I tell you, one was enough. Two was more than plenty. I don't know what got into me to try it a third time.

MURIEL: You were sick, and you were too tight to hire a nurse so you married me.

HERBERT: I got well. Why didn't I kick you out?
    Muriel starts to cry.
Now don't cry. You know I don't mean it. You were always crying. Cried buckets at our son's wedding. Took on something awful.

MURIEL: We didn't have any children. And I don't cry. That was Mary. I'm Muriel.

HERBERT: It's no wonder I'm confused . . . which I'm not. But you all the time saying "Grace . . . Mary . . . Muriel."

MURIEL: I'm just trying to straighten you out.

HERBERT: What difference does it make? I answer when you call me Bernie.

Muriel remembers Bernie not at all; Herbert remembers him as the man Muriel was carrying on with when Herbert met her. But maybe it was Grace that was carrying on with Bernie . . . . Bernie Walters! Muriel exclaims, but then a moment later she repeats that she has never heard of any Bernie.

It was Harry in Venice, Muriel admits. Herbert fumbles among his memories: was it Grace who was gentle and kind, and who died—or was it Mary? Was it Mary who drove Herbert crazy—"two young colts prancing around in the nude"—or was it Grace? Was Grace the one who was cold and wouldn't allow herself to be seen naked—or was it Mary? Herbert has never seen Muriel naked.

MURIEL: You married me at seventy . . . and you were through then . . . Except for dreaming.
HERBERT: You're lying. We had some good go's together, down by the beach.
MURIEL: You and I were never near a beach. And you were never near me in that way.
HERBERT: Old women forget . . . forget the joys of the flesh. Why is that?
MURIEL: I don't forget Bernie?
HERBERT: Who?
MURIEL: Bernie Walters.
HERBERT: Never heard of him.

Herbert remembers some wickedness under a willow tree with Mary, or Muriel . . . Herbert's mind started slipping a long time ago, Muriel reminds him, just before they went to Florida, he in his pongee suit. Herbert insists he's never been to Florida or owned a pongee suit.

Muriel tells Herbert (whom she calls Harry) to relax until he gets everything straight in his mind: he is Herbert, she is Grace. They went to Chicago once, for the funeral of their daughter. Now it is Herbert who insists they had no children together, but Muriel insists they conceived Ralph—Herbert's stepson—under a willow tree.

Muriel urges Herbert to close his eyes and rest.

MURIEL: . . . . . Let's not argue, George.
HERBERT: I'm Harry.
MURIEL: Yes, yes. All right. We'll just hold hands here, and try to doze a little . . . and think of happier days . . .
         She takes his hand . . . and they close their eyes and rock . . .
HERBERT *(after a long moment . . .):* Mmmmm . . . Venice.
MURIEL *(dreamy):* Yes . . . Oh, yes . . . Wasn't that lovely . . . Oh, you were so gallant . . . if slightly shocking . . . *(She laughs, remembering.)*
HERBERT: The beach . . .
MURIEL: . . . The willow tree . . .
HERBERT *(smiling):* You running around naked . . . Oh, lovely . . . lovely . . .
MURIEL: Yes . . . lovely . . .
         They go on rocking and smiling . . . holding hands . . . as the lights dim . . . Curtain.

A GRAPHIC GLANCE

PETER BULL, GERALDINE PAGE, LYNN REDGRAVE, MICHAEL CRAWFORD,

DONALD MADDEN AND CAMILA ASHLAND IN "BLACK COMEDY"

LOUISE TROY, GRETCHEN VAN AKEN, SHARON DIERKING, GEORGE ROSE
AND NORMAN WISDOM IN "WALKING HAPPY"

BARBARA HARRIS AS EVE, PASSIONELLA AND PRIN-
CESS BARBÁRA IN "THE APPLE TREE"

CONSTANCE TOWERS (UPPER LEFT), STEPHEN DOUGLASS, WILLIAM WARFIELD, DAVID WAYNE AND BARBARA COOK IN THE REVIVAL OF "SHOW BOAT" AT THE MUSIC THEATER OF LINCOLN CENTER

MELINA MERCOURI AND ORSON BEAN IN "ILLYA DARLING"

MARY MARTIN AND ROBERT PRESTON IN "I DO! I DO!"

JANET FOX, DOLORES GRAY, CLIVE REVILL AND ELIZABETH ALLEN IN "SHERRY!"

BARBARA SHARMA AND ALLEN CASE (UPPER LEFT), ALAN WEEKS, WINSTON DEWITT HEMSL

LESLIE UGGAMS, LILLIAN HAYMAN AND ROBERT HOOKS IN "HALLELUJAH, BABY!"

HARRY TOWB AND SHELLEY WINTERS IN "UNDER THE WEATHER"

PLAYS PRODUCED
IN THE
UNITED STATES

PLAYS PRODUCED ON BROADWAY

Figures in parentheses following a play's title indicate number of performances. Plays marked with an asterisk (*) were still running on June 1, 1967, and their number of performances is figured from opening night through May 31, 1967, not including extra non-profit performances. In a listing of a show's numbers—dances, sketches, musical numbers, etc.—the titles of songs are identified by their appearance in quotation marks (").

HOLDOVERS FROM PREVIOUS SEASONS

Plays which were running on June 1, 1966 are listed below. More detailed information about them is to be found in previous *Best Plays* volumes of appropriate years. Important cast changes are recorded in a section of this volume.

* **Barefoot in the Park** (1,502). By Neil Simon. Opened October 23, 1963.

* **Hello, Dolly!** (1,406). Musical suggested by Thornton Wilder's *The Matchmaker;* book by Michael Stewart; music and lyrics by Jerry Herman. Opened January 16, 1964.

Any Wednesday (982). By Muriel Resnik. Opened February 18, 1964. (Closed June 26, 1966)

* **Funny Girl** (1,312). Musical with book by Isobel Lennart; music by Jule Styne; lyrics by Bob Merrill. Opened March 26, 1964.

* **Fiddler on the Roof** (1,122). Musical based on Sholom Aleichem's stories; book by Joseph Stein; music by Jerry Bock; lyrics by Sheldon Harnick. Opened September 22, 1964.

Luv (901). By Murray Schisgal. Opened November 11, 1964. (Closed January 7, 1967)

* **The Odd Couple** (928). By Neil Simon. Opened March 10, 1965.

Half a Sixpence (511). Musical based on H.G. Wells' *Kipps;* book by Beverley Cross; music and lyrics by David Heneker. Opened April 25, 1965. (Closed July 16, 1966)

Generation (299). By William Goodhart. Opened October 6, 1965. (Closed June 25, 1966)

The Impossible Years (670). By Bob Fisher and Arthur Marx. Opened October 13, 1965. (Closed May 27, 1967)

On a Clear Day You Can See Forever (272). Musical with book and lyrics by Alan Jay Lerner; music by Burton Lane. Opened October 17, 1965. (Closed June 11, 1966)

The Royal Hunt of the Sun (261). By Peter Shaffer. Opened October 26, 1965. (Closed June 11, 1966)

Skyscraper (241). Musical based on Elmer Rice's *Dream Girl;* book by Peter Stone; music by James Van Heusen; lyrics by Sammy Cahn. Opened November 13, 1965. (Closed June 11, 1966)

* Man of La Mancha (633). Musical suggested by the life and works of Miguel de Cervantes y Saavedra; book by Dale Wasserman; music by Mitch Leigh; lyrics by Joe Darion. Opened November 22, 1965.

You Can't Take It With You (255). Revival of the comedy by Moss Hart and George S. Kaufman. Opened November 23, 1965. (Closed June 18, 1966 after 239 performances) Returned in repertory February 10, 1967 (see its entry in this volume's Broadway listing).

* Cactus Flower (614). By Abe Burrows; based on a play by Pierre Barillet and Jean-Pierre Gredy. Opened December 8, 1965.

* Sweet Charity (556). Musical based on the screenplay *Nights of Cabiria* by Federico Fellini, Tullio Pinelli and Ennio Flaiano; book by Neil Simon; music by Cy Coleman; lyrics by Dorothy Fields. Opened January 29, 1966.

Wait Until Dark (373). By Frederick Knott. Opened February 2, 1966. (Closed December 31, 1966)

Philadelphia, Here I Come! (326). By Brian Friel. Opened February 16, 1966. (Closed November 26, 1966)

Hostile Witness (156). By Jack Roffey. Opened February 17, 1966. (Closed July 2, 1966)

Wait a Minim! (456). Musical revue by Leon Gluckman. Opened March 7, 1966. (Closed April 15, 1967)

Mark Twain Tonight! (85). One-man performance by Hal Holbrook. Opened March 23, 1966. (Closed June 11, 1966)

The Caucasian Chalk Circle (93). By Bertolt Brecht; English version by Eric Bentley. Opened March 24, 1966. (Closed June 18, 1966)

"It's a Bird It's a Plane It's SUPERMAN" (129). Musical based on the comic strip "Superman"; book by David Newman and Robert Benton; music by Charles Strouse; lyrics by Lee Adams. Opened March 29, 1966. (Closed July 17, 1966)

Ivanov (47). Revival of the play by Anton Chekhov. Opened May 3, 1966. (Closed June 11, 1966)

A Time for Singing (41). Musical based on Richard Llewellyn's novel *How Green Was My Valley;* book and lyrics by Gerald Freedman and John Morris; music by John Morris. Opened May 21, 1966. (Closed June 25, 1966)

* Mame (427). Musical based on the novel *Auntie Mame* by Patrick Dennis and the play by Jerome Lawrence and Robert E. Lee; book by Jerome Lawrence and Robert E. Lee; music and lyrics by Jerry Herman. Opened May 24, 1966.

Where's Charley? (15). Musical revival based on Brandon Thomas' *Charley's Aunt;* book by George Abbott; music and lyrics by Frank Loesser. Opened May 23, 1966. (Closed June 5, 1966)

Annie Get Your Gun (125). Musical revival with book by Herbert and Dorothy Fields; music and lyrics by Irving Berlin. Opened at Lincoln Center May 31, 1966. (Closed July 9, 1966 after 47 performances) Reopened on Broadway September 21, 1966. (Closed November 26, 1966 after 78 performances; see its return engagement entry in this volume's Broadway listing)

PLAYS PRODUCED JUNE 1, 1966—MAY 31, 1967

The New York City Center Light Opera Company spring season of four Frank Loesser musical revivals: *How to Succeed in Business Without Really Trying, The Most Happy Fella, Where's Charley?* (see their entries in 1965-66 *Best Plays* volume) and **Guys and Dolls** (23). Based on a story and characters by Damon Runyon; book by Jo Swerling and Abe Burrows; music and lyrics by Frank Loesser. Produced by The New York City Center Light Opera Company, Jean Dalrymple director, at New York City Center. Opened June 8, 1966. (Closed June 26, 1966)

Nicely-Nicely Johnson ....Dale Malone	Nathan Detroit ....Jan Murray
Benny Southstreet ....Joe Ross	Angie the Ox ....Roger Brown
Rusty Charlie ....Edward Becker	Miss Adelaide ....Vivian Blaine
Sarah Brown ....Barbara Meister	Sky Masterson ....Hugh O'Brian
Arvide Abernathy ......Clarence Nordstrom	Mimi ....Rita O'Connor
Mission Band ....Jeanne Schlegel,	General Matilda B. Cartwright Claire Waring
Clarence Nordstrom, Carl Nicholas,	Big Jule ....B. S. Pully
Susan Cogan, Jeanne Frey	Drunk ....Eddie Phillips
Harry the Horse ....Tom Pedi	Waiter ....Marvin Goodis
Lt. Brannigan ....Frank Campanella	

Singers: Susan Cogan, Edward Becker, Roger Brown, Joe Bellomo, Reese Burns, Richard Ensslen, Paul Flores, Marvin Goodis, Joseph Gustern, Mark Howard, Doug Hunt, Robert Maxwell, Sean Walsh.

Dancers: Diane Arnold, Nephele Buecher, Marilyn D'Honau, Judith Dunford, Mercedes Ellington, Shelly Frankel, Altovise Gore, Rose Holotik, Joan Lindsay, Rita O'Connor, Melissa Stoneburn, Maria Strattin, Gerard Brentte, Frank Coppola, Vito Durante, Philip Filiato, Mark Holliday, Bob La Crosse, Teak Lewis, Carlos Macri, Mitchell Nutick, Paul Owsley, Dom Salinaro, Marc Scott.

Standby: Miss Blaine—Iva Withers. Understudies: Mr. O'Brian—Joe Bellomo; Miss Meister— Jeanne Frey; Messrs. Malone, Ross—Doug Hunt; Mr. Nordstrom—Carl Nicholas; Miss Waring— Jeanne Schlegel; Mr. Becker—Richard Ensslen.

Directed by Gus Schirmer; choreography, Ralph Beaumont; musical director, Irving Actman; Jo Mielziner's original scenery designs adapted by Peter Wolf; costumes, Frank Thompson;

lighting, Peggy Clark; associate conductor, Abba Bogin; production stage managers, Herman Shapiro, Chet O'Brien; stage manager, George Rondo: press, Homer Poupart.

Guys and Dolls was first produced on November 24, 1950, by Feuer and Martin at the Forty-sixth Street Theater for 1,200 performances. It was named a Best Play of its season and won the New York Drama Critics Circle award for best musical. It has been revived by the City Center in 1955, by Jean Dalrymple at the Hudson Celebration Theater in Central Park in 1959 and by the City Center in 1965.

Synopsis of scenes and list of musical numbers in *Guys and Dolls* appear in its Broadway entry on page 329 of the 1950-51 *Best Plays* volume.

Music Theater of Lincoln Center. Schedule of two musical revivals: *Annie Get Your Gun* (see its entry in 1965-66 *Best Plays* volume; also entry as Broadway return engagement elsewhere in this list) and **Show Boat** (63). Based on the novel by Edna Ferber; book and lyrics by Oscar Hammerstein II; music by Jerome Kern. Produced by Music Theater of Lincoln Center, Richard Rodgers president and producing director, at the New York State Theater of Lincoln Center for the Performing Arts. Opened July 19, 1966. (Closed September 10, 1966)

Rubberface	Bob La Crosse	Congress of Beauties	Emilina Escariz,
Captain Andy	David Wayne		Rita O'Connor, Nancy Van Rijn,
Windy	David Thomas		Carol Hanzel
Joe	William Warfield	Fatima	Sally Neal
Queenie	Rosetta LeNoire	Landlady; Old Lady on Levee	Helen Noyes
Ellie	Allyn Ann McLerie	Ethel	Joyce McDonald
Frank	Eddie Phillips	Sister	Frances Haywood
Parthy Ann Hawks	Margaret Hamilton	Mother Superior	Mary Manchester
Pete	Bob Monroe	Kim	Maureen McNabb
Julie	Constance Towers	Jake	Clyde Walker
Steve	William Traylor	Man with Guitar	Paul Adams
Gaylord Ravenal	Stephen Douglass	Doorman at Trocadero	Edward Taylor
Vallon; Jim	Barton Stone	Drunk	John Roberson
Magnolia	Barbara Cook	Lottie	Martha Danielle
Backwoodsman; 3d Barker	Neil McNelis	Dolly	Trudy Wallace
Jeb	Jess Green	Sally	Frances Buffalino
1st Barker	George McWhorter	Maisie	Judith Keller
Strong Woman	Doug Spingler	A Girl	Barbara Lindner
2d Barker	Garrett Morris	A Man	Dale Westerman

Singers: Phyllis Bash, Frances Buffalino, Jane Coleman, Martha Danielle, Dolores Godwin, Frances Haywood, Ernestine Jackson, Judith Keller, Mary Manchester, Barbara Lindner, Joyce McDonald, Estella Munson, Geraldine Overstreet, Lorice Stevens, Trudy Wallace, Paul Adams, Donald Coleman, Ray Duval, Scott Gibson, Jess Green, Vincent Henry, Richard Kahn, James Kelley, James Kennon-Wilson, George McWhorter, Laried Montgomery, Garrett Morris, Garwood Perkins, John Roberson, Alan Sanderson, Richard Sparks, Edward Taylor, Clyde Walker, Dale Westerman, Joe Williams, Lee Winston.

Dancers: Emilina Escariz, Lois Etelman, Carol Hanzel, Vivian Houston, Eileen Lawlor, Sally Neal, Rita O'Connor, Carol Perea, Nancy Van Rijn, Bryant Baker, Allan Byrns, Peter DeNicola, Ronald Dennis, Bob Hall, Bob La Crosse, Donald Mark, Robert St. John, Doug Spingler.

Children: Paul Dwyer, Michael Grady, Lisa Huggins, Jeanne Ladomirak, William Sims.

Directed by Lawrence Kasha; choreography, Ronald Field; musical director, Franz Allers; scenery, Oliver Smith; costumes, Stanley Simmons; lighting, Jean Rosenthal; associate conductor, William H. Brohn; orchestrations, Robert Russell Bennett; dance arrangements, Richard De Benedictis; production stage manager, William Ross; stage manager, Henry Velez; press, Richard Maney.

Show Boat was first produced on December 27, 1927, by Florenz Ziegfeld at the Ziegfeld Theater for 572 performances. It was revived at the Ziegfeld Theater by its librettist, Oscar Hammerstein II, on January 5, 1946, for 170 performances.

Act I, Scene 1: The Levee at Natchez on the Mississippi in the 1880s. Scene 2: Kitchen pantry of the "Cotton Blossom" five minutes later. Scene 3: Auditorium and stage of the

"Cotton Blossom" one hour later. Scene 4: Box office on the foredeck three weeks later. Scene 5: Auditorium and stage during the third act of *The Parson's Bride* that night. Scene 6: Stage door. Scene 7: The top deck later that night. Scene 8: The Levee at Greenville the next morning. Act II, Scene 1: The Midway Plaisance, Chicago World's Fair, 1893. Scene 2: A room on Ontario Street, 1904. Scene 3: Trocadero Music Hall, a few days later. Scene 4: St. Agatha's Convent, about the same time. Scene 5: Trocadero Music Hall, just before midnight on New Year's Eve 1905. Scene 6: The "Cotton Blossom" at the Greenville levee, 1927.

ACT I

(In previous Broadway productions of *Show Boat* the numbers "Queenie's Ballyhoo" and "Life Upon the Wicked Stage" in Act I were reversed in position, as were the reprises of "You Are Love" and "Ol' Man River" in Act II. "I Might Fall Back on You" was cut from this production in rehearsal.)

"Cotton Blossom" ....Ensemble
"Show Boat Ballyhoo" ....Captain Andy, Show Boat Troupe, Townspeople
"Only Make Believe" ....Ravenal, Magnolia
"Ol' Man River" ....Joe, Stevedores
"Can't Help Lovin' Dat Man" ....Julie, Queenie, Magnolia, Joe, Quartet
("I Might Fall Back on You") ....Ellie, Frank)
"Queenie's Ballyhoo" ....Queenie, Captain Andy, Ensemble
"Life Upon the Wicked Stage" ....Ellie, Ensemble
"You Are Love" ....Magnolia, Ravenal
Cakewalk and Finale ....Entire Company

ACT II

"At the Fair" ....Sightseers, Barkers, Ushers
"Why Do I Love You" ....Magnolia, Ravenal, Ensemble
"Bill" (Lyric by P. G. Wodehouse) ....Julie
"Can't Help Lovin' Dat Man" (Reprise) ....Magnolia
Service and Scene Music—St. Agatha's Convent
 "Only Make Believe" (Reprise) ....Ravenal
"Goodbye, My Lady Love"—Cakewalk ....Frank, Ellie
Magnolia's Debut in Trocadero Music Hall
 "After the Ball" ....Magnolia
"You Are Love" (Reprise) ....Ravenal
"Ol' Man River" ....Joe
Finale ....Entire Company

A Hand Is on the Gate (21). Program of poetry and folk music by American Negroes. Produced by Ivor David Balding for the Establishment Theater Company, Inc. (directors—Ivor David Balding, Peter Cook, Joseph E. Levine) with Rita Fredricks at the Longacre Theater. Opened September 21, 1966. (Closed October 8, 1966)

Leon Bibb
Roscoe Lee Browne
Gloria Foster
Moses Gunn

Ellen Holly
James Earl Jones
Josephine Premice
Cicely Tyson

Musicians: Stuart Scharf, guitar; Bill Lee, bass; Floyd Williams, percussionist; Sheldon Powell, flutist.

Arranged and directed by Roscoe Lee Browne; lighting consultant, Jules Fisher; production manager, Charles Maryan; associate producer, Stephen Aaron; musical arrangements, Bill Lee and Stuart Scharf; stage manager, Ed Cambridge; press, Dorothy Ross, Richard O'Brien, Michael Gershman.

This collection of readings from works by Negro authors and renditions of Negro songs was first presented for one performance on August 15, 1966, by the New York Shakespeare Festival at the Delacorte Theater.

PART I

AUTHOR	SELECTION	PERFORMER
George Moses Horton	On Liberty and Slavery	Jones
Langston Hughes	The Negro Speaks of Rivers	Miss Holly
Robert Hayden	Frederick Douglass	Gunn
Paul Laurence Dunbar	We Wear the Mask	Miss Tyson
Arna Bontemps	Southern Mansion	Bibb
Melvin Tolson	The Dark Symphony: Lento Grave	Miss Premice
James Weldon Johnson	O Black and Unknown Bards	Jones, Miss Foster, Browne
(Traditional)	"Buked and Scorned"	Bibb
Countee Cullen	From the Dark Tower	Jones
Langston Hughes	Mother to Son	Miss Holly
Sterling Brown	An Old Woman Remembers	Miss Foster
Claude McKay	If We Must Die	Browne
James Weldon Johnson	My City	Gunn
James Weldon Johnson	The Glory of the Day Was in her Face	Miss Premice
Paul Laurence Dunbar	A Death Song	Bibb
James Weldon Johnson	Sence You Went Away	Miss Foster
Paul Laurence Dunbar	When Malindy Sings	Miss Tyson
John Holloway	Miss Melerlee	Bibb
Paul Laurence Dunbar	"A Negro Love Song"	Browne
(Traditional children's song)	"Hey-ey-ey-ey Jane Jane"	Ensemble
Sterling Brown	Ol' Lem	Jones, Gunn
Frank Marshall Davis	Robert Whitmore	Miss Holly
Robert Hayden	Runagate Runagate	Miss Foster, Jones
Fenton Johnson	Tired	Browne
(Traditional)	" 'Buked and Scorned" (Reprise)	Bibb
Margaret Walker	October Journey	Miss Premice
Gwendolyn Brooks	The Crazy Woman	Miss Tyson
Sterling Brown	After Winter	Gunn
Margaret Walker	Molly Means	Misses Tyson, Foster, Holly, Premice
(Traditional)	"Little Boy, Little Boy"	Miss Premice, Bibb
Countee Cullen	For a Lady I Know	Miss Tyson
Countee Cullen	Saturday's Child	Miss Foster
Waring Cuney	No Images	Jones
Ted Joans	Why Try	Browne
Armand Lanusse	Epigram	Miss Premice
Waring Cuney	Conception	Miss Tyson
LeRoi Jones	As a Possible Lover	Gunn
G. C. Oden	As When Emotion Too Far Exceeds Its Cause	Jones
Gwendolyn Brooks	To Be in Love	Miss Foster
Frank Yerby	Wisdom	Bibb
W. C. Handy	"Careless Love"	Miss Premice
Frank Yerby	Calm After the Storm	Miss Foster
Binga Dismond	At Early Morn	Jones
Jessie Fauset	La Vie C'Est La Vie	Miss Holly
James Emanuel	The Treehouse	Gunn
Gwendolyn Brooks	A Lovely Love	Miss Tyson
Frank Yerby	Weltschmerz	Browne
Roscoe Lee Browne	On Neglect	Miss Holly
(Traditional)	"Dink's Song"	Miss Premice

PART II

AUTHOR	SELECTION	PERFORMER
James Vaughn	Four Questions Addressed to His Excellency, the Prime Minister	Browne
Gwendolyn Brooks	Mentors	Miss Holly
Myron O'Higgins	To a Young Poet	Miss Foster
Owen Dodson	Counterpoint	Bibb
Bruce McM. Wright	Journey to a Parallel	Gunn
Margaret Danner	The Elevator Man Adheres to His Form	Miss Premice
Roscoe Lee Browne	Ontogeny Recapitulates	Jones
Margaret Danner	Far From Africa: Four Poems	Misses Holly, Tyson, Foster, Premice
M. Carl Holman	Notes for a Movie Script	Jones
Gwendolyn Brooks	. . .Meanwhile a Mississippi Mother Burns Bacon	Miss Holly
Anne Spencer	Letter to My Sister	Miss Tyson
Langston Hughes	Bound No'th Blues	Miss Foster
Sterling Brown	Ma Rainey "Backwater Blues"	Miss Premice
James Emanuel	Get Up, Blues	Miss Tyson
Mari Evans	The Rebel	Miss Tyson
Julian Bond	Look at That Gal	Browne
Langston Hughes	"Harlem Sweeties"	Bibb, Gunn, Jones, Browne
Gwendolyn Brooks	A Street in Bronxville: Kitchenette	Miss Premice
Wesley Curtright	Heart of the Woods	Miss Holly
Gwendolyn Brooks	The Ballad of Rudolph Reed	Miss Tyson
Robert Hayden	Letters from The South	Gunn
Richard Wright	Between the World and Me	Jones
Jonathan Brooks	My Angel	Bibb
Arna Bontemps	The DayBreakers	Miss Foster
Robert Hayden	Witch Doctor	Browne
(Traditional)	"Glory, Glory"	Miss Premice, Bibb
Donald Hayes	Appoggiatura	Gunn
LeRoi Jones	Preface to a 20-Volume Suicide Note	Bibb
James Emanuel	The Voyage of Jimmy Poo	Gunn
Samuel Allen	A Moment Please	Jones, Browne
Calvin Hernton	The Distant Drum	Browne
Margaret Walker	We Have Been Believers	Miss Foster
(Traditional)	"Oh Shenandoah"	Bibb
Gwendolyn Brooks	Piano After War	Gunn
Mari Evans	When in Rome	Miss Tyson
Samuel Allen	American Gothic: To Satch	Jones
(Traditional)	"Eas' Man"	Bibb
Waring Cuney	My Lord, What a Morning	Miss Foster
Owen Dodson	Tell Rachel, He Whispered	Miss Holly
Donald Hayes	Alien	Bibb
Gwendolyn Brooks	The Preacher Ruminates	Miss Foster
Langston Hughes	Personal	Browne
	Blues	Miss Premice, Jones, Bibb
Myron O'Higgins (Collected by Alan Lomax; arranged by Leon Bibb)	Sunset Horn	Browne
	"Rocks and Gravel"	Bibb

Annie Get Your Gun (78). Return engagement of the musical revival (see its entry in the 1965-66 *Best Plays* volume) with book by Herbert and Dorothy Fields; music and lyrics by Irving Berlin. Produced by Music Theater of Lincoln Center, Richard Rodgers president and producing director, at the Broadway Theater. Opened September 21, 1966. (Closed November 26, 1966)

Little Boy; Indian Boy .... Jeffrey Scott	Mrs. Little Horse; Mrs. Sylvia
Little Girl .... Deanna Melody	Potter-Porter .... Mary Falconer
Charlie Davenport .... Jerry Orbach	Mrs. Black Tooth .... Eva Marie Sage
Dolly Tate .... Benay Venuta	Mrs. Yellow Foot .... Kuniko Narai
Iron Tail .... Brynar Mehl	Conductor .... Jim Lynn
Yellow Foot .... Gary Jendell	Porter .... Beno Foster
Mac; Mr. Clay .... John Dorrin	Waiter .... David Forssen
Foster Wilson; Mr. Schuyler	Major Gordon Lillie
Adams .... Ronn Carroll	(Pawnee Bill) .... Jack Dabdoub
Frank Butler .... Bruce Yarnell	Chief Sitting Bull .... Harry Bellaver
The Shy Girl .... Diana Banks	The Wild Horse .... Tony Catanzaro
Annie Oakley .... Ethel Merman	Pawnee's Messenger;
Little Jake (Her Brother) ... David Manning	Mr. T. L. C. Keeler .... Walt Hunter
Her Sisters:	Major Domo .... Ben Laney
Nellie .... Donna Conforti	Mrs. Schuyler Adams .... Patricia Hall
Jessie .... Jeanne Tanzy	Dr. Ferguson .... Marc Rowan
Minnie .... Holly Sherwood	Mrs. Ferguson .... Bobbi Baird
Col. Wm. F. Cody	Mr. Ernest Henderson ..... Grant Spradling
(Buffalo Bill) .... Rufus Smith	Mrs. Ernest Henderson ...... Lynn Carroll

Singers: Bobbi Baird, Chrysten Caroll, Lynn Carroll, Audrey Dearden, Lynn Dovel, Mary Falconer, Patricia Hall, Florence Mercer, Susan Terry, Kenny Adams, John Dorrin, David Forssen, Beno Foster, Walt Hunter, Ben Laney, Jim Lynn, Marc Rowan, Grant Spradling.

Dancers: Diana Banks, Joanne DiVito, Carolyn Dyer, Rozann Ford, Barbara Hancock, Ruth Lawrence, Kuniko Narai, Eva Marie Sage, Evelyn Taylor, Bjarne Buchtrup, Frank Derbas, Ronn Forella, Marcelo Gamboa, Gary Jendell, Daniel Joel, Brynar Mehl, Gene Myers.

Standbys: Miss Merman—Eileen Rodgers; Mr. Yarnell—Jack Dabdoub. Understudies: Mr. Bellaver—Ronn Carroll; Miss Venuta—Iris O'Connor; Mr. Orbach—Jim Lynn; Mr. Dabdoub—Walt Hunter; Mr. Smith—John Dorrin; Mr. Catanzaro—Ronn Forella; Master Manning—Jeffrey Scott; Miss Sherwood—Joanne DiVito; Misses Tanzy, Conforti—Deanna Melody; Messrs. Carroll, Hunter—David Forssen; Mr. Dorrin—Ben Laney; Mr. Foster—Grant Spradling; Messrs. Forssen, Laney—Marc Rowan; Mr. Lynn—Kenny Adams; Misses Falconer, Hall—Susan Terry.

Directed by Jack Sydow; dances and production numbers staged by Danny Daniels; musical director, Jonathan Anderson; scenery, Paul McGuire; costumes Frank Thompson; lighting, Peter Hunt; orchestations, Robert Russell Bennett; dance arrangements, Richard De Benedictis; production stage manager, William Ross; stage managers, J. P. Regan, Iris O'Connor; press, Richard Maney.

Annie Get Your Gun was first produced May 16, 1946 by Richard Rodgers and Oscar Hammerstein II at the Imperial Theater with Ethel Merman creating the role of Annie Oakley. It ran for 1,147 performances. It was last revived by the New York City Center Light Opera Company on February 19, 1958. For this Music Theater of Lincoln Center revival Irving Berlin added one new number to Act II (as recorded below)—"Old Fashioned Wedding," sung by Miss Merman—and eliminated the number "Who Do You Love, I Hope." Minor book revision by Dorothy Fields included the elimination of a secondary romantic interest.

ACT I

Scene 1: The Wilson House, a summer hotel on the outskirts of Cincinnati, Ohio, in July
"Colonel Buffalo Bill" .... Charlie, Dolly, Ensemble
"I'm a Bad, Bad Man" .... Frank, Girls
"Doin' What Comes Natur'lly" .... Annie, Children, Wilson
"The Girl That I Marry" .... Frank
"You Can't Get a Man With a Gun" .... Annie

"There's No Business Like Show Business" ....Annie, Frank, Buffalo Bill, Charlie
Scene 2: A Pullman parlor in an Overland Steam Train six weeks later
"They Say It's Wonderful" ....Annie, Frank
"Moonshine Lullaby" ....Annie, Trio, Children
Scene 3: The Fair Grounds at Minneapolis, Minn., a few days later
Wild West Pitch Dance ....The Wild Horse, Dancers
"There's No Business Like Show Business" (Reprise) ....Annie
"My Defenses Are Down" ....Frank, Boys
Scene 4: The arena of the big tent, later that night
Ceremonial Dance ....The Wild Horse, Indian Braves
"I'm an Indian Too" ....Annie
Adoption Dance ....Annie, The Wild Horse, Braves
"You Can't Get a Man With a Gun" (Reprise) ....Annie

ACT II

Scene 1: The deck of a cattle boat, eight months later
"Lost in His Arms" ....Annie, Singers
Scene 2: The ballroom of the Hotel Brevoort, the next night
"There's No Business Like Show Business" (Reprise) ....Frank, Dolly, Pawnee Bill,
Mr. & Mrs. Schuyler Adams
"I Got the Sun in the Morning" ....Annie, Company
"Old Fashioned Wedding" ....Annie, Frank
"The Girl That I Marry" (Reprise) ....Frank
Scene 3: Aboard a ferry en route to Governor's Island, next morning
Scene 4: Governor's Island, near the Fort, immediately following
"Anything You Can Do" ....Annie, Frank
"There's No Business Like Show Business" (Reprise) ....Ensemble
Finale: "They Say It's Wonderful" ....Entire Company

A Delicate Balance (132). By Edward Albee. Produced by Theater 1967 (Richard Barr and Clinton Wilder) at the Martin Beck Theater. Opened September 22, 1966. (Closed January 14, 1967)

Agnes	Jessica Tandy	Harry	Henderson Forsythe
Tobias	Hume Cronyn	Edna	Carmen Mathews
Claire	Rosemary Murphy	Julia	Marian Seldes

Understudy: Miss Seldes—Jane Lowry.
Directed by Alan Schneider; scenery, William Ritman; costumes, Theoni V. Aldredge; lighting, Tharon Musser; production stage manager, Mark Wright; stage manager, Joseph Cali; press, Howard Atlee, David Roggensack.
Time: Now. Place: Living room of a large and well-appointed suburban house. Act I: Friday night. Act II, Scene 1: Early the following evening. Scene 2: Later that evening. Act III: Early the next morning.
A middle-aged husband and wife are forced to re-evaluate their relationships with and responsibilities toward those they love best, when their comfortable, serene environment is invaded by an alcoholic sister, a daughter who has made a mess of her fourth marriage and close friends panicked by the nothingness of their lives, all seeking refuge.
A Best Play; see page 143

Dinner at Eight (127). Revival of the play by George S. Kaufman and Edna Ferber. Produced by Elliot Martin, Lester Osterman, Alan King and Walter A. Hyman Ltd. at the Alvin Theater. Opened September 27, 1966. (Closed January 14, 1967)

Gustave	John Randolph Jones	Ricci	Joseph Mascolo
Dora	April Shawhan	Hattie Loomis	Ruth Ford
Millicent Jordan	June Havoc	Miss Copeland	Lucille Patton
Oliver Jordan	Walter Pidgeon	Mr. Fosdick	Daniel Keyes
Paula Jordan	Judith Barcroft	Carlotta Vance	Arlene Francis

Dan Packard	Robert Burr	Mr. Hatfield	Wally Peterson
Kitty Packard	Pamela Tiffin	Miss Alden	Marilyn Clark
Tina	Niki Flacks	Lucy Talbot	Mindy Carson
Dr. J. Wayne Talbot	Jeffrey Lynn	Mrs. Wendel	Blanche Yurka
Larry Renault	Darren McGavin	Jo Stengel	John Carpenter
The Bellboy	Jack Pickett	Mr. Fitch	Edward Holmes
The Waiter	Kenneth Frankel	Ed Loomis	Daniel Keyes
Max Kane	Phil Leeds		

Understudies: Misses Havoc, Ford—Marilyn Clark; Misses Shawhan, Barcroft, Tiffin—Niki Flacks; Messrs. Jones, Mascolo—Jack Pickett; Messrs. Pidgeon, Lynn—Edward Holmes; Misses Francis,Yurka—Lucille Patton; Messrs. Burr, McGavin—John Carpenter; Misses Patton, Flacks, Clark, Carson—Marjorie Martin.

Directed by Tyrone Guthrie; scenery and lighting, David Hays; costumes, Ray Diffen; original music composed by Mark Lawrence; associate producers, Leonid Kipnis and Fred J. Antkies; production stage manager, Frederic deWilde; stage managers, Frank Hamilton, Wally Peterson; press, Nat and Irvin Dorfman.

Time: November 1930. Place: Manhattan. *Dinner at Eight* was first produced October 22, 1932 by Sam H. Harris at the Music Box for 232 performances. It was named a Best Play of its season and was made into a film by M-G-M. This production is its first Broadway revival.

John Carpenter replaced Darren McGavin 11/28/66 through 1/1/67.

Help Stamp Out Marriage! (20). By Keith Waterhouse and Willis Hall. Produced by Theater Guild Productions, Inc. with Peter Bridge at the Booth Theater. Opened September 29, 1966. (Closed October 15, 1966)

David Lord	Roddy Maude-Roxby	Stuart Wheeler	Francis Matthews
Sarah Lord	Valerie French	Valerie Pitman	Ann Bell

Standby: Misses French, Bell—Joanna Morris. Understudies: Messrs. Maude-Roxby, Matthews—Ronald Drake.

Directed by George Abbott; original production design, J. Hutchinson Scott; design supervision and lighting, Lloyd Burlingame; costumes, Julia Sze; stage manager, Wally Engelhardt; press, Joe Wolhandler, Marianne Mackay.

Time: the present. Place: the flat of David and Sarah Lord, the lobby of their building and outside the pub around the corner, the Hussar, in London. Act I: About 7 o'clock on a Friday evening. Act II: Thirty minutes later.

Comedy about a small apartment and two couples, one engaged in an illicit love affair and one married. A foreign play previously produced in London.

The City Center Drama Company. American Playwrights Series of three revivals. **The Country Girl** (22). By Clifford Odets. Opened September 29, 1966. (Closed October 16, 1966) **The Rose Tattoo** (76). By Tennessee Williams. Opened October 20, 1966. (Closed December 31, 1966) **Elizabeth the Queen** (14). By Maxwell Anderson. Opened November 3, 1966 (Closed November 13, 1966). Produced by The City Center Drama Company, Jean Dalrymple director, at New York City Center.

THE COUNTRY GIRL

Bernie Dodd	Rip Torn	Nancy Stoddard	Robin Strasser
Larry	Walter Allen	Frank Elgin	Joseph Anthony
Phil Cook	Jack Somack	Georgie Elgin	Jennifer Jones
Paul Unger	Richard Beymer	Ralph	Walter Lott

Standbys: Miss Jones—Nina Wilcox; Mr. Anthony—Will Hare. Understudies: Messrs. Allen, Beymer, Lott—Will Gregory; Miss Strasser—Annie Laurie Glass.

Directed by Martin Fried; production supervised by Lee Strasberg; scenery and lighting, Feder; costumes, Audré; production stage manager, Herman Shapiro; stage manager, George Rondo; press, Homer Poupart.

Time: The present. Place: New York and Boston. *The Country Girl* was first produced

November 10, 1950 by Dwight Deere Wyman at the Lyceum Theater for 235 performances. It was named a Best Play of its season. This is its first Broadway revival.

THE ROSE TATTOO

Salvatore ....Sonny Rocco	Father De Leo ....Dino Terranova
Vivi ....Elena Christi	A Doctor ....Kevin O'Morrison
Bruno ....Peter Falzone	Miss Yorke ....Barbara Townsend
Assunta ....Nina Varela	Flora ....Gina Collens
Rosa Delle Rose ....Maria Tucci	Bessie ....Peggy Pope
Serafina Delle Rose ....Maureen Stapleton	Jack Hunter ....Christopher Walken
Estelle Hohengarten ....Marcie Hubert	The Salesman ....L. M. Gibbons
The Strega ....Georgia Simmons	Alvaro Mangiacavallo .....Harry Guardino
Giuseppina ....Rossetta Vencziani	Lucia ....Gloria Tofano
Peppina ....Jo Flores Chase	Giovana ....Dorothy Raymond
Violetta ....Ruth Manning	Children ....Joanna Sandra Malatzky,
Mariella ....Anna Berger Malatzky	Susan Carol Malatzky
Teresa ....Honey Sanders	

Directed by Milton Katselas; scenery, David Ballou; costumes, Frank Thompson; lighting, Peggy Clark; assistant to Mr. Katselas, Michael Montel; stage manager, Ray Laine; press (at Billy Rose Theater), Arthur Cantor, Artie Solomon.

Time: The present. Place: A village populated mostly by Sicilians somewhere along the Gulf Coast between New Orleans and Mobile. *The Rose Tattoo* was first produced February 3, 1951 by Cheryl Crawford at the Martin Beck Theater for 306 performances. It was named a Best Play of its season. This production, its first Broadway revival, played 14 performances at the City Center, closing October 30, 1966; then it moved to the Billy Rose theater where it resumed its run November 9, 1966 for 62 more performances.

Jane Gregory replaced Maria Tucci 11/29/66.

ELIZABETH THE QUEEN

Sir Walter Raleigh ....William Roerick	Councillor ....Jon Richards
Penelope Gray ....Anne Meacham	Man-at-Arms ....Austin Colyer
Captain Armin ....Drew Eliot	Marvel ....Robert Crawley
Sir Robert Cecil ....Michael Lombard	A Courier ....Donald Marlatt
Francis Bacon ....John Baragrey	A Captain of the Guards .....David Haine
Lord Essex ....Donald Davis	A Courtier ....Jeremy Jones
Elizabeth ....Judith Anderson	A Herald ....Alec Murphy
Lord Burghley ....Don McHenry	Burbage ....David Doyle
The Fool ....Gene Nye	Hemmings ....David Anderson
Mary ....Joan Tyson	Poines ....Douglas Easley
Tressa ....Cinda Siler	Ladies-in-Waiting ....Patricia Sinnott,
Ellen ....Diane Gray	Lois deBanzie

Courtiers, Guards, Men-at-Arms: John Buck Jr., Austin Colyer, Richard Esckilsen, David Groh, J. Patrick Hart, Ted Nils Hoen, Ken Kliban, Jay Lanin, Alec Murphy, Robert Rodan.

Standby: Miss Anderson—Jacqueline Brookes. Understudies: Messrs. Davis, Crawley—Jay Lanin; Mr. Roerick—Douglas Easley; Miss Meacham—Patricia Sinnott; Mr. Lombard—Austin Colyer; Mr. Baragrey—Drew Eliot; Mr. McHenry—Jon Richards; Mr. Nye—Alec Murphy; Mr. Anderson—John Buck Jr.; Mr. Easley—David Haine; Mr. Marlatt—Jeremy Jones.

Directed by Herbert Machiz; scenery and lighting, Feder; costumes, Stanley Simmons; production associate, Gus Schirmer; song "May the Merry Month," by Max Marlin; assistant designer, Ronnie Baldwin; production stage manager, Herman Shapiro; stage manager, George Rondo.

Elizabeth the Queen was first produced November 3, 1930 by the Theater Guild at the Guild Theater. It was named a Best Play of its season.

The Investigation (103). By Peter Weiss; English version by Jon Swan and Ulu Grosbard. Produced by Alan King and Walter A. Hyman, Ltd., Eugene V. Wolsk and Emanuel Azenberg at the Ambassador Theater. Opened October 4, 1966. (Closed December 31, 1966)

The Accused	Wendell K. Phillips Sr.	Graham Jarvis
Russell Baker	Dan Priest	John Marley
Peter Brandon	Wallace Rooney	Vivian Nathan
Richard Castellano	John Servetnik	Defense Attorney
Gordon B. Clarke	Witnesses for the Accused	Leon B. Stevens
Ivor Francis	Leslie Barrett	Judge
Tom Gorman	Henry Oliver	Will Hussung
Ferdi Hoffman	Witnesses for the Prosecution	Prosecuting Attorney
Paul Larson	Ward Costello	Franklin Cover
Tom Pedi	Alice Hirson	

Understudies: Mitchell Jason, Rose Gregorio, Curt Dempster.
Directed by Ulu Grosbard; scenery, Kert Lundell; costumes, Anna Hill Johnstone; lighting, Martin Aronstein; production stage manager, Del Hughes; stage manager, Curt Dempster; press, Merle Debuskey, Violet Welles, Lawrence Belling.
Time: 1964-65 and 1941-45. Place: A courtroom and the German concentration camp of Auschwitz. Act I: The Platform; The Camp. Act II: The Swing; The End of Lili Tofler; S.S. Corporal Stark. Act III: Phenol; The Bunker Block; Cyklon B; The Fire Ovens; The Possibility of Survival.
The Investigation is a group recitation of the court record at the trial of 21 persons for the death of 4,000,000 people at the Auschwitz concentration camp. The trial was held by a German court in Frankfurt form January, 1964 to August 1965. Its record was distilled by the playwright but no dialogue or other words were invented for this recapitulation of gigantic criminality. Actors playing the accused represented single individuals, but those playing witnesses spoke as many different persons. A foreign play previously produced in East and West Germany.

The Killing of Sister George (205). By Frank Marcus. Produced by Helen Bonfils and Morton Gottlieb by arrangement with Michael Codron in association with Bernard Delfont at the Belasco Theater. Opened October 5, 1966. (Closed April 1, 1967)

Alice "Childie" McNaught	Eileen Atkins	Mrs. Mercy Croft	Lally Bowers
June Buckridge (Sister George)	Beryl Reid	Madame Xenia	Polly Rowles

Standbys: Misses Bowers, Rowles—Paddy Croft; Miss Atkins—Anne Murray.
Directed by Val May; foreign production designed by Catherine Browne; American production supervised by William Ritman; costumes supervised by Jane Greenwood; production stage manager, Warren Crane; stage manager, Anne Murray; press, Dorothy Ross, Richard O'Brien, Michael Gershman.
Time: The present. Place: The living room of June Buckridge's flat in Devonshire Street, London. Act I: An afternoon in late September. Act II, Scene 1: A week later. Scene 2: The same day, evening. Act III: Two weeks later, morning.
Comedy about a radio actress, her clinging blonde roommate and her coveted role of Sister George, the nurse-heroine of a B.B.C. soap opera, who is "killed" out of the serial. A foreign play previously produced in London.
A Best Play; see page 165

The Loves of Cass McGuire (20). By Brian Friel. Produced by David Merrick Arts Foundation at the Helen Hayes Theater. Opened October 6, 1966. (Closed October 22, 1966)

Mother	Frances Brandt	Tessa	Mary Greaney
Dom	Don Scardino	Pat Quinn	Arthur O'Sullivan
Alice	Sylvia O'Brien	Trilbe Costello	Brenda Forbes
Harry	Liam Redmond	Mr. Ingram	Dennis King
Cass	Ruth Gordon	Mrs. Butcher	Dorothy Blackburn

Understudies: Misses Gordon, Forbes, Blackburn—Eleanor Phelps; Messrs. Redmond, King, O'Sullivan—Tom McDermott; Miss Greaney—Lesley Hunt; Mr. Scardino—Gary Barton.

Directed by Hilton Edwards; scenery and lighting, Lloyd Burlingame; costumes, Noel Taylor; associate producer, Samuel Liff; production stage manager, Mitchell Erickson; stage manager, Lesley Hunt; press, Harvey B. Sabinson, Lee Solters, Jay Russell.

Time: The present. Place: Ireland. Act I: Two weeks before Christmas. Act II: One week before Christmas. Act III: Christmas Eve.

A boozy but gallant woman comes back to her home in Ireland after 42 years in America. Instead of helping to bind up her wounds, her disapproving family banishes her to a home for the aged. A foreign (Irish) play which had its world premiere in this production.

New York City Opera. Fall repertory included revival of work which originated on Broadway: **The Consul** (2). Words and music by Gian Carlo Menotti. Opened October 6, 1966. (Closed October 30, 1966) Produced by New York City Opera at New York State Theater of Lincoln Center.

John Sorel ....David Clatworthy	The Foreign Woman ....Julia Migenes
Magda Sorel ....Patricia Neway	Anna Gomez ....LaVergne Monette
The Mother ....Evelyn Sachs	Vera Boronel ....Charlotte Povia
Secret Police Agent ....Joseph Fair	The Magician
1st Plainclothesman ....Philip Erickson	(Nika Magadoff) ....Gene Bullard
2d Plainclothesman ....Richard Park	Assan ....Jack Bittner
The Secretary ....Beverly Evans	The Voice on the Record ....Mabel Mercer
Mr. Kofner ....David Smith	

Directed by Gian Carlo Menotti; conductor, Charles Wilson; scenery, Horace Armistead; stage director, Francis Rizzo; stage managers, Dan Butt, Chris Goodyear; press, Nat and Irvin Dorfman.

Time: The present. Place: Somewhere in Europe. Act I, Scene 1: The home, early morning. Scene 2: The consulate, later the same day. Act II, Scene 1: The home, in the evening, a month later. Scene 2: The consulate, a few days later. Act III, Scene 1: The consulate, late afternoon, several days later. Scene 2: The home, that night.

The Consul was first presented March 15, 1950 at the Ethel Barrymore Theater for 269 performances. It was last revived for 3 performances in the 1965-66 season by New York City Opera. Its musical numbers have never been identified by individual titles in its theater presentations.

* The Repertory Theater of Lincoln Center for the Performing Arts. Season of four plays. **The Alchemist** (52). Revival of the play by Ben Jonson. Opened October 13, 1966. (Closed November 26, 1966) **Yerma** (60). Revival of the play by Federico Garcia Lorca; new translation by W.S. Merwin. Opened December 8, 1966. (Closed January 28, 1967) **The East Wind** (60). By Leo Lehman. Opened February 9, 1967. (Closed April 1, 1967) *** Galileo** (56). Revival of the play by Bertolt Brecht; adapted by Charles Laughton. Opened April 13, 1967. All four plays produced by The Repertory Theater of Lincoln Center, under the direction of Herbert Blau and Jules Irving, at the Vivian Beaumont Theater.

NOTE: So relatively few actors played more than one important role during Lincoln Center's season that the casts are listed separately here.

THE ALCHEMIST

Subtle ....Michael O'Sullivan	Ananias ....Earl Montgomery
Jeremy Butler, alias Captain, alias Lungs,	Tribulation Wholesome ....Aline MacMahon
alias Ulen Spiegel ....Robert Symonds	Kastril ....Robert Phalen
Dol Common ....Nancy Marchand	Dame Pliant ....Elizabeth Huddle
Dapper ....Lee Goodman	Lovewit ....Philip Bosco
Abel Drugger ....Ray Fry	Parson ....Glenn Mazen
Sir Epicure Mammon ....George Voskovec	Officers ......Robert Haswell, Peter Nyberg
Pertinax Surly ....Michael Granger	

Neighbors: Frank Bayer, Marketa Kimbrell, Beatrice Manley, Glenn Mazen, Peter Nyberg, Priscilla Pointer, Judith Propper, Tom Rosqui, Shirley Jac Wagner, Ronald Weyand, Erica Yohn.

Understudies: Mr. O'Sullivan—Ray Fry; Miss Marchand—Shirley Jac Wagner; Messrs. Goodman, Granger—Glenn Mazen; Mr. Fry—Frank Bayer; Mr. Bosco—Robert Haswell; Mr. Voscovec—Earl Montgomery; Miss MacMahon—Beatrice Manley; Messrs. Montgomery, Haswell, Nyberg—Ronald Weyand; Mr. Phalen—David Sullivan; Miss Huddle—Priscilla Pointer; Mr. Mazen—Peter Nyberg.

YERMA

Yerma	Gloria Foster	2d Sister-in-law	Ruth Manning
Victor	Tom Rosqui	Dolores	Nancy Marchand
Juan	Frank Langella	1st Neighbor	Ruth Attaway
Maria	Maria Tucci	2d Neighbor	Virgilia Chew
Alegria	Aline MacMahon	Male Mask	Arthur C. Thompson
Village Woman	Margo Ann Berdeshevsky	Female Mask	Barbara Conrad
Dolores' Daughter	Pamela Dunlap	Soloist	Nina Dova
1st Sister-in-law	Beatrice Manley	(Child)	Ronnie Misa, Barry Symonds

Villagers: Marketa Kimbrell, Vera Lockwood, Anthony Mainionis, Glenn Mazen, Peter Nyberg, Michael Parish, Robert Phalen, Priscilla Pointer, Judith Propper, Emily Ruhberg, John P. Ryan, Erica Yohn.

Musicians: Stanley Silverman, guitar; Michael Sahl, harpsichord; John Bergamo, percussion; Buell Niedlinger, bass.

Understudies: Miss Foster—Elizabeth Huddle; Miss Tucci—Pamela Dunlap; Mr. Langella—Robert Phalen; Mr. Rosqui—John P. Ryan; Miss MacMahon—Virgilia Chew; Miss Dunlap—Beatrice Manley.

THE EAST WIND

Zauber	Michael Granger	Mrs. Bamberg	Marketa Kimbrell
Konarski	George Voskovec	Marteau	Ronald Weyand
Mrs. Humphreys	Aline MacMahon	Mr. Crockett	Earl Montgomery
Vitek	Tom Rosqui	Waitress	Shirley Jac Wagner
Lowacki	Robert Haswell	Jack	Philip Bosco
Bamberg	Michael Gorrin	Doris	Estelle Parsons

People of London in *The East Wind*: Roberta Callahan, Jennifer Gaus, Robert Haswell, Marketa Kimbrell, Beatrice Manley, Glenn Mazen, Robert Phalen, Priscilla Pointer, Tom Rosqui, Shirley Jac Wagner, Ronald Weyand.

Understudies for *The East Wind*: Mr. Granger—Michael Gorrin; Mr. Voskovec—Robert Haswell; Misses Parsons, Wagner—Priscilla Pointer; Messrs. Bosco, Haswell, Montgomery—Glenn Mazen; Mr. Gorrin—Earl Montgomery; Miss Kimbrell—Beatrice Manley; Messrs. Rosqui, Weyand—Robert Phalen; Miss MacMahon—Shirley Jac Wagner.

Robert Symonds replaced Michael Granger 2/23/67.

GALILEO

Ballad Singer	George S. Irving	Federzoni	Robert Symonds
(Ballad Singer's Wife)	Kate Hurney, Judith Hastings	Matti	John Carpenter
		The Doge; Lord Chamberlain	Glenn Mazen
(Ballad Singer's Child)	Robert Puleo, Robert Harwood	(Prince Cosimo de Medici)	Charles Abruzzo, Robert Puleo
Galileo Galilei	Anthony Quayle	Old Lady	Shirley Jac Wagner
Mrs. Sarti	Aline MacMahon	Young Lady	Roberta Callahan
(Andrea Sarti as a child)	Alan Cabel, Donnie Melvin	Philosopher	Ronald Weyand
Ludovico Marsili	Charles Siebert	Mathematician; Informer	Earl Montgomery
Priuli	Fred Stewart	Fat Prelate	Ronald Bishop
Virginia	Estelle Parsons	Furious Monk; Peasant	Robert Phalen
Sagredo	Philip Bosco	Old Cardinal	Edgar Daniels
		Attendant Monk	Peter Nyberg

Christopher Clavius ....Warren Wade   Cardinal Bellarmine ...Ted van Griethuysen
Little Monk ....Frank Bayer   Cardinal Barberini ....George Voskovec
Clerk; Monk ....Ralph Drischell   Cardinal Inquisitor .....Shepperd Strudwick
Clerk ....Richard Levy   Andrea Sarti as a man ......Stephen Joyce

(Parentheses indicate role in which the actor alternated)

Senators, clergy, ladies, townspeople: Christopher Bernau, Carl Esser, Judith Hastings, Robert Haswell, Joseph Hindy, Russell Horton, Marketa Kimbrell, Bryan Marks, Don Mc-Govern, William Pardue, Michael Parish, Priscilla Pointer, Judith Propper, Arthur Roberts, George Van Den Houten.

Musicians: Sophie Sollberger, flute; Efraim Guigui, clarinet; Roland Gagnon, harpsichord.

Understudies: Mr. Quayle—Robert Symonds; Mr. Irving—John Carpenter; Miss Mac-Mahon—Shirley Jac Wagner; Mr. Siebert—Christopher Bernau; Mr. Stewart—Ted van Grie-thuysen; Miss Parsons—Roberta Callahan; Messrs. Bosco, Strudwick—Ralph Drischell; Mr. Symonds—Ronald Weyand; Messrs. Bishop, Daniels—Earl Montgomery; Messrs. Bayer, Joyce—Robert Phalen; Mr. van Griethuysen—Ronald Bishop; Mr. Voskovec—Robert Haswell.

THE ALCHEMIST directed by Jules Irving; scenery and costumes, James Hart Stearns; lighting, John Gleason; music composed by George Rochberg; musical director, Stanley Silver-man; production stage manager, James Kershaw; stage managers, David Sullivan, Kenneth Haas; press, Bill Doll & Co.

Time: 1610. Place: Lovewit's House in London.

The Alchemist was well received in its first presentation at the Globe Theater in 1610. Its most recent New York revivals took place off Broadway in the season of 1957-58 and at the Gate Theater September 14, 1964 for 46 performances.

YERMA directed by John Hirsch; scenery and lighting, David Hays; costumes, James Hart Stearns; music composed by Stanley Silverman; choreography, Jean Erdman; stage manager, Timothy Ward.

Time: The recent past over a period of five and one-half years. Place: Spain. Scene 1: Juan's house. Scene 2: A field near the village, one year later. Scene 3: By a stream. Scene 4: On the patio of Juan's house, two years later. Scene 5: The house of Dolores, later that evening. Scene 6: A hermitage in the mountains, October of the same year. In this production Yerma was performed without intermission.

In Yerma a barren peasant wife suffers more and more from the loneliness and frustration of her unfulfilled state. When she learns that her husband has never wanted a child, she strangles him. A foreign play first produced in Madrid in 1935. It was produced off Broadway in 1952 by Circle in the Square.

THE EAST WIND directed by Robert Symonds; scenery, James F. Göhl; costumes, James Hart Stearns; lighting, Martin Aronstein; music, John Herbert McDowell; production stage manager, James Kershaw; stage manager, Kenneth Haas.

Time: The twenty years beginning with World War II. Place: A delicatessen shop at 11 Bloomsbury Place, London, and other places in Europe, Asia, Africa and Australia. The action is divided into three acts.

In The East Wind, two refugees from a Central European town, one a pragmatist and one a dreamer, manage to survive war and persecution and finish as partners in a London deli-catessen, a resolution which delights the pragmatist but drives the dreamer to suicide. A foreign (British) play which had its world premiere in this production.

GALILEO directed by John Hirsch; scenery, Robin Wagner; costumes, James Hart Stearns; lighting, Martin Aronstein; music, Hanns Eisler; additional music, Stanley Silverman; con-ductor and vocal director, Roland Gagnon; masks, Ralph Lee; stage managers, Timothy Ward, James Kershaw.

Time: 1609-1642. Place: Italy. Scene 1: A humble study in Padua. Scene 2: The great arsenal of Venice, by the harbor. Scene 3: Galileo's work-room in Padua. Scene 4: Galileo's house in Florence. Scene 5: Hall of the Collegium Romanum in Rome. (Intermission followed Scene 5) Scene 6: Cardinal Bellarmine's house in Rome. Scene 7: The palace garden of the Florentine Ambassador in Rome. Scene 8: Galileo's house in Florence. (Intermission followed Scene 8) Scene 9: A marketplace in Florence. Scene 10: The Medici Palace in Florence. Scene 11: An apartment in the Vatican. Scene 12: The palace garden of the Florentine Ambassador in Rome. Scene 13: A country house near Florence.

Dramatization of the astronomer Galileo's battle for intellectual freedom against the church, which forced him to recant his theory of the movement of the planets around the sun. A foreign play first produced in German in Zurich in 1943; produced in Paris in 1949 and in Berlin in 1956. This Charles Laughton translation was produced in Los Angeles in 1947 and off Broadway for 6 performances in the Experimental Theater sponsored by T. Edward Hambleton and ANTA.

Herbert Blau resigned as co-director of Lincoln Center Repertory on January 13, 1967, leaving Jules Irving in sole charge for the remainder of the season.

* **The Apple Tree** (260). Musical based on *The Diary of Adam and Eve* by Mark Twain, *The Lady or the Tiger?* by Frank R. Stockton and *Passionella* by Jules Feiffer; book by Sheldon Harnick and Jerry Bock; additional book material by Jerome Coopersmith; music by Jerry Bock; lyrics by Sheldon Harnick. Produced by Stuart Ostrow at the Sam S. Shubert Theater. Opened October 18, 1966.

PART I—THE DIARY OF ADAM AND EVE

Adam	Alan Alda	Snake	Larry Blyden
Eve	Barbara Harris		

PART II—THE LADY OR THE TIGER?

Balladeer	Larry Blyden	Captain Sanjar	Alan Alda
King Arik	Marc Jordan	Guard	Robert Klein
Princess Barbára	Barbara Harris	King Arik's Court	Jackie Cronin, Barbara
Prisoner	Jay Norman		Lang, Mary Louise, Michael Davis,
Prisoner's Bride	Jaclynn Villamil		Neil F. Jones
Nadjira	Carmen Alvarez		

PART III—PASSIONELLA

Narrator	Larry Blyden	Producer	Marc Jordan
Ella and Passionella	Barbara Harris	Flip, The Prince Charming	Alan Alda
Mr. Fallible	Robert Klein		

Subway Riders, El Morocco Patrons, Fans, Flip's Following, Movie Set Crew: Carmen Alvarez, Jackie Cronin, Michael Davis, Neil F. Jones, Marc Jordan, Robert Klein, Barbara Lang, Mary Louise, Jay Norman, Jaclynn Villamil.

Standby: Messrs. Alda, Blyden—Ken Kercheval. Understudies: Miss Harris—Carmen Alvarez; general understudies—Bill Reilly, Ceil Delli.

Directed by Mike Nichols; additional musical staging, Herbert Ross; choreography, Lee Theodore; musical direction and vocal arrangements, Elliot Lawrence; scenery and costumes, Tony Walton; lighting, Jean Rosenthal; orchestrations, Eddie Sauter; animation film sequence of Miss Harris by Richard Williams; additional scoring, Elliot Lawrence; production stage manager, Jerry Adler; stage managers, George Thorn, Tom Porter; press, Harvey B. Sabinson, Lee Solters, Harry Nigro.

THE DIARY OF ADAM AND EVE—Time: Saturday, June 1. Place: Eden. Adam and Eve's discovery of life in the Garden of Eden bears many resemblances to any couple's adventures among the new, daily problems of marriage.

THE LADY OR THE TIGER?—Time: A long time ago. Place: A semi-barbaric kingdom. A warrior who dares to love his Princess is put to the test of opening one of two doors behind which he will find either a beautiful girl whom he must marry or a tiger. The Princess tips her warrior which door to open—but to which fate will she surrender her lover, a feminine rival or the tiger?

PASSIONELLA—Time: Now. Place: Here. Satire on dreams of glamor, as a chimney sweep who longs to become a movie star achieves her ambition by means of a trick (a fairy godmother), only to discover that her idolized Prince Charming in his black leather jacket is also a phony.

Phyllis Newman replaced Barbara Harris at all matinee performances beginning 11/23/66. Ken Kercheval replaced Alan Alda 3/27/67. Hal Holbrook replaced Ken Kercheval 4/6/67.

A Best Play; see page 213

THE DIARY OF ADAM AND EVE
"Here in Eden"	Eve
"Feelings"	Eve
"Eve"	Adam
"Friends"	Eve
"The Apple Tree" ("Forbidden Fruit")	Snake

"Beautiful, Beautiful World" ....Adam
"It's A Fish" ....Adam
"Go To Sleep Whatever You Are" ....Eve
"What Makes Me Love Him" ....Eve

THE LADY OR THE TIGER?
"I'll Tell You A Truth" ....Balladeer
"Make Way" ....King's Court, King Arik
"Forbidden Love" (In Gaul) ....Princess Barbára, Captain Sanjar
"The Apple Tree" (Reprise) ....Balladeer
"I've Got What You Want" ....Princess Barbára
"Tiger, Tiger" ....Princess Barbára
"Make Way" (Reprise) ....King's Court
"Which Door?" ....Captain Sanjar, Princess Barbára, King Arik, Court
"I'll Tell You A Truth" (Reprise) ....Balladeer

PASSIONELLA
"Oh, To Be a Movie Star" ....Ella
"Gorgeous" ....Passionella
"(Who, Who, Who, Who) Who Is She?" ....The Company
"Wealth" ....Passionella
"You Are Not Real" ....Flip, The Company
"George L." ....Ella, Flip

We Have Always Lived in the Castle (9). By Hugh Wheeler; based on the novel by Shirley Jackson. Produced by David Merrick at the Ethel Barrymore Theater. Opened October 19, 1966. (Closed October 26, 1966)

Merricat	Heather Menzies	Mrs. Clarke	Doris Rich
Jonas	William Sims	Mrs. Wright	Murial Williams
Constance	Shirley Knight	Charles	Phillip Clark
Uncle Julian	Alan Webb		

Standbys: Mr. Webb—Rex Williams; Mr. Clark—William Jordan; Misses Rich, Williams—Virginia Downing.
Understudies: Louise Schaeffer, Donna Fern, Kevin Featherstone.
Directed by Garson Kanin; scenery and lighting, David Hays; costumes, Noel Taylor; associate producer, Samuel Liff; associate director, David Pardoll; stage manager, Rex Williams; press, Harvey B. Sabinson, Lee Solters, Robert Ullman.
Time: The present. Place: The Blackwood home outside a small Vermont village. The play is divided into three acts.
A teen-ager, her older sister and her aged uncle are all that remain of a family decimated by poison one fearful evening; the survivors shut themselves up in their old house but the world nevertheless impinges on their lives and forces the disclosure that the teen-ager was the poisoner.

How's the World Treating You? (40). By Roger Milner. Produced by Elaine Perry and Charles Hollerith Jr. at the Music Box. Opened October 24, 1966. (Closed November 26, 1966)

Captain Mike Holden; Geoff Horton;
  Jack Robinson ....John Tillinger
Corporal Clark; Stephanie Cork;
  Miss Clegg ....Denise Huot
Frank More ....James Bolam

The Colonel; Mr. Cross;
  Mr. Scace ....Peter Bayliss
Violet; Nell; Rover ......Patricia Routledge
Diedre ....Margaret Linn

Standby: Miss Routledge—Margaret Braidwood. Understudies: Messrs. Bolam, Tillinger, Russell Horton. Misses Huot, Linn—Veronica Castang.
Directed by Philip Grout; scenery and lighting, Ben Edwards; costumes, Jane Greenwood; incidental music, Ian Kellam; production stage manager, John Drew Devereaux; stage manager, Wayne Carson; press, Bill Doll, Midori Tsuji, Ted Goldsmith, Virginia Holden.
Time: 1946-1966, twenty years in the life of Frank More. Place: England. Act I: A demobilization center in the North of England, 1946. Act II: The home of Mr. and Mrs. Cross, ten years later. Act III: The living room of Mr. and Mrs. Scace, ten years later.

Comedy about a born loser's misadventures in three key episodes of his life—the army, courtship and marriage failure—with the same actors playing the different characters in each episode. A foreign play previously produced in London.

Under the Weather (12). By Saul Bellow. Produced by Theodore R. Brauer in association with Creative Trio, Inc. at the Cort Theater. Opened October 27, 1966. (Closed November 5, 1966)

PART I

Harry Faufill ....Harry Towb   Flora Sharkey ....Shelley Winters
A Cop ....Hazen Gifford

PART II

Marcella Vankuchen ....Shelley Winters   Solomon Ithimar ....Harry Towb

PART III

Pennington ....Harry Towb   Hilda ....Shelley Winters

Standbys: Miss Winters—Doris Roberts; Mr. Towb—Hazen Gifford.
Directed by Arthur Storch; scenery and costumes, Kert Lundell; lighting, Roger Morgan; production stage manager, Harry Young; stage manager, Robert Hewitt; press, Frank Goodman, Martin Shwartz, Ruth Cage.
Time: The present. Place: Part I—The weather picture for the Northeast. Bethpage, Long Island is bucking a blizzard. Out here are the numb, frozen suburbs. Part II—The weather picture for the Southeast. The present hurricane started east of Cuba. It is now expected in Florida. Miami is all puckered up. Part III—The weather picture for the Midwest. Rain . . . Chicago . . . Gary . . . worst of all Indiana Harbor. The air (a misleading word meaning a lot of industrial chemicals) gets misty.
Under the Weather is a program of three one-act comedies entitled (in tryout productions in Europe at Glasgow, London and Spoleto) *Out From Under, The Wen* and *Orange Souffle.* In Part I, a widower connives to avoid remarriage. In Part II, a Nobel Prize scientist travels to Florida to persuade a childhood playmate to show him a wen he remembers seeing, once, on an intimate part of her body. In Part III, a prostitute tries to seduce her 87-year-old friend into a warmer relationship, but she fails.

The Threepenny Opera (13). Marionette version of the musical based on John Gay's *The Beggar's Opera;* book and lyrics by Bertolt Brecht; music by Kurt Weill; English version by Marc Blitzstein. Produced by Jay K. Hoffman in the production of The Stockholm Marionette Theater of Fantasy, Michael Meschke founder and artistic director, at the Billy Rose Theater. Opened October 27, 1966. (Closed November 6, 1966)

A Street Singer; Filch ....Haken Serner
(Arne Hogsander)
Mr. J.J. Peachum ....Ingvar Kjellson
(Ulf Hakan Jansson)
Mrs. Peachum ....Ulla Sjoblom
(Zanza Lidums)
Polly Peachum ....Helena Brodin
(Ellika Linden)
Macheath (Mack the Knife) Goran Graffman
(Per Nielsen)

Jenny ....Ulla Sjoblom (Ellika Linden)
Tiger Brown, Commissioner of
    Police ...Jan Blomberg (Arne Hogsander)
Lucy Brown ......Meta Velander (Lydia de
    Lind van Wijngaarden)
Mack's Gang
    Matt ....Jan Blomberg
    Jake ....Heinz Spira
    Bob ....Folke Tragardh
    Walt ....Michael Meschke

(The "marionettes" of this production were not dolls but actors behind cutout figures or costumed three-dimensionally. Above, these players' names appear in parentheses; the other names designate the actors who supplied the marionette characters' voices)

Directed by Michael Meschke; puppets, masks and scenery, Franciszka Themerson; lighting, Jules Fisher; choreography, Holger Rosenquist; assistant to the producer, Agneta Pauli; press, Artie Solomon, Deborah Steinfirst.

The Threepenny Opera is a foreign play first performed in Berlin in 1928. A 1953 revival of the work off Broadway ran for 2,611 performances.

Gilbert Becaud on Broadway (19). One-man program of songs, most of them in the French language, sung by Gilbert Becaud. Lyrics by Pierre Delanoe, Louis Amade, Maurice Vidalin, Charles Aznavour, Jean Broussolle, Mack David, Gilbert Becaud; music by Gilbert Becaud. Produced by Norman Twain at the Longacre Theater. Opened October 31, 1966. (Closed November 20, 1966)

Musical director, Raymond Bernard; scenery and lighting, Ralph Alswang; production coordinator, Jean Silly; production stage manager, Martin Gold; press, Max Eisen, Carl Samrock. A foreign show previously produced in Paris and South America.

PART I: "Je T'Attends," "Viens Dans La Lumiere," "Les Jours Meilleurs," "C'etait Mon Copain," "Age Tendre Et Tetes De Bois," "Le Bateau Blanc," "Rosy and John," "Forever," "Quand Il Est Mort Le Poete," "T'es Venu De Loin," "Le Pianiste De Varsovie," "La Corrida."

PART II: "Alors Raconte," "Mon Arbre," "Mademoiselle Lise," "Sand and Sea," "L'Oiseau De Toutes Les Couleurs," "The Other Three," "L'Orange," "Nathalie," "Le Jour Ou La Pluie Viendra," "Et Maintenant," "La Ballade Des Baladins."

Let's Sing Yiddish (107). Musical in the Yiddish language based on Yiddish folklore, humor and art songs by Itsik Manger, Mordecai Gebirtig, Morris Rosenfeld, M. Nudelman and Wolf Younin. Produced by Ben Bonus at the Brooks Atkinson Theater. Opened November 9, 1966. (Closed January 29, 1967)

PART I—ONCE UPON A SHTETL

Girl; Shaindele	Susan Walters	Organ Grinder	Shmulik Goldstein
Shadchen; Berl	Max Bozyk	Drummer	Bernard Sauer
Neighbor; Mother	Rose Bozyk	Yosl-Ber; Actor	Ben Bonus
Minstrel; Baile	Mina Bern		

The Fibich Dancers: Donna Shadden, James May, Martha Pollak, Tamara Woshak, Tony Masullo, Dan Tylor.

Musical numbers, Part I: Shadchen Dance and Wedding Dance by the Fibich Dancers. "Let's Sing Yiddish" (Hassidic Melodies) by Ben Bonus and Ensemble.

PART II

Castle Garden (Susan Walters, Bernard Sauer, Mina Bern, Shmulik Goldstein); Life in the Shop (Ben Bonus, Fibich Dancers, Mina Bern, Susan Walters, Bernard Sauer, Shmulik Goldstein); On the Subway (Rose Bozyk, Max Bozyk, Fibich Dancers); Encounter in the Park (Rose and Max Bozyk); Wishful Thinking (Mina Bern, Ben Bonus, Fibich Dancers); American in Israel (Mina Bern, Bernard Sauer and Ensemble); "Let's Sing Yiddish" (Reprise).

Directed by Mina Bern; choreographer and assistant director, Felix Fibich; music arranged and conducted by Renee Solomon; assistant choreographer, Judith Fibich; literary supervision, Wolf Younin; Shtetl envisioned by Sylvia Younin, Naomi Hoffman; production supervisor, Bernard Sauer; press, Max Eisen, Jeanne Gibson Merrick, Carl Samrock.

Part I—Time: Before the two World Wars. Place: A shtetl, or small town, in Europe. Part II—Time: Immediately following and continuing to the present. Place: America.

The first part of the musical is a series of typical incidents of love, work and worship in a small European village. The second part takes place in America and deals with immigration, the sweat shop and, finally cultural sophistication.

D'Oyly Carte Opera Company. Repertory of five operetta revivals with librettos by W.S. Gilbert; music by Arthur Sullivan. **The Pirates of Penzance** (7). Opened November 15, 1966. **The Mikado** (9). Opened November 17, 1966. **Ruddigore** (4). Opened November 22, 1966. **H.M.S. Pinafore** (8). Opened November 23, 1966. **Patience** (4). Opened November 29, 1966. Produced by S. Hurok at New

York City Center. Repertory opened November 15, 1966. (Closed December 11, 1966)

PERFORMER	"THE PIRATES OF PENZANCE"	"THE MIKADO"	"RUDDIGORE"	"H.M.S. PINAFORE"
Donald Adams	Pirate King	Mikado	Sir Roderic	Dick Deadeye
George Cook	Sergeant	Go-To	Adam Goodheart	Bill Bobstay
Ann Hood			Rose Maybud	Josephine
Peggy Ann Jones	Edith	Pitti-Sing	Mad Margaret	
Thomas Lawlor		Pish-Tush		Capt. Corcoran
Beti Lloyd-Jones		(Katisha)		
Jennifer Marks	Isabel		Zorah	
Valerie Masterson	Mabel	Yum-Yum		
Christene Palmer	Ruth	(Katisha)	Dame Hannah	Little Buttercup
David Palmer			Richard Daunt-less	Ralph Rackstraw
Philip Potter	Frederic	Nanki-Poo		
Anthony Raffell	Samuel			Bob Becket
John Reed	Maj.-Gen. Stanley	Ko-Ko	Sir Ruthven	Adm. Porter
Kenneth Sandford		Pooh-Bah	Sir Despard	
Pauline Wales	Kate	Peep-Bo	Ruth	Hebe

(Parentheses indicate role in which the actor alternated)

PATIENCE

Colonel Calverley ....Donald Adams
Major Murgatroyd ....Alfred Oldridge
Lieut. The Duke of Dunstable ..Philip Potter
Reginald Bunthorne ....John Reed
Archibald Grosvenor .....Kenneth Sandford
Mr. Bunthorne's Solicitor ...James Marsland
Lady Angela ....Peggy Ann Jones
Lady Saphir ....Pauline Wales
Lady Ella ....Jennifer Marks
Lady Jane ....Christene Palmer
Patience ....Ann Hood

Small parts, Understudies and Chorus: Glyn Adams, John Banks, Neville Grave, John Hugill, Peter Lodwick, Gordon Mackenzie, Ralph Mason, Clifford Parkes, David Rayson, John Webley, Howard Williamson, Adrienne de Winters, Katherine Dyson, Mercia Glossop, Abby Hadfield, Beti Lloyd-Jones, Susan Maisey, Marian Martin, Norma Millar, Alison Parker, Abigail Ryan, Vera Ryan, Anne Sessions, Anna Vincent.

Produced under the personal supervision of Bridget D'Oyly Carte; musical director, Isidore Godfrey; associate conductor and chorus master, James Walker; director of productions, Herbert Newby; scenery, Peter Goffin; stage manager, Peter Riley; press, Martin Feinstein, Michael Sweeley.

MIKADO production directed by Anthony Besch; costumes, Charles Ricketts; Nanki-Poo Act I costume, Disley Jones. RUDDIGORE costumes, Peter Goffin. H.M.S. PINAFORE Little Buttercup costume, Anne and Janet Grahame-Johnstone. PATIENCE directed and designed by Peter Goffin.

The last Broadway visit of the D'Oyly Carte Opera Company from the Savoy Theater, London, was November 17, 1964 under S. Hurok's management at New York City Center. The repertory was the same, except that *Iolanthe* and *Trial by Jury* were given instead of *Patience*.

The Apparition Theater of Prague (21). Musical pantomime, ballet and drama show in the Czech language conceived by Jiri Srnec. Produced by Carroll and Harris Masterson and Norman Twain at the Cort Theater. Opened November 16, 1966. (Closed December 3, 1966)

PART I: Out West (Frantisek Kratochvil, Eva Schoberova, Milan Molzer, Alexej Okunev); Orpheus (Milada Danhelova, Alexej Okunev, Milan Molzer, Eva Schoberova, Emma Navratilova); The Cane (Frantisek Kratochvil); Calisthenics (Frantisek Kratochvil); Ghosts (Frantisek Kratochvil, Milan Molzer, Alexej Okunev).

PART II: Fishing (Frantisek Kratochvil); The Photographer (Eva Macalikova, Milada Danhelova, Frantisek Kratochvil); Suitcases (Jiri Anderle, Frantisek Kratochvil); Arena (Jiri Srnec); The Hunter (Jiri Anderle, Emma Navratilova, Frantisek Kratochvil, Eva Schoberova, Milan Molzer, Eva Macalikova, Alexej Okunev, Milada Danhelova).

Directed by Jiri Srnec; music, Jimmy Giuffre Quartet; production coordinator, Ivan Englich; press, Max Eisen, Carl Samrock.

An entertainment based principally upon a special stage effect using performers dressed in black against black backdrops to "animate" objects covered with luminous paint. A foreign show previously produced in Prague.

Les Ballets Africains (85). Dance and musical show in the French language by the National Ensemble of the Republic of Guinea. Produced by David H. McIlwraith by arrangement with Stephen W. Sharmat at the Ethel Barrymore Theater. Opened November 16, 1966. (Closed January 28, 1967)

Mademoiselles
  Sadio Bah
  Oumou Bangoura
  Mariama Barry
  Moussoukoura Camara
  Nalo Camara
  Namassa Camara
  Rouguiatou Camara
  Manou Fofana
  Jeanne Macauley
  Fanta Kaba
  Kankou Kouyate
  Aissata Toure
  Arafran Toure
  Sene Kady
  Goundo Souare

Messieurs
  Edouard Bangoura
  Ali Camara
  Ibrahima Camara

Faouly Camara
Moriba Camara
Damany Conde
Sekou Conde
Noumba Conde
Ibrahima Conte
Karamoko Fofana
Koca Sale Diabate
Secou Diabate
Almany Dioubate
Bakary Keita
Mamady Kourouma
Tamba Kourouma
Moussa Kone
Mamady Mansare
Bakary Mara
Guila Traore
Gbamou Vomo
Konate Famodou
Cisse M' Ma Ma Nana

Directed by David H. McIlwraith; general manager, Sekou Sakho; artistic managers, Hamidou Bangoura, Italo Zambo; stage manager, Salifou Bangoura; press, Max Eisen, James O'Rourke.

A collection of folk dances, songs and legends, with native instrumental music, from the Republic of Guinea. It was last presented on Broadway in 1959 at the Martin Beck Theater for 80 performances. A foreign show previously produced in Guinea and on a 19-year world tour.

PART I: Bagatai (legend of the God of the Bagas); The Forest (story dance, seduction and punishment); "Toutou Diarra" (song of a king's court); Midnight (illustration of a poem).

PART II: Konkoba (harvest dance); "Soundiata" (song of Emperor Soundiata); Doundoumba (warrior dance); Tiranke (satire); Finale (history of Guinea folkore).

* Don't Drink the Water (223). By Woody Allen. Produced by David Merrick in association with Jack Rollins and Charles Joffe at the Morosco Theater. Opened November 17, 1966.

Father Drobney ....Dick Libertini
Ambassador
  James F. Magee ....House Jameson
Kilroy ....Gerry Matthews
Axel Magee ....Anthony Roberts
Marion Hollander ....Kay Medford
Walter Hollander ....Lou Jacobi
Susan Hollander ....Anita Gillette
Krojack ....James Dukas

Burns ....Curtis Wheeler
Chef ....Gene Varrone
The Sultan of Bashir ....Oliver Clark
Sultan's 1st Wife ....Donna Mills
Kaznar ....John Hallow
Countess Bordoni ....Sharon Talbot
Novotny ....Luke Andreas
Waiter ....Jonathan Bolt

Standbys: Miss Medford—Merle Albertson; Mr. Jacobi—Don De Leo. Understudies: Mr. Roberts—Jonathan Bolt; Miss Gillette—Donna Mills; Messrs. Jameson, Wheeler, Libertini—John Hallow; Messrs. Dukas, Clark, Varrone—Luke Andreas; Messrs. Matthews, Hallow—Jim Stevenson.

Directed by Stanley Prager; scenery and lighting, Jo Mielziner; costumes, Motley; associate producer, Samuel Liff; stage manager, Jim Stevenson; press, Harvey B. Sabinson. Lee Solters, Jay Russell.

Time: The present. Place: An American Embassy somewhere behind the Iron Curtain. Act I, Scene 1: At a late summer afternoon. Scene 2: Later the same day. Scene 3: Several days later. Scene 4: Late that night. Scene 5: Several days later. Act II, Scene 1: The next day. Scene 2: Two days later. Scene 3: That night. Scene 4: The next morning.

Comedy about a Newark caterer, his wife and his daughter travelling behind the Iron Curtain, suspected of being spies and forced to take refuge in the American Embassy.

* Cabaret (221). Musical based on John van Druten's play *I Am a Camera* and stories by Christopher Isherwood; book by Joe Masteroff; music by John Kander; lyrics by Fred Ebb. Produced by Harold Prince in association with Ruth Mitchell at the Broadhurst Theater. Opened November 20, 1966.

Master of Ceremonies ....Joel Grey	Boockvor, Roger Briant, Edward Nolfi
Clifford Bradshaw ....Bert Convy	Frau Wendel ....Mara Landi
Ernst Ludwig ....Edward Winter	Herr Wendel ....Eugene Morgan
Custom Official ....Howard Kahl	Frau Kruger ....Miriam Lehmann-Haupt
Fraulein Schneider ....Lotte Lenya	Herr Erdmann ....Sol Frieder
Herr Schultz ....Jack Gilford	Kit Kat Girls
Fraulein Kost ....Peg Murray	Maria ....Pat Gosling
Telephone Girl ....Tresha Kelly	Lulu ....Lynn Winn
Kit Kat Band ....Maryann Burns, Janice	Rosie ....Bonnie Walker
Mink, Nancy Powers, Viola Smith	Fritzie ....Marianne Selbert
Maitre D' ....Frank Bouley	Texas ....Kathie Dalton
Max ....John Herbert	Frenchie ....Barbara Alston
Bartender ....Ray Baron	Bobby ....Jere Admire
Sally Bowles ....Jill Haworth	Victor ....Bert Michaels
Two Ladies .....Mary Ehara, Rita O'Connor	Greta ....Jayme Mylroie
German Sailors ....Bruce Becker, Steven	Felix ....Robert Sharp

Understudies: Miss Haworth—Jayme Mylroie; Mr. Gilford—Sol Frieder; Mr. Convy—Edward Winter; Miss Lenya—Peg Murray; Mr. Grey—Bert Michaels; Miss Murray—Mara Landi; Mr. Winter—John Herbert.

Directed by Harold Prince; dances and cabaret numbers, Ronald Field; musical direction, Harold Hastings; scenery, Boris Aronson; costumes, Patricia Zipprodt; lighting, Jean Rosenthal; orchestrations, Don Walker; dance arrangements, David Baker; production stage manager, Ruth Mitchell; stage manager, James Bronson; press, Mary Bryant, Ellen Levene.

Time: 1929-30, before the start of the Third Reich. Place: Berlin in Germany.

Cabaret re-tells Christopher Isherwood's stories about a young author in decadent pre-Hitler Berlin; he meets, loves and loses a young night club entertainer. John van Druten's straight dramatization of this story, *I Am a Camera*, was first produced November 28, 1951 by Gertrude Macy in association with Walter Starke at the Empire Theater for 214 performances. It was named a Best Play of its season and won the New York Drama Critics Circle award for Best American Play.

Peg Murray replaced Lotte Lenya 3/6/67 to 3/18/67.

A Best Play; see page 209

ACT I

"Willkommen" ....Master of Ceremonies, Company
"So What?" ....Fraulein Schneider
"Don't Tell Mama" ....Sally, Girls
"Telephone Song" ....The Company
"Perfectly Marvelous" ....Cliff, Sally
"Two Ladies" ....M.C., Two Ladies
"It Couldn't Please Me More" ....Fraulein Schneider, Herr Schultz
"Tomorrow Belongs to Me" ....M.C., Waiters
"Why Should I Wake Up?" ....Cliff, Sally
"The Money Song" ....M.C., Girls
"Married" ....Fraulein Schneider, Herr Schultz

"Meeskite" ....Herr Schultz
"Tomorrow Belongs to Me" (Reprise) ....Fraulein Kost, Ernst, Guests

ACT II

"If You Could See Her" ....M.C., Girls
"Married" (Reprise) ....Fraulein Schneider, Herr Schultz
"If You Could See Her" (Reprise) ....M.C., Bobby
"What Would You Do" ....Fraulein Schneider
"Cabaret" ....Sally
Finale ....Cliff, Sally, Fraulein Schneider, Herr Schultz, M.C., Company

* **The Association of Producing Artists (APA) Repertory Company.** Repertory of seven plays. **The School for Scandal** (48). Revival of the play by Richard Brinsley Sheridan. Opened November 21, 1966. **Right You Are** (42). Revival of the play by Luigi Pirandello; English version by Eric Bentley. Opened November 22, 1966. **We Comrades Three** (11). By Richard Baldridge; from the works of Walt Whitman. Opened December 20, 1966. * **The Wild Duck** (41). Revival of the play by Henrik Ibsen; translated by Eva Le Gallienne. Opened January 11, 1967. **You Can't Take It With You** (16). Reopening of the 1965-66 APA revival of the comedy by Moss Hart and George S. Kaufman. Opened February 10, 1967. * **War and Peace** (40). Adaptation of Leo Tolstoy's novel by Alfred Neumann, Erwin Piscator and Guntram Prufer; English version by Robert David MacDonald. Opened March 21, 1967. Produced by APA-Phoenix (a project of Theater Incorporated), T. Edward Hambleton managing director, at the Lyceum Theater.

PERFORMER	"THE SCHOOL FOR SCANDAL"	"RIGHT YOU ARE"	"WE COMRADES THREE"
Esther Benson	(Lady Sneerwell)	(Sras. Sirelli, Agazzi, Ponza)	(Mother)
Dan Bly	Numps; (Careless)	(Governor)	(Walt Whitman)
Joseph Bird	Rowley; (Sir Oliver)	Centuri; (Agazzi)	
Olivia Cole	Sip; (Lisp; Maria)	(Dina; Sra. Ponza)	(Young Woman)
Patricia Conolly	(Lady Teazle)	Signora Sirelli; (Sra. Ponza)	Young Woman
Clayton Corzatte	Charles	(Laudisi)	(Young Walt)
Keene Curtis	Sir Oliver	Sirelli	
Anita Dangler	(Mrs. Candour)	Signora Nenni; (Sra. Cini)	
Alan Fudge	Nod; (Trip)		(Walt)
Will Geer	(Sir Peter)	(Governor)	Walt Whitman
Gordon Gould	(Crabtree; Rowley)	Governor; (Ponza; Butler)	
James Greene	Snake	Butler; (Centuri)	
Jennifer Harmon	Maria	Dina	(Young Woman)
Rosemary Harris	Lady Teazle; Epilogue	(Sra. Ponza)	(Young Woman)
Helen Hayes	Mrs. Candour	Signora Frola	Mother
Nikos Kafkalis	Nip		
Michael Alan MacDonald	Slap		
Nicholas Martin	Backbite	(Butler)	
Betty Miller	(Maria)	Signora Cini; (Sra. Frola)	
Donald Moffat	(Joseph)	Laudisi	
George Pentecost	Careless; (Backbite)	(Sirelli)	
Stephen Peters	Trip; (William)		
Christine Pickles	(Lady Sneerwell; Mrs. Candour)	(Sra. Nenni)	

PERFORMER	"THE SCHOOL FOR SCANDAL"	"RIGHT YOU ARE"	"WE COMRADES THREE"
Ellis Rabb	Joseph	(Governor)	
Nat Simmons	Nap		
Marco St. John	(Charles)		Young Walt
James Storm	Slip		
Joel Stuart	William; (Snake)		
Dee Victor	Lady Sneerwell	Signora Agazzi	
Sydney Walker	Sir Peter	Ponza	Walt
Paulette Waters	Lisp		
Richard Woods	Crabtree	Agazzi	

PERFORMER	"THE WILD DUCK"	"YOU CAN'T TAKE IT WITH YOU"	"WAR AND PEACE"
Esther Benson	Mrs. Sörby		
Dan Bly	Kasperson; (Graaberg; Hjalmar)	(G-Man)	
Joseph Bird	Relling; (Lt. Ekdal)	DePinna; (Grandpa)	Alpatich
Olivia Cole		(Rheba; Gay)	Lisa
Patricia Conolly	(Hedvig)	(Alice; Essie; Gay)	
Clayton Corzatte	Gregers	(Tony)	Narrator
Keene Curtis	(Molvik; Balle)	Boris	Napoleon; (Pierre)
Anita Dangler		(Gay; Olga; Penny)	
Gwyda Donhowe		Gay	
Anne Francine		Olga	
Alan Fudge	Gentleman	G-Man	Dolokhov
Will Geer	(Lt. Ekdal)		
Stefan Gierasch			Pierre
Gordon Gould	Petterson; (Gregers; Werle)	Ed; (Mr. Kirby)	Kusmich
James Greene	Gentleman; (Molvik; Balle; Relling; Petterson; Kasperson)	Henderson; (DePinna; Paul)	Karatayev; Kutusov
Jennifer Harmon	Hedvig	(Essie)	
Rosemary Harris	(Gina)	Alice	Natasha
Nikos Kafkalis	Gentleman	(G-Man)	
Michael Alan MacDonald	(Gentleman)	(G-Man)	
Nicholas Martin	Molvik; (Graaberg)	(Boris)	
Betty Miller	Gina	Mrs. Kirby	
Donald Moffat	Hjalmar	Grandpa	Andrei
George Pentecost	Balle; (Molvik)	G-Man; (Henderson; Ed)	Rostov
Stephen Peters	Gentleman; (Jensen; Graaberg)	(G-Man)	
Christine Pickles		Essie	Maria
Ellis Rabb	(Gregers)	(Boris)	
Nat Simmons		Donald	Soult
Marco St. John		Tony	Kuragin
James Storm	Jensen	G-Man	Alexander I
Joel Stuart	Graaberg; (Kasperson; Jensen)	(G-Man; Henderson)	
Dee Victor	(Mrs. Sörby)	Penny	Countess Rostova
Sydney Walker	Lt. Ekdal	Paul	Bolkonski
Paulette Waters		Rheba	
Richard Woods	Werle	Mr. Kirby	

(Parentheses indicate role in which the actor alternated following the opening night performance, whose roles are listed above without parentheses)

Soldiers, Peasants, Servants in *War and Peace:* Kermit Brown, Alexander Courtney, Kenneth W. Freeman, Reuben Greene, Harley Hackett, Roger Harkenrider, Ken Kliban, Michael Alan MacDonald, Hancel McCord, John Merensky, Don Parker, Stephen Peters, Gastone V. Rossilli Jr., James Sullivan, James Whittle.

Artistic director of APA Repertory Company, Ellis Rabb; scenery, James Tilton; costumes, Nancy Potts; lighting, Gilbert V. Hemsley Jr.; stage managers, Dan Bly, George Darveris, Sean Gillespie, Robert Alan Gold, Bruce A. Hoover, Robert Moss; press, Ben Kornzweig, Reginald Denenholz.

THE SCHOOL FOR SCANDAL directed by Ellis Rabb; associate director, Hal George.

Time: 1777. Place: London.

The first of *The School for Scandal's* many New York productions took place December 12, 1785. The Sheridan comedy entered APA repertory the summer of 1961 and was presented off Broadway by APA in the spring of 1962. Its last Broadway revival was January 24, 1963, staged by John Gielgud at the Majestic Theater for 60 performances.

Anne Francine replaced Helen Hayes, 2/13/67 to 3/29/67.

RIGHT YOU ARE directed by Stephen Porter; music, Conrad Susa.

Time: 1916. Place: A room in Councillor Agazzi's apartment.

This Pirandello work, sometimes presented under its longer title *Right You Are If You Think You Are,* entered APA repertory in the fall of 1960 and was last produced in New York by APA March 4, 1964, off Broadway. The play's only Broadway production of record was on March 2, 1927 by the Theater Guild at the Guild Theater for 48 performances.

WE COMRADES THREE directed by Ellis Rabb and Hal George.

The play, adapted from Walt Whitman's works, ranges through time and place to recreate the events of Whitman's life and his relation to his era which included the Civil War. Whitman appears throughout the play as three continuing and contiguous characters: himself as a young man, as a man of 40 and as an old man. *We Comrades Three* entered APA repertory in the fall of 1962 and made its New York debut in this production.

THE WILD DUCK directed by Stephen Porter.

Time: The 1880s. Place: Werle's house and later Hjalmar Ekdal's studio in Christiania, Norway.

Ibsen's *The Wild Duck* entered APA repertory last season. It was last revived on Broadway December 26, 1951 at the New York City Center for 15 performances.

YOU CAN'T TAKE IT WITH YOU directed by Ellis Rabb; assistant director, Jack O'Brien.

Time: 1936. Place: The home of Martin Vanderhof in New York.

You Can't Take It With You entered APA repertory last season and was brought to Broadway November 23, 1965, for a run of 239 performances ending June 18, 1966. This is a return engagement, in repertory, of that production.

WAR AND PEACE directed by Ellis Rabb; assistant director, Jack O'Brien.

Time: 1805-1812. Place: Europe between the Rhine and the Mitischi.

This adaptation of Tolstoy's novel was first produced at the Schiller Theater in Berlin in 1955. The English version entered APA repertory in Ann Arbor in the fall of 1964 and was presented by the APA off Broadway at the Phoenix theater January 11, 1965 for 71 performances.

Those That Play the Clowns (4). By Michael Stewart. Produced by David Black in association with Nathan Friedman at the ANTA Theater. Opened November 24, 1966. (Closed November 26, 1966)

1st Soldier	Patrick Gorman	Fru Gerdes; Queen	Grayson Hall
2d Soldier; Guard	Edward Rudney	1st Drover; Captain	Lloyd Battista
3d Soldier	John J. Holzman	2d Drover; Sergeant	Alfred Toigo
Priest; Sergeant	Taldo Kenyon	Anna Sophie; Lady in Waiting	Jane Draper
Judge Lander	Eduard Franz	Tall Man	Larry Swanson
Peddler; King	Leslie Litomy	Kaj	Edgar Stehli
Helge; Lady in Waiting	Myrna LaBow	Henning	Thayer David
Eva; Minister's Daughter	Fredricka Weber	Valentina Ponti	Joan Greenwood
Jens	Jerry Dodge	Soren Brandes	Alfred Drake
Hr. Blixen; Minister	Arn Weiner	Prince	Stephen Joyce
Fru Blixen; Lady in Waiting	Michele Evans		

Standbys: Mr. Drake—Alfred Toigo; Miss Greenwood—Grayson Hall; Mr. Franz—Leslie Litomy. General Understudies: Lloyd Battista, Jane Draper, Michele Evans, Patrick Gorman, John J. Holzman, Taldo Kenyon, Myrna LaBow, Leslie Litomy, Edward Rudney, Fredricka Weber, Arn Weiner.

Directed by Robin Midgley; scenery and costumes, Michael Annals; lighting, Martin Aronstein; scenic supervisor, Lawrence Reehling; associate producer, Mary Sharmat; production manager, Jose Vega; percussion, Herbert Harris; stage manager, Donald Buka; press, Frank Goodman, Martin Shwartz.

Time: In the days of Prince Hamlet. Place: Zealand near the Baltic Sea. Act I: A country inn. Act II, Scene 1: The wine cellar of a nearby castle. Scene 2: The main hall of the castle. Act III: The inn—a short while after. Scene 2: The east road at dawn.

About the strolling players in Hamlet; how they came to Elsinore and how they put on the play-within-the-play.

Walking Happy (161). Musical based on Harold Brighouse's play *Hobson's Choice;* book by Roger O. Hirson and Ketti Frings; music by James Van Heusen; lyrics by Sammy Cahn. Produced by Feuer and Martin by arrangement with Lester Linsk at the Lunt-Fontanne Theater. Opened November 26, 1966. (Closed April 16, 1967)

Henry Horatio Hobson ....George Rose	Footman ....Steven Jacobs
George Beenstock ....Ed Bakey	Tubby Wadlow ....Gordon Dilworth
Minns ....Thomas Boyd	Will Mossop ....Norman Wisdom
Denton ....Casper Roos	Ada Figgins ....Jane Laughlin
Tudsbury ....Carl Nicholas	Mrs. Figgins ....Lucille Benson
Heeler ....Michael Quinn	The Figgins Brothers ....Ian Garry, Al Lanti
Maggie Hobson ....Louise Troy	Customer ....Eleanor Bergquist
Alice Hobson ....Sharon Dierking	Handbill Boy ....Richard Sederholm
Vickie Hobson ....Gretchen Van Aken	Thief ....Bert Bier
Albert Beenstock ....James B. Spann	Policeman ....Chad Block
Freddie Beenstock ....Michael Berkson	Beggar ....Richard Korthaze
Mrs. Hepworth ....Emma Trekman	

Townsmen: Burt Bier, Chad Block, Thomas Boyd, Ian Garry, Gene Gavin, Steven Jacobs, Richard Korthaze, Al Lanti, Carl Nicholas, Don Percassi, Michael Quinn, Casper Roos, Richard Sederholm, Dan Siretta.

Townswomen: Eleanor Bergquist, Diane L. Blair, Sandra Brewer, Ellen Graff, Marian Haraldson, Jane Laughlin, Marie Patrice O'Neill, Nada Rowand, Anne Wallace.

Standby: Mr. Wisdom—Byron Mitchell. Understudies: Miss Troy—Eleanor Bergquist; Mr. Rose—Michael Quinn; Mr. Bakey—Casper Roos; Mr. Dilworth—Burt Bier; Miss Trekman—Nada Rowand; Miss Dierking—Sandra Brewer; Miss Van Aken—Jane Laughlin; Mr. Berkson—Richard Sederholm; Mr. Spann—Dan Siretta.

Directed by Cy Feuer; dances and musical numbers staged by Danny Daniels; musical direction and vocal arrangements, Herbert Grossman; scenery and lighting, Robert Randolph; costumes, Robert Fletcher; orchestrations, Larry Wilcox; dance music arranged by Ed Scott; production stage manger, Phil Friedman; stage manager, Jack Leigh; press, Merle Debuskey, Violet Welles, Lawrence Belling.

Time: 1880. Place: Salford, an industrial town in Lancashire, England.

A shoemaker's daughter determines to marry her father's cringing apprentice, in whom she discerns special possibilities. She sets out to make a master shoemaker and a husband of her runty catch.

ACT I

"Think of Something Else" ....Hobson, Beenstock, Townsmen
"Where Was I" ....Maggie
"How D'ya Talk To A Girl" ....Will, Tubby
"Clog and Grog" ....Townsmen
"If I Be Your Best Chance" ....Will
"A Joyful Thing" ....Will, Mrs. Figgins, Ada Figgins, Townspeople
"What Makes It Happen" ....Will
"Use Your Noggin" ....Maggie, Vickie, Alice

ACT II

"You're Right, You're Right" ....Maggie
"I'll Make a Man of The Man" ....Maggie
"Walking Happy" ....Will, Maggie, Townspeople
"I Don't Think I'm In Love" ....Will, Maggie
"Such A Sociable Sort" ....Hobson, Friends
"It Might As Well Be Her" ....Will, Tubby
"People Who Are Nice" ....Hobson
"You're Right, You're Right" (Reprise) ....Will, Maggie, Hobson
"I Don't Think I'm In Love" (Reprise) ....Will

Hail Scrawdyke! (8). By David Halliwell. Produced by Si Litvinoff, Inc. in association with Jerry Leiber, Mike Stoller and Gil Garfield, by arrangement with Michael Codron, Ltd. at the Booth Theater. Opened November 28, 1966. (Closed December 3, 1966)

Malcolm Scrawdyke	..........Victor Henry	Dennis Charles Nipple	..........Tim Preece
Irwin Ingham	............Austin Pendleton	Ann Gedge	..........Ann Stockdale
John "Wick" Blagden	........Drewe Henley		

Understudies: Messrs. Henry, Pendleton—Lawrence Block; Messrs. Preece, Henley—Ian Jenkins; Miss Stockdale—Jane Farnol.

Directed by Alan Arkin; scenery, Peter Larkin; costumes, Willa Kim; lighting, Jules Fisher; associate producer, Max L. Raab; production stage manager, Randall Brooks; press, Dorothy Ross, Richard O'Brien, Jane Friedman.

Time: January, 1965. Place: Scrawdyke's studio in Huddersfield, an industrial town in the North of England. Act I is divided into two scenes, Act II into three scenes and Act III takes place in one scene.

A misfit art student organizes a few of his friends into an ineffectual fantasy rebellion against the establishment. A foreign play previously produced in Dublin and London under the title *Little Malcolm and His Struggle Against the Eunuchs.*

* I Do! I Do! (162). Musical based on Jan de Hartog's play *The Fourposter;* book and lyrics by Tom Jones; music by Harvey Schmidt. Produced by David Merrick at the Forty-sixth Street Theater. Opened December 5, 1966.

She (Agnes) ....Mary Martin He (Michael) ....Robert Preston

Directed by Gower Champion; scenery, Oliver Smith; costumes, Freddy Wittop; lighting, Jean Rosenthal; musical director, John Lesko; orchestrations, Philip J. Lang; assistant to director, Lucia Victor; pianists, Woody Kessler, Albert Mello; stage manager, Wade Miller; press, Ben Washer.

Time: Fifty years of a marriage, beginning just before the turn of the century. Place: A bedroom.

The emotional crescendos of a happy but occasionally stormy marriage are depicted in a series of bedroom scenes between husband and wife. The play on which this musical was based, *The Fourposter,* was first produced on Broadway October 24, 1951 for 632 performances and was named a Best Play of its season.

ACT I

Prologue ....Both
 "All the Dearly Beloved"
 "Together Forever"
 "I Do! I Do!"
"Good Night" ....Both
"I Love My Wife" ....He
"Something Has Happened" ....She
"My Cup Runneth Over" ....Both
"Love Isn't Everything" ....Both
"Nobody's Perfect" ....Both
"A Well Known Fact" ....He

"Flaming Agnes" ....She
"The Honeymoon Is Over" ....Both

ACT II

"Where Are the Snows" ....Both
"When the Kids Get Married" ....Both
Another Wedding
  "The Father of the Bride" ....He
  "What Is a Woman" ....She
"Someone Needs Me" ....She
"Roll up the Ribbons" ....Both
"This House" ....Both

My Sweet Charlie (31). By David Westheimer; adapted from his novel. Produced by Bob Banner Associates at the Longacre Theater. Opened December 6, 1966. (Closed December 31, 1966)

Marlene Chambers ....Bonnie Bedelia   Jack Larrabee ....Gar Wood
Charles Roberts ....Louis Gossett   Mr. Treadwell ....John Randolph
Laurie Larrabee ....Sarah Cunningham   Doctor Kercheval ....David Tabor

Standbys: Mr. Gossett—James Spruill; Miss Bedelia—Margaret Ladd.
Directed by Howard Da Silva; scenery and lighting, Jo Mielziner; costumes, Jack Martin Lindsay; production supervisor, H.R. Poindexter; production stage manager, Norman Grogan; stage manager, Maxine Taylor; press, Seymour Krawitz.
Time: The present. Place: A summer cottage on the Gulf Coast. Act I, Scene 1: An evening in late fall. Scene 2: Three days later, late afternoon. Scene 3: Dawn the next morning. Act II, Scene 1: Later the same day. Scene 2: One week later, early evening. Act III, Scene 1: A week before Christmas, afternoon. Scene 2: The same day, early evening. Scene 3: Later the same night.
A Northern Negro lawyer on the run after killing a white man in self-defense meets another outcast: a pregnant poor-white-trash girl in hiding in an empty summer home on the Gulf Coast. Their relationship progresses from hostility to affection, and finally the lawyer sacrifices his life to help the girl.

Agatha Sue I love you (5). By Abe Einhorn. Produced by Judith Abbott and Edwin Wilson in association with Tommy Valando and John Pransky at Henry Miller's Theater. Opened December 14, 1966. (Closed December 17, 1966)

Jack ....Corbett Monica   Agatha Sue ....Lee Lawson
Eddie ....Ray Walston   Sheila ....Reneé Taylor
Mrs. Gordon ....Betty Garde

Understudies: Messrs. Walston, Monica—Robert Kasparian. Misses Lawson, Taylor—Jean McClintock Hickey.
Directed by George Abbott; scenery and lighting, William and Jean Eckart; costumes, Patton Campbell; "Agatha Sue" song composed by Sid Ramin; stage manager, Robert Kasparian; press, Mary Bryant, Lila King.
Time: The present. Place: A room in the Great White Way Hotel, New York City. Act I, Scene 1: Evening. Scene 2: 3 a.m. the next morning. Act II: that evening.
Comedy about two horse players, broke and trying to raise another stake with the help of the pretty young folk singer in the hotel room next door.

A Joyful Noise (12). Musical based on Borden Deal's novel *The Insolent Breed;* book by Edward Padula; music and lyrics by Oscar Brand and Paul Nassau. Produced by Edward Padula and Slade Brown in association with Sid Bernstein at the Mark Hellinger Theater. Opened December 15, 1966. (Closed December 24, 1966)

Shade Motley ....John Raitt   Walter Wishenant ....George Mathews
Brother Locke ....Clifford David Jenny Lee ....Susan Watson

Sam Fredrickson ....Art Wallace
Miss Jimmie ....Leland Palmer
Saw Mill Boys and The Motley Crew
    De Witt ....Eric Weissberg
    Freddy ....Martin Ambrose
    Jaybird ....Charles Morley
    Oscar ....Oatis Stephens
    Tommy ....Tommy Tune
Bliss Stanley ....Swen Swenson

Stage Manager ....Jack Fletcher
Director ....Ken Ayers
Mary Texas ....Karen Morrow
Boys ....Paul Charles, Scott Pearson,
                        Alan Peterson, Barry Preston
Announcer ....Jack Metté
Bailey ....Jo Jo Smith
John Tom ....Shawn Campbell

Ensemble singers: Veronica McCormick, Jessica Quinn, Diane Tarleton, Linda Theil, Jamie Thomas, Ken Ayers, Jack Fletcher, Stuart Mann, Eric Mason, Jack Metté, Darrell Sandeen.

Ensemble dancers: Christine Bocchino, Susan Donovan, Baayork Lee, April Nevins, Diane Phillips, Joy Serio, Melissa Stoneburn, Carol Lynn Vazquez, Bonnie Ano, Paul Charles, Winston DeWitt Hemsley, Scott Pearson, Alan Peterson, Barry Preston, Steven Ross, Jo Jo Smith, Tommy Tune.

Understudies: Mr. Raitt—Jack Metté; Misses Watson, Morrow—Jamie Thomas; Mr. David —Jack Fletcher; Mr. Mathews—Darrell Sandeen; Miss Palmer—Christine Bocchino; Mr. Campbell—Vone O'Fallon; Saw Mill Boys—Tommy Tune.

Directed by Edward Padula; dances and musical numbers staged by Michael Bennett; musical director, Rene Wiegert; scenery and lighting, Peter Wexler; costumes, Peter Joseph; orchestrations and vocal arrangements, William Stegmeyer; dance music, Lee Holdridge; assistant choreographers, Leland Palmer, Jo Jo Smith; assistant musical director, Rudolph Bennett; production supervisor, Jeb Schary; production stage manager, Edward Julien; stage manager, Howard Perloff; press, Sol Jacobson, Lewis Harmon.

Time: Yesterday and today. Place: Macedonia and Nashville, Tennessee. Act I, Scene 1: A clearing in the hills. Scene 2: The town square. Scene 3: A clearing. Scene 4: The saw mill. Scene 5: The field. Scene 6: The top of the valley. Act II, Scene 1: Backstage, Nashville. Scene 2: A clearing in Macedonia. Scene 3: The Grand Ole Opry. Scene 4: The recording studio. Scene 5: The state fair. Scene 6: The town square.

A wandering singer is run out of a small Tennessee town by the irate father of the girl he loves. When he returns he has become a popular folk-singing idol but chooses to return to his former existence as an itinerant minstrel.

ACT I

"Longtime Travelin' " ....Shade
"A Joyful Noise" ....Shade, Townspeople
"I'm Ready" ....Jennie Lee, Miss Jimmie, The Girls
"Spring Time of the Year" ....Shade
"I Like To Look My Best" ....Shade, Sam, The Saw Mill Boys
"No Talent" ....Bliss
"Not Me" ....Jenny Lee, Miss Jimmie
"Until Today" ....Shade, Jenny Lee
"Swinging a Dance" ....Shade, Company
"To the Top" ....Bliss, Shade

ACT II

"I Love Nashville" ....Mary Texas and Her Boys
"Whither Thou Goest" ....Brother Locke
"We Won't Forget To Write" ....Miss Jimmie, Sam, The Saw Mill Boys
Grand Ole Opry
    "Ballad Maker" ....Shade, Mary, The Motley Crew, Ensemble
    "Barefoot Gal" ....Mary Texas
    "Clog Dance" ....Dance Ensemble
    "Fool's Gold" ....Shade, Mary, The Motley Crew, Ensemble
"The Big Guitar" ....Bliss
"Love Was" ....Jenny Lee
"I Say Yes" ....Shade, The Motley Crew, Ensemble
"Lord, You Sure Know How To Make a New Day" ....Shade
"A Joyful Noise" (Reprise) ....Shade, Townspeople

Carousel (22). Musical revival based on Ferenc Molnar's *Liliom;* book and lyrics by Oscar Hammerstein II; music by Richard Rodgers. Produced by The New York City Center Light Opera Company, Jean Dalrymple director, at New York City Center. Opened December 15, 1966. (Closed January 1, 1967)

Carrie Pipperidge	Nancy Dussault	Hannah	Jenny Workman
Julie Jordan	Constance Towers	Boatswain; Carnival Boy	Darrell Notara
Mrs. Mullin	Louise Larabee	Second Policeman	Gene Albano
Billy Bigelow	Bruce Yarnell	Captain	William R. Miller
First Policeman	Paul Adams	Heavenly Friend (Joshua)	Jay Velie
David Bascombe	Alexander Clark	Starkeeper	Parker Fennelly
Nettie Fowler	Patricia Neway	Louise	Sandy Duncan
Enoch Snow	Jack De Lon	Enoch Snow Jr.	Dennis Cole
Jigger Craigin	Michael Kermoyan	Principal	Philip Ewart

Townspeople: Phyllis Bash, Jane Coleman, Mona Elson, Maria Hero, Joyce McDonald, Estella Munson, Marie O'Kelley, Joyce Olson, Eleanor Shaw, Maggie Task, Paul Adams, Gene Albano, Darrell Askey, Bob Barbieri, Austin Colyer, Gordon Cook, Philip Ewart, Marvin Goodis, William R. Miller, Laried Montgomery, Joe R. Rhyne, Joseph Williams, Jerry Wyatt.

Dancers: Karen Brock, Linda Caputi, Alice Condodina, Joanna Crosson, Lois Etelman, Carol Flemming, Joanne Geahry, Mickey Gunnersen, Lucia Lambert, Gilda Mullett, Toodie Wittmer, Roy Barry, Joseph Carow, Reese Haworth, Curtis Hood, Paul Olson, Vernon Wendorf. Dance Captain: Dennis Cole.

Standbys: Mr. Yarnell—Nolan Van Way; Miss Larabee—Betty Hyatt Linton. Understudies: Miss Towers—Estelle Munson; Miss Dussault—Maria Hero; Miss Neway—Maggie Task; Mr. De Lon—Joe R. Rhyne; Mr. Kermoyan—Bob Barbieri; Mr. Fennelly—Jay Velie; Mr. Clark—William R. Miller.

Directed by Gus Schirmer; Agnes de Mille dances restaged by Gemze de Lappe; musical director, Jonathan Anderson; scenery, Paul C. McGuire; costumes, Stanley Simmons; lighting, Feder; production stage managers, Herman Shapiro, Chester O'Brien; stage manager, George Rondo; press, Homer Poupart.

Time: 1873-1888. Place: The New England Coast. Act I, Scene 1: Prelude: an amusement park on the New England Coast, May. Scene 2: A tree-lined path along the shore, a few minutes later. Scene 3: Nettie Fowler's Spa on the ocean front, June. Act II, Scene 1: On an island across the bay, that night. Scene 2: Mainland waterfront, an hour later. Scene 3: Up there. Scene 4: Down here on a beach, fifteen years later. Scene 5: Outside Julie's cottage. Scene 6: Outside a schoolhouse, same day.

Carousel was first produced on Broadway April 19, 1945 by the Theater Guild at the Majestic Theater for 890 performances. It has been revived at New York City Center three times: January 25, 1949 (by the Theater Guild) for 48 performances, June 2, 1954 (by New York City Center Light Opera Company) for 79 performances and September 11, 1957 for 24 performances. It was revived August 10, 1965 by the Music Theater of Lincoln Center for 48 performances.

ACT I

Prelude: Waltz suite "Carousel" .... Ensemble
"You're a Queer One, Julie Jordan" .... Carrie, Julie
"When I Marry Mr. Snow" .... Carrie
"If I Loved You" .... Billy, Julie
"June Is Bustin' Out All Over" .... Nettie, Carrie, Ensemble (Dance by
Dancing Ensemble led by Lucia Lambert)
"When I Marry Mr. Snow" (Reprise) .... Carrie, Mr. Snow, Girls
"When the Children Are Asleep" .... Mr. Snow, Carrie
"Blow High, Blow Low" .... Jigger, Billy, Male Chorus (Hornpipe led by
Jenny Workman, Darrell Notara)
"Soliloquy" .... Billy
Finale

ACT II

"This Was a Real Nice Clambake" ....Carrie, Nettie, Julie, Mr. Snow, Ensemble
"Geraniums in the Winder" ....Mr. Snow
"There's Nothin' So Bad for a Woman" ....Jigger, Ensemble
"What's the Use of Wond'rin?" ....Julie
"You'll Never Walk Alone" ....Nettie
"The Highest Judge of All" ....Billy
Ballet: Louise—Sandy Duncan; A Younger Miss Snow—Toodie Wittmer; The Brothers and
   Sisters Snow—Linda Caputi, Lois Etelman, Karen Agello, Lorraine Cullen, Dean Crane;
   Badly Brought-Up Boys—Reese Haworth, Curtis Hood; A Young Man Like Billy—Darrell
   Notara; A Carnival Woman—Jenny Workman; Members of the Carnival Troupe—Karen
   Brock, Carol Flemming, Lucia Lambert, Gilda Mullett, Roy Barry, Joseph Carow, Paul Ol-
   son, Vernon Wendorf.
"If I Loved You" (Reprise) ....Billy
"You'll Never Walk Alone" (Reprise) ....Entire Company
Finale

* **The Star-Spangled Girl** (186). By Neil Simon. Produced by Saint-Subber at the Plymouth Theater. Opened December 21, 1966.

Andy Hobart ....Anthony Perkins   Sophie Rauschmeyer ....Connie Stevens
Norman Cornell ....Richard Benjamin

   Understudies: Messrs. Perkins, Benjamin—William Bogert; Miss Stevens—Melinda Plank.
   Directed by George Axelrod; scenery, Oliver Smith; costumes, Ann Roth; lighting, Jean
Rosenthal; production stage manager, William Dodds; stage manager, Wisner Washam; press,
Harvey B. Sabinson, Lee Solters, Harry Nigro.

   Time: The present. Place: A duplex studio apartment in San Francisco. Act I, Scene 1:
Late afternoon, early summer. Scene 2: Three days later. Act II, Scene 1: The next day, about
5 p.m. Scene 2: A few days later. Act III: The next day, early afternoon.
   Comedy about two roommates, editors of a small but rebellious magazine, whose intellectual
preoccupations are disarranged by the pretty blonde in the next apartment.

At the Drop of Another Hat (104). Two-man program performed by Michael Flanders and Donald Swann; words by Michael Flanders; music by Donald Swann. Produced by Alexander H. Cohen in A Nine O'Clock Theater Production at the Booth Theater. Opened December 27, 1966. (Closed April 8, 1967)

   Associate producer, Sidney Lanier; designed by Ralph Alswang; production stage manager,
Jake Hamilton; stage manager, Paul Maloney; press, Bill Doll & Co., Midori Tsuji, Ted Goldsmith, Virginia Holden.
   The program is a series of songs, mostly in duet, with Swann at the piano, and with comments and one monologue by Flanders. A foreign play previously produced in London and on
a world tour.

   PART I: "The Gasman Cometh," "From Our Bestiary," "P** P* B**** B** D******,"
"Bilbo's Song" (lyric by J.R.R. Tolkien), "Slow Train," "Thermodynamic Duo," "Sloth,"
"More Songs for Our Time," "In the Desert," Los Olvidados, "Motor Perpetuo," "A Song of
Patriotic Prejudice."
   PART II: "All Gall," "Horoscope," "Armadillo Idyll," "Twenty Tons of T.N.T.," "Ill Wind"
(music by Mozart), "Food for Thought," "Prehistoric Complaint," "Twice Shy."

The Persecution and Assassination of Jean-Paul Marat as Performed by the In-mates of the Asylum of Charenton Under the Direction of the Marquis de Sade (55). Revival of the play by Peter Weiss; English version by Geoffrey Skelton; verse adaptation by Adrian Mitchell. Produced by Zev Bufman in The National Players Company Production at the Majestic Theater. Opened January 3, 1967. (Closed February 18, 1967)

M. Coulmier ....Stephen Elliott
Mme. Coulmier ....Barbara Cason
Marquis de Sade ....William Roerick
Herald ....Douglas Watson
Jean-Paul Marat ....Dennis Patrick
Simonne Evrard ....Shellie Feldman
Charlotte Corday ....Verna Bloom
Duperret ....Jered Barclay
Jacques Roux ....Robert Fields
Cucurucu ....Leonard Drum

Polpoch ....Igors Gavon
Kokol ....Gerard Russak
Rossignol ....Christine Norden
Mad Animal ....Abe Vigoda
Schoolmaster ....James Cahill
Mother ....Fay Chaiken
Father ....Peter Blaxill
Voltaire ....John Tormey
Lavoisier ....Alan Louw

Patients: Fayne Blackburn, Imogene Bliss, Beatrice Brooks, Madlyn Cates, (Louise Clay), Zola Long, Helen F. Ross, Carol Teitel, Geri Wolcott. Nuns: John Toland, Edmond Varrato. Guards: Sam Kirkham, (Robert Keegan). (Actors whose names are listed in parentheses are non-members of the National Players Company)

Standby: Misses Bloom, Feldman—Carol Teitel. Understudies: Mr. Patrick—Robert Fields; Messrs. Russak, Gavon, Drum—Edmond Varrato; Mr. Elliott—Alan Louw; Mr. Barclay— James Cahill; Mr. Watson—Peter Blaxill; Mr. Fields—John Tormey.

Musicians: guitar, Bernie Moore; flute-piccolo, Roberta Russell; percussion, Patrick Harrison; trumpet, Frank Emerson.

Directed by Donald Driver; scenery, Edward Burbridge; costumes, Lewis Brown; lighting, Martin Aronstein; music composed by Richard Peaslee; musical director, Rod Derefinko; assistant to the director, Rudy Tronto; stage manager, Robert Keegan; assistant stage manager, Louise Clay; press, Seymour Krawitz, Stan Brody.

Time: The Napoleonic Era. Place: The insane asylum at Charenton in France.

The Royal Shakespeare Company production of this play appeared on Broadway December 27, 1965 for 144 performances. Its title is commonly abbreviated *Marat/Sade* or *Marat/de Sade*. Marat's first name "Jean-Paul" was not included in the full-length title in its previous Broadway production.

* **The Homecoming** (168). By Harold Pinter. Produced by Alexander H. Cohen, by arrangement with the governors of the Royal Shakespeare Theater, Stratford-Upon Avon, England and by arrangement with Theater Guild Productions, Inc., in the Royal Shakespeare Company production at the Music Box. Opened January 5, 1967.

Max ....Paul Rogers
Lenny ....Ian Holm
Sam ....John Normington

Joey ....Terence Rigby
Teddy ....Michael Craig
Ruth ....Vivien Merchant

Understudies: Miss Merchant—Lynn Farleigh; Messrs. Rogers, Normington—Denis Holmes; Messrs. Holm, Craig—Michael Jayston; Mr. Rigby—Lloyd Battista.

Directed by Peter Hall; designed by John Bury; produced in association with Gerry Geraldo; production stage manager, Jake Hamilton; press, James D. Proctor, Max Gendel, Lawrence Belling.

Time: The present, summer. Place: An old house in North London. Act I: Evening. Act II: Afternoon.

A college professor brings his wife home to meet his father (a retired butcher) and his brothers (a pimp and a boxer). She is a mother-wife-whore symbol who is persuaded not to return home with her husband, but to remain in this household to be enjoyed by all its men. A foreign play previously produced in London.

Lynn Farleigh replaced Vivien Merchant 4/24/67. Michael Jayston replaced Ian Holm 4/24/67.

A Best Play; see page 260

The Astrakhan Coat (20). By Pauline Macaulay. Produced by David Merrick at the Helen Hayes Theater. Opened January 12, 1967. (Closed January 28, 1967)

James ....Brian Bedford
Twins
    Barbara ....Carole Shelley
    Alain . ...Job Stewart

Claud ....Roddy McDowall
Mrs. Tuffin ....Jean Cameron
Inspector Rogers ....James Coco
Sergeant Harris ....Patrick Tull

Standby: Messrs. McDowall, Bedford—D.J. Sullivan. Understudies: Miss Cameron—Margaret Braidwood; Miss Shelley—Carole Gister.

Directed by Donald McWhinnie; scenery and costumes, Lloyd Burlingame; lighting, Martin Aronstein; associate producer, Samuel Liff; production stage manager, Mitchell Erickson; stage manager, Geoffrey Johnson; press, Harvey B. Sabinson, Lee Solters, Jay Russell.

Time: The present. Place: London. Act I, Scene 1: An apartment in a smart block, early evening. Scene 2: A bed-sitting room in World's End, an afternoon some days later. Scene 3: The apartment, that evening. Act II, Scene 1: A room, the next day. Scene 2: A police station, the same evening. Scene 3: The Bed-sitting room, later that night.

A thrill-seeking thief and killer and his twin assistants make a fall guy out of a gullible young waiter and leave him to take the blame for their crimes. A foreign play previously produced in Nottingham, England.

Come Live With Me (4). By Lee Minoff and Stanley Price. Produced by Helen Bonfils and Morton Gottlieb at the Billy Rose Theater. Opened January 26, 1967. (Closed January 28, 1967)

Joanna	Marion Gray	Colette	Yvonne Constant
Chuck Clark	Soupy Sales	Milton Rademacher	Sorrell Booke
Tristram Hawkins	Michael Allinson	A Visitor	Nan Martin
Ingeborg	Hanne Bork		

Standby: Miss Gray—Susan Willis. Understudies: Misses Bork, Constant—Marion Gray; Messrs. Allinson, Booke—Eugene Stuckmann.

Directed by Joshua Shelley; production associate, Jonathan Miller; scenery and lighting, William Ritman; costumes, Patton Campbell; production stage manager, Warren Crane; stage manager, Eugene Stuckmann; press, Dorothy Ross, Mort Nathanson, Michael Gershman.

Time: The present, summer. Place: Chuck Clark's living room, London S.W. 1. Act I, Scene 1: A morning. Scene 2: An early evening. Act II, Scene 1: Later that same evening. Scene 2: The next morning.

Comedy about a writer living in London in a flat also occupied by a beautiful aupair; then visited, most inconveniently, by his divorced wife.

The Paisley Convertible (9). By Harry Cauley. Produced by Michael Ellis at Henry Miller's Theater. Opened February 11, 1967. (Closed February 18, 1967)

Amy Rodgers	Joyce Bulifant	Meg Tynan	Marsha Hunt
Charlie Rodgers	Bill Bixby	Sylvia Greer	Betsy von Furstenberg
Ralph Keppleman	Jed Allan		

Understudies: Miss Hunt—Jen Nelson; Misses von Furstenberg, Bulifant—Mary Rausch; Messrs. Bixby, Allan—Richard Hoffman.

Directed by James Hammerstein; scenery and lighting, Jo Mielziner; costumes, Alvin Colt; production stage manager, Perry Bruskin; press, David Rothenberg, Joel Kudler.

Time: The present. Place: The one-room apartment of Charlie and Amy Rodgers in the East Seventies, in New York City. Act I: June, 4 p.m. Act II: Later that day. Act III: Early the next morning.

Comedy of newlyweds (he's an interne) coping with their former fiances and the bride's mother.

* Black Comedy and White Lies (125). By Peter Shaffer. Produced by Alexander H. Cohen at the Ethel Barrymore Theater. Opened February 12, 1967.

WHITE LIES

Sophie: Baroness Lemberg	Geraldine Page	Tom	Michael Crawford
Frank	Donald Madden		

BLACK COMEDY

Brindsley Miller	Michael Crawford	Harold Gorringe	Donald Madden
Carol Melkett	Lynn Redgrave	Schuppanzigh	Pierre Epstein
Miss Furnival	Camila Ashland	Clea	Geraldine Page
Colonel Melkett	Peter Bull	Georg Bamberger	Michael Miller

Standbys: Miss Page (as Sophie)—Margaret Phillips; Mr. Madden—Alan Mixon. Understudies: Mr. Crawford—John Horn; Misses Redgrave, Page, Ashland—Nancy Reardon; Messrs. Bull, Epstein—Michael Miller.

Directed by John Dexter; scenery and costumes, Alan Tagg; lighting, Jules Fisher; production associate, Hildy Parks; associate producer, Sidney Lanier; production supervisor, Jerry Adler; production stage manager, Randall Brooks; stage manager, Robert Borod; press, James D. Proctor, Max Gendel, Lawrence Belling.

WHITE LIES—Time: The present, around six o'clock in the evening, mid-September. Place: The Fortune Teller's Parlor of Sophie, Baroness Lemberg, on the promenade of a run-down seaside resort on the south coast of England. BLACK COMEDY—Time: 9:30 on a Sunday night. Place: Brindsley Miller's apartment in South Kensington, London.

WHITE LIES, the opening play written expressly for this Broadway production, is about a fortune teller bribed to influence a client but discovering to her dismay that the "secrets" told her in advance are lies invented by the client himself. BLACK COMEDY is a comedy about the romantic and career problems of a harried young artist. In it (as in a famous classical Chinese theater scene), the lighting reverses reality. The play opens on a pitch dark stage on which the characters can "see" perfectly. Shortly afterward, a fuse blows, and the stage becomes fully lighted to the audience but is now "dark" to the stumbling characters. *Black Comedy* is a foreign play commissioned by the National Theater of Great Britain and previously produced in London.

Jennifer Tilston replaced Lynn Redgrave 4/10/67

A Best Play; see page 278

Love in E-Flat (24). By Norman Krasna. Produced by Alfred de Liagre Jr. at the Brooks Atkinson Theater. Opened February 13, 1967. (Closed March 4, 1967)

Howard	Hal Buckley	Stanley	Joe Ponazecki
Amy	Kathleen Nolan	Mr. Cooper	Charles Lane
Bea	Marcia Rodd	Mitchell	Morty Gunty

Understudies: Misses Nolan, Rodd—Gillian Spencer; Messrs. Buckley, Gunty, Ponazecki—Jonathan Bolt; Mr. Lane—Arthur Marlowe.

Directed by George Seaton; scenery and lighting, Donald Oenslager; costumes, Julia Sze; production stage manager, Ben Janney; stage manager, Arthur Marlowe; press, Ben Washer.

Time: The present, mid-June. Place: A converted brownstone on the East Side of New York City. Act I, Scene 1: 10 a.m. Sunday. Scene 2: 1 a.m. the next morning. Act II, Scene 1: 10 p.m. that night. Scene 2: Thursday noon.

Comedy about two lovers, an interne and a school teacher, monitoring each other's apartments with listening devices.

Bristol Old Vic. Repertory of three revivals of plays by William Shakespeare. **Measure for Measure** (7). Opened February 14, 1967. **Hamlet** (9). Opened February 16, 1967. **Romeo and Juliet** (8). Opened February 21, 1967. Produced by S. Hurok at New York City Center. (Repertory closed March 5, 1967).

PERFORMER	"MEASURE FOR MEASURE"	"HAMLET"	"ROMEO AND JULIET"
Jane Asher	Julietta		Juliet
Georgine Anderson	Mariana	1st Court Lady; (Gertrude)	Lady Capulet
Frank Barrie	Lucio	Horatio	Mercutio
Richard Jones Barry	Barnardine	Sailor	Page to Paris
Arthur Blake	Elbow	Rosencrantz	Capulet
Christopher Burgess	Provost	Ghost; 1st Player; Player King	Tybalt
Timothy Davies	Messenger	Francisco	Gregory
Tom Durham	Servant to Angelo	Voltimand	Friar John
Norman Eshley	1st Gentleman	Fortinbras	Paris
Gawn Grainger	Claudio	Laertes	Romeo
Roger Hockley		Cornelius	
Anthony Kyle		Messenger	Apothecary

PERFORMER	"MEASURE FOR MEASURE"	"HAMLET"	"ROMEO AND JULIET"
Barbara Leigh-Hunt	Isabella	Ophelia	
Richard Glyn Lewis	2d Gentleman	Guildenstern	Benvolio
Charles McKeown	Justice		Balthasar
Frank Middlemass	Pompey	Polonius	Chorus; Friar Lawrence
Christopher Miles			Abraham
Joan Morrow		Player Queen; (Ophelia)	
Richard Pasco	Angelo	Hamlet	
John Franklyn Robbins	Duke	Claudius	
Bryan Robson	Friar Thomas	Marcellus; Osric	Escalus
Madge Ryan	Mistress Overdone	Gertrude	Nurse
Christopher Serle	Froth	2d Gravedigger	Peter
Desmond Stokes	Escalus	Barnardo; 1st Gravedigger	Montague
Philip Taylor	Abhorson	Captain	Sampson
Francis Wallis		Player Murderer	
Marcia Warren	Francisca	Lady-in-Waiting	Lady Montague

(Parentheses indicate roles which the actor understudies)

Monks, Gaolers, Courtiers, Magnificos, Prisoners, Whores in *Measure for Measure:* Joan Morrow, Judy Matheson, Janet Key, Diana Berriman, Francis Wallis, Clark Kirby, Christopher Miles, Richard Jones Barry, Anthony Kyle, Tom Durham, Timothy Davies, Roger Hockley, Philip Taylor, Charles McKeown, Norman Eshley, Richard Glyn Lewis.

Courtiers, Soldiers, Messengers, Players in *Hamlet:* Judy Matheson, Janet Key, Diana Berriman, Joan Morrow, Francis Wallis, Clark Kirby, Christopher Miles, Richard Jones Barry, Anthony Kyle, Tom Durham, Timothy Davies, Roger Hockley, Philip Taylor, Charles McKeown, Norman Eshley, Christopher Serle.

Citizens, Kinsfolk of both Houses, Guards, Watchmen, Servants and Attendants in *Romeo and Juliet:* Tom Durham, Anthony Kyle, Christopher Miles, Roger Hockley, Timothy Davies, Charles McKeown, Philip Taylor, Patrick Black, Joan Morrow, Janet Key, Diana Berriman, Francis Wallis, Clark Kirby, Judy Matheson.

Bristol Old Vic director, Val May; general manager, Douglas Morris; lighting, Kenneth Vowles; production stage manager, John L. Moorehead; stage manager, Derek Rye; press, Martin Feinstein, Michael Sweeley.

MEASURE FOR MEASURE directed by Tyrone Guthrie; scenery and costumes, Graham Barlow; assistant to director, Rob Knights; music arranged by John Oxley.

Measure for Measure was produced in New York previously this season, by the New York Shakespeare Festival at the Delacorte Theater. Off-Broadway productions took place in 1957, 1959-60 and 1963.

HAMLET directed by Val May; scenery, Graham Barlow; costumes, Audrey Price; fights, Patrick Crean.

Recent Hamlets in New York were Richard Burton's on Broadway in 1964 and Alfred Ryder's, later Robert Burr's, in the New York Shakespeare Festival 1964 summer outdoor production.

ROMEO AND JULIET directed by Val May; scenery and costumes, Catherine Browne; fights, Patrick Crean; music, Sidney Sager; dance arranged by Bob Stevenson; assistant to director, Rob Knights.

Romeo and Juliet was last presented on Broadway in 1962 by the Old Vic. It was produced in the summer of 1965 in a Spanish-language mobile unit production by the New York Shakespeare Festival.

Of Love Remembered (9). By Arnold Sundgaard. Produced by Arthur Cantor and Nicholas Vanoff (Ltd.) at the ANTA Theater. Opened February 18, 1967. (Closed February 25, 1967)

Lars	William Traylor	The Father	George Gaynes
Ansgar	Toralv Maurstad	Karl	James Olson
Inga	Ingrid Thulin	Hazel	Janet Ward

Understudies: Misses Thulin, Ward—Pat Sales; Messrs. Maurstad, Gaynes, Traylor—Douglas Easley; Mr. Olson—John Kramer.

Directed by Burgess Meredith; scenery and lighting, Eldon Elder; costumes, Saul Bolasni; original music, Michel Legrand; associate director, David Winters; production manager, Stephen Gardner; production associate, Barbara Rhodes; produced in association with Santa Fe Productions, Inc.; stage manager, William Chambers; press, Artie Solomon, Irene Pinn.

Time: Beginning with the present. Place: Minnesota in the present and Norway in the past. The action takes place without intermission.

Drama of fifty years in the lives of a Norwegian family, which has moved to St. Paul, Minn., is focussed on a woman's three loves.

The Natural Look (1). By Lee Thuna. Produced by David Black and Lorin E. Price in association with Susan Slade, in Helen Harvey's production at the Longacre Theater. Opened and closed at the evening performance March 11, 1967.

Reedy Harris	Brenda Vaccaro	Edna	Doris Roberts
Dr. Barney Harris	Gene Hackman	Countess	Ethel Griffies
Norman Carmichael	Patrick Baldauff	Jane Fenice	Zohra Lampert
Stever Kenny	Dolph Sweet	Addison Demas	Andreas Voutsinas
Malcolm	Jerry Orbach		

Directed by Martin Fried; scenery, Ed Wittstein; costumes, Patton Campbell; lighting, Jules Fisher; production manager, Jose Vega; stage manager, Gene Perlowin; press, Frank Goodman, Martin Shwartz.

Time: The present. Place: The bedroom of the Harris' apartment on Park Avenue and Reedy's office at Contessa Cosmetics, Inc. Act I, Scene 1: The middle of the night, between Sunday and Monday. Scene 2: The next morning. Scene 3: That evening. Act II, Scene 1: The next morning. Scene 2: The next morning. Scene 3: That afternoon. Scene 4: That evening.

Comedy about a working wife, in the beauty business, striving to hold both job and husband.

* You Know I Can't Hear You When the Water's Running (92). Program of four one-act plays by Robert Anderson: *The Shock of Recognition, The Footsteps of Doves, I'll Be Home for Christmas* and *I'm Herbert*. Produced by Jack Farren and Gilbert Cates at the Ambassador Theater. Opened March 13, 1967.

THE SHOCK OF RECOGNITION

Jack Barnstable	George Grizzard	Dorothy	Melinda Dillon
Herb Miller	Joe Silver	Richard Pawling	Martin Balsam

THE FOOTSTEPS OF DOVES

Salesman	George Grizzard	George	Martin Balsam
Harriet	Eileen Heckart	Jill	Melinda Dillon

I'LL BE HOME FOR CHRISTMAS

Chuck	Martin Balsam	Clarice	Melinda Dillon
Edith	Eileen Heckart		

I'M HERBERT

Herbert	George Grizzard	Muriel	Eileen Heckart

Standbys: Miss Heckart—Frances Sternhagen; Miss Dillon—Carolyn Groves; Mr. Grizzard—Robert Darnell.

Directed by Alan Schneider; scenery, Ed Wittstein; costumes, Theoni V. Aldredge; lighting, Jules Fisher; production stage manager, Mark Wright; stage manager, Robert D. Currie; press, Lee Solters, Harvey B. Sabinson, Robert Ullman.

Time: The present. Place: *The Shock of Recognition*—A producer's office. *The Footsteps of Doves*—A basement showroom of a bedding store. *I'll Be Home for Christmas*—An apartment living room and kitchen. *I'm Herbert*—A side porch.

In *The Shock of Recognition*, a playwright wants to place a naked man on the stage and interviews an eager-beaver actor for the role. In *The Footsteps of Doves*, a middle-aged wife drives her husband into a younger woman's arms by insisting on switching from a double to twin beds. *I'll Be Home for Christmas* is a husband-wife quarrel in which the emptiness of a marriage is exposed as they fight over the welfare and discipline of their children. *I'm Herbert* is a rocking-chair reminiscence by an aged couple who can remember love but not the identity of their former lovers.

A Best Play; see page 314

That Summer—That Fall (12). By Frank D. Gilroy. Produced by Edgar Lansbury at the Helen Hayes Theater. Opened March 16, 1967. (Closed March 25, 1967)

Angelina Capuano	Irene Pappas	Josie	Tyne Daly
Steve	Jon Voight	Victor	Richard Castellano
Zia	Elena Karam		

Standby: Miss Pappas—Eileen Yohn. Understudies: Mr. Castellano—Peter Gumeny; Mr. Voight—Robert Gentry; Miss Daly—Elizabeth Berger.

Directed by Ulu Grosbard; scenery and lighting, Jo Mielziner; costumes, Theoni V. Aldredge; music composed and conducted by David Amram; produced in association with TDJ Productions Inc.; production stage manager, Del Hughes; press, Samuel J. Friedman, Marvin Kohn.

Time: The present. Place: New York City. Act I, Scene 1: Part of a playground in Lower Manhattan. Scene 2: The Capuanos' apartment. Scene 3: 3 a.m. the next morning. Scene 4: Afternoon, a week later. Scene 5: 11 a.m. the next morning. Scene 6: 5 p.m. the same day. Scene 7: Midnight, several days later. Scene 8: Several nights later. Act II, Scene 1: 8 p.m. the night of the dance. Scene 2: Three hours later. Scene 3: The next morning. Scene 4: Late that night. Scene 5: The playground.

The tragedy of Phaedra transposed to a modern Italian family; the wife falls in love with her stepson and kills herself, then the stepson follows her in death.

Sherry! (72). Musical based on *The Man Who Came to Dinner* by George S. Kaufman and Moss Hart; book and lyrics by James Lipton; music by Laurence Rosenthal. Produced by Lee Guber, Frank Ford and Shelly Gross at the Alvin Theater. Opened March 27, 1967. (Closed May 27, 1967)

Daisy Stanley	Mary Loane	Harriet Stanley	Paula Trueman
Miss Preen	Janet Fox	Bert Jefferson	Jon Cypher
John	Merritt Smith	Lorraine Sheldon	Dolores Gray
Sarah	Barbara Webb	Cosette	June Lynn Compton
Maggie Cutler	Elizabeth Allen	Beverly Carlton	Byron Webster
Ernest W. Stanley	Donald Burr	Westcott	Haydon Smith
Dr. Bradley	Cliff Hall	Banjo	Eddie Lawrence
Sheridan Whiteside	Clive Revill	Ginger	Leslie Franzos

Ensemble: Diane Arnold, Edie Cowan, Carol Estey, Leslie Franzos, Altovise Gore, Carol Hanzel, Carol Perea, Peter De Nicola, Frank De Sal, Luigi Gasparinetti, Roger Allan Raby, Haydon Smith, Doug Spingler, Ted Sprague, Lucille Blackton, June Lynn Compton, Rita Metzger, Jeannette Seibert, Trudy Wallace, Herb Fields, Del Hinkley, Joe Kirkland, Duane Morris, Clyde Williams, Denise Nickerson, Glenn Dufford, Robert Fitch.

Standbys: Mr. Revill—Byron Webster; Misses Gray, Allen—Roberta MacDonald. Understudies: Mr. Cypher—Del Hinkley; Mr. Webster—Duane Morris; Miss Fox—June Lynn Compton; Messrs. Hall, Burr—Joe Kirkland; Miss Trueman—Jeannette Seibert; Miss Loane—Rita Metzger; Miss Webb—Altovise Gore; Mr. Smith—Clyde Williams; Mr. Lawrence—Herb Fields.

Directed by Joe Layton; scenery and lighting, Robert Randolph; costumes, Robert Mackintosh; musical direction and vocal arrangements, Jay Blackton; dance arrangements, John Morris; associate producer, Marvin A. Krauss; production stage manager, Michael Thoma; stage manager, John Actman; press, Saul Richman.

Time: Between December 10 and Christmas Day, 1938. Place: Mesalia, Ohio.

The Kaufman-Hart comedy version of this story of an international literary celebrity stranded in suburban Ohio opened October 16, 1939. It was named a Best Play of its season and played 739 performances.

ACT I

Scene 1: The Stanley living room
"In the Very Next Moment" ....Maggie, Daisy, John, Sarah, Ensemble
"Why Does the Whole Damn World Adore Me?" ....Whiteside
Scene 2: Township of Mesalia
"Maggie's Date" ....Maggie, Bert, Ensemble
Scene 3: Exterior Stanley residence
"Maybe It's Time for Me" ....Maggie
Scene 4: The Stanley library
"How Can You Kiss Those Good Times Goodby" ....Whiteside, Maggie
Scene 5: A jewelry shop
"With This Ring" ....Maggie, Bert, Whiteside
Scene 6: The Stanley living room
"Sherry" ....Lorraine, Whiteside
"Au Revoir" ....Beverly
Scene 7: Mansion House Hotel in Mesalia
"Proposal Duet" ....Lorraine, Beverly
"Listen Cosette" ....Lorraine, Cosette
Scene 8: The Stanley living room
"Christmas Eve Broadcast" ....Whiteside, Lorraine, Ensemble

ACT II

Scene 1: Billy's tavern
"Putty in Your Hands" ....Lorraine, Ensemble
Scene 2: The Stanley solarium
"Imagine That" ....Maggie, Whiteside
Scene 3: The Stanley library
"Marry the Girl Myself" ....Whiteside, Maggie, Banjo, Ginger, Ensemble
Scene 4: The Stanley living room
"Putty in Your Hands" (Reprise) ....Lorraine, Whiteside, Banjo
"Harriet Sedley" ....Whiteside, Banjo, Mr. Stanley
"Sherry" (Reprise) ....Company

Hello, Solly! (68). American Yiddish musical revue. Produced by Hal Zeiger at Henry Miller's Theater. Opened April 4, 1967. (Closed May 28, 1967)

Mickey Katz   Stan Porter
Larry Best   Little Tanya
Michael (Getzel) Rosenberg

Musical director, Al Hausman; press, David Lipsky, Lisa Lipsky.
Act I, Scene 1: Overture. Scene 2: Mickey Katz. Scene 3: Little Tanya. Scene 4: Larry Best. Act II, Scene 1: Stan Porter. Scene 2: Michael Rosenberg. Scene 3: Finale.
A collection of acts in the vaudeville tradition, with a few Yiddish phrases contained in the occasional dialogue (in English).

* The New York City Center Light Opera Company spring season of three musical revivals. **Finian's Rainbow** (23). Book by E.Y. Harburg and Fred Saidy; music by Burton Lane; lyrics by E.Y. Harburg. Opened April 5, 1967 (Closed April 23, 1967). **The Sound of Music** (23). Book by Howard Lindsay and Russel Crouse; suggested by *The Trapp Family Singers* by Maria Augusta Trapp; music by Richard Rodgers; lyrics by Oscar Hammerstein II. Opened April 26, 1967. (Closed May 14, 1967). *** Wonderful Town** (17). Book by Joseph Fields and Jerome Chodorov; music by Leonard Bernstein; lyrics by Betty Comden and

Adolph Green. Opened May 17, 1967. Produced by The New York City Center Light Opera Company, Jean Dalrymple director, at New York City Center.

FINIAN'S RAINBOW

Sunny (Harmonica Player) ....Elliot Levine	1st Geologist ....Ronald B. Stratton
Buzz Collins ....Ronn Carroll	2d Geologist ....Clark Salonis
Sheriff ....Howard Fischer	Howard ....Jim McMillan
1st Sharecropper ....John Dorrin	Diane ....Ellen Hansen
2d Sharecropper ....Laried Montgomery	Mr. Robust ....Austin Colyer
Susan Mahoney ....Sandy Duncan	Mr. Shears ....Paul Adams
Henry ....Kevin Featherstone	1st Passion Pilgrim Gospeler .....Jerry Laws
Maude ....Carol Brice	2d Passion Pilgrim Gospeler ...Tiger Haynes
Finian McLonergan ....Frank McHugh	3d Passion Pilgrim Gospeler ..John McCurry
Sharon McLonergan ....Nancy Dussault	1st Deputy ....Paul Eichel
Woody Mahoney ....Stanley Grover	2d Deputy ....Joey Carow
Og (A Leprechaun) ....Len Gochman	John The Preacher ....Garwood Perkins
Senator Billboard Rawkins ..Howard I. Smith	

Singers: Barbara Christopher, Jane Coleman, Mary Falconer, Ellen Harris, Ernestine Jackson, Mina Jo King, Joyce McDonald, Dixie Stewart, Alyce Elizabeth Webb, Paul Adams, Austin Colyer, John Dorrin, Paul Eichel, Doug Hunt, Elliot Levine, Laried Montgomery, Garrett Morris, Garwood Perkins, Clark Salonis, Grant Spradling.

Dancers: Mary Barnett, Josetta Cherry, Joanna Crosson, Joanne De Vito, Ruth Lawrence, Sally Lou Lee, Joy Serio, Toodie Wittmer, Mary Zahn, Guy Allen, Bjarne Buchtrup, Joey Carow, Dennis Edenfield, Jerry Fries, Garold Gardner, Ted Goodridge, Mark Holliday, Bob La Crosse, Ronald B. Stratton, Mark Scott.

Children: Ellen Hansen, Lisa Huggins, Tom Brooke, Kevin Featherstone, William Sims.

Standby: Mr. Gochman—Art Ostrin. Understudies: Mr. McHugh—Ronn Carroll; Miss Dussault—Ellen Harris; Mr. Grover—Paul Eichel; Miss Brice—Alyce Webb; Miss Duncan—Ruth Lawrence; Mr. Fischer—John Dorrin; Mr. Smith—Howard Fischer; Mr. Carroll—Laried Montgomery; Mr. McMillan—Ted Goodridge; Mr. Featherstone—William Sims.

Directed by Gus Schirmer; music director, Jonathan Anderson; choreographer, Betty Hyatt Linton; scenery, Howard Bay; costumes, Frank Thompson; lighting, Peggy Clark; production stage manager, Herman Shapiro; stage managers, Forrest Carter, Herman Magidson; press, Homer Poupart.

Time: The present. Place: Rainbow Valley, Missitucky, U.S.A. Act I, Scene 1: The Meetin' Place. Scene 2: The same, that night. Scene 3: The Colonial estate of Senator Billboard Rawkins, the next morning. Scene 4: The Meetin' Place, the following day. Scene 5: A path in the woods. Scene 6: The Meetin' Place, next morning. Act II, Scene 1: Rainbow Valley, a few weeks later. Scene 2: A wooded section of the hills. Scene 3: The Meetin' Place. Scene 4: Just before dawn.

Finian's Rainbow was first produced January 10, 1947 at the Forty-sixth Street Theater for 725 performances. It was revived for 27 performances April 27, 1960 by The New York City Center Light Opera Company.

ACT I

"This Time of Year" ....Singing Ensemble
Dance ....Susan, Dance Ensemble
"How Are Things in Glocca Morra?" ....Sharon
"Look to the Rainbow" ....Sharon, Woody, Singing Ensemble
"Old Devil Moon" ....Woody, Sharon
"How Are Things in Glocca Morra?" (Reprise) ....Sharon
"Something Sort of Grandish" ....Og, Sharon
"If This Isn't Love" ....Woody, Sharon, Finian, Singing, Dancing Ensembles
Dance ....Susan
   (Three Couples—Joy Serio, Garold Gardner, Mary Zahn, Bjarne Buchtrup, Joanna Crosson, Joey Carow; The Chase Couple—Sally Lou Lee, Dennis Edenfield; The Adolescents—Joanne De Vito, Mark Scott; The Timids—Toodie Wittmer, Ronald B. Stratton; The Hep Cats—Josetta Cherry, Ted Goodridge; Triangle—Sandy Duncan, Ruth Lawrence, Sally Lou Lee, Bjarne Buchtrup, Dennis Edenfield, Bob La Crosse; Others—Mary Barnett, Joy Serio, Guy Allen, Joey Carow)

"Something Sort of Grandish" (Reprise) ....Og
"Necessity" ....Maude, Singing Ensemble
"Great Come-and-Get-It Day" ....Woody, Sharon, Singing, Dancing Ensembles

ACT II

"When the Idle Poor Become the Idle Rich"
  Dance ....Susan, Dance Ensemble
  Song ....Sharon, Singing Ensemble
"Old Devil Moon" (Reprise) ....Sharon, Woody
Dance of the Golden Crock ....Susan
"The Begat" ....Three Passion Pilgrim Gospelers
"Look to the Rainbow" (Reprise) ....Sharon, Woody, Singing Ensemble
"When I'm Not Near the Girl I Love" ....Og, Susan
"If This Isn't Love" (Reprise) ....Entire Ensemble
Finale: "How Are Things in Glocca Morra?" (Reprise) ....Sharon, Entire Company

THE SOUND OF MUSIC

Maria Rainer	Constance Towers	Brigitta	Dawn Sherwood
Sister Berthe	Jessica Quinn	Marta	Mindy Sherwood
Sister Margaretta	Nadine Lewis	Gretl	Robin Sherwood
The Mother Abbess	Eleanor Steber	Rolf Gruber	Reid Klein
Sister Sophia	Bernice Saunders	Elsa Schraeder	M'el Dowd
Captain Georg von Trapp	Bob Wright	Ursula	Alison Sherwood
Franz	Jim Oyster	Max Detweiler	Christopher Hewett
Frau Schmidt	Helen Noyes	Herr Zeller	Larry Swanson
Liesl	Sandy Duncan	Baron Elberfield	Grant Gordon
Friedrich	Gary Hamilton	A Postulant	Kyle Sherwood
Louisa	Holly Sherwood	Admiral von Schreiber	Jay Velie
Kurt	Eric Hamilton		

Neighbors, Nuns, Novices, Postulants, Contestants in Festival Concert, Storm Troopers: Mona Elson, Susan Feldon, Barbara Gregory, Joy Ellyn Holly, Oksana Iwaszczenko, Patti Kogin, Estella Munson, Marilyn Murphy, Joyce Olson, Candida Pilla, Mary Ann Rydzeski, Ellen Shade, Ann Tell, Beverley Jane Welch, Maggie Worth, Bill Galarno, Garold Gardner.

Standby: Mr. Wright—Webb Tilton. Understudies: Miss Quinn—Ellen Shade; Miss Towers— Estella Munson; Miss Saunders—Joyce Olson; Miss Lewis—Beverley Jane Welch; Miss Steber —Nadine Lewis; Messrs. Swanson, Velie—Grant Gordon; Miss Noyes—Ann Tell; Miss Duncan —Kyle Sherwood; Messrs. Gary and Eric Hamilton—Kevin Hamilton; Misses Holly, Dawn, Mindy and Robin Sherwood—Alison Sherwood; Mr. Klein—Bill Galarno; Miss Dowd—Maggie Worth; Mr. Hewett—Jay Velie; Mr. Gordon—Garold Gardner.

Directed by John Fearnley; musical numbers staged by Reid Klein; musical director, Frederick Rudolph Dvonch; scenery, Oliver Smith; costumes, Stanley Simmons; lighting, Peggy Clark; orchestrations, Robert Russell Bennett; choral arrangements, Trude Rittman; production stage manager, Chet O'Brien; stage managers, Bill Field, Sean Cunningham.

Time: 1938. Place: Austria.

The Sound of Music was first produced November 16, 1959 at the Lunt-Fontanne Theater and became Broadway's fourth longest-run musical, with 1,443 performances. This is its first revival.

Synopsis of scenes and list of musical numbers in *The Sound of Music* appear in its Broadway entry beginning on page 303 of the 1959-60 *Best Plays* volume.

WONDERFUL TOWN

Guide	Austin Colyer	Ruth	Elaine Stritch
Appopolous	Ted Thurston	A Strange Man	Richard Miller
Lonigan	Ronn Carroll	Drunks	Ben Laney, Henry Lawrence
Helen	Betsy von Furstenberg	Robert Baker	Nolan Van Way
Wreck	Jack Knight	Associate Editors	Paul Adams,
Violet	Betty Hyatt Linton		Michael Harrison
Speedy Valenti	George Marcy	Mrs. Wade	Claire Waring
Eileen	Linda Bennett	Frank Lippencott	Jack Fletcher

Chef ....Marvin Goodis	Shore Patrolman ....Edward Taylor
Waiter ....Henry LeClair	1st Cadet ....Tim Ramirez
Delivery Boy ....Ronny Headrick	2d Cadet ....Vito Durante
Chick Clark ....Richard France	Ruth's Escort ....Stokely Gray

Greenwich Villagers—Singers: Maria Bradley, Jacqueline Dean, Mona Elson, Joan Nelson, Barbara Miller, Susan Stockwell, Peggy Walthen, Alyce Elizabeth Webb, Maggie Worth, Paul Adams, Austin Colyer, Marvin Goodis, Stokely Gray, Michael Harrison, Ben Laney, Henry Lawrence, Henry LeClair, Richard Miller, Edward Taylor. Dancers: Bonnie Ano, Patty Cope, Judith Dunford, Shelley Frankel, Judith Haskell, Ellie Knowles, Ina Kurland, Kuniko Narai, Mary Ann Niles, Guy Allen, Rodd Barry, George Bunt, Vito Durante, Raphael Gilbert, Ronny Headrick, Dan Joel, Tim Ramirez, Tony Stevens.

Understudies: Messrs. Colyer, Taylor—Paul Adams; Mr. Thurston—Ronn Carroll; Miss von Furstenberg—Maria Bradley; Mr. Knight—Richard Miller; Miss Linton—Mary Ann Niles; Mr. Marcy—Vito Durante; Miss Bennett—Joan Nelson; Miss Stritch—Evelyn Page; Mr. Van Way—Stokely Gray; Messrs. Adams, Harrison—Ben Laney; Miss Waring—Maggie Worth; Messrs. Fletcher, Gray—Austin Colyer; Mr. Headrick—Tony Stevens; Mr. France—George Marcy.

Directed by Gus Schirmer; musical numbers and dances staged by Ralph Beaumont; musical director, Irving Actman; scenery, Raoul Pène du Bois; lighting, Peggy Clark; costumes, Frank Thompson; production stage manager, Herman Shapiro; stage managers, Bill Field, Forrest Carter.

Time: The 1930s. Place: New York City. Act I, Scene 1: Christopher Street. Scene 2: The studio. Scene 3: The street. Scene 4: Baker's office. Scene 5: The street. Scene 6: The backyard. Scene 7: The Navy Yard. Scene 8: The backyard. Act II, Scene 1: The jail. Scene 2: The street. Scene 3: The studio. Scene 4: The street in front of the Vortex. Scene 5: The Vortex.

Wonderful Town is based on the play *My Sister Eileen* by Joseph Fields and Jerome Chodorov, and on stories by Ruth McKenny. It was first produced on Broadway by Robert Fryer on February 25, 1953, for 559 performances. It was revived by The New York City Center Light Opera Company March 5, 1958 for 16 performances and February 13, 1963 for 16 performances.

ACT I

"Christopher Street" ....Guide, Tourists, Villagers
"Ohio" ....Ruth, Eileen
"Conquering New York" ....Ruth, Eileen, Villagers
"One Hundred Easy Ways" ....Ruth
"What a Waste" ....Robert Baker, Associate Editors
Story Vignettes (By Miss Comden and Mr. Green)
    Rexford ....Stokely Gray
    Mr. Mallory ....Henry LeClair
    Danny ....Marvin Goodis
    Trent ....Austin Colyer
and Elaine Stritch

"A Little Bit in Love" ....Eileen
"Pass the Football" ....Wreck, Villagers
"Conversation Piece" ....Ruth, Eileen, Frank Lippencott, Robert Baker, Chick Clark
"A Quiet Girl" ....Robert Baker
"Conga" ....Ruth, Cadets

ACT II

"My Darlin' Eileen" ....Eileen, Police
"Swing" ....Ruth, Villagers
"Ohio" (Reprise) ....Ruth, Eileen
"It's Love" ....Robert Baker, Villagers
"Village Vortex Blues" ....Villagers
"Wrong Note Rag" ....Ruth, Eileen, Villagers
"It's Love" (Reprise) ....The Company

* **Illya Darling** (59). Musical based on the movie *Never on Sunday;* book by Jules Dassin; music by Manos Hadjidakis; lyrics by Joe Darion. Produced by Kermit Bloomgarden in association with United Artists at the Mark Hellinger Theater. Opened April 11, 1967.

Yorgo	Titos Vandis	Forward Sailor	Joseph Corby
Costa	Thomas Raskin	Timid Sailor	Robert La Tourneaux
Workman	Dom Angelo	Vassily	Joe E. Marks
Tonio	Nikos Kourkoulos	Voula	Lou Rodgers
Captain	Rudy Bond	Kiki	Sandy Ellen
Illya	Melina Mercouri	Cassandra	Gloria Lambert
Homer Thrace	Orson Bean	Playgoer	Nick Athas
Waiter	Harold Gary	Drama Critic	Fred Burrell
Garbage	William Duell	Wife	Del Green
Despo	Despo	No Face	Hal Linden
Musician	Joe Alfasa	Bodyguard	Harry Kalkanis
Little Man; Bodyguard	Gerrit de Beer	The Other Girl	Ann Barry

Ensemble: Ann Barry, Sandy Ellen, Del Green, Eileen Joy Haber, Suzanne Horn, Robert La Tourneaux, Urylee Leonardos, Lou Rodgers, Arthur Shaffer, Maria Strattin, Martin Allen, Dom Angelo, Lonnie Davis, Marcelo Gamboa, Louis Genevrino, Nat Horne, Harry Kalkanis, Robert Karl, Juleste Salve, Bill Starr, Mitch Thomas, Terry Violino, Nick Athas, Edward Becker, Alvin Cohen, Joseph Corby, Gerrit de Beer, Johnny LaMotta, Stephen Lardas, Thomas Raskin, Loukas Skipitaris.

Standby: Miss Mercouri—Fleury D'Antonakis. Understudies: Mr. Bean—Fred Burrell; Messrs. Vandis, Bond, Linden—Harold Gary; Mr. Kourkoulos—Hal Linden; Despo—Gloria Lambert; Messrs. Duell, Marks—Joe Alfasa.

Directed by Jules Dassin; dance and musical numbers staged by Onna White; musical direction, Karen Gustafson; scenery, Oliver Smith; lighting, Jean Rosenthal; costumes, Theoni V. Aldredge; orchestrations, Ralph Burns; dance music arranged by Roger Adams; assistant choreographer, Tommy Panko; production stage manager, Don Doherty; bouzouki soloist, Harry Lemonopoulos; stage manager, Bert Wood; press, James D. Proctor, Max Gendel, Lawrence Belling.

Time: The present. Place: The port of Piraeus in Greece. Act I, Scene 1: A shipyard in Piraeus. Scene 2: A bouzouki place. Scene 3: Illya's bedroom. Scene 4: Outside Illya's house. Scene 5: Seaside. Scene 6: Shipyard. Scene 7: Illya's apartment. Scene 8: The Acropolis. Scene 9: The bouzouki place. Scene 10: Illya's bedroom. Act II, Scene 1: Illya's apartment. Scene 2: Outside Illya's house. Scene 3: Illya's bedroom. Scene 4: A street in Piraeus. Scene 5: Illya's apartment. Scene 6: Street of the Girls. Scene 7: The bouzouki place. Scene 8: The port.

The musical's book is based on Jules Dassin's 1960 movie *Never on Sunday* about a popular Greek prostitute (also played on the screen by Melina Mercouri) and the American schoolteacher who tries to "rescue" her from the life she loves.

ACT I

"Po, Po, Po" .... Homer, Tonio
Dance .... Ensemble
"Zebekiko" .... Yorgo
"Piraeus, My Love" .... Illya, Men
"Golden Land" .... Homer, Ensemble
"Zebekiko" (Reprise) .... Yorgo
"Love, Love Love" .... Illya
"I Think She Needs Me" .... Homer
"I'll Never Lay Down Any More" .... Despo
"After Love" .... Tonio
"Birthday Song" .... Tonio, Captain, Men
"Medea Tango" .... Illya, Men
"Illya Darling" .... Illya, Yorgo, Ensemble

ACT II

"Dear Mr. Schubert" ....Illya
"The Lesson" ....Illya, Homer
"Never on Sunday" ....Illya, Ensemble
"Piraeus, My Love" (Reprise) ....Illya
"Medea Tango" (Reprise) ....Tonio
Dance ....Illya, Homer, Yorgo, Tonio, Captain, Vassily, Waiter, Ensemble
"Ya Chara" ....Company

A Warm Body (1). By Lonnie Coleman. Produced by Jeff Britton at the Cort Theater. Opened and closed at the evening performance April 15, 1967.

Kate	Lois Markle	Charles	Franklin Cover
Mrs. Finn	Doris Rich	Sally	Rita McLaughlin
Alan	Will Gregory	Benjamin	Anthony Loder
Audrey	Evelyn Russell	Lola	Dorothy Sefton
Homer	Kevin McCarthy		

Directed by Porter Van Zandt; scenery and lighting, Robert T. Williams; costumes, Anna Hill Johnstone; production associate, Gerald Thomas; production stage manager, Tom Sawyer; stage manager, Mark Healy; press, David Lipsky, Marian Graham.
Time: The present. Place: Kate Moorehead's New York apartment. Act I: 6 p.m. Saturday, early spring. Act II: Late Sunday morning.
A charming and successful archeologist spends the night in the apartment of a cautious and equally successful newspaperwoman.

Little Murders (7). By Jules Feiffer. Produced by Alexander H. Cohen at the Broadhurst Theater. Opened April 25, 1967. (Closed April 29, 1967)

Kenny Newquist	David Steinberg	Alfred Chamberlain	Elliott Gould
Marjorie Newquist	Ruth White	Rev. Henry Dupas	Richard Schaal
Carol Newquist	Heywood Hale Broun	Lt. Miles Practice	Phil Leeds
Patsy Newquist	Barbara Cook		

Guests: Hy Anzell, Elizabeth Huddle, Glenn Kezer, Roy London, Charles Welch, Kate Wilkinson, Ellen Wittman.
Understudies: Miss Cook—Elizabeth Huddle; Mr. Gould—Richard Schaal; Miss White—Kate Wilkinson; Mr. Broun—Glenn Kezer; Messrs. Leeds, Schaal—Charles Welch; Mr. Steinberg—Roy London.
Directed by George L. Sherman; scenery, Ming Cho Lee; costumes, Theoni V. Aldredge; lighting, Jules Fisher; associate producer, Sidney Lanier; production supervisor, Jerry Adler; production associate, Hildy Parks; production stage manager, Jake Hamilton; press, James D. Proctor, Tom Trenkle, Lawrence Belling.
Time: The present. Place: The Newquist apartment in a big city. Act I, Scene 1: An afternoon in February. Scene 2: Two months later. Act II, Scene 1: Four hours later. Scene 2: Six months later.
The world closes in on Carol Newquist and his family, corrupting his son, mating his daughter to a pacifist son-in-law he cannot dominate; finally, bullets fly in through the windows and the Newquists begin to shoot back.

* Hallelujah, Baby! (43). Musical with book by Arthur Laurents; music by Jule Styne; lyrics by Betty Comden and Adolph Green. Produced by Albert W. Selden and Hal James, Jane C. Nusbaum and Harry Rigby at the Martin Beck Theater. Opened April 26, 1967.

Georgina	Leslie Uggams	Calhoun; Bus Driver	Lou Angel
Momma	Lillian Hayman	Mary	Barbara Sharma
Clem	Robert Hooks	Mister Charles; Timmy	Frank Hamilton
Provers	Clifford Allen, Garrett Morris,	Mrs. Charles; Mistress;	
	Kenneth Scott, Alan Weeks	Ethel; Dorothy	Marilyn Cooper
Harvey	Allen Case	Tip and Tap	Winston DeWitt Hemsley,
Captain Yankee	Justin McDonough		Alan Weeks

Cuties ....Hope Clarke, Sandra Lein,
                    Saundra McPherson
Prince ....Bud Vest
Princess ....Carol Flemming
Sugar Daddy; Master ......Darrell Notara
Bouncer; Official ....Chad Block

Director ....Alan Peterson
Brenda ....Ann Rachel
G.I.s ....Winston DeWitt Hemsley, Kenneth
                Scott, Alan Weeks, Clifford Allen
Maid ....Hope Clarke

Ensemble: Clifford Allen, Barbara Andrews, Lou Angel, Chad Block, Hope Clarke, Norma Donaldson, Carol Flemming, Nat Gales, Maria Hero, Lee Hooper, Alan Johnson, Sandra Lein, Justin McDonough, Saundra McPherson, Garrett Morris, Darrell Notara, Paul Reid Roman, Suzanne Rogers, Kenneth Scott, Ella Thompson, Bud Vest.

Standbys: Miss Uggams—Norma Donaldson; Miss Hayman—Alma Hubbard. Understudies: Mr. Hooks—Nat Gales; Mr. Case—Justin McDonough; Miss Sharma—Suzanne Rogers.

Directed by Burt Shevelove; dances and musical numbers staged by Kevin Carlisle; scenery, William and Jean Eckart; costumes, Irene Sharaff; lighting, Tharon Musser; musical direction and vocal arrangements, Buster Davis; orchestrations, Peter Matz; dance orchestrations, Luther Henderson; associate producer, Joe Linhart; assistant choreographers, William Guske, Marie Lake; production stage manager, James Gelb; stage manager, Ernest Austin; press, Merle Debuskey, Violet Welles, Faith Geer.

Time: From the turn of the century until now. Place: In this country.

A determined and talented Negro girl struggles from the kitchen to celebrity and affluence (and, symbolically, to greater freedom) over a period of sixty-odd years in which neither she, her doubting mother, her two lovers (Negro and white) or the other characters age.

ACT I

Introduction
    Prologue ....Georgina
The 1900s: The kitchen
    "Back in the Kitchen" ....Momma
    "My Own Morning" ....Georgina
    "The Slice" ....Clem, Provers
    "Farewell, Farewell" ....Mr. Calhoun, Betty Lou, Captain Yankee, Georgina, Harvey
The 1920s: A cabaret
    "Feet Do Yo' Stuff" ....Georgina, Chorines, Tip and Tap
    "Watch My Dust" ....Clem
    "Smile, Smile" ....Clem, Georgina, Momma
The 1930s: The bread line
    "Witches' Brew" ....Georgina, Mary, Ethel, Company
    Breadline Dance ....Bums
    "Another Day" ....Harvey, Clem, Mary, Georgina
    "I Wanted to Change Him" ....Georgina
    "Being Good Isn't Good Enough" ....Georgina

ACT II

The 1940s: An Army camp; outside a night club
    Dance Drill ....Tip and Tap, G.I.s
    "Talking to Yourself" ....Georgina, Clem, Harvey
    Limbo Dance ....Night Club Patrons
The 1950s: A night club
    "Hallelujah, Baby!" ....Georgina, Tip and Tap
    "Not Mine" ....Harvey
    "I Don't Know Where She Got It" ....Momma, Clem, Harvey
    "Now's the Time" ....Georgina
The 1960s: An apartment
    "Now's the Time" (Reprise) ....Entire Company

The National Repertory Theater. Repertory of three revivals. **The Imaginary Invalid** (6). By Molière; translated by Miles Malleson. Opened May 1, 1967. **A Touch of the Poet** (5). By Eugene O'Neill. Opened May 2, 1967. **Tonight at 8:30**

(5). Program of three one-act plays by Noel Coward: *Ways and Means, Still Life* and *Fumed Oak*. Opened May 3, 1967. Produced by The American National Theater and Academy and Michael Dewell and Frances Ann Dougherty at the ANTA Theater. Repertory closed May 13, 1967)

PERFORMER	"THE IMAGINARY INVALID"	"A TOUCH OF THE POET"	"TONIGHT AT 8:30" Ways and Means	Still Life
Les Barkdull	Apothecary	Paddy O'Dowd	Gaston	Young Man
Joan Bassie	Angelica		Stella	Mildred
John Church	Cleante		Toby	Stanley
Denholm Elliott	Dr. Diaforus	Cornelius		Alec
Joan Force			Nanny	Dolly
Herbert Foster	M. Bonnefoy	Nicholas	Stevens	
Geoff Garland	Dr. Purgon	Mickey		Bill
Patricia Guinan	Louise		Princess	Beryl
Jeanne Hepple	Beline	Sara	Olive	Myrtle
Priscilla Morrill		Nora		Laura
Sloane Shelton	Toinette	Deborah		
Geddeth Smith	Dr. Thomas	Patch	Chaps	Johnnie
John Straub	M. Beralde	Dan	Murdoch	
G. Wood	M. Argan	Jamie		Albert

TONIGHT AT 8:30—*Fumed Oak*

Doris Gow	Sloane Shelton	Mrs. Rockett	Joan Force
Elsie Gow	Patricia Guinan	Henry Gow	Geoff Garland

ALL PLAYS: Scenery, Will Steven Armstrong; costumes, Alvin Colt; lighting, Tharon Musser; production manager, William Armitage; assistant producer, Gina Shield; music, Dean Fuller; stage manager, James Haire; press, Mary Bryant, Bob Pasolli.

THE IMAGINARY INVALID—Directed by Jack Sydow. Time: 1672. Place: The sitting-room of Monsieur Argan's house in Paris. Molière's 17th-century comedy was last performed in New York in French as part of the repertory of Le Théâtre du Nouveau Monde beginning April 29, 1958.

A TOUCH OF THE POET—Directed by Jack Sydow. Time: July 27, 1828. Place: Melody's Tavern in a village a few miles from Boston. This O'Neill play was first produced Oct. 2, 1958 for 284 performances. This is its first Broadway revival.

TONIGHT AT 8:30—*Ways and Means* directed by Nina Foch. Time: 1927. Place: The Villa Zephyr on the Cote d'Azur. *Still Life* directed by Jack Sydow. Time: 1937. Place: Milford Junction Station. *Fumed Oak* directed by G. Wood. Time: 1947. Place: The Gows' house in South London. The program *Tonight at 8:30* was first produced in New York by John C. Wilson on November 24, 1936, for 118 performances (time of the plays is updated for this production). It was revived in the 1945-46 season off Broadway and on Broadway February 20, 1948 for 26 performances.

Sing Israel Sing (14). Musical in the Yiddish language; based on texts and music by Asaf Halevi, Moishe Broderson, M.M. Warshavsky, Wolf Younin, M. Neu, Shlomo Weisfisch, Joel Chayes, E. Kishon, H. Kon; special material by M. Nudelman. Produced by Ben Bonus at the Brooks Atkinson Theater. Opened May 11, 1967. (Closed May 21, 1967—see Note)

PART I—IN THE KIBBUTZ

Guards	Itamar, Ben Bonus
Kibbutz Girls	Mina Bern, Susan Walters
Kibbutz Men	Daniel Franklin, Bernard Sauer
Oldtimers	Max Bozyk, Rose Bozyk

Kibbutzniks ....Hadassah Badoch, Melita Ross, Donna Shadden, Marsha Wolfson,
                    Edward Effron, Tony Masullo, Ralph Nelson, Dance Ensemble
Dora ....Rose Bozyk
David ....Daniel Franklin
Accordionist ....Ami Gilad
The Dream ....Itamar, Hadassah Badoch
  Mazal, The Bride ....Susan Walters
  Companions of The Bride ....Dance Ensemble
  "Only I and You" ....Susan Walters, Daniel Franklin
Encounter No. 1 ....Shmulik Goldstein, Mina Bern
  Bus Station ....Bernard Sauer, Mina Bern
  Dance of The Rain ....Dance Ensemble
  "Song of The Rain" ....Ben Bonus
Encounter No. 2 ....Shmulik Goldstein, Mina Bern
The Law Is the Law
  Policewoman ....Rose Bozyk
  Kibbutznik ....Max Bozyk
  "Meeting" ....Entire Ensemble
  "Sing Israel Sing" ....Ben Bonus

PART II—KUMZITS (A JOYFUL GET-TOGETHER)

Boys' Dance (Debka) ....Itamar, Daniel Franklin, Bernard Sauer, Dance Ensemble
"The Bride Sings" ....Susan Walters
Economists ....Max Bozyk, Shmulik Goldstein
"Reminiscing" ....Ben Bonus
Dances of Many Lands ....Dance Ensemble
Two American Business Women ....Mina Bern, Rose Bozyk
"Bride's Side" ....Hadassah Badoch, Itamar, Tony Masullo, Melita Ross, Donna
              Shadden, Marsha Wolfson, Edward Effron, Ralph Nelson, Dance Ensemble
"Groom's Side"
  Musicians ....Rose Bozyk, Mina Bern, Susan Walters, Shmulik Goldstein
  Fathers-in-Law ....Max Bozyk, Bernard Sauer
  Bride and Groom ....Susan Walters, Daniel Franklin
  Mothers-in-Law ....Mina Bern, Rose Bozyk
"Wedding Dance" ....Entire Ensemble
"Guard of Israel" ....Ben Bonus

Directed by Mina Bern; assistant director and choreographer, Felix Fibich; music arranged
and conducted by Ami Gilad; assistant conductor, Renee Solomon; assistant choreographer,
Judith Fibich; libretto, Wolf Younin; kibbutz envisioned by Sylvia Younin; costume planning,
Judith; production supervisor, Bernard Sauer; press, Max Eisen, Carl Samrock.
  Sing Israel Sing is a mixture of Yiddish and Israeli folklore, humor and art songs tied to-
gether as events taking place in a kibbutz in Israel.
NOTE: Performances of Sing Israel Sing were suspended 5/21/67 to translate the book into
English and add material, for an anticipated reopening in June.

The Girl in the Freudian Slip (4). By William F. Brown. Produced by Michael
Ellis, Frank J. Hale and James B. McKenzie at the Booth Theater. Opened May
18, 1967. (Closed May 20, 1967)

Dr. Dewey Maugham	.........Alan Young	Peter Wellman	...............Bruce Hyde
Paula Maugham	...........Marjorie Lord	Dr. Alec Rice	...............Russell Nype
Leslie Maugham	...........Heather North	Barbara Leonard	.............Susan Brown

Standbys: Messrs. Young, Nype—Peter Turgeon; Misses Lord, Brown—Julie Wilson; Miss
North—Bernadette Peters.
  Directed by Marc Daniels; scenery, Leo B. Meyer; lighting, Clarke Dunham; costumes,
Julia Sze; production stage manager, Gene Perlowin; press, Mary Bryant, Ellen Levene.
  Time: The present, two weeks in March. Place: The New York office-apartment of Dr.
Dewey Maugham. The action is divided into two acts with two scenes in each.
  Comedy about a psychiatrist with sex problems in his home and office life.

PLAYS WHICH CLOSED
PRIOR TO BROADWAY OPENING

Productions which were organized in New York for Broadway presentation, but which closed during their tryout performances out of town or in New York previews, are listed below.

Chu Chem. Musical conceived and written by Ted Allan; music by Mitch Leigh; lyrics by Jack Haines and Jack Wohl. Produced by Cheryl Crawford and Mitch Leigh in a pre-Broadway tryout at the Locust Theater in Philadelphia. Opened November 15, 1966. (Closed November 19, 1966)

The Inhabitants of Kaifeng Fu ....Alvin Ing, Sumiko Murashima, Franklin Siu, Maureen Tionco, Barbara-Jean Wong
The Elder ....Khigh Dhiegh
The Prompter ....Yuki Shimoda
His Assistants .....Chao-li, Haruki Fujimoto, Joel Galietti, Murphy James, Tom Matsusaka
Pink Cloud ....Reiko Sato
Black Cloud Bride ....Tisa Chang
Daffodil ....Joanne Miya
Cherry Stone ....Virginia Wing
Children ...Heather-Jean Lee, Dana Shimizu, Mona Lee Soong, Tracy Michele Lee
The Occidental Actors

Chu Chem ....Menasha Skulnik
Rose ....Henrietta Jacobson
Lotte ....Marcia Rodd
The Mongols
Lord Hoo Hah ....Jack Cole
His Henchmen ....Buzz Miller, J.C. McCord
His Acrobats ....Daniel Cartagena, Bill Starr
The Inhabitants of Ming Province
Prince Eagle ....James Shigeta
His Brother ....Robert Ito
His Bodyguards .....Chuck Morgan, Man Mountain Dean Jr., Leon Spelman

Standbys: Mr. Skulnik—Lou Gilbert; Miss Rodd—Lette Reynolds. Understudies: Mr. Shigeta—Robert Ito; Mr. Cole—Buzz Miller; Misses Wing, Miya—Maureen Tionco; The Acrobats —Murphy James; The Wrestlers—Leon Spelman.

Directed by Albert Marre; choreography, Jack Cole; musical director, Howard Cable; scenery and lighting, Howard Bay; costumes, Willa Kim and Howard Bay; dance and vocal arrangements, Neil Warner; musical arrangements, Music Makers, Inc.; Mr. Leigh's production associate, Milton Herson; production stage manager, James S. Gelb; stage manager, Joseph Olney; press, Harvey B. Sabinson, Lee Solters, Robert Larkin.

Molly Picon played the role of Rose until 11/14/66, when Miss Jacobson replaced her.

About a Jewish family arriving in Kaifeng Fu and becoming interested in Chen Buddhism. In an attempt to create a casual impression almost of improvisation, individual scenes and musical numbers were not identified as such at the request of the authors.

Breakfast at Tiffany's. Musical based on the novel by Truman Capote; adapted by Edward Albee; music and lyrics by Bob Merrill. Produced by David Merrick in a pre-Broadway tryout at the Forrest Theater in Philadelphia. Opened October 15, 1966. (Closed December 14, 1966 during preview performances at the Majestic Theater, New York)

Jeff Claypool ....Richard Chamberlain
Holly Golightly ....Mary Tyler Moore
Mr. Buckley ....James Olson
Mr. Moss ....William Stanton
Voice ....John Anania
O.J. Berman ....Martin Wolfson
O.J.'s Assistant ....Richard Terry
Guests ....John Anania, Justin McDonough,

Henry LeClair, John Aman, Scott Schultz, Feodore Tedick, Robert Donahue
Rusty Trawler ....Thayer David
Mag Wildwood ....Sally Kellerman
Cat ....Louis
Doc Golightly ....Art Lund
Joe Howard ....Charles Welch
Messenger ....John Sharpe

Bar Patrons .... William Stanton, John Sharpe, Mitchell Thomas
Carlos .... Larry Kert
Patrick O'Connor .... Robert Donahue
Sheila Fezzonetti .... Paula Bauersmith
Announcer .... Justin McDonough
Hospital Attendant .... Paul Solen
Giovanni's Girls ...... Sally Hart, Maryann Kerrick, Marybeth Lahr
Giovanni .... Paul Michael

Singers: Sally Hart, Lee Hooper, Maryann Kerrick, Marybeth Lahr, John Anania, Henry LeClair, Robert Donahue, Bob Gorman, Justin McDonough, Richard Terry, John Aman, Scott Schultz, Feodore Tedick.

Dancers: Barbara Beck, Trudy Carson, Judith Dunford, Carolyn Kirsch, Priscilla Lopez, Debe Macomber, Pat Trott, Bud Fleming, Teak Lewis, Dom Salinaro, John Sharpe, Paul Solen, William Stanton, Kent Thomas, Mitchell Thomas.

Understudies: Miss Moore—Sally Kellerman, Sally Hart; Mr. Chamberlain—Justin McDonough; Mr. Lund—Robert Donahue; Miss Kellerman—Maryann Kerrick.

Directed by Joseph Anthony; musical staging, Michael Kidd; scenery, Oliver Smith; costumes, Freddy Wittop; lighting, Tharon Musser; vocal arrangements and musical direction, Stanley Lebowsky; orchestrations, Ralph Burns; dance music arrangements, Marvin Laird; assistant choreographer, Tony Mordente; associate producer, Samuel Liff; stage manager, Harry Clark; press, Harvey B. Sabinson, Lee Solters, David Powers.

Time: The present. Place: New York City.

Based on Truman Capote's story of Holly Golightly (the musical was originally adapted and directed by Abe Burrows and entitled *Holly Golightly*), a bachelor girl-about-town. In this version Holly is a character in a young writer's story who comes to life from the printed page, in the author's imagination.

ACT I

Scene 1: Tiffany's
"Holly Golightly" .... Jeff
Scene 2: Brownstone exterior
"Breakfast at Tiffany's" .... Holly
Scene 3: Jeff's apartment
"When Daddy Comes Home" .... Holly
"Freddy Chant" .... Holly
Scene 4: Holly's apartment
"Lament for Ten Men" .... Holly, Guests
"Lament for Ten Men" (Reprise) .... Holly's Guests
Scene 5: Holly's apartment, next day
"Home for Wayward Girls" .... Holly, Mag
"Who Needs Her?" .... Jeff
Scene 6: Brownstone exterior
"You've Never Kissed Her" .... Doc
"You've Never Kissed Her" (Reprise) .... Jeff
Scene 7: The bar
"Lulamae" .... Doc, Jeff, Holly
Scene 8: Holly's apartment

ACT II

Scene 1: The bar
"Who Needs Her?" .... Holly, Jeff
Dance .... Holly, Three Bar Patrons
Scene 2: Rusty's house
"Stay With Me" .... Carlos
Scene 3: Holly's apartment
"I'm Not the Girl" .... Holly, Jeff
"Grade 'A' Treatment" .... Holly, Carlos
Scene 4: TV newsreel
Scene 5: Prison hospital
"Ciao, Compare" .... Giovanni, His Girl Friends
"Breakfast at Tiffany's" (Reprise) .... Holly
Scene 6: Holly's apartment
"Better Together" .... Jeff
"Same Mistakes" .... Holly
Scene 7: The street
"Holly Golightly" (Reprise) .... Jeff

Two Weeks Somewhere Else. By Herman Raucher. Produced by the Theater Guild and Jerry Gershwin and Elliott Kastner in a pre-Broadway tryout at the Wilbur Theater in Philadelphia. Opened December 26, 1966. (Closed January 7, 1967)

Maimonides Cohen	David Kossoff	Cliff Scofield	Bruce Glover
Willie Werber	Philip Bruns	Abby Docker	Alix Elias
Gloria Martinson	Pat Englund	Irving Greenthal	George S. Irving

Standbys: Misses Englund, Elias—Janis Young; Mr. Kossoff—Lou Gilbert.

Directed by Harvey Medlinsky; scenery and lighting, David Ballou; costumes, Theoni V. Aldredge; production stage manager, Wally Engelhardt; stage manager, Wayne Carson; press, Nat & Irvin Dorfman.

Time: Today, spring. Place: A New York City brownstone. Act I: Tuesday night. Act II: The following Thursday. Act III: The following Tuesday.

Comedy about the mistaken identity of an art dealer who borrows a psychiatrist's apartment and tries gamely to help the many callers who seem to be troubled.

The Hemingway Hero. By A.E. Hotchner; based on the writings of Ernest Hemingway. Produced by William Court Cohen, Seymour Vall and Ralph Alswang in a pre-Broadway tryout at the Shubert Theater in New Haven. Opened February 21, 1967. (Closed at the Wilbur Theater in Boston March 4, 1967)

Robert Jordan	Gary Merrill	Pablo	Norman Rose
John; Lumberjack; Orderly; Waiter;		Alice; Guest	Patricia Fay
Enrique; MacWalsey;		Frances; Brett; Helen	Jennifer West
Anselmo	Stephen Joyce	Catherine; Diane; Dorothy;	
Bill; Orderly; Officer; Guest; Phil;		Maria	Lois Nettleton
Paco; Barman; Rafael	Ira Lewis	Guest; Pilar	Carol Gustafson
Cook; Major; Count; Husband;			

Understudies: Misses Nettleton, West, Gustafson—Martha Galphin; Messrs. Joyce, Lewis—John Garces; Mr. Rose—Howard Fischer; Mr. Merrill—Stephen Joyce.

Directed by Charles Aidman; living screen designed and lighted by Ralph Alswang; costumes, Michael Travis; associate producer, Rick Mandell; production supervisor, Nelle Nugent; production stage manager, Hal Halvorsen; stage manager, Howard Fischer; press, Seymour Krawitz.

Time: Beginning with the Spanish Civil War. Place: Beginning in the Escorial Mountains north of Madrid in Spain.

Many of Hemingway's male heroes are combined into one, in a collection of Hemingway episodes.

What Do You Really Know About Your Husband? By Michael V. Gazzo. Produced by Albert W. Selden and Hal James in a pre-Broadway tryout at the Shubert Theater in New Haven. Opened March 9, 1967. (Closed March 11, 1967)

The Writer's Wife	Kate Reid	Francis	Murvyn Vye
Marion	Betty Bruce	Donald Wallace Jr.	Roy R. Scheider
Ann Hall	Helen Martin	Little Alfy	Abe Vigoda
The Writer	Dennis O'Keefe	Maude	K.C. Townsend
Eddie Colby	Alfred Leberfeld	Mary-Alice	Nancie Phillips
Harry	Frank Campanella	Doctor Winters	Richard Bengal

Standbys: Mr. O'Keefe—Stephen Elliott; Miss Reid—Gaylee Byrne. Understudies: Messrs. Vye, Campanella, Vigoda—Howard Mann; Messrs. Leberfeld, Scheider, Bengal—Norman Shelly; Misses Bruce, Martin—Margaret Draper.

Directed by Sherwood Arthur; scenery and lighting, Ben Edwards; costumes, Jane Greenwood; production stage manager, Leonard Auerbach; stage manager, Norman Shelly; press, Merle Debuskey, Violet Welles, Faith Geer.

Time: The present. Place: An apartment on New York City's West Side. Act I: Christmas Eve. Act II: Three days later. Act III, Scene 1: The following night. Scene 2: Two hours later.

Comedy about a writer who tries to get out of financial difficulty by staging a fake testimonial dinner for a gangster.

PLAYS PRODUCED OFF BROADWAY

Figures in parentheses following a play's title indicate number of performances. Plays marked with an asterisk (*) were still running on June 1, 1967, and their number of performances is figured from opening night through May 31, 1967, not including extra non-profit performances. In a listing of a show's numbers—dances, sketches, musical numbers, etc.—the titles of songs are identified by their appearance in quotation marks (" ").

HOLDOVERS FROM PREVIOUS SEASONS

Plays which were running on June 1, 1966 are listed below. More detailed information about them appears in previous *Best Plays* volumes of appropriate years. Important cast changes are recorded in a section of this volume.

* **The Fantasticks** (2,955). Musical suggested by the play *Les Romantiques* by Edmund Rostand; book and lyrics by Tom Jones; music by Harvey Schmidt. Opened May 3, 1960.

A View From the Bridge (780). Revival of the play by Arthur Miller. Opened January 28, 1965. (Closed December 11, 1966)

The American Savoyards (109). Repertory of five Gilbert & Sullivan operetta revivals. **The Pirates of Penzance** (26) opened May 23, 1966. **Princess Ida** (27) opened May 26, 1966. *The Mikado, Trial by Jury* and *H.M.S. Pinafore* opened after May 31, 1966, see their entries in this volume. (Repertory closed September 4, 1966)

Pick a Number XV (400). Cabaret revue conceived by Julius Monk. Opened October 14, 1965. (Closed June 4, 1966)

Just for Openers (395). Cabaret revue conceived by Rod Warren. Opened November 3, 1965. (Closed June 11, 1966)

Hogan's Goat (607). By William Alfred. Opened November 11, 1965. (Closed April 23, 1967)

Happy Ending and **Day of Absence** (504). Program of two one-act plays by Douglas Turner Ward. Opened November 15, 1965. (Closed January 29, 1967)

* **The Pocket Watch** (601). By Alvin Aronson. Opened January 5, 1966.

* **The Mad Show** (723). Musical revue based on *Mad Magazine;* book by Larry Siegel and Stan Hart; lyrics by Marshall Barer, Larry Siegel and Steven Vinaver; music by Mary Rodgers. Opened January 9, 1966.

Serjeant Musgrave's Dance (135). By John Arden. Opened March 8, 1966. (Closed July 3, 1966)

The World of Günter Grass (80). Adaptation by Dennis Rosa of selections from Günter Grass' *The Tin Drum, Dog Years* and *Selected Poems*. Opened April 26, 1966. (Closed July 3, 1966)

PLAYS PRODUCED JUNE 1, 1966—May 31, 1967

The American Savoyards. Repertory of five Gilbert & Sullivan operetta revivals. **The Mikado** (28) opened June 1, 1966. **Trial by Jury** and **H.M.S. Pinafore** (28) opened June 7, 1966. *The Pirates of Penzance* opened May 23, 1966 and *Princess Ida* opened May 26, 1966; see their entries in the 1965-66 *Best Plays* volume. Produced by American Gilbert and Sullivan Presentations, Inc., Jeff G. Britton managing director, Dorothy Raedler artistic director, at the Jan Hus Playhouse. (Repertory closed September 4, 1966)

PERFORMER	"THE MIKADO"	"TRIAL BY JURY"	"H.M.S. PINAFORE"
Arden Anderson-Broecking	Pitti-Sing		Hebe
Helene Andreu	Peep-Bo	1st Bridesmaid	Tom Tucker
Ron Armstrong		Usher	Bob Becket
Richard Best	Pooh-Bah		
Robert Brink	Ko-Ko	Judge	Sir Joseph Porter
Donald Chapman		Counsel	
William Copeland	Pish-Tush		Capt. Corcoran
Donna Curtis	Yum-Yum		Josephine
Sandra Darling		Plaintiff	
Don Derrow		Associate	
Nell Evans	Katisha		Little Buttercup
Don Junod	Nanki-Poo	Defendant	
Theodore Morrill			Ralph Rackstraw
William Tost		Foreman	Bill Bobstay
Don Yule	Mikado		Dick Deadeye

Chorus: Dick Cerasani, Sheila Coleman, Bill Collins, Nina Gervais, Bill Gibbens, Carl John, Karl Patrick Krause, Dorothy Lancaster, Jack Lines, Regina Lynn, Naomi Robin, Joyce Weibel, Dennis Carpenter, Craig Palmer.

Directed by Dorothy Raedler; scenery, Henry Heyman; musical director, Kenneth Bowen; production stage manager, David Bamberger; press, Ben Kornzweig, Reginald Denenholz.

Undercover Man (21). By Norman Kennelly. Produced by Shepard Traube, Dina and Alexander E. Racolin and Jim Mendenhall Productions at the Actors Playhouse. Opened June 2, 1966. (Closed June 19, 1966)

Jerome Pendleton ....Robert Elston   Connie Bontempo ....Rebecca Darke

Directed by Edward Morehouse; scenery, Marc Gingold; lighting, Michael Allen McDonald; presented in association with Romar Productions; stage manager, Mark Lonow; press, Lenny Traube.

Time: The present. Place: An apartment on West End Avenue in New York City. Act I: A Saturday evening in late November. Act II, Scene 1: Immediately following. Scene 2: Early the next morning.

Comedy about a man who cannot be persuaded to get out of bed.

The Kitchen (137). By Arnold Wesker. Produced by Rita Fredricks and Paul Stoudt with The Establishment Theater Company, Inc. (Ivor David Balding executive producer) in a New Theater Workshop production at the 81st Street Theater. Opened June 13, 1966. (Closed October 9, 1966)

Mangolis	Akila Couloumbis	Jackie	Hortensia Colorado
Max	Conrad Bain	Monique	Sylvia Miles
Bertha	Madlyn Cates	Alfredo	Michael Enserro
Betty	Joy Hatton	Head Waiter	P. Ray Marunas
Winnie	Lee Addoms	Michael	Danny Frankel
Paul	Colgate Salsbury	Gaston	Morris Erby
Raymond	Alek Primrose	Hans	John Kramer
Hettie	Mari Gorman	Kevin	Peter Rogan
Violet	Pamela Saunders	Nicholas	Peter Deanda
Anne	Leslie Weldon	Peter	Rip Torn
Daphne	Susan Dorlen	Frank	James Harder
Gwen	Constance Clarke	Chef	David Clarke
Cynthia	Lee Roscoe	Marango	Muni Seroff
Dimitri	Ernesto Gonzalez	Tramp	Martin Garner
Molly	Mary Hara		

Directed by Jack Gelber; scenery, Ed Wittstein; lighting, Jules Fisher; production stage manager, John Paul Austin; press, Dorothy Ross.

Time: The present. Place: The kitchen in a restaurant. Rush hour behind the scenes in a glamorous restaurant. A foreign play previously produced in London.

Until the Monkey Comes . . . (56). By Venable Herndon. Produced by Slade Brown and the Mannhardt Theater Foundation, Inc. by arrangement with David Black at the Martinique Theater. Opened June 20, 1966. (Closed July 31, 1966)

Cassy	Susan Tyrrell	Billie-Mae	Norma Donaldson
Sonny	Philip Carlson	Philip	Gordon Addison
Jack	Don Amendolia	Luke	Russell Drisch

Directed by Robert Haddad; designed by Bil Mikulewicz; stage manager, Charles Kindl; press, Shirley Herz.

Time: The present. Place: Sonny's apartment in Sutton Point South, New York City. Act I: The last day of the year. Act II: The same, a few moments later. About spoiled, rich, cynical members of the younger generation.

Below the Belt (186). Cabaret revue conceived by Rod Warren. Produced by Rod Warren at the Downstairs at the Upstairs. Opened June 21, 1966. (Closed October 8, 1966)

Richard Blair	Robert Rovin
Genna Carter	Lily Tomlin
Madeline Kahn	

Production supervised by Rod Warren; directed by Sandra Devlin; musical direction and arrangements, Michael Cohen; stage manager, George Curley; press, Dorothy Ross, Richard O'Brien.

The musical numbers were collected and updated from previous Rod Warren revues: *And in This Corner, The Game Is Up* and *Just for Openers*.

Command Performance (14). Program of four one-act plays by Montgomery Hare: *Pin Up, Venus-Shot, The Child and the Dragon* and *Miracle in Brooklyn*. Produced by Quartet Productions at the Maidman Playhouse. Opened June 23, 1966. (Closed July 3, 1966)

Directed by Clinton Atkinson; scenery, Mark Simont; lighting, Carl Seltzer; production stage manager, Michael Schultz; press, Seymour Krawitz. With Marc Alaimo, Elizabeth Berger, Jacqueline Bertrand, Joseph W. Kapfer, Tom McDermott, Herbert Nelson. *Pin Up* is about two old men living in a cellar, and their nude pin-up. *Venus Shot* tells of the honeymoon of a young man who helps build spacecraft. *The Child and the Dragon* is about a child telling his uncle something he shouldn't. *Miracle in Brooklyn* is about a pair of lovers in a Brooklyn park interrupted by another pair of lovers—fantasies from the 17th century.

Mardi Gras! (54). Return engagement of the musical with book by Sig Herzig; music and lyrics by Carmen Lombardo and John Jacob Loeb. Produced by Guy Lombardo at the Jones Beach Marine Theater. Opened July 8, 1966. (Closed September 4, 1966)

John Laffity; Jean Lafitte; Lucky Laffity ....David Atkinson	Mr. Buzárd ....Joel Grey
George Baxter; Capt. Benedict Baxter; Arnold Baxter ....Ralph Purdum	Anne; Annette; Anna ....Gail Johnston
Peggy Willard; Marguerite de Villiers; Meg ....Karen Shepard	Katie; Katherine; Marie Le Veau ....Barbara Ann Webb
Caroline Willard; Madame de Villiers; Carrie Nation ......Fran Stevens	Jacques ....Edmund Walenta
Buzz Lamont; Dominique You;	Vesta ....Doris Galiber
	Lulu ....Maggie Worth
	Father Time ....Peter Costanza

In person: Louis Armstrong and his All Stars; Guy Lombardo and his Royal Canadians.

Understudies: John Laffity—Adam Petroski; Peggy Willard—Marsha Tamaroff; Buzz Lamont —Norman Shelly; George Baxter—Leslie Meadow; Caroline Willard—Maggie Worth; Annette —Sherry Lambert; Katie—Doris Galiber.

Singers: Katherine Barnes, Doris Galiber, Sherry Lambert, Leonore Lanzillotti, Carol Marraccini, Mildred Petroski, Laurette Raymon, Mary Ann Rydzeski, Eileen Sarafis, Marsha Tamaroff, Elise Warner, Maggie Worth, Gilbert Adkins, Irving Barnes, Michael Bloom, Eddie Carr, Peter Clark, Peter Costanza, Nino Galanti, Leslie Meadow, Robert Monteil, Adam Petroski, Jerome Toti, Edmund Walenta.

Dancers: Jean Adams, Lynn Broadbent, Helen Butler, Lynda Christ, Joanna Crosson, Kathy Dalton, Juliette Durand, Jean Einwick, Mimi Funes, Peggy Marie Haug, Debe Macomber, Joan Paige, Lucinda Ransom, Renee Rose, Geri Spinner, Patti Watson, Fred Benjamin, Henry Boyer, Roger Briant, Myron Curtis, Fred Gockel, Ted Goodridge, Dennis Lynch, Mario Maroze, Pat Matera, Luis Montero, Guy Naples, Ed Nolfi, James Piersall, Don Strong, Tommy Thornton, Kip Watson.

Production supervised by Arnold Spector; direction and choreography, June Taylor; musical direction, Shepard Coleman; scenery, George Jenkins; costumes, Winn Morton; lighting, Peggy Clark; orchestrations, Philip J. Lang; production stage manager, Mortimer Halpern; dance arrangements, Milt Sherman; press, Saul Richman.

Time: 1815, 1905 and 1966. Place: New Orleans. Act I, Scene 1: New Orleans, 1966, the Grand Ballroom. Scene 2: Katie's Voodoo Shack. Scene 3: Smuggler's Cove, 1815. Scene 4: Belle Ile, the pirate village. Act II, Scene 1: Katie's Voodoo Shack. Scene 2: New Orleans, 1905, a street. Scene 3: Lucky Laffity's Bar on Basin Street. Scene 4: The Bayou St. John. Scene 5: In orbit. Scene 6: Peggy Willard's boudoir. Scene 7: The Mardi Gras, 1966.

Mardi Gras! was produced at Jones Beach Marine Theater June 26, 1965 for 68 performances. Musical numbers (with the addition of a setpiece by Louis Armstrong and his All Stars in Act II of this production) appear in the 1965-66 *Best Plays* volume.

The Long Christmas Dinner, Queens of France and **The Happy Journey to Trenton and Camden** (72). Program of three one-act play revivals by Thornton Wilder. Produced by Theater 1967 (Richard Barr, Clinton Wilder and Edward Albee), a project of Albarwild Theater Arts Inc., at the Cherry Lane Theater. Opened September 6, 1966. (Closed November 6, 1966)

THE LONG CHRISTMAS DINNER

Lucia ....Leora Dana	Genevieve ....Cynthia Harris
Mother Bayard ....Paula Trueman	Leonora ....Marian Hailey
Roderick ....John Beal	Ermengarde ....Bette Henritze
Cousin Brandon ....James Noble	Sam ....Stephen Cooke
Nurse ....Guinevare Breeding	Lucia II ....Vicki Blankenship
Charles ....Michael Lipton	Roderick II ....John Horn

QUEENS OF FRANCE

Marie-Sidonie Cressaux ....Marian Hailey	Mlle. Pointevin ....Bette Henritze
M. Cahusac ....John Beal	Old Lady ....Guinevare Breeding
Mme. Pugeot ....Paula Trueman	Boy ....Alan Cabal

THE HAPPY JOURNEY TO TRENTON AND CAMDEN

Stage Manager	James Noble	Caroline	Susan Towers
Ma Kirby	Paula Trueman	Pa Kirby	John Beal
Arthur	Alan Cabal	Beulah	Cynthia Harris

Directed by Michael Kahn; scenery, Ed Wittstein; costumes, Betty Williams; lighting, Sean O'Brien; stage manager, Phil Koch; press, Howard Atlee.

THE LONG CHRISTMAS DINNER—Time: Christmas Day. Place: The dining room of the Bayard home. Comedy-drama-fantasy about 90 years in the life of a family, including birth and death, in the context of a single Christmas episode. *The Long Christmas Dinner* was first produced in New Haven in 1931. QUEENS OF FRANCE—Time: 1896. Place: A lawyer's office in New Orleans. Comedy about a con man deceiving gullible ladies, first produced at the University of Chicago in 1932. THE HAPPY JOURNEY TO TRENTON AND CAMDEN—Time: 1930s, a summer day. Place: The old family Chevrolet. A family drive from Newark to Camden, first produced in New Haven in 1931.

Program moved to the Orpheum Theater 10/4/66.

The Israeli Mime Theater (63). Evening of mime created by Claude Kipnis under the title *Men and Dreams*. Produced by Luben Vichey (Vichey Attractions, Inc.) at the Theater de Lys. Opened September 6, 1966. (Closed October 30, 1966)

Original score, Noam Sheriff; decor, Amiram Shamir; costumes, Dinah Kipnis; lighting, Marshall Spiller; produced by arrangement with Lucille Lortel Productions, Inc.; stage manager, Dinah Kipnis; press, Samuel J. Friedman, Shirley Herz. A foreign show previously produced in Israel and elsewhere.

PART I: Introduction, The Hobo (dreams of a Parisian *clochard*), Eve and the Serpent (story of an apple), The Village (recollections of a Jewish village), Fantasy in Wax (the thief and the mannequin), The Hooligan (a bad boy kills time), The Cabinet Minister (spends a weekend as a commoner in his Kibbutz). PART II: The Lifeguard (on a crowded beach), The Bottle (fantasy on alcohol), Main Street (in Tel Aviv—or anywhere), Jacob and the Angel (man's fight against divine power), The Bus (in Israel), Finale.

My Wife and I (8). Musical with book, music and lyrics by Bill Mahoney. Produced by Katydid Productions at Theater Four. Opened October 10, 1966. (Closed October 22, 1966)

Directed by Tom Ross Prather; musical direction and arrangements, James Reed Lawlor; musical numbers stage by Darwin Knight; scenery and lighting, Robert Green; production stage manager, George Cavey; press, David Rothenberg. With Helon Blount, Carol Leigh Jensen, Ron Leath, Denise Norden, Edward Penn, Karen Schuck, Greg Stone, Debbie Thomas, Robert R. Wait.

Time: Before television—1939. Place: Michael's home and on a street outside. A boy runs away from his home but returns safely.

Match-Play and **A Party for Divorce** (7). Program of two one-act plays by Lee Kalcheim. Produced by Theater 1967 (Richard Barr, Clinton Wilder and Michael Kasdan) at the Provincetown Playhouse. Opened October 11, 1966. (Closed October 16, 1966)

Directed by Robert Livingston; scenery and lighting, Clarke Dunham; costumes, Mopsy; press, Howard Atlee, Anne Woll. With Rudy Bond, Tony Musante, Beverly Ballard, Nicholas Pryor, Philip Sterling, Rebecca Darke.

MATCH-PLAY—Time: The present. Place: A large home in Riverdale. A rich spoiled child finds that his father's influence can't get him out of being drafted. A PARTY FOR DIVORCE—Time: The present. Place: A New York apartment. A wife deliberately picks a fight with her husband to help him work off repressions.

A Whitman Portrait (71). By Paul Shyre; adapted from the works of Walt Whitman. Produced by Ira Skutch and Allan Frank at the Gramercy Arts Theater. Opened October 11, 1966. (Closed January 11, 1967)

The Man	Alan Mixon	The Woman	Carolyn Coates
The Young Man	Wayne Maxwell	Walt Whitman	Alexander Scourby

Directed by Paul Shyre; scenery and lighting, Eldon Elder; costumes, Sara Brook; music, Robert Rines; press, Lee Solters.

Act I: Youth and the Civil War. Act II: Take My Leaves, America.

Who's Got His Own (19). By Ronald Milner. Produced by The American Place Theater, Sidney Lanier president, Wynn Handman artistic director, at St. Clement's Church. Opened October 12, 1966. (Closed October 29, 1966)

Tim Jr.	Glynn Turman	Reverend Calver	L. Errol Jaye
Clara	Barbara Ann Teer	1st Deacon	Sam Laws
Mother	Estelle Evans	2d Deacon	Roger Robinson

Directed by Lloyd Richards; scenery and costumes, Kert Lundell; lighting, Roger Morgan; production stage manager, Peter Galambos; press, John Springer Associates, Walter Alford, Louise Weiner.

Time: Continuing past. Place: Detroit-Central City. Act I: Afternoon. Act II: Evening. Act III: Morning. A young Negro comes home to Detroit for his father's funeral; he becomes a victim of his own consuming hatred of society.

Eh? (233). By Henry Livings. Produced by Theodore Mann at Circle in the Square. Opened October 16, 1966. (Closed May 24, 1967)

Price	Dana Elcar	Valentine Brose	Dustin Hoffman
Aly	Carl Gabler	Reverend Mort	Joseph Maher
Mrs. Murray	Elizabeth Wilson	Betty Dorrick	Alexandra Berlin

Directed by Roger Short; scenery and costumes, Rouben Ter-Arutunian; lighting, Jules Fisher; production stage manager, Joseph Kapfer; press, Merle Debuskey, Violet Welles, Lawrence Belling.

Time: The present. Place: The boiler room of a dye works. Comedy about a harebrained nonentity who deliberately pushes the wrong buttons, revolting against a complex industrial organization. A foreign play previously produced in London.

MacIntyre Dixon replaced Dustin Hoffman 2/21/67.

Eh? alternated performances with *Drums in the Night* 5/11/67-5/24/67.

The Butter and Egg Man (32). Revival of the play by George S. Kaufman. Produced by Theater 1967 (Richard Barr, Clinton Wilder and Edward Albee), a project of Albarwild Theater Arts Inc., at the Cherry Lane Theater. Opened October 17, 1966. (Closed November 13, 1966)

Joe Lehman	Philip Bruns	Cecil Benham	Robert Downing
Jack McClure	Tom Aldredge	Bernie Sampson	Jeff David
Fanny Lehman	Vicki Cummings	Peggy Marlowe	Carole Ann Lewis
Jane Weston	Tyne Daly	Kitty Humphreys	Vicki Blankenship
*Mary Marvin	Christine Norden	Oscar Fritchie	Walter A. Dunnett III
Peter Jones	David Christmas	A. J. Patterson	Wyman Pendleton
Waiter	Joseph Palmieri		

* In the original production, this character was named Mary Martin.

Directed by Burt Shevelove; scenery, Peter Harvey; lighting, Sean O'Brien; stage managers, Charles Kindl, Donald Wesley; press, Howard Atlee, Anne Woll.

Time: 1925. Place: New York City and Syracuse. *The Butter and Egg Man* was first produced September 23, 1925, for 243 performances and was named a Best Play of its season.

* **Mixed Doubles** (320). Cabaret revue conceived by Rod Warren. Produced by Upstairs at the Downstairs at Upstairs at the Downstairs. Opened October 19, 1966.

Judy Graubart	Robert Rovin
Madeline Kahn	Janie Sell
Larry Moss	Gary Sneed

Production supervised by Rod Warren; directed and choreographed by Robert Audy; musical direction, Michael Cohen; music arranged and performed by Michael Cohen, Edward Morris; lighting, Richard Mensoff; stage manager, Richard Mensoff; press, Dorothy Ross, Richard O'Brien.

ACT I

"Mixed Doubles" ....The Company
  Lyric, Rod Warren; music, Bach
"New York Is a Festival of Fun" ....Misses Kahn, Sell, Messrs. Rovin, Sneed
  Lyric and music, Gene Bissell
The Honeymooners ....Miss Graubart, Moss
  By Marshall Brickman
"Questions" ....Miss Kahn, Rovin, Sneed
  Lyric, Drey Shepard; music, Ed Kresley
"Mixed Marriages" ....Miss Sell, Moss
  Lyric, David Finkle; music, Bill Weeden
Man With a Problem ....Miss Graubart, Rovin
  By John Boni
"Walter Kerr" ....Sneed
  Lyric, Michael McWhinney, Rod Warren; music, Rod Warren
"Sartor Sartoris" ....Moss, Rovin
  Lyric and music, Franklin Underwood
Fashion Show ....Misses Kahn, Graubart, Mr. Sneed
  By Sid Davis
"Bon Voyeur" ....Moss
  Lyric and music, James Rusk
"Ronald Reagan" ....The Ladies
  Lyric, Drey Shepard; music, Ed Kresley
"More Questions" ....Misses Graubart, Kahn, Messrs. Moss, Rovin
"Physical Fitness" ....Miss Sell
  Lyric and music, James Rusk
"Spoleto" ....The Company
  Lyric, Michael McWhinney; music, Jerry Powell

ACT II

"And a Messenger Appeared" ....Miss Kahn, The Company
  Lyric and music, Gene Bissell
"Brittania Rules" ....Miss Graubart
  Lyric, Rod Warren; music, Jerry Powell
Brief Encounter ....Misses Kahn, Sell, Messrs. Rovin, Sneed
  By Bill Kaufman and Paul Koreto
"Friendly, Liberal Neighborhood" ....The Gentlemen
  Lyric and music, June Reizner
"Still More Questions" ....Misses Graubart, Kahn, Sell, Messrs. Moss, Sneed
"Holden and Phoebe" ....Miss Graubart, Rovin
  Lyric, Michael McWhinney; music, Michael Cohen
"In Old Chicago" ....Miss Kahn
  Lyric, Tony Geiss; music, Michael Cohen
Civilian Review Board ....Miss Sell, Sneed
  By Michael McWhinney
"Bobby the K" ....Rovin
  Lyric, Michael McWhinney; music, Richard Robinson
"And a Few More Questions" ....Most of The Company
"Best Wishes" ....The Company
  Lyric, John Meyer; music, Steven Lawrence

Autumn's Here! (80). Musical based on Washington Irving's *Legend of Sleepy Hollow;* book, music and lyrics by Norman Dean. Produced by Bob Hadley at the Bert Wheeler Theater. Opened October 25, 1966. (Closed December 31, 1966)

Diedrich Knickerbocker ....Leslie Wilkinson	Ben ....Les Freed
Brom Bones ....Fred Gockel	Douglas ....John Johann
Katrina ....Karin Wolfe	Etta ....Zona Kennedy
Ichabod Crane ....Bob Riehl	Will ....Dan Leach
Mr. Van Tassel ....Allan Lokos	Dora ....Regina Lynn
Mrs. Van Tassel ....Joyce Lynn	Della ....Pamela Privette
Jo ....Joyce Devlin	Lew ....Gordon Ramsey

Directed and choreographed by Hal Le Roy; scenery, Robert Conley; lighting, Arthur Ter-
jeson; musical direction, Gordon Munford; costumes, Eve Henriksen; orchestrations, Norman
Dean; stage manager, Ross Hertz; press representative, David Rothenberg.

Time: 1819. Place: Sleepy Hollow, N.Y. The story of the schoolmaster Ichabod Crane, his
rivalry with Brom Bones for the hand of Katrina Van Tassel and his disappearance after an
encounter with the legendary, fearful Headless Horseman.

ACT I

Scene 1: Sleepy Hollow
"Sleepy Hollow" ....The Company
Scene 2: Race Track in Tarrytown
"Boy Do I Hate Horse Races" ....The Boys and The Girls
"Me and My Horse" ....Brom
"Autumn's Here" ....Katrina
Scene 3: School Room
"Song of the 13 Colonies" ....The Boys and The Girls
"Patience" ....Ichabod
Scene 4: Old Dutch Church
"For the Harvest Safely Gathered" ....The Company
"Who Walks Like a Scarecrow" ....Brom, The Company
Scene 5: The Van Tassel Home
"This is the Girl For Me" ....Ichabod
"Do You Think I'm Pretty?" ....Katrina, Ichabod, Mr. and Mrs. Van Tassel
"Fine Words and Fancy Phrases" ....Mr. and Mrs. Van Tassel, Katrina
Scene 6: A Country Lane
"Private Hunting Ground" ....Ben, Lew, Will
"It's a Long Road Home" ....Ben, Etta
"Brom and Katrina" ....Della, Etta, Jo, Brom
Scene 7: The Village Square
"Dark New England Night" ....The Company
(Danced by Della, Douglas, Jo)

ACT II

Scene 1: The Van Tassel Farm
"Dutch Country Table" ....The Company
"You Never Miss the Water" ....Brom, Ben, Lew, Will
"Any Day Now" ....Katrina
"You May Be The Someone" ....Katrina, Ichabod
"Beware as You Ride Through the Hollow" ....The Company
Scene 2: In the Forest
"The Chase" ....The Company
Scene 3: Sleepy Hollow
"Sleepy Hollow" (Reprise) ....The Company

This Here Nice Place (6). By Howard Otway. Produced by Theater 80 St. Marks
at Theater 80 St. Marks. Opened November 1, 1966. (Closed November 6, 1966)

Directed by Howard Otway; stage manager, Edward Royce; press, Max Eisen, Jeanne Gibson Merrick. With Harold Cherry, Griff Evans, Gaylord Mason, James Spruill, Eugene R.
Wood. Time: The Present. Place: A Bar. A seedy barroom is visited by a representative of a
mystical power.

* America Hurrah (234). Program of three one-act plays by Jean-Claude van
Itallie: *Interview, TV,* and *Motel.* Produced by Stephanie Sills Productions at the
Pocket Theater. Opened November 6, 1966.

INTERVIEW

First Interviewer ....Cynthia Harris   Third Interviewer ....Brenda Smiley
First Applicant ....Conard Fowkes   Third Applicant ....Henry Calvert
Second Interviewer ....James Barbosa   Fourth Interviewer ....Bill Macy
Second Applicant ....Ronnie Gilbert   Fourth Applicant ....Joyce Aaron

TV

Hal ....Conard Fowkes   Television people ....Joyce Aaron, James
Susan ....Brenda Smiley   Barbosa, Henry Calvert, Ronnie Gilbert,
George ....Bill Macy   Cynthia Harris

MOTEL

Dolls ....Conard Fowkes, James Barbosa,   Motel Keeper's Voice ....Ruth White
                Brenda Smiley

TV and Motel directed by Jacques Levy; Interview directed by Joseph Chaikin; costumes, Tania Leontov; lighting, James Dwyer; incidental music, Marianne du Pury; song "Drivin' " sung by The Mushrooms; press, Howard Atlee.

All plays—Time: The present, in three views of the U.S.A. INTERVIEW—Place: An employment agency. Well-qualified job seekers are rejected by the cold interview process and then harangued by such public spokesmen as a politician and a priest. TV—Place: The viewing room of a television rating company. Reminders of the world's daily problems, including the Viet Nam war, are contrasted with a cacophony of cheerful TV shows. MOTEL—Place: A motel room. A jolly papier-mache-doll of a motel keeper describes the comforts of her establishment, while two grotesque guest-dolls scribble obscenities on the walls and wreck the place.

A Best Play; see page 240

* **Man With a Load of Mishief** (235). Musical adapted from the play by Ashley Dukes; book by Ben Tarver; music by John Clifton; lyrics by John Clifton and Ben Tarver. Produced by Donald H. Goldman at the Jan Hus Playhouse. Opened November 6, 1966.

The Innkeeper ....Tom Noel   The Man ....Reid Shelton
His Wife ....Lesslie Nicol   The Lady ....Virginia Vestoff
The Lord ....Raymond Thorne   The Maid ....Alice Cannon

Directed by Tom Gruenewald; choreography, Noel Schwartz; musical direction, Sande Campbell; scenery and lighting, Joan Larkey; costumes, Volavkova; orchestrations, John Clifton; production stage manager, Richard Moss; press, Nat & Irvin Dorfman.

Time: Early 19th century. Place: England, a wayside inn. Act I, Scene 1: Late afternoon, the inn. Scene 2: Immediately following, the lady's bedroom. Scene 3: Immediately following, the inn. Scene 4: Immediately following, the garden. Scene 5: That evening before dinner, the inn. Scene 6: That evening after dinner, the inn. Scene 7: That night, the garden. Act II, Scene 1: The next morning, the inn. Scene 2: Immediately following, the courtyard.

The Prince's mistress has a romantic rendezvous with a nobleman but falls in love instead with his valet. The play The Man With a Load of Mischief was produced on Broadway in 1925 for 16 performances.

Man With a Load of Mischief transferred to the Provincetown Playhouse 5/14/67.

ACT I

"Wayside Inn" ....Innkeeper
"The Rescue" ....Wife
"Entrance Polonaise" ....The Company
"Goodbye, My Sweet" ....Lady
"Romance!" ....Innkeeper, Wife, Lord, Maid
"Lover Lost" ....Lady
"Once You've Had a Little Taste" ....Maid
"Hulla-Baloo-Balay" ....Man

"Once You've Had a Little Taste" (Reprise) ....Maid, Wife, Innkeeper
"Dinner Minuet" ....The Company
"You'd Be Amazed" ....Lord, Lady, Man
"A Friend Like You" ....Lady, Lord
"Masquerade" ....Man
"Man With a Load of Mischief" ....Lady
"Masquerade" (Reprise) ....Man

ACT II

"What Style!" ....Innkeeper
"A Wonder" ....Lady
"Make Way for My Lady!" ....Man
"Forget" ....Lord
"Any Other Way" ....Wife, Innkeeper
"Little Rag Doll" ....Maid
"Romance!" (Reprise) ....Lady
"Sextet" ....The Company
"Make Way for My Lady!" (Reprise) ....Man, Lady

Three Hand Reel (72). Program of three one-act plays by Paul Avila Mayer: *The Frying Pan, Eternal Triangle* and *The Bridal Night*. Based on stories by Frank O'Connor. Produced by The Irish Players in association with Oscar Zurer, Bernice Kleppel and Red Barn Theater, Ltd. at the Renata Theater. Opened November 7, 1966. (Closed January 1, 1967)

THE FRYING PAN

Bill Whitton ....Liam Gannon
Una Whitton ....Helena Carroll   Father Jerome Fogarty ....John Cullum

ETERNAL TRIANGLE

Tom Dorgan ....John Cullum   Man ....Neil Fitzgerald
Mary Cummins ....Helena Carroll   English Soldier ....Don Billett
Irish Soldier ....Liam Gannon

THE BRIDAL NIGHT

Mrs. Sullivan ....Brid Lynch   Sean Donaghue ....Neil Fitzgerald
Miss Regan ....Helena Carroll   Danny Donaghue ....Don Billett
Denis Sullivan ....John Cullum   Doctor ....Liam Gannon

Standby: Miss Carroll—Patricia Fay.
Directed by William Hunt; scenery and lighting, Walter S. Russell; stage manager, Richard Herr; press, Howard Atlee.
THE FRYING PAN—Time: The present. Place: Living-room of a small middle-class home in the village of Kilmulpeter, Ireland. A woman's husband wishes he were a priest—and the priest wishes he were her husband. ETERNAL TRIANGLE—Time: Easter Sunday, 1916, and the following morning. Place: A tramcar in Dublin Square, Ireland. A prostitute's tragic encounter during the Easter Rebellion. THE BRIDAL NIGHT—Time: The present. Place: A tiny two-room cottage and nearby exterior areas high above a harbor on the west coast of Ireland. A prim school teacher makes a major sacrifice for the demented youth who loves her.

Javelin (14). By Owen Rachleff. Produced by Stella Holt at the Actors Playhouse. Opened November 9, 1966. (Closed November 20, 1966)

Directed by Amnon Kabatchnik; scenery, Tadeusz Gesek; costumes, Ted Van Griethuysen; lighting, James Gore; stage manager, William Davidson; press, David Lipsky, Marlan Graham. Story of Saul, David and Jonathan in the first book of Samuel.

Viet Rock (62). By Megan Terry. Produced by Jordan Charney, Nancy Cooper-stein and David Rothenberg in association with Stanley Swerdlow at the Martinique Theater. Opened November 10, 1966. (Closed December 31, 1966)

Seth Allen	Paul Giovanni
Kay Carney	Marcia Jean Kurtz
Shami Chaikin	Roy London
Jordan Charney	Muriel Miguel
Joseph Daly	Gerome Ragni
Fred Forrest	Barbara Ralley
Sharon Gans	

Directed by Megan Terry; lighting, Gil Wechsler; musical accompaniment, incidental music, Marianne de Pury; stage manager, Jerome Michael; press, David Rothenberg.
Series of vignettes in protest against the Viet Nam war.

The Infantry (8). By Andy and Dave Lewis. Produced by Arthur Joel Katz at the 81st Street Theater. Opened November 13, 1966. (Closed November 20, 1966)

Directed by Andy Lewis; scenery and lighting, Clarke Dunham; production stage manager, Richard Hamilton; press, Joe Wolhandler. In the kitchen of a German house in 1945, a platoon of American soldiers express their individual frustrations, even toying with the idea of torture and rape.

Blitzstein! (7). Program of songs with words and music by Marc Blitzstein. Produced by Herbert Dorfman and Stage Associates at the Provincetown Playhouse. Opened November 30, 1966. (Closed December 4, 1966)

Directed by Ellen Pahl; scenery, Cynthia Bernardi; lighting, Thomas Kelly; production stage manager, Christopher Kelly; press, David Lipsky, Marian Graham. Singers: Mira Gilbert, Norman Frieden. Piano: Peter Basquin.

The Ox Cart (83). By Rene Marques; translated by Charles R. Pilditch. Produced by George P. Edgar in a Stella Holt production at the Greenwich Mews Theater. Opened December 19, 1966. (Closed February 26, 1967)

Chaguito	Jose Perez	Lito	Ruben Figueroa
Dona Gabriela	Lucy Boscana	Matilde	Carla Pinza
Juanita	Miriam Colon	Dona Isa	Corina Magureanu
Don Chago	William Myers	Paco	Jose Ocasio
Luis	Raul Julia	Lidia	Mary Tahmin
Germana	Teodorina Bello		

Directed by Lloyd Richards; scenery, Douglas Schmidt; lighting, James Gore; costumes, Joseph Aulisi; production manager, Walter Mason; press, David Lipsky, Marian Graham.
Time: The present. Place: Puerto Rico and New York City. Act I: A rural district outside San Juan, Puerto Rico, 5 o'clock on a September afternoon. Act II: "The Pearl," slum district beside the ancient fortress of El Morro in San Juan, one year later. Act III: Puerto Rican district in the Bronx, one year later, a cold, gray autumn day with a threat of snow. Puerto Rican family strives to find a better life in the cities. Previously produced in Puerto Rico.

The Penny Friend (32). Musical based on a play by J. M. Barrie; book, music and lyrics by William Roy. Produced by Thomas Hammond at Stage 73. Opened December 26, 1966. (Closed January 22, 1967)

Charles Bodie	Michael Wager	Mrs. Maloney	Georgia Creighton
Policeman	Jamie Ross	Maudie	Terry Forman
Kate Bodie	Charlotte Fairchild	Lady	Sherill Price
Cinderella	Bernadette Peters	George	Dewey Golkin
Mr. McGill	Bill Drew	Hans	Jeffrey Golkin
Mr. Jennings	John Senger	Invite	Jimmy Rivers

Directed by Benno D. Frank; designed by Ben Shecter; musical numbers staged by Lou Kristofer; technical coordinator, Charles Miller; lighting, Robert L. Steele; press, Karl Bernstein.

As in the Barrie play *A Kiss for Cinderella* on which this musical is based, the story concerns a cockney shopgirl who imagines she is a modern Cinderella.

ACT I

"The Penny Friend" ....Ensemble
"She Makes You Think of Home" ....Charles
"Who Am I, Who Are You, Who Are We?" ....Charles
"Mrs. Bodie" ....Cinderella
"I Am Going to Dance" ....Cinderella
"Feet" ....Cinderella
"She Makes You Think of Home" ....Policeman
"The Great Unknown" ....Cinderella
"The Penny Friend" ....Mrs. Maloney, McGill, Jennings
"How Doth the Apple Butterfly" ....Cinderella
"The Diagnostician" ....Kate

ACT II

"Won't You Come to the Party" ....Ensemble
"The Grand Parade" ....Ensemble
"A Very Full and Productive Day" ....Cinderella, Charles, David, Kate
"The Penny Friend" ....Charles, Cinderella
"The World Today" ....Kate, David
"The Great Unknown" ....Kate
"The Penny Friend" ....Ensemble

Night of the Dunce (47). By Frank Gagliano. Produced by Theater 1967 (Richard Barr, Clinton Wilder and Edward Albee), a project of Albarwild Theater Arts Inc., at the Cherry Lane Theater. Opened December 28, 1966. (Closed February 5, 1967)

Malcolm Supley	James Noble	David Byron	Tony Musante
Geraldine La Mossa	Elaine Hyman	Mr. Crowley	Alfred Hinckley
Connie	Robert Salvio	Young Man	Terry Kiser
Mrs. Vickers	Anne Revere	Max Kupreef	Salem Ludwig

Directed by Joseph Hardy; designed by William Ritman; production supervised by Michael Kasdan; stage managers, Charles Kindl, Donald Wesley; press, Howard Atlee.

Time: The present, an early September evening. Place: Road's End Branch Public Library. A library and its staff are besieged by a gang of toughs bent on destroying the building and everything in it.

The Displaced Person (18). By Cecil Dawkins; adapted from short stories by Flannery O'Connor. Produced by The American Place Theater at St. Clement's Church. Opened December 29, 1966. (Closed January 14, 1967)

Mrs. Hopewell	Frances Sternhagen	Sledgewig	Linda Thomas
Mr. Shortley	David Clarke	Mr. Guisac	Zito Kerras
Joy	Dixie Marquis	Mrs. Guisac	Sandra Lucot
Scofield	William Jordan	Randall	Robertearl Jones
Mrs. Shortley	Bette Henritze	Sulk	Woodie King Jr.
Wesley	Russell Horton	Bible Salesman	James Hall
Father Finn	Tom Ahearne	Dr. Block	Edwin Cooper
Rudolph	Alan Nistikakis		

Directed by Edward Parone; scenery and costumes, Kert Lundell; lighting, Neil Peter Jampolis; production stage manager, Peter Galambos; press, John Springer Associates, Walter Alford, Louise Weiner.

Time: Middle to late summer, 1953. Place: A dairy farm in South Georgia. Act I, Scene 1: Morning. Scene 2: Three weeks later. Scene 3: The next afternoon. Act II, Scene 1: The following morning. Scene 2: A week later. Scene 3: The end of August, afternoon and night; morning, September 1. Series of episodes concerning the residents of an unprosperous Southern farm.

Young People's Repertory Theater. Repertory of one new play and one revival. **When Did You Last See My Mother?** (11). By Christopher Hampton. Opened January 4, 1967. **Antigone** (4). Revival of the play by Sophocles in the Dudley Fitts-Robert Fitzgerald version. Opened January 14, 1967. Produced by Young People's Repertory Theater, Terese Hayden artistic director, at the Sheridan Square Playhouse. (Repertory closed January 16, 1967)

Designed by Michael Harwood; lighting, Joe Pacitti; production stage manager, Penelope H. Parkhurst; press, Max Eisen, Carl Samrock. WHEN DID YOU LAST SEE MY MOTHER?— With Gregory Reese, Robert Fielding, Elaine Aiken, Sheryl Blevins, Steven Mencher. A young man is emotionally involved with both his roommate and his roommate's mother. A foreign play previously produced in London. ANTIGONE—With Sima Gelbert, Gregory Reese.

Kicking the Castle Down (23). By Robert Kornfeld. Produced by Tricorn Productions, Ltd. at the Gramercy Arts Theater. Opened January 18, 1967. (Closed February 5, 1967)

Karl	Peter Simon	Pat	Trish Van Devere
Freddie	Wayne Geis	Carola	Catherine Gaffigan
Nance	Jo Anne Jameson	Mrs. Kane	Gale Sondergaard

Directed by David Young; scenery and lighting, Elmon Webb and Virginia Dancy; costumes, Lee Smith; production stage manager, Duke Houze; press, Arthur Cantor, Artie Solomon.

Time: New Year's Eve. Place: Karl's room. A tortured young man assails family and friends with his personal feelings and views.

By Jupiter (118). Musical revival with book by Richard Rodgers and Lorenz Hart, based on Julian F. Thompson's *The Warrior's Husband;* additional material by Fred Ebb; music by Richard Rodgers; lyrics by Lorenz Hart. Produced by Robert Cherin in association with Christopher Hewett at Theater Four. Opened January 19, 1967. (Closed April 30, 1967)

Theseus	Robert R. Kaye	Huntress	Alice Glenn
Homer	Emory Bass	3d Sentry; Trumpeter	Joyce Maret
Hercules	Charles Rydell	Caustica	Ronnie Cunningham
Herald	Richard Marshall	Heroica	Norma Doggett
Achilles	Ben Gerard	Pomposia	Irene Byatt
Buria	Rosemarie Heyer	Trumpeter; Runner	Debra Lyman
Sergeant; Penelope	Renata Vaselle	Hippolyta	Jackie Alloway
1st Sentry	Fayn Le Veille	Sapiens	Bob Dishy
2d Sentry; Messenger;		Antiope	Sheila Sullivan

Amazon and Greek Women: Violetta Landek, Fayn Le Veille, Alice Glenn, Renata Vaselle, Joyce Maret, Debra Lyman. Greek Warriors and Amazon Men: Hamp Dickens, Ronn Forella, Richard Natkowski, Ben Gerard.

Understudies: Miss Alloway—Renata Vaselle; Miss Sullivan—Rosemarie Heyer; Mr. Kaye— Richard Marshall; Mr. Dishy—Ben Gerard; Miss Byatt—Fayn Le Veille; Misses Doggett, Cunningham—Debra Lyman; Mr. Bass—Richard Natkowski; Mr. Marshall—Fred Kimbrough; Mr. Rydell—Hamp Dickens; Miss Heyer—Fayn Le Veille.

Directed by Christopher Hewett; choreography and musical numbers staged by Ellen Ray; musical director, Milton Setzer; scenery, Herbert Senn and Helen Pond; costumes, Winn Morton; lighting, Robert L. Steele; orchestrations, Abba Bogin; dance arrangements, Lee Holdridge; associate producers, James Love, Fritz Holt; production stage manager, Fritz Holt; stage manager, Fred Kimbrough; press, Samuel J. Friedman, Marvin Kohn.

By Jupiter was first produced on Broadway June 3, 1942 at the Shubert Theater by Dwight Deere Wiman and Richard Rodgers with Richard Kollmar, for 427 performances.

ACT I

Scene 1: The Greek Camp
"For Jupiter and Greece" ....Theseus, Homer, Hercules, Herald, Greek Men
Scene 2: The Amazon Palace
"Ride Amazon Ride" ....Buria, Amazons

"Jupiter Forbid" ....Hippolyta, Pomposia, Caustica, Heroica, Amazon Warriors, Men
"Life With Father" ....Sapiens, Amazon Men
"Nobody's Heart" ....Antiope
"In the Gateway of the Temple of Minerva" ....Theseus
Ballet
  Minerva ....Renata Vaselle
  Greek Chorus ....Ronnie Cunningham, Norma Dogett, Fayn Le Veille
  Maiden Statuettes ....Violetta Landek, Alice Glenn
  Satyrs ....Debra Lyman, Joyce Maret
  Sacrificial Slaves ....Hamp Dickens, Ronn Forella, Ben Gerard, Richard Natkowski
Finale ....Hippolyta, Pomposia, Sapiens, Caustica, Heroica, Amazon Warriors, Men

ACT II

Scene 1: The Greek Camp, Three Weeks Later
  "Wait Till You See Her" ....Theseus, Homer, Herald, Hercules, Greek Men
Scene 2: The Amazon Camp
  "The Boy I Left Behind Me" ....Buria, Amazons
  "Nobody's Heart" (Reprise) ....Sapiens
  "Ev'rything I've Got" ....Hippolyta, Sapiens
  "Bottoms Up" ....Hippolyta, Antiope, Herald, Homer, Achilles, Caustica,
                                      Heroica, Amazon Warriors, Greek Warriors
  "Careless Rhapsody" ....Antiope, Theseus
  "Finaletto" ....Hippolyta, Sapiens, Pomposia, Caustica, Heroica, Amazon Warriors
Scene 3: The Greek Camp
  "Ev'rything I've Got" (Reprise) ....Hippolyta
Scene 4: Inside Theseus' Tent
  "Now That I've Got My Strength" ....Sapiens, Camp Followers, Greek Men
Finale ....Entire Company

The Wicked Cooks (16). By Günter Grass; translated by A. Leslie Willson. Produced by Vaslin Productions at the Orpheum Theater. Opened January 23, 1967. (Closed February 5, 1967)

Petri ....John Coe	Other Cooks ....Bruce Comer, Isaac Dostis,
Benny ....Martin Shakar	Bayne Ellis, Henry Proach, Charles Ferrall
Green ....Sy Travers	Count ....Norman Rose
Stock ....Jara Kohout	Martha ....Linda Noyes
Vasco ....Martin Sheen	Aunt Theresa;
Kletterer ....Eugene Heller	Mrs. Coldwater ....Nina Varela

Directed by Vasek Simek; scenery and lighting, Clarke Dunham; music, Harold Seletsky; costumes, Joseph Aulisi; original slides, Dorothea Moos-Hake and Lloyd Greenberg; stage manager, Bud Coffey; press, William Greenblatt.

A parable and enigma of German confusion, smugness and guilt. A foreign play previously produced in Bonn, in a workshop production.

The Golden Screw (40). Musical with book, music and lyrics by Tom Sankey. Produced by Pandora Productions in association with Delancey Productions at the Provincetown Playhouse. Opened January 30, 1967. (Closed March 5, 1967)

Janet Day   Patrick Sullivan
Murray Paskin

Musicians: Tom Sankey and Jack Hopper. Members of the Inner Sanctum: Kevin Michael, Gerry Michael, Vince Taggart, Frank Thumhart.

Directed by David Eliscu; designed by C. Murawski; musical director, David Lucas; stage manager, Len Ross; press, Dorothy Ross, Mort Nathanson.

Understudies: Messrs. Sullivan, Paskin—Len Ross. Miss Day—Laurie Eliscu.

Dramatization of a rock 'n' roll singer's rise to the top, with folk music in the first half and hard rock in the second half.

ACT I—"Hard Times—Good Times," "New Evaline," "2,000 Miles," "Jesus Come Down," "You Won't Say No," "Beautiful People," "I Heard My Mother Crying," "I Can't Make It Anymore," ACT II—"Trip Tick Talking Blues," "Can I Touch You," "That's Your Thing, Baby," "I Can't Remember," "Bottom End of Bleecker Street," "Little White Dog."

The Deer Park (128). By Norman Mailer. Produced by Supreme Pix Inc. (Garen-Mailer-Walsh) at the Theater de Lys. Opened February 1, 1967. (Closed May 21, 1967)

Sergius O'Shaugnessy	.........Gene Lindsey	Elena Esposito	.............Rosemary Tory
Marion Faye	....................Rip Torn	Teddy Pope	................Joe McWherter
Bobby	.....................Marsha Mason	Tony Tunner	.............Gary Campbell
Lulu Meyers	..............Beverly Bentley	Dorothea O'Faye	.........Margret O'Neill
Charles Francis Eitel	.......Hugh Marlowe	Don Beda	.................Bernard Farbar
Carlyle Munshin	.............Mickey Knox	Zenlia	......................Mara Lynn
Teppis	........................Will Lee		

Directed by Leo Garen; scenery and lighting, Will Steven Armstrong; costumes, Ann Roth; music supervised by Charles Gross; production, James Walsh; production stage manager, Paul John Austin; press, James D. Proctor, Larry Belling, Max Gendel.

Time: Some undefined time after the Second World War; offers echoes of all the decades. Place: A resort in Southern California called Desert D'Or, or in the drunken memories of Sergius O'Shaugnessy's brain, or in some not quite definable estate or existence of hell. The human comedy expressed through Hollywood characters—the star, the world-weary director, the paternalistic studio head, etc.—mostly in terms of sexual adventures.

Diane Rousseau replaced Beverly Bentley 4/4/67. Richard Shepard replaced Rip Torn 4/18/67.

Les Femmes Savantes (9). Revival of the comedy by Molière performed in the French language. Produced by Jacques Courtines and Seff Associates Ltd., by special arrangement with Jean de Rigault, with the cooperation of La Comédie de L'Ouest, in Le Tréteau de Paris production at the Barbizon-Plaza Theater. Opened February 6, 1967. (Closed February 18, 1967)

Armande	.................Marie-Ange Roux	Philaminte	..............Jeannette Granval
Henriette	..................Catherine Broe	Trissotin	..................Michel Garland
Clitandre	..................Gerard Paquis	L'Epine	..................Jacques Daniaud
Belise	.....................Denise Bonal	Vadius	...................Michel Chasseing
Ariste	..............Jean-Claude Bouillaud	Julien	......................Francois Perez
Chrysale	...................Pierre Bolo	Le Notaire	................Francis Aubert
Martine	..................Antonine Mai		

Directed by Guy Parigot; scenery and costumes, Claude Bessou; production, Jean de Rigault; produced under the sponsorship of the Government of the French Republic; production stage manager, Jacques Daniaud; press, Arthur Pine Associates.

Die Brücke. German overseas ensemble in three plays in the German language. **Nathan der Weise** (3). By von Gotthold Ephraim Lessing. Opened December 8, 1966. **Bürger Schippel** (2). By Carl Sternheim. Opened December 11, 1966. **Kennen Sie die Milchstrasse?** (2). By Karl Wittlinger. Opened December 13, 1966. Produced by Gert Von Gontard and Felix G. Gerstman in association with Deutches Theater, N.Y., under the auspices of the Goethe Institute, at the Barbizon-Plaza Theater. (Series closed December 14, 1966).

NATHAN DER WEISE— Directed by Ernst Seiltgen; scenery and costumes, Ekkehard Grübler. Inspirational, poetic legend of a Jewish family living in Jerusalem. BÜRGER SCHIPPEL— Directed by Walter Vorberg; scenery, Ekkehard Grübler. Comedy about the rise of a humble flautist in the world of music and in society. KENNEN SIE DIE MILCHSTRASSE? (Do You Know the Milky Way?)—Directed by Joost Siedhoff. Symbolic drama of man's inhumanity to man, about a mental patient who believes he was born on another planet. All plays: press, Max Eisen. With Dieter Brammer, Joost Siedhoff, Peter Lühr, Gardy Brombacher, Inge Rassaerts, Christine Wodetzky, Heinz Baumann, Bruno Dallansky, Jörg von Liebenfels, Klaus Reents. Die Brücke is a travelling German troupe whose home base is Frankfurt.

Sometime Jam Today (33). By F. Story Talbot. Produced by Tanyasara Productions at the Bouwerie Lane Theater. Opened February 12, 1967. (Closed March 12, 1967)

Smith ....Ron Seka   T.C. ....Lise Beth

Directed by Mr. Talbot; scenery and lighting, Adam Ritchie; special music, Tom Wing; played by The Nickel Bag; production stage manager, Sydney Gregg; press, William Greenblatt.
Time: Late afternoon and next morning. Place: A pad in the East Village. Act I: The roof, late afternoon. Act II: The pad, the next morning. Hip girl from the East Village meets boy who is seemingly square but turns out to be the one who knows best how to cope.

* **Bil and Cora Baird's Marionette Theater.** Repertory of two marionette shows. *****People Is the Thing That the World Is Fullest Of** (105). Marionette revue conceived by Bil Baird. Opened February 20, 1967. *****Davy Jones' Locker** (11). Revival of the marionette musical based on a story by Bil Baird; with book by Arthur Birnkrant and Waldo Salt; music and lyrics by Mary Rodgers. Opened April 19, 1967. Produced by The American Puppet Arts Council, Inc., Arthur Cantor executive producer, at the Bil Baird Theater.

PEOPLE IS THE THING THE WORLD IS FULLEST OF—Directed by Burt Shevelove; design consultant, Will Steven Armstrong; lighting consultant, Peggy Clark; costumes, Fania Sullivan, Marianne Harms; music arranged and conducted by Alvy West; press, Artie Solomon, Irene Pinn. With Bil Baird, Cora Baird, Frank Sullivan, Franz Fazakas, Carl Harms, Jerry Nelson, Phyllis Nierendorf, Robin Kendall, Byron Whiting.
ACT I—Overture; "People, People" (music by Buster Davis); It's a Sin to Tell a Lie; "Asia"; "Conformity"; Slugger Ryan; Man and Woman; Science Fiction; "Bill Bailey"; Lover; "Old Abe Lincoln Had a Farm" (music by Buster Davis). ACT II—Overture; Pollution; Bil Baird; Africa; Words; Saloon Talk; The Family Danced; Crazy, Man, Crazy; In the Beginning, God . . . ; "The Population Explosion."

DAVY JONES' LOCKER

Nick; Paddlefoot ....Franz Fazakas	Mr. Merriweather;	
Billy; Capt. Fletcher Scorn;	Davy Jones ....Frank Sullivan	
The Sea Monster ....Bil Baird	Miranda ....Cora Baird	

Assorted Fishes, Ghosts, Pirates and Things: Jerry Nelson, Phyllis Nierendorf, Byron Whiting, Robin Kendall.
Directed by Burt Shevelove; musical arrangements, Alvy West; production manager, Carl Harms.
Davy Jones' Locker was originally produced in 1959. In this 1967 production it played only matinees and was augmented with a variety program entitled *A Pageant of Puppetry. Davy Jones' Locker* was also presented in December 1966 for 20 special children's performances.

The Rimers of Eldritch (32). By Lanford Wilson. Produced by Theater 1967 (Richard Barr, Clinton Wilder and Edward Albee), a project of Albarwild Theater Arts Inc. at the Cherry Lane Theater. Opened February 20, 1967. (Closed March 19, 1967)

Wilma Atkins ....Dena Dietrich	Eva Jackson ....Amy Taubin
Martha Truit ....Kate Wilkinson	Josh Johnson ....Walter Hadler
Nelly Windrod ....Blanche Lee	Skelly Mannor ....John O'Leary
Judge—Preacher ....James Noble	Peck Johnson ....Alfred Hinckley
Mary Windrod ....Bette Henritze	Evelyn Jackson ....Elizabeth Moore
Robert Conklin ....Don Scardino	Lena Truit ....Katherine Bruce
A Trucker ....Richard Orzel	Mavis Johnson ....Helen Stenborg
Cora Groves ....Ruth Manning	Patsy Johnson ....Susan Tyrrell
Walter ....Kevin O'Connor	

Directed by Michael Kahn; designed by William Ritman; stage managers, Charles Kindl, Donald Wesley; press, Howard Atlee.
Time: The present. Place: Eldritch, a town in the Middle West. Likeable small-towners allow themselves to lapse into an incident of intolerance and injustice.

* **MacBird!** (113) By Barbara Garson. Produced by John Curtis and David Productions at the Village Gate. Opened February 22, 1967.

Prologue; Chamberlain; Spectator; Egg of Head; Conspirator ......Dalton Dearborn
Beatnik Witch; Spectator;
  MacBird Daughter ....Jennifer Darling
Muslim Witch;
  Conspirator ....Cleavon Little
Revolutionary Witch;
  Spectator ....Tony Capodilupo
John Ken O'Dunc;
  Wayne of Morse ....Paul Hecht
Robert Ken O'Dunc ....William Devane

Ted Ken O'Dunc ....John Pleshette
MacBird ....Stacy Keach
Crony ....David Spielberg
Aide; Spectator;
  Crony's Crony ....Joel Zwick
Lady MacBird ....Rue McClanahan
Earl of Warren;
  Conspirator ....John Clark
Secretary; Spectator; MacBird Daughter;
  Messenger ....Deborah Gordon

Directed by Roy Levine; scenery, Clarke Dunham; costumes, Jeanne Button; lighting, Robert Brand; songs and music, John Duffy; production stage manager, Russell McGrath; press, Dorothy Ross, Leo Stern, Jane Friedman.

Act I, Scene 1: Prologue. Scene 2: Behind the Convention Hall. Scene 3: Ken O'Dunc's headquarters. Scene 4: The MacBird ranch. Scene 5: The Coronation. Scene 6: The MacBird ranch. Scene 7: The parade. Scene 8: The Capitol. Act II, Scene 1: The office of the President. Scene 2: Bobby's headquarters. Scene 3: MacBird's chamber. Scene 4: By the railroad tracks. Scene 5: Bobby's headquarters. Scene 6: MacBird's banquet hall. Scene 7: Bobby's headquarters. Scene 8: Outside the Convention Hall.

Parody of *Macbeth* used as a political cartoon of the relationship between President Lyndon B. Johnson and the Kennedy brothers, particularly in the supposed deadly political rivalry between President Johnson and Senator Robert Kennedy.

* **Fortune and Men's Eyes** (112). By John Herbert. Produced by David Rothenberg and Mitchell Nestor in association with The Little Room at Actors Playhouse. Opened February 23, 1967.

Rocky ....Victor Arnold
Mona ....Robert Christian
Queenie ....Bill Moor

Guard ....Clifford Pellow
Smitty ....Terry Kiser

Directed by Mitchell Nestor; designed by C. Murawski; costumes, Jan; music and sound effects, Terry Ross; press, David Rothenberg.

Time: The present. Place: The dormitory cell of a Canadian penal institution. The strange releases of emotional pressures in prison life, including homosexuality.

William Martel replaced Clifford Pellow 5/7/67.

The Harold Arlen Songbook (41). Program of musical numbers with music by Harold Arlen; lyrics by Truman Capote and Harold Arlen, Dorothy Fields, Ira Gershwin, E.Y. Harburg, Ted Koehler, Dory Langdon, Johnny Mercer, Leo Robin and Billy Rose. Produced by Ray Ramirez and Robert Elston at Stage 73. Opened February 28, 1967. (Closed April 2, 1967)

Pamela Hall
Jerry Holmes
Marcia Mohr

Ray Ramirez
Major Wiley

Production conceived and directed by Robert Elston; musical direction and vocal arrangements, George Taros; orchestrations, Lee Holdridge; lighting, Tony Quintavalla; stage manager, Bud Jarvis; assistant to director, Terry Crawford; press, Michael F. Goldstein Inc.

ACT I

Opening ....All
"Little Biscuit" ....Ramirez
Medley ....All

"Let's Take a Walk Around the Block" .... Miss Mohr
"In the Shade of the New Apple Tree" .... Holmes
Medley .... All
"Ridin' on the Moon" .... Ramirez
"Out of This World" .... Miss Hall
"We're Off to See the Wizard" .... All
Medley .... All
"Bubbles" .... All
"Merry Old Land of Oz" .... Wiley
"Push De Button" .... All
"I Wonder What Became of Me" .... Miss Hall
"So Long, Big Time" .... Ramirez
"Man That Got Away" .... Miss Mohr
"For Ev'ry Man There's a Woman" .... Holmes
"Anyplace I Hang My Hat Is Home" .... Wiley

ACT II

Medley .... All
"T'morra, T'morra" .... Wiley
"Love Held Lightly" .... Miss Hall
"Game of Poker" .... Holmes
"It's Only a Paper Moon" .... Miss Mohr
"I Had Myself a True Love" .... Miss Hall
"House of Flowers" .... Ramirez
"Willow in the Wind" .... Holmes
Medley .... All

Shoemakers' Holiday (6). Musical with book and lyrics by Ted Berger; music by Mel Marvin. Produced by Ken Costigan in association with R. Robert Lussier at the Orpheum Theater. Opened March 3, 1967. (Closed March 5, 1967)

Directed by Ken Costigan; musical staging and choreography, Myrna Gallé; musical direction, arrangements, Elman Anderson; scenery, Robert Conley; costumes, Whitney Blausen; press, David Lipsky, Marian Graham, Lisa Lipsky. With Jerry Dodge, Tom Lacy, Gary Oakes, Penny Gaston, Sue Lawless, Gail Johnston, Judy Knaiz, Robert Ronan, Garnett Smith, Lana Caradimas, Lynn Martin, George Cavey, Tom Urich, John Keller, Marcia Wood.

Time: The 16th Century. Place London. A musicalization of the Elizabethan comedy *The Shoemaker's Holiday* by Thomas Dekker.

* You're a Good Man Charlie Brown (98). Musical based on the comic strip "Peanuts" by Charles M. Schulz; book, music and lyrics by Clark Gesner. Produced by Arthur Whitelaw and Gene Persson at Theater 80 St. Marks. Opened March 7, 1967.

Linus .... Bob Balaban   Schroeder .... Skip Hinnant
Charlie Brown .... Gary Burghoff   Snoopy .... Bill Hinnant
Patty .... Karen Johnson   Lucy .... Reva Rose

Directed by Joseph Hardy; scenery and costumes, Alan Kimmel; lighting, Jules Fisher; musical supervision, arrangements and additional material, Joseph Raposo; piano, Ronald Clairmont; percussion, Lou Nazarro; stage manager, Ed Royce; press, Max Eisen, Carl Samrock, Jeanne Gibson Merrick.

Time and place: An average day in the life of Charlie Brown. Songs and sketches about Charlie Brown's problems with kiting, redheads, baseball, school—and Lucy.

A Best Play; see page 298

ACT I

"You're a Good Man Charlie Brown" .... Entire Company
"Schroeder" .... Lucy, Schroeder
"Snoopy" .... Snoopy, Charlie Brown
"My Blanket and Me" .... Linus
"Kite" .... Charlie Brown

"Dr. Lucy (The Doctor Is In)" ....Lucy, Charlie Brown
"Book Report" ....Charlie Brown, Lucy, Linus, Schroeder

ACT II

"The Red Baron" ....Snoopy
"T.E.A.M. (The Baseball Game)" ....Entire Company
"Glee Club Rehearsal" ....Entire Company
"Little Known Facts" ....Lucy, Linus, Charlie Brown
"Suppertime" ....Snoopy
"Happiness" ....Entire Company

* **Hamp** (101). By John Wilson; based on an episode from the novel by J. L. Hodson. Produced by Theater Vanguard and Stanwyck Ventures, Ltd. in association with Joseph H. Shoctor at the Renata Theater. Opened March 9, 1967.

Private Arthur Hamp	........Robert Salvio	President of the Court	......Leslie Redford
Corporal of the Guard	.........Ian Edward	Captain	......................Don Silber
Guard Private	...............Gary Britton	Lt. Prescott	..................Peter Bosche
Lt. William Hargreaves	.....Michael Lipton	Padre	......................Leslie Barrett
Lt. Tom Webb	.................Jess Osuna	Capt. O'Sullivan	........Francis Bethencourt
Lt. Midgley	..............David S. Howard	Orderly Officer	...............Henry Avery

Directed by Arthur A. Seidelman; scenery, Joseph Morton; lighting, Howard Becknell; costumes, Fran Brassard; music consultation, William Inglis; associate producer, Robert J. Gibson; production stage manager, Andy M. Rasbury; press, David Rothenberg.
Time: 1917. Place: The Western Front during the battle of Passchendaele. About judgement passed and executed upon a feckless British private who has deserted after three years at the front. A foreign play previously produced in Edinburgh and London.
A Best Play; see page 190

Dynamite Tonite (7). Revival of the musical play with words by Arnold Weinstein; music by William Bolcom. Produced by Paul Libin at the Martinique Theater. Opened March 15, 1967. (Closed March 19, 1967)

Directed by Paul Sills; scenery, Paul Short; lighting, F. Mitchell Dana; costumes, Thom Peterson; press, David Rothenberg. With Bill Alton, Alvin Epstein, Mark Epstein, Ben Hayeem, George Gaynes, Lou Gilbert, Allyn Ann McLerie, Gene Troobnick. Revised version of a play with music decrying war as absurd and cruel, previously presented off Broadway at Actors Studio Theater for one performance March 15, 1964.

Not a Way of Life (7). By James Rush. Produced by Thomas T. Kilhenny at the Sheridan Square Playhouse. Opened March 22, 1967. (Closed March 26, 1967)

Directed by Curt Dempster; designed by Kert Lundell; lighting, Neil Jampolis; stage manager, Robert Cline; press, Samuel J. Friedman, Marvin Kohn. With George Cotton, Dana Glenn, Sam Groom, Kate Harrington, Dirk Kooiman, Ryan MacDonald, Gretchen Walther. About the Roman Catholic Church's position on birth control.

The Diary of a Madman (4). One-man performance by Roger Coggio in a dramatization of the book by Nikolai Gogol; adapted by Sylvie Luneau and Roger Coggio; English translation by Ralph Manheim. Produced by Jacques Courtines, Ninon Tallon Karlweis, Jean de Rigault and Martin Rubin at the Orpheum Theater. Opened March 23, 1967. (Closed March 25, 1967)

Directed by Francois Perrot and Roger Coggio; music, Georges Delerue; scenery and costumes, Jacques Carelman; lighting, Daniel Barrau; press, Artie Solomon, Arthur Cantor. Drama of a lonely clerk's disintegration into madness. A foreign play previously produced in France.

Carricknabauna (21). By Padraic Colum; dramatized by Padraic Colum and Basil Burwell; music by Harriet Bailin. Produced by Greenwich Players, Inc. in a Stella

Holt production at Greenwich Mews Theater. Opened March 30, 1967. (Closed April 16, 1967)

Martyn Green	Rosemary McNamara
Neil Fitzgerald	Mark Jenkins
Hal Norman	Olive Murphy
Anne Draper	Brid Lynch
Tanny McDonald	Christopher Strater
Denise Huot	

Directed by Larry Arrick; assistant director, Rhoda Levine; scenery, lighting, costumes, Jock Stockwell; production stage manager, Robert Buzzell; press, David Lipsky, Marian Graham.

An adaptation of Padraic Colum's poetry and ballads in the form of a folk play with music. A foreign play previously presented, in part, in Dublin under the title *The Road Round Ireland*.

PART I

The Old Poet ....Neil Fitzgerald
"When You Were a Lad" ....Hal Norman, Christopher Strater, Mark Jenkins
"I Went Out in the Evening" ....Martyn Green
Fern's Castle ....Jenkins
The Crows ....Jenkins
Queen Gormlai ....Brid Lynch
"Carricknabauna" ....Fitzgerald, Norman, Jenkins, Strater
"For a Bride You Have Come" ....Rosemary McNamara, Denise Huot
The Well ....Jenkins
The Charm ....Strater
Dirge of the Lone Woman (by Mary Colum) ....Tanny McDonald
Dermott Donn MacMorna ....Miss Huot
"Tonight You See My Face" ....Miss McDonald
"No Bird That Sits" ....Miss McNamara
"Sean O'Dwyer" ....Green
Old Scholar ....Fitzgerald
"Sojourner" ....Norman
Old Woman of the Roads ....Miss Lynch
"Cheap Jack" ....Green
"The Lannan Shee" ....Misses Lynch, Huot, McNamara, McDonald
"The Fiddles Were Playing" ....Anne Draper

PART II

Stations of the Cross .....Green, Strater, Jenkins, Misses McDonald, McNamara, Huot, Lynch
"One Came Before Her" ....Miss McNamara, Strater
"Toymaker" ....Green
"County Mayo" ....Fitzgerald
Raftery ....Green
Raftery's Repentence ....Fitzgerald
An Drinaun Donn ....Miss Huot
"The Terrible Robber Men" ....Norman, Strater, Miss McNamara
"The Cradle Song" ....Miss McDonald
"Spanish Lady" ....Martyn Green
White Faced Throng ....Miss Lynch
"Seumas-a-Ree" ....Miss Huot
The Rebel ....Green
"The Birds That Left the Cage" ....Norman, Strater, Fitzgerald, Jenkins,
                                                  Misses Huot, McDonald, McNamara
O'Connell Bridge ....Jenkins
"Meditation" ....Miss Draper
Age of Bronze ....Miss Draper, Jenkins
"Over the Hills and Far Away" ....Green, Entire Company

Skits-oh-Frantics! (17). Musical revue with words and music by Bernie Wayne; additional material by Charles Naylor and Ken Welch. Produced by Bob Hadley at the Bert Wheeler Theater. Opened April 2, 1967. (Closed April 16, 1967)

Directed by Hank Ladd; musical staging, Frank Westbrook; scenery and lighting, Carleton Snyder; costumes, Eve Henriksen; musical director, Bernie Wayne; additional choreography, Patti Karr; orchestra leader, Walter Fleisher; production manager, Jack Saunders; producer associates, Thomas G. Abernathy, Freeman Parks; supplementary lyrics, Marvin Moore, Lee Morris; press, Max Eisen. With Hank Ladd, Irving Harmon, Bobbi Baird, Bes-Arlene, Mona Crawford, Patti Karr, Barney Martin, Robert Weil, Geene Courtney-James. A revue of songs, dances, stand up monologues and burlesque routines.

Chocolates (8). By Ian Bernard. Produced by Lynn Loesser in association with Manon Enterprises, Inc. at the Gramercy Arts Theater. Opened April 10, 1967. (Closed April 16, 1967)

Directed by Ian Bernard; scenery and lighting, Michael Allen Hampshire; press, Karl Bernstein. With Virginia Kiser, J. Frank Lucas, George Randall, Hope Stansbury. An old-fashioned individualist struggles against conformity in the world of the future.

* Gorilla Queen (42). By Ronald Tavel. Produced by Paul Libin at the Martinique Theater. Opened April 24, 1967.

Venus Fly Trap ....Jo Ann Forman	Clyde ....James Hilbrandt
Brute ....George Harris II	Taharahnugi White Woman ...Quinn Halford
Glitz Ionas ......Adrienne de Antonio, Mary	Chimney Sweep ....David Kerry Heefner
Duke, Norman R. Glick, John Harrill,	Sister Carries ....Eddie McCarti
George Harris III, Dick Lipkin,	Paulet ....Barbara Ann Camp
Norman Soifer	Queen Kong .....Norman Thomas Marshall
Mais Oui ....Selena Williams	Intern ....Harvey Tavel
Karma ....Paula Shaw	

Directed by Lawrence Kornfeld; scenery, Jerry Joyner; costumes, Linda Sampson; music, Robert Cosmos Savage; lighting, John P. Dodd, Deborah Lee; incidental songs "Frickadellin," "Cockamanie," "Pyromania" and "Ay Yi Yi" by Al Carmines; production stage manager, Roland Turner; press, Michael F. Goldstein Inc.

Campy takeoff of Hollywood jungle movies, with various sex deviations comically represented.

To Clothe the Naked (30). Revival of a play by Luigi Pirandello; translated by William Murray. Produced by David Black and Lorin E. Price at the Sheridan Square Playhouse. Opened April 27, 1967. (Closed May 21, 1967)

Ersilia Drei ....Kathleen Widdoes	Franco Laspiga ....Alex Cort
Ludovico Nota ....Louis Zorich	Emma ....Brenda Lesley
Mrs. Onoria ....Helen Craig	Grotti ....Joseph Mascolo
Alfredo Cantavalle ....Tony Capodilupo	

Directed by Jonathan Black; scenery and lighting, Joan Larkey; costumes, Jack Edwards; sound, Mike Sahl; production supervisor, Jose Vega; production stage manager, Lewis S. Rosen; press, Frank Goodman, Martin Shwartz.

Time: 1912. Place: Combination study and living room of the writer, Ludovico Nota in Rome. Act I: Afternoon. Act II: The following morning. Act III: Late that afternoon. Melodrama about a young servant girl, embroiled with three men and telling lies in an attempt to set them free of her. This play was last revived under the title *Naked* off Broadway in 1950 by Studio 7, and on Broadway in 1926 (in English) and 1924 (in French).

Follies Burlesque '67 (16). Musical with book by Stanley Richman; music and lyrics by Sol Richman. Produced by Richman-Maurer-Richards at the Players Theater. Opened May 3, 1967. (Closed May 14, 1967)

Libby Jones	Cathy Collins
Mickey Hargitay	Bill Drew
Claude Mathis	Frank Silvano
Count Gregory	Julie Taylor
Joe Tempo	Toni Karrol

Directed by Dick Richards; choreography, Paul Morokoff; lighting, Ricardo; costumes, S. Binder; press, Max Eisen, Carl Samrock.

A musical in the burlesque style, with a book about the visit of a group of women to Paris. Scheduled to reopen at the Bert Wheeler Theater in June 1967.

ACT I

"Burlesque Is a Stamping Ground" ....Entire Company
Parisian Street Scene ....Entire Company
  "Oooh Lah Lah"
The Title ....Count Gregory, Frank Silvano, Libby Jones
Exotic ....Julie Taylor
The Transformer ....Cathy Collins, Mickey Hargitay, Claude Mathis, Libby Jones
Exotic Dance Team ....Toni Karrol, Dick Richards
Comedy in Stripping ....Cathy Collins
The Stand-in ....Mickey Hargitay, Frank Silvano, Bill Drew
"Scratch-My-Back" ....Cathy Collins, Girls

ACT II

"The Rabbit Habit" ....Cathy Colins, Joe Tempo, Girls
"The More I Hold You" ....Frank Silvano
"Buono Notte" ....Frank Silvano
Tappin' In ....Bill Drew
"Tell Me" ....Libby Jones
Exotic ....Julie Taylor
"The Spiritual" ....Frank Silvano, Girls
Crazy Horse ....Claude Mathis, Mickey Hargitay, Cathy Collins, Girls
Libby ....Libby Jones
Finale ....Entire Company

Les Fourberies de Scapin (4). Revival of the comedy by Molière in the French language. Produced by The Hunter College Concert Bureau in association with Mel Howard under the auspices of the French Government and with the cooperation of the French Cultural Services in the United States and in conjunction with Les Productions d'Aujourd'hui of Paris at the Hunter College Playhouse. Opened May 7, 1967. (Closed May 10, 1967)

Argante ....Jacques Plee
Géronte ....Fred Personne
Octave ....Pierre Yves Coustere
Léandre ....André Widmer
Zerbinette ....Evelyne Istria

Hyacinte ....Claude Cendra
Scapin ....Claude Leveque
Sylvestre ....Jean-Marie Richier
Nérine ....Dominique Dullin
Carle ....Philippe Jarry

Directed by Edmond Tamiz; assistant director, Philippe Jarry; scenery and costumes, Christiane Lücke; music, Modern Jazz Quartet.

Time: 1671. Place: Naples. *Les Fourberies de Scapin* was last presented in New York in APA repertory, in English, March 9, 1964. This production was mounted in Paris at the Théâtre de Récamier in 1965.

The Experiment (16). By David Halliwell and David Calderisi. Produced by Robert Fowler at the Orpheum Theater. Opened May 8, 1967. (Closed May 21, 1967)

Gwendolyn Van Drysdale ....Joy Martin
Michael Ellsworthy ....Rik Pierce
Nicholas Tyler ....Peter Maloney
Jean Biggs ....Barbara Ann Teer
Aylmer Demune ....Sheldon Baron

Arthur Rose ....Jack Kassabian
Eugenie Thorpe ....Margaret Ladd
Celia Browne ....Paula Shaw
Jackson McIver ....Ray Stewart

Directed by Ian Lindsay; film sequences by Robert Downey; production stage manager, David Bamberger; press, Howard Atlee.

A director is searching for the ultimate in absurd style as he marshals his actors in a scene depicting the assassination of President Garfield. A foreign play which grew out of actors' improvisations and was previously produced in London.

Harold and **Sondra** (8). Program of one-act plays by Frederick Feirstein. Produced by Mari Saville at the Provincetown Playhouse. Opened May 9, 1967. (Closed May 14, 1967)

Directed by Vasek Simek; set supervision and lighting, Charles Ard; costumes, Ann Froman; press, Reuben Rabinovitch. With Michael Baseleon, Nancy Cushman, Martin Huston, Linda Noyes, Sasha von Scherler, Jennifer West, Ben Yaffee. *Sondra* is about two partying couples who ignore the cries of a woman being raped and murdered. *Harold* is about a family reunion of people who bicker so much that they ignore their son dying of bronchial pneumonia.

The Party on Greenwich Avenue (6). By Grandin Conover. Produced by Theater 1967 (Richard Barr, Clinton Wilder and Edward Albee), a project of Albarwild Theater Arts Inc., at the Cherry Lane Theater. Opened May 10, 1967. (Closed May 13, 1967)

Directed by Richard Altman; designed by Rouben Ter-Arutunian; press, Howard Atlee. With Joyce Aaron, Carolyn Coates, James Hall, Tresa Hughes, Philip Sterling, Clarence Williams III. A middle-class couple from New Jersey becomes the object of sadistic jokes and assaults.

* The Coach with the Six Insides (24). Revival of the play by Jean Erdman, inspired by James Joyce's *Finnegans Wake*. Produced by The-Here-We-Are-Again-Gaieties Corporation in association with Richard Herd at the East 74th Street Theater. Opened May 11, 1967.

Anna Livia Plurabelle ....Jean Erdman	Daughter—Iseult ....Gail Ryan
(Margaret Beals)	Elder Twin—Shaun ....Michael Prince
Wife and Charwoman ....Anita Dangler	Younger Twin—Shem ....Van Dexter

Written, directed and choreographed by Jean Erdman; slide projection designs, Milton Howarth; music, Teiji Ito; costumes, Gail Ito; lighting, Carol Hoover; decor, Dan Butt; musicians, Peter Berry, director, Herb Bushler, Harold Vick; production stage manager, Carol Hoover; press, Betty Lee Hunt, Fred Weterick.

Act I Time: Past present (harry me)—The fall, wake and reappearance of a certain party. Act II Time: Future present (marry me)—Chips off the old block. Act III Time: Future past (bury me)—His gadabout in her day. This comedy was previously presented off Broadway for 114 performances in the 1962-63 season, when it won Obie and Vernon Rice Awards.

The Death of the Well-Loved Boy (8). By John Farris. Produced by Susan Richardson at St. Marks Playhouse. Opened May 15, 1967. (Closed May 21, 1967)

Directed by Patricia Carmichael; scenery, Peter Harvey; costumes, Lohr Wilson; lighting, V.C. Fuqua; original music and sound, Don Heckman; press, Dorothy Ross. With Barbara Cason, Keith Charles, Elizabeth Franz, Diane Kagan, Nelson Phillips, James Noble, John Marriott, Mina Jo King, Kermit Brown, M. Emmet Walsh, Larry Blauvelt. The tragic effect of the death of a Southern family's son.

To Bury a Cousin (5). By Gus Weill. Produced by David Lawlor at the Bouwerie Lane Theater. Opened May 16, 1967. (Closed May 21, 1967)

Directed by Philip Oesterman Jr.; scenery, Douglas W. Schmidt; costumes, Terry Leong; lighting, James Gore; press, Sol Jacobson, Lewis Harmon. With Mary Boylan, Rosalind Cash, Edwin Cooper, Janet Dowd, Elliot Levine, J. Frank Lucas; John Scanlan, Arn Weiner, Mildred Weitz. A famous playwright returns to his home for a cousin's funeral and investigates why this cousin had accomplished nothing in his 50 years of life.

* Drums in the Night (15). By Bertolt Brecht; adapted by Frank Jones. Produced by Theodore Mann at Circle in the Square. Opened May 17, 1967.

Carl Balicke ....Hector Elizondo	Maid; Marie ....Lynne Lipton
Emily Balicke ....Peggy Feury	Anna Balicke ....Joanna Miles

Frederick Murk ....Ed Setrakian	2d Man; Bulltrotter ....Jack Kehoe
Babusch ....Michael Egan	Piccadilly Cafe Owner;
Andrew Kragler ....Ralph Waite	Glubb ....George Stauch
Piccadilly Bar Manke;	Drunk ....Charles Creasap
His Brother ....Martin Siegel	Augusta ....Roxanne Smith
1st Man; Newsboy ....Neil Peckett	

Directed by Theodore Mann; lighting, Mark D. Healy; scenery, John Annus; musical supervision and translation of "The Ballad of a Dead Soldier," Will Holt; stage manager, Penelope Court; press, Merle Debuskey, Violet Welles, Faith Geer.
Time: 1918. Place: Berlin. Act I: Africa—the Balicke's house. Act II: Pepper—the Piccadilly Bar. Act III: The Booze Dance—a small gin mill. Act IV: The Bed—a city street. Disillusionment and social injustice in the story of a soldier's return home in post-World War I Germany. A foreign play previously produced in Munich, Berlin and elsewhere.
Drums in the Night alternated with *Eh?* at the Circle in the Square, 5/17/67-5/24/67.

An Evening with the Times Square Two (10). Two-man musical revue with Mycroft Partner and Andrew i. Produced by Roger Euster at the Gramercy Arts Theater. Opened May 19, 1967. (Closed May 28, 1967)

Directed by Saul Gottlieb; musicians, Sara Hart, Marrin Sklar; special staging, Paul McDowell; press, David Lipsky, Marian Graham, Larry Gore. Program of satirical songs, juggling, jokes, etc.

* Absolutely Free (13). Musical revue with music and lyrics by Frank Zappa. Produced by Herb Cohen at the Garrick Theater. Opened May 24, 1967.

With the Mothers of Invention: Mr. Zappa, Don Preston, Ray Collins, Jimmy Clark Black, Bunk Gardner, Roy Estrada, Billy Mundi. Program made up mostly of songs and instrumental numbers.

* A Time for the Gentle People (7). By Tom Coble. Produced by Tosi Productions in association with Jim Borland. Opened May 25, 1967.

Bob Verducci ....Jack Dabdoub	Jane Young ....Jeanne Carberry
Sue Garlin ....Diane Tarleton	Betty Carbone ....Leslie Jane Borland
Joe Verducci ....Tom Coble	

Directed by Tom Coble; scenery, Giasulo Studio; lighting, Michael Velenti; press, Max Eisen. An Ole Miss football star tries to become an actor in New York.

Some Additional Productions

The American Place Theater. Subscription series of four plays produced by The American Place Theater at St. Clement's Church. *Who's Got His Own* and *The Displaced Person* (see their individual entries in the off-Broadway list) and the following programs presented to subscribers only:

LA TURISTA (29). By Sam Shepard; directed by Jacques Levy; lighting, Roger Morgan. With Joyce Aaron, Lawrence Block, Michael Lombard, Joel Novack, Sam Waterston. Opened March 4, 1967. (Closed April 1, 1967)

* POSTERITY FOR SALE (21). By Niccolo Tucci; directed by Rocco Bufano; scenery and costumes, Kert Lundell; lighting, Roger Morgan. With Salome Jens, Sam Waterston, Anne Draper, Eric Elgar, Brendan Fay, George Gaynes. Opened May 11, 1967.

ANTA Matinee Theater Series. The Greater New York Chapter of ANTA's Matinee Theater Series, under the direction of Lucille Lortel, presented four productions on Monday evenings and Tuesday afternoons, plus one production for members only, at the Theater de Lys.

SEVEN AGES OF BERNARD SHAW (2). One-woman program of Shavian writings performed by Margaret Webster. November 21, 1966 (evening) and November 22 (matinee).

COME SLOWLY, EDEN (A portrait of Emily Dickinson) (2). By Norman Rosten. December 5, 1966 (evening) and December 6 (matinee). Directed by Thomas Skelton. With Kim Hunter, Jacqueline Brookes, Robert Elston, Robert Moberly, William Roerick, David J. Stewart, Douglass Watson.

THE DEADLY ART (2). Stage swordplay through the ages, with Rod Colbin and Vincent Milana. December 12, 1966 (evening) and December 13 (matinee). Special program for subscribers.

A PROGRAM OF NEW AMERICAN PLAYS (2). Program of two plays. January 9, 1967 (evening) and January 10 (matinee). The Viewing written and directed by Lyle Kessler; lighting, Timmy Harris. With Michael Fischetti, Will Hare, Eleanor Lynn. Conditioned Reflex by Curtis Zahn; directed by Edward Morehouse. With Leslie Barrett and Robert Elston.

WILLIE DOESN'T LIVE HERE ANYMORE (2). Adapted by Robert Kamlot from a play by Gert Hofmann. February 6, 1967 (evening) and February 7 (matinee). Directed by William Archibald. With Mildred Dunnock, Conrad Bain, Julie Follansbee, Walter McGinn, Renee Taylor, Sasha von Scherler.

Equity Theater. The following plays were produced by Equity Theater at the Master Theater.

YOU NEVER CAN TELL (9). By George Bernard Shaw. October 21, 1966. Directed by Edward Morehouse. With Richard Graham, William Grannell, Glenn Kezer, John Le Grand, Mark Lonow, Susan Monson, Richard Morse, Arlene Nadel, Dorothy Price, Lucille Saint-Peter.

ALL THE KING'S MEN (9). By Robert Penn Warren. Directed by Ben Benoit. With Jay Barney, Dorothy Chace, Stanley Brock, Verna Bloom, James Davis, James Douglas, Ray Durand, John Glover, George Harris II, William Leet, Zola Long, Frank A. Lutz III, P. L. Pfeiffer, Don Phelps, Frank Rohrbach, Janet Sarno, Barry Simpson, Jerry Trichter, Allister Whitman, Ian Crosby.

ALL IN LOVE (14). Musical with book and lyrics by Bruce Geller; music by Jack Urbont. Directed and choreographed by Roger Sullivan and Dania Krupska. With Ernestine Barrett, Stephen Bolster, George Cavey, Robert Dagny, Nell Evans, Nina Gervais, Linda Gregg, Janet Hayes, Don Jay, Peter Johl, Dorothy Lancaster, Del Lewis, Robert Meyer, Joan Nelson, Gregg Nickerson, Dodi Protero, Ted Pugh, Reva Rose, Evan Thomas, Pascual Vaquer, Noel Craig.

THE NIGHT OF THE IGUANA (9). By Tennessee Williams. Directed by Tom Brennan. With Ray Arlen, Bob Berger, Jane Culley, Barbara Hollis, Antoinette Kray, Ric Mancini, Dean McIlnay, Donna Pearson, Alek Primrose, Donald Ross, Marc Sachs, Anthony Serchio, Ingrid Severson, Fern Sloan.

ONCE UPON A MATTRESS (14). Musical with book by Jay Thompson, Marshall Barer and Dean Fuller; music by Mary Rodgers; lyrics by Marshall Barer. Directed by Dolores Ferraro. With Joe Alfasa, Harriet All, Bonnie Boland, Dennis Carpenter, Steve Ciosek, George Comtois, Frank Coppola, Stephan De Ghelder, Jean Even, Susan Feldon, Danny Fortus, Avril Gentles, Pamela Gruen, Elinor Ellsworth, Ed Hatton, Jo Henderson, Don Jacob, Joan Jaffe, David Jarrett, Christopher Lloyd, Alan McCarter, Martin Ross, Sondra Wolf.

THE WOOD DEMON (9). By Anton Chekhov; translated by Alex Szogyi. Directed by William Woodman. With Bo Brundin, Ronn Carroll, Lance Cunard, Lee Elliott, Lewis Jacobson, Andrew Johns, Cam Kornman, Donald Marlatt, Ralph Nilson, Charles Seals, Guy Spaull, Sunja Svenson, Betsy Thurman, Ralph Wainright.

THE HOSTAGE (9). By Brendan Behan. Directed by Lester Robin. With Michael Baybak, Harry Bergman, Dorothy Chace, Grant Code, Aurelia De Felice, William Jay, Marilyn Madderom, Peter Maloney, Thom Molyneau, Carmel Signa, Sasha von Scherler, Bill Wiley, Curt Williams, Barbara Young.

DAMN YANKEES (14). Musical with book by George Abbott and Douglass Wallop; music and lyrics by Richard Adler and Jerry Ross. Directed by Leland Ball; choreography, Frank Pietri. With Diaan Ainslee, Alice Beardsley, John Bernabei, Frank Borgman, Larry Burns, Vela Ceres, Frank Damis, Don Dolan, Martha Greenhouse, Peter Harris, Herbert Jefferson, Jay Kirsch, James LeVaggi, Lynn Martin, Neil McNelis, Frank Pietri, Hansford Rowe, Clifton Steere, Andrea Stevens, Robert Tananis, Bill Wiley, Kent Wood.

INVITATION TO A MARCH (10). By Arthur Laurents. Directed by George Wojtasik. With Laura Addams, Doris Brent, Gene R. Coleman, Ron Leath, Joan Lowell, Edward Penn, Marjorie Stapp, Jeff Stuart.

Equity Theater Informals at the Library and Museum of Performing Arts at Lincoln Center took place as follows:

THE WEARY BLUES (3). Adapted by Woodie King Jr. from poetry and prose of Langston Hughes. October 31, 1966.

PAST MIDNIGHT! PAST THE MORNING STAR! (3). Adapted by Julia Beals from the poetry and letters of Emily Dickinson. November 28, 1966.

ONE PERFECT ROSE: An Evening With Dorothy Parker (3). Adapted and directed by Gail Bell. December 12, 1966.

AN EVENING WITH SUE & PUGH (3). Musical revue by and with Sue Lawless and Ted Pugh. January 16, 1967.

ROBERT MOLNAR (3). Program of pantomime. January 23, 1967.

THE GENTLE ART OF MAKING ENEMIES (3). Adapted and directed by Joel Friedman from writings of James McNeill Whistler. March 13, 1967.

FROM DISTANT ROOMS (3). A memory of Jean Cocteau adapted by T. Diane Anderson; conceived and directed by Mark Mason. April 3, 1967.

DIVISION STREET: AMERICA (3). Adapted from the book by Studs Terkel. April 10, 1967.

EXPERIMENTS IN DANCE-THEATER (3). Choreography by Joan Baker and Rudy Perez. April 24, 1967.

The Blackfriars' Guild. Three new plays produced by the Blackfriars' Guild (Rev. Thomas F. Carey, Moderator) at the Blackfriars' Guild.

GO, GO, GO, GOD IS DEAD! (61). By Mary Drahos. October 11, 1966. Directed by Walter Cool; scenery, T. Fabian; lighting, Allen Edward Klein; costumes, Alice Merrigal. With Ann D'Andrea, Lawrence J. Buckley, Barbara Coggin, Evelyn Denon, Richard Egan, Fred Hodges, Bob Macke, Mitchell McGuire, John F. Rush, Kathleen Tighe. A comedy about the moral values of high schoolers.

THE MAN WHO WASHED HIS HANDS (33). By William C. Thompson. February 15, 1967. Directed by Walter Cool; scenery and lighting, Allen Edward Klein; costumes, Alice

Merrigal. With Ann D'Andrea, Frank Benedetto, Reb Buxton, Ben Greer, Frank Praino, Frank Salmonese, Dennis Johnson and Pat Girvan. An existential treatment of Pontius Pilate.

THE HAPPY FACULTY (34). By Joan and Philip Nourse; directed by Walter Cool; scenery and lighting, T. Fabian; costumes, Alice Merrigal. With Madeleine Fisher, Winston May, Patrick McCullough, Ruth Ann Norris, John F. Rush, Reuben Schafer, Jim Parker. Romantic comedy about certain college administrative practises.

The New Theater Workshop. Monday Night Play Series of productions at the New Theater.

THE PEACE CREEPS (3). By John Wolfson. Directed by John Stix. December 5, 1966. With Pamela Bekolay, James Earl Jones, John Birrell, Pat Corley, Malcolm Cowles, Al Pacino, Connie Scott, Don Scardino.

CAFE UNIVERS (3). By David Karp. Directed by Stephen Aaron. March 13, 1967. With Salem Ludwig, Michael Enserro, John Brinkley, Paul Carson, William Cox, Michael Egan, Peggy Elcar, Michael Fishchetti, Mi-

chael Greene, Dennis Helfend, David Jackson, John Pavelko.

A FEW OF THE USUAL NUDES (3). By Robert Cessna; music by William Brohn. April 13, 1967. Directed by Charles Maryan. With Barbara Casson, Simm Landres, Gabor Morea, Sarah Sanders, Joe Sicari.

ARF! (3). By Dan Greenburg; directed by Larry Arrick. May 16, 1967. With Robert Barend, Richard Schaal, Judi West.

CAST REPLACEMENTS AND TOURING COMPANIES

The following is a listing of some of the more important cast replacements in productions which opened in previous years, but which were still playing in New York during a substantial part of the 1966-67 season; or were still on a national tour; or opened in 1966-67 and cast a touring company in that same season. The name of the character is listed in italics beneath the title of the play in the first column, and in the second column appears the name of the actor who created the role and, immediately beneath, his subsequent replacements. The third column gives information about touring companies of these productions. Where there is more than one roadshow company (not including bus-truck troupes), #1, #2, and #3 appear before the name of the performer who created the role in those companies. Their subsequent replacements, if any, are listed beneath. A note on bus-truck tours appears at the end of this section.

BAREFOOT IN THE PARK

	NEW YORK COMPANY	TOURING COMPANIES
Corie Bratter	Elizabeth Ashley 10/23/63	Joan Van Ark 7/28/64
	Penny Fuller 6/8/64	Christina Crawford 9/6/65
	Joan Van Ark 5/23/66	Beverly Penberthy 10/31/65
		Geraldine Court 7/4/66
Paul Bratter	Robert Redford 10/23/63	Richard Benjamin 7/28/64
	Robert Reed 9/7/64	Philip Clark 9/6/65
	Anthony Roberts 4/5/65	
	Joel Crothers 8/29/66	
Mrs. Banks	Mildred Natwick 10/23/63	Myrna Loy 7/28/64
	Eileen Heckart 9/20/65	
	Ilka Chase 5/23/66	
	Sylvia Sidney 4/4/67	
Victor Velasco	Kurt Kasznar 10/23/63	Sandor Szabo 7/28/64
	Charles Korvin 9/20/65	
	Jules Munshin 2/21/66	

CACTUS FLOWER

Stephanie	Lauren Bacall 12/8/65	
	Betsy Palmer 10/17/66	
	Lauren Bacall 10/24/66	
Julian	Barry Nelson 12/8/65	
	Kevin McCarthy 5/8/67	
	Barry Nelson 5/29/67	
Toni	Brenda Vaccaro 12/8/65	
	Ethelyne Dunfee 12/19/66	

A DELICATE BALANCE

Tobias	Hume Cronyn 9/22/67	Hume Cronyn 2/13/67
Agnes	Jessica Tandy 9/22/67	Jessica Tandy 2/13/67

THE FANTASTICKS

The Narrator	Jerry Orbach 5/3/60	
	Gene Rupert	
	Bert Convy	
	John Cunningham	

	NEW YORK COMPANY	TOURING COMPANIES
	Don Stewart 1/8/63	
	David Cryer	
	Keith Charles	
	John Boni 1/13/65	
	Jack Mette 9/14/65	
	George Ogee	
	Keith Charles	
	John Boni	
The Girl	Rita Gardner 5/3/60	
	Carla Huston	
	Liza Stuart	
	Eileen Fulton	
	Alice Cannon	
	Royce Lenelle	
	B.J. Ward 12/1/64	
	Leta Anderson 7/13/65	
	Carol Deems 12/5/66	
The Boy	Kenneth Nelson 5/3/60	
	Gino Conforti	
	Jack Blackton	
	Paul Giovanni	
	Ty McConnell	
	Richard Rothbard	
	Gary Krawford	
	Bob Spencer 9/5/64	
	Erik Howell	

FIDDLER ON THE ROOF

Tevye	Zero Mostel 9/22/64	Luther Adler 4/11/66
	Luther Adler 8/15/65	
	Herschel Bernardi 11/8/65	
Golde	Maria Karnilova 9/22/64	Dolores Wilson 4/11/66

FUNNY GIRL

Fanny Brice	Barbra Streisand 3/26/64	Marilyn Michaels 10/8/65
	Mimi Hines 12/27/65	
Nick Arnstein	Sydney Chaplin 3/26/64	Anthony George 10/8/65
	George Reeder	
	Johnny Desmond 7/5/65	

GENERATION

Jim Bolton	Henry Fonda 10/6/65	Robert Young 8/17/66
		Don Porter 10/22/66

HALF A SIXPENCE

Arthur Kipps	Tommy Steele 4/25/65	Dick Kallman 7/26/66
	Tony Tanner 3/21/66	
	Dick Kallman 7/4/66	
Ann Pornick	Polly James 4/25/65	Anne Rogers 7/26/66
	Anne Rogers 7/4/66	Ann Wakefield 11/28/66

HAPPY ENDING and DAY OF ABSENCE

Arthur; Mayor	Douglas Turner Ward 11/15/65	Douglas Turner Ward 12/16/66
	James Earl Jones 12/16/66	
	Douglas Turner Ward 1/24/67	

HELLO, DOLLY!

Mrs. Dolly Gallagher Levi	Carol Channing 1/16/64	#1 Mary Martin 4/17/65
	Ginger Rogers 8/9/65	Dora Bryan 5/14/66
	Martha Raye 2/27/67	#2 Carol Channing 9/6/65
		#3 Betty Grable 11/3/65

	NEW YORK COMPANY	TOURING COMPANIES

		#4 Ginger Rogers 4/19/67
Horace Vandergelder	David Burns 1/16/64	#1 Loring Smith 4/17/65
	Max Showalter 3/13/67	Replaced 5/14/66
		#2 Horace McMahon 9/6/65
		Milo Boulton
		#3 Max Showalter 11/3/65
		#4 David Burns 4/19/67

HOGAN'S GOAT

Edward Quinn	Tom Ahearne 11/11/65
	Dolph Sweet 12/6/66
	Michael Hogan 2/28/67
Matthew Stanton	Ralph Waite 11/11/65
	Richard Mulligan 2/1/66
	Ralph Waite 5/5/66
	Gene Rupert 10/18/66
Kathleen Stanton	Faye Dunaway 11/11/65
	Kay Chevalier 1/22/66
	Karen McCrary 5/17/66

HOSTILE WITNESS

Simon Crawford	Ray Milland 2/17/66	Ray Milland 9/6/66

THE IMPOSSIBLE YEARS

Dr. Jack Kingsley	Alan King 10/13/65
	Ed McMahon 1/17/66
	Alan King 1/24/66
	Sam Levene 8/22/66

LUV

Harry Berlin	Alan Arkin 11/11/64	Herbert Edelman 9/6/65
	Gabriel Dell 8/24/65	
	Gene Wilder 6/13/66	
Milt Manville	Eli Wallach 11/11/64	Tom Bosley 9/6/65
	Larry Blyden 2/28/66	
	Robert Darnell 6/27/66	
Ellen Manville	Anne Jackson 11/11/64	Dorothy Loudon 9/6/65
	Barbara Bel Geddes 2/28/66	

MAME

Mame	Angela Lansbury 5/24/66
	Sheila Smith 2/13/67
	Angela Lansbury 2/27/67
Vera Charles	Beatrice Arthur 5/24/66
	Sheila Smith 3/27/67
	Beatrice Arthur 4/10/67
Young Patrick	Frankie Michaels 5/24/66
	Stuart Getz 5/8/67

MAN OF LA MANCHA

Don Quixote (Cervantes)	Richard Kiley 11/22/65	José Ferrer 9/24/66
	José Ferrer 5/28/66	Richard Kiley 4/11/67
	John Cullum 2/24/67	
	José Ferrer 4/11/67	
Aldonza	Joan Diener 11/22/65	Maura K. Wedge 9/24/66
	Marion Marlowe 1/17/67	Joan Diener 4/11/67
	Maura K. Wedge 4/11/67	

MARAT/SADE

Marquis de Sade	William Roerick 1/3/67	William Roerick 2/20/67
Jean-Paul Marat	Dennis Patrick 1/3/67	Robert Fields 2/20/67
Charlotte Corday	Verna Bloom 1/3/67	Verna Bloom 2/20/67

	NEW YORK COMPANY	TOURING COMPANIES
THE ODD COUPLE		
Oscar Madison	Walter Matthau 3/10/65	#1 Dan Dailey 12/27/65
	Jack Klugman 11/8/65	#2 Phil Foster 8/1/66
	Pat Hingle 2/28/66	
	Mike Kellin 10/3/66	
Felix Unger	Art Carney 3/10/65	#1 Richard Benjamin 12/27/65
	Eddie Bracken 10/25/65	Elliott Reid 9/19/66
		#2 George Gobel 8/1/66

	NEW YORK COMPANY	TOURING COMPANIES
ON A CLEAR DAY YOU CAN SEE FOREVER		
Daisy Gamble	Barbara Harris 10/17/65	Linda Lavin 9/5/67
Dr. Mark Bruckner	John Cullum 10/17/65	Van Johnson 9/5/67

	NEW YORK COMPANY	TOURING COMPANIES
PHILADELPHIA, HERE I COME!		
Gareth O'Donnell		
In public	Patrick Bedford 2/16/66	Patrick Bedford 11/28/66
In private	Donal Donnelly 2/16/66	Donal Donnelly 11/28/66

	NEW YORK COMPANY	TOURING COMPANIES
SWEET CHARITY		
Charity	Gwen Verdon 1/29/66	Juliet Prowse 12/29/67
	Helen Gallagher 7/11/66	
	Gwen Verdon 7/25/66	

	NEW YORK COMPANY	TOURING COMPANIES
A VIEW FROM THE BRIDGE		
Eddie	Robert Duvall 1/28/65	
	Richard Castellano 6/8/65	
	Robert Duvall 9/14/65	
	Richard Castellano 10/19/65	
	Jack Somack 9/13/66	
Beatrice	Jeanne Kaplan 1/28/65	
Rodolpho	Jon Voight 1/28/65	
	Wayne Geis 10/19/65	
Catherine	Susan Anspach 1/28/65	
	Susan Kapilow 8/31/65	

	NEW YORK COMPANY	TOURING COMPANIES
WAIT UNTIL DARK		
Susy Hendrix	Lee Remick 2/2/66	Shirley Jones 1/16/67
		Ann Blyth 5/15/67
Harry Roat Jr.	Robert Duvall 2/2/66	Jack Cassidy 1/16/67
	James Tolkan 5/66	James Tolkan 5/15/67

	NEW YORK COMPANY	TOURING COMPANIES
WALKING HAPPY		
Will Mossop	Norman Wisdom 11/26/66	Norman Wisdom 4/25/67
Maggie Hobson	Louise Troy 11/26/66	Anne Rogers 4/25/67
	Anne Rogers 4/4/67	

BUS-TRUCK TOURS: Nine major bus-truck troupes visited 505 cities from coast to coast during the 1966-67 season. These are productions designed for maximum mobility and ease of handling in one-night and split-week stands (with occasional engagements of a week or more). The nine were as follows: *The Odd Couple* with Lyle Talbot and Harvey Stone, 107 cities, 10/7/66-4/22/67; *Half a Sixpence* with Kenneth Nelson, 104 cities, 8/22/66-3/18/67; *Generation* with Hans Conried, 65 cities, 1/15/67-4/30/67; *Luv* with Nancy Walker and Scott McKay, 53 cities, 10/1/66-12/18/66 and with Eileen Brennan and Roy Shuman, 38 cities, 2/2/67-4/8/67; *Porgy and Bess* with Laverne Hutcherson, Joyce Bryant, Avon Long and Val Pringle, 52 cities, 12/26/66-3/20/67; *Barefoot in the Park* with Sylvia Sidney, 23 cities, 10/13/66-12/10/66; *The Royal Hunt of the Sun* with W.B. Brydon and Clayton Corbin, 32 cities, 10/11/66-1/21/67; *The Exception and the Rule* and *The Elephant Calf* (double bill), 20 colleges, 4/3/67-4/29/67; *The Coach With the Six Insides* with Jean Erdman, 11 colleges, 4/7/67-4/22/67.

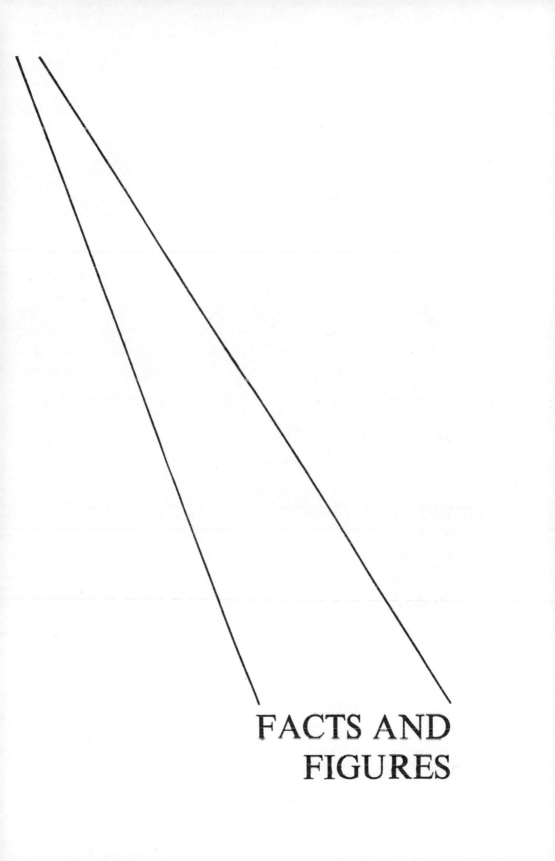

FACTS AND
FIGURES

LONG RUNS ON BROADWAY

(500 or more performances)

THROUGH MAY 31, 1967

(PLAYS MARKED WITH ASTERISK WERE STILL PLAYING JUNE 1, 1967)

Plays	Number Performances		
Life with Father	3,224	Kiss and Tell	957
Tobacco Road	3,182	*The Odd Couple	928
My Fair Lady	2,717	The Moon Is Blue	924
Abie's Irish Rose	2,327	Bells Are Ringing	924
Oklahoma!	2,212	Luv	901
Harvey	1,775	Can-Can	892
South Pacific	1,694	Carousel	890
Born Yesterday	1,642	Hats Off to Ice	889
Mary, Mary	1,572	Fanny	888
The Voice of the Turtle	1,557	Follow the Girls	882
*Barefoot in the Park	1,502	Camelot	873
Arsenic and Old Lace	1,444	The Bat	867
The Sound of Music	1,443	My Sister Eileen	865
How to Succeed in Business		White Cargo	864
Without Really Trying	1,417	Song of Norway	860
*Hello, Dolly!	1,406	A Streetcar Named Desire	855
Hellzapoppin	1,404	Comedy in Music	849
The Music Man	1,375	You Can't Take It With You	837
*Funny Girl	1,312	La Plume de Ma Tante	835
Angel Street	1,295	Three Men on a Horse	835
Lightnin'	1,291	The Subject Was Roses	832
The King and I	1,246	Inherit the Wind	806
Guys and Dolls	1,200	No Time for Sergeants	796
Mister Roberts	1,157	Fiorello!	795
Annie Get Your Gun	1,147	Where's Charley?	792
The Seven Year Itch	1,141	The Ladder	789
*Fiddler on the Roof	1,122	Oliver	774
Pins and Needles	1,108	State of the Union	765
Kiss Me, Kate	1,070	The First Year	760
Pajama Game	1,063	Two for the Seesaw	750
The Teahouse of the August		Death of a Salesman	742
Moon	1,027	Sons o' Fun	742
Damn Yankees	1,019	Gentlemen Prefer Blondes	740
Never Too Late	1,007	The Man Who Came to Dinner	739
Any Wednesday	982	Call Me Mister	734
A Funny Thing Happened on		West Side Story	732
the Way to the Forum	964	High Button Shoes	727
Anna Lucasta	957	Finian's Rainbow	725

431

	Number		Number
Plays	*Performances*	*Plays*	*Performances*
Claudia	722	The Student Prince	608
The Gold Diggers	720	Bye Bye Birdie	607
Carnival	719	Broadway	603
The Diary of Anne Frank	717	Adonis	603
I Remember Mama	714	Street Scene	601
Tea and Sympathy	712	Kiki	600
Junior Miss	710	Flower Drum Song	600
Seventh Heaven	704	Wish You Were Here	598
Gypsy	702	A Society Circus	596
The Miracle Worker	700	Blossom Time	592
Cat on a Hot Tin Roof	694	The Two Mrs. Carrols	585
Li'l Abner	693	Kismet	583
Peg o' My Heart	692	Detective Story	581
The Children's Hour	691	Brigadoon	581
Dead End	687	No Strings	580
The Lion and the Mouse	686	Brother Rat	577
Dear Ruth	683	Show Boat	572
East Is West	680	The Show-Off	571
Come Blow Your Horn	677	Sally	570
The Most Happy Fella	676	Golden Boy	568
The Doughgirls	671	One Touch of Venus	567
The Impossible Years	670	Happy Birthday	564
Irene	670	Look Homeward, Angel	564
Boy Meets Girl	669	The Glass Menagerie	561
Beyond the Fringe	667	Wonderful Town	559
Who's Afraid of Virginia Woolf?	664	Rose Marie	557
Blithe Spirit	657	Strictly Dishonorable	557
The Women	657	A Majority of One	556
A Trip to Chinatown	657	*Sweet Charity	556
Bloomer Girl	654	Toys in the Attic	556
The Fifth Season	654	Sunrise at Campobello	556
Rain	648	Jamaica	555
Witness for the Prosecution	645	Stop the World—I Want to Get	
Call Me Madam	644	Off	555
Janie	642	Ziegfeld Follies	553
The Green Pastures	640	Floradora	553
Auntie Mame	639	Dial "M" for Murder	552
A Man for All Seasons	637	Good News	551
*Man of La Mancha	633	Let's Face It	547
The Fourposter	632	Milk and Honey	543
The Tenth Man	623	Within the Law	541
Is Zat So?	618	The Music Master	540
Anniversary Waltz	615	Pal Joey	540
*Cactus Flower	614	What Makes Sammy Run?	540
The Happy Time	614	What a Life	538
Separate Rooms	613	The Unsinkable Molly Brown	532
Affairs of State	610	The Red Mill	531
Star and Garter	609		

Plays	Number Performances	Plays	Number Performances
A Raisin in the Sun	530	The New Moon	509
The Solid Gold Cadillac	526	The World of Suzie Wong	508
Irma La Douce	524	Shuffle Along	504
The Boomerang	522	Up in Central Park	504
Rosalinda	521	Carmen Jones	503
The Best Man	520	The Member of the Wedding	501
Chauve Souris	520	Panama Hattie	501
Blackbirds	518	Personal Appearance	501
Sunny	517	Bird in Hand	500
Victoria Regina	517	Room Service	500
Half a Sixpence	511	Sailor, Beware!	500
The Vagabond King	511	Tomorrow the World	500

LONG RUNS OFF BROADWAY

Plays	Performances	Plays	Performances
*The Fantasticks	2,955	The Trojan Women	600
The Threepenny Opera	2,611	Krapp's Last Tape and The Zoo Story	582
The Blacks	1,408		
Little Mary Sunshine	1,143	The Dumbwaiter and The Collection	578
Leave It to Jane	928		
A View From the Bridge	780	The Crucible	571
The Boy Friend	763	The Iceman Cometh	565
*The Mad Show	723	The Hostage	545
The Connection	722	Six Characters in Search of an Author	529
The Knack	685		
The Balcony	672	Happy Ending and Day of Absence	504
Hogan's Goat	607		
*The Pocket Watch	601	The Boys From Syracuse	500

DRAMA CRITICS CIRCLE VOTING 1966-67

The New York Drama Critics Circle voted *The Homecoming* the best play of the season by 32 points against 19 for *A Delicate Balance*, 14 for *You Know I Can't Hear You When the Water's Running*, 12 for *America Hurrah*, 5 for *The Killing of Sister George*, 4 for *Black Comedy* and one each for *The Deer Park*, *How's the World Treating You?* and *My Sweet Charlie*.

The critics voted *Cabaret* the best musical of the season by 28 points against 19 for *I Do! I Do!*, 13 for *You're a Good Man Charlie Brown*, 11 for *The Apple Tree*, 3 for *Annie Get Your Gun* and 2 for *Dynamite Tonite*.

No candidate in either category won the required three-fourths majority of first choices on the first ballot, so that the voting went to second ballots on which a point system was used. Each critic could list a first choice (3 points), a second choice (2 points) and a third choice (1 point), with the plays which received the greatest number of points winning the awards. Some dissatisfaction was expressed among the critics at this particular application of the point system, because those who omitted to list a second or third choice thereby gave more weight, intentionally or unintentionally, to their first choice.

A motion by Henry Hewes to vote an additional award for Best American Play was defeated.

SECOND BALLOT FOR BEST PLAY

Critic	1st Choice (3 pts.)	2d Choice (2 pts.)	3d Choice (1 pt.)
Whitney Bolton—*Morning Telegraph*	You Know I Can't Hear You When the Water's Running		
John Chapman—*Daily News*	A Delicate Balance	Black Comedy	Water's Running
Harold Clurman—*The Nation*	The Homecoming		
Ethel Colby—*Journal of Commerce*	The Homecoming	Water's Running	The Killing of Sister George
Richard Cooke—*Wall Street Journal*	The Homecoming		
Jack Gaver—UP	Water's Running	Black Comedy	The Deer Park
Richard Gilman—*Newsweek*	The Homecoming		
William H. Glover—AP	A Delicate Balance	The Homecoming	Water's Running
Martin Gottfried—*Women's Wear Daily*	The Homecoming	America Hurrah	How's the World Treating You?
Henry Hewes—*Saturday Review*	The Homecoming	A Delicate Balance	My Sweet Charlie
Ted Kalem—*Time*	The Homecoming	America Hurrah	Sister George
Walter Kerr—*Times*	America Hurrah		
Emory Lewis—*Cue*	The Homecoming	A Delicate Balance	
John McCarten—*The New Yorker*	(Abstain)		
Hobe Morrison—*Variety*	Sister George		

434

Critic	1st Choice (3 pts.)	2d Choice (2 pts.)	3d Choice (1 pt.)
Norman Nadel— *World Journal Tribune*	America Hurrah	The Homecoming	Water's Running
George Oppenheimer —*Newsday*	A Delicate Balance	The Homecoming	Water's Running
William Raidy—Newhouse Papers	A Delicate Balance	America Hurrah	Water's Running
Richard Watts Jr.— *Post*	A Delicate Balance	The Homecoming	Water's Running

SECOND BALLOT FOR BEST MUSICAL

Critic	1st Choice (3 pts.)	2d Choice (2 pts.)	3d Choice (1 pt.)
Whitney Bolton	Cabaret		
John Chapman	The Apple Tree	I Do! I Do!	Cabaret
Harold Clurman	(Abstain)		
Ethel Colby	Cabaret	The Apple Tree	I Do! I Do!
Richard Cooke	Cabaret		
Jack Gaver	Cabaret	I Do! I Do!	The Apple Tree
Richard Gilman	(Abstain)		
William H. Glover	I Do! I Do!	You're a Good Man Charlie Brown	
Martin Gottfried	I Do! I Do!	Dynamite Tonite	
Henry Hewes	Annie Get Your Gun	I Do! I Do!	Charlie Brown
Ted Kalem	(Abstain)		
Walter Kerr	Cabaret		
Emory Lewis	Cabaret	Charlie Brown	The Apple Tree
John McCarten	(Abstain)		
Hobe Morrison	I Do! I Do!		
Norman Nadel	Cabaret	The Apple Tree	Charlie Brown
George Oppenheimer	Charlie Brown	I Do! I Do!	The Apple Tree
William Raidy	Cabaret	Charlie Brown	The Apple Tree
Richard Watts Jr.	Cabaret	Charlie Brown	I Do! I Do!

Choices of some other critics:

Critic	BEST PLAY	BEST MUSICAL
Judith Crist—"Today"	America Hurrah	Cabaret
Thomas P. Dash—*Show Business*	The Homecoming	Cabaret
Tom Prideaux—*Life*	The Homecoming	The Apple Tree
Leonard Harris—WCBS-TV	The Homecoming	Cabaret
Edwin Newman—WNBC-TV	The Homecoming	Cabaret
Stanley Kauffmann—WNDT	The Homecoming	Cabaret
Ted Hoffman—Westinghouse Broadcasting	The Homecoming	Cabaret

NEW YORK DRAMA CRITICS CIRCLE AWARDS

Listed below are the New York Drama Critics Circle Awards, classified as follows: (1) Best American Play, (2) Best Foreign Play, (3) Best Musical, (4) Best, regardless of category.

1935-36—(1) Winterset

1936-37—(1) High Tor

1937-38—(1) Of Mice and Men, (2) Shadow and Substance

1938-39—(1) No Award, (2) The White Steed

1939-40—(1) The Time of Your Life

1940-41—(1) Watch on the Rhine, (2) The Corn Is Green

1941-42—(1) No Award, (2) Blithe Spirit

1942-43—(1) The Patriots

1943-44—(1) No Award, (2) Jacobowsky and the Colonel

1944-45—(1) The Glass Menagerie

1945-46—(1) No Award, (2) No Award, (3) Carousel

1946-47—(1) All My Sons, (2) No Exit, (3) Brigadoon

1947-48—(1) A Streetcar Named Desire, (2) The Winslow Boy

1948-49—(1) Death of a Salesman, (2) The Madwoman of Chaillot, (3) South Pacific

1949-50—(1) The Member of the Wedding, (2) The Cocktail Party, (3) The Consul

1950-51—(1) Darkness at Noon, (2) The Lady's Not for Burning, (3) Guys and Dolls

1951-52—(1) I Am a Camera, (2) Venus Observed, (3) Pal Joey (Special citation to Don Juan in Hell)

1952-53—(1) Picnic, (2) The Love of Four Colonels, (3) Wonderful Town

1953-54—(1) The Teahouse of the August Moon, (2) Ondine, (3) The Golden Apple

1954-55—(1) Cat on a Hot Tin Roof, (2) Witness for the Prosecution, (3) The Saint of Bleecker Street

1955-56—(1) The Diary of Anne Frank, (2) Tiger at the Gates, (3) My Fair Lady

1956-57—(1) Long Day's Journey Into Night, (2) Waltz of the Torreadors, (3) The Most Happy Fella

1957-58—(1) Look Homeward, Angel, (2) Look Back in Anger, (3) The Music Man

1958-59—(1) A Raisin in the Sun, (2) The Visit, (3) La Plume de Ma Tante

1959-60—(1) Toys in the Attic, (2) Five Finger Exercise, (3) Fiorello!

1960-61—(1) All the Way Home, (2) A Taste of Honey, (3) Carnival

1961-62—(1) The Night of the Iguana, (2) A Man for All Seasons, (3) How to Succeed in Business Without Really Trying

1962-63—(4) Who's Afraid of Virginia Woolf? (Special citation to Beyond the Fringe)

1963-64—(4) Luther, (3) Hello, Dolly! (Special citation to The Trojan Women)

1964-65—(4) The Subject Was Roses, (3) Fiddler on the Roof

1965-66—(4) The Persecution and Assassination of Marat as Performed by the Inmates of the Asylum of Charenton Under the Direction of the Marquis de Sade, (3) Man of La Mancha

1966-67—(4) The Homecoming, (3) Cabaret

PULITZER PRIZE WINNERS

1917-18—Why Marry?, by Jesse Lynch Williams

1918-19—No award.

1919-20—Beyond the Horizon, by Eugene O'Neill

1920-21—Miss Lulu Bett, by Zona Gale

1921-22—Anna Christie, by Eugene O'Neill

1922-23—Icebound, by Owen Davis

1923-24—Hell-bent for Heaven, by Hatcher Hughes

1924-25—They Knew What They Wanted, by Sidney Howard
1925-26—Craig's Wife, by George Kelly
1926-27—In Abraham's Bosom, by Paul Green
1927-28—Strange Interlude, by Eugene O'Neill
1928-29—Street Scene, by Elmer Rice
1929-30—The Green Pastures, by Marc Connelly
1930-31—Alison's House, by Susan Glaspell
1931-32—Of Thee I Sing, by George S. Kaufman, Morrie Ryskind, Ira and George Gershwin
1932-33—Both Your Houses, by Maxwell Anderson
1933-34—Men in White, by Sidney Kingsley
1934-35—The Old Maid, by Zoë Akins
1935-36—Idiot's Delight, by Robert E. Sherwood
1936-37—You Can't Take It with You, by Moss Hart and George S. Kaufman
1937-38—Our Town, by Thornton Wilder
1938-39—Abe Lincoln in Illinois, by Robert E. Sherwood
1939-40—The Time of Your Life, by William Saroyan
1940-41—There Shall Be No Night, by Robert E. Sherwood
1941-42—No award
1942-43—The Skin of Our Teeth, by Thornton Wilder

1943-44—No award
1944-45—Harvey, by Mary Chase
1945-46—State of the Union, by Howard Lindsay and Russel Crouse
1946-47—No award.

1947-48—A Streetcar Named Desire, by Tennessee Williams
1948-49—Death of a Salesman, by Arthur Miller
1949-50—South Pacific, by Richard Rodgers, Oscar Hammerstein II and Joshua Logan
1950-51—No award
1951-52—The Shrike, by Joseph Kramm
1952-53—Picnic, by William Inge
1953-54—The Teahouse of the August Moon, by John Patrick
1954-55—Cat on a Hot Tin Roof, by Tennessee Williams
1955-56—The Diary of Anne Frank, by Frances Goodrich and Albert Hackett
1956-57—Long Day's Journey into Night, by Eugene O'Neill
1957-58—Look Homeward, Angel, by Ketti Frings
1958-59—J. B., by Archibald MacLeish
1959-60—Fiorello!, by Jerome Weidman, George Abbott, Sheldon Harnick and Jerry Bock
1960-61—All the Way Home, by Tad Mosel
1961-62—How to Succeed in Business Without Really Trying, by Abe Burrows, Willie Gilbert, Jack Weinstock and Frank Loesser
1962-63—No award
1963-64—No award
1964-65—The Subject Was Roses, by Frank D. Gilroy
1965-66—No award
1966-67—A Delicate Balance, by Edward Albee

ADDITIONAL PRIZES AND AWARDS, 1966-1967

The following is a list of major prizes and awards for theatrical achievement:

MARGO JONES AWARDS. HARLAN P. KLEIMAN and JON JORY of the Long Wharf Theater in New Haven, Conn., "for courage in disregarding easy and comfortable policy by presenting, in fully professional productions, a festival of new plays." A University Award to PROFESSOR ARTHUR BALLET of the University of Minnesota and its Office for Advanced Drama Research.

KELCEY ALLEN AWARD. MAYOR JOHN V. LINDSAY for his cooperation with the theater industry and preserving New York City's reputation for cultural sophistication by permitting African dancers to perform topless. Special Citation to ABRAHAM MANDLESTAM for

his many years of service to the Award and to its committee.

GEORGE JEAN NATHAN AWARD (for drama criticism). ERIC BENTLEY for his articles "Il Tragico Imperatore" and "An Un-American Chalk Circle," published in the Tulane Drama Review.

CLARENCE DERWENT AWARDS (for best non-featured performances). REVA ROSE for You're a Good Man Charlie Brown. AUSTIN PENDLETON for Hail Scrawdyke! Special award to PHILIP BOSCO for The Alchemist.

DRAMA DESK-VERNON RICE AWARDS (for off-Broadway achievement). JEAN-CLAUDE VAN ITALLIE, author of *America Hurrah*, and LANFORD WILSON, author of *The Rimers of Eldritch*. DUSTIN HOFFMAN for his performance in *Eh?* STACY KEACH for his performance in *MacBird!* BILL HINNANT for his performance in *You're a Good Man Charlie Brown*. WILL LEE for his performance in *The Deer Park*. JOSEPH HARDY for his direction of *You're a Good Man Charlie Brown*.

BRANDEIS CREATIVE ARTS AWARDS. JEROME ROBBINS, choreographer and director, and ELLEN STEWART, off-off-Broadway producer at Cafe La Mama.

JOSEPH MAHARAM FOUNDATION AWARDS. BORIS ARONSON, scene designer, for *Cabaret*. JEANNE BUTTON, costume designer, for *MacBird!*

OBIE AWARDS (for off-Broadway excellence). Distinguished plays: *Futz* by Rochelle Owens; *Eh?* by Henry Livings; *La Turista* by Sam Shepard. Best actor: SETH ALLEN in *Futz*. Best director: TOM O'HORGAN for *Futz*. Distinguished performances: TOM ALDREDGE and BETTE HENRITZE in *Measure for Measure;* ROBERT BONNARD in *The Chairs;* ALVIN EPSTEIN in *Dynamite Tonite;* NEIL FLANAGAN in *The Madness of Lady Bright;* STACY KEACH in *MacBird!;* TERRY KISER in *Fortune*

and Men's Eyes; EDDIE MCCARTY in *Kitchenette;* ROBERT SALVIO in *Hamp;* RIP TORN in *The Deer Park*. Joseph Cino Memorial Award to JEFF WEISS, author of *And That's How the Rent Gets Paid* and *A Funny Walk Home*. Citations to the La Mama troupe for presenting repertory to European audiences; to the Open Theater for its laboratory work; to TOM SANKEY for authorship of *The Golden Screw*, in which he also acted; to the Second Party Players for superior production standards; to John Dood for lighting.

OUTER CIRCLE AWARDS (voted by critics who cover N.Y. theater for out-of-town periodicals). *Cabaret, You're a Good Man Charlie Brown, America Hurrah* and *You Know I Can't Hear You, etc.;* ALEXANDER H. COHEN, producer of *The Homecoming* and *Black Comedy*, and for his work in revitalizing the Tony Awards; MARTIN BALSAM for his performance in *You Know I Can't Hear You, etc.;* MELINA MERCOURI in *Illya Darling* and LESLIE UGGAMS of *Hallelujah, Baby!* as outstanding new personalities; JOHN HIRSCH, director of *Galileo;* CONSTANCE TOWERS for her performance in *The Sound of Music* revival; BIL and CORA BAIRD for establishing a permanent puppet theater.

SAM S. SHUBERT AWARD. VINCENT SARDI SR.

VARIETY'S POLL OF NEW YORK DRAMA CRITICS

Each year, representative first-string New York drama critics are polled by *Variety* to learn their choices for bests in categories other than best play or musical. Fifteen critics participated in the balloting on the 1966-67 season: John Chapman, Richard P. Cooke, Jack Gaver, William Glover, Martin Gottfried, Leonard Harris, Henry Hewes, Allan Jefferys, Theodore Kalem, Walter Kerr, Emory Lewis, John McCarten, Norman Nadel, Edwin Newman, Tom Prideaux. The names of those who were cited in the various categories appear below together with the number of critics' votes they received. The winner in each category is listed in **bold face type.**

MALE LEAD—Straight Play. **Paul Rogers** (6) in *The Homecoming*, Martin Balsam (4) in *You Know I Can't Hear You When the Water's Running*, Hume Cronyn (3) in *A Delicate Balance*, Michael Crawford (1) in *Black Comedy*, Anthony Quayle (1) in *Galileo*.

FEMALE LEAD—Straight Play. **Beryl Reid** (6) in *The Killing of Sister George*, Vivien Merchant (5) in *The Homecoming*, Eileen Atkins (1) in *Sister George*, Rosemary Harris (1) in APA-Phoenix repertory, Maureen

Stapleton (1) in *The Rose Tattoo*, Patricia Routledge (1) in *How's the World Treating You?*

MALE LEAD—Musical. **Robert Preston** (10) in *I Do! I Do!*, Joel Grey (2) in *Cabaret*, Clive Revill (2) in *Sherry!*, Norman Wisdom (1) in *Walking Happy*.

FEMALE LEAD—Musical. **Barbara Harris** (10) in *The Apple Tree*, Mary Martin (3) in *I Do! I Do!*, Ethel Merman (1) in *Annie*

Get Your Gun, Leslie Uggams (1) in *Halle-lujah, Baby!*

ACTOR SUPPORTING ROLE. **Joel Grey** (7) in *Cabaret*, Ian Holm (5) in *The Home-coming*, Donald Madden (2) in *Black Com-edy*, Jack Gilford (1) in *Cabaret*.

ACTRESS SUPPORTING ROLE. **Rosemary Murphy** (4) in *A Delicate Balance*, Marian Seldes (3) in *A Delicate Balance*, Eileen At-kins (1) in *Sister George*, Lally Bowers (1) in *Sister George*, Lillian Hayman (1) in *Hal-lelujah, Baby!*, Lotte Lenya (1) in *Cabaret*, Vivien Merchant (1) in *The Homecoming*, Geraldine Page (1) in *Black Comedy*, Maria Tucci (1) in *The Rose Tattoo*, Janet Ward (1) in *Of Love Remembered*.

MOST PROMISING NEW BROADWAY ACTOR. **Michael Crawford** (4) in *Black Comedy*, Richard Benjamin (2) in *The Star-Spangled Girl*, Ian Holm (2) in *The Home-coming*, Allen Case (1) in *Hallelujah, Baby!*, Bruce Hyde (1) in *The Girl in the Freudian Slip*, Jon Voight (1) in *That Summer—That Fall*, **No Choice** (4).

MOST PROMISING NEW BROADWAY ACTRESS. **Leslie Uggams** (5) in *Hallelujah, Baby!*, Bonnie Bedelia (4) in *My Sweet Charlie*, Patricia Routledge (2) in *How's the World Treating You?*, Jill Haworth (1) in *Cabaret*, Ingrid Thulin (1), No Choice (2).

DIRECTOR. **Peter Hall** (8) for *The Home-coming*, John Dexter (3) for *Black Comedy*, Gower Champion (1) for *I Do! I Do!*, Milton

Katselas (1) for *The Rose Tattoo*, Harold Prince (1) for *Cabaret*, Alan Schneider (1) for *You Know I Can't Hear You, etc.*

SCENE DESIGNER. **Boris Aronson** (8) for *Cabaret*, Robert Randolph (2) for *Sherry!* and *Walking Happy*, John Bury (1) for *The Homecoming*, William and Jean Eckart (1) for *Hallelujah, Baby!*, Jo Mielziner (1) for *That Summer—That Fall*, Oliver Smith (1) for *Illya Darling*, No Choice (1).

COSTUME DESIGNER. **Patricia Zipprodt** (7) for *Cabaret*, Irene Sharaff (4) for *Halle-lujah, Baby!*, Nancy Potts (2) for *War and Peace* and *The Wild Duck*, James Hart Stearns (1) for *Galileo*, No Choice (1).

COMPOSER. **John Kander** (6) for *Cabaret*, Harvey Schmidt (3) for *I Do! I Do!*, Jerry Bock (2) for *The Apple Tree*, Oscar Brand and Paul Nassau (1) for *A Joyful Noise*, Jule Styne (1) for *Hallelujah, Baby!*, No Choice (2).

LYRICIST. **Fred Ebb** (7) for *Cabaret*, Tom Jones (3) for *I Do! I Do!*, Sheldon Harnick (2) for *The Apple Tree*, Betty Comden and Adolph Green (1) for *Hallelujah, Baby!*, No Choice (2).

MOST PROMISING PLAYWRIGHT. Jules Feiffer (4) for *Little Murders*, Woody Allen (2) for *Don't Drink the Water*, Frank Mar-cus (2) for *Sister George*, Leo Lehman (1) for *The East Wind*, David Westheimer (1) for *My Sweet Charlie*, **No Choice** (5).

THE TONY AWARDS

The Antoinette Perry (Tony) Awards are voted upon by members of The League of New York Theaters and the governing bodies of The Dramatists Guild, Actors Equity and the Society of Stage Directors and Choreographers and the official first and second night press lists. Below were the nominations in the various categories, made by a nominating committee composed of Leonard Harris, Henry Hewes, Max Lerner, Stuart W. Little, Richard Watts Jr. and John Wingate. The winner in each category appears in **bold face type.**

BEST PLAY (award goes to both producer and author). *A Delicate Balance*, produced by Theater 1967 (RICHARD BARR, CLINTON WILDER), written by EDWARD ALBEE. *Black Comedy*, produced by ALEXANDER H. COHEN, written by PETER SHAFFER; **The Homecom-ing**, produced by **Alexander H. Cohen**, written by **Harold Pinter**; *The Killing of Sister George*, produced by HELEN BONFILS

and MORTON GOTTLIEB, written by FRANK MARCUS.

BEST MUSICAL PLAY (award goes to both producer and author). **Cabaret**, produced by Harold Prince, book by Joe Masteroff. *I Do! I Do!*, produced by DAVID MERRICK, book by TOM JONES. *The Apple Tree*, pro-duced by STUART OSTROW, book by SHELDON

HARNICK and JERRY BOCK. *Walking Happy*, produced by CY FEUER and ERNEST MARTIN, book by ROGER O. HIRSON and KETTI FRINGS.

ACTOR—Dramatic Star. HUME CRONYN in *A Delicate Balance*. DONALD MADDEN in *Black Comedy*. DONALD MOFFAT in *Right You Are* and *The Wild Duck*. **Paul Rogers** in *The Homecoming*.

ACTRESS—Dramatic Star. EILEEN ATKINS in *The Killing of Sister George*. VIVIEN MERCHANT in *The Homecoming*. ROSEMARY MURPHY in *A Delicate Balance*. **Beryl Reid** in *The Killing of Sister George*.

ACTOR—Musical Star. ALAN ALDA in *The Apple Tree*. JACK GILFORD in *Cabaret*. **Robert Preston** in *I Do! I Do!* NORMAN WISDOM in *Walking Happy*.

ACTRESS—Musical Star. **Barbara Harris** in *The Apple Tree*. LOTTE LENYA in *Cabaret*. MARY MARTIN in *I Do! I Do!* LOUISE TROY in *Walking Happy*.

ACTOR—Dramatic Featured or Supporting. CLAYTON CORZATTE in *The School for Scandal*. STEPHEN ELLIOTT in *Marat/Sade*. **Ian Holm** in *The Homecoming*. SYDNEY WALKER in *The Wild Duck*.

ACTRESS—Dramatic Featured or Supporting. CAMILA ASHLAND in *Black Comedy*. BRENDA FORBES in *The Loves of Cass McGuire*. **Marian Seldes** in *A Delicate Balance*. MARIA TUCCI in *The Rose Tattoo*.

ACTOR—Musical Featured or Supporting. LEON BIBB in *A Hand Is on the Gate*. GORDON DILWORTH in *Walking Happy*. **Joel Grey** in *Cabaret*. EDWARD WINTER in *Cabaret*.

ACTRESS—Musical Featured or Supporting. **Peg Murray** in *Cabaret*. LELAND PALMER in *A Joyful Noise*. JOSEPHINE PREMICE in *A Hand Is on the Gate*. SUSAN WATSON in *A Joyful Noise*.

DIRECTOR—Play. JOHN DEXTER for *Black Comedy*. DONALD DRIVER for *Marat/Sade*. **Peter Hall** for *The Homecoming*. ALAN SCHNEIDER for *A Delicate Balance*.

DIRECTOR—Musical Play. GOWER CHAMPION for *I Do! I Do!* MIKE NICHOLS for *The Apple Tree*. **Harold Prince** for *Cabaret*. JACK SYDOW for *Annie Get Your Gun*.

COMPOSER AND LYRICIST. JERRY BOCK and SHELDON HARNICK for *The Apple Tree*. SAMMY CAHN and JAMES VAN HEUSEN for *Walking Happy*. TOM JONES and HARVEY SCHMIDT for *I Do! I Do!* **John Kander** and **Freb Ebb** for *Cabaret*.

SCENIC DESIGNER. **Boris Aronson** for *Cabaret*. JOHN BURY for *The Homecoming*. OLIVER SMITH for *I Do! I Do!* ALAN TAGG for *Black Comedy*.

COSTUME DESIGNER. NANCY POTTS for *The Wild Duck* and *The School for Scandal*. TONY WALTON for *The Apple Tree*. FREDDY WITTOP for *I Do! I Do!* **Patricia Zipprodt** for *Cabaret*.

CHOREOGRAPHER. MICHAEL BENNETT for *A Joyful Noise*. DANNY DANIELS for *Walking Happy*. **Ronald Field** for *Cabaret*. LEE THEODORE for *The Apple Tree*.

1966-67 PUBLICATION
OF RECENTLY-PRODUCED PLAYS

The Apple Tree. (Musical) Book by Jerry Bock and Sheldon Harnick, additional book material by Jerome Coopersmith, based on stories by Mark Twain, Frank R. Stockton and Jules Feiffer, music by Jerry Bock, lyrics by Sheldon Harnick. Random House.

Cabaret. (Musical) Book by Joe Masteroff, based on the play *I Am a Camera* by John van Druten and stories by Christopher Isherwood, music by John Kander, lyrics by Fred Ebb. Random House.

The Deer Park. Norman Mailer. Dell.

A Delicate Balance. Edward Albee. Atheneum.

Eight Plays From Off-Off-Broadway: The General Returns From One Place to Another by Frank O'Hara; *The Madness of Lady Bright* by Lanford Wilson; *Chicago* by Sam Shepard; *The Great American Desert* by Joel Oppenheimer; *Balls* by Paul Foster; *America Hurrah* by Jean-Claude van Itallie; *The Successful Life of 3* by Maria Irene Fornes; *Calm Down Mother* by Megan Terry; edited by Nick Orzel and Michael Smith. Bobbs-Merrill.

Hail Scrawdyke! David Halliwell. Grove Press.

The Homecoming. Harold Pinter. Grove Press.

The Investigation. Peter Weiss, English version by Jon Swan and Ulu Grosbard. Atheneum.

The Journey of the Fifth Horse and *Harry, Noon and Night.* Ronald Ribman. Little, Brown.

The Killing of Sister George. Frank Marcus. Random House.

The Lion in Winter. James Goldman. Random House.

The Loves of Cass McGuire. Brian Friel. Farrar, Straus & Giroux.

MacBird! Barbara Garson. Grove Press.

Mame. (Musical) Book by Jerome Lawrence and Robert E. Lee, based on their play and the book *Auntie Mame* by Patrick Dennis, music and lyrics by Jerry Herman. Random House.

Man of La Mancha. (Musical) Book by Dale Wasserman, music by Mitch Leigh, lyrics by Joe Darion. Random House.

The Odd Couple. Neil Simon. Random House.

On a Clear Day You Can See Forever. (Musical) Book and lyrics by Alan Jay Lerner, music by Burton Lane. Random House.

Philadelphia, Here I Come! Brian Friel. Farrar, Straus & Giroux.

Rooms: Better Luck Next Time and *A Walk in Dark Places.* Stanley Mann. Random House.

Sweet Charity. (Musical) Book by Neil Simon, based on the screenplay *Nights of Cabiria* by Federico Fellini, Tullio Pinelli, and Ennio Flaiano, music by Cy Coleman, lyrics by Dorothy Fields. Random House.

Where's Daddy? William Inge. Random House.

A SELECTED LIST OF OTHER PLAYS PUBLISHED IN 1966–1967

Beatrice Cenci. Alberto Moravia, translated by Angus Davidson. Farrar, Straus & Giroux.

Flesh and Blood. William Hanley. Random House.

Four Plays: The Ham Funeral, The Season at Sarsaparella, A Cheery Soul and *Night on a Bald Mountain.* Patrick White. Viking.

Herakles. Archibald MacLeish. Houghton Mifflin.

The Innocent Party. John Hawkes. New Directions.

Juliet in Mantua. Robert Nathan. Knopf.

Plays for a New Theater: The Long Night of Medea by Corrado Alvaro, *Methusalem or Eternal Bourgeois* by Yuan Goll, *The Wax Museum* by John Hawkes, *The Assault upon Charles Sumner* by Robert Hivnor, *Knackery for All* by Boris Vian. New Directions.

The Plebians Rehearse the Uprising. Günter Grass, translated by Ralph Manheim. Harcourt, Brace & World.

Suite in Three Keys: A Song at Twilight, Shadows of the Evening and *Come Into the Garden Maud.* Noel Coward. Doubleday.

Summer Is a Foreign Land. E. M. Broner. Wayne State University Press.

Three Plays: Never, Never Ask His Name, A Little Night Music and *The Weekend That Was.* Mark Van Doren. Hill and Wang.

ORIGINAL CAST ALBUMS
OF NEW YORK SHOWS

The following albums were issued during the 1966-67 season. The first number appearing after each title is the number of the monaural version, the second the number of the stereo version.

Annie Get Your Gun (revival). RCA Victor. LOC-1124; LSO-1124.
The Apple Tree. Columbia. KOL-6620; KOS-3020.
By Jupiter (revival). RCA Victor. LOC-1137; LSO-1137.
Cabaret. Columbia. KOL-6640; KOS-3040.
Fiddler on the Roof (Bernardi). Columbia. OL-6610; OS-3010.
Fiddler on the Roof (Israeli cast). Columbia. OL-6650; OS-3050.
Hallelujah, Baby! Columbia. KOL-6690; KOS-3090.
A Hand Is on the Gate. Verve/Folkways. 9040-2-OC; s-9040-2-OC.
I Do! I Do! RCA Victor. LOC-1128; LSO-1128.
Illya Darling. United Artists. UAL-8910; UAS-9901.
MacBird! Grove (Evergreen). RM-0004; RS-0004.
Man With a Load of Mischief. Kapp. 4508; 5508.
Walking Happy. Capitol. VAS-2631; (S)2631.
You're a Good Man Charlie Brown. MGM. 1E9; S1E9.

THE BEST PLAYS, 1894-1966

The following lists in alphabetical order all those plays that have appeared in previous volumes of the Best Plays Series. Opposite each title is given the volume in which the play appears, its opening date and its total number of performances, and those plays marked with asterisks were still playing on June 1, 1967. Adaptors and translators are indicated by (ad) and (tr), and the symbols (b), (m) and (l) stand for the author of book, music and lyrics in the case of musicals.

PLAY	VOLUME	OPENED	PERFS.
ABE LINCOLN IN ILLINOIS—Robert E. Sherwood	38-39	Oct. 15, 1938	472
ABRAHAM LINCOLN—John Drinkwater	19-20	Dec. 15, 1919	193
ACCENT ON YOUTH—Samson Raphaelson	34-35	Dec. 25, 1934	229
ADAM AND EVA—Guy Bolton, George Middleton	19-20	Sept. 13, 1919	312
AFFAIRS OF STATE—Louis Verneuil	50-51	Sept. 25, 1950	610
AFTER THE FALL—Arthur Miller	63-64	Jan. 23, 1964	208
AH, WILDERNESS!—Eugene O'Neill	33-34	Oct. 2, 1933	289
ALIEN CORN—Sidney Howard	32-33	Feb. 20, 1933	98
ALISON'S HOUSE—Susan Glaspell	30-31	Dec. 1, 1930	41
ALL MY SONS—Arthur Miller	46-47	Jan. 29, 1947	328
ALL THE WAY HOME—Tad Mosel, based on James Agee's novel A Death in the Family	60-61	Nov. 30, 1960	334
ALLEGRO—(b, l) Oscar Hammerstein, II, (m) Richard Rodgers	47-48	Oct. 10, 1947	315
AMBUSH—Arthur Richman	21-22	Oct. 10, 1921	98
AMERICAN WAY, THE—George S. Kaufman, Moss Hart	38-39	Jan. 21, 1939	164
AMPHITRYON 38—Jean Giraudoux, (ad) S. N. Behrman	37-38	Nov. 1, 1937	153
ANDERSONVILLE TRIAL, THE—Saul Levitt	59-60	Dec. 29, 1959	179
ANDORRA—Max Frisch, (ad) George Tabori	62-63	Feb. 9, 1963	9
ANGEL STREET—Patrick Hamilton	41-42	Dec. 5, 1941	1,295
ANIMAL KINGDOM, THE—Philip Barry	31-32	Jan. 12, 1932	183
ANNA CHRISTIE—Eugene O'Neill	21-22	Nov. 2, 1921	177
ANNA LUCASTA—Philip Yordan	44-45	Aug. 30, 1944	957
ANNE OF THE THOUSAND DAYS—Maxwell Anderson	48-49	Dec. 8, 1948	286
ANOTHER LANGUAGE—Rose Franken	31-32	Apr. 25, 1932	344
ANOTHER PART OF THE FOREST—Lillian Hellman	46-47	Nov. 20, 1946	182
ANTIGONE—Jean Anouilh, (ad) Lewis Galantière	45-46	Feb. 18, 1946	64
ARSENIC AND OLD LACE—Joseph Kesselring	40-41	Jan. 10, 1941	1,444
AS HUSBANDS GO—Rachel Crothers	30-31	Mar. 5, 1931	148
AUTUMN GARDEN, THE—Lillian Hellman	50-51	Mar. 7, 1951	101
AWAKE AND SING—Clifford Odets	34-35	Feb. 19, 1935	209
BAD MAN, THE—Porter Emerson Browne	20-21	Aug. 30, 1920	350
BAD SEED—Maxwell Anderson, adapted from William March's novel	54-55	Dec. 8, 1954	332
BARBARA FRIETCHIE—Clyde Fitch	99-09	Oct. 23, 1899	83
BAREFOOT IN ATHENS—Maxwell Anderson	51-52	Oct. 31, 1951	30
* BAREFOOT IN THE PARK—Neil Simon	63-64	Oct. 23, 1963	1,502
BARRETTS OF WIMPOLE STREET, THE—Rudolf Besier	30-31	Feb. 9, 1931	370
BECKET—Jean Anouilh, (tr) Lucienne Hill	60-61	Oct. 5, 1960	193
BEGGAR ON HORSEBACK—George S. Kaufman, Marc Connelly	23-24	Feb. 12, 1924	224
BEHOLD THE BRIDEGROOM—George Kelly	27-28	Dec. 26, 1927	88
BELL, BOOK AND CANDLE—John van Druten	50-51	Nov. 14, 1950	233
BELL FOR ADANO, A—Paul Osborn, based on John Hersey's novel	44-45	Dec. 6, 1944	304
BERKELEY SQUARE—John L. Balderston	29-30	Nov. 4, 1929	229
BERNARDINE—Mary Coyle Chase	52-53	Oct. 16, 1952	157
BEST MAN, THE—Gore Vidal	59-60	Mar. 31, 1960	521

443

PLAY VOLUME OPENED PERFS.

MAN FROM HOME, THE—Booth Tarkington, Harry Leon Wilson ..99-09..Aug. 17, 1908.. 406
*MAN OF LA MANCHA—(b) Dale Wasserman, suggested by the
life and works of Miguel de Cervantes y Saavedra, (1) Joe
Darion, (m) Mitch Leigh ....65-66..Nov. 22, 1965.. 633
MAN WHO CAME TO DINNER, THE—George S. Kaufman, Moss
Hart ....39-40..Oct. 16, 1939.. 739
MARGIN FOR ERROR—Clare Boothe ....39-40..Nov. 3, 1939.. 264
MARY, MARY—Jean Kerr ....60-61..Mar. 8, 1961..1,572
MARY OF SCOTLAND—Maxwell Anderson ,.....................33-34..Nov. 27, 1933.. 248
MARY ROSE—James M. Barrie ....20-21..Dec. 22, 1920.. 127
MARY THE 3RD—Rachel Crothers ....22-23..Feb. 5, 1923.. 162
MATCHMAKER, THE—Thornton Wilder, based on Johann Nes-
troy's Einen Jux will es sich Machen, based on John Oxen-
ford's A Day Well Spent ....55-56..Dec. 5, 1955.. 486
ME AND MOLLY—Gertrude Berg ....47-48..Feb. 26, 1948.. 156
MEMBER OF THE WEDDING, THE—Carson McCullers, adapted
from her novel ....49-50..Jan. 5, 1950.. 501
MEN IN WHITE—Sidney S. Kingsley ....33-34..Sept. 26, 1933.. 351
MERRILY WE ROLL ALONG—George S. Kaufman, Moss Hart ....34-35..Sept. 29, 1934.. 155
MERTON OF THE MOVIES—George S. Kaufman, Marc Connelly,
based on Harry Leon Wilson's novel ....22-23..Nov. 13, 1922.. 381
MICHAEL AND MARY—A. A. Milne ....29-30..Dec. 10, 1929.. 246
MILK TRAIN DOESN'T STOP HERE ANYMORE, THE—Tennessee
Williams ....62-63..Jan. 16, 1963.. 69
MINICK—George S. Kaufman, Edna Ferber ....24-25..Sept. 24, 1924.. 141
MISTER ROBERTS—Thomas Heggen, Joshua Logan, based on
Thomas Heggen's novel ....47-48..Feb. 18, 1948..1,157
MOON FOR THE MISBEGOTTEN, A—Eugene O'Neill ....56-57..May 2, 1957.. 68
MOON IS DOWN, THE—John Steinbeck ....41-42..Apr. 7, 1942.. 71
MORNING'S AT SEVEN—Paul Osborn ....39-40..Nov. 30, 1939.. 44
MOTHER COURAGE AND HER CHILDREN—Bertolt Brecht, (ad)
Eric Bentley ....62-63..Mar. 28, 1963.. 52
MOURNING BECOMES ELECTRA—Eugene O'Neill ....31-32..Oct. 26, 1931.. 150
MR. AND MRS. NORTH—Owen Davis, based on Frances and Rich-
ard Lockridge's stories ....40-41..Jan. 12, 1941.. 163
MRS. BUMSTEAD-LEIGH—Harry James Smith ....09-19..Apr. 3, 1911.. 64
MRS. McTHING—Mary Coyle Chase ....51-52..Feb. 20, 1952.. 350
MRS. PARTRIDGE PRESENTS—Mary Kennedy, Ruth Hawthorne ....24-25..Jan. 5, 1925.. 144
MY FAIR LADY—(b, 1) Alan Jay Lerner, based on Bernard
Shaw's Pygmalion, (m) Frederick Loewe ....55-56..Mar. 15, 1956..2,717
MY SISTER EILEEN—Joseph A. Fields, Jerome Chodorov, based
on Ruth McKenney's stories ....40-41..Dec. 26, 1940.. 865
MY 3 ANGELS—Sam and Bella Spewack, based on Albert Hus-
son's play La Cuisine des Anges ....52-53..Mar. 11, 1953.. 341

NATIVE SON—Paul Green, Richard Wright, based on Mr.
Wright's novel ....40-41..Mar. 24, 1941.. 114
NEST, THE—Paul Geraldy, Grace George ....21-22..Jan. 28, 1922.. 152
NEXT TIME I'LL SING TO YOU—James Saunders ....63-64..Nov. 27, 1963.. 23
NICE PEOPLE—Rachel Crothers ....20-21..Mar. 2, 1921.. 247
NIGHT OF THE IGUANA, THE—Tennessee Williams ....61-62..Dec. 28, 1961.. 319
NO MORE LADIES—A. E. Thomas ....33-34..Jan. 23, 1934.. 162
NO TIME FOR COMEDY—S. N. Behrman ....38-39..Apr. 17, 1939.. 185
NO TIME FOR SERGEANTS—Ira Levin, adapted from Mac Hy-
man's novel ....55-56..Oct. 20, 1955.. 796

O MISTRESS MINE—Terence Rattigan ....45-46..Jan. 23, 1946.. 452
*ODD COUPLE, THE—Neil Simon ....64-65..Mar. 10, 1965.. 928
OF MICE AND MEN—John Steinbeck ....37-38..Nov. 23, 1937.. 207
OF THEE I SING—(b) George S. Kaufman, Morrie Ryskind,
(1) Ira Gershwin, (m) George Gershwin ....31-32..Dec. 26, 1931.. 441
OH DAD, POOR DAD, MAMMA'S HUNG YOU IN THE CLOSET AND

NECROLOGY

JUNE 1, 1966—MAY 31, 1967

PERFORMERS

Gilbert Adkins—May 26, 1967
Edythe Angell (68)—July 25, 1966
Harry Antrim (72)—Jan. 18, 1967
Mischa Auer (62)—Mar. 5, 1967
Billy Austin (59)—Jan. 4, 1967
Dora Barton—Sept. 13, 1966
Jennie Batcheller (70)—Aug. 23, 1966
Gertrude Berg (66)—Sept. 14, 1966
Count Bernivici (82)—July 12, 1966
Aline Berry (62)—April 3, 1967
Violet Fisher Blake (70)—Jan. 5, 1967
Edward Blincoe (28)—Mar. 21, 1967
Millard Briggs (59)—Mar. 18, 1967
James Brockman (80)—May 22, 1967
George Brookes (68)—Jan. 7, 1967
Wilson A. Brooks (57)—Nov. 19, 1966
Noel Burns (67)—Sept. 27, 1966
Walton Butterfield (68)—Aug. 22, 1966
George J. Byrne (62)—Dec. 15, 1966
Carvel Carter (31)—Jan. 27, 1967
Liza Chapman (37)—Jan. 21, 1967
Michael Charles (26)—Mar. 24, 1967
Sydney Chatton (48)—Oct. 6, 1966
Bessie Clifford—May 11, 1967
Montgomery Clift (45)—July 23, 1966
Philip Coolidge (58)—May 23, 1967
Grace Cunard (73)—Jan. 19, 1967
Jeanne De Casalis (70)—Aug. 19, 1966
Crahan Denton (52)—Dec. 4, 1966
Raymond Duncan (91)—Aug. 14, 1966
Emma Dunn (91)—Dec. 14, 1966
Jane Eccles (70)—summer 1966
Carl Emory (59)—Aug. 30, 1966
Billy Engle (77)—Nov. 28, 1966
Jules Epailly (80s)—Apr. 29, 1967
Greek H. Evans (77)—Jan. 23, 1967
Judith Evelyn (54)—May 7, 1967
Lucille Fenton (50s)—Oct. 17, 1966
Eric Fleming (41)—Sept. 28, 1966
Arthur F. Foran (55)—Jan. 30, 1967
Wallace Ford (68)—June 11, 1966
Irwin Franklyn (62)—Sept. 7, 1966
Michael Garrison (43)—Aug. 17, 1966
Gene Gauntier (80s)—Dec. 18, 1966
Margaret and Mary Gibb (54)—Jan. 12, 1967
Rose Goldberg (78)—Oct. 6, 1966
Mandane Phillips Halley (87)—May 18, 1967
Gardner Halliday (56)—Sept. 6, 1966
Gordon Harker (81)—Mar. 2, 1967
Averell Harris—Sept. 25, 1966

Harry Hines (78)—May 3, 1967
Baliol Holloway (84)—Apr. 15, 1967
E. Mason Hopper (82)—Jan. 3, 1967
Lulu Mae Hubbard (59)—Oct. 21, 1966
Dorothy Jardon (83)—Sept. 30, 1966
Lillian Julie—Nov. 8, 1966
Helen Kane (62)—Sept. 26, 1966
Al Kelly (67)—Sept. 6, 1966
Jan Kiepura (60)—Aug. 15, 1966
Joe Landis—Oct. 16, 1966
Wilfred Lawson (66)—Oct. 10, 1966
George Lehrer (77)—Aug. 25, 1966
Elsie Leslie—Oct. 31, 1966
John N. MacBryde (84)—June 22, 1966
Claire McDowell (88)—Oct. 24, 1966
Thomas J. McElhany (75)—July 22, 1966
Harry McNaughton (70)—Feb. 26, 1967
Walter Macken (51)—Apr. 22, 1967
Sylvia Manon (56)—Aug. 24, 1966
Joseph Anthony Mayo (36)—Nov. 12, 1966
Clara Melroy (62)—Nov. 17, 1966
Nina Melville (56)—Dec. 23, 1966
Joe Mercedes (77)—July 6, 1966
Douglass Montgomery (58)—July 23, 1966
Danny Murphy (75)—Dec. 30, 1966
William Newell (73)—Feb. 21, 1967
Donald Novis (60)—July 23, 1966
George Oakes (69)—June 25, 1966
William O'Gorman (63)—Aug. 30, 1966
Frank Overton (49)—Apr. 24, 1967
Kim Peacock (65)—Dec. 26, 1966
Frederic J. Persson (74)—Sept. 16, 1966
Joe Phillips (78)—Dec. 16, 1966
Claude Rains (77)—May 30, 1967
Hazel Reading—Aug. 17, 1966
Roy Rice (79)—Dec. 29, 1966
Katharine Witchie Riggs (80)—Apr. 19, 1967
Bradford Ropes (60)—Nov. 21, 1966
Marion Ross (68)—July 23, 1966
Sig Rumann (82)—Feb. 14, 1967
Nathaniel Sack (84)—July 2, 1966
Sammy Sales (61)—Feb. 18, 1967
Madge Saunders (72)—Mar. 5, 1967
Al Schenk (61)—Nov. 20, 1966
Oscar Shaw (76)—Mar. 6, 1967
Ann Sheridan (51)—Jan. 21, 1967
Cecile Sorel (92)—Sept. 2, 1966
Frank S. Stevens (43)—June 20, 1966
David J. Stewart (52)—Dec. 23, 1966
George E. Stone (64)—May 26, 1967
Earle E. Styres (69)—Aug. 4, 1966
Evelyn Nesbit Thaw (82)—Jan. 18, 1967

Phyllis Schuyler Thaxter (74)—July 31, 1966
Arthur J. Thornton—Mar. 27, 1967
Al Trahan (69)—Dec. 14, 1966
Emerson Treacy (66)—Jan. 10, 1967
Maury Tuckerman (61)—Oct. 23, 1966
Daphne Vane (49)—Dec. 15, 1966
Frank Wallace (73)—Oct. 15, 1966
Kitty Watson (80)—Mar. 3, 1967
Clifton Webb (72)—Oct. 13, 1966
Desmondoe Wheeler (67)—Aug. 8, 1966
Sadie Burt Whiting—Dec. 6, 1966
Richard Whorf (60)—Dec. 14, 1966
Betty Williams—spring 1967
Walter Wills (86)—Jan. 18, 1967
Rini Zarova Willson (54)—Dec. 6, 1966
Jack Wilson (49)—Dec. 18, 1966
Roland Wood (70)—Feb. 3, 1967
Ed Wynn (79)—June 19, 1966

PLAYWRIGHTS

Darragh Aldrich (85)—Mar. 31, 1967
Azorin (93)—Mar. 2, 1967
Anne Morrison Chapin—Apr. 7, 1967
Francis Edwards Faragoh (71)—July 25, 1966
Louis Freiman (75)—Jan. 30, 1967
Celestino Gorostiza (62)—Jan. 11, 1967
Elmer Harris (88)—Sept. 6, 1966
Langston Hughes (65)—May 22, 1967
Orin Jannings (48)—Oct. 24, 1966
Harry Kalmanovitch (80)—Oct. 11, 1966
Alfred Kreymborg (82)—Aug. 15, 1966
Norma Mitchell—May 29, 1967
James H. Montgomery (78)—June 17, 1966
Anne Nichols (67)—Oct. 12, 1966
Ernest Pascal (70)—Nov. 4, 1966
Steve Passeur (67)—Oct. 12, 1966
Elmer Rice (74)—May 8, 1967
Harlan Thompson (76)—Oct. 29, 1966
Brandon Tynan (91)—Mar. 19, 1967

PRODUCERS, DIRECTORS AND CHOREOGRAPHERS

Sidney Bernstein (56)—July 22, 1966
Laurence Feldman (40)—Mar. 9, 1967
Nat Goldstone (62)—July 24, 1966
Jack Landau (42)—Mar. 16, 1967
Norman Loring (79)—Mar. 9, 1967
Anthony Mann (60)—Apr. 29, 1967
John Moses (60)—Apr. 2, 1967
Milton J. Shubert (66)—Mar. 7, 1967
Helen Tamiris (64)—Aug. 4, 1966

DESIGNERS

Frank Cambria (83)—Sept. 17, 1966
Henry Edward Gordon Craig (94)—July 29, 1966
Ernest de Weerth (73)—Mar. 29, 1967
Raymond Sovey (72)—June 25, 1966

COMPOSERS AND LYRICISTS

Vittorio Giannini (63)—Nov. 28, 1966
Tot Seymour (70s)—Aug. 31, 1966
Deems Taylor (80)—July 3, 1966

CONDUCTORS

Leonid Leonardi (65)—Mar. 3, 1967
James N. Peterson (55)—Apr. 25, 1967
Leo Troostwyk (75)—Sept. 13, 1966

CRITICS

Stanley K. Anderson (50)—Jan. 13, 1967
  Cleveland *Press*
John W. Gassner (64)—Apr. 2, 1966
John McClain (63)—May 3, 1967
  New York *Journal-American*
Ward Morehouse (67)—Dec. 7, 1966
  Newhouse Papers
John Rosenfeld Jr. (66)—Nov. 25, 1966
  Dallas *Morning News*

OTHERS

John E. Baker—Nov. 16, 1966
  Director of Nashua, N. H. Players and St.
  Christopher Players
Sherman Billingsley (68)—Oct. 4, 1966
  Owner of The Stork Club
Ward Bishop (66)—July 30, 1966
  Production stage manager
Herbert Carlin (70)—May 25, 1967
  Theatrical press agent
Saul Colin (58)—Apr. 21, 1967
  President of Senior Dramatic Workshop,
  translator of Gide
Arthur F. Driscoll (82)—May 4, 1967
  Theatrical attorney
Louis Dreyfus (89)—May 2, 1967
  President Chappell & Co., music publishers
Lajos Egri (79)—Feb. 7, 1967
  Teacher and author of *The Art of Dramatic
  Writing*
Sir Fordham Flower (62)—July 9, 1966
  Chairman, Royal Shakespeare Company
Harry Forwood (62)—Jan. 16, 1967
  Theatrical press agent
Joey Gold—June 14, 1966
  Ticket Broker
Harold M. Goldblatt (75)—Sept. 20, 1966
  Theatrical attorney
E. M. Jacobs (85)—June 30, 1966
  Boston booking agent
Annette Schein Jaslow (79)—Jan. 27, 1967
  Theater publicity and promotion agent (ret.)
Mike Kavanagh (80)—Mar. 6, 1967
  General manager Shubert Theater, Boston
Kenneth MacSarin (55)—Jan. 17, 1967
  Theatrical press agent

Yale Meyer (49)—Dec. 11, 1966
  Teacher of speech and acting
J. P. Mitchelhill (87)—Aug. 6, 1966
  British manager and impresario
Blanche Patch (87)—Oct. 10, 1966
  Secretary to George Bernard Shaw
Rollo Peters (74)—Jan. 21, 1967
  Actor, scenic designer, director, producer
  and a founder of the Theater Guild
John H. Potter (78)—summer 1966
  Talent manager
Edward C. Raftery (69)—May 15, 1967
  Theatrical attorney
Edd X. Russell (88)—Nov. 17, 1966

Former West Coast representative of Actors'
Equity
Lee Simonson (78)—Jan. 23, 1967
  Scenic designer and a founder of the Thea-
  ter Guild
Albert Sirmay (85)—Jan. 15, 1967
  Composer, conductor and chief editor of
  Chappell & Co., music publishers
Anne Sloper (44)—July 25, 1966
  Company manager
Kirk Willis (60)—Nov. 17, 1966
  Coordinating director of the Cleveland Play
  House

INDEX

Bold face page numbers refer to pages where Cast of Characters may be found.